2750

‖‖‖‖‖‖‖‖‖‖‖‖‖‖‖‖‖‖‖‖‖‖‖‖

S0-AJM-876

ANNUAL REVIEW OF
BEHAVIOR THERAPY
THEORY AND PRACTICE

VOLUME 9

G. TERENCE WILSON
Rutgers University

CYRIL M. FRANKS
*Carrier Foundation and
Rutgers University*

KELLY D. BROWNELL
University of Pennsylvania

PHILIP C. KENDALL
University of Minnesota–Twin Cities

THE GUILFORD PRESS
New York   London

©1984 G. Terence Wilson, Cyril M. Franks, Kelly D. Brownell, and Philip C. Kendall

Published by The Guilford Press
A Division of Guilford Publications, Inc.
200 Park Avenue South, New York, N.Y. 10003

Printed in the United States of America

Library of Congress Catalog Card No. 76-126864
ISBN 0-89862-618-8
ISSN 0091-6595

It is a popular delusion that the scientific enquirer is under an obligation not to go beyond generalisation of observed facts . . . but anyone who is practically acquainted with scientific work is aware that those who refuse to go beyond the facts, rarely get as far.

THOMAS HUXLEY

PREFACE

Volume 9 in this series is the second volume of the "new look" *Annual Review of Behavior Therapy*. In contrast to the founding format that mixed reprinted articles with commentary by Franks and Wilson, the present volume consists entirely of original commentary by the current four-author team. Each author covers the same topic areas that he discussed in Volume 8 last year, thereby providing continuity of commentary.

The Preface to the first volume in this series (1973) began by borrowing from Ebbinghaus (cited in Boring, 1950) to observe that behavior therapy has a long past but a short history. The reference, of course, was to the relatively recent emergence of behavior therapy in the latter half of the 1950s as a formal, systematic alternative to traditional psychodynamic approaches to assessment and treatment. One of the consequences of this short history has been that the founding fathers of behavior therapy are not only alive but have also continued to play active roles in the development and refinement of the field. Inevitably, however, time will have its inexorable way, our history will grow longer, and the familiar figures, who once led the way, will pass from the scene. In this connection, we sadly note here the deaths of two major contributors to what we know as behavior therapy today.

Edmund Jacobson passed away on January 7, 1982. It is hard, indeed inconceivable, to imagine contemporary behavior therapy without the widespread uses of relaxation training as a therapeutic method in its own right and as a component of systematic desensitization. When Joseph Wolpe adapted Jacobson's methods to his own purposes in developing the landmark technique of systematic desensitization he also ensured that Jacobson would have an important place in the history of behavior therapy. As has often been pointed out, the relaxation training that has become second nature to behavior therapists, and that has come to play such an important role in behavioral medicine, is quite different from the lengthy and complex method described by Jacobson. Ironically then, we note a comprehensive review of the literature on relaxation training this past year by Lehrer (1982) in *Behaviour Research and Therapy* in which he reaches the following conclusion: "I think that it is time for us to reread Jacobson's work. When reduction of physiological arousal is therapeutically important, we might well be advised to return to studying and using the method in the manner that Jacobson intended it to be done" (p. 425).

O. Hobart Mowrer died in June 1982. Among his many accomplishments during a brilliant academic career, Mowrer emerged as one of the genuine innovators and leaders of the field of learning theory. By extension, his theoretical contributions to behavior therapy have been seminal. Especially for those of us involved in research on fear and fear reduction techniques, it is impossible to conceive of behavioral treatment methods without his renowned two-factor theory of fear and avoidance behavior. Planned exposure and response prevention, which today are generally accepted as the preferred and usually effective means of treating phobic and obsessive–compulsive disorders, derived directly from Mowrer's theory—a stunning achievement. Although two-factor theory is currently the focus of criticism as an adequate explanation of the demonstrably successful techniques to which it gave birth, as described in Chapters 3 of this and last year's volume of the *Annual Review*, it still has its prominent proponents and is still "the theory to improve upon." And finally, the lives of countless children and families have been immeasurably enhanced by Mowrer's imaginative development (with his wife) of a safe, simple, and successful method for curing enuresis—the famous bell-and-pad device. It is an extraordinary tribute to Mowrer that we can say that he lastingly changed the nature of theory, research, and practice in experimental clinical psychology.

By way of acknowledgments, GTW is indebted to Barbara Honig of the Rutgers Alcohol Behavior Research Laboratory for her unstinting help in typing his chapters in this volume. Preparation of these chapters was made possible, in part, by National Institute of Alcohol Abuse and Alcoholism Grant AA00259-13. CMF thanks Alleen Pusey and Carol Martin of the Carrier Foundation for their tireless efforts in typing his two chapters in this volume. KDB is grateful to Patricia Mitchell of the University of Pennsylvania for her secretarial help. Preparation of his chapters was supported by Research Scientist Development Award #MH00319 from the National Institute of Mental Health. PCK acknowledges the secretarial staff of the Department of Psychology, University of Minnesota, for their cooperative spirit and willingness to adjust to shifting priorities and deadlines. Preparation of his chapters was supported by a grant from the National Institute of Mental Health.

As always, we are especially grateful to our wives, Elaine, Violet, Mary Jo, and Sue, for their support and encouragement in the writing of this volume.

G. Terence Wilson
Cyril M. Franks
Kelly D. Brownell
Philip C. Kendall

CONTENTS

   PRACTICE OF BEHAVIOR THERAPY   309
   G. TERENCE WILSON
     Surveys of Trends in the Practice of
       Behavior Therapy   309
     Professional Issues: Models of Training, Delivery of Services,
       and the Peer Review Process   312
     Applying What We Know and Knowing How to Do This   324
     Clinical Issues   328

     References   345
     Author Index   407
     Subject Index   423

CHAPTER

1

BEHAVIOR THERAPY: AN OVERVIEW

CYRIL M. FRANKS

INTRODUCTION

Behavior therapists typically question their identity, conduct surveys, review the literature, and engage in ceaseless soul searching (if readers will pardon the expression). This year's crop of articles provides many opinions and much data but little that can be construed as even a minor breakthrough.

It is easy, if no longer valid, to criticize behavior therapy as being manipulative, limited, mechanistic, and dehumanizing. Unfortunately, such arguments tend to obscure more serious issues. For example, many behavior therapists are confused about values, we have not yet developed a viable philosophy of man, and there now is a danger of losing our identity as we strive to expand our domain (Franks, 1981; Kazdin & Hersen, 1980; Woolfolk & Richardson, 1981).

In 1971, Krasner identified some 15 diverse streams within psychology and related disciplines that cohered during the 1950s and 1960s to form the approach generally known as behavior therapy. (See Franks, 1983, for a more detailed appraisal of these streams in the light of contemporary developments. If behavior therapy was diverse then, it is hardly surprising that the "promiscuous expansionism" of the late 1970s and early 1980s results now in even greater diffusion and existential concerns about a fading identity.)

Farkas (1981) also traces the early development of behavior therapy and relates it to the pluralistic models that now prevail. The broad cohesiveness of our formative years, argues Farkas, has outlived its purpose. According to Farkas, the drive toward preservation of the

1

label "behavior therapy," "which is more symbol than substance," is maintained by such powerful motivating forces as the prestige more easily achieved by recognition within a delimited reference group; the inertia and resistance to change that characterize most organizations and individuals; the material rewards that are more likely to be generated within an identifiable and homogeneous market; and the greater opportunities to influence both policy and people within a structured group.

At a more sanguine level, Matarazzo (1980, 1982) implicitly propels behavior therapy into the age of behavioral health rather than the by now more customary behavioral medicine. As Evans (1982) points out, far from devoting its sophisticated methodological heritage to meaningful socioeconomic issues, behavioral medicine seems determined to ape such detrimental features of modern medicine as iatrogenic screening programs and the symptomatic management of stress. Matarazzo's call for a behavior therapy of health rather than of medicine is courageous, timely, and refreshing. These developments are also reflected in the policies and promised contents of two new journals: the *International Journal of Behavioural Social Work and Abstracts* and the *International Journal of Behavioral Geriatrics*.

Another interesting development is the abandonment of reductionism within behavior therapy. Peele (1981) draws attention to the seductive appeal of behavioral reductionism—the notion that human behavior can be meaningfully ordered into its biological components. Any psychological intervention that fails to take account of such individualized determinants as personality structure, subjective needs, and situational and cultural variables is probably incomplete. In its formative years, behavior therapy, with its understandably simplistic emphasis on S-R learning theory, fell into this category. If anything characterizes behavior therapy of the 1980s, it is the recognition of the complex and subtle elements that determine our behavioral future (Michelson, Hersen, & Turner, 1981b).

This is not to say that, as certain critics (e.g., Marks, 1981c) suggest, conditioning has had its day. On February 26, 1980, Horsley Gantt died at the age of 87. The writings of Gantt are rarely cited in the behavior therapy literature these days. For many individuals, usually young practitioners rather than aging scholars, the stimulus "Gantt" evokes either historical interest or, regrettably, no response at all. For those of us who were in at the start, so to speak, Gantt was the pioneer of conditioning who translated Pavlov's works into English, laid the foundations of behavioral psychopharmacology, developed numerous clinically useful conditioning procedures, and urged the return to experimental tradition in the field of mental health (Franks, in press; Reese, 1982). We honor his memory.

These accolades notwithstanding, conditioning alone is no longer an adequate conceptual basis for behavior therapy (Wilson, 1982d). But it is premature to throw out the proverbial baby with the bath water. As Wolpe (1982) notes, the relevance of genetic, biological, cognitive, and environmental variables merely delimits the occurrence of conditioning; it does not contradict it. Even more to the point, conditioning is still alive and vital. Each year issues formerly believed to be settled are reexamined as new data emerge. For example, with the notable exception of Razran (1956), it was generally accepted as axiomatic that backward conditioning does not occur. There is now mounting evidence to suggest that this conclusion is premature and that backward conditioning, in which the onset of the CS follows that of the US, is an experimentally and clinically meaningful concept and not a matter of pseudoconditioning, as was the prevailing belief until very recently (Spetch, Wilkie, & Pinel, 1981).

If one had to single out one review article for 1982, it would probably be Kazdin's (1982e) "The Token Economy: A Decade Later." In 1972, Kazdin and Bootzin identified certain key obstacles to the effective application of token economies and suggested possible research strategies for enhancing program efficacy, training staff, overcoming client resistance, and promoting long-term maintenance and transfer of behavior. Kazdin's 1982 update pinpoints advances toward these goals. The major thrust seems to be toward the incorporation of societal parameters into the overall model. In this context, Fawcett, Matthews, and Fletcher's (1980b) notion of an "appropriate technology" compatible with the context, resources, philosophy, and values of the settings in which a procedure is to be used is of significance.

It is with such perspectives in mind that I turn to a brief discussion of the topic areas reviewed last year. It will be noticed that although, in the main, we follow similar headings in this volume, there are certain exceptions. For example, this year there is no specific discussion of black psychology. The clarion call of Hayes in 1972 for a radical black behaviorism is still not echoed by a peal of data, and until this happens there is little to comment upon.

Similarly, last year we noted the role of cognition in behavior therapy and the movement toward an integration of behavior therapy and psychodynamics. Interim developments, or lack thereof, to be more precise, no longer warrant such a section. While behavior therapists continue to debate the nature of cognition and the role of free will, the literature continues to remain long on speculation and understandably short on data. Despite Royce's (1982) call for action, it is difficult to see how a problem that is ultimately philosophical can ever be resolved by experiment. What we can do is clarify our thinking about these matters and abandon the simplistic conceptions of cognition that still prevail.

Increasingly, informed and thoughtful behavior therapists are abandoning the mechanistic assumption that cognitions are the lineal causal antecedents of other psychological phenomena (e.g., Coyne, 1982).

This unavoidable lack of philosophic closure is particularly frustrating for those who take time to consider the implications of Bandura's (1982) fashionable reciprocal determinism (Franks & Barbrack, 1983; F. C. Richardson, 1981). In trying to encompass free will and determinism at one and the same time, the social learning theorist is trying to eat his or her cake and have it too. Individuals are free, at least to some degree, to control their own behaviors; yet at the same time environmental events can reciprocally influence human actions. How this comes about is not clear. It could be that the role of reciprocal determinism is to create an illusion of free will, whatever this is.

Other individuals propose different solutions. For Grossberg (1981), there is no problem at all other than a verbal failure to communicate. Lieberman (1979) advocates a partial return to introspection in the study of self-control, and others (e.g., Moore, 1980; Zettle & Hayes, 1983) argue for a radical behaviorism that includes private events. Levey and Martin (in press) propose a partial resolution in which two innate mechanisms related to adaptive behavior coexist, with neither "superior" to the other. In a sense, all of these researchers seem to be trying to eat their philosophic cake and have it, too.

In 1973, Morgan and Bass reported that there was no good evidence in favor of self-reinforcement. A decade later, Sohn and Lamal (1982) reviewed the subsequent literature and came to the same conclusion. They find no reason to believe that an organism can freely and with full volition exercise control over any situation without evoking some form of external contingency. If self-reinforcement is an illusion, then therapy predicated upon this illusory notion, if it works at all, does so for reasons other than those generally posited (Franks & Wilson, 1977b, p. 93ff.; see also Kanfer & Karoly, 1982; Nelson & Hayes, 1981; and Rachlin, 1974, for further discussion of these matters).

The rest of this chapter should be read with these introductory observations in mind.

THE RELATIONSHIP BETWEEN RESEARCH
AND CLINICAL PRACTICE IN BEHAVIOR THERAPY

Last year I drew attention to the burgeoning gap between fundamental research and technological application in behavior therapy. Paralleling this gap, there is a gulf between what clinicians say they know and believe, on the one hand, and what they actually do, on the other. Regrettably, the naive expectations for behavior therapy generated in its formative years have been only partially realized. Clinical research seems to have little influence on clinical practice.

It may be, as Raush pointed out as long ago as 1974, that the lack of accord between research and practice is due primarily to the failure of these research methods to meet the clinical needs of the practitioner. Foremost among these limitations are the practical difficulties of conducting meaningful clinical research using traditional experimental between-group and within-group methodology. Either inappropriate analogue studies have to be employed or inadequately matched groups have to be utilized. Another problem to which Barlow (1981a) draws attention is the continued reliance on theoretically meaningful but clinically naive statistical tests and measures of significance by authors of basic texts. No wonder then that practicing clinicians have learned to disregard statistical significance, since it says little about clinical improvement in real-life situations. The goal of the clinician is and should be to get specific clients better as quickly as possible, whereas in research this does not necessarily apply. Procedures that produce some change on the average are not necessarily clinically meaningful or appropriate for application to the individual client. Experimental validation without social validation is of limited utility.

Most clinicians seem to acquire their techniques by watching trained therapists. But there is also what Barlow (1981a), modeling himself after Cronbach (1975), calls "intensive local observation applied to clinical investigation." In addition to the more customary methodological criteria, this entails careful attention to uncontrolled conditions, personal characteristics, and unexpected events that occur during the assessment or intervention process. The exception is taken as seriously as the rule, a method that directs attention to clinical successes and failures unique to a particular locale, rather than to statistical significance.

Such an approach, argues Barlow, points the way to a meaningful role for the practicing clinician that would provide data missing from traditional clinical research. Inferential statistics derived from large-scale studies would establish higher-order interactions; procedures developed in clinical research could then become the domain of the clinician. Clinicians should not be expected to carry out the complex and costly manipulations involved in the more formal research design (see also Kazdin, 1981b; Nelson, 1981).

Possibly unrealistically, Barlow envisions clinicians collecting data on hundreds of thousands of cases over the years, noting both improvements and failures, and feeding back this information to large clinical research centers for investigation of specific hypotheses under more systematic conditions. As Barlow wisely cautions, this would require a major reevaluation of training programs to include more empirical approaches to clinical practice and the creative use of case studies, single experimental designs, and time series methodology (Hayes, 1981). How realistic this proposal is, how it is to be implemented, and whether it will close the scientist–practitioner and theory–application gaps remain questions that can only be answered in the future. A "two-way street" between laboratory and clinic (Woolfolk & Lazarus, 1979) is easier argued for than realized.

To see if behavior therapy, presumably devoted to methodological rigor, had indeed conformed to the expectations of an earlier era, Agras and Berkowitz (1980) examined a randomly chosen sample of articles from behavior therapy journals and compared their findings with those derived from an earlier examination of two research-oriented medical journals (Fletcher & Fletcher, 1979). With one notable exception, behavior therapy fares well; behavior therapists consistently employ far better designs. But the exception is major: a mean of 26 weeks of follow-up for medicine and 4 weeks for behavior therapy.

A second and closely related study reported in the same article is likewise encouraging. Behavior therapy researchers are increasingly concerned with significant clinical problems and research is continually expanding to consider new problems. Nevertheless, emphasis is still placed on issues surrounding immediate outcome, and there is a paucity of studies devoted to generalization, maintenance, follow-up, dissemination of results to the practicing clinician, and examination of the effectiveness of therapy in actual clinical practice. By these standards, Agras and Berkowitz reluctantly conclude that "the field is indeed only halfway there."

If the problem is in part attributable to the rapid development of behavior therapy, there are a variety of other fairly obvious contributing factors that militate against long-term research, such as the academic need to publish and the restrictions imposed by limited financial resources. When Kendall and Ford (1979) asked a representative sample of contributors to the *Journal of Consulting and Clinical Psychology* to report on their motivations for conducting studies that had been published in that journal, the results indicated that

> the primary motivation of these clinical researchers was to build on prior theory and research through the gathering and analysis of new data to answer socially significant applied-clinical questions. More immediate pragmatic considerations (e.g., tenure, funding, degree or job requirements, and availability of subjects) were reported to be of secondary, but nevertheless significant, importance. (p. 99)

What Kendall and Ford do not tell us is the relationship between these noble motivations as reported and what was really going on in the respondents' minds.

A number of surveys report discrepancies between behavior therapy as represented in research and behavior therapy as practiced (e.g., Ford & Kendall, 1979b; Swan & MacDonald, 1978). The gap between theoretical guidelines and practical implementations is great (Ford & Kendall, 1979a). More recently, Kendall, Plous, and Kratochwill (1981b) surveyed a decade of research comprising 1000 investigators publishing in four leading behavior therapy journals to determine the motivations for clinical research. Bearing in mind the bias of self-report, the declared reasons for research paralleled those noted above. Answering clinical questions, working on problems posed in the literature, and studying new treatment procedures emerged as central. Reputation was not a high priority in the reported motivations.

This section is concluded with a brief discussion of an important issue raised by Samelson (1980). In an earlier volume I commented briefly upon Harris's (1979) discussion of Watson's classic "Little Albert" experiment on conditioned fear responses and its subsequent fate in the psychological literature. Samelson now provides some additional historical information needed to put this classic study into perspective and links it with the celebrated twin studies of Burt (e.g., 1958, 1966, 1972) in order to raise some cogent questions about the status and treatment of such articles in the social process of psychology as a science.

In 1940, Hilgard and Marquis concluded that subsequent investigators had been unsuccessful in duplicating the Watson study. But nevertheless, as both Harris and Samelson note, the lesson was apparently lost on the writers of the assorted textbooks that followed. Watson's study could not have become enshrined as the paradigm for human conditioning on the basis of a hard look at the evidence. The extraordinary appeal of Little Albert, argues Samelson, must have come from the fact that it was "a beautiful illustration of an idea already congenial to its audience."

At a different level, Samelson draws attention to the unreliability of secondary sources, the problematic nature of some primary sources, and the occasional uncritical reading of all of these resources. As Samelson points out, it is simply not good enough to put the blame on human weaknesses—to call Watson a propagandist rather than a scientist and Burt deliberately dishonest in defense of his strong convictions. Why were so many of us so willing to give these data an evidentiary status they did not deserve? It is easier to pose such questions than to answer them, but answer them we must.

THE IMAGE OF BEHAVIOR THERAPY

Each year we consistently report an association by the general public, and even certain professionals, between behavior therapy and negative adjectives such as "inhuman," "mechanistic," and "simplistic." So-called solutions have ranged from rejection of these "false" images (e.g., Wolpe, 1981a), through improvement of public relations (e.g., Turkat, 1979), to the provision of more informative behavioral education for beginning psychology students (e.g., Knapp & Delprato, 1980). This year has seen the customary spate of minor surveys and inconsequential proposals for remediation, but little that can be construed as constructive implementation.

The weakest study of the year is probably that of Gochman, Allgood, and Geer (1982), who base their conclusions on an analysis of 45 questionnaires completed by members of the Association for Advancement of Behavior Therapy (AABT). Presumably to make their results appear more impressive, they use percentages in their categorical breakdowns. Most of their respondents report themselves as eclectic, rational–emotive, or cognitive–behavioral rather than strictly behavioral. The authors also note that "most have not had personal therapy." What Gochman et al. infer from this is uncertain. A possible clue may be gleaned from their conclusion that "behavior therapists are apparently become more flexible in their attitudes . . . and use a variety of behavioral techniques." I suspect that these authors differ radically from the authors of this volume with respect to the nature of behavior therapy (see Chapter 8).

Previous research suggests that the label "behavior therapy" in itself leads to less favorable lay perceptions (e.g., Woolfolk, Woolfolk, & Wilson, 1977) and that the public finds psychoanalytic and client-centered conceptualizations less "scientific" but nevertheless more attractive (e.g., Fancher & Gutkin, 1971). These impressions notwithstanding, there is reason to believe that in reality behavior therapists display at least as much concern, interpersonal contact, and empathy as other clinicians (e.g., McGovern, Fernald, & Calhoun, 1980). Unfortunately, many mental health professionals think otherwise and, by implication, psychiatrists sometimes relate these misperceptions to their notions about the role of psychologists. For example, when approximately one-half of all psychiatric residents in Canada were surveyed, some 40% felt that psychologists were primarily helpful in cases involving the use of behavior therapy, reflecting preconceived stereotypes about both psychologists and behavior therapy.

Turkat, Harris, and Forehand's (1979) examination of the perceptions of college students led to the conclusion that behavior modification is viewed neither as threatening nor as good. But they failed to demonstrate that the students' definitions of behavior modification were similar to those of the investigators. No distinction was made between behavior modification and psychological therapies in general. Thus it is unclear whether disagreement with the use of behavior modification to change a specific problem such as homosexuality reflected rejection of behavior therapy per se or a belief in the inappropriateness of changing homosexual behavior on any account.

Noting these limitations, Young and Patterson (1981) examined 475 undergraduates and 49 nonpsychology faculty members at the University of Mississippi. In marked contrast to the results of Turkat *et al.*, their respondents generally accepted behavior modification as applicable to virtually all problems evaluated. Nevertheless, Young and Patterson draw cold comfort from these findings. A substantial proportion of their respondents misidentified such procedures as brainwashing, electroconvulsive therapy, and mind control drugs as behavior modification. Only 11% recognized time out as behavior modification, and less than one-third successfully identified systematic desensitization as falling into this category. Between one-third and one-half of all students believed behavior modification to be unethical and dehumanizing.

Even if little is done about it, concern continues to be expressed about negative connotations and misuse of the term "behavior modification" (e.g., Barling, 1979; Turkat & Forehand, 1980). Studies such as that of Woolfolk *et al.* (1977) and replications demonstrating the negative connotations evoked by behavior modification (e.g., Barling & Wainstein, 1979; Woolfolk & Woolfolk, 1979) are interpreted as evidence of labeling bias against behavior modification. A labeling bias may well exist, but, as Kazdin and Cole (1981) point out, this cannot be inferred from the investigations cited above. It could be the content of the procedures and the manner in which this content is presented rather than the label per se that accounts for the negative evaluation. Most of the previous research in this area confounds the effects of label, content, and language used to describe the content.

Three experiments specifically designed to resolve these confounds led Kazdin and Cole to the conclusion that the content of the teaching method consistently contributed to the evaluation of the procedure. Behavior modification was evaluated negatively when compared to humanistic and neutral procedures, but these evaluations were not influenced by the presence or absence of the label "behavior modification." Not altogether surprisingly, procedures were rated more favorably if they were described in jargon. Students seem to be the same the world over. It may be that relabeling is not sufficient and that alternative strategies need to be considered. At this stage, we can hazard only the vaguest of guesses as to their nature.

ETHICS, GUIDELINES, AND VALUE SYSTEMS
IN BEHAVIOR THERAPY

Last year the focus was on guidelines. This year I look at some of the ethical and philosophical implications underlying these guidelines. One solution is to avoid the issue altogether and focus on pragmatics. For example, Knight's (1981) no-nonsense guiding precepts (he calls them "moral insights") range from homilies about treating individuals as persons, and as ends in themselves, through the law of reciprocity (do unto others . . .), to favoring the individual over the collective and preserving the "fidelity of the covenant" in the doctor–patient relationship. Curl (1982) likewise arrives at a list of down-to-earth procedures, considerations, and principles to be applied in given situations. Unfortunately, disregard of philosophical and ethical belief systems does not necessarily lead to relevant guidelines for action (McCann, 1982).

Behavior therapists who are ethical relativists argue that value judgments are relative to individuals and their cultures. Ethical skepticism, a closely related position, is the view that it is not possible to decide objectively which value is better than another. Either way, behavior therapists make value judgments and, for consistency of action, they should be able to justify them (Kitchener, 1979). Our own position has been by no means static in these respects. For example, in 1973 we maintained that behavior therapy is a conceptual system that is independent of ethics (Franks & Wilson, 1973). In 1975, we stated that "refuge may no longer be taken in the cliché that the technology of behavior modification is ethically neutral" (Franks & Wilson, 1975). With Kitchener, I now conclude that, whether we like it or not, it is desirable to make and justify value judgments. As Kitchener repeatedly observes, behavior therapists can give up ethical relativism only if they also abandon certain other cherished views: for example, that values are no more than positive reinforcers, that values are individual subjective preferences, and that value judgments need not and cannot be rightly defended. This of course is but one of several defensible positions. In his effective reply to critics such as Ward (1980), Kitchener (1980b) seems to imply that there is some kind of official directive or approved philosophical policy for behavior therapists. Would that this were so: It would make the writing of these chronicles much easier!

Tymchuk (1981) draws attention to the lag between the rise of new techniques and the development of guidelines for their application. In the absence of such guidelines, there is a possibility of abrogation of the rights of individuals or groups. Lacking explicit guidelines, psychologists resort to whatever value systems, ethical statements, laws, and research findings are available. Although all of these are useful under certain circumstances, each has shortcomings. For example, the

AABT (1977) guidelines presuppose the acceptance of certain specific behavioral tenets. Other guidelines are functions of the prevailing economic system (that the interests of the individual are going to take precedence over fees under the system prevailing in the United States is most unlikely). Instead of specific guidelines for ethical behavior, Tymchuk opts for the development of a decision-making model that would allow for systematic examination of relevant influences.

Finally, but with no sense of closure, I note the need to distinguish carefully between ethical and legal imperatives. Coming at times from different models of humankind, the two do not necessarily have to be in accord (Farkas, 1980, 1981). For example, the most effective therapy can be at variance with the least restrictive alternative. Effective therapy may involve the contingent application of primary reinforcers that are legally provided for only on a noncontingent basis. In an age of accountability, behavior therapists can conscientiously avoid neither their legal nor ethical obligations, nor, in the long run, the philosophical implications of their decisions (Sheldon-Wildgen, 1982).

PROFESSIONAL TRAINING IN BEHAVIOR THERAPY

In 1977 Marzillier found that only 2% of recently trained British clinical psychologists had failed to obtain training in behavior therapy, as contrasted with over 30% of those trained 10 or more years earlier. Of those respondents who qualified more than 10 years ago, 77% reported their training in behavior therapy to be highly inadequate as contrasted with only 30% of those trained within the 2 years preceding the study. In this country, Wolpe continues to lament the fact (as he sees it) that few behavior therapists have received "adequate supervised training" (Wolpe, 1981b). The problem is that not everyone would agree with Wolpe's criteria for adequacy.

Adequacy of training in behavior therapy implies a data-oriented, research-awareness base—an obligation violated more than observed (Barlow, 1980). For the most part, behavior therapists are no more inclined to integrate research, even clinical research, into their practices than are their nonbehavioral confreres. As possible alternatives to the clearly inadequate scientist-practitioner model, it has been suggested that professionals be trained to understand the workings of science and become consumers of research rather than researchers per se (e.g., Peterson, 1976).

Some 67% of APA-approved clinical psychology programs now offer training in ethics, as contrasted with 9% 25 years ago (Tymchuk, Drapkin, Ackerman, Major, Coffman, & Baum, 1979). When Tymchuk, Drapkin, Major-Kingsley, Ackerman, Coffman, and Baum (1982) surveyed a large random sample of members of the APA Division of Clinical Psychology, some 89% felt that training in ethics should be required of all psychology graduate students. What there was far less consensus about was the content of this training.

To have training conducted by trained peers rather than by outside consultants (pyramid training) is cost effective and potentially thera-peutic for trainer and trainee alike. Furthermore, the ready availability of the peer facilitates maintenance of the newly acquired skills (Black, Keane, Garvin, Gross, & Richter, 1980). Pyramid training seems particu-larly appropriate for institutions (Page, Iwata, & Reid, 1982), and it is too bad that research in this area has been neglected to date.

For Bernstein (1982), effective training rests upon an interactive and functional ecobehavioral framework. The traditional triadic model of service provision involves a consultant, defined as anyone with pertinent knowledge; a mediator, defined as anyone who offers rein-forcers to the target; and the target, or client, defined as anyone whose behavior the consultant agrees to have modified. According to Bernstein, the interactive model featured in Figure 1-1 accurately describes current approaches to behavioral services. In this model, the client is anyone whose behavior the behavior engineer agrees to modify, the behavior manager is anyone who implements agreed-upon change procedures, the behavior engineer is anyone who designs and adjusts the change procedures, and the consultant is the troubleshooter and resource pro-vider who assists the behavior engineer with program design and the behavior manager with program implementation. These positions, it should be noted, describe functions rather than people or professions.

FIG. 1-1.

An interactive model of behavioral service delivery. (From "Training Behavior Change Agents: A Conceptual Review" by G. S. Bernstein, *Behavior Therapy*, 1982, *13*, 1–23. Copyright 1982, Association for Advancement of Behavior Therapy. Reprinted by permission.)

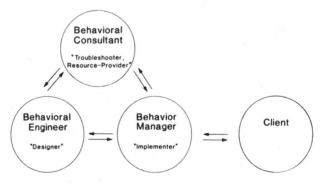

Much of the recent behavioral training literature pertains to the training of those who are not primarily behavior therapists in their role identifications. In the United Kingdom alone, there are at least three behavior therapy training courses for nurses (Feldman, 1980). Bird, Marks, and Lindley (1979) offer a detailed review of these developments, the controversies generated, and their implications. Hafner, Hatton, and Larkin (1981) draw attention to what they view as a fundamental deficiency of such programs: the tendency to reduce therapy to a series of behavioral techniques. Unfortunately, their systems-based remedy offers a promise but little more. Only 12 patients, few or no objective measures, the absence of any form of control group, and follow-up restricted to 1 month are not calculated to inspire confidence in any study!

While behavior therapy is the preferred orientation of approximately one-third of all social workers in this country (Jayaratne, 1978) and training in behavior therapy is now a focus part of many social work programs (Thyer & Bronson, 1981), evaluation of this training is rare and lacking in rigor (e.g.,, McAuley, 1981). With the notable exception of the Draper Correctional Center, a maximum security state institution located in Alabama and the setting for an impressive series of studies in behavioral training over the years (Smith, Milan, Wood, & McKee, 1976), the behavioral training of correction officers fares little better. To increase effectiveness, behavior therapy is being taught to probation officers working with juvenile delinquents. But here too, with one or two exceptions (e.g., Wood, Green, & Bry, 1982), the field is characterized by programs based on impressions rather than data.

Prior to the mid-1960s, institutional in-service staff training programs were the exception rather than the rule. As service delivery systems shifted emphasis from custody to habilation and rehabilitation, administrators became faced with the need to deliver these services in a cost-effective fashion. It became apparent that this was more likely to be achieved if direct-care staff could be trained to provide a substantial proportion of the habilitation process. As yet, the evidence with respect to the efficacy of these programs remains inconclusive (Ziarnik & Bernstein, in press). Relatively little is known about what programs to apply under what circumstances, what skills are most amenable to training, and what are the most useful ingredients in such programs. In-service and preservice training need to be coordinated. In this respect, those responsible for preservice training programs would be well to examine with care the social validation model developed by Marchetti, Rusch, and Lamson (1981). (See also L. M. Miller, 1978, for a discussion of performance expectations in training, and Mealies & Duffy, 1980, for additional discussion of pitfalls in training.)

Finally, we draw attention to the behavioral training of paraprofessionals. Behavior therapists were among the first to employ nonprofessionals and paraprofessionals as therapeutic agents. The training of
nonprofessional behavior therapists is beginning to emerge as an area
of specialization based upon a psychosocial rather than a medical
model (Jeger & McClure, 1980). Paraprofessionals can be as effective as
professionals in bringing about therapeutic change in numerous clinical problems (Durlak, 1979), and psychology undergraduates can be
successfully trained in community-oriented intervention (Jason, 1981b).
So far, most of these demonstrations are small scale and somewhat
contrived in their structure.

COMPLIANCE AND NONCOMPLIANCE

This is the first year that compliance has been singled out for review in
this chapter (see Chapters 7 and 8 as well). Compliance and noncompliance seem to be in behavioral vogue. At least three very good
books (DiMatteo & DiNicola, 1982; Haynes, Taylor, & Sackett, 1979;
Shelton & Levy, 1981a) and one indifferent book (Withersty, 1980) deal
exclusively with this topic. The Withersty text is primarily a poor
compilation of second-hand impressions.

A plethora of definitions can be found in the literature. As yet,
there is little agreement with respect to what should or should not be
included under the rubric of compliance and noncompliance. For
example, compliance might be restricted to specific medical problems
or might include failure to obey regulations such as those pertaining to
seat-belt buckling or smoking. There are at least three divergent models
of compliance in current usage. Learning theorists assume that the
determinants of compliance are sets of antecedents and consequences
surrounding the classes of behavior that the clinician would call compliance or noncompliance. Others hold tendentiously to quite different
models. Few have the benefit of substantiating data.

The ethics of compliance are equally debatable, and a variety of
fundamental issues await clarification. For example, does compliance
reflect an overly authoritative approach to patient care and thereby
imply a questionable obligation for the patient to follow orders blindly
(DiMatteo & Friedman, 1982)? And what of the impoverished elderly
who spend much money on health care, often with little benefit and
sometimes with considerable detriment? How desirable is compliance
when there is little evidence for the necessity for this activity (Chillag,
1980)? An individual has the right to refuse treatment in all but a few
legally defined situations (see Haynes et al., 1979).

Solutions to specific problems must take into account these under-lying complexities (e.g., Gunter-Hunt, Ferguson, & Bole, 1982). Com-pliance and noncompliance may be more than mirror images of each other (Tryon, 1981). Much clearer outcome studies might result if subjects were to be divided into those who complied and those who did not. Ensuring that the independent variable or treatment is applied consistently is known as procedural reliability (Billingsley, White, & Munson, 1980). The relationship of procedural reliability to treatment compliance is just beginning to be studied (Johnson, Wildman, & O'Brien, 1980).

Do professionals consistently comply with treatment regulations? In one study, cited by Ley (1981), 54 out of 64 qualified psychologists made major errors, frequently basic ones, in the scoring of submitted test protocols. In other studies, 10% of pharmacists made serious mis-takes in writing down directions for use as recommended by the physi-cian, 21% of pediatricians and 76% of general physicians were found not to use antibiotics properly, and 21 out of 22 nurses would have given patients twice the stated maximum permissible daily doses of medicines in response to a telephone request alone. As Ley temperately concludes from his careful survey of some 17 studies of compliance and non-compliance, there is cause for concern.

There are few systematic studies of the roles of memory and under-standing in compliance. According to Ley (1979), failure to recall medical advice is a complex function of the amount of advice pre-sented, the patient's medical knowledge, anxiety, and possibly of age level, but not of intelligence. It might be expected that better informa-tion would facilitate comprehension and thereby lead to increased patient satisfaction, but support from the experimental literature is not as strong as correlational surveys indicate (Ley, 1980a). Increased com-prehension usually but not invariably leads to increased satisfaction (Ley, 1980b, 1982).

Predicting noncompliance is rarely possible. All that can be done, given the present lack of knowledge and closure, is to focus upon specific determinants relevant to a particular setting. For example, Demetral, Gipson, Irvin, Anderson, and Catania (1981) systematically compared the compliance consequences of a special unit-dosage pack-aging system and verbal reinforcement in chronic psychiatric out-patients who required medication.

Shelton and Levy (1981a) make the possibly premature assump-tion that there are three reasons for failure to comply with instructions: lack of necessary skills or knowledge, cognitions that interfere with completion of the assignment, and a restrictive environment. Based on these assumptions, the following 11 recommendations are offered to the therapist to help ensure maximum compliance:

1. Be sure assignments contain specific detail regarding response and stimulus elements relevant to the desired behavior.
2. Give direct skill training when necessary.
3. Reinforce compliance.
4. Begin with small homework requests and gradually increase assignments.
5. Use cueing.
6. Have the client make a public commitment to comply.
7. Help the client develop a private commitment to comply.
8. Use cognitive rehearsal strategies to improve successful assignments.
9. Try to anticipate and reduce the negative effects of compliance.
10. Closely monitor compliance with as many sources as possible.
11. Use paradoxical strategies when necessary.

FROM INSTITUTION TO DEINSTITUTIONALIZATION

Chronic wards are still characterized by lack of stimulation and widespread apathy on the part of patients and staff members alike. Traditional approaches such as milieu and occupational therapy have made little headway. Token economies and social-skills training remain the mainstay of what behavior therapy has to offer the institutionalized patient (Kazdin, 1982e).

According to Fraser (1983), it cannot necessarily be assumed that a specific token contingency is the main factor in changing behavior in any particular token economy setting. Target behaviors seem to show most changes when instructions are combined with prompting and verbal reinforcement delivered by the nursing staff. It may well be that the token economy achieves its effects primarily through the elaborate social information system that is involved in its application and that conditioning theory as such is of relatively little significance.

The need to adapt to different environments, even within the same institution, may also produce complex and little understood changes in the overall situation, sometimes for better and sometimes for worse. For example, Spreat and Isett (1981) examined the developmental progress of 49 institutionalized mentally retarded persons who had been recently transferred to different cottages, as contrasted with progress achieved by a matched group of 49 residents who had not been moved. At least temporarily, the nontransferred group gained, whereas the transferred group regressed.

Despite a spate of recent reviews (e.g., Cipani, 1982; Curran & Monti, 1982; Grantham & Joslyn, 1981; Hersen, 1979; McFall, 1982;

Michelson & Wood, 1980; Wallace, Nelson, Liberman, Aitchison, Lukoff, Elder, & Ferris, 1980), there is still little agreement as to what constitutes social skills. Curran, Wessberg, Farrell, Monti, Corriveau, and Coyne (1982) come to the conclusion from their well-designed study that different researchers are indeed measuring different constructs. No wonder, then, that a large number of people are carrying out social skills training without clear notions as to what it is that they are training or even how to measure it (Curran & Mariotto, 1980). Operational definitions vary in their emphasis upon the inclusion of specific outcome, content, and process variables. Current behavioral models range from exclusive reliance upon observable variables (e.g., Bellack, Hersen, & Lamparski, 1979) to complex mediational models based on social learning theory (e.g., Galassi & Galassi, 1978). Most current models focus on the individual, but others (e.g., Strain & Fox, 1981b) emphasize an entire social system in describing social-skills functions.

If there is little consensus with respect to definition and model, there is even less when it comes to assessment. Empirical answers are needed to questions concerning situation, sex, age, person, and other variables of relevance to the acquisition of social skills (see Greenwood, Walker, Todd, & Hops, 1981; La Greca, 1981; Trower, 1980).

Despite the effectiveness of social-skills training in changing topographical features within the institution and reducing self-reports of anxiety, these changes rarely result in substantial differences in the quality of life (Wallace et al., 1980). The technology is promising, but it must be expanded to include as "social skills" clinically meaningful behavior applicable across a wide range of interpersonal interactions (Authier, Gustafson, Fix, & Daughton, 1981).

If the goal is successful adjustment in the community, then more attention needs to be given to socially appropriate skills and their maintenance outside the institution (P. Brown, 1980; Matson, Zeiss, Zeiss, & Bowman, 1980). In 1977, Lehrer and Lanoil developed a program to maintain involvement in the transition from institution to community. They described a setting, called "The Club," that concentrated on natural or intrinsic reinforcers. Programs were designed to avoid any opportunity for failure, and there was no time requirement or limitation for participation. Natural consequences (e.g., attention, recognition, and status) were used to motivate attendance and participation in prevocational activities.

When C. A. Kiesler (1982) reviewed ten studies of psychiatric patients randomly assigned either to inpatient or some alternative mode of outpatient care, in no instance was the outcome of hospitalization more positive than alternative treatment. Typically, the alternative care was more effective with respect to psychiatric evaluation, probability of eventual employment, independent living arrangements, staying in school, and direct costs. But despite a national policy of deinstitutionalization, Kiesler concludes that the episodic rate of hospitalizing mental patients has increased in the last 20 years, a finding that Kiesler simplistically interprets as evidence of the self-perpetuating of hospitalization in mental patients. In seeming contrast, Dellario and Anthony (1981) conclude from their review that there is little appreciable difference between subjects treated in institutions and those treated in community-based alternatives. The *where* of service delivery may be of less importance than the *what* and *how*. What is needed are systematic studies of the comparative effects of institutionalization and alternative modes of care.

An adequate study should possess certain methodological characteristics: First, all participants should be judged as seriously disturbed, so that hospitalization would be the normal modal treatment. Second, there should be random assignment to conditions of treatment, including some patients admitted by chance to the hospital with others assigned to some alternative treatment mode, even if only an untreated condition. Third, the characteristics of the patient population and the details of professional treatment should be specified (C. A. Kiesler, 1982).

Social costs should be at least as important as economic considerations. As part of a series of controlled comparisons of community living programs and short-term hospitalization plus aftercare, Stein and Test examined the social costs of alternatives to hospitalization (Stein & Test, 1980; Test & Stein, 1980; Weisbrod, Test, & Stein, 1980). While the specific details of their findings are possibly of less immediate relevance than their methodology, their results are not without interest: For example, an experimental community program for the treatment of severely disturbed patients resulted in no more burden on either the family or the community than the traditional approach.

On the other side of the coin, P. Brown (1980) draws attention to the failure of most deinstitutionalization programs to meet their promises with respect to humane care, prevention, and rehabilitation. It is his contention that these failures have produced the beginning of a "delegitimization" of the new look in mental health. In times of economic crisis, it is tempting to use deinstitutionalization programs to chip away at social service. This reinforces reliance on cost-effective plans that do not benefit clients and poses the danger of increasing the numbers of persons among the marginal group classified as psychological misfits.

In her thoughtful review of institutional versus community-based programs for juvenile and adult offenders, Sarri (1981) asks why it is that public policy has turned away from rehabilitation to punishment and retribution. Political decisions about incarceration, she concludes, are made without reference to available knowledge. The prevailing ideology associated with incarceration, punishment, and deterrents precludes the serious consideration of community-based alternatives. As Berkson and Romer (1981) and Gurland, Bennett, and Wilder (1981) independently point out, psychology is not sufficient; the deinstitutionalization movement must also be studied within its ideological, fiscal, and demographic contexts.

BEHAVIOR THERAPY AND MENTAL RETARDATION

The advent of operant conditioning gave new life to programs for the mentally handicapped. New books, articles, and conference proceedings continue to flow at a rate that prohibits comprehensive review; it is therefore necessary to be selective.

N. R. Ellis (1981) points out that behavior modification research in mental retardation is still largely the product of clinical psychologists working in their spare time with limited financial support, under trying conditions, and with few back-up resources. Under these circumstances, it is not surprising that, in aggregate, this research reflects both lack of creative innovation and serious methodological deficit. Matson and McCartney's (1981) *Handbook* is a case in point: It epitomizes the best that is available and a little of the worst.

In this *Handbook*, Whitman and Scibak (1981) review some 280 studies and come to the conclusion that, for the most part, the subjects included in these investigations were not randomly selected. This makes it difficult to generalize from the findings. As for the findings themselves, the undisciplined use of a wide array of behavior change techniques in complex combinations often made it difficult to unravel the specific contributions of the components. Other serious deficits noted include limited reliability data, an emphasis upon short-term effects, inadequate attention to follow-up and maintenance, and a neglect of social validation.

An example of an exemplary study is a recent investigation by Senatore, Matson, and Kazdin (1982). Matched groups, adequate controls, and a 6-month follow-up lead systematically to questions for future resolution as well as to answers. For example, although their study suggests that active practice and rehearsal enhance the treatment effects of social skills training, it raises the questions of the specific factors responsible for the improved outcome and the circumstances surrounding their manifestation (the type of activity, involving clients in quasi-therapist roles, having therapists leave the treatment sessions so that the treatment can be practiced by the clients under more natural conditions, etc.).

What may seem the simplest of operations, such as learning to open doors or ascend stairs safely, may present formidable obstacles for the seriously retarded (e.g., Cipani, Augustine, & Blomgrem, 1982, in press). To maintain even simple skills, concerned staff involvement is highly desirable, but this is not always easy to maintain (e.g., Faw, Reid, Schepis, Fitzgerald, & Welty, 1981). Sometimes peer groups themselves can be constructively involved in this process (e.g., Gola, Holmes, & Holmes, 1982).

Until Ellis's (1963) theoretical analysis of the S-R principles involved, the problem of incontinence was viewed as virtually insoluble. It was assumed that severely mentally handicapped institutionalized individuals could not learn toileting skills, or any other skills for that matter, and they were treated (or not treated) accordingly. Since 1963, numerous studies have demonstrated that toileting can be taught, and much has been learned. Nevertheless, as McCartney and Holden (1981) note, the sophisticated research needed to establish the relevant parameters of toilet training for such individuals has yet to be conducted. In so doing, it is important not to neglect certain practicalities: Whoever conducts the training has to be well supervised and highly motivated; the resident–staff ratio needs to be low, which is easier said than done; finally, the trainer has to consider the specific characteristics of the subject, especially the adaptive behaviors (e.g., if a client cannot follow a simple command, then the technique has to be modified accordingly).

Comparison studies within institutions for the retarded are rare. For some reason, most investigations of this kind have been confined to outpatients. For example, Matson and Senatore (1981) found that a social-skills training package involving instructions, performance feedback, modeling-role playing, and social reinforcement was more effective than traditional therapy for mild to moderately retarded outpatients.

Self-injurious behavior is a serious problem for the institutionalized retarded, presenting management problems out of all proportion to the estimated frequency of 3 to 10% of the patient population in whom it is reported to occur (Haywood, Meyers, & Switzky, 1982). As the AABT task force on the treatment of self-injurious behavior in the retarded reports, the focus of behavioral research in this area has been upon intervention rather than etiology (Favell & Associates, 1982). As yet, there is no adequate behavioral formulation to account for either the genesis or the maintenance of self-injurious behavior. Methodologically sound studies are lacking, there is little agreement with respect to the concise definition of the response, and we have inadequate knowledge of the parameters controlling generalization. Nevertheless, as Favell and her associates note, there is a general behavioral treatment strategy that does seem to be well substantiated. The details are outlined by Favell and her associates (1982) in their AABT report together with guidelines for implementation.

Of necessity, punishment is a focal part of the treatment of self-injurious behavior. Each year we discuss the issues involved in the use of punishment and the establishment of guidelines. Total rejection of punishment techniques would seem to be unethical and possibly illegal (Repp & Deitz, 1978). A more appropriate policy would be to design specific criteria for the application of punishment procedures. In addition to social and experimental validation, practical demands, staff training, institutional policies, and the availability of viable behavioral alternatives to punishment need to be addressed (Matson & Kazdin, 1981). For example, Homer and Peterson (1980) report the application of differential reinforcement to reduce undesired behavior as a preferred response-elimination procedure.

The move toward community placement of the mentally retarded has gained considerable momentum in recent years. As part of this "normalization" process, it is important not to focus upon specific skills research at the expense of either delivery systems or enlightening the general public and professionals about the mentally retarded, and parent and staff training (Marchetti & Matson, 1981). Successful integration into the community also requires "real life" vocational and social survival skills, and a growing number of investigators are challenging traditional efforts to develop work behaviors in sheltered settings (Rusch & Schutz, 1981). The thrust now seems to be toward ecologically and socially significant behaviors in more naturalistic environments, a much more complicated process than the acquisition of vocational skills within some form of sheltered workshop setting.

Acceptable vocational functioning is important, but other behaviors affect job maintenance as well. For example, there is the ability to communicate basic needs, the ability to move safely about the workshop, and the ability to participate. Skills must be socially relevant. As part of this thrust toward "independence training," Matson (in press) has developed a program for the teaching of shopping skills. Thompson, Braam, and Fuqua (1982) focus upon laundry skills—mundane subjects, perhaps, but very necessary for successful living in the outside world. Schleien, Wehman, and Kiernan (1981) show how to teach leisure skills to the mentally handicapped, and Van Den Pol, Iwata, Ivancic, Page, Neef, and Whitley (1981) concern themselves with the social activities involved in eating in public places.

The growing trend toward normalization mandates training in skills that are likely to enhance community acceptance. Social validation is one way of approaching this problem (Kazdin & Matson, 1981). At a more specific level, Sutter and her associates attempt to pinpoint what it is about the community that brings about placement failure. In three interesting studies, caretakers and homes from which deinstitutionalized community-placed clients had been returned to the institution were compared with homes from which no client had been returned (Sutter, 1980; Sutter, Mayeda, Call, Yanagi, & Yee, 1980; Sutter, Mayeda, Yee, & Yanagi, 1981). Better matching could lead us one step further on the path to ecological harmony (see also Haywood & Newbrough, 1981; S. A. Richardson, 1981).

COMMUNITY, SOCIETY, AND BEHAVIOR THERAPY

By now, behavioral community psychology is firmly established and there are numerous publications to underscore the point. Most of the recent journal articles deal competently enough with circumscribed but important problems of everyday living (e.g., safety belt use: Geller, Johnson, & Pelton, 1982a; jaywalking: Jason & Liotta, 1982). Among the significant new books, the following may be singled out: Baum and Singer's (1981) study of energy conservation, and Geller, Winett, and Everett's (1982b) searching evaluation of over 150 behavioral studies of environmental problems. To do all these reports justice would require an extra volume. My alternative here is to focus upon general trends and issues that seem to herald what lies ahead.

Environmental psychology deals with relationships between persons and environment: Russell and Ward's (1982) "place specificity." As we move from one place or system to another, our behavior changes in accord with many determinants. The complexities involved form the basis of contemporary behavioral community psychology. Conservation, for example, involves attitude change, economics, politics, systems theory, traditional behavior modification, and environmental psychology (e.g., Cook & Berrenberg, 1981; Hake & Zane, 1981; Winkler & Winett, 1982).

Traditional service delivery models have many shortcomings (Jason & Bogat, 1983). Developments in the community mental health movement and preventive psychology lead to alternative approaches and to the several streams of behavioral community psychology as currently practiced (Jason & Glenwick, 1980; Jason, 1981a; Winett, 1979). Behavioral technologies are enticingly inexpensive, decentralized, flexible, and sustainable (Fawcett et al., 1980b). But their incorporation into a viable behavioral community model requires ingenuity, vision, and experience with a variety of related disciplines. Unresolved technical issues include evaluation criteria, problems of cost effectiveness, the current lack of long-term follow-up, and the methodological difficulties involved in the extension of small-scale demonstrations to the community at large (Jason, 1981a; Kazdin, 1980c). At a more practical level, it is necessary to contend with institutional and bureaucratic constraints; political, economic, and administrative pressures; the absence of a common language among disciplines, and more. The choice of procedures, target populations, and problems, and the selection of the decision makers, raise ethical as well as practical issues (Meyers, Meyers, & Craighead, 1981).

People and resources determine community participation and social interaction and thereby contribute to psychological problems (O'Donnell, 1983). It is important, therefore, not only to design ways to bring people together but also to provide the necessary psychological and material resources. Environmental psychology can pinpoint and correct such physical problems as sound proofing and the provision of adequate facilities. Behavioral and community psychologists stress more psychologically oriented constructs, such as social networks and manning theory. Social networks emphasize the structure of interpersonal links, and manning theory pertains to the effects of the number of individuals available in particular settings upon social participation.

The community buzz phrase of the year seems to be "behavioral ecology." Consider, for example, such impressive-sounding titles as "Behavioral Ecology: A Social Systems Approach to Environmental Problems" (Hake, 1981) and *Community Mental Health and Behavioral-Ecology: A Handbook of Theory, Research and Practice* (Jeger & Slotnick, 1982). In the biological sciences, "ecology" is generally defined as the study of functional relationships between organisms and their environments. In the behavioral sciences, the word "ecology" implies an interdependence among environments, people, and behavior. It follows from this transactional emphasis that there are, in any absolute sense, neither good nor bad persons or environments. Instead, the notion of a person–environment "fit" is more appropriate. Thus, in contrast with a medical or public health mode ("treatment" of "mental illness" and "prevention" of "disease"), behavioral ecologists seek to optimize human development by enhancing coping skills, increasing self-efficacy and self-esteem, and marshalling organizational and community strengths to improve the quality of life (McClure, Cannon, Allen, Belton, Connor, D'Ascoli, Stone, Sullivan, & McClure, 1980).

Staging raffles to promote recycling and employing individual prompts to reduce energy consumption are hardly likely to have large-scale effects. To expand the behavioral horizons, Nietzel, Winett,

MacDonald, and Davidson (1977) recommend first that behaviorally oriented professionals be committed advocates for the populations they serve; second that interdisciplinary knowledge bases be incorporated into the model (with contributions from economics, science, sociology, and areas of psychology other than learning theory); and third that behavior therapists adopt an extended view of community service in which professionals serve as program planners, consultants, and trainers rather than direct service providers.

If ecology stresses the natural environment, behavior modification provides the necessary technology and theoretical base from which to launch the intervention (Hake, 1981). This may necessitate a shift in the domain of behavior modification and especially in that branch known as applied behavior analysis. For Greene (1981), community behavior analysis implies commitment on at least three levels. At a personal level, behavior analysts need to establish networks of consumer groups and agencies that operate in the public interest. At the level of graduate training, major revisions will be necessary to add breadth to the programs offered. Finally, professional organizations that represent community behavior analysis (such as AABT and ABA) should sponsor work periods in public organizations.

CRIME, DELINQUENCY, AND BEHAVIOR THERAPY

The application of learning principles to the modification of delinquents and criminal behavior has received considerable notoriety (Stumphauzer 1981a, 1981b). Public opinion oscillates between reform and punishment for adult offenders, and it is not surprising that behavior modification, which can be applied to both these goals, reflects these vacillations. With juveniles, reform is a more consistently held theme and it is therefore understandable that positive reinforcements predominate. In appraising progress, it is important to avoid both therapeutic nihilism (nothing works) and uncritical optimism (Feldman, in press).

The Eleventh Banff International Conference (Stuart, 1981) focused upon social learning processes in the control, management, and treatment of violence. It is not possible to predict future violence exclusively from a knowledge of violence in the past. To this must be added an assessment of current reinforcers. Fixsen, Phillips, Dowd, and Palmer (1981) make this point dramatically in terms of the violent behavior that can occur in an environment that is impoverished and with a custodial staff that is abusive. Dangerousness is a behavioral concept that is closely related to violence, and, as for violence, a variety of definitions have emerged (Shah, 1978, 1981a). Fortunately, legal usage is tending toward greater specification and the concept of dangerousness is gradually being incorporated into behavioral models of crime (Shah, 1981b).

Applied behavior analysis usually focuses upon easily identifiable problems of a relatively simple nature, with individual subjects as the target rather than complex social systems. This is an example of what Watzlawick, Weakland, and Fisch (1976) term "first-order change." First-order change takes place when a problem is conceptualized in terms of rearranging specific parts of the system rather than altering the functioning of the system as a whole. Second-order change is brought about by modifying the functioning of the system itself, thereby solving the presenting problem. Applied behavior analysis directs itself to the study of crime, primarily in terms of first-order change. This is necessary but insufficient (Wardlaw, 1981). Equally limiting are those studies that focus on correlational rather than causal relationships (see Gaffney & McFall, 1981).

Locking up delinquents, especially young delinquents, is not necessarily a satisfactory solution. Nevertheless, if we are going to continue locking them up, it is necessary to have effective programs, and this continues to present a challenge to behavior modifiers. Two programs compared by Stumphauzer (1981a, 1981b), behavior modification and transactional analysis, turned out to be similar in their effectiveness, and neither was more than marginally superior to regular and comparable institutionalization programs. Generalization might have been enhanced, speculates Stumphauzer, if some form of after care or follow-through component to continue while the youth was on parole had been instituted. Neither program had such a stipulation built into it.

Both programs were successful in several respects and yet both were terminated. Program continuation rightly depends upon research validation, but the *realpolitik* of funding, political expedience, public acceptance, and what Stumphauzer terms the enthusiasm of perhaps one particular program administrator are probably of equal importance. These factors become even more relevant as the intervention strategy shifts from institution to community. Each year we discuss new developments in so-called half-way house programs, such as Achievement Place and Learning House. Each year we are forced to conclude that the need for social validation and sociopolitical considerations to go hand in hand with research practice is given less than its due. A recent otherwise comprehensive outcome evaluation study of Teaching Family group home treatment programs for juvenile offenders by Kirigin, Braukmann, Atwater, and Wolf (1982) is a case in point.

The Draper Correctional Center offers what is probably the most humane, comprehensive, and systematically studied residential program to date (see previous volumes in this series). Educational opportunities, institutional job training, and behavioral counseling are readily available. Nevertheless, even this program has major shortcomings. For example, to prepare residents for the outside world, real job placement services and transitional employment may be needed (Lehrer, 1975). Perhaps for this reason among others, an 18-month follow-up by Stumphauzer (1981a, 1981b) showed the Draper program to be no more effective in reducing further law violation than a no-treatment control condition.

It is possible that, at least for juveniles, effective correctional services can be provided more humanely and more cost efficiently in community-based settings. But there is little consensus and even less data with respect to the principles to be followed in the provision of such services (Coates, 1981). The trend in this area, as elsewhere in behavior therapy, seems to be toward a marriage of sophisticated methodology with conceptual innovation, based on a consideration of systems and social forces rather than the individual alone (e.g., Stumphauzer, Veloz, & Aiken, 1981). Kiessling and Andrews's (1980) promising new approach to correctional theory and practice is based upon a synthesis of systems and behavioral and management principles that goes far beyond the goal of law-abiding behavior alone. For such programs to be effective and for program organizers and policy makers to determine which aspects need to be modified or stabilized, data are required (Barton & Sarri, 1979). At present there seem to be more questions than answers in the behavior therapy of crime and delinquency.

BEHAVIOR THERAPY IN INDUSTRY
AND THE MARKETPLACE

It is customary in this section to lament the continuing lack of research sophistication. At last, this is starting to change. The mainstream of behavior therapy is beginning to take note of this new world to explore. For example, *The Behavior Therapist*, an official publication of AABT, has just completed a three-part introduction to behavior modification in business and industry (definition, development, and current status, Frederiksen, 1982; behavior modification and the organization, Bourdon, 1982; the perspectives of an outsider called in, Komaki & Penn, 1982). For more critical appraisal see Andrasik, Heimberg, and McNamara

(1981b) and McNamara and Andrasik (1981). At the textbook level, there is a workman-like introduction to organizational behavior modification (OBM) by Rambo (1982) and a more general industrial handbook edited by O'Brien, Dickinson, and Roscow (1982). (For a recent review of behavioral developments in the nonprofit sector, see Prue, Krapfl, Noah, Cannon, & Maley, 1980.)

The term "behavior modification" is no longer treated with opprobrium by practicing managers. Kreitner (1981) invited 210 executives to evaluate a specially constructed on-the-job behavior modification program alternatively labeled as "behavior modification" or "human relations" and as a "high success" program or a "low success" program. The managers responded significantly more favorably to the high-success condition and, contrary to expectation, were not adversely affected by the label "behavior modification." It seems then that, at least as far as this study is concerned, the term "behavior modification" does not elicit a negative reaction from practicing managers. Managers are results oriented and to them it is success that counts. (What is meant by success and from whose perspective it is viewed are topics to which I shall return shortly.) Given certain duly recognized methodological limitations, Kreitner is correct in drawing the implication that those whose concern is with the introduction of behavior modification to managers should focus upon successes and practical application rather than conceptual issues.

In his discussion of the ethics of OBM, Berthold (1982) spells out six guiding principles. These emphasize the use of positive rather than negative techniques and candor with respect to outcomes and goals. But as Landy (1982) notes in his perceptive review of Lawler's (1981) *Pay and Organization Development*, it is not good enough, in this day and age, to reinvent industrial social Darwinism in the belief that workers exist for the good of the organization. It could be that the organization also exists for the worker. Making things more fair, less secretive, and more systematic in order to identify and keep the "better workers" is what Landy terms "Ersatz humanism." While this is probably an oversimplified analysis, it does draw attention to the need to think these matters through further.

I begin this selective review with a brief discussion of performance feedback. Because it is inexpensive and straightforward, rarely requires complicated training, and stresses positive rather than negative consequences, performance feedback is understandably regarded as an attractive industrial intervention technique (Prue & Fairbank, 1981). Unfortunately, most of the seemingly positive findings consist of uncontrolled case reports. Precisely how feedback differs from other consequation strategies remains unclear. All consequences include a feedback component and all feedback is potentially rewarding or punishing (Andrasik *et al.*, 1981b).

Of industry-based studies reported in the *Journal of Organizational Behavior Management* since its inception some four years ago, 60% employed "performance feedback." As Prue and Fairbank (1981) note, the term is indiscriminantly applied to behavioral interventions that have little in common. Even when usage seems similar, the relevant parameters and the circumstances of their contributions to performance remain unknown. For example, feedback could be provided either privately (with performance information shared only with the target individual) or publicly (with information provided additionally to others). In practice, the degree to which feedback is made public or private varies on a continuum.

Extrinsic rewards may have long-term deleterious effects on attitudes and performance (the overjustification effect). Salient, tangible reinforcements undermine intrinsic motivation. In previous years we have drawn attention to the meticulous investigations carried out by Deci and his associates and the disputed conclusion that contingent pay can cause a decrease in intrinsic motivation (see Deci, 1975). Deci (1976) cautions educators and managers alike against the indiscriminate use of extrinsic rewards. But the matter is far from resolved. It is still not clear that reward per se is the critical causal agent that produces the overjustification effect.

Williams (1980) manipulated four levels of behavior constraint–reinforcement in fourth- and fifth-grade children: attractive reward for target activity performance; unattractive reward; unrewarded request to play with a particular toy; and a no-reward, no-request control. Only the unattractive reward and request groups showed the performance decrements that suggest an overjustification effect. According to Williams, extrinsic reinforcement does not necessarily cause the overjustification effect. The behavior-constraining aspect of a contingency produces the effect, whereas the reinforcement or "reward value" aspect leads to the opposite effect—an increase in interest and postcontingency performance. For obvious reasons, caution should be extended in extrapolating these findings to the industrial setting.

The overjustification effect seems to be more in evidence in laboratorylike settings than elsewhere. For example, Fisher's (1979) well-controlled study of an ongoing token economy for chronic psychiatric patients failed to detect any sign of overjustification. Equally unreinforcing findings have been reported by Mawhinney and Taylor (1981) in a more directly work-related milieu.

Organizational psychologists generally conceptualize motivation in operant rather than drive terms, and studies of pay schedules readily lend themselves to this way of thinking. But, as with overjustification, it is not easy to give real-life investigations of reinforcement schedules the precision of laboratory studies. Job simulation analogues are rarely adequate. For example, Pritchard, Hollenback, and DeLeo (1980) used newspaper advertisements to recruit high school students for what the students thought was a real job of 5 days' duration but was really a contrived activity involving a self-paced programmed text in electronics. Their conclusion, that partial schedules are no more effective in maintaining task performance than continuous piece-rate schedules, is at variance with prevailing impressions. But once again we are confronted with the hazards of extrapolating from even the best of analogue studies to real situations.

As two recent behavioral reviews testify, few areas could be more "real life" than the marketplace (Nord & Peter, 1980; Rothschild & Gaidis, 1981). Jason and Frasure's (1980) attempt to modify customer buying reactions and managerial purchasing behavior in supermarkets indirectly highlights a recurring theme of this chapter: the constraints imposed on traditional behavior modification activities by bureaucratic and other sociopolitical factors. As a first step, it may be more strategic to introduce behavior modification into such settings by way of problems that are of more pressing concern to management.

Shoplifting, for example, is one of the most frequent crimes in the United States, and as such it is the major profit killer for retailers. It has been estimated that approximately three-fourths of the $4.8 to $6 billion stolen annually is taken by employees, which still leaves over $1 billion of theft each year by the public at large (Andrasik et al., 1981b). Most behavior modification programs take the form of conspicuously placed signs or response-cost procedures involving punishment and reward contingencies (e.g., Geller, Koltuniak, & Shilling, in press). According to Andrasik et al., while such procedures are effective in reducing theft in the short run, the durability of these effects and the feasibility of administration are at present unknown. Furthermore, significant generalization across different categories of merchandise does not seem to occur.

We turn now to a different area, finding a job. Traditionally, vocational counseling has been steeped in motivational psychology, and the transition to a behavioral model is still in its early stages. As an example of this new look in vocational counseling, the work of Azrin and his associates (e.g., Azrin & Besalel, 1980) is exemplary, and we have had repeated occasion to refer to these developments over the years. One of their more innovative programs is the job-finding club. Potential applicants are informed of job possibilities, how to search for employment, how to dress and groom themselves, how to behave in an interview, how to prepare a résumé, and more. Each participant is paired with a buddy in order to generate additional sources of encouragement.

Social skills training has been successfully utilized to modify the job interview performance of formerly hospitalized psychiatric patients, mentally retarded persons, predelinquent boys, employed teenage mothers, college seniors, and clients in various vocational rehabilitation settings (Gillen & Heimberg, 1980; Heimberg, Cunningham, Stanley, & Blankenberg, 1982). Most of these studies are analogous in nature and virtually all demonstrate improvement. However, few report whether their subjects were actually able to obtain employment as a result of the training, and only one attempted to monitor interview performance in another setting (Kelly, Wildman, & Berler, 1980). The findings are further limited by the small number of subjects typically employed and by the fact that subjects are usually informed that no offer of employment will be forthcoming from the interviews. Thus the reality of these situations is limited and the impact of social skills training on real job interview performance remains largely unevaluated.

Heimberg *et al.* (1982) utilized social skills training in a federally funded Youth Employee Training Program. Participants receive social skills training in four-session or two-session packages or were placed in one of two control conditions. Training focused on the development of behavioral skills reported as important in preliminary interviews with previous program participants, their counselors, and employers. The impact of the training was evaluated in role-played interviews and competitive employment interviews for real jobs. Social skills training resulted in superior role-play performance, as indicated by group differences in overall ratings and specific behavioral measures.

At the other end of the spectrum, there is the problem of preparation for retirement. Traditional retirement counseling takes the form of leisure training and an examination of motivation in drive terms. One of several possible behavioral approaches is to modify pertinent work contingencies on a gradual and systematic basis directly within the employment setting. If operationally defined and otherwise acceptable job modifications were to be made available, older workers could coordinate planning for retirement with a restructuring of their customary work patterns. Job modification may thus represent not only an alternative to retirement but also a means of implementing a second career for the later years (Shkop & Shkop, 1982).

I conclude this section with a brief review of things to come as seen through the eyes of selected experts. Andrasik and McNamara (1982) draw attention to the need to develop appropriate behavior modification strategies that introduce high-technology systems into the work force. McNamara's (1980) "synergistic" intervention model fuses behavior modification with other systems. The premise, which remains to be tested, is that fusion of principles and techniques derived from the integration of two conceptual systems is likely to be more effective than each used independently. As an example, McNamara points to the fusion of behavioral psychology and human engineering. Another example might be economics and behavior modification, as advocated by Winkler (1983). Assessing the need for training is also likely to become part of the cost-conscious organizations of the future. Andrasik *et al.* (1981b) draw attention to the supplementing of more traditional self-report training by sophisticated assessment-center methodologies and the on-line computerized recording of employee behavior (see Komaki, Collins, & Thoene, 1980).

Two opinion polls pertaining to the future of behavior modification in industry have been reported. Andrasik, McNamara, and Edlund (1981c) solicited predictions from members of the editorial board of the *Journal of Organizational Behavior Management* and a small number of individuals engaged in research in this area. Respondents were specifically asked to identify the future needs of business and government and the kinds of approaches likely to meet these needs. Frederiksen and Lovett (1980) questioned 159 members of OBM subgroups within two leading behavior modification associations with respect to future opportunities for the practice of OBM in their respective work settings. Table 1-1, compiled by Andrasik and McNamara (1982), tabulates specific areas of future application in the rank order of their mention in these two studies. What is particularly striking is that the areas of predicted importance for tomorrow tend to overlap with the dominant interests of today.

BEHAVIOR THERAPY AND THE ELDERLY

Patterson and Jackson (1981) offer several reasons why the practice of behavior therapy with the elderly is likely to grow in the immediate future: The number of people in the United States age 65 and older is expected at least to double in the next 50 years; the problems related to aging are primarily behavioral in nature (poor eating and exercise habits, retirement adjustment, smoking, etc.); the behavior of the elderly is demonstrably changeable.

Older people are still discriminated against in our youth-oriented society. Medical care of the elderly is still occasionally characterized by negativism, defeatism, and professional antipathy. Gerontophobia, or ageism, are two well-chosen terms to describe the prevailing negative

TABLE 1-1.

Future Applications of OBM: Comparisons between Two Surveys on the Basis of Rank Order

Application	Andrasik, McNamara, & Edlund (1981c)	Frederiksen & Lovett (1980)
Increase individual employee productivity	1	1
Improve employee training procedures	2	3
Help produce and direct organizational change	3	3
Improve employees' abilities to self-manage	5	—
Train specialists in OBM	5	—
Modification of anti-health behaviors	5	—
Increase conservation of energy	8.5	—
Improve the climate of organizations	8.5	—
Increase staff communication with management	8.5	7.5
As a basis for job descriptions/job evaluations	8.5	3
Increase consumer satisfaction	14.5	9.5
Increase use of safety precautions	14.5	11
Establishment of cost control procedures	14.5	5
Increase the productivity of the entire organization	14.5	6
Assist employees in developing satisfying leisure-time activities	14.5	—
Increase employee morale	14.5	9.5
Provide behavioral counseling to employees with personal problems	14.5	—
Improve customer service behavior	14.5	—
Increase attendance/reduce tardiness	—	7.5

Note. From "Future Directions for Industrial Behavior Modification" by F. Andrasik and J. R. McNamara, in R. M. O'Brien, A. M. Dickinson, and M. R. Rosow (Eds.), *Industrial Behavior Modification: A Management Handbook.* Copyright 1982, Pergamon Press. Reprinted by permission.

attitudes that still obtain, and we now have at least one objective measuring device for the study of health professional–geriatric patient interactions. Adelson, Nasti, Sprafkin, Marinelli, Primavera, and Gorman (1982) developed ten operationally defined behavioral categories for the measurement of the attitudes and potential behavior of health professionals engaged in the care of geriatric patients.

In the past, behavior therapy has had limited impact on the elderly, an observation noted over a decade ago and now once again by Patterson and Jackson. By way of partial explanation, these authors invoke what they call the "law of the instrument": investigators tend to find new applications for old techniques primarily because these techniques exist rather than because they are suitable. According to Patterson and Jackson, the majority of studies of behavior modification with the elderly fall into this category. Only now are we beginning to witness the modification of existing techniques in terms of the specific needs of old people.

The spring of 1982 saw the emergence of *The International Journal of Behavioral Geriatrics*. In 1981 a new discipline appeared on the behavioral horizon: behavioral thanatology, the application of behavioral principles to the problems of the dying patient, the family, and the members of the treatment team. (As Thorpe, 1982, notes, the arid phrase "behavioral thanatology" seems calculated to raise the hackles of its opponents. It is therefore encouraging to see recent behavioral texts in geriatrics and gerontology stress the compatibility of behavioral principles and humanism; e.g., Sobel, 1981.)

It was once thought that safety and comfort constituted the ideal institutional environment for the elderly. It is now recognized that excessive dependency and conformity may well develop in such settings. A more desirable environment may be one that combines activities and life styles that foster independence and decision making with appropriate safety and comfort. Contemporary behavior therapy could be the ideal vehicle to achieve this goal.

Sometimes a simple modification, such as the introduction of an organized activity, is all that is required to lead to a generalized increase in activity level and social interaction (e.g., Burrows, Jason, Quattrochi-Tubin, & Lavelli, 1981). Mechanical devices such as signs improve facilities but are not sufficient in themselves to produce the desired increase in activity. It is necessary to involve the professional staff and volunteers in a personal reaching out (Reinke, Holmes, & Denny, 1981; Reitz & Hawkins, 1982).

As Hussian and Lawrence (1981) found in a well-controlled study of the institutionalized elderly, an increase in activity alone will not necessarily result in long-term reduction in depression. While they are initially useful, activity programs in long-term-care facilities additionally need to include a problem-solving approach if improvement is to be maintained. In even the best nursing homes, an institutional atmosphere can engender a downward spiral of increasing dependence and learned helplessness in its elderly residents. Overprotection can lead to a loss of dignity, enhanced depression, greater physical illness, and decline (Lieff & Brown, 1981).

Sometimes minor changes in the physical environment are all that is needed to reduce apathy (Hanley, 1981). Inactivity and apathy may be as much artifacts of the institutional facilities as a manifestation of some "disease" process. Melin and Götestam (1981), for example, found that moving the furniture around and changing simple meal-time routines lead to increased communication and improved table manners among patients formerly considered to be senile and other-wise intractable.

Social ecology has much to contribute to behavior therapy, and nowhere is this more evident than in determining optimum residential care settings for the elderly (Moos, 1980, 1981). Social ecologists view environmental resources in terms of four major domains: physical and architectural, policy and program, residents and staff, and social-environmental. Attempts to focus upon only one (e.g., altering the interior design of nursing homes [Smetak & Jason, 1983], or modify-ing the behavior of institutionalized elderly patients by the introduc-tion of artificial stimuli such as specific color patterns or cues [Hussian, 1980]) are of limited value. Finally, Moos (1981) makes the point that, to the extent that this is feasible, the residents themselves must have input into the decision-making process.

In the best of institutions, residents tend to be socially isolated, with little or no exposure to everyday living. Institutions that facilitate successful resident adaptation are characterized by a relatively high degree of community integration and by "permeable boundaries" be-tween institution and the community (David, Moos, & Kahn, 1981). Data accumulated by David et al. suggest that one key to integration with the community is the removal of social barriers to full participa-tion. Social barriers are easier to modify than are architectural struc-tures or physical disabilities. Sometimes a simple rearrangement of staff time and responsibilities is all that is required. More often, a major reordering of staff attitudes and values is indicated. The expecta-tion that it is reasonable and natural for residents to engage in extra-mural activities requires drastic restructuring of the value systems held by most of those who care for the elderly.

Institutionalization is usually a less satisfactory solution to the problems of aging than integration within the community. Aging persons can function very adequately within the community if pro-vided with the necessary physical and social supportive services (Delisle, 1982; Engstrom-Poulin, 1982). Unfortunately, most evaluations of community programs for the elderly tend to rely primarily upon anecdotal responses and lack adequate controls. They manage to avoid any form of outcome evaluation or follow-up.

Refreshingly, Bogat and Jason (1980) circumvent many of these methodological heresies. In their study, elderly community residents in the Chicago area were assigned to one of three groups: a network-building student visiting program that reinforced and encouraged involvement in community settings; a relationship-oriented visiting program that emphasized empathy and concern; or a nonequivalent control group. All groups were given appropriate pre- and posttesting involving a variety of measures ranging from questionnaires, telephone calls, and ratings to direct observation. Weekly activities and fortnightly quality-of-life ratings were collected for the two experimental groups. At the program's end, although few significant differences were found, the network-building group evidenced directionally higher means on most variables. Regrettably, intervention lasted only 3 months, the sample was small, the control group was nonequivalent, and there was no follow-up.

A variety of community alternatives to institutionalization for older people exist. These run the gamut from independent or congregate housing, through mobile homes, to small-scale residences. Other things being equal, older people prefer to remain in the community (Lawton, 1981). This is an area of research that remains largely unexplored by behavior therapists.

We conclude this section with a caution. The elderly are particularly vulnerable to exploitation by investigators, no matter how well-intentioned. In 1977, the National Institute on Aging convened a conference on the protection of elderly research subjects. Issues considered included the determination of risk–benefit criteria, a variety of methodological constraints, review procedures, the obligation to ensure privacy, and the process of informed consent (see Patterson & Jackson, 1981, for a more detailed report on this conference).

CONCLUSIONS

Two interwoven themes run through recent developments in behavior therapy. On the one hand, there is a trend toward rigorous and methodologically sophisticated intervention. On the other hand, there is a movement toward comprehensive, multimodal, interdisciplinary interventions that cut across psychological, sociological, economic, political, and even philosophical boundaries. Whether behavior therapy can retain its conceptual integrity under these circumstances remains an issue for the future to determine. (See Franks, 1981, for a more extensive discussion of these matters.)

For Farkas (1981) the solution is clear: Abandon partisanship in favor of a pluralistic psychology of behavior change. It is time for behavior therapy to relinquish its flagging identity and move toward some form of pluralism that is independent of theoretical bias. There is, however, another alternative: to adapt the hard-won advantages of a rigorous behavioral approach to the exigencies of contemporary society.

In their excellent discussion of the foundations of behavior therapy, Woolfolk and Richardson (1981) draw attention to the fact that behavior therapy is both an intellectual force and a cultural movement. It cannot stand in isolation from its historical, social, and philosophical origins. To understand behavior therapy and appreciate its distinctive character, argue Woolfolk and Richardson, it is essential to take a broad view of its foundations. Much more than social learning theory must be included among its underpinnings. There is a prevailing ideology, a philosophical "faith" that stems back to the modernity of the scientific revolution, with its dedication to the autonomy and integrity of human reason, to ethical ideals, to the enhancement of human liberty, and to an opposition to irrational authority and arbitrary privilege.

In the early years of behavior therapy, this renaissance took the form (among other developments) of a departure from a controlling medical model to one in which clients were taught to be responsible for their own lives (e.g., Michie, 1981). But eventually it became quite evident that, while virtually always necessary, intervention at the level of the individual is rarely sufficient. Life does not develop in a vacuum: Contextual factors are as essential targets for analysis and intervention as is the behavior of individuals (Sarason, 1981). Drawing attention to this point, Winett (in press) stresses the dangers of placing emphasis on individual responsibility at the expense of an analysis in terms of systems, politics, and economics. A somewhat similar point is made by Brechner and Linder (1981) in their pithy analysis of the "social trap," the classic confrontation between private and public welfare. A strategy that maximizes an individual's short-term gains may in the long run prove disastrous to society as a whole and therefore to each individual's long-term best interests. The emerging notion of behavioral health and the development of a positive rather than a negative focus (Matarazzo, 1982) is also relevant here.

Certain developments in and around behavior therapy impinge on these trends more than others do. McDowell's (1982) reformulation of Herrnstein's 10-year-old mathematical statement of the law of effect in terms of its implications for contemporary behavior therapy is a case in point. As McDowell reminds us, Herrnstein's equation is considerably more descriptive of the environment than was Skinner's earlier view of reinforcement. Sources of reinforcement other than those in direct contact with the behavior in question need to be taken into consideration. It is this broader view of reinforcement, argues McDowell, that makes the application of operant principles to complex environments more feasible.

The Society for Risk Analysis is a relatively new organization dedicated to the interdisciplinary analysis of risk. Its members include statisticians, engineers, systems analysts, social psychologists, policy makers, and many other professionals, but as yet few behavior therapists. It would seem that, as the complexity of behavior therapy increases, so the need for systematic cost–benefit evaluation in terms of risk is likely to assume greater importance. Somewhat related, Wahler and Fox (1981) draw attention to the need to examine the potential side, or unintended, effects of behavioral intervention.

In an elaborate theoretical statement, Staats (1981) argues convincingly for the emergence of a unified theory in psychology. Some individuals view cognitive-behavior therapy as an attempt to fuse together two formerly separate and competing entities, cognition and behavior. Cognitions, argues Schwartz (1982a), are attributes to be studied in their own right in terms of their effects on behavior, as with the study of drugs or genetics. An interactive approach that incorporates cognition, behavior, and affect is the logical future in this area. To what extent this "ecumenicalism" is either meaningful or feasible to implement remains uncertain. Kazdin's (1982b) note of caution with respect to the premature tendency to promulgate cognitive-behavior therapy as a general approach needs to be taken most seriously.

Bandura's (1982) notions about unification are somewhat different. In his own words,

> Efficacy in dealing with one's environment is not a fixed act or simply a matter of knowing what to do. Rather, it involves a generative capability in which component cognitive, social and behavioral skills must be organized into integrated courses of action to serve innumerable purposes. A capability is only as good as its execution. Operative competence requires orchestration and continuous improvisation of multiple subskills to manage ever-changing circumstances. (p. 122)

From this broad statement, Bandura slips almost imperceptibly into "collective efficacy." People, argues Bandura, do not live their lives as social isolates; the challenges and difficulties they face reflect group problems that often require sustained collective efforts to produce significant change. The strength of these social structures, which include nations, lies in part in a sense of collective efficacy and the belief that it is possible to solve problems and improve lives through concerted efforts. Modern life is regulated by complex physical technologies that most individuals neither comprehend nor believe they can do much to influence.

In advocating collective efficacy, Bandura calls for broad and comprehensive research effort, including the development of suitable tools for measuring group perceptions of efficacy and for systematic investigation of the means by which factional interests can be incorporated into the common goal of shared purpose. Regrettably, while Bandura calls for a commitment to collective effort rather than "litanies of powerlessness that instill in people beliefs of inefficacy to influence conditions that shape the course of their lives," he does not tell us how this is to be accomplished.

Community behavior therapists continually stress the need to respond to social determinants. But the understandable, and in many ways defendable, tendency to focus upon specific strategies rather than national and international developments remains (e.g., Baum & Singer, 1981). Geller's (1982) sophisticated, large-scale intervention model does not fall into this category. The information and resources now exist for a concerted application of applied behavioral interventions on a nationwide basis, argues Geller, and he establishes a series of guidelines for an interdisciplinary Energy Conserving Community System to prove his point. As yet, the proof is more in print than practice.

Persuading the powers that be to adopt validated innovative technologies is likely to tax the ingenuity and forbearance of a behavioral saint. (See King, 1981, and Stolz, 1981, for a discussion of ten manipulable variables that could lead to the adoption of such technologies by government and other agencies.) The important question that Stolz asks in her plaintive lament, "Does Anybody Care?" is as follows: Do we care enough about the adoption of behavioral innovation to develop the behavioral technology necessary to shape these adoptions? One hopes that the answer is yes, but only the coming years will produce the necessary resolution (see Chapter 8). It is of interest that the beginning appears to emerge as much from public health as from behavior therapy. For example, McGuire (1980) lists seven steps in the design of an effective public health communication campaign to win the acceptance of both the public and those who mold and make decisions. Perhaps behavior modifers will take their cue from McGuire, Stolz, and others and focus upon molding the opinions of decision makers as well as developing specific intervention programs per se. On this cautionary but positive note I conclude this overview of recent developments in behavior therapy for the year.

CHAPTER

2

BEHAVIORAL ASSESSMENT AND METHODOLOGY

PHILIP C. KENDALL

As I reflect over the research reported during the recent past, it is thoroughly pleasing to see the widespread use of behavioral assessments for the evaluation of psychological intentions. Naturalistic observations for programs in classrooms, marriage treatment dyads, and family groups, as well as simulations and role plays for the entire range of disorders, evidence the comfortable acceptance of behavioral data in therapy outcome evaluations. Behavioral assessment remains central to clinical research (see Cone & Foster, 1982) and, indeed, this role was the topic of an entire special issue of *Behavioral Assessment* (Vol. 3, Nos. 3 and 4, 1981). Also, Cone and Foster (1982) provide a carefully considered list of the considerations necessary when one is contemplating the use of direct behavioral assessment methodologies. The continued vitality of behavioral assessment is evidenced by the appearance or planned appearance of second editions of texts on behavioral assessment (e.g., Ciminero, Calhoun, & Adams, in press; Hersen & Bellack, 1982), the continued success of two journals (*Behavioral Assessment* and the *Journal of Behavioral Assessment*) that published their fourth volumes in 1982, and the ongoing interest in training in behavioral assessment. Several papers describing training have appeared.

I do not think that I was unique when, upon being asked to teach a section on behavioral assessment, I sought out and carefully read the curriculum published by Evans and Nelson in the *American Psychologist* (1974). At that time, behavioral assessment was emerging and new courses were being developed to provide graduate students in several different types of degree programs with the needed exposure to the strengths and weaknesses of these nascent methods. Now, a decade later, training in behavioral assessment remains an important part of many graduate programs and it is a rare program in which it is not met with. Three recent articles on courses for behavioral assessment (Hay, 1982; Jackson, 1982; Prinz, 1982) perhaps best serve to illustrate the established place of behavioral assessment within clinical training.

Based on these descriptions of the courses, behavioral assessment encompasses a wide range of methods, including naturalistic observation, role plays, self-monitoring, and self-report inventories. More impressive than its breadth, however, is the obvious focus of behavioral assessment courses on clinical intervention and application. In each of the course outlines, participants are described as users of the behavioral assessment methods and not merely as students of the behavioral assessment literature. For example, in the program described by Hay (1982), students complete a self-monitoring project and serve as independent observers at a school for autistic children. Prinz (1982) notes that each student conducts two comprehensive assessments (one adult, one child), with home and school visits providing the opportunity to apply (and learn the difficulties involved in) naturalistic observation procedures. Students also conduct and report the results of a pretreatment assessment as part of the course outlined by Jackson (1982). The use of behavioral assessment methods as part of the professional management of clinical cases stands as a most commendable training strategy.

In keeping with the applied emphasis seen within the teaching of behavioral assessment, there is a notable focus on functional analysis and outcome evaluation (single-case designs). While single-case designs are not without criticisms, the conscious connection of assessment to treatment evaluation is meritorious.

Perhaps our sense of behavioral assessment as a flourishing enterprise is misleadingly positive. The articles describing the courses appeared in *Behavioral Assessment*, not in an adversarial journal, and the course descriptions are from university training programs where the behavioral influence has been apparent. The views of instructors of traditional assessment courses and the course descriptions from programs lacking a behavioral tradition would shed additional light on the current status of the acceptance of behavioral assessment. Nevertheless, instructors interested in modifying or improving their own courses in behavioral assessment, either to broaden the scope or to take a more applied stance, are directed to Hay (1982), Jackson (1982), and Prinz (1982).

Behavioral assessment is not, however, a panacea. Complex assessment problems require more than behavioral assessment (Hersen, 1981), and some disorders, by their nature, require reliance on other types of assessments. Thus behavioral assessment deserves continual attention, but not to the point of neglect of all other measurement methods.

RELIABILITY

As noted in last year's *Annual Review*, the "turning inward" that has taken place within behavioral assessment has led to a greater interest in the psychometric features, specifically reliability and validity, of our measures. These features continue to be important.

For instance, following behavioral assessors' dismissal of their unquestioning satisfaction with percentage agreement estimates of interobserver reliability, Cohen's (1960) κ has been applied with increasing frequency. Green (1981) briefly describes three methods of indexing interobserver reliability: proportion of agreement, G index, and κ. Although Green himself does not unequivocally support κ, its intentional and successful accounting for chance agreements makes it the prime candidate for index of choice. In a related paper, Brennan and Prediger (1981) identify and discuss common uses and misuses of coefficient κ and provide considerations of alternate κ-like statistics.

The effects of different manipulations on the accuracy of observational data has experienced a renewed burst of interest and a corresponding expanse of archival space. The list of manipulated variables gives the appearance of being comprehensive, if not exhaustive. For instance, the effects of settings, instructions, length of session, frequency of behavior, sex of observer, methods of calculation, and data recording have all been examined and reported (Boykin & Nelson, 1981; Cunningham & Tharp, 1981; Horn & Haynes, 1981; Smith, Madsen, & Cipani, 1981). Examining sex effects, Horn and Haynes (1981) asked whether male and female observers differed in their observational recordings or subjective ratings of disruptive child behavior. On both of these indices, there were no apparent biases, although female observers rated the target children (of both sexes) as more normal than did male observers. Could it be that women have a more positive and accepting cognitive set and therefore see less deviance? Nevertheless, the authors justly conclude that, within the constraints of their study, their data support the internal validity of past research that used observers of predominately one sex.

Cunningham and Tharp (1981) varied the setting and observational method and examined the effects on the accuracy and reliability of behavioral observations. Settings were manipulated ingeniously; subjects viewed one of four videotapes in which the target child behaved similarly while the behavior of nontarget children varied. Thus the behavior of nontarget children was manipulated to vary the setting of target behaviors. The two observational methods were (1) global—watching the entire tape, and (2) systematic interval sampling. At the completion of the study it was determined that the global method of observation, but not the systematic sampling method, resulted in subjects being biased by the behaviors of the nontarget children. Also, subjects using the sampling method produced more reliable and more accurate data.

The effects of instructions and calculation procedures on observers' accuracy, agreement, and the correctness of calculations was reported by Boykin and Nelson (1981). Accuracy referred to the extent to which observers concurred with an expert (consensually validated criterion); agreement was interobserver agreement; correctness had to do with the calculated scores. The manipulation of instructions involved telling subjects (observers) that either accuracy or agreement was the important criterion for evaluating their observations. A number of interesting outcomes emerged from this complex experiment. First, it was found that students erroneously inflated agreement levels for their own data and deflated data that had been contrived to appear to have been collected by others. Second, the manipulation of instructions affected outcome: Observers told that interobserver agreement was important obtained higher agreement scores than accuracy scores, while observers told that accuracy was important obtained higher accuracy scores than agreement scores. Assuming for the moment that these results were not caused by blatantly mischievous intentions, it is interesting to begin to speculate about the biases in thinking or information processing that affect observational data.

A comparison of three recording methods was reported by Smith, Madsen, and Cipani (1981). The three methods of recording were (1) observers watched and recorded behaviors during every 10-second interval, (2) observers watched and recorded behaviors in the first five 10-second intervals and rested during the next 10-second interval, and (3) observers watched during one 10-second interval and recorded the occurrences during the next 10-second interval. No differences were found in the reliabilities across the three recording methods.

A number of these reports add supportive evidence to previous studies. For instance, the inflation of observers' self-calculations of agreement had been reported previously (e.g., Kent, O'Leary, Diament, & Dietz, 1974); importantly, the recent results underscore the necessity of having the experimenter (as opposed to the biased observers) calculate reliabilities. Similarly, the behaviors of nontarget children (as a setting variable) can affect observational data, instructions can affect reliability estimates, and systematic sampling is considered to be superior to global methods. Each of these issues requires attention when any of the forms of naturalistic observations are undertaken. Future research might find it interesting, though perplexing, to begin to try to unknot the processes that are involved (within the observer) in the data distortions that have been documented.

Regarding the special considerations of interobserver agreement in duration recording, Lambourne and Wheldall (1982) describe a microcomputer approach. When one wants to assess the duration of somewhat continuous behavior, these authors point out, stopwatches employed by two observers can be checked for reliability, but these data are usually a summary of the "whole session." A more accurate assessment of reliability would be possible if each session was divided into smaller segments. By using a computer, the intervals can be made as short as necessary. As Lambourne and Wheldall (1982) point out, each observer can be given a pushbutton connected to the computer, to be held down when the observer considers the subject to be emitting the target behavior. The computer can then divide the session into brief time intervals and determine the proportion of time that neither button was pressed, one or the other button was pressed, or both buttons were pressed. If there is relative ease of access to microcomputers, in the lab and now sometimes in the clinic, this approach might be implemented without great difficulty.

VALIDITY

According to the American Psychological Association standards for psychological measures, there are three major types of validity: content, criterion-related, and construct. Although these concepts have typically been applied to psychological tests, their meaning has relevance to the range of behavioral assessments as well. Ignoring for the moment any of the unwanted associations these concepts might have, validity coefficients are time-honored and worthy of review. It is not that these concepts are unknown, but that a refresher may be valuable.

"Content validity" refers to the degree to which an assessment taps a representative sample of the universe of behaviors relevant to the variable being measured. When assessing social skill, a content valid measure would tap all, as opposed to only select, dimensions of the construct of social skill. "Criterion-related validity" refers to either concurrent criterion-related validity or predictive criterion-related validity. The two are distinguished by time: In concurrent validity estimates the two measures are taken at the same time, whereas predictive validity indicates the extent to which future behavior is predicted by current measures.

"Construct validity" is more demanding than other validities. A measure or concept is said to have construct validity only when the accumulated results of a number of studies are integrated and judged to be supportive. For construct validity to be evident, characteristics of high and low scores must conform to expected relationships on several measures. Convergent validity and discriminant validity contribute to construct validation. "Intelligence" or "ego" might come to mind first as constructs, and it might seem foreign for behavioral assessors to be concerned with these topics. Perhaps so. However, concepts central to behavioral assessment can also be studied to examine their construct validity. For instance, hyperactivity, self-control, depression, and anxiety are concepts that can be examined for convergent and discriminant validity. Do the concepts of anxiety and depression have established construct validity? Problems develop when self-report assessments of these two concepts are correlated in the .7 range. Behavioral assessments can play an important role in efforts to establish the construct validity of the concepts of current interest.

The validity of role-play tests, a topic that has been under consideration (see Volume 8), continues to attract research interest. Working with elementary-school-aged children, Van Hasselt, Hersen, and Bellack (1981) examined role-play tests of social skills and reported generally low-magnitude relationships between role-play behavior and criterion situations. An ancillary finding deserves mention: Test–restest reliability of their role-play procedures was considered "unacceptable." While these data are consistent with the already reported lack of correspondence between behavior on role-play tests and in naturalistic situations with adult subjects, they also point to the potential need for lengthening role plays. Can we expect that a person will display "key" (predictive) behaviors in the brief role plays we create? As Van Hasselt *et al.* (1981) noted, brief role-play formats may be overly restrictive and consequently may fail to evoke critical responses.

We can learn a lesson here from our psychological colleagues in personnel selection, where role-play tests (of sorts) are undertaken for periods of days. For instance, you are hired to choose from among three candidates the one who will make the best new police chief for your city. You employ behavioral assessments in order to make your hiring recommendation. Do you use a 5-minute role play? Probably not. Rather, you confront the candidates with all of the challenges that are likely to confront a police chief within a period of a day or two and have raters, at various levels of employment in the police department (e.g., sergeants, captains, secretaries), observe and report their satisfaction or dissatisfaction with each candidate's behavior. The challenges may include a press conference, a crisis in need of immediate action, a racially loaded issue, and so forth. In essence, you get a sample of behavior from each candidate. This is a solid procedure not lacking in predictive criterion validity. But why do role-play tests come up short? Because they are short? Increasingly lengthy data bases are necessary to ensure that critical responses emerge and thereby acquire the desired validation. Industry literally buys such assessment procedures, and if we are to market behavioral assessment role plays, they too will have to employ more extended and convincing experiences.

At least two recent reports scrutinized the validity of some form of the Marital Interaction Coding System (MICS; Jones, Reid, & Patterson, 1975), thus continuing the line of research discussed in last year's *Annual Review*. The original MICS, according to Jacobson, Elwood, and Dallas (1981), consisted of 29 codes of verbal and nonverbal behavior (e.g., verbal: agree, criticize, interrupt; nonverbal: attention, positive physical contact). Typically, the MICS is used to code the behavior of couples in a standardized, laboratory problem-solving situation. Several a priori clusters of codes are also used. However, different sources may describe the clusters differently. According to Margolin and Wampold (1981) the commonly used a priori clusters are problem solving, verbal positive, nonverbal positive, verbal negative, nonverbal negative, and neutral.

The criterion-related validity of behavioral and self-report measures of problem solving and communication skills was examined and reported by Robin and Weiss (1980). They contrasted known groups of distressed and nondistressed mother–adolescent dyads as the criterion and used a modification of the MICS, an issues checklist, and a conflict behavior questionnaire as predictors. Based on the MICS, 12 of the 23 categories of behavior differentiated the criterion groups. The issues checklist and the conflict behavior questionnaire also discriminated distressed and nondistressed dyads. Given that the numerous codes of the MICS have been used in outcome research, Robin and Weiss's suggestion to use a single composite score (of the 12 discriminating categories) seems potentially useful. Cross-validation and additional inquiry into the hit rate of the assessments could buttress this recommendation.

Robin and Weiss (1980) pointed out that while the self-report and behavioral measures were not directly compared in terms of their ability to discriminate the known groups, both types of measures were successful at the task. The MICS composite score, however, explained 25% more of the variance than the other two measures.

Margolin and Wampold (1981) compared distressed and nondistressed couples using the MICS but took the method of analysis one step further than usual. These authors examined sequential communications with some methodological improvements over other sequential analyses. Subjects completed 1-hour interviews, self-report questionnaires, and two negotiation sessions. Videotapes of the negotiations were coded using a modified version of the MICS. Analyses of the behavioral rates indicated that nondistressed couples emit higher rates of problem-solving, verbal and nonverbal positive, and neutral behaviors than distressed couples. The sequential analysis indicated that positive reciprocity (reciprocity implies that behavior from one person will increase the probability that the other person will deploy the same behavior at a later time) characterized both distressed and nondistressed couples. However, negative reciprocity was significantly more likely in distressed than nondistressed couples. As the authors noted,

> The sequential findings surrounding negative behaviors are particularly notable in view of the lack of significant findings regarding negative base rates. That is, nondistressed couples emitted negative behaviors at a rate similar to that of distressed couples but not in a contingent fashion. In distressed couples, emitting an aversive action increased the probability of receiving a similar response and also reduced the probability of a positive reaction. (p. 565)

Although there were some limitations (e.g., the two samples came from different locations), the study continues to advance the social learning analysis of couples interactions and marital adjustment. It is troubling, however, to note that while self-reports were correlated among themselves and some MICS data were internally related, there were no significant correlations between self-report and MICS data.

The main theme of a study by Haynes, Jensen, Wise, and Sherman (1981) was the validity of a marital intake interview, but the MICS was employed as part of the study. The Haynes *et al.* interview was structured and lasted 20 minutes, with spouses interviewed either separately or together according to a counter-balanced schedule. Self-report questionnaires and 10-minute communication assessment (coded with the MICS) were also employed. Satisfied and dissatisfied couples were examined. It should be noted, however, that this comparison was between couples seeking marital enhancement (satisfied) and those seeking marital therapy (dissatisfied) and that this is different from the more typical distressed/nondistressed comparisons, where one group is seeking therapy and the other is not seeking help in any form.

Haynes *et al.*'s results provided strong support for the discriminant validity of the marital intake interview, with the discriminant function analysis correctly diagnosing 49 of 54 individuals. A second important finding was that the presence or absence of a spouse affected verbal reports during the interview and the criterion-related validities for separate interviews were higher than for joint interviews. Also along these lines, the criterion-related validities of the separate and joint interviews were mediated by the social sensitivity of the interview items. Sensitive items, such as sexual satisfaction, were more influenced by the single versus joint interview format than were nonsocially sensitive items such as demographics. Haynes *et al.* find that while it appears true that separate interviews may elicit more valid information, the joint interview also provides the clinician with an opportunity to gather a sample of actual marital interaction. Overall validity and clinical utility may be enhanced by conducting first separate and then joint interviews when working with couples seeking marital assistance. Readers interested in the MICS and a review of the assessment of the marital dysfunction literature in general might also refer to Jacobson *et al.* (1981).

Other clinical arenas have benefited from systematic behavioral observation systems, not the least of which are child clinical investigations (see Mash & Terdal, 1981). Robinson and Eyberg (1981) added, however, that the available observation systems are often too cumbersome for practicing clinicians who do not have access to equipment, coders, or lengthy home observation periods. These authors recently reported on the development of the Dyadic Parent–Child Interaction Coding System (DPICS)—a system of assessment intended to be clinically practical.

Robinson and Eyberg's (1981) DPICS consists of 22 parent and child behavior categories in parent-directed interaction and 19 categories in child-directed interaction. Sample parent behaviors include direct command, indirect command, labeled praise, unlabeled praise, and descriptive question. Sample child behaviors include whine, yell, and noncompliance. Behavioral sequences were also considered, such as the parent's response following a child's response to parental command. Other variables were also created from the observation categories (e.g., total deviant behavior = whine + cry + physical negative + smart talk + yell + destructive).

Two observations were taken by four observers, both in a clinic setting. The observations produced total frequency data per 5-minute interval, with a total of 10 minutes of observation available from the two observations (1 week apart). Average interrater reliabilities, defined as the correlation between the behavioral frequencies of two observers during 244 of the 276 5-minute observations, were .91 (parent behaviors) and .92 (child behaviors).

Known groups were compared. Conduct-problem families were 20 referred families with a problem child aged 2 to 7 (and with at least one sibling aged 2 to 10, and not retarded or severely disordered). There were 22 nondisturbed families recruited by advertisement. These families had at least two appropriately aged children but no child with a history of behavior problems and no family member in psychotherapy. Analyses of the behavioral observations evidenced that referred children engaged in higher rates of noncompliant behavior than normal children, and their parents were more critical and directive than normal parents. Using the DPICS, Robinson and Eyberg were able to correctly classify 94% of the families.

While the DPICS was successful in discriminating the known groups, results were based on only a brief sample (10 minutes) of behavior. Robinson and Eyberg (1981) point out that the structure of the situations allowed parents and children to behave under varying degrees of parental control and suggest that this structural feature maximized the opportunity to observe dysfunctional behavior.

The technology and observational methodology for behavioral assessments have been noticeably advanced over their short history. However, we are far from a definitive statement about the length of behavioral assessment necessary to achieve a desired level of predictive criterion-related validity. Research evaluating the validity of variations in the duration of observation is much needed. Potentially, this line of inquiry could provide recommendations regarding the optimal duration of behavioral observations. It is of interest to note that criterion-related validity can apply not only to discriminating known groups but also to accurately predicting successful versus unsuccessful treatment outcomes.

SELECTED ASSESSMENT TARGETS

Although I now turn away from the direct commentary on issues of reliability and validity per se and turn toward a discussion of specific targets of assessment, I fully anticipate that reliability and validity issues will resurface. Indeed, most assessment research within each content area pertains to the psychometric credentials of the assessments. Four content areas are examined in the pages that follow: depression, social skills, assertion, and hyperactivity.

Depression

Perhaps it can be said to be paradoxical, but the topic of depressed mood has captured the unveiled energy and enthusiasm of numerous clinical researchers. Already we have been witness to the presentation of diverse etiological models and the proliferation of methods and evaluations of psychotherapeutic strategies. Recent research reports document the nearly unbridled vitality of the interest in the assessment of depression.

Depression is a multifaceted pattern with symptoms as varied as psychomotor retardation, loss of appetite, dejected mood, crying spells, indecisiveness, sleep disturbance, and cognitive distortion, and the methods of assessment include behavioral observations (see Lewinsohn & Lee, 1981), the Hamilton Rating Scale (Hamilton, 1960), and self-report inventories (e.g., the Beck Depression Inventory [BDI; Beck, Ward, Mendelson, Mock, & Erbaugh, 1961] and the Depression scale of the MMPI). Apparently the BDI is of particular interest, for much archival space has been allotted to recent research on this measure.

As described in Lewinsohn and Lee's (1981) discussion of the behavioral assessment of affective disorders, the BDI consists of 21 items to which subjects respond the way they feel "today"; that is, "right now." (Note also that the scale is based on an interview procedure.) The scale appears often in studies of the etiology and treatment of depressive disorders. Nevertheless, many questions about the psychometric qualities of the BDI have long remained unexamined.

Sacco (1981) has recently challenged the test–retest reliability of the BDI. The challenge was based on Sacco's research experience with college students who were classified at one level of depression on one day but would not be similarly classified upon another assessment. Although some reported test–retest reliability coefficients have been acceptable (e.g., 75 in Rehm, 1976; .79 and .86 in Gallagher, Nies, & Thompson, 1982), what of the reliability of the classification of subjects as "not depressed," "mildly depressed," "moderately depressed," and "severely depressed"? Hammen (1980) reported that 79% of college students classified as moderately depressed were no longer so classified after 2 to 3 weeks. Recently, Hatzenbuehler, Parpal, and Matthews (1982) reported that students scoring high on the BDI were not reliably classified upon retesting, even when retesting was done on the same day. In a second study, these authors found less reliable classification for the more-depressed subjects. Hatzenbuehler *et al.* recommended that the BDI instructions require that subjects report their feelings and symptoms over the past week rather than just for today.

For purposes of research, subjects can be initially screened by large-group administration of the BDI, but the subjects should be readministered the scale just before their actual participation in experiments. This reassessment seems essential, for journal reviewers continually point to this potential methodological flaw. Sacco's (1981) conclusion was quite telling: "Failure to reassess depression level immediately prior to beginning the experiment results in sufficient ambiguity to seriously threaten the validity of the interpretation of results . . ." (pp. 145–146).

A report by King and Buchwald (1982) investigated sex differences and the effects of public versus private administration of the BDI. It is first valuable to recall that epidemiological evidence documents that depression is more common among women than among men. Women may actually be more depressed, may live in more depressing circumstances, or may be more likely to admit depressive symptoms than men. King and Buchwald identified the context of BDI administration as a potentially explanatory factor. For instance, King and Buchwald (1982) reported that Beck (1967) found that women scored significantly higher than men in a sample of 606 psychiatric patients, but that Hammen and Padesky (1977) did not find sex differences in a sample of 2272 college students. King and Buchwald went on to report that Beck administered the BDI in an interview, whereas Hammen and Padesky used a paper-and-pencil questionnaire. Based on these data, the authors sought to examine the effects of the disclosure situation on sex differences in depression.

In their first experiment, King and Buchwald (1982) studied 106 male and 104 female college students who either endorsed a self-report BDI or responded to BDI questions in a face-to-face interview. Methodological problems, such as the absence of random assignment and the fact that the self-report questionnaire was given in groups (and perhaps not seen as "private"), undermined the authors' findings. In their second study these problems were remedied. Somewhat surprisingly, however, the results of both studies did *not* confirm that women would report more depression than men in an interview situation whereas the sex differences would not emerge from a questionnaire administration. King and Buchwald did report that there was a greater willingness to admit more symptoms to a same-sex person. Given our focus on the BDI as an assessment device, it is important to point out that these results "indicate that deviation from Beck's prescribed interview format in the form of questionnaire presentation does not generally depress or inflate scores, at least among college students" (p. 968).

Psychometric properties of the BDI with psychiatrically hospitalized adolescents are reported to be satisfactory (Strober, Green, & Carlson, 1981). Coefficient α (internal consistency) was .79, test–retest reliability (5-day interval) was .69 (.74 for patients with affective diagnoses and .51 for patients with nonaffective diagnoses), and BDI scores were correlated .67 with global clinical ratings of depression. Using a cutoff score of 16 and above, the BDI correctly identified 81% of the sample. Using a sample of older adults (over 60 years of age), Gallagher et al. (1982) reported test–retest reliabilities over a 6-to-21-day interval. For normal elderly subjects test–retest reliability was .86, for depressed elderly subjects it was .79. Estimates of interval consistency were between .58 and .91.

Reynolds and Gould (1981) examined the BDIs of 163 methadone maintenance patients and reported an internal consistency of .85. These authors also studied the short form of the BDI (13 items) and reported an internal consistency of .83. Both the long form and the short form were significantly correlated with another self-report scale of depression and a loneliness scale. The long form and the short form were correlated .93. The authors concluded that both the standard and short forms of the BDI were found to be reliable and valid measures. However, correlations between long and short forms of a test are insufficient for evaluating the short form. For instance, it is possible that even when highly significant long–short form correlations exist, the short form may be inaccurate in assigning individual subjects to categories of depression. A more rigorous test of the utility of short forms would require that both forms be used to designate levels (categories) of depression (e.g., moderate, severe) and subsequently to examine the percentage agreement.

Although Lewinsohn and Teri (1982) did not use the BDI, their research has direct bearing on the question of the accuracy of "labeling" or "diagnosing" depression based on a single administration of a self-report measure. Lewinsohn and Teri (1982) used (1) the Center for Epidemiological Studies—Depression Scale (CES-D; Radloff, 1977), (2) a 5-point Likert rating of depression for self-labeling, and (3) a Schedule for Affective Disorders and Schizophrenia (SADS) interview categorized in Research Diagnostic Criteria (RDC; Spitzer, Endicott, & Robins, 1978a).

Lewinsohn and Teri (1982) reported different degrees of accuracy for categorizing depressed and nondepressed subjects. Nondepressed subjects were classified with 82% accuracy using CES-D scores < 17. A score ≥ 17 resulted in an accuracy rate of only 34%. Successive CES-D administrations increased accuracy (to 49% for four administrations). The authors appropriately conclude that "self-report measures can adequately classify nondepressed subjects, yielding a very small false negative rate," but that "classification of subjects as depressed cannot be accomplished by reliance on self-report measures alone" (p. 591).

Social Skills Assessment

A recent review (Curran & Wessberg, 1981) concluded that "social skills assessment is at a very primitive level, with no one instrument adequately validated" (pp. 406–407). Part of the problem is no doubt the result of inadequate conceptual systems guiding social skills assessments. But, as Curran and Wessberg propose and as I agree, the conceptualization of the problem can be improved and the construct more reasonably studied with the aid of traditional assessment methodologies. Curran and Wessberg do not refer here to specific traditional tests or test procedures but to the traditional methodological issues of incremental validity, nomological networks, taxometric research, and construct validation.

Curran and his associates have reported investigations of the generalizability of a behavioral role-play measure of social skills called the Simulated Social Interaction Test (SSIT). The SSIT (see Curran, Monti, Corriveau, Hay, Hagerman, Zwick, & Farrell, 1980) consists of four practice simulations followed by the eight SSIT simulations. Each simulation involves a narrator, who reads a script describing the social situation, and a confederate, who issues prompts. In the Curran et al. (1980) report, the generalizability of the SSIT across judges, items, and methods was examined. The authors reported "good" agreement between judges and "good" discriminant validity between social skills and social anxiety. Social skills were evaluated differently across different situations and there was a lack of convergent validity between the judges' SSIT ratings and two self-ratings.

Two experiments on the external validity of the SSIT were reported by Wessberg, Curran, Monti, Corriveau, Coyne, and Dziadosz (1981). In the first project, the performances of psychiatric patients and National Guardsmen on the SSIT were compared. Judges rated the guardsmen as less anxious and more socially skilled than the patients. The second study examined the relationship of the judges' ratings of the psychiatric patients' social skills with others' perceptions of the social skills of these same individuals. These "others" included "the patients themselves, five nurses on an inpatient unit, two trained raters who observed subjects during a noontime meal, a research assistant who recruited and escorted these subjects to our research laboratory, and two senior members of our research team who conducted a structured interview examining each subject's developmental social history" (p. 215). The correlations (corrected for the unreliability of the non-SSIT ratings) between SSIT ratings and the other ratings (with the exception of the ward ratings at the noontime meal) were significant and in the moderate range.

Although the external validity of role-play tests has been questioned (e.g., Bellack, Hersen, & Lamparksi, 1979; Bellack, Hersen, & Turner, 1978; see also Volume 8 of this *Annual Review*), Wessberg *et al.*'s (1981) data provided moderate support for the external validity of the SSIT. What might explain the apparent inconsistency in these conclusions? Wessberg *et al.* (1981) suggest that their use of molar ratings in comparison to Bellack and associates' use of molecular ratings accounts for the discrepancy. They quote Wiggins (1973), who noted that "narrowly defined behavioral attributes run the risk of a high degree of specificity, which may preclude the possibility of generalizability to criterion behaviors" (Wessberg *et al.*, p. 218). I propose that investigators conduct a direct study of the external validity of ratings that vary along the specific–global dimension, though Wessberg *et al.*'s (1981) recommendation to seek midrange units may already have both a reasonable rationale and indirect research support.

Curran, Wessberg, Farrell, Monti, Corriveau, and Coyne (1982) also addressed generalizability but asked whether different social skills laboratories are measuring the same construct. The researchers shared the videotapes of 20 psychiatric patients and 20 National Guardsmen used in the Wessberg *et al.* (1981) report; the videotapes included short role-play scenes from the SSIT and a longer extended interaction (the "longer extended interaction" was 2 minutes long). Six different laboratories known for research on social skills were involved. Curran *et al.* (1982) reported, though this summary loses some of the complexities of the study, moderate degrees of generalizability across laboratories based on the brief role plays. Based on the longer interactions, generalizability was found for the anxiety ratings but relative differences were found for the social skills ratings. The findings are somewhat equivocal. However, the authors report being encouraged, since there are numerous factors working against generalizability across laboratories.

Despite the fact that the findings are less than clear cut, a few positive features of the work of Curran and his associates work are noteworthy. First, there is a cognizance of the need to examine more than one construct: The authors examine both social skills and social anxiety and thereby allow for differentiation of two constructs and perhaps the discovery of construct-specific phenomena. When one finds and reports differences between subjects who differ on social skills alone, readers may question whether social skills were the meaningful individual difference variable or whether some other concept, such as social anxiety, might account for the observed differences. By using two constructs, the Curran and associates group-model appropriate assessment methodologies.

Second, Curran and his colleagues have put generalizability theory and methods (see Cronbach, Gleser, Nanda, & Rajaratnam, 1972) to good use. Similarly, some of the solid traditional assessment methodologies are evident in this research, and they document the applicability of advances in assessment in general to the advancement of behavioral assessment in particular. The collaboration of traditional psychometrics and behavioral assessment is one of the successful integrations within behavior therapy (Kendall, 1982d). However, the criticism of the brevity of role plays (2 minutes in duration) pertains here as well as anywhere, and future research with lengthier role plays is due.

Additional quality social skills assessment research has appeared in the recent past. For instance, Gaffney and McFall (1981) developed a social skills assessment for discriminating delinquent and nondelinquent girls. Their measure, the Problem Inventory for Adolescent Girls (PIAG), correctly assigned 85% of subjects to their appropriate delinquent or nondelinquent group. Based on the discriminating and non-discriminating items, the authors suggested that delinquency seemed more closely related to skill deficits in interacting with adult authority figures than to skill deficits with peers. It is interesting to note that some of the interventions with similar populations (e.g., Sarason & Sarason, 1981; see also Chapter 4) have worked specifically to teach adolescents how to interact with adult figures (on job interviews, for example). This illustration is but one of the many ties between systematic assessments and their outcomes and the enhancement of intervention procedures.

Assessing Assertion

As mentioned in Chapter 4, where the treatment of nonassertiveness is considered, psychological research on the construct of assertion continues to earn its share of archival space. In last year's *Annual Review* (Volume 8), literature on measuring assertion seemed to share the common ground of issues of validity; this year's review discovered that the role of cognition in the assessment of assertion attracted notice. While this trend clearly reflects the larger drift toward and interest in cognition, it also reflects the contemporary penchant away from intervention evaluations and toward more careful examination of the nature of the disorder one is trying to treat. Indeed, my perception is that the future trend across all major topic areas is toward the detailed study of the cognitive distortions and deficits associated with specific patterns of disordered behavior. I hasten to add, however, that the implications for treatment that these results would provide remain a primary source of motivation.

The question of whether nonassertiveness is a function more of skill deficits or of selective self-evaluation was addressed by Alden and Cappe (1981). Using students who scored significantly differently from a normative sample (both assertive and nonassertive), the researchers asked their subjects to role play a series of assertion situations as assertively as possible. These performances were videotaped and rated by both trained observers and the subjects themselves. Subjects and trained observers also rated the performances of assertive, nonassertive, and aggressive models.

Based on the trained observers' ratings, assertive and nonassertive subjects did not differ in behavioral competence while role playing. Also, the assertive and nonassertive subjects did not differ in their ratings of the models' performances. However, the nonassertive participants rated themselves as less assertive, less effective, and more anxious than the assertive participants rated themselves. In terms of the agreement between trained observers' ratings and subjects' self-ratings, nonassertive subjects were generally in agreement with observers. In contrast, assertive subjects were significantly more positive about their performance than the observers were. Alden and Cappe (1981) continued by pointing out that "the nonassertive subjects functioned more like trained raters using stringent evaluation standards while the assertive subjects were more self-accepting" (p. 113). These findings are consistent with others' conclusions that nonassertiveness concerns cognitive-evaluative difficulties as opposed to behavioral inability.

Of the other researchers who have drawn similar conclusions, the work of Schwartz and Gottman (1976) is often cited. A paper by Bruch (1981) reports on a replication and extension of this line of research. Subjects (both male and female) of high, moderate, and low assertiveness completed self-report and role-play assessments. As part of an extension of earlier work, subjects were also assessed for measures of information-processing style and interpersonal problem-solving ability. (Information processing and assertiveness are addressed by Rudy, Merluzzi, & Henahan, 1982; see the section on schemata.) Although Bruch (1981) did not support the earlier finding that knowledge of appropriate assertive responses did not differentiate levels of assertion, he did replicate the finding that moderate- and low-assertion subjects did not, within themselves, differ with regard to positive and negative thinking but that high-assertion subjects did. The nature of the differences within the high-assertion group was an absence of negative thinking (see also the section on powers of nonnegative thinking).

The information-processing dimension referred to cognitive complexity (as exemplified by a paragraph completion test; see Hunt, Butler, Noy, & Rosser, 1978), and it was reported that subjects high on assertiveness received high cognitive-complexity scores (see also Bruch, Juster, & Heisler, 1982). High scorers, according to Schroder, Driver, and Streufert (1967), and as cited in Bruch (1981), view situations from multiple perspectives and use self-standards to make decisions, while low scorers use categorical judgments and rely on external authority in decision making. This finding seems to relate to Alden and Cappe's (1981) work, in which subjects who differed in level of assertion also differed in terms of standards for self and other judgments.

On a less conceptual level, studies by Andrasik, Heimberg, Edlund, and Blankenship (1981) and Rock (1981) are pertinent. Andrasik *et al.* rated and reported the reading levels (readability scores) of 11 often-used self-report assertion inventories. The measures were typically of 7th-to-10th grade level and the test instructions were 8th-to-12th grade level. Apparently, most individuals will be able to comprehend the instructions and items on assertion inventories. Rock (1981) examined the social desirability of two self-report assertion inventories and suggested, based on the results, that caution be exercised when interpreting scores on the assertion measures studied.

Hyperactivity

What might you expect of a topic such as hyperactivity? A simple and calm dialogue? Not likely. Consistent with the early emphasis on excessive motor activity within hyperactivity research, you might expect that the topic would appear "all over the place." A scattered pattern emerged in Volume 8 of this series, with hyperactivity receiving deserved attention in both the chapter on children and adolescents and the chapter on behavioral medicine. Adding to the mobility of the topic, I consider it here as well as I focus on behavioral assessment.

The main theme of contemporary hyperactivity assessment research has been efforts to determine the association between the construct of hyperactivity and the concept of aggression. In a sense, researchers (e.g., Milich, Loney, & Landau, 1982; O'Leary & Steen, 1982; Prinz, Connor, & Wilson, 1981; Roberts, Milich, Loney, & Caputo, 1981) have been seeking to determine the characteristics of hyperactivity that are essentially independent of aggression. This line of inquiry is often traced to Loney and her colleagues' paper on subgrouping hyperactive children (Loney, Langhorne, & Paternite, 1978). The results reported at that time indicated that it was feasible to separate the behavioral patterns of hyperactivity and aggression. That is, a factor analysis of judges' ratings of the frequency and severity of symptoms of hyperactivity resulted in two factors: hyperactivity and aggression. I will now turn to some recent research that bears on this issue.

Roberts *et al.* (1981) conducted a multitrait–multimethod analysis of teacher ratings of aggression, hyperactivity, and inattention. Their results provided reasonable convergent and discriminant validity and documented that teachers could distinguish the dimensions of aggression, hyperactivity, and inattention.

Hyperactivity and aggression was also studied by Prinz *et al.* (1981), who examined 109 first- to third-graders. Teachers provided daily evaluations on a daily behavior checklist that included 11 aggressive (e.g., argued in an angry way) and 11 hyperactive (e.g., ran around room during work or quiet time) behaviors. A subgroup of children was selected: These children exhibited both hyperactive and aggressive behavior at rates greater than 98% of their classmates. This subgroup was found to score significantly higher on teacher ratings using the Conners scale (Conners, 1973) than an alternate subgroup who showed hyperactive but not aggressive behaviors. Apparently, high scores on the often-used Conners scale indicate greater frequencies of aggressive as well as hyperactive behaviors. The clarity of the construct assessed by the Conners is in question.

To further the validational evidence for the differentiation of hyperactive and aggressive dimensions, Milich *et al.* (1982) examined observational data gathered in a playroom situation. The subjects were 90 boys referred to an outpatient psychiatry service. By DSM-III diagnoses, 22 had attention deficit disorder, 22 conduct disorder, 8 had received both of these diagnoses, and 38 were assigned other diagnoses.

The 90 boys participated in two 15-minute playroom observation periods: a free-play situation and a restricted, academic situation. The playroom floor was marked into grids and several behaviors were coded (e.g., grid crossing, out-of-seat, fidgeting, attention shifts). Chart ratings similar to those employed in Loney *et al.* (1978) were examined (e.g., frequency/severity of attention problems, impulsivity, aggressive interpersonal), and mother and teacher ratings were gathered.

Factor analysis yielded three factors: hyperactivity, anxiety/depression, and aggression. Regarding demographic data, socioeconomic status was related to the aggression factor but not the hyperactivity factor. The hyperactivity factor helped account for variations in mothers' and teachers' ratings of hyperactivity and inattention but did not add to the prediction of conduct problems. Similarly, the hyperactivity factor added to the prediction of the observation data beyond the common variance with the aggression factor. Milich *et al.* (1982) concluded that the two factors do not provide redundant information and that the separation of the two dimensions provides valuable information. It is important to note here that the earlier study by Loney *et al.* (1978) had been criticized for using a homogeneous sample of hyperactive subjects. In the Milich *et al.* report, however, the two dimensions were identified with a heterogeneous sample.

The apparent replication and the assumed clearing of the air may not hold, as the air turns smoggy again when we consider additional evidence provided by O'Leary and Steen (1982). These authors provided a direct examination of the issue of the homogeneity/heterogeneity of subjects. Three samples of children were used: a heterogeneous group, the hyperactive sample of the heterogeneous group, and another sample of hyperactive children. Factor and correlational analyses produced separate hyperactivity and aggression dimensions in both samples of hyperactive children but not in the heterogeneous sample of children. The O'Leary and Steen methods were operationally different from those of Loney et al. (O'Leary & Steen used the Stony Brook scale for assessing symptom ratings), but conceptually they were a replication. With the exception of the heterogeneous sample, the O'Leary and Steen findings further document that hyperactivity and aggression are independent dimensions of behavior within hyperactive children.

Although it is speculative at this time, it seems reasonable to hypothesize that the degree of independence between the two dimensions is in part the direct result of the accuracy of the original referral and referral agent. Given the popular acceptance of methylphenidate as a successful treatment for hyperactivity and given the psychological naivete of some referral agents, it is not unlikely that "problem kids," classroom nuisances, or old-fashioned "brats" are sent off for medication to calm them down. It may not be a great psychological insight, but the dimensions that have emerged from current research may be related to the reasons for referral. Nevertheless, the feasibility and desirability of differentiating hyperactivity and aggression takes on extra importance when there are associated advances in the prediction of meaningful individual reactions—for instance, when the separation of the two dimensions helps predict response to medications and the likelihood of delinquency (Loney, Kramer, & Milich, 1983). Untempered enthusiasm is not yet called for, as the evidence is inconclusive and the research results remain equivocal (e.g., Lahey, Green, & Forehand, 1980).

Some of the studies discussed in this section have addressed the question of what is being measured by the often-used scales of hyperactivity. More specifically, they have inquired about the concept of aggression within assessments of hyperactivity. Kendall and Brophy (1981) asked a similar question: "What is being measured by the often-used Conners scale of hyperactivity?" but they were interested in the motor activity-versus-attentional-problems distinction. According to DSM-III, hyperactivity is a portion of the attention deficit disorder. But do teacher ratings on the Conners scale reflect excessive motor activity or attentional problems? Based on teacher ratings, mechanical measures of activity, and observations of attention behavior in a testing situation, Kendall and Brophy (1981) reported that teachers' ratings were meaningfully related only to the indices of activity. The failure of the teacher rating scales to tap the attentional component suggests that additional measurements of attentional deficits and capacities are required for accurate determination of attentional deficiencies.

Other Topics Briefly Noted

BEHAVIORAL INTERVIEW TRAINING

Interviews remain one of the most often used and near universally appropriate methods of assessment, and several studies have examined the effects of various types of interview training. In an early study, Bailey, Deardorff, and Nay (1977) compared role playing, video feedback, and modeling to no-treatment controls. Subjects were undergraduates who were learning basic interviewing procedures. Bailey et al. (1977) found that modeling was generally associated with the greatest gains in "positive therapist behavior," followed by feedback and role playing. The authors described the effects of role playing as a poor third-place finish. These results, while generally consistent with the authors' hypotheses, are somewhat surprising, since role playing has an enactive performance-based component and might not be the candidate for third place.

In a more recent study, Keane, Black, Collins, and Vinson (1982) compared behavioral rehearsal, modeling, and a no-treatment control. Subjects were clinical pharmacy students learning behavioral interviewing (for conducting functional analyses). Keane et al.'s behavioral rehearsal group not only saw a modeling film but also received 3 hours of rehearsal with feedback and cue cards. The modeling group observed the videotape in groups. Based on analyses of content (number of areas explored regarding seizures and mediation compliance) and style (e.g., use of open-ended questions, minimizing interviewer talk time), both treatment groups increased the number of content areas; behavioral rehearsal produced significantly greater gains. Behavioral rehearsal was the only treatment to improve interview style. Moreover, the pharmacists reported being extremely satisfied with the behavioral rehearsal program. Thus, unlike Bailey et al., the more performance-based training led to more improved interviewing. It may be the case that the role-play training in the Bailey et al. study was relatively ineffective because it did not include the modeling or directive feedback components as the Keane et al. study did.

Using a multiple baseline across subjects, Brown, Kratochwill, and Bergan (1982) studied the effects of a multicomponent interview training program. Interview students were taught verbal skills to aid in specifying, observing, and summarizing problem behaviors and behavior settings. Based on observation, desired changes were evident as a result of training.

MEASURES OF SEXUAL AROUSAL

In a paper discussing psychophysiological issues in behavioral psychotherapy, Sartory (1981) provides a brief discussion of measures of sexual arousal. For males, a strain gauge has been used to measure penile circumference and a plethysmograph to measure penile volume changes. Sartory mentions that the former technique is simpler but the latter has been shown to be more sensitive within the range of mild sexual arousal. For women, in contrast, assessments have not progressed as rapidly. However, vaginal engorgement has been monitored in some studies. Research by Earls and Jackson (1981) suggests that temperature does not affect the assessment of penile tumescence, and Davidson, Malcolm, Lanthier, Barbaree, and Ho (1981) provided suggestions for operating the Parks plethysmograph.

COGNITIVE–BEHAVIORAL ASSESSMENT

A great deal of contemporary research concentrates on cognition: the role of self-statements in the onset of disordered behavior patterns, the processing of information, the structure of our organizing systems, the role of cognition distortions in normal and pathological behavior patterns, and the evaluation of cognitive change within behavioral change. As noted last year, even the disinterested observer must readily recognize the striking and persistent vigor of behavior therapy's interest in the role of cognition. Outlines and discussions of the methods for the measurement of cognition have appeared (see Kendall & Hollon, 1981b; Merluzzi, Glass, & Genest, 1981), and recent research conspicuously exhibits the application of all kinds of assessment strategies: think aloud (e.g., Waern, 1980), thought listing (e.g., Last, Barlow, & O'Brien, 1982), thought sampling (e.g., Hunt & Rosen, 1981), and self-statement inventories (e.g., Glass, Merluzzi, Biever, & Larsen, 1982; Harrell, Chambless, & Calhoun, 1981; Hollon & Kendall, 1980; Klass, 1981; Ryon & Harrell, 1982). This year's review examines the following topics: the power of nonnegative thinking, self-efficacy, schemata, self-statements, self-control, and a pot-luck blend of cognitive topics serving as food for thought.

The Power of Nonnegative Thinking

Norman Vincent Peale, a minister, in collaboration with Smiley Blanton, a psychiatrist, ran Marble Collegiate Church (a religiopsychiatric clinic) on Fifth Avenue in New York. Riding the crest of the post-Korean War revival of religion, Peale gained an audience. He is perhaps best known for his book *The Power of Positive Thinking* (1952), which promises personal gains through the power of self-encouragement. This theme is also evident in children's tales, such as the story of the train that was struggling to reach the top of the mountain while chanting "I think I can, I think I can." Current research evidence, however, does not support such a simplistic conceptualization. In contrast, evidence suggests that various operationalizations of psychological adjustment are related not so much to positive thinking as to the absence of negative thinking. I have elsewhere referred to this as "the power of nonnegative thinking" (Kendall & Hollon, 1981a; Kendall & Korgeski, 1979).

Although equivocal in the conclusions that are reached, the distinction between positive and negative self-talk continues to be one of the dominant dichotomies employed in the scoring of cognitive assessments. The dichotomy appeared early on (e.g., Schwartz & Gottman, 1976), has been replicated (e.g., Bruch, 1981), and continues to date (e.g., Galassi, Frierson, & Sharer, 1981a). Importantly, the application of the positive thinking versus negative thinking dichotomy has crossed assessment methodologies with self-statement inventories (e.g., Kendall, Williams, Pechacek, Graham, Shisslak, & Herzoff, 1979), thought checklists (e.g., Galassi *et al.*, 1981a), and thought listing (e.g., Cacioppo, Glass, & Merluzzi, 1979) being recent examples.

Gormally, Sipps, Raphael, Edwin, and Varvil-Weld (1981) compared a clinical sample of anxious men and a group of competent daters and reported that "the tendency to hold irrational beliefs and the construction of social overtures as quite risky, discriminated between confident and anxious men" (p. 301). The authors went on to state that the greater the subjects' tendency to engage in cognitions that are maladaptive (negative), the less self-confidence they reported in social encounters.

In a study of the treatment of debilitating performance anxiety (Kendrick, Craig, Lawson, & Davidson, 1982; see also discussion in Chapter 4) the authors examined variations in positive and negative self-talk and their associations with improvement. They reported that "therapeutic gains were largely associated with reductions in negative self-statements." In a case report of the exposure treatment of an agoraphobic, Last *et al.* (1982) reported that exposure resulted in behavioral improvement and a worsening of the client's cognitive style. However, at 1-year follow-up the cognitive style had improved. Consistent with my notion of the power of nonnegative thinking, the improvement was seen in a near absence of maladaptive thoughts, but without the appearance of positive thoughts. Cognitive change followed behavioral change, with the cognitive change being seen in the reduction of negative thinking.

An interesting parallel emerges when we consider the positive-versus-negative dichotomy and the power of nonnegativity, not with cognitions but with behaviors. Data presented by Margolin and Wampold (1981) are germane. Margolin and Wampold's study dealt with a sequential analysis of behaviors associated with conflict and accord in distressed and nondistressed marital partners (see also discussion on pp. 45–46). The results of current interest pertain to the sequencing of positive and negative behaviors. Positive reciprocity characterized both distressed and nondistressed couples, and both distressed and nondistressed couples emitted negative behaviors at a similar rate; however, negative reciprocity and negative reactivity were more likely to occur in distressed couples. Negative reciprocity differentiated distressed and nondistressed couples, with the nondistressed couples not showing negative reciprocity.

Self-Efficacy

In Volume 8 of the *Annual Review* self-efficacy was seen as a conceptual framework that had captured the interest of behaviorally oriented applied psychologists. The observation remains true this year, as an impressive variety of researchers initiate or continue assessments of self-efficacy and examinations of self-efficacy theory. Indeed, the concept has not gone unnoticed, nor has it gone unquestioned.

Bandura's theory of self-efficacy (1977a) proposes that self-efficacy is a cognitive mechanism, common across behavior change methods, for mediating behavioral responses. Behavioral choices and the persistences toward coping or completion also are influenced by self-efficacy. Given comparable skills and motivation, self-efficacy is the determinant of behavior. In a recent paper Bandura (1982) states that "perceived self-efficacy is concerned with judgments of how well one can execute courses of action required to deal with prospective situations" (p. 122). Four sources of information provide the basis for judgments of self-efficacy: performance attainments, vicarious (observational) experiences, verbal persuasion, and physiological states. Enactive attainments provide the most influential source of efficacy information (Bandura, 1982).

Although Bandura and his colleagues have been some of the most productive and supportive researchers examining self-efficacy (e.g., see Bandura, 1982; Bandura, Reese, & Adams, 1982), other researchers in other labs have provided supportive evidence as well. In the review of self-efficacy in human agency by Bandura (1982) we learn of the influential role of self-efficacy judgments across topical domains. For instance, in addition to the confirmatory evidence that different modes of influence affect perceptions of efficacy (e.g., Bandura & Adams, 1977; Bandura, Adams, & Beyer, 1977; Bandura, Adams, Hardy, & Howells, 1980) and that behavior corresponds to reported efficacy regardless of the mode of influence, we are also exposed to literature on the role of self-efficacy judgments in the process of relapse from self-regulatory training, the enhancement of postcoronary rehabilitation, the selection of career interests, the factors that undermine personal efficacy, and the social influences of collective efficacy. Since it is outside the scope of the present work to review all of the self-efficacy studies, I refer readers to Bandura's (1982) paper for an up-to-date review. This more circumscribed discussion will merely note some interesting research findings regarding self-efficacy and mention related issues of assessment.

In one of the more compelling and comprehensive reports (Bandura et al., 1982), fearful subjects' self-efficacy levels were enhanced and coping behavior was changed correspondingly. This "efficacy–action relationship was replicated across different modes of efficacy induction, different types of behavioral dysfunction, and in both intergroup and intrasubject comparisons" (Bandura et al., 1982, p. 5). Assessments of behavioral avoidance (e.g., snake and spider phobic approach tests) and fear arousal accompanied self-reported judgments of self-efficacy. Strength of self-efficacy was rated on a 100-point scale with 10-unit intervals. Level of self-efficacy was the number of performance tasks that subjects judged as having a self-efficacy over 20. In later studies also included in this report, heart rate and blood pressure data were gathered.

In an intriguing, if not complex, application of path analysis, Feltz (1982) examined the causal contribution of self-efficacy to performance in a sports endeavor (back diving). Heart rates, self-reported anxiety and diving efficacy, and qualified judgments of performance were gathered and multiple performance trails included. The self-efficacy assessment concerned subjects' ratings of their strength of belief that they could accomplish the back dive at four different heights of the diving board. The customary 100-point scale with 10-unit intervals was employed. However, since there were only four diving heights, the level of self-efficacy was not assessed (generality of self-efficacy was also not measured). Feltz reported that an imbalanced reciprocal cause-

and-effect relationship emerged between self-efficacy and back-diving performance: As one gained experience with the performance task, performance had a greater influence on self-efficacy than self-efficacy had on performance. Feltz's modified model, where performance and efficacy were predictions, explained greater portions of the variance.

The recent studies of self-efficacy provide solid models for methodology in general and for assessment methodology in particular. In each case behavioral performance assessments, physiological reactions, and self-efficacy judgments were gathered and their interrelationships scrutinized carefully. Assessments of behavior, physiology, and cognition are the hallmark of comprehensive measurement. It is also pleasing to acknowledge that precautions are being taken to reduce any unwanted effects from assessing self-efficacy in a public, as compared to a private, fashion. In Feltz (1982), for example, subjects folded and slipped questionnaire measures into a box to reduce experimenter influence.

Without going into detail about the experimental procedures and findings, we can review several recent reports that document the versatility of the assessment of self-efficacy. For example, Condiotte and Lichtenstein (1981) developed a pretreatment confidence questionnaire designed to assess the magnitude, strength, and generality of efficacy expectations in smoking situations. The scale included 48 items (situations), and subjects were asked to indicate the probability that they would be able to resist the urge to smoke in each situation. DiClemente (1981) also reported a measure of self-efficacy for smoking avoidance consisting of 12 situations. The development of physical self-efficacy scale was reported by Ryckman, Robbins, Thornton, and Cantrell (1982).

Schunk (1982) has assessed self-efficacy with 7- to 10-year-old children in a study demonstrating that effort-attributional feedback for past achievement led to more rapid mastery of new tasks and higher perceptions of self-efficacy. Importantly, children were given practice with the procedure of rating self-efficacy. The 100-point scale (10-unit intervals) was applied to a jumping task (10 = not sure, 40 = maybe, 70 = pretty sure, and 100 = real sure). Jumping distances ranged from a few inches to 10 yards. Thus, children were given meaningful experience with the scale and with the notion of estimating confidence. Keyser and Barling (1981) did not use a pretraining experience yet were successful in assessing sixth-grade children's scholastic efficacy beliefs on a 20-item 5-point Likert scale. A lack of variability in efficacy judgments was reported as problematic in another study of children's self-efficacy (Zimmerman & Ringle, 1981). Given that a certain level of cognitive development is necessary for understanding the concept of self-efficacy or confidence, and given that children may not be familiar with the standard anchors and descriptions on rating scales, extreme care is required for assessing children's self-efficacy expectations. The training experience provided by Schunk (1982) to familiarize children with the measure is applauded and future research would no doubt profit from such precaution.

One final paper on self-efficacy requires attention here, for it speaks to a somewhat methodological concern. Are efficacy judgments differentially meaningful for different types of tasks? Variations in the characteristics of the tasks for which self-efficacy expectations were assessed led Kirsch (1982) to conclude that "efficacy ratings have different meanings depending on whether they are made in response to nonaversive skill tasks or to tasks requiring approach to a feared stimulus" (p. 316). Fifty male and female subjects who had indicated "terror" of snakes provided efficacy estimates (strength and magnitude) for a skill task and a fear task. The skill task involved tossing paper into a wastebasket at increasing distances. The fear task involved approaching a snake. The role of incentives in efficacy assessments was also examined, with subjects being offered an incentive ($5) to perform the first behavior that had not been endorsed "can do" on an experimental questionnaire. Kirsch (1982) reported that the meaning of self-efficacy ratings differs for different tasks: When a subject provides efficacy judgments regarding paper tossing (a skill task), the data represent each subject's belief in his or her ability. In this case, an incentive does not meaningfully alter self-efficacy. However, when a subject provides efficacy judgments regarding approach behavior (a fear task), the data represent what subjects are willing to do and can be altered by incentives. Kirsch (1982) provides examples of subjects' own explanations about the differential effects of incentives: for example, "One's a matter of skill which I don't have. One is just my own fear which I could do to get the money." While this and the other anecdotal reports are consistent with Kirsch's position, one might wonder about the veridicality of the initial fear assessment: If $5 is enough incentive to achieve a mastery response, then we might well be advised simply to pay phobics to improve. The Kirsch data do suggest some cautions, but the sample studied must have had a rather high initial efficacy in order to achieve mastery so quickly. Readers interested in theoretical and methodological difficulties in self-efficacy theory are referred to Eastman and Marzillier (1982).

EFFICACY EXTREMES

With the explicit intention of stimulating research, I ask: What are the effects of inflated yet inaccurate perceptions of self-efficacy? Interviewing an alcoholic about his or her self-perceived ability to control drinking may be one near surefire way to uncover unrealistically inflated self-efficacy expectations. Many alcoholics have the inaccurate belief that they can stop drinking at any time (I put aside for the moment the important question of whether or not they actually can). Even in cases where they have an unsuccessful record of quit attempts, efficacy expectations can resound with confidence. Persons with such unrealistic efficacy expectations may carry with them certain as yet unspecified variations in cognitive processing, schematic interpreting, or patterns of behaving that can have theoretical and applied impact. Accordingly, our assessments of self-efficacy should make more of an effort to leave open the ceiling and allow for grandiose judgments of confidence.

Marked differences between two clinical cases[1] further illustrate the potential richness of studying other types of efficacy extremes. At the most simplistic level, both of the clients to be discussed have problems with speech or public-speaking fears. One, a civil service employee, experiences an inability to approach or interact with people in a friendly manner. His life is lonely, his mistrust of others is high, and he speaks little more than to his therapist. He does, however, hold a job successfully and maintain an apartment, a car, and a competitive athletic schedule. His life is not a disaster, but his self-efficacy is extremely low, not just within the domain of communication and interpersonal skills, but in all areas. An inability or deficit in one area has generalized to the self-perception of total incompetence.

The second client is the president of a major bank conglomerate. He claims to be able to accomplish almost anything, and he very nearly can. He is a mover and a shaker, and when he actually gives a speech, it is forceful, sincere, and very well received. His list of recognized accomplishments is impressive. This client entertains and is entertained by governors, international stars, and business and sports luminaries. But don't ask him to appear on the *McNeill–Lehrer Report* or tell that "old story about _____." The anxiety associated with formal, prepared presentations or on-the-spot requests for a performance can be considered nothing less than painful. In this case, self-efficacy is unquestionably and justifiably near its zenith in all areas of functioning except one.

What I have suggested in these brief descriptions is that there may be important information associated with the extremes of self-efficacy expectations. Inflated yet inaccurate, deflated yet overgeneralized, and accurately high yet marred efficacy expectations may share the same cognitive distortion: a failure to process accurately past experiences

---

1. Nonessential portions of the client descriptions have been changed to protect their identities.

and their outcomes. The drunk who claims he can stop drinking does not process his past failures, whereas the successful business executive does not assimilate his uniform successes. To what extent can a common processing distortion account for such variations in behavior?

Schemata

The general thrust of theory concerning schemata is that sets of information serve to guide and flavor our perceptions, understandings, and recollections. These schemata, or cognitive sets, are more often described as structures than as processes (see Turk & Speers, 1983, for further discussion of structures and processes). Thorndyke and Hayes-Roth (1979) described a schema as "a prototypical abstraction of the complex concept it represents." Neisser (1976) referred to a schema as a format, in the computer sense. Within the clinical arena the schema has been considered a template that guides our cognitive processing. There are studies of schemata in human memory and self-perception, and there are studies of social and interpersonal schemata. All of these "templates" serve to modulate and mediate the following: (1) the impact of the therapeutic experiences that we, as therapists, provide for clients, (2) the clients' perceptions of these experiences, (3) what is learned as a result of these experiences, and (4) what future stimuli will be attended to in related situations. Perhaps the following question best illustrates my concern: What relevant cognitive template (schema) guides phobic clients' perceptions and learning as they pass through *in vivo* exposure? (Readers interested in suggestions for clinical intervention based on the notion of schemata are referred to Goldfried & Robins, 1983; those interested in methods for recovering social schemata are referred to Rudy *et al.*, 1982; those interested in prototypes as cognitive organizations are referred to Horowitz, Weckler, & Doren, 1983; Horowitz, Wright, Lowenstein, & Parad, 1981).

Assuming that schemata are important in the processing of therapeutic experiences, how are they assessed? Descriptions of various strategies for assessing schemata are available in the literature (e.g., Landau & Goldfried, 1981; see also Rudy *et al.*, 1982).

Markus (1977) has studied self-schemata and describes them as generalizations (structural constellations) about the self, derived from past experience, that organize and guide the processing of information about one's own behavior across a variety of situations. Current experiences and information about the self are assimilated (or fail to be assimilated) based on reference to the self-schema. In Markus's (1977) study she identified individuals who saw themselves as independent,

dependent, or aschematic. Independents rated themselves at the extreme of at least two relevant dimensions (e.g., independent–dependent; leader–follower), rated these dimensions as important, and checked "independent" as a self-description on a separate adjective checklist. Dependent individuals completed these measures indicating a dependent style. Aschematics were neither independent nor dependent. That is, independent and dependent subjects choose the independent–dependent dimension as the one on which they characterized themselves as most extreme.

A variety of tasks and measures were then studied, including content and latency of self-description, provision of behavioral evidence for self-description, predictions of the likelihood of behavior, and interpretations of new information. In each instance, it was found that subjects with an independent self-schema used this schema to organize, summarize, and explain behavior.

Landau (1980) used semantic judgments and multidimensional scaling procedures to examine reactions of dog-phobic and non-dog-phobic subjects. He found that while both groups employed the categories of size and ferocity in making judgments about dogs, the dog phobics' dog schema overemphasized information that discriminated in terms of size. Perhaps, as Landau and Goldfried (1981) suggested, the information present in phobic individuals' schema of the feared object is such that avoidance behavior may be a reasonable course of action consistent with their interpretation of the environment.

Via an intriguing use of multidimensional scaling procedures, Rudy et al. (1982) studied how people cognitively represent social situations involving assertion. The researchers recovered these schemata (cognitive representations) by examining how subjects rated the similarity of difficulty of responding as they imagined themselves in situations described by vignettes.

These results evidenced that three dimensions characterized subjects' scaling of the positive situations (emotional/arousal, interpersonal/ social intelligence, safe vs. unpredictable situations). These dimensions were of different degrees of importance for the subjects at different levels of assertion. For instance, dimension 2 (interpersonal/social intelligence) was significantly more important for high-assertive subjects and significantly less important for low-assertive subjects. Importantly, the low-assertive subjects appeared to use only the emotional/arousal schema in their ratings, whereas the high and moderate assertion groups used all three to some degree. Nonassertiveness seems to be associated with unischematic interpretations or representations of positive social situations.

Negative situations were characterized by four dimensions: status level of the target, arousal due to violation of social norms, plausibility of the situation, and intensity of the situation. Again, differences were evident for subjects differing in assertiveness. Social appropriateness was more important for low-assertive and client groups than for middle- or high-assertive groups. Plausibility (or familiarity) of the situation was more important for the middle and high assertiveness groups than for the other groups. Status level of the target of the assertive responses was, generally speaking, an important dimension for all groups. Based on these findings, we can now recognize that social situations are perceived in different ways by individuals with varying degrees of assertiveness. Stated differently, level of assertion has associated with it a social schema that moderates the processing of information regarding social situations. The application of information-processing efforts to research in psychopathology merits our energy, support, and reading time.

The influence of schemata such as those studied by Landau (1980), Markus (1977), and Rudy *et al.* (1982) has implications for behavior therapy. For example, a sexually anxious client probably has a well-articulated schema for sexual encounters. The client's cognitive schema about sexuality will help to organize and summarize new information about members of the opposite sex and marital relationships. When such a client engages in sexual contact, he or she may not report less fear (or more pleasure) as a result of this single experience. Why? Because the schema is involved in processing the new behavior and the schema does not change based on an isolated event. In contrast, if an individual does not have a well-formulated schema pertinent to sexuality, then a single experience may be seen as powerful evidence that the person is capable of sexual contact. An individual who has a well-established schema about a feared situation or object will require greater numbers of experiences before we can expect to disconfirm expectations and produce behavior change.

Because cognitive–behavioral strategies focus upon the correction of reasoning processes, Greenberg and Safran (1981) comment that one may then fail to correct the client's initial (and inaccurate) perceptions. They go on to state that a client "may realize that the world as perceived is a product of faulty reasoning processes and yet still retain dysfunctional perceptions" (p. 168). Going one step further, Greenberg and Safran suggest that it is not enough to treat irrationality or negative thinking—perceptual attention should be tackled therapeutically.

Interestingly, schemata play an important role in perceptual attention: The schema sets the stage for what will be perceived. A worker who has heard negative feedback repeatedly, this schema will set the perceptual stage, and the person might perceive negative feedback even upon the approval of a supervisor. This outcome could occur despite the feedback being neutral or positive. Schemata offer an elusive yet intriguing conceptualization of perception.

Self-Statements

For some cognitive-behavior therapists, self-statements are specific sentences that reflect an individual's underlying beliefs, schemata, expectations, and so forth. In this one sense, various measures of self-referent speech—self-statements (see Kendall & Hollon, 1981a)—have been used to operationalize "cognition." Approaches to the measurement of self-statements include inventories, thought-listing forms, thought-sampling procedures, and videotape construction, to mention a few.

Perhaps one of the most successful and most often used approaches to the assessment of self-statements has been the self-statement inventory. Typically, self-statement inventories provide (often 25 or 30) "thoughts" that subjects are asked to endorse on a 5-point rating scale to indicate how often they have thought each of the self-statements provided. As noted in Volume 8, separate inventories have been developed for the study of assertiveness (Schwartz & Gottman, 1976), anxiety (Glass et al., 1982), depression (Hollon & Kendall, 1980), and stress due to invasive medical procedures (Kendall et al., 1979). We add at this time that by having separate inventories for separate topics, the self-statement inventory methodology acknowledges that cognitive assessment is often geared toward cognitive activities that are specific to types of disorder or types of situations, and this awareness of specificity is to be applauded.

In contrast, however, there are three methodological concerns that require additional attention. First, we have been puzzled by the lack of attention given the individual meaning of self-statements (see Arnkoff & Glass, 1982; Kendall & Hollon, 1981a). As William James noted, the magic of words depends not on the words but on the minds using the words (quoted in Meyer, 1980, p. 264). We must move beyond *prima facie* validity and toward an understanding of the personal meaning of self-talk. That is, researchers will have to inquire to identify the meaning that each specific self-statement has for a given subject, rather than to assume that each self-statement has the same personal meaning for all subjects involved. Meaning can also vary within individual clients. That is, behavioral procedures may change the subjective meaning of self-statements (and the associated behavior), so that clients continue to repeat the same self-statement but employ the thought differently (e.g., as a cue for newly learned skills).

Although we are considering here, as I have elsewhere, that the personal meaning of self-statements may influence their functional role, there are data to assuage our anxieties about this potential short-coming. In a discussion with R. M. Schwartz (1982b), we concluded that there may have been a bit too much concern over idiosyncratic self-talk since the often-used method of development of self-statement inventories included a process of selecting only those self-statements that received high degrees of consensual validation. That is, a large number of self-statements is generated as potential items for the self-statement inventory, but a small sample is actually used. The sample is selected because a group of judges agree (often 90% to 100% agreement) on their judgment about the self-statement (such as a judgment about whether a self-statement is helpful or hindering in task performance). At least for the dimension on which the judgment was made, there is more consensual agreement than idiosyncrasy in meaning.

A second potentially valuable consideration in the assessment of self-statements concerns the sequence of the self-statements. That is, are there significant differences between individuals who self-correct their negative or unrealistic thinking and those whose negative or unrealistic thoughts are left uncorrected? It is possible that a mere count of certain types of self-statements may not be as predictive as the sequence of the person's internal dialogue.

Glass and Arnkoff (1982) argued that a content analysis of thoughts fails to describe how thoughts fit together, whereas a sequential analysis comes much closer to an understanding of the process of an internal dialogue. Drawing on the statistical technique of sequential analysis (e.g., Gottman & Notarius, 1978; Notarius, 1981), the authors illustrate how researchers can examine different sequential patterns of thought.

Another method of assessing sequences of positive and negative self-statements has been employed by Schwartz and Gottman (1976) and Bruch (1981). Citing from Bruch (1981), subjects can be asked to select one of four sequences that best describes the pattern of their thinking; the four sequences included unshaken confidence (positive at first and throughout), coping (negative at first but positive as time goes on), giving up (positive at first but negative as time goes on), and unshaken doubt (negative at first and throughout). In Bruch's (1981) research on assertiveness, high-assertive subjects were more likely to use either of the two adaptive sequences rather than the maladaptive ones. Further, Bruch (1981) replicated Schwartz and Gottman's study (1976) and reported that an assessment of assertive and nonassertive subjects' self-statements replicated the finding that assertive individuals focus on positive thoughts while less assertive persons engage in more negative thinking about their actions.

Two emerging trends within the assessment of self-statements give rise to a third concern. First, a diversity of approaches to the measurement of self-statements is appearing in the literature. Second, researchers are employing only one of these methods in any given investigation. Method variance is the emerging concern. Data can be more influenced by the method used to collect them than by variations in the topic being assessed. Unless measured by several different procedures, one cannot isolate and remove from the total variability that which is attributable to method variance. For instance, research using self-statement inventories and focusing on deficits associated with non-assertion has supported Schwartz and Gottman's (1976) finding that an "internal dialogue of conflict" characterizes nonassertive, as opposed to assertive, individuals.

Although Chiauzzi and Heimberg (1982) did not directly test the role of method variance, they examined the positive and negative self-talk of assertive and nonassertive subjects and did not find the more typical outcome that nonassertive subjects have an internal dialogue of conflict (Schwartz & Gottman, 1976). Chiauzzi and Heimberg, however, did not use a self-statement inventory as had previous researchers. These authors had subjects engage in postperformance videotape reconstruction. Their results included nonmeaningful differences between assertive and nonassertive subjects in terms of the positive/negative dimension of self-talk. The failure to replicate the "internal dialogue of conflict" when using videotape reconstruction, despite the apparent strength of the finding when self-statement inventories are used, underscores the need to consider method variance and, importantly, the need to compare the methods of cognitive assessment (Kendall & Korgeski, 1979). Since the inventory method is more private than performance on videotape reconstruction, and since the inventory method provides both positive and negative thoughts (as opposed to letting the subject generate and report thoughts), the self-statement inventory may be a more sensitive measurement strategy. Nevertheless, the method of assessment may affect the data; correspondingly, comparisons of the self-statement assessment methods are the current mandate.

Galassi, Frierson, and Sharer (1981b) provide an excellent example of the methodological inquiries needed in cognitive–behavioral assessment. Using a structured questionnaire, Galassi et al. (1981b) investigated whether retrospective and concurrent cognitive assessments in a test-taking situation would yield comparable data. The authors studied the subjects' positive and negative thoughts, units of distress, and reported bodily sensations and found that there were no significant differences between concurrent and retrospective assessment on any of these measures. In addition, concurrent assessment did not alter test performance.

Self-Control

The assessment of self-control was one of the topic areas included in Volume 8. The Self-Control Rating Scale (SCRS; Kendall & Wilcox, 1979), for children, and the Self-Control Schedule (SCS; Rosenbaum, 1980), for adults, were discussed. Since that time, several reports using the SCRS have come to my attention. The inequality of the number of reports dealing with one instrument rather than another is not so much a function of relative merit as of my involvement in the development of the SCRS.

Robin, Fischel, and Brown (1981) examined the validity of the SCRS, using parents as raters, with 4- to 18-year-old lower-class subjects. The SCRS significantly differentiated distressed (psychiatric) from nondistressed (medical) clinical cases, and the results were replicated on two samples. Among the distressed children, the SCRS discriminated hyperactives (lacking self-control) from those with other disorders not involving self-control. The means for parent raters approximated those for teacher raters. Robin *et al.* (1981) concluded that the SCRS was "useful for assessing self-control across socioeconomic levels and with either teachers or parents as raters" (p. 3). Kendall and Braswell (1982b) reported a .66 correlation between parent and teacher ratings. Apparently, in addition to discriminating psychologically distressed from nondistressed subjects and hyperactives from other disorders, the SCRS can be employed by parents as well as by teachers. These data support the continued use of the SCRS.

Two other studies deserve brief mention. Myers (1981) studied 30 (15 male, 15 female) fourth- to sixth-graders and their mothers. SCRS ratings and interpersonal problem-solving scores were found to be significantly related to intensity of maternal punishment, with decreasing self-control and problem-solving associated with an increased intensity of maternal punishment. Israel, Stolmaker, and Prince (1982) reported a moderate correlation between SCRS ratings and eating style in third- to fifth-graders. Here a behavioral measure of total interruptions while eating was related to teacher ratings of self-control. As the literature on the SCRS expands (see also Kendall, Zupan, & Braswell, 1981), it is important to keep discriminant as well as convergent validity in mind. A scale that is valuable both for research and clinical practice shows meaningful relationships with similar concepts but is not correlated with everything. Understanding the nomological network associated with self-control in children requires a matrix of interrelationships.

Humphrey (1982) reported on the development of parallel scales of children's self-control: forms for teachers and for children. The teachers' scale contained 15 items, while the children's self-report scale contained 11 items. The Teachers' Self-Control Rating Scale (TSCRS) was based on Kendall and Wilcox's (1979) SCRS and maintained their cognitive–behavioral conceptualization of self-control. Humphrey reported that "for systems-oriented interventions, a 33-item scale is too long for teachers to complete on all children in a class" (p. 625). Items were deleted from the SCRS and some new items were added: The 7-point rating format was changed to a 5-point format. The Children's Perceived Self-Control Scale (CPSCS) was designed with content paralleling that of the TSCRS.

Although the correlation between the two scales was low, teachers' ratings were meaningfully correlated with behavioral observations in the classroom taken when children worked in small groups (4 to 8 children) with the teacher. Children's self-reports were "less robustly related to the external criteria" (Humphrey, 1982, p. 630). The relative limitations of the children's self-reports were consistent with earlier research, in which for instance, teacher ratings evidenced treatment gains whereas self-report by children showed no change (e.g., Kendall & Finch, 1978). The teachers' scale produced two factors, cognitive/personal and behavioral/interpersonal self-control, that were found to be stable across subsamples. Similar to the data on the SCRS, Humphrey's data provided support for the construct validity of measures of self-control in children. Questions regarding the correlation between the TSCRS and its parent, the SCRS, and the sensitivity of the new scales to treatment effects require research attention. Although the TSCRS requires somewhat less time to complete, the lengthier SCRS, with its 7-point metric, provides for greater variations in self-control ratings.

Food for Thought

As a writer for this *Annual Review* I collect stacks of preprints, reprints, and lists of relevant citations (and numerous self-directing notes to see this and that paper) that are a part of the literature of the approximately 1-year period to be reviewed. Unfortunately, the stacks accumulated to such a sizable task that simply reading all of the material, let alone organizing the labyrinth and preparing the review, would exceed the work boundaries of a 9-day week. Organization and inclusion or exclusion decisions must be made, and certain topics or articles may not make it past one of the several required cuts. Despite space and time limitations, the following topics simply could not be bypassed. However, only brief tastes of several topics are offered as food for thought.

THE "NEED" FOR COGNITION

Cacioppo and Petty (1982) bring new life to the notion of individual differences in the tendency to engage in and enjoy thinking. They reported four studies: (1) a known-groups comparison, (2) a factor analysis, (3) a correlational study including convergent and discriminant variables, and (4) a study examining predictive validity. Together, the data provided evidence for the reliability and validity of the Need for Cognition Scale. In the first study, people who perform repetitive, monotonous tasks (assembly-line workers) were compared to individuals who are thought to enjoy thinking (university faculty). Only those items that discriminated these groups were kept for further study. The final scale included 34 items. Study 2 employed a large sample of subjects and involved factor analysis. The one-factor structure that emerged replicated the structure based on a factor analysis of study 1 responses. In study 3, convergent and discriminant validity was suggested by Need for Cognition Scale correlations with cognitive style, close-mindedness, and general intelligence. Need for Cognition Scale scores were not meaningfully correlated with measures of test anxiety and social desirability. In the final study, individual differences in need for cognition were associated with differences on a laboratory task: None of the subjects reported having enjoyed the task, but people with high need for cognition found the task more unpleasant when a simple (as opposed to complex) rule was to be followed, whereas subjects with low need for cognition found the complex task more unpleasant.

The Cacioppo and Petty paper is of interest for several reasons. First, it offers an impressive series of studies that contrast with the more typical single-study reports. Second, it proposes an individual difference variable concerning cognition that may have application for clinicians seeking to make accurate prescriptions of the most effective treatment or predictions of treatment outcome. For instance, clients who differ in need for cognition may respond with dissimilar reactions to a therapist's persuasive argument. Cacioppo (1982) suggested that people high in need for cognition can appreciate the fact that an externally provided argument is cogent, but for their own self-generated reasons, they are not more persuaded than people low in need for cognition.

While the scale was designed for clinical clients and research subjects, the responses of clinicians and researchers and the relationship of their scores to their research interests might prove unintentionally illuminating.

COGNITIVE DISTORTIONS IN AGGRESSIVE BOYS

In a series of recent studies, Dodge and his colleagues (Dodge, 1980; Dodge & Frame, 1982; Dodge & Newman, 1981) have conducted analyses of inference of hostile intention, the process of decision making, and the preference for certain causal attributions that are associated with children's aggression. For instance, Dodge (1980) documented that aggressive and nonaggressive youngsters differed in their perception of hostile intent: In a neutral situation aggressive children responded as if a peer had acted with hostile intent, whereas nonaggressive children responded as if the peer acted with benign intent. Subsequently, Dodge and Newman (1981) determined that the decision-making speed of aggressive boys was implicated in their bias toward attributing hostility to peers in unwarranted situations. Dodge and Newman reported that aggressive boys "responded more quickly and with less attention to available social cues than nonaggressive boys" and that "aggressive boys overattributed hostility to peers in unwarranted circumstances, but only when they responded quickly" (p. 375).

Three studies were included in the most recent report (Dodge & Frame, 1982). In my brief summary I feel it is important to point out that the biased attribution of hostility was found to be restricted to attributions of a peer's behavior toward an aggressive boy but not toward a second peer. Attributional analyses have found meaningful applications in two timely areas—children and aggression. Speaking as one who has experienced a renewed interest in the function of cognitive deficiencies and distortions in the development of psychological disturbances in children, I eagerly await further discoveries.

MOOD AND MEMORY

Velten's (1968) laboratory task for inducing mood states has come under fire for several reasons (e.g., Buchwald, Strack, & Coyne, 1981). For instance, Teasdale (in press) points out that the experimental instructions often include strong encouragement to the subjects to get into the appropriate mood state—thus confounding demand characteristics with the effects of the self-statements (see also study 3 in Snyder & White, 1982).

Other variations in induction procedures have gathered interest. For example, Teasdale and Taylor (1981) examined the effects of mood-induction procedures that either do or do not make reference to life situations and experiences on the accessibility of positive and negative cognitions. Their results indicated that differences in accessibility of memory result from the induced mood and not the mood-induction procedure. Studying a related topic, Natale and Hantas (1982) used a hypnotic mood-induction procedure and Teasdale (1982) described the merits of playing prerecorded musical selections to induce affective states.

Teasdale (in press) summarizes a series of mood and memory studies by stating that mood state differentially affects the accessibility of positive and negative cognitions, positive cognitions being less accessible in depressed moods than in elated moods and negative cognitions being relatively more accessible in depressed moods. Although this relationship seems reasonably well accepted among researchers and clinicians, the question of causality remains an enigma (see also Golin, Sweeney, & Shaeffer, 1981; Lewinsohn, Steinmetz, Larson, & Franklin, 1981). Correspondingly, Teasdale's notion of a vicious cycle (reciprocal relationship) and Bower's (1981) associative network theory contain propositions that may help untangle the interesting but challenging causal knot.

METHODOLOGY

The majority of, if not all, practitioners and scientists have one or several topic areas of interest to them. These topics are typically content oriented—child abuse, alcoholism, depression, schizophrenia. Occasionally, however, one finds a methodologist—a scholar not of a content area but of the procedure for investigating content areas. Because methodology serves as the foundation for all content areas, it deserves special attention. Surprisingly, until recently, single sources on clinical research methodology were lacking. The *Handbook of Research Methods in Clinical Psychology* (Kendall & Butcher, 1982) and *Research Design in Clinical Psychology* (Kazdin, 1980d) were prepared to fill the gap by providing the current status of research methodologies employed in the study of human behavior and clinical services associated with the assessment and treatment of psychological dysfunctions. Behavioral influences on research methods are apparent in both books (overriding the fact that theoretical boundaries were intentionally not drawn in the *Handbook*). The expansion of behavioral methods into new arenas and the integration of behavioral methodologies into contemporary clinical research methods is apparent.

Single-Subject Methodologies

Discussions of how best to operationalize the empirical clinician continue (see also Volume 8). While it is uniformly agreed that the goal is desirable, it remains controversial whether the clinical employment of single-case analyses can be the single solution to the problem of research versus practice. Consistent with efforts to move toward the further advancement of single-subject procedures, I observe in recent journals instances of the clinical use of single-subject designs to make treatment decisions (e.g., Wells, Conners, Imber, & Delamater, 1981), to illustrate treatment evaluation via cognitive and behavioral channels (e.g., Kendall & Urbain, 1981), to examine generalization (e.g., Johnson & Cuvo, 1981), and to document the merits (e.g., Ollendick, Shapiro, & Barrett, 1981) and demerits (e.g., Shapiro, Kazdin, & McGonigle, 1982) of the alternating-treatment design. Discussion articles, such as that on the uses of mixed single-subject designs (e.g., Wong & Liberman, 1981) also serve to further the single-subject methodologies. Although they have not yet fully infiltrated clinical practice, scholars have worked to strengthen the applicability of single-subject designs.

The alternating-treatment design has received substantial contemporary interest as a clinical evaluation tool. The alternating-treatment design is described as an intrasubject replication methodology intended for the comparison of the relative effects of different treatments. While it is always a challenge to compare two treatments applied to an individual case, recent studies do suggest advances for the methodology. For instance, in addition to the comparison of different treatments, Barlow and Hayes (1979) and Kazdin and Hartmann (1978) recommended that a no-treatment condition be included in the design from the outset. Ollendick *et al.* (1981) employed such a strategy in their comparison of physical restraint and positive practice overcorrection procedures for the treatment of stereotypic behaviors in retarded children and found that both treatments were more effective than no treatment. In addition, the treatments were found to have differential impact, with some subjects responding better to one active treatment than to the other.

Shapiro *et al.* (1982) state that the alternating-treatment design avoids the problems of order and sequence effects that are encountered when alternate treatments are compared in reversal or multiple baseline designs but that it is susceptible to multiple-treatment interference effects. To study the influence of multiple-treatment interference, these authors examined the effects of a specific intervention when paired with one of two other interventions (the alternate treatments). Their specific intervention was a token reinforcement program, and the alternate conditions were baseline and response cost. Multiple treatment interference was reported to exist. For example, mean levels of on-task behavior during token reinforcement were found to be slightly higher when the alternate condition was baseline rather than response cost. As Shapiro *et al.* note, "it is essential to recognize that juxtaposing alternative treatments in the simultaneous or alternating-treatments design may affect the conclusions that are reached about the specific interventions" (p. 114). It seems plausible to speculate that these multiple-treatment interference effects are "contrast effects" similar to those seen in other related research (e.g., Burchard & Barrera, 1972; Johnson, Bolstad, & Lobitz, 1976; Kendall, Nay, & Jeffers, 1975). Contrast effects involve the differential effects of one procedure depending upon the prior history or concurrent occurrences of other procedures against which the first procedure is "contrasted."

After comparing three durations of facial screening using an alternating-treatment design, Singh, Beale, and Dawson (1981) also noted the potential involvement of contrast effects. Further research is needed on the effects one intervention has on the potency of another intervention. It seems valuable, if not essential, that we begin to learn whether or not, and if so when, specific treatments are hampered or supplemented by the history or presence of other treatments. Contrast effects or multiple-treatment interferences may not be so much methodological noise as evidence for the potency or enhancement effects of concurrent treatments.

Statistical analyses play a central role in all forms of research, yet the application of statistical tests within the single-subject methodologies remains a source of discussion and, according to Kazdin (1982d), a matter of considerable controversy. On the side of endorsing statistical evaluation, Kazdin (1982d) suggests that when the requirements of single-case research are not met, as in the case of nonstable baseline data, or when an investigator is beginning a new area of single-case research, statistical analyses may be especially useful. Limitations of statistical evaluation are also described, such as the potential to identify statistically significant but clinically meaningless findings and the increased demands placed on the investigator. Lastly, most of the statistical tests for single-case research have described a comparison of baseline to treatment, but such a comparison would not ensure that the intervention was responsible for change (i.e., would not eliminate some rival sources of internal invalidity), since the logic of the single-case approach is based on the pattern of data across several phases.

Edgington has been one of the proponents of statistical tests for single-subject research evaluation and has addressed the issue of randomization (Edgington, 1980). In a recent paper, Edgington discusses the use of nonparametric tests for single-subject, multiple-schedule research (Edgington, 1982). Multiple-schedule experiments are defined as those in which there is more than one possible source of treatment and the source alternates during the course of the intervention. The effects under these differing conditions are then examined using non-parametric tests. It should be kept in mind that statistical tests assume some type of random assignment of the treatment to clients, occasions for treatment, or behaviors to be treated. The four nonparametric tests discussed by Edgington (1982) are (1) the Wilcoxon matched-pairs signed-ranks test, (2) the Mann–Whitney U test, (3) the sign test, and (4) Fisher's exact test. The application of Revusky's (1967) randomization test (Rn) was described in an appropriately cautious article by Wolery and Billingsley (1982).

This review of the latest single-subject literature has thus far considered the alternating-treatment design and statistical analysis. A paper by Kratochwill and Levin (1980) brings the two topics together as they discuss, among related topics, the applicability of data analysis procedures to the alternating-treatment design. Kratochwill and Levin (1980) argue that there are problems with the use of analysis-of-variance procedures and recommend nonparametric randomization tests. When large effects are apparent, visual analysis may be a sufficient evaluation. However, when effects are not apparent, as when there is an absence of consensual agreement of the visual inspection, statistical tests may be necessary. Because these instances do occur, the issues, concerns, and applications of statistical tests will continue to be an important topic for consideration.

As seen in Volume 8 of the *Annual Review*, there have been several recent studies of the reliability of the visual analysis of intrasubject data, and their outcomes have documented that the judges were not particularly reliable. In a report by Wampold and Furlong (1981) the process of visual inspection was studied by comparing two groups: (1) students of single-subject research methods who had been exposed to prototypes of single-subject designs, and (2) students of multivariate analysis who had no formal exposure to prototypical single-case designs. It was hypothesized that subjects with experience with proto-types would judge treatment effects based on large absolute changes and would ignore variation. In contrast, it was hypothesized that multivariate-trained subjects would attend more to the size of change in relation to variation. The authors' abstract condensed the findings nicely: "Subjects primarily trained in visual inference . . . attended to large changes between phases in a time series regardless of the relative variation; subjects trained in multivariate statistics, on the other hand, did not demonstrate this bias" (p. 79). It should be kept in mind, as the authors note, that subjects were not randomly assigned and that train-ing was not manipulated experimentally. Nevertheless, the meaningfulness of data depends on accurate inspection and analysis and continued research into these processes is essential.

Also noted in Volume 8 was a methodology for assessing generalization using single-subject designs. Two papers relate to this development. For instance, Johnson and Cuvo (1981) used design with a multiple baseline across subjects to demonstrate treatment control and a multiple baseline across responses to examine response generalization. Also, Rusch and Kazdin (1981) discussed design options that are potentially useful for investigating response maintenance. The single-subject strategies, despite the associated controversies, continue to merit consideration as a means of conducting clinical evaluations.

Normative Comparisons

One might assume that as therapy outcome research methods are improved, clinical researchers will be capable of conducting more convincing tests of psychological therapies. To a degree, this assumption is true. Increasingly sophisticated research methods have contributed to a reduction of the sources of internal invalidity likely to undermine the conclusions of a research report, clinical samples have enhanced the external generalizability of the research data, and advances in design and analysis have allowed researchers to ask and answer increasingly difficult yet more meaningful questions. However, the advances in therapy outcome research have been largely within the same domain: niceties of the internal design of the study. The pejorative connotation of the word "niceties" is only partially intended, for refinements in the development of control group, the provision of controls for expectancy and therapy credibility, the inclusion of multiple measures of treatment outcomes, and the careful application of subject-selection criteria are welcomed as routine procedural requirements. Nevertheless, with the exception of social validation procedures (e.g., Kazdin, 1977), these and other increasingly sophisticated methodologies do not address the convincingness of the outcome data. In other words, these methods help assure us that the researcher can state with greater certainty that the therapeutic manipulation was responsible for certain specific changes, but they do not address or advance our ability to quantify the extent of the impact of the intervention. True and convincing demonstrations of therapeutic efficacy must evidence that once troubled and disordered clients are now, after treatment, not distinguishable from a meaningful and representative nondisturbed reference group. Normative comparisons provide a methodology for documenting such changes.

The specifics of normative comparisons were outlined briefly in last year's review (Volume 8) and discussed and illustrated in somewhat greater detail in Kendall and Norton-Ford (1982). The present commentary is intended to provide current examples of their use with both children and adults and to encourage their further application.

An early example of normative comparisons was provided by Patterson (1974). In this instance, the data were behavioral observations. Patterson examined changes in deviant behavior from baseline to treatment and follow-up using visual inspection of the time series, but also demonstrated that the rate of behavior was reduced to within a normal range. More recently, Kendall and Braswell (1982b) employed normative comparisons on behavioral observations and other data (e.g., rating scale data). The frequency of observed behavior of treated children was compared against the frequency of nontreated children (matched for age and sex and approximately matched for IQ) in the same classroom. Blind teacher ratings were gathered on a sample of all children in the target grades, and treatment effects were determined, in part, by whether target problem children were returned to within the normal range of ratings. Rickel and Lampi (1981) examined changes at follow-up by comparing the at-risk and treated children to a group of low-risk children. Their problem-solving intervention moved the treated children toward a level of performance comparable to that of the low-risk children. Working with nonassertive adults, Kazdin employed normative comparisons to support his treatment effects (e.g., Kazdin, 1982d). Kazdin gathered behavioral role-play data on treated subjects and compared them to similar data from subjects not lacking in assertiveness. Thus, behavioral observations, ratings, and role plays, as well as other dependent measures, can be examined by comparisons with nondisturbed samples.

Statistical tests can be used to determine whether the treated group is significantly different from the normative group. In these comparisons it is desirable that the differences be nonsignificant—no meaningful differences between treated and normative samples. Based on these results, the average treated child is not meaningfully different on the measure used from average normal subjects and the investigator can make more encouraging claims about the impact of the treatment.

Follow-Ups

There has been a laudatory increase in the reporting of relatively lengthy (e.g., 1-year) follow-ups, a trend that is evident in a diversity of content areas. With adult clients, there have been reports in the area of alcohol or other substance abuse (Cannon, Baker, & Wehl, 1981; La

Porte, McLellan, Erdlen, & Parente, 1981; Olson, Ganley, Devine, & Dorsey, 1981) and self-control programs for study-skills improvement (e.g., Kirschenbaum, Malett, Humphrey, & Tomarken, 1982).

One of the attendant vicissitudes of conducting longitudinal (follow-up) research is the almost inevitable reduction in sample size that occurs with the passing of time. Potential sources of subject attrition include geographical relocation, lack of willingness to co-operate, death, inability to contact, and many others. Are follow-up samples representative of the sample in the original study? This is a reasonable question, given the difficulty of gathering follow-ups. Regarding response to treatment, La Porte et al. (1981) asked, "Do subjects who are more difficult to follow up have poorer treatment outcomes?" to which clinical lore might unabashedly answer "yes." La Porte et al. (1981) followed up substance abuses and grouped their subjects according to the difficulty in completing the follow-up. Based on 18 assessments, neither alcohol or drug samples produced meaningful differences. Apparently, based on this report, there is no difference in the outcome status of subjects more difficult to contact for follow-up.

Regarding the outcome of some of the alcohol treatments, Olson et al. (1981) obtained follow-up phone interviews during five periods ranging from 6 months to 4 years. The behavioral treatment, covert sensitization and relaxation (a cognitive-behavioral hybrid), was meaningfully superior to transactional analysis at 6 months and 18 months after treatment, but not thereafter. These authors stressed the need for even lengthier follow-ups. Cannon et al. (1981) reported 6-month and 12-month follow-ups of their aversion-treated clients.

Several follow-up reports of treatment with children and adolescents have appeared. Rickel and Lampi (1981) provided 2-year follow-up support for their problem-solving preventive mental health program, and Kendall provided follow-up support for his cognitive-behavioral self-control therapy (see Chapter 4), but some other data were less supportive (Kendall & Braswell, 1982b). Methodologically, these studies included tests to determine whether the follow-up sample was comparable to the original sample on important variables (e.g., initial problem sensitivity, intellectual ability). Graziano and Mooney (1982) report 2½- to 3-year maintenance of gains for the treatment of night fears in children. Lastly, Sarason and Sarason (1981) provided support for their cognitive and social skills training. The Sarasons' follow-up of their low-achieving at-risk high school students was especially valuable, since archival, ecologically valid, and downright convincing measures were taken: absences, tardiness, and behavior referrals during the year. It is reassuring to see an evaluation based on such solid indices of treatment impact, and it is particularly reassuring when the data are supportive.

In a 5-year follow-up, Markman (1981) found that the more positively premarital couples had rated their communication, the more
satisfied they were with their relationship 5½ years later. This finding
was consistent with an earlier follow-up report and added further
support to the social learning hypothesis that communication and
problem-solving deficits are etiologically related to marital distress.
Follow-ups are important to show that we have helped our clients in a
meaningful way, but an overemphasis or exclusive focus on long-term
change has several potential dangers (see Brownell, 1982a).

A paper published in 1980 by Cross, Sheehan, and Khan raised the
question of alternative advice and counsel in psychotherapy. That is, to
what extent do clients seek aid outside the efforts of the therapist? Cross
et al. (1980) stated that members of control groups, if denied treatment,
as well as members of treatment groups, may seek alternative sources of
aid, and they asked to what extent clients seek alternative counsel and
whether this potential confounds affect outcome. Cross et al. (1980)
administered the Alternative Counsel Scale (ACS), a scale based on the
work of Paul (1967a), and gathered data on "the seeking of advice, the
acceptance of advice, and the number of times that advice was offered
from various help sources in the community" (p. 617). Cross et al.
(1982) also provided behavioral and insight-oriented treatment to non-
psychotic psychiatric outpatients and compared changes to those seen
in waiting-list controls. While I do not agree with all of Cross et al.'s
conclusions, a few methodological points warrant our attention. First,
the waiting-list controls in this instance behaved as controls and,
according to the ACS results, did not seek or use alternative counsel.
This finding can be said to support the validity of waiting-list controls.
Second, both the behavioral and insight-oriented treatment groups
showed an increase in the amount of informal support over the treatment period relative to the controls.

The important question emerging from this study at this time
pertains to the seeking and following of alternative counsel and the
effects of such actions on the validity of follow-up reports. Although
the Cross et al. (1980) report did not address this specifically, there were
conflicting implications. Based on the appropriateness of the control
subjects in not seeking alternative counsel, one could speculate that
subjects do not seek outside help during follow-up intervals. In contrast, based on the behavior of the treated subjects, one could expect
that clients would seek and listen to alternative advice during the
follow-up. The question of the "alternate advice seeking" behavior of
treated clients during follow-up intervals is as critical as, if not more
critical than, the necessity of follow-ups per se. Research designed to
answer these and related questions would be a valued addition to the
literature.

Comparability of Subjects from Different Sources

Berrier, Galassi, and Mullinix (1981) state the issue clearly—there are questions about the value of analogue research as a means of increasing knowledge about the effects of therapy. They go on to note that one of the major concerns is that subjects in analogue studies differ from clinical samples on such treatment-related characteristics as problem severity, level of psychological distress, and motivation for change. Two studies report on relevant data. Berrier *et al.* (1981) compared low-assertive subjects from university classes (analogue) and low-assertive university counseling-center clients. Subjects were matched on sex and self-reported assertiveness. The results indicated sex differences. Female subjects from both sources were comparable on a behavioral assertion test and on measures of psychological adjustment. Male subjects from different sources were also comparable on the behavioral test, but male subjects from the clinic were less well adjusted on three of four adjustment measures.

Solicited and nonsolicited depressive female subjects were compared in a report by Hersen, Bellack, and Himmelhoch (1981). Nonsolicited subjects sought help by going to an outpatient clinic, whereas solicited subjects responded to newspaper and radio advertisements. Analyses of self-report, observer, and behavioral measures for depression, assertiveness, and social adjustment did not reveal significant differences. Marital status and other demographic variables also did not show significant differences.

Taken together, these studies suggest that female subjects who come from different sources to participate in treatment research can be considered comparable. This comparability refers to level of adjustment and problem severity. However, it is not clear that this holds true for male subjects, nor whether there are differences in motivation for change. Berrier *et al.*'s data would suggest that male clients from analogue versus clinical samples are different. Future research is needed to address the potential effects of possible differences in motivation and treatment outcome. Moreover, since social supports are often implicated in the maintenance of treatment effectiveness, it seems essential that analogue and clinic samples be compared on their respective access to and quality of social support systems.

META-ANALYSIS: THE SECOND TIME AROUND

What do "motivational biases in attributions," "sex differences in social influence," "the effects of goal structures on achievement," "models of leadership effectiveness," and "the effects of psychotherapy" have in common? The answer: Each has been meta-analyzed (Burger, 1981; Eagly & Carli, 1981; Johnson, Maruyama, Johnson, & Nelson, 1981; Smith & Glass, 1977; Strube & Garcia, 1981). Judging from the diversity of topics examined, the procedures of meta-analysis have spanned the tentative boundaries between areas of psychology and have fostered meta-analysis as an area of inquiry unto itself. For example, Hsu (1980) proposed a statistical procedure for testing the differences between effect sizes in independent studies and Kraemer and Andrews (1982) argued that effect sizes should be calculated following a non-parametric technique. In contrast, Hedges (1982) criticized Hsu's procedure for rejecting the small hypotheses of equal effect sizes too often, whereas Yeaton and Sechrest (1981) asked for indices of change more meaningful than effect size.

The meta-analytic procedures are not the only source of controversy: Conclusions drawn from the metawork have been criticized. For example, the meta-analytic literature on self-serving attributions (e.g., Arkin, Cooper, & Kolditz, 1980) has received cautious scrutiny (e.g., Cook & Leviton, 1980) in terms of (1) loss of relevant information, (2) bias in the samples of studies reviewed, and (3) ignoring statistical interactions (see also Cooper & Arkin, 1981; Leviton & Cook, 1981). The merits of these writings notwithstanding, the application of the procedures of meta-analysis to the outcomes of psychotherapy are my main concern.

The methods used to evaluate psychotherapy are indeed diverse. Equally if not more so are the journals and books in which the therapy outcome literature appears. How does one accumulate, assimilate, and evaluate all of the resources? Two potential solutions have appeared in the literature: the "voting" or "box score" method (e.g., Luborsky, Singer, & Luborsky, 1975) and the statistical operations called "meta-analysis" (e.g., Smith & Glass, 1977). By way of a brief review, Smith and Glass (1977) included nearly 400 studies in their cumulative evaluation of psychotherapy. These authors calculated "effect sizes" for each of the dependent variables reported in the studies reviewed. Effect sizes indicate, in a manner that can be accumulated across studies, the degree to which treated subjects improve in relation to control subjects. There are several ways to calculate effect sizes (Cohen, 1977): Smith and Glass (1977) calculated their effect sizes by subtracting the mean of the control group from the mean of the treatment group and dividing that difference by the standard deviation of the control group.

The authors then proceeded to compare the effect sizes of various types of psychotherapy and the effect sizes resulting from the different dependent measures employed. The statistical integration of the data from numerous studies led Smith and Glass to conclude that "the findings provide convincing evidence of the efficacy of psychotherapy" (p. 752). The authors also conclude that the behavioral and nonbehavioral therapies were not meaningfully different from one another in producing therapeutic effects.

The methods and conclusions of Smith and Glass (1977) have not gone without criticism. For instance, Rachman and Wilson (1980) stated that "the claim is often made that poor data are better than no data at all. However, poor data from faulty studies can mislead and confuse" (p. 256). The unselected nature of the studies included by Smith and Glass led Kendall and Norton-Ford (1982) to question seriously the gamble that "hundreds of sows' ears can be statistically processed into a silk purse" (p. 454). Additional criticisms appeared early on, including Presby's (1978) call for more specific subcategories of psychotherapy, Gallo's (1978) commentary on the appropriateness of Smith and Glass's conclusions, and Eysenck's (1978) disagreements with several of the authors' assumptions and procedures. Glass and Smith (1978) have replied to Eysenck. Further critical commentaries have also appeared (e.g., Strube & Hartmann, 1983; Wilson & Rachman, 1983; see also the seven articles on this topic in the February 1983 issue of the *Journal of Consulting and Clinical Psychology*, Vol. 51, No.1).

In their call for a less impassioned review of meta-analysis, Shapiro and Shapiro (1982a) claim that powerful professional allegiances, the inherent complexity of the task, and the potential for subjective bias combine to reduce the likelihood of a balanced view. While I agree that it is possible to identify aroused reactions in the literature, the majority of comments have served to clarify the complexities, improve the methodology, and, if we proceed with a sense of optimism, lead to more appropriate cumulative evaluations. Shapiro and Shapiro (1982a) provided a discussion of (1) the numerical combination of results from independent studies, (2) the procedures for searching and criteria for including studies in meta-analyses, and (3) the coding of the features of the source studies. A consideration of each follows.

Regarding the combining of results from independent studies, Shapiro and Shapiro (1982a) concluded that "there is no justification for the *a priori* assumption that generalizations of the kind sought by meta-analysts and any other literature reviewers are, or are not, possible." With proper caution, however, Shapiro and Shapiro add that any attempt at a generalization (here referring to a general statement about the effects of therapy) should be conducted in such a way as to permit the identification of exceptions to the generalization. We would add that the analyses go beyond "permitting" the identification of exceptions to the generalization and focus directly on these more specific findings. "Does therapy work?" has been recognized as an unanswerable question. We must address the specifics of the mandate (platitudinous as it now sounds): What type of therapy for what type of disorder provided by what agent produces what effects?

A somewhat consistent concern with meta-analysis has been the appropriateness of the inclusion criteria employed in the selection of the target studies. In the section of their paper on this topic, Shapiro and Shapiro (1982a) offer a review of the commentaries of several earlier critics (notably Rachman & Wilson, 1980) of Smith and Glass's meta-analysis. While they are correct in pointing out that Smith and Glass's report did not include certain key behavioral treatment reports and in describing the presumably nonpartisan selection method they used in their own subsequent report (Shapiro & Shapiro, 1982b), Shapiro and Shapiro (1982a) unfortunately perpetuate the misperception that studies without control groups can or should be included in meta-analytic reports. Despite the authors' separation of the questions of the efficacy and *relative* efficacy of forms of psychotherapy, research studies without proper control conditions must yield information that is subject to other interpretations besides the interpretation that the treatment produced the change. For this most basic reason, as well as for a host of others, some form of methodological section appears necessary to guarantee that the results of cumulative analysis are based on valid individual studies.

Coding the features of the source studies is essential in order to break down any general conclusion into reasonable, specific conclusions. Disaggregation offers promise for the future of meta-analysis. But the methods of coding for disaggregation can be problematic. For instance, caution is paramount in meta-analyses in which various studies are said to provide evidence that some form of treatment is superior to another or to a control condition. The exact nature of the "treatment" and the "control" condition in each specific outcome study must be examined, especially in the case of attention-placebo controls. This caution arises from the use of misleading labels to describe treatments and the indefinite definition of control groups. That is, one researcher's attention control might be similar to another researcher's treatment condition. An example from my own work illustrates the need to examine control conditions carefully before including them in meta-analysis. In a comparison of cognitive–behavioral treatment and a patient-education intervention for reducing the stress of invasive medical procedures (Kendall et al., 1979), a current conditioned control and an attention-placebo control were employed. Patients in the attention-placebo condition participated in individual, nondirective discussions during which the therapist actively listened and accurately reflected the feelings that the patient expressed. Does this control condition not resemble a Rogerian client-centered intervention? Coding, or subclassifying the studies in order to disaggregate the results in terms of type of therapy, requires extremely careful (and documentedly reliable) assignments. This comment is not intended to imply that all disaggregations are troublesome: Quite the contrary— disaggregations are important, and when the coding of the source studies can be accomplished with reliability and validity they are to be encouraged.

The Second Time Around: Replications and Refinements

Two reports of meta-analysis of the therapy outcome literature, following the lead of Smith and Glass (1977; see also Smith, Glass, & Miller, 1980) have appeared in the recent literature. In each instance, the authors acknowledge some of the strengths and weaknesses of the meta-analytic method and proceed to conduct a meta-analysis taking into account their prior criticisms. The work of Landman and Dawes (1982) illustrates this move to replicate and refine. In the authors' own words, their study "was designed to address more directly [than the correlations reported by Glass & Smith, 1978] the continuing questions concerning the influence of methodological quality of the component studies on the resulting size of effect in the meta-analysis of psychotherapy" (p. 506). Landman and Dawes (1982) set out to determine whether or not the results reported by Smith and Glass (1977) would be replicated when a select subset of the original studies (all of uniformly high quality) were reanalyzed. Two additional goals were set forth by Landman and Dawes: (1) to determine the magnitude of the placebo effect and (2) to examine the influence of statistical nonindependence of data points on the results obtained by Smith and Glass (1977).

Landman and Dawes (1982) proceeded by first randomly selecting a subset of the studies used in Smith and Glass (1977). This subset consisted of 65 studies. Of these, 42 were judged to be of sufficient methodological merit to be included. The design of the 42 studies included random assignment of subjects to a treatment or a no-treatment control group. Of this subset of sufficiently controlled studies, those that had placebo controls were also reanalyzed as a separate group. To examine the influence of statistical nonindependence, (1) the "study" (as opposed to the measure) was used as the unit of analysis, and (2) the results obtained at three different points in time were examined separately.

The quality of the studies included in the meta-analysis was found not to inflate the index of therapeutic effectiveness. The mean effect size for the methodologically sound studies was .78 (Landman & Dawes, 1982), somewhat larger than that obtained by Smith and Glass (.68) when the methodologically unsound studies were included. The interpretation of the .78 effect size is that, on the average, members of the therapy conditions were .78 standard deviation better than members of the control condition on combined measures of outcome.

The average effect size for placebo conditions (relative to no treatment) was .18, the average effect size for placebo relative to treatment was .38, and the average effect size for therapy (relative to no treatment) was .56. It seems reasonable to conclude that the effects of placebo conditions were less than that of therapy.

The results of the analyses to determine if statistical nonindependence affected the conclusions drawn by Smith and Glass indicated that neither the use of the entire study (as opposed to each measure) as the unit of analysis nor the separation of the determination of effect sizes for the three different points in time had any meaningful effects on the outcomes and conclusions. Based on these data, and others, Landman and Dawes (1982) concluded that

> the results of this reanalysis of the meta-analysis executed by Smith and Glass consistently support the conclusions drawn by the original authors. When studies without adequate controls are omitted from analysis, the magnitude of effectiveness of psychotherapy remains moderately high. . . . Moreover, it appears on the basis of these results that placebo "treatment" is responsible for a minuscule degree of improvement over and above that associated with no treatment. (p. 511)

Detailed replications and refinements deserve the praise of inquisitive readers, eternal optimists, and curious critics alike. To a degree, Landman and Dawes's report is praiseworthy. However, I can hardly generate enthusiastic praise for a report that fails to recognize the mandate for psychotherapy research that has prevailed for over a decade and a half: What treatment for what disorder, in what settings and provided by what change agent, produces what effects? (Kiesler, 1966; Paul, 1967b). Landman and Dawes report only on the answer to the question "Does psychotherapy work?"—a question that is unanswerable without reference to the moderating effects of the factors identified above. The fact that variations in the type of disorder being treated will affect the conclusions of meta-analytic research was noted in the Landman and Dawes report. They divided their sample into two rough categories: less severe problems (e.g., test anxiety), and severe problems (e.g., schizophrenia, depression). The average effect size for the less severe cases was 1.11, for the severe cases, .68. The difference between an effect size of 1.11 and .68 is quite large in relation to the differences between other average effect sizes reported in either the Smith and Glass or the Landman and Dawes reports. For its careful selection of studies to be included in the meta-analysis, for its look at placebo effects, and for its examination of the influence of nonindependence, the Landman and Dawes report is commendable. For failing to include, in what will likely be an often-cited report, sufficient analysis of the differential effects of types of therapy and their efficacy on different types of aberrant behavior problems, much commendation must be withheld.

Meta-analysis might be perceived by some as a statistical procedure that removes unwanted subjectivity from traditional reviews. Such a perception is not veridical, for the procedures of meta-analysis contain subjective components. Wilson and Rachman (1983) describe several areas where subjectivity can enter and perhaps bias the cosmetic appearance of statistical objectivity. For instance, selecting the studies for inclusion in meta-analysis and classifying the studies for disaggregation. It should be noted that Shapiro and Shapiro (1982b) reported that coding studies into categories was at least 80% reliable. (But I might point out that up to 20% were not reliable.) Subjectivity is a part of the process. Strube and Hartmann (1983) also contend that "meta-analysis consists of a series of complex, subjective, and sometimes arbitrary-seeming decisions" (p. 25). These authors go on to warn that the meta-analyst should not be "seduced by the quantitative nature of the approach" (p. 25).

Smith and Glass (1977) conclude that psychotherapies are effective and that there are negligible differences among the treatment methods, and recent efforts have claimed additional support for these conclusions. Wilson (1982b) concluded quite the contrary: that meta-analytic methods are not a cure-all for the process of cumulative review and that the conclusions of meta-analysis can be misleading. However, it does appear that others are accepting the "all have won" conclusion and that it has provided them with reassurance. To reiterate an important point, distinctions among types of treatment are often associated with the problem for which they were intended, and no cumulative conclusion can justifiably obscure the effectiveness of matching treatments and target problems.

Let us now turn to the second meta-analytic replication and refinement. Specifically, Shapiro and Shapiro (1982b) conducted their meta-analysis in a manner designed to take into account some of the criticisms advanced by Kazdin and Wilson (1978) and Rachman and Wilson (1980). For instance, Shapiro and Shapiro included only those studies that made comparisons between two or more treatments and a control group, and they excluded difficult-to-locate unpublished dissertations. Shapiro and Shapiro also took a more detailed look at the differential effects of different types of treatment for different target problems. In an effort to remove or reduce subjectivity in selecting studies, Shapiro and Shapiro took as a representative sample all published, controlled comparisons between treatments located by means of a manual search of the *Psychological Abstracts*, 1975–1979. They chose to include analogue research but to eliminate studies with children under 16 years of age and with within-subjects comparisons. Shapiro and Shapiro's (1982b) search turned up 143 studies.

The 143 studies were then coded according to the type of treatment provided (15 categories), the target problem (5 categories), and the method of measurement (4 categories). The major treatment categories were behavioral, cognitive, dynamic/humanistic, mixed, unclassified, and minimal. The behavioral category was further divided into rehearsal/self-control/self-monitoring, biofeedback, covert behavioral, flooding, relaxation, systematic desensitization, reinforcement, modeling, social skills training, and study skills training. The major target problem categories were anxiety/depression, phobias, physical/habit problems, social/sexual problems, and performance anxieties.

Both authors coded 70 studies and reported at least 80% agreement on each coding dimension. Overall effect sizes were calculated and correlated with parameters such as treatment and therapist variables, client variables, contextual variables, measurement variables, and design variables.

The space limitations of the present review dictate that my examination of the detailed but cumbersome results be somewhat cursory. I will, however, highlight the main data and their implications. The overall effect size reported by Shapiro and Shapiro (1982b) was .93—the average treated client scored at the 82nd percentile of untreated clients. Regarding the nature of the studies in their sample, the predominant mode of therapy was group (52%), therapists had an average of 3 years of experience, and treatment typically lasted 7 hours. The most common problems were anxieties and habit problems.

The effects of different treatment methods on effect sizes was significant and accounted for approximately 11% of the variance. The largest effect sizes were for behavioral (1.06), cognitive (1.00), and mixed (described mainly as behavioral, 1.42). Another category of treatment methods, labeled "unclassified" but described as mainly behavioral, had an effect size of .78. Of the behavioral treatment methods (1.06), modeling (1.43) and covert behavioral (1.52) methods had the highest effect sizes, whereas study skills (.26) and social skills training (.85) had the lowest effect sizes.

Individual therapy was more successful (1.12) than group treatment (.89). More experienced therapists obtained lower effect sizes than novices, but the novices were found to have worked with the types of client problems that had the greatest effect sizes. An otherwise troublesome conclusion, that experienced therapists do worse, was examined carefully and clarified.

Differences in the target of treatment accounted for 20% of the variance in effect sizes, with large effect sizes reported for phobias and small effect sizes for anxiety and depression. Measurement factors also affected effect sizes, with weaker effects seen on achievement and personality measures and stronger effects on more specific measures.

Shapiro and Shapiro (1982b) concluded that their finding of an effect size approaching one standard deviation was consistent with the largely independent survey by Smith *et al.* (1980). Unfortunately, these authors persist in the line of thinking set forth by the original data analysis and conclude that there is some meaning in an effect size that is averaged across types of treatment, types of problems, and so forth. This remains puzzling. On the positive side, however, the authors provide more specific conclusions by noting that their data reveal a modest but undeniable superiority of behavioral and cognitive methods and a corresponding relative inferiority of dynamic and humanistic ("verbal") methods (p. 31).

The Shapiro and Shapiro (1982b) report took a more detailed look at an issue of particular importance—the effects of different types of therapy or different types of target problems. It also identified some interesting differences in effect sizes attributable to variations in measurement factors and types of problems treated. Accordingly, this report may be considered the strongest of the weak lot of meta-analyses of treatment outcome. The authors' methodological conclusion merits restatement: "No meta-analysis can transcend the limitations of the data gathered by researchers undertaking its source studies" (p. 32). Apparently, Shapiro and Shapiro do not see meta-analysis as a cure-all. I concur, and I add that meta-analyses would be best considered worthless unless, at least, (1) the studies included are select in terms of adequate methodology, (2) the disaggregations are conducted in a demonstratedly reliable fashion, and (3) the conclusions sought are specific to types of problems treated and types of treatments used.

In another paper, Shapiro and Shapiro (1983) contend that the studies that were a part of their meta-analysis were not representative of clinical practice. That is, the therapists had an average of 3 years' experience, treatment lasted 7 hours, and the most common problems were anxieties and habit problems. Add to this the reported finding "that only 17% of the treated groups comprised individuals who had sought the aid of a clinician, or whose problems were of clinical severity" (p. 17) and that "61% of the groups had a mean age of 20 years or less." The authors go on to argue that these descriptive data document how unrepresentative of clinical practice the outcome literature is. They use these data to suggest that the studies lack external validity. Before such claims can be accepted, however, it is essential to know the descriptive data for clinical practice. There is also a pejorative connotation associated with the "unrepresentativeness" comment— research therapy lasts only 7 hours, whereas real clinical treatments are longer, and longer is better. Treatment duration is an important empirical question. But before we can assume that the duration is unrepresentative we need to know what duration is necessary and sufficient.

Let us digress, for a moment, to the issue of treatment duration and the representativeness of outcome research as clinical practice. Before we can state that any treatment duration is or is not too long or too short we must first undertake research on the duration of treatment to criterion. The criterion would be some desired level of outcome (e.g., a reduced anxiety score, such as from 58 to 27 on a scale with a mean of 36 and an SD of 9). We must then treat a sample of clients until they reach the criterion. The average duration of the treatment to criterion would provide the standard against which we could then make judgments about the appropriateness of the duration of treatments in outcome research. If the duration of treatment to criterion was determined to be 12 sessions, then we would conduct 12-session treatments in our outcome studies. Although we propose this strategy as an ancillary discussion, its potential contribution is important.

Early negative reactions to the initial meta-analytic efforts were justified—the process is not a statistical panacea and it does not eliminate subjectivity or reduce the merits and necessity of scholarship in reviewing related literatures. Since that time, however, we have become aware of the limitations of the meta-analytic methods and we have seen the methods modified and slightly improved. As the claims for the method are reduced, as the actual procedures are improved, and as the specificity of the questions asked are advanced, some of the criticisms may well deserve to be tempered. Future refinements are necessary.

CHAPTER

3

FEAR REDUCTION METHODS AND THE TREATMENT OF ANXIETY DISORDERS

G. TERENCE WILSON

PHOBIC DISORDERS

Research on phobic disorders has been a mainstay of behavior therapy from the beginning. The past year, not surprisingly, marked the active continuation of this emphasis in behavior research and therapy. Among the more enticing offerings of a rich literature were two important books: *Agoraphobia*, by Mathews, Gelder, and Johnston (1981), and *Learning Theory Approaches to Psychiatry*, a volume edited by Boulougouris (1982) containing papers delivered at an international symposium in Crete in 1980. As in the past, the best source of original articles on the assessment and treatment of fears and phobias was *Behaviour Research and Therapy*, although publications on the topic appeared in a wide range of journals. Studies focused on the development of phobias, on the therapeutic outcome of individual treatment techniques, on the procedural elements that promote success, and on comparisons between behavioral and cognitive methods. Analyses of theoretical mechanisms in fear reduction featured prominently in the behavioral literature, and important clinical themes such as the interpersonal context of therapy received further attention.

Therapy Outcome Research

BEHAVIORAL VERSUS COGNITIVE METHODS

Evaluation of the cognitive restructuring techniques that have risen to prominence within behavior therapy has been limited largely to the treatment of the interpersonal, test, and public-speaking anxiety. Applied to these particular problems, methods such as rational restructuring (Goldfried, 1979) and self-instructional training (Meichenbaum, 1977) have generally produced favorable results (Rachman & Wilson, 1980). In contrast, the application of cognitive restructuring methods to the more complex and severe disorder of agoraphobia has failed to show significant therapeutic benefits (Emmelkamp, Kuipers, Eggeraat, 1978; Williams & Rappoport, 1983). Emmelkamp *et al.* (1978), for example, found that *in vivo* exposure was superior to cognitive restructuring on a behavioral measure of phobic behavior as well as on clinical ratings of phobic anxiety and avoidance. Cognitive restructuring alone had little effect. However, as the authors themselves have pointed out, a mere five sessions conducted over only 1 week cannot be said to be a convincing test of cognitive restructuring in the treatment of a complex anxiety disorder. Ellis (1979) was quick to object to the adequacy of the cognitive restructuring treatment, arguing that in his rational–emotive therapy approach, homework assignments involving *in vivo* exposure would be an integral part of therapy.

A recent study by Emmelkamp and Mersch (1982) provides a more comprehensive and, in some ways, improved analysis of the effects of cognitive restructuring in the treatment of agoraphobia. The subjects of the study were 27 agoraphobics. As in most studies of agoraphobics, the majority of the patients were women ($n = 22$). All patients had been agoraphobic for at least 1 year, the average duration of their problem being 8.7 years. Patients were assigned, in order of their application for therapy, to one of three treatment conditions: (1) *in vivo* exposure; (2) cognitive restructuring; and (3) a combination of *in vivo* exposure and self-instructional training. The *in vivo* exposure treatment replicated that employed by Emmelkamp *et al.* (1978) in their earlier investigation and consisted of eight 2-hour group sessions. Therapists accompanied patients during exposure tasks during the first three sessions but thereafter met with the group only for discussion before and after performance of the exposure tasks. No systematic homework assignments were prescribed between therapy sessions, although "patients' own initiative to practice was encouraged" (Emmelkamp & Mersch, 1982, p. 80). The cognitive restructuring condition was essentially identical to that of the previous investigation, comprising relabeling of anxiety reactions, insight into irrational beliefs, and self-instructional training. Homework assignments emphasized identification and rational disputation of anxiety-eliciting thoughts. Aside from the greater number of therapy sessions over a longer period of time, the only difference between this treatment and that used in the Emmelkamp *et al.* (1978) study was that "more emphasis was placed on insight into unproductive thinking or irrational beliefs" (Emmelkamp & Mersch,

1982, p. 80). The combined treatment began with three sessions of relabeling and self-instructional training. In subsequent sessions, *in vivo* exposure followed a 15-minute period of self-instructional training. Clients were asked to use rational self-talk during *in vivo* exposure. In contrast to the cognitive restructuring treatment, insight into irrational beliefs received no formal attention. The therapists were advanced clinical psychology graduate students with specific training in behavior therapy.

The results at the end of therapy replicated those of the previous study by Emmelkamp *et al.* (1978). *In vivo* exposure and the combined procedure (self-instructional training plus exposure *in vivo*) were clearly superior to cognitive restructuring on clinical ratings of phobic anxiety and avoidance and on a measure of actual behavioral avoidance, although the difference between exposure and cognitive restructuring on the latter measure was nonsignificant. Self-instruction did not enhance the effects of exposure *in vivo*. On no variable was the combined procedure found to be more effective than exposure *in vivo*. A 1-month follow-up revealed that the between-group differences had disappeared. In a consistent trend across different outcome measures over this 1-month period, the combined group maintained its improvement, the *in vivo* exposure group showed some deterioration, and the cognitive restructuring group continued to improve. On a measure of assertiveness, the Adult Self-Expression Scale (Gay, Hollandsworth, & Galassi, 1975), the cognitive restructuring treatment was significantly superior to the *in vivo* exposure condition.

Emmelkamp and Mersch (1982) are cautious in interpreting these results, although they do suggest that the study indicates that cognitive restructuring may produce clinically meaningful effects. This conclusion was based on the limited effects of cognitive restructuring at the 1-month follow-up. Even here, however, it must be noted that the combined treatment was not significantly superior to *in vivo* exposure alone. It might be tempting to attribute this finding to the absence of the insight component in the combined treatment. Another possibility is that this result is simply another instance of the not uncommon phenomenon of a combined treatment condition faring more poorly than either of its constituent parts when evaluated alone (see Franks & Wilson, 1977a, pp. 360–362). These uncertainties call for further investigation of cognitive restructuring in the treatment of agoraphobic disorders, with still longer follow-ups.

One additional result from this study might be mentioned. Correlations between the behavioral avoidance measure and clients' own ratings of their phobic anxiety and avoidance ranged from a modest .55 to .65. The failure to obtain higher correlations between these measures argues against the view that clinical ratings alone suffice to evaluate the effects of behavioral treatment. It would seem, rather, that there is good reason to try to include both clinical ratings and actual measures of avoidance behavior in the evaluation of treatment outcome.

Two other investigations pitted behavioral against cognitive methods in the treatment of simple and social phobics. Biran and Wilson (1981) randomly assigned 22 simple phobics with fears of either heights, elevators, or darkness to either a guided *in vivo* exposure or a cognitive restructuring treatment. Both treatments entailed five sessions of individual therapy, over a 2–3-week period, following extensive assessment of the clients' problems. Based on social learning theory (Bandura, 1977b), several strategies were used to ensure that the *in vivo* exposure would produce maximal and enduring reductions in fear and avoidance. For example, performance aids were introduced whenever subjects exhibited inhibitions or anxiety in face of certain activities. These included using a rope when approaching the edge of the roof and talking on the phone with the therapist while staying in a darkened room. As treatment progressed, the supplementary aids were eliminated. As each behavioral task was successively mastered, clients were encouraged to engage in self-directed performances to facilitate self-attribution of change and generalization of treatment effects. Therapists interacted with the subjects in a supportive and encouraging manner and verbally reinforced self-directed performance and self-mastery. They never pushed subjects toward better performance, and they adapted themselves to the pace of each subject. Communication was focused around performance issues rather than around cognitions and feelings. The importance of practicing homework assignments (i.e., rehearsal of *in vivo* exposure between sessions) was emphasized and monitored throughout treatment. The cognitive restructuring treatment was closely modeled after that used by Emmelkamp *et al.* (1978).

The therapists were four advanced graduate students in clinical psychology. All had 2–3 years of experience in conducting therapy. Therapist training was conducted in four 2-hour group sessions and in six individual meetings with the investigators. The therapists were supplied with manuals, and training sessions consisted mainly of role-playing exercises.

Evaluation at posttreatment showed that the guided-exposure treatment was significantly superior to cognitive restructuring across multiple measures of outcome. These comprised actual avoidance behavior, self-report of fear during the behavioral avoidance test, self-efficacy ratings (which are discussed in greater detail later in this chapter), and physiological indices of autonomic arousal. Taken before and after treatment, the latter consisted of heart rate and skin potential measures during imagination of neutral and phobic scenes. The striking superiority of guided exposure is evident in the following data. Clients who could perform all of the tasks on the behavioral test were considered maximal performers. Of the 11 subjects in the guided-exposure treatment, 9 achieved maximal performance, compared to only 1 subject in the cognitive restructuring treatment.

A 1-month follow-up, employing all of the posttreatment measures, showed impressive maintenance of treatment effects. Generalization of treatment effects to clients' daily lives, based on interviews with each client, revealed substantial improvements among those who had received guided exposure. For example, several former acrophobics could now enjoy recreational activities such as skiing and mountain climbing. A female client who had been afraid of darkness could now enjoy night driving. Improvement in other specific problem areas, however, was not reported. Thus some former acrophobics could now climb stairs and look down from windows but still found it difficult to drive over bridges. Clients treated with cognitive restructuring, aside from the individual who had achieved maximal performance on the behavioral avoidance test at posttreatment, reported no change in their specific phobias or in other fears. Nevertheless, in contrast to their counterparts in the guided-exposure treatment, cognitive restructuring clients reported improvements in the social area. They experienced more self-confidence in social situations, felt more optimistic about life in general, and reported that treatment supplied them with a strategy by which they could cope with and better control anxiety.

At the 1-month follow-up, the 10 clients who had shown little improvement were offered additional treatment using guided exposure. The 7 who accepted and then received guided exposure showed comparable improvement to those clients initially treated in this manner; 6 achieved maximal performance on the behavioral avoidance test. This intrasubject analysis indicates that the poor showing of cognitive restructuring on the behavioral measure cannot be attributed to specific characteristics of the subjects who were assigned to this treatment condition. A 6-month follow-up, once again using the posttreatment measures, showed good maintenance of treatment effects for all clients who had received guided exposure. In fact, there was some evidence of continued improvement. All 11 clients in the original guided-exposure condition now achieved maximal performance on the behavioral avoidance test, and there was further reduction of self-reported fear. The remaining 4 clients from the cognitive restructuring condition,

who had declined supplementary treatment, showed no sign of any further progress. A 2-year follow-up showed continued maintenance of improvement in successfully treated clients (Biran, 1982).

Interpretation of these results is aided by two additional findings. Both treatments were considered equally credible by subjects, a finding that satisfies one of the important conditions laid down by Kazdin and Wilcoxon (1976), among others, for interpreting comparative treatment outcome results unambiguously. Similarly, analysis of subjects' compliance with homework assignments showed that the two treatment groups engaged in different activities consistent with the procedural requirements of the respective treatments.

These results reaffirm the efficacy and efficiency of exposure treatment for simple phobias in otherwise well-adjusted clients. They provide little support for cognitive restructuring, however. Although within-groups analyses indicated that the latter treatment did produce some improvement on the behavioral avoidance test, this was distinctly modest and confined to what Biran and Wilson, following Bandura (1977a), termed the "familiar threat," namely, the same behavioral avoidance test used in pretreatment assessment. No improvement was registered on the unfamiliar threat or novel behavioral measure of phobic avoidance. And, of course, the absence of an appropriate attention-placebo control treatment makes it impossible to attribute this modest improvement to cognitive restructuring per se. The only apparent advantage of cognitive restructuring lay in clients' reported gains in social functioning and in their general attitudes. Even here, however, without better measures, firm conclusions are ruled out.

As in the case of the Emmelkamp et al. (1978) study with agoraphobics, it can be plausibly argued that five sessions of cognitive restructuring are simply insufficient for effective treatment. While a lengthier course of treatment might prove more effective, guided exposure would still enjoy a decisive edge, simply on the grounds of its greater efficiency. Another caveat that must be issued is that the form of cognitive restructuring employed by Biran and Wilson cannot be taken to be representative of all forms of cognitive restructuring. In particular, it might not have constituted a fair test of Ellis's RET. Nevertheless, the specific procedure used by Biran and Wilson does seem to be reasonably representative of some popular cognitive methods, such as rational restructuring (Goldfried & Davison, 1976).

Most studies of the behavioral treatment of phobic disorders have focused on simple phobias and agoraphobia, with relatively little attention paid to social phobias (Barlow & Wolfe, 1981). Using a single-case experimental design, Biran, Augusto, and Wilson (1981) evaluated the comparative efficacy of guided exposure and cognitive restructuring in the treatment of three clients with a debilitating fear of signing documents in public. This problem entails both highly circumscribed avoidance behavior as well as more generalized social anxiety about being exposed to the scrutiny of other people. All three clients experienced intense physiological symptoms of anxiety when confronted with their phobic situations, and all used minor tranquilizers (with no benefit) quite regularly. In addition, all clients reported general apprehensiveness in different social situations in addition to their specific phobia. They were highly sensitive to being evaluated or watched closely while performing different activities. This was reflected in their scores on the Fear of Negative Evaluation (FNE; Watson & Friend, 1969) questionnaire and the Rathus Assertiveness Scale (1973). The rationale for comparing *in vivo* exposure with cognitive restructuring was that the former appeared to be the treatment of choice for eliminating the avoidance behavior associated with this social phobia, while the latter would be well-suited to the self-consciousness and negative self-evaluation associated with the problem. Both treatments were essentially the same as those used by Biran and Wilson (1981), as described above.

Following baseline assessment, two of the clients received five sessions of cognitive restructuring followed by five sessions of *in vivo* exposure. The third subject completed the exposure treatment immediately after three baseline assessments. *In vivo* exposure was found to be superior to cognitive restructuring in enhancing approach behavior, both on the behavioral posttest and in daily-life situations. For example, the clients were now able to use credit cards and to write checks in public at stores and banks. As a result of treatment, two of the clients found it possible to secure full-time jobs, while the third became involved in volunteer work. Caution must be exercised in interpreting these data, given the limitations of the experimental methodology. Only three clients were included in this single-case experimental design, thereby restricting the necessary points of comparison between therapist-assisted exposure and cognitive restructuring to only two instances. Nevertheless, a comparison between guided exposure and cognitive restructuring in a fourth client with the same social phobia, employing double the number of sessions of cognitive restructuring, yielded identical results (Biran & Niaura, 1983).

One other finding in the Biran *et al.* (1981) study is worthy of mention: the desynchrony, over time, between behavioral and self-report measures of fear. At a 1-month follow-up behavioral improvement was accompanied by marked reductions in self-reports of fear. At the 9-month follow-up the behavioral improvement had been maintained, but self-reports of fear had steadily increased. At this stage of the study, subjects were obliged to continue forcing themselves to perform certain activities. It might be said that what therapy had taught them was how to be courageous in spite of their fear. This desynchrony is a common finding in research on fears and phobias (Lang, 1969; Rachman & Hodgson, 1974). One would expect subjective fear to decrease with repeated exposure, so that over time there would be better concordance of fear and avoidance behavior. Hypothesis 4 of Hodgson and Rachman's (1974) analysis of desynchrony in measures of fear states that the "degree of concordance between measures in different response systems, after a treatment intervention, will increase during the follow-up period" (p. 322).

This desynchronous pattern of results stands in marked contrast to Biran and Wilson's (1981) findings with simple phobics. In that study, synchrony between measures of behavioral avoidance and self-reports of fear actually increased from posttreatment to the 6-month follow-up. Moreover, a subsequent 12-month follow-up showed no sign of any erosion in this synchronous pattern of improvement (Biran, 1982). The discrepancy between the two studies is not easily explained. One factor accounting for it might be the differences in target problems. Whereas with a simple phobia the avoidance and the fear are both relatively circumscribed, with a social phobia such as this, the fear is much broader than a simple fear of writing. What seems to underlie the fear of writing is a more general social apprehensiveness, of which fear of writing is only one manifestation. Indeed, Biran et al. (1981) reported that all three clients expressed a general concern about being observed and judged by other people. The authors note:

> These results suggest that in treating a social phobia of the kind described here it is necessary to take into consideration the different dimensions of the problem rather than focusing narrowly on a specific phobic response. A priori, cognitive restructuring would seem to have been suitable for reducing the generalized social anxiety associated with this phobia (see Goldfried, 1979). Yet little effect was noted on either questionnaire measures of generalized social anxiety and assertiveness, or specific self-reports of anxiety during performance of the avoidance behavior. (p. 531)

The apparent ineffectiveness of cognitive restructuring in complementing exposure treatment is puzzling. Of course, the method used here might have been too brief or too narrowly focused. It can be fairly argued then that cognitive structuring has not been evaluated under more optimal conditions. Subsequent studies that overcome the limitations of the cognitive restructuring methods described above might yield better results. In the meantime, it must still be concluded that cognitive methods have yet to be shown to be effective in treating severe phobic disorders.

PARADOXICAL INTENTION VERSUS IN VIVO EXPOSURE

According to Ascher (1981), behavior therapists have been remiss in overlooking the therapeutic potential of paradoxical intention. He emphasizes two reasons for paying more attention to this approach. First, it is based on exposure to anxiety-eliciting situations, which is usually the common denominator in the effective treatment of phobic disorders. Second, it lends itself to self-administration and therefore promises to reduce time-consuming and costly participation by the therapist in behavioral treatment. The latter assertion derives from Ascher's assumption that whereas paradoxical intention has elements in common with flooding, it requires "little or no direct supervision of the client" (p. 534). Flooding, involving as it does the elicitation of prolonged and intense anxiety, requires careful and immediate monitoring by the therapist.

Ascher (1981) compared paradoxical intention to graded *in vivo* exposure, using a creative combination of single-case and between-groups experimental designs. The ten agoraphobics who consented to the assessment and treatment strategies of the study were assigned to one of two groups. Clients in group A, following a variable baseline period ranging from 4 to 8 weeks, received a standard 6-week graded *in vivo* exposure treatment. This was followed by paradoxical intention treatment (as described in the following paragraphs). Clients in group B received paradoxical intention treatment immediately after the baseline period. The variable baseline period made it possible for Ascher to use a multiple-baseline design across clients within each of the two groups. (The difficulties with developing behavioral measures of agoraphobia were discussed in Chapter 3 of Volume 8 in this series.) Ascher came up with a different behavioral measure from other studies. Taking the inevitable practical considerations into account (e.g., time and distance from home), two maximally difficult (defined by clients' experiencing 100 subjective units of distress on Wolpe's [1973] scale) tasks were devised for each client. Both tasks were then divided into 10 hierarchical units. Each item on each task was considered completed when clients were able to remain in the situation until they felt "comfortable." Clients were instructed to try to complete as much of these two designated tasks as they could once a week throughout treatment.

The graded exposure treatment was based on that described by Emmelkamp (1974) as "self-observation." Clients were instructed to make no more than two attempts a day, 5 days a week, to advance as far as they could on the two behavioral tasks. Weekly individual therapy sessions focused on a review of clients' progress and problems with the homework assignments. It is most important to emphasize the particular type of *in vivo* exposure treatment that was evaluated in this study. To adapt an old saying, graded exposure is not graded exposure is not graded exposure! In Ascher's treatment, clients were explicitly instructed *to return home as soon as they experienced anxiety.* Instructions to avoid anxiety in this manner are not necessarily characteristic of other graded *in vivo* treatment methods, as Ascher himself notes. For example, the treatment manuals that are detailed in the Mathews *et al.* (1981) text provide clients with information and strategies (described more fully later) for coping with anxiety rather than avoiding it. This emphasis characterized the graded *in vivo* exposure treatments in the studies by Biran and Wilson (1981) and Biran *et al.* (1981). Indeed, it can be argued that learning to cope with ("work through") mainly mild to moderate levels of anxiety in a constructive manner so that clients do not avoid or withdraw from threatening situations is a significant aspect of thorough therapy (Wilson, 1983). Clients' knowledge that they are able to cope with unpredictable anxiety symptoms (i.e., possessing a strong yet realistic sense of personal efficacy) may be crucial to the maintenance of treatment success over time.

The rationale for the paradoxical intention treatment emphasized the following points: (1) that avoidance, or withdrawal, from feared situations strengthens the phobia; (2) that experiencing anxiety is "not necessarily bad and need not be avoided at all costs"; (3) that attempts to control anxiety can actually increase discomfort and aggravate the problem; and (4) that the preferred alternative to trying to control anxiety is to focus "on the most prominent aspect of the physiological experience of anxiety and to try to increase this symptom in an attempt to court the anticipated disastrous consequence" (Ascher, 1981, p. 536). Clients were instructed to apply the paradoxical intention principle whenever they reached a point at which they experienced what they considered to be too much discomfort to carry on. They were to apply the principle until they felt comfortable performing that particular task. Paradoxical intention treatment was continued until clients could complete all the items on both tasks within the same week. In all, this treatment ranged from 2 to roughly 16 weeks in duration.

The results were straightforward. In group A, a within-subjects statistical analysis indicated that the graded-exposure treatment failed to produce significant change from baseline. The same analysis for group B, using the first 6 weeks of paradoxical intention treatment, showed a significant improvement. The comparison between the effects of graded exposure in group A with those during the first 6 weeks of paradoxical instruction in group B showed the statistically significant superiority of the latter treatment. These statistical analyses are strongly supported by visual analysis of the individual outcomes. The multiple-baseline design shows that it was only when paradoxical treatment was introduced that marked changes in phobic avoidance became evident.

The limitations of this study include the absence of multiple measures of outcome. It must also be stressed that the behavioral outcome measure in this study was apparently derived second-hand from clients' reports to the therapist. It would have been informative to have systematic reports of subjective anxiety throughout the treatment process. This would seem especially pertinent given that the presumed mechanism of action of paradoxical intention is the way in which anxiety is emotionally processed. In this connection it is unfortunate that we have no data on clients' compliance with therapeutic instructions. Did they reliably try to exacerbate their anxiety? Clinical experience would suggest several problems with compliance with such demanding requirements. Did the paradoxical technique ever lead to increased anxiety? Were there any panic attacks? What did the clients make of all of this? Without answers to these questions it is impossible to know why the paradoxical treatment apparently worked so well. Moreover, the therapist is not provided with information about potential problems and pitfalls in the application of this technique.

FLOODING

Volume 8 in this series (Chapter 3) summarized the results of a study by Chambless, Foa, Groves, and Goldstein (1979) in which flooding in imagination, with the concurrent administration of Brevital, a quick-acting barbiturate, was compared to flooding only and to an attention-placebo control condition. The purpose of this study was to examine the effect on treatment outcome of the degree of anxiety clients experience during exposure treatment. Allowing for the limitations of the measures of treatment outcome, the non-drug flooding group showed greater improvement than the flooding group that received concurrent administration of Brevital. The authors concluded that the non-drug flooding group had experienced greater anxiety during treatment and that this exposure to higher levels of anxiety was the reason for the group's superiority. In a more recent paper, Chambless, Foa, Groves, and Goldstein (1982) not only report the effects of additional treatment over a 4-month follow-up period but also provide a reanalysis of their earlier findings that cause them to alter one of their previous conclusions.

In the extended report of this study, only 21 of the original 27 clients were included in the data analysis. The remaining 6 clients were excluded from the analysis because they did not participate in the follow-up phase of the study. The reasons for their lack of participation are not given. Examination of clients' subjective anxiety during flooding, based on the smaller sample ($n = 21$) of clients, indicated that contrary to the authors' predictions, the non-drug group failed to report higher anxiety than the group that received Brevital. Indeed, at the end of the eight sessions of therapy, the Brevital group reported significantly greater levels of anxiety than the non-drug group, a finding completely at odds with the hypothesis of the study. Moreover, the data indicated that whereas anxiety levels decreased over treatment sessions for the non-drug group, they steadily increased over the same period for the Brevital group. The problem that this pattern of results poses for Chambless et al.'s original interpretation of their data is clear. As they now note, "since the non-drug group was not consistently more anxious during flooding, its greater improvement cannot be attributed to differential exposure to interoceptive cues of anxiety" (Chambless et al., 1982, p. 227). Taking a different tack, Chambless et al. suggest that the relative inferiority of the Brevital flooding group was related to absence of between-session habituation of anxiety in that group. They further point out the parallel between this relationship and Foa's (1979) findings that between-sessions habituation of anxiety characterizes successful outcomes in obsessive-compulsive clients treatment with in vivo exposure. However, invoking the notion of habituation across sessions is simply a description of decreased reports of anxiety. Both the habituation and the subsequent treatment outcome still remain to be explained.

Chambless et al. (1982) speculate as follows:

> The relationship between across-session habituation and treatment outcome may be mediated by self-appraisal processes. Clients who observed themselves responding with less anxiety to flooding scenes as treatment proceeds may have had heightened expectancy of change outside the sessions. Conversely, the anxious drug group clients may have taken note of their continued anxiety response to phobic imagery and . . . have concluded they were unimproved. This perception, then, might have led to less vigorous efforts at self-initiated exposure and continued expectations of fearful response to phobic situations. (p. 228)

But what is still unanswered is why the Brevital-flooding group, to a greater extent than the non-drug group, continued to show anxiety during treatment sessions. One plausible explanation of these results draws on what in attribution theory is referred to as the "augmentation principle." This principle states: "If for a given effect, both a plausible inhibitory cause and a plausible facilitative cause are present, the role of the facilitative cause in producing the effect will be judged greater than if it alone were present as a plausible cause for the effect" (Kelley, 1972, p. 12). Translated in terms of Chambless et al.'s procedures, clients in the Brevital-flooding group were faced with explaining their continued anxiety in response to the phobic imagery in terms of an external inhibitory cause (the drug) and an internal facilitative cause (their anxiety). It might be argued that the clients did not discount the inhibitory cause (i.e., they believed that Brevital is a powerful anxiety-reducing agent). Instead, they might have surmised that their continuing anxiety, despite the ostensibly powerful antianxiety drug, indicated the severity of their problems. As a result, they would react to this interpretation of their personal experience with still greater anxiety.

In the extended study, the original non-drug flooding group received weekly hour-long individual treatment sessions over a 4-month period following posttreatment evaluation at the end of the initial eight sessions of flooding. The treatment is described as "communications training" and was geared to helping clients cope with problematic interpersonal situations that were believed to trigger anxiety reactions. The additional treatment, in the absence of further flooding, had no impact on any of the different outcome measures. This finding must call into question some of the clinically popular assumptions about the factors that cause and maintain agoraphobia. For example, it is widely held that agoraphobic symptoms are causally related to interpersonal, usually marital, conflict (Chambless & Goldstein, 1980). This issue is discussed further in a following section.

Both the original flooding and Brevital group and the attention-placebo group received 4 months of additional treatment consisting of both communications training and *in vivo* exposure. This enabled Chambless *et al.* (1982) to compare the effects of imaginal flooding during the first phase of the study with those of *in vivo* flooding during the second phase. Contrary to what would be expected, the *in vivo* treatment was not significantly superior to the imaginal treatment. As the authors point out, this finding is similar to that of Mathews, Johnston, Lancashire, Munby, Shaw, and Gelder (1976). In that earlier study, however, careful monitoring of clients' progress during treatment revealed that clients in the imaginal treatment condition carried out self-directed *in vivo* exposure that plausibly accounted for their improvement. Unfortunately, Chambless *et al.* did not collect data that would have made possible a comparable analysis. Future outcome studies would do well to obtain such information. Data on the degree to which clients comply with treatment instructions or engage in potentially therapeutic activities on their own initiative are vital if we are to interpret unambiguously the results of comparative outcome studies.

The potential problems with clinical rating scales have been referred to in discussion of the Emmelkamp and Mersch (1981) study. Chambless *et al.* (1982) issue the specific warning that their failure to find differences between the imaginal and *in vivo* flooding treatments might be attributable to measurement problems that obscured actual differences. They note that agreement between client and therapist ratings was not high (correlations ranged from .35 to .88, with a mean of .62). Moreover, contrary to Marks and Mathews (1979), fear and avoidance ratings did not correlate highly—correlations ranged from .24 to .69, with a low mean of .47. Appropriately, Chambless *et al.* analyzed their fear and avoidance ratings separately. In making comparisons with other studies in this area it is important to realize that fear and avoidance ratings are sometimes combined.

Chambless *et al.* (1982) concluded the report of their study with the warning that behavior therapists might "be abandoning" imaginal flooding in favor of *in vivo* exposure. Indeed, there appears to be a consensus about the superiority of the latter in the treatment of most phobic and compulsive disorders (Bandura, 1977a; Marks, 1981c; Rachman & Hodgson, 1980; Wilson, 1982a). Whatever the validity of Chambless *et al.*'s admonition about imaginal flooding with agoraphobics, the method is clearly applicable when *in vivo* exposure is impossible for practical reasons. A persuasive illustration of the value of imaginal flooding is provided by Keane and Kaloupek (1982) in the treatment of a Vietnam veteran suffering from a posttraumatic stress disorder. In a model case study, Keane and Kaloupek demonstrated the efficacy of the method on the basis of detailed psychophysiological assessment throughout the course of therapy. Follow-up measures over 1 year produced additional evidence of clinical success, such as job status, emotional involvement, and the absence of nightmares and flashbacks. This particular problem would seem to be well suited to imaginal flooding.

Theoretical Considerations

In last year's volume in this series, I noted a welcome increase in the attention devoted to elucidating the basic mechanisms involved in fear reduction. In addition to traditional conditioning principles, cognitive formulations such as self-efficacy theory and still newer concepts of emotional processing had been advanced as explanations for the effects of the various symbolically based and performance-based treatment methods used by behavior therapists. During the past year, much of the experimental analysis of fear-reduction processes has been guided by Bandura's (1977a) self-efficacy theory. Some important discussions of conditioning formulations were published, and the argument that greater attention should be addressed to exploring affective processes that possibly go beyond existing conditioning or cognitive models was put forward by Rachman (1981a).

In a commentary on the Albany conference on the behavioral treatment of anxiety disorders (Barlow & Wolfe, 1981), Wolpe (1981b) suggests that the conferees viewed behavioral methods as "conceptually rootless." He goes on to assert that many behavior therapists have lost sight of the laboratory origins of these techniques, with the result that laboratory research on theoretical mechanisms is ignored. As he puts it:

> The indifference to the laboratory is quite general: No awareness is shown of important phenomena that have been studied for years by innovative experimental psychologists—most notably, Richard Solomon. . . . Since the distinctive feature of behavior therapy is its foundation in experimentally established principles, it ought ceaselessly to be nourished by the fruits of laboratory research. (p. 604)

It seems that Wolpe is referring to a particular type of laboratory research, namely studies of classical conditioning in laboratory animals. The direct influence of basic laboratory research, using human subjects, is clearly seen in self-efficacy theory, as indicated below. Other examples of the concern with and impact of experimental research on basic mechanisms in behavioral treatments of anxiety disorders are documented in Boulougouris's (1982) book, and it is to these considerations that I now turn.

SELF-EFFICACY THEORY

Bandura (1982) published a major statement of his self-efficacy theory in which he developed the concept and presented new experimental evidence on the relationship of efficacy expectations to avoidance behavior and fear arousal. One line of research from his laboratory has sought to establish a causal link between the construct of self-efficacy and behavior (Bandura, Reese, & Adams, 1982). To this end, snake-phobic subjects were treated with what Bandura terms "enactive mastery" (essentially the same method Biran and Wilson, 1981, called "guided exposure"). Treatment was continued until subjects reached predetermined levels of low, moderate, or high self-efficacy. This was accomplished by assessing subjects' efficacy levels following the completion of each task on the hierarchically arranged behavioral avoidance test. Finally, increasing levels of self-efficacy were successively induced within the same subjects. Both intergroup and intragroup experimental designs showed that approach behavior varied as a function of self-efficacy, covariation that Bandura interprets as establishing the causal nature of perceived efficacy.

A key characteristic of self-efficacy theory is its claim to comprehensiveness, to providing a unifying conceptual framework within which the effects of diverse treatment methods on fear reduction can be understood and predicted. A major assumption is that the ability to approach previously feared situations corresponds closely to level (or strength) of self-efficacy, irrespective of the means by which efficacy expectations are induced. Consistent with this fundamental and ambitious assumption, a number of studies from Bandura's laboratory have shown highly congruent relationships between perceived efficacy and approach behavior in snake-phobic subjects treated with such different techniques as enactive mastery (guided exposure), vicarious modeling, imaginal systematic desensitization, and covert (cognitive) modeling. A finding that is discrepant with this otherwise uniformly supportive set of studies is contained in the Biran and Wilson (1981) study. As described earlier, this investigation compared cognitive restructuring to guided exposure in the treatment of simple phobics. It represented the first systematic analysis of self-efficacy theory with respect to cognitive restructuring as a treatment for phobic disorders. A microanalysis of congruence between self-efficacy and performance, using the assessment procedures identical to those used by Bandura and his colleagues, revealed that self-efficacy proved to be an accurate predictor of individual task performance in the guided exposure group both with regard to the familiar (96%) and the unfamiliar (92%) threats. For the cognitive restructuring groups the levels of congruence were 71% and 64%, respectively. These levels are significantly lower than those obtained for the guided-exposure treatment. The implications of this finding are unclear, although Biran and Wilson (1981) suggest that the data "may indicate that the cognitive treatment is less effective in providing clients with reliable information about their coping ability in phobic situations than are other nonperformance techniques" (p. 898). Cognitive restructuring as employed in this and other studies relies preeminently on verbal operations. As such, it is an example of the "verbal persuasion" mode of influence on self-efficacy in Bandura's scheme of things. This mode of influence has not been empirically tested in the fear-reduction studies completed by Bandura. Given the important consequences for the theory's claim to providing a unifying framework for different methods of fear reduction, additional analyses of the relationship between self-efficacy and actual behavior in clients treated with cognitive restructuring methods are clearly called for.

Appropriately, much of the initial attention was devoted to the relationship between self-efficacy and avoidance behavior (e.g., Rachman, 1978b). It has always been a tenet of the theory, however, that perceived self-efficacy is closely related to subjective fear. Bandura (1982) puts it as follows: "Because stress-inducing thought plays a paramount role in human arousal, self-percepts of coping efficacy can reduce the level of arousal before, during, and after a trying experience" (p. 137). More specifically, perceived self-efficacy is viewed as a cognitive mechanism by which controllability reduces fear arousal. The data from Bandura's own laboratory provide impressive support for this aspect of the theory. In the different studies of the effects of enactive mastery, vicarious modeling, covert modeling, and systematic desensitization, subjects reported the strength of their perceived efficacy in performing different tasks varying in threat value. During later behavioral tests they reported the intensity of fear arousal that they experienced in anticipation of performing each task and again while they were performing the activity. The results showed that at low levels of self-efficacy subjects experienced high anticipatory and performance fear arousal. As their levels of self-efficacy increased, their fear began to decrease. At high strengths of efficacy, the previously feared tasks were performed with little or no fear (see Bandura, 1982). The same relationship was demonstrated in those experiments by Bandura *et al.* (1982) in which low, moderate, or high levels of self-efficacy were induced in different subjects or successively in the same subjects.

Biran and Wilson (1981) failed to obtain support for this aspect of self-efficacy theory. In their study, both level and strength of self-efficacy were highly correlated with avoidance behavior, but not with verbal expressions of either anticipatory or performance fear. In separate correlational analyses of the results of each of the two treatments, significant negative correlations were found between level of self-efficacy and anticipatory and performance fear. This was not true of the guided-exposure treatment. This discrepancy between the two different forms of treatment, as well as between self-efficacy and self-report of subjective fear in the guided-exposure method, raises questions for further investigation.

The foregoing analyses of the relationship between self-efficacy and fear arousal were limited to self-report measures of fear. Bandura *et al.* (1982) expanded their usual methodology in an experiment with severe spider phobics in which they assessed heart rate and blood pressure during both the anticipation and performance of threatening tasks that corresponded to low, medium, and high levels of self-efficacy. In a subsequent phase of the experiment, high levels of self-efficacy were induced in subjects and the same autonomic measures of these tasks assessed once more. At high levels of self-efficacy the spider phobics showed little autonomic arousal. On tasks on which they had rated themselves as only moderately efficacious, however, both heart rate and blood pressure increased sharply. When high levels of self-efficacy were induced through additional treatment, however, these same tasks were performed with considerably reduced autonomic arousal. These results provide strong support for the theory. In sum, with the single exception of Biran and Wilson's (1981) study, the evidence reviewed here is consistent with the assumption that fear arousal is closely and negatively correlated with levels of perceived self-efficacy.

Self-efficacy, as Rosenthal (1982) points out, is a capsule construct that subsumes different subprocesses such as attention and attribution. Thus changes in perceptions of efficacy will occur only to the extent that an individual attributes therapeutic improvement to himself or herself. One of the problems in treating some complex phobic disorders, such as agoraphobia, is that clients often discount successful instances of nonphobic behavior, explaining them away as "luck" or as one of those rare but real "good days" that agoraphobics experience. To overcome these therapeutic difficulties one must address the client's cognitive processing of information. Clients with complex disorders, including some agoraphobics, typically show distortions in the way in which they appraise personal and situational information. They attend selectively to cues, mislabel internal sensations, misinterpret events, recall selected information in a cognitively biased manner that emphasizes negative features, and may minimize or ignore evidence of accomplishment (see Wilson, 1983). Indeed, the fact that perceived efficacy is not merely an isomorphic reflection of past performance, and emphasizes the importance of cognitive processing, is one of the minitheory's major theoretical and clinical attractions. These clinical realities introduce theoretical as well as therapeutic complications that were not major factors in the treatment of the relatively well-adjusted simple phobics who were subjects in the studies of Bandura et al. (1982) and Biran and Wilson (1981). The subjects of the latter study appear to have rationally derived the appropriate information from the planned exposure experiences that disconfirmed their fearful expectations, boosted self-efficacy, and thereby led to reductions in avoidance behavior. Of course, it need hardly be repeated that the controlled laboratory studies of the kind conducted by Bandura are ideally suited to developing theories of behavior change and for testing their cardinal assumptions (Rachman & Wilson, 1980). Now that the concept has been shown to be of value, it is time to focus on the niceties of cognitive processing, the "inferential process in which the relative contribution of personal and situational factors must be weighted and integrated" (Bandura, 1982, p. 124).

In his recent statement, Bandura (1982) touches upon the nature of the cognitive processing of efficacy expectations. "Preliminary explorations," he reports, indicate that individuals' self-efficacy increases when their

> experiences disconfirm misbeliefs about what they fear and when they gain new skills to manage threatening activities. They hold weak self-percepts of efficacy in a provisional status, testing their newly acquired knowledge and skills before raising judgments of what they are able to do. If in the course of completing a task, they discover something that appears intimidating about the undertaking or suggests limitations to their mode of coping, they register a decline in self-efficaciousness despite their successful performance. (pp. 125–126)

Therapists will be familiar with the common experience of agoraphobics, who despite an apparently successful venture into feared territory, such as a supermarket, will come away from the event as fearful as ever because of some unexpected and unnerving feeling of anxiety. Bandura addresses the same issue in his mention of factors that may account for discrepancies between efficacy percepts and behavior. Discrepancies are said to be the result of "faulty self-knowledge, misjudgment of task requirements, unforeseen situational constraints on action, disincentives to act on one's self-percepts of efficacy, ill-defined global measures of perceived self-efficacy in the time elapsing between probes of self-efficacy and action" (p. 129).

Elsewhere I have suggested that a clinical conceptualization of the cognitive processing of efficacy information, based on Beck's (1976) cognitive–behavioral treatment, provides useful therapeutic leads (Wilson, 1983). The cognitive distortions or errors that Beck and other cognitive therapists have identified describe the difficulties that may occur at any or all of the different subprocesses of cognitive processing, such as attention, perception, encoding, storage, and retrieval. Particularly important in this regard is the influential role that affect plays in biasing cognitive processing. The importance of affect in this connection is elaborated upon below.

To reiterate a point I have made in the past (e.g., Wilson, 1982c), one's theory of fear-reduction processes and behavior change will significantly influence both choice of treatment methods and even how the same method will be implemented. For example, exposure treatment informed by a social learning perspective (one that includes but also goes beyond self-efficacy theory) will necessarily include emphasis on cognitive restructuring in the service of increasing motivation, facilitating compliance, and prompting appropriate interpretation of success and failure experiences. I have argued that descriptions of exposure treatment in the literature might have minimized the importance of these strategies or relegated them to the dumping ground of nonspecific influences (Wilson, 1980). A careful analysis of actual treatment, however, as discussed later in this chapter, reveals the important role these broader treatment processes play.

In this connection, it is well to draw attention to an observation recorded by Gelder (1982) in his discussion of whether or not exposure is necessary and sufficient for the successful treatment of agoraphobia. He notes that "when behaviour therapy was first introduced into Europe in the 1950s, the standard method for agoraphobia was a form of exposure treatment known as graded retraining. This gave very limited results . . ." (p. 87). Gelder attributes the increased efficacy of current exposure-based techniques to subsequent research developments. Referring to the eminently successful clinical research of his group of investigators at Oxford University, Gelder states that

> exposure is sufficient, but in this treatment it is not used alone but combined both with anxiety management techniques and with considerable efforts to replace attitudes of helplessness with those of self-efficacy. If we remember the limited results which were obtained years ago with graded retraining, in which exposure treatment was used without these two additional measures, then we would be unwise to conclude that exposure is a sufficient condition. One way of interpreting this is to suppose that the behavioural procedure of exposure to avoided situations does not, by itself, produce the cognitive changes which are required for complete recovery; and that the additional measures are necessary to induce these cognitive changes. (p. 92)

The clinical wisdom of this assertion would be hard to dispute. The general thinking behind self-efficacy theory begins to map out the nature of the cognitive changes Gelder refers to.

RELATIONSHIPS BETWEEN EMOTION AND COGNITION

In Volume 8 mention was made of Zajonc's (1980) thesis that "affect and cognition are under the control of separate and partially independent systems that can influence each other in a variety of ways, and that both constitute independent sources of effects in information processing" (p. 151). Recently Rachman (1981a) published a commentary on Zajonc's views, drawing out its implications for assessment and treatment in behavior therapy. Understandably, Rachman finds in Zajonc's analysis support for the three-systems model of fear. If the affective or emotional system is largely inaccessible to cognitive influences, then means must be found for modifying affect directly. Cognitive methods, the hallmark of rational and other verbal psychotherapies, will be unsuitable and ineffective. In general, this position is consistent with the available evidence on the effects of psychological therapies (Rachman & Wilson, 1980). The problem for both the three-systems model and Lazarus's (1976) multimodal therapy, however, as discussed in detail in Chapter 8 of last year's volume, is that the most effective treatment methods do not necessarily have to be in the same modality as the disorder to which they are applied. The outstanding example of this absence of an isomorphic relationship between treatment and problem modality is the well-documented success of behavioral procedures in altering both cognitive and emotional functioning. While we would be well-advised to heed Rachman's suggestion that we search for more effective ways of modifying affective reactions directly, the evidence indicates that behavioral methods are the best available. Zajonc (1980) and Rachman (1981a) have both helped to clarify an issue of importance to behavior therapists, but neither paper suggests specific treatment procedures beyond those currently in use.

Rachman also draws on Zajonc's analysis in proposing an alternative solution to what he terms "Bandura's therapeutic paradox." The latter is Bandura's (1977a) persuasive observation that "on the one hand, it is performance based treatments that are proving most powerful in effecting psychological changes. Regardless of the method involved, the treatments implemented through actual performance achieve results consistently superior to those in which fears are eliminated to cognitive representations of threats" (p. 78). The explanation that Bandura offers is that behavioral procedures produce changes in cognitive mediating mechanisms, such as self-efficacy. Rachman, accepting the view that there is partial independence between affective and cognitive systems, proposes that the efficacy of behavioral methods could be caused by their primary impact on affective processes. This view fits in with his own work and with Lang's (1979) concept of emotional processing, a topic that was discussed in last year's volume and has seen little systematic development during the past year.

The evidence showing the primary influence of affect on psychological functioning cannot be lightly dismissed. As I indicated in Chapter 3 of Volume 8, however, possibly the most sensible view to adopt is to accept that there are at least two sources of fear reactions (see Bandura, 1969, and Rachman, 1977, for details of this framework). The first is emotional arousal that is self-generated by distressing thoughts. Self-efficacy theory primarily addresses this aspect of functioning. The second is the emotional arousal that appears to be more directly elicited by threatening stimuli. Zajonc's (1980) comments on the primacy of affect would be directly relevant to this set of fear reactions, as are the assumptions and methods of conditioning theory.

It is frequently assumed by cognitive therapists that it is possible to identify anxiety-eliciting thoughts immediately prior to the onset of an attack. The belief is that these frightening cognitions trigger the anxiety attack (e.g., Beck, Laude, & Bohnert, 1974). Yet I would argue that clinical experience amply supports Rachman's (1981a) observation that even the most searching of clinical interviews and assessments often fail to identify reliable patterns of thought that reliably cause anxiety attacks. The reason, Rachman suggests, is that these cases probably reflect emotional changes that are part of an affective system that is relatively inaccessible to cognitions. Given this view, he proposes that

> less time and effort should be devoted to searching for putative S-R relationships, especially in treating anxiety states, "free-floating" anxiety, agoraphobias and disorders in which mood disturbances are prominent. . . . Given that the determinants of affective reactions are likely to be vague, global and gross, the role of meticulous behavioral or S-R analyses in carrying out affect modification might be slight and not useful. (p. 289)

CONDITIONING AND ATTRIBUTION

Conditioning research is hardly moribund, and Eelen (1982), in a thoughtful paper, directs our attention to relevant features of current thinking on this topic. Intriguingly, he suggests useful ways of linking conditioning principles with avowedly cognitive attribution theory. The behavior therapy literature has traditionally pitted these two conceptual views against each other as part of the conditioning-versus-cognition controversy. Eelen begins by emphasizing that modern, sophisticated conceptualizations of classical conditioning are usually ignored in the behavior therapy literature in favor of manifestly inadequate and outmoded views. Summarizing the evidence on phenomena such as blocking, latent inhibition, and the role of contingency, he reaches the following conclusion:

> The mere coincidence of two events is not a sufficient condition for the learning of a relation between two events. . . . Instead of an automatic process within a passive organism, classical conditioning seems to postulate an active information-processing organism. (p. 7)

The problem with this view is neatly expressed by MacIntosh (1978):

> It is one thing, however, to say that the information-processing machinery that an organism brings to the world is designed to be sensitive to contingent relations rather than to coincidentally occurring events. But this tells us relatively little about the exact nature of that machinery. (p. 173)

It might be, as Eelen points out, that "being influenced by a correlative relation between events, does not imply that the organism has any 'idea' of the correlation at all" (p. 7). This last point allows Eelen to build a bridge to attribution theory.

Attribution theory addresses the process of making causal inferences about different events. Typically, the unobservable process of inference has been studied through the person's verbal report. But as Eelen shows, the validity of these verbalized attributions has been seriously questioned. Aside from citing Nisbett and Wilson's (1977) conclusion that the cognitive mediating processes on which attribution theory rests are not accessible to introspection, Eelen quotes other researchers to the same effect. Consider the following quote from Langer (1978):

> Much psychological research relies on a theoretical model that depicts the individual as one who is cognitively aware most of the time, and who consciously, constantly, and systematically applies "rules" to incoming information about the environment in order to formulate interpretations and courses of actions. Attribution theorists rely on this model in attempting to uncover the sources of regularities in human behaviour. But if in fact it can be demonstrated that much complex human behaviour can and does occur without these assumed cognitive assessments, then we must question both the pervasiveness of attribution making as a cognitive process and the assumption made by most psychologists. (p. 35)

In sum, Eelen proposes that there is much in common about the way in which infrahuman and human organisms discover the causal network of their environment, and that conditioning and attribution research are both addressing this broader question. He calls for the integration of current cognitive theories within behavior therapy, but not at the cost of forgetting our roots. Thus he is quick to point out the problems with current cognitive–behavioral treatment approaches:

> In the past ten years, behaviour therapy has been "going cognitive" and within this new look, it is even becoming old-fashioned to show any interest in such simple phenomena as conditioning. But just as in early attribution research, too much emphasis is given by cognitive therapists to conscious or semiconscious private "self-talks" of their clients. These self-talks are epiphenomena, "surface structures," which might or might not be congruent with some deeper epistemic knowledge of their world. (p. 15)

THE ACQUISITION OF PHOBIC REACTIONS

In his critical evaluation of the conditioning theory of the acquisition of fears and phobias, Rachman (1977) concluded that there are three pathways to fear: (1) direct conditioning, (2) vicarious learning (modeling), and (3) verbal instruction. In elaborating upon this framework for the acquisition and maintenance of fear and phobic reactions, Rachman (1978a) put forward a number of hypotheses about response patterns among the three pathways. These included the following: (1) "In fears acquired by a conditioning process . . . the components that will be most prominent are the psychophysiological and behavioral" (p. 198); (2) "where fears have been transmitted indirectly (vicariously or informationally) we might expect the subjective aspect to be predominant" (p. 198); and (3) "fears acquired informationally are more likely to be mild than severe" (p. 194). These hypotheses have been put to the test in a large-scale study by Ost and Hugdahl (1981).

The subjects for this wide-ranging investigation were 110 phobic patients who had received or were receiving treatment for the phobias as part of a treatment program directed by Ost and his colleagues. They were classified as animal phobias ($n = 41$), social phobias ($n = 34$), and claustrophobia ($n = 35$). A comprehensive questionnaire, containing items about experiences bearing on Rachman's three pathways, items tapping the experience of physiological fear reactions, and items assessing anticipatory (subjective) fear reactions, was sent to all animal and social phobics. The return rates were an impressive 97.6% and 91.2%, respectively. The claustrophobics completed the questionnaire during the course of their treatment. In addition, Ost and Hugdahl were able to draw on the detailed pretreatment assessments they had made of all patients. These measures, described fully in Ost, Jerremalm, and Johansson (1981), included objective behavioral measures, heart-rate responses, and specific self-ratings of fear during the behavioral tests. For the animal phobics the behavioral test was the typical avoidance task, for the claustrophobics it was how long they remained in a small test chamber, and for the social phobics it was reliable behavioral ratings of their anxiety.

The results showed that a large majority (58%) of the patients attributed their phobias to conditioning experiences, while 17% recalled vicarious experiences, 10% recalled instructions or information, and 15% could not recall any specific onset circumstances. Contrary to Rachman's hypotheses about differential patterning of the response components across fears acquired via the three pathways, no clearcut relationships were found between ways of acquisition and behavioral, physiological, and subjective components of fear. Nor did fears acquired through conditioning prove to be more severe than those acquired through the other pathways. The only exception to this trend was for the animal phobics, for whom conditioned fears were more severe than those acquired via modeling and instructions.

Preparedness theory (Seligman, 1971) has been invoked by some theorists (e.g., Eysenck, 1982; Rachman, 1977) to account for some of the problems the conditioning theory of the development phobias has run up against. Foremost among these problems is the nagging question of why phobic reactions do not extinguish naturally. The persistence of phobias is inconsistent with laboratory evidence showing that classically conditioned fears extinguish readily once the unconditioned stimulus is removed. Preparedness theory presents a partial explanation in that it assumes that phobic reactions are biologically prepared responses that are uniquely resistant to extinction. Thus far the strongest experimental support for the preparedness theory of phobias has been the elegant series of studies by Öhman and his colleagues (see Volume 7 of the *Annual Review*, pp. 46–48, for a review of some of these studies in particular, Öhman, Frederikson, & Hugdahl, 1980; Hygge & Öhman, 1978; and Hugdahl, 1978). Their major finding has been that fear responses conditioned to prepared or "fear-relevant" stimuli are more resistant to extinction than those conditioned to unprepared or "fear-irrelevant" stimuli. This finding, however, does not necessarily demonstrate that it is biological preparedness that makes the difference. Accounts that emphasize the person's previous learning history provide a plausible alternative (e.g., Bandura, 1977b; Delprato, 1980).

McNally and Reiss (1982) modified Öhman's conditioning paradigm to test preparedness theory in a novel way. If Seligman's (1971) theory is correct, they argued, then it should be more difficult to establish a fear-relevant stimulus (a snake) as a conditioned safety signal than a fear-irrelevant stimulus (a flower). The results of their study showed that both stimuli could be established as safety signals, with no apparent difference between them. They conclude that the "finding that disassociations between pictorial snakes and electric-shock can be readily learned is, thus, inconsistent with the notion of a species-wide 'belongingness' between snakes and aversive stimuli" (p. 158). At the same time, however, it must be noted that their finding is also inconsistent with the alternative social learning interpretation of previous studies from the laboratory of Öhman and his group. Nonetheless, McNally and Reiss's study adds to the weight of evidence suggesting that preparedness theory is of questionable value in explaining the phenomena of phobic reactions (Delprato, 1980; Wilson & O'Leary, 1980).

Clinical Considerations

INSTRUCTIONAL MANUALS

Analyses of the pros and cons of self-help manuals have been the subject of discussion on more than one occasion in this series (e.g., Volume 5). Given the many problems with so many of these manuals (no empirical support, irresponsible claims, and so on), the publication of Mathews *et al.*'s (1981) book on agoraphobia is particularly welcome. Included as appendices in this comprehensive and scholarly volume are the two self-help manuals that formed the basis for this group's innovative and effective home-based treatment program for agoraphobia (Mathews, Teasdale, Munby, Johnston, & Shaw, 1977; reprinted in Volume 6 of this series). One manual is written for the agoraphobic, the other for the spouse who assists in treatment under the overall guidance of the therapist. They are clearly written, consistent with the best research evidence on the treatment of agoraphobia, and they provide the necessary procedural details for easy use. Among the many excellent features of these manuals, therapists will find the instructions on how the spouse might relate to his or her agoraphobic partner in a consistent and constructive fashion to be of particular value. Many therapists are all too quick to jump on the spouse of the agoraphobic, ferreting out flimsy evidence of his or her deliberate (and usually unconscious) collusion in the etiology and maintenance of the disorder. While there are instances in which the spouse is inextricably linked to the maintenance of the problem, and appropriate therapeutic strategies that go beyond exposure treatment are called for, it is also evident that in many instances the spouse simply does not know how to act. Living with an agoraphobic is a difficult and trying experience, and it should hardly be necessary to add that signs of marital strain (where they exist, and this is by no means always the case) may be the result rather than the cause of the phobic problem.

Mathews *et al.* (1981) have done the field a great service by laying out in detail the therapeutic methods they use. "Exposure treatment" is usually discussed in the literature as though it were a uniform and standardized procedure that was directly comparable from one study to the next. This assumption is probably untenable. Although exposure treatment is a straightforward method, its effective use frequently depends on success in dealing with clinical issues such as increasing motivation, facilitating compliance, coping with anticipated anxiety attacks during exposure sessions, and overcoming cognitive distortions of the kind referred to in the previous section (Wilson, 1983). These often critically important clinical strategies tend to be ignored or relegated to the status of "nonspecific factors" in necessarily abbreviated journal accounts of behavioral studies. Thanks to Mathews *et al.* (1981), it is possible to examine, in procedural detail, the sort of strategies they have followed in their successful treatment studies. This detail ensures that therapists will be apprised of the clinical nuances and strategies that are vital in implementing exposure treatment and enables researchers to replicate this procedure and analyze its components.

Not surprisingly, the manuals contain strategies that are particularly relevant to the clinical issues noted above. The treatment program cannot be encompassed by simply describing it as an extinction technique aimed at producing habituation of fear. In addition to prescribing the basic behavioral tasks of gradually approaching phobic situations, Mathews *et al.* (1981) offer suggestions for coping with thoughts and feelings that would otherwise undermine therapeutic progress. Detailed considerations of these treatment manuals is beyond the scope of the present chapter, but the point at issue here can be illustrated with reference to their suggestions for coping with what they call "setbacks."

Consider the following advice:

> Hardly anyone recovers from agoraphobia without having at least one "setback." Feelings vary, sometimes from day to day, and what you did successfully yesterday may seem impossible today. Even then, you could make real progress. What counts is how you cope with whatever feelings you experience. So, a little done on a bad day can be worth more than a lot done on a good day. (1981, p. 184)

Here and elsewhere in the manual Mathews *et al.* (1981) help clients to interpret (others might say "reframe") critical events in constructive rather than negative, self-defeating ways. By anticipating the possibility of a "setback" at some point in the future, they explicitly attempt to defuse the otherwise detrimental effects of an unexpected anxiety attack just when clients feel they are improved. Little or no mention is made of such specific interventions in the literature on agoraphobics, but it is plain to see that Mathews *et al.* are engaging in what Marlatt (in press), in the field of addictive disorders, has described as the cognitive–behavioral technique or relapse-prevention training. Mathews *et al.* even provide clients with a short set of summary rules about what to do if a panic strikes. These include the following: "1. The feelings are normal bodily reactions; 2. They are not harmful; 3. Do not add frightening thoughts; . . . 9. Plan what to do next . . ." (p. 183). The parallel to relapse-prevention training, in which clients are provided very similar "rules" that bear on attributional processes, and coping strategies is striking. Specifying treatment interventions (including cognitive and behavioral components) and relating progress in one area to developments in another, as now seems possible, constitutes a major therapeutic advance.

MARITAL SATISFACTION AND THE TREATMENT OF AGORAPHOBIA

The issues of the marital satisfaction of agoraphobics and the interaction between marital satisfaction and the treatment of agoraphobia behavior continue to attract considerable clinical attention. Major reviews of these issues by Brehony and Geller (1981), Mathews *et al.* (1981), and Vandereycken (in press) cover the wide range of opinions on the role of interpersonal influences, particularly marital factors, in the etiology, maintenance, and treatment of agoraphobia. As Mathews *et al.* (1981) demonstrate, however, much of the literature in this area reduces to mere opinion, with infrequent attempts at empirical confirmation. Methodological inadequacies in the majority of studies preclude anything but the most tentative conclusions. The problems, so ably documented by Mathews *et al.* (1981) and Vandereycken (in press), include the small number of patients that comprise many studies, the absence of appropriate control groups, and correlational and retrospective studies. Inadequate and inconsistent measurement of the quality of marital relationships presents numerous difficulties. For the most part, assessment has been limited to single and simple self-report scales, many of unknown reliability and validity. The use of different measures in different studies makes comparison of results particularly hazardous. Improved assessment of marital functioning must be a high priority in future research in this important area.

An exception to the overall trend of poorly designed correlational studies in the area is a well-controlled study by Buglass, Clarke, Henderson, Kreitman, and Presley (1977). They compared 30 married agoraphobic women with "normal" controls matched for age, sex, social class, and marital status. Besides semistructured, conjoint, and separate interviews with husband and wife, all participants (including the spouses) were administered a variety of questionnaires. Contrary to clinical stereotypes about the allegedly pathological quality of agoraphobics' marital relationships, Buglass *et al.* found no significant differences between the two groups across a wide range of measures, including decision making, domestic organization, social relationships, and problems in their children. Both husbands and wives of each group described their marriages in similar terms before the onset of agoraphobia or during the comparable period among the control group. Nor could Buglass *et al.* unearth evidence indicating that spouses were reinforcing dependency in the agoraphobic partners—no joy here for the systems theorists and their communications conceptions of agoraphobia. To sum up, the results of this well-controlled study indicate that agoraphobia is an isolated problem that emerges independently from the interpersonal (marital) context.

In view of the lack of convincing evidence about pathology in agoraphobics' marriages, and the data to the contrary from one of the rare well-controlled investigations in this area, the question that remains is: Why the tenacity of the clinical belief in disordered marriages among agoraphobics? Somewhat cynically, it might be noted that persistent clinical convictions that fly in the face of empirical evidence are all too common in the field of psychotherapy as a whole. A plausible explanation of this particular instance of apparent bias is offered by Mathews *et al.* (1981). They speculate that the assumption that major difficulties are commonly present in married agoraphobics derives "from a relatively small number of striking cases in which prominent marital problems cause so much difficulty in treatment that they are remembered long after less complicated cases are forgotten" (p. 7). One can go beyond this observation and suggest how it is that relatively few but "striking" cases make such a disproportionate and lasting impression on clinicians. In Chapter 8 of last year's volume (pp. 318–319), I discussed recent research in cognitive-social psychology that demonstrates how highly probative data-summary information sometimes is ignored while less probative case-history information has a substantial impact on inferences. The magnitude of this phenomenon in clinical psychology, and its consequences for the field, has yet to be fully appreciated.

In the discussion of these issues in last year's volume it was pointed out that allegations that *in vivo* exposure treatment of agoraphobic behavior had resulted in increases in marital dissatisfaction (Milton & Hafner's [1979] ill-considered charge of symptom substitution) had proved to be groundless. Similarly, the notion that agoraphobics could not be successfully treated for their phobic disorder if the marital relationship was distressed was also found to be in error (Barlow, Mavissakalian, & Hay, 1981; Marks, 1981c). Mathews *et al.*'s (1981) authoritative and empirically based analysis convincingly supports this position. Additional data bearing on this question were reported by Bland and Hallam (1981).

On the basis of the combined patient–spouse scores on the Stuart Marital Pre-Counseling Inventory, which was completed prior to therapy, and on the therapist's own rating of the couple at the initial interview, 16 married agoraphobics were classified as having good or bad marriages. Following the initial interview 4 subjects dropped out of the study, leaving a final number of 10 female and 2 male subjects. Each subject received six 2-hour sessions of therapist-guided exposure treatment. Assessments of marital satisfaction, phobic behavior (based on clinical ratings), and neurotic symptoms were made before and after treatment and at 1- and 3-month follow-up intervals. Subjects in the good-marriage group responded well to treatment and maintained their improvement at both follow-ups. Their counterparts in the poor-marriage group showed a different pattern. They improved initially but later lost most of the gains and reported no change in general neurotic symptoms. Patients' dissatisfaction with their spouses, measured before therapy, predicted outcome in the sample as a whole, whereas spouses' dissatisfaction with the patient was not predictive.

This finding reinforces the now widely held view in behavior therapy (e.g., Barlow & Wolfe, 1981) that for some clients, *in vivo* exposure therapy must be supplemented by additional treatment methods, such as marital therapy, following careful individual assessment. The other major finding that emerged from this study further refutes Milton and Hafner's (1979) claim that improvement in phobic behavior leads to negative changes in the marriage. As Bland and Hallam (1981) noted, there were no data "to indicate that spouses took a negative view of patients' improvements or felt less satisfied with the marriage as a result. Dissatisfied spouses remained dissatisfied; satisfied spouses tended to become more satisfied as the patient's phobia improved" (p. 338).

The literature is replete with different views, not only about whether to address the interpersonal (marital) context of agoraphobics in therapy but also about when and how to do this (see Vandereycken's [in press] review of these divergent views). In view of the available evidence, Vandereycken outlines what appears to be the most sensible clinical approach. He suggests that the therapist initiate *in vivo* exposure treatment aimed at the phobic disorder with the active involvement of the spouse, if possible, following the procedure described by Mathews *et al.* (1981). According to Vandereycken, several advantages attach to this approach, especially in cases where phobic and marital problems appear to co-exist:

> 1. The exposure treatment may well be expected to improve both agoraphobia and marital relationship; further or separate marital therapy may be unnecessary (see, e.g., Cobb *et al.*, 1980). . . . 2. In other cases the exposure treatment may result in symptom removal or improvement, at least, but existing marital problems either remain unchanged or become more prominent or even worsen; the partial symptom-treatment success may motivate the couple to engage in a marital therapy they would probably have rejected if it had been offered before phobia-treatment. . . . 3. Finally, in some cases exposure treatment may fail in every respect; meanwhile the marital relationship, however, may have reached a crisis . . . or a supportive and non-threatening therapeutic relationship may have been established so that the patient and/or the spouse have become more willing to accept an approach that is aimed at their marital interaction.

TREATMENT OF AGORAPHOBIA AND SELF-HELP GROUPS

The previous section addressed the use of *in vivo* exposure treatment for agoraphobics within the context of a specific social support system, marriage. Sinnott, Jones, Scott-Fordham, and Woodward (1981) have extended the concept of social support for the implementation of exposure treatment by forming neighborhood self-help groups. In prompting agoraphobic clients to complete homework assignments, Sinnott *et al.* noticed that these clients had lost social contacts because of their long-standing phobic symptoms. As a result, "they lacked realistic targets which could serve as the basis for practice of short journeys from the home culminating in rewarding social contact. This seemed to reduce incentive and decreased the likelihood of successful completion of homework targets" (p. 339). This gave the researchers the idea of creating new social contacts through neighborhood self-help groups.

Sinnott *et al.* assigned 30 agoraphobic clients to the following three treatment groups: *in vivo* exposure for selected clients who lived within a 1-mile radius (the "zoned" group); *in vivo* exposure for "unzoned" subjects who, on average, lived several miles apart from each other; and a no-treatment control condition. Because 9 clients failed to complete treatment, 8, 7, and 6 clients were left in the three respective groups. Group discussions prior to graded exposure tasks were devoted to developing group cohesiveness. Homework assignments were prescribed between sessions, and spouses and significant others "were encouraged to attend with the subjects to promote their involvement in homework" (p. 340). Clients in the zoned group "were encouraged to use each other as target destinations e.g. by attending a meeting at the home of another group member or by meeting another subject at an agreed half-way point etc." (p. 341).

Both treated groups showed significantly greater improvement than the no-treatment control, as measured by their progress along a standardized hierarchy of journeys ranging from a short accompanied walk to an unaccompanied bus trip. Only clients in the zoned group, however, reported significant reductions in the anxiety they experienced while performing the tasks on the avoidance hierarchy. Moreover, only subjects in this group increased their number of social contacts at posttreatment. Measures of social contact were taken from Buglass *et al.* (1977). The failure of clients in the unzoned group to increase their range of social contact, despite reductions in avoidance behavior and consequently increased geographic range is noteworthy, suggesting that specific steps might be necessary to improve this facet of agoraphobics' functioning. Improvements were maintained at a 3-month follow-up.

Particularly important in view of the study's rationale is the finding that the zoned subjects completed their homework assignments more regularly, often with other clients in their zone as encouraged by the therapists. Sinnott *et al.* did not include a measure of group cohesiveness, but they report anecdotally that the clients in the zoned group were more cohesive. A potentially useful clinical observation by Sinnott *et al.* concerns the reactions of clients who suffered from social anxiety in addition to their primary agoraphobic disorder. They resisted group involvement:

> In one case an apparent intensification of agoraphobic symptoms occurred which seemed to reflect the patient becoming less willing to venture out of the house because this would have exposed her to the interactional demands of neighbourhood group participation. (p. 346)

Sinnott *et al.* recommend prior screening of candidates for adjunctive self-help groups for social anxiety that might undermine the advantages of the group experience.

OBSESSIONS AND COMPULSIONS

Unwanted Intrusive Cognitions

The most recent developments in Rachman's influential program of research on obsessional disorders are to be found in his monograph on unwanted intrusive cognitions (Rachman, 1981b). These troublesome cognitions, defined as "repetitive, unwanted, intrusive thoughts of internal origin," were the subject of an initial investigation by Rachman and DeSilva (1978) that focused on the nature of unwanted intrusive cognitions, their relationship to the obsessions of clinical patients, and their origins. In their recently published monograph, Parkinson and Rachman (1982b) summarize the results of a large-scale study that sought to replicate and extend the findings of the initial investigation. The volunteers, 60 nonpatient adults who reported having clear intrusive ideas at least twice a month, participated in detailed interviews and extensive psychometric testing. The results were reassuringly consistent with those reported earlier by Rachman and DeSilva (1978). The form and content of unwanted intrusive cognitions were similar to that of clinically defined obsessions, with themes of death, doing harm to oneself or one's family, sex, and aggression predominating. These cognitions were, however, less intense and less disturbing than clinical obsessions. What Rachman refers to as the dismissability of intrusive thoughts was related to their intensity and distressing qualities. The more distressing a thought, the harder it is to banish. Finally, the study revealed that external precipitants featured prominently as the cause of unwanted intrusive thoughts.

A second study by Parkinson and Rachman (1982a) replicated earlier findings that naturally occurring stress reliably increases distressing, intrusive thoughts. The behavior and thoughts of a group of mothers whose children had been admitted to the hospital for surgery were compared to those of a control group. Mothers under stress reported significantly greater anxiety and a greater number of intrusive cognitions. They performed poorly on a cognitive (arithmetic) task and showed heightened sensitivity to words relevant to their immediate stress. In a second study, Sutherland, Newman, and Rachman (1981) experimentally induced happy or sad moods in nonclinical subjects who were then asked to dismiss selected intrusive or neutral thoughts. Their hypothesis that depressed mood makes it more difficult to control or remove intrusive thoughts was supported. In an engaging literary touch, the authors remind the reader of Samuel Johnson's observation that "the mind drives away painful fancies, except when melancholic notions take the form of duty."

The monograph also contains an analysis of reasons for the persistence of intrusive unwanted cognitions. Rachman summarizes the relevant findings as follows:

> Factors [that] seem to contribute to the persistence of intrusive unwanted cognitions [are]: dysphoria, exposure to stress, the emotional significance of the cognitive material, the frequency of occurrence of external provocations, and other unnamed factors. On the other side, unwanted intrusive cognitions tend to decrease in frequency when—threats or stresses are removed, when the subject is relaxed, when the material produces little or no emotional reaction, when the external triggers are diminished or removed, and during stable or pleasant mood states. (p. 96)

In addition to the content of Rachman's research program, the methods of study are worthy of note. A major problem confronting behavioral researchers in the field of obsessional disorders is the assessment and measurement of thoughts, which, by their nature, are unobservable. Parkinson and Rachman (1982a) wisely turned to the technology of cognitive psychology for guidance in developing measures other than verbal report. For example, in a creative attempt to operationalize intrusiveness of thoughts, they devised an auditory recognition task based on dichotic listening: "The degree of intrusiveness is assessed by the auditory level at which the interruption takes place e.g. a particularly intrusive stimulus will be capable of interrupting an ongoing activity even at low level of volume" (p. 97). There are, of course, numerous assessment possibilities suggested by information-processing models, an instance of which was discussed in Chapter 3 in last year's volume (Burgess, Jones, Robertson, Radcliffe, & Emerson, 1981), and we may anticipate further advances in this area in the future.

Treatment of Obsessions

While reasonably effective methods have been developed for the modification of compulsive rituals, successful treatments for obsessions have remained elusive (Rachman & Hodgson, 1980). Encouragingly, behavioral researchers are now trying to remedy this situation, as evidenced by the publication of the following studies this past year.

Emmelkamp and Giesselbach (1981) evaluated the effects of one treatment method that has shown some promise in helping obsessional patients: prolonged exposure in imagination to their obsessional thoughts. More specifically, they compared exposure to relevant versus irrelevant cues. Six patients received six 1-hour therapy sessions of each form of imaginal exposure in the context of a crossover design. Assessments were made before and after each treatment. In the relevant cue condition, patients were asked to imagine scenes that triggered their obsessions, with the therapist making frequent checks to ensure that the scenes were eliciting the desired anxiety. In the irrelevant-cue condition, patients were instructed to imagine scenes that elicited anxiety but were unrelated to their obsessions (e.g., being burned to death, eaten by a tiger, or dying in a plane crash).

Exposure to relevant cues produced greater improvement, as measured by daily counts of obsessions and ratings of daily distress, than exposure to irrelevant cues. Indeed, the latter led to an increase in daily distress ratings. These results contradict the findings of a similar comparison with agoraphobics by Watson and Marks (1971). The small number of patients requires that caution be maintained in interpreting these results. It would also be well to heed the authors' warning about the need for additional treatment in four of the cases and their observation that the one patient who derived no benefit from exposure treatment failed to show any anxiety in response to imaginal presentation of cues.

Rachman's (1977) satiation or habituation technique for treating obsessions (reprinted in Volume 5 of this series) is a form of prolonged exposure in imagination. Vogel, Peterson, and Broverman (1982) assert that a problem with this method is its reliance on the patient being able to generate his or her obsessions during therapy sessions. According to these authors, an obsession generated on demand will differ in emotional quality from the spontaneous experience of the obsession in the patient's natural environment. Although this is possible, the authors present no evidence to support their claims. Moreover, it is after all an empirical question whether Rachman's technique is effective or not. Nevertheless, Vogel et al. propose a modification of the basic technique. Briefly, they require the active cooperation of a friend or family member with whom the patient spends a good deal of time. This "surrogate therapist" (ST) is instructed to ask the patient whether he or she is thinking of the obsession "whenever the patient seems to be distracted, preoccupied, or troubled" (p. 102). If the response is affirmative, the patient follows the therapist's instructions and describes the details of the obsession. The ST listens attentively but makes no comment. If the answer is negative, the ST reinforces the patient's ostensible thought control.

Vogel *et al.* report three successes and three failures with this method, providing only anecdotal observations about each. The considerable demands such a method places on dutiful compliance by the patient, let along that required of the ST, would appear to make this procedure less feasible than Rachman's original formulation.

Treatment of Compulsions

Emmelkamp (1982) investigated the merits of involving the obsessive-compulsive's partner in the therapeutic process. The basic treatment consists of self-controlled *in vivo* exposure. In this method, a hierarchy of stimuli that elicit compulsive rituals is developed by the therapist. At each session patients are instructed to complete homework assignments consisting of items from the hierarchy. Patients are asked to expose themselves to situations that trigger their compulsions and to desist from engaging in their rituals. As Emmelkamp notes, this method is best described as gradual exposure *in vivo* plus self-imposed response prevention. The 12 obsessive–compulsive patients were randomly assigned either to self-exposure treatment alone or to self-exposure with the active assistance of a partner. In the patient-alone condition, the partner "was neither involved in the discussions with the therapist, nor in the execution of the homework assignments. Family members were instructed to be absent during the practice hours" (p. 120). In the couple condition, "the partner had to accompany the patient each treatment session. After the rationale was explained to the couple, the patient received instructions for self-controlled exposure. He had to carry out his homework assignments with his partner present. The task of the partner was to encourage the patient and to have him confront the stimuli which distressed him" (p. 120). Treatment was comprised of 4 "information" sessions and 10 treatment sessions.

The preliminary results of this study show that both treatments produced significant improvement, although the couple condition was superior. These data should be viewed cautiously, however. The only outcome measure reported was a self-rating anxiety scale in which "data for the main obsessive–compulsive and the other obsessive–compulsive problems have been combined" (p. 120). The limitations of clinical rating scales of this nature, and the problems of combining measures of different behaviors, were discussed in Volume 8 (pp. 85–86). With regard to the discussion of marital satisfaction and exposure treatment earlier in this chapter, it is worth noting Emmelkamp's comment that "even in cases with clear marital discord the partner could be involved in the treatment without disrupting treatment progress" (p. 120). He also remarks on the apparent improvement in patients' marital relationships following *in vivo* exposure treatment directed at compulsive rituals. Doubtless the ease with which an obsessive–compulsive's partner can be involved in treatment will vary from patient to patient. In many instances, trying to obtain the constructive support of the obsessive–compulsive's family is itself a large part of the therapy. Clinical experience suggests that therapeutic strategies designed to alter family relationships are often necessary supplements to exposure methods.

As is now well known, *in vivo* exposure appears to be an effective method for treatment of phobic and compulsive disorders, but we are not sure why it works. Evidence from research with both infrahuman (Baum, 1976) and human subjects (Borkovec, 1974, 1982) has shown that what organisms do during exposure to anxiety-eliciting stimuli is an important determinant of fear reduction. With patients this question centers importantly on what they do cognitively. In an analysis of cognitive activity during exposure to anxiety-eliciting stimuli, Grayson, Foa, and Steketee (1982) compared the effects of distraction with those of attention focusing. The subjects were 16 obsessive-compulsives whose rituals were triggered by specific contaminating stimuli. In the context of a crossover design, each subject received one 90-minute session of each type of exposure *in vivo* to his or her anxiety-eliciting objects. In the distraction condition, subjects "were asked to hold the contaminating object in one hand while playing video games with their therapist." In the attention-focusing condition, "the therapist engaged the subject in the conversation about the contaminant he/she was holding and the discomfort it aroused. Patients' attempts to discuss related issues were stopped and conversation was redirected to the contaminating object" (p. 324). Measures of heart rate and subjective units of disturbance were obtained at different intervals during the exposure.

Habituation of both heart rate and verbal report of fear was obtained during exposure under both distraction and attention focusing. However, greater between-sessions habituation and greater synchrony between the psychophysiological and the subjective measures of anxiety were observed when attention focusing preceded distraction. The authors interpret these data as showing that "separate mechanisms are involved in the two types of habituation and that it is primarily cognitive factors which affect between-session habituation" (p. 327). Attention to the stimuli that trigger anxiety reactions or compulsive rituals appears to facilitate exposure treatment. But what still remains to be explained is the mechanism or process whereby fear reduction (habituation) takes place once attention is engaged.

Finally, Queiroz, Motta, Madi, Sossai, and Boren (1981) described detailed case reports of the treatment of obsessive–compulsive disorders in children and adults in which they highlight the importance of making a thorough functional analysis of the presenting problems. Reminding us that fine-grained assessment of the individual patient's particular problem is a cardinal feature of the behavioral approach, Queiroz *et al.* illustrate how different functional analyses lead to widely differing therapeutic strategies. In some cases, direct treatment of the obsession or compulsion using exposure in imagination or *in vivo* might suffice. In others, however, what the authors refer to as "indirect" treatments are required. Pointing out the clinical reality that many obsessive–compulsive patients have "many behavioral deficits and grossly inadequate conditions to maintain normal behavior," Queiroz *et al.* draw attention to the value of techniques such as assertion training and the alteration of social (family) reinforcement contingencies. These observations are endorsed by Emmelkamp (1982) in his observations on the clinical treatment of obsessive–compulsive disorders.

CHAPTER

4

COGNITIVE PROCESSES AND PROCEDURES IN BEHAVIOR THERAPY

PHILIP C. KENDALL

The history of cognitive–behavioral approaches to psychotherapy is surprisingly short. Nevertheless, writers have been active in the attempt to capture accurately the transitions in the field and describe its current status. It is public record that cognitive–behavioral strategies have been labeled a "shotgun wedding," an "oxymoron," and, less pejoratively, a rational integration of procedures with demonstrated efficiencies. The changes in the status of cognitive–behavior therapy have been dramatic: from radical criticisms of its mentalistic and theoretically weak foundations, to its endorsement as the second most dominant theoretical orientation (eclecticism aside) among clinical and counseling psychologists (Smith, 1982).

If, like the present authors, you partake in and enjoy the tracking and tracing of the history of movements within the field, you no doubt recognize the remarkable growth of cognitive–behavioral interventions, a trend that has been documented in earlier volumes of the *Annual Review*. A closer look at the Smith (1982) report and a related report by Heesacker, Heppner, and Rogers (1982) provides extra enlightenment. Smith (1982) essentially followed the lead of Garfield and Kurtz (1974, 1976, 1977) and conducted a survey of the attitudes and orientations of psychologists. However, unlike Garfield and Kurtz, who surveyed only clinical psychologists, Smith surveyed both clinical and counseling psychologists. Seeking a random sample of 800 subjects (200 Division 12 members, 200 Division 12 Fellows; 200 Division 17 members, 200 Division 17 Fellows) from the American Psychological Association,

Smith mailed his one-page questionnaire to selected individuals. Of the 437 questionnaires that were returned (55% return rate), 422 provided usable information.

Of the 13 theoretical orientations offered the respondents, the largest group of subjects identified themselves as eclectic (171 of 415 subjects, or 41.2%). This somewhat expected result was consistent with (though less extensive than) the earlier reports by Garfield and Kurtz (1974, 1976, 1977) and Kelly (1961). In Smith's sample, the major theoretical orientation was psychoanalytic (45 out of 415 subjects, or 10.84%) followed very closely by cognitive–behavioral (43 out of 415 subjects, or 10.36%). The difference between them is nonmeaningful. The next largest groups endorsed the theoretical orientations "other" (38 subjects, or 8.67%) and behavioral (28 subjects, or 6.75%).

Yet another data set provided evidence that the cognitive–behavioral orientation is one of the major trends in psychotherapy. Smith (1982) requested that his respondents identify persons they considered to be most influential in current psychotherapy trends, and he reported the weighted scores for the 10 most influential psychotherapists. Smith noted that "cognitive–behavioral and/or rational-emotive was the predominant representation among the 10 most influential therapists" (4 out of 10) (p. 807).

The Heesacker et al. (1982) report is relevant here, for their data also evidenced the impact of cognitive–behavioral writers. Working with the frequency of citations in articles published in three counseling psychology journals for a period of 2 years (approximately 14,000 citations) the authors identified major contributions before and since 1957. Fully one-half of the post-1957 list of "emerging major contributions" were cognitive–behavioral and one-third of the "emerging classic books" were cognitive–behavioral.

An important and informative aggregation of the Smith data involves the combining of alternate views on the behavioral orientation. Although Smith did not aggregate his data in this way, the behavioral (6.75%) and cognitive–behavioral (10.36%) orientations can form a cohesive grouping that would account for 17.11% of the respondents. Thus this more generic behavior therapy orientation surpasses the psychoanalytic orientation and would be second only to eclecticism.

Smith (1982) was also interested in the viability of "schools of psychotherapy"—are the days of schools of therapy virtually over? Based on his survey data, he reported that "the heyday of schools of psychotherapy has past [sic]" (p. 808) and that there is a move toward integration (see also Goldfried, 1982; Kendall, 1982d; and the miniseries in the November issue of Behavior Therapy, 1982). I need not repeat the strong arguments against the integration of behavior therapy and psychoanalytic approaches (see Franks & Wilson, 1979), but one should recognize that a more generic behavior therapy has already integrated the contributions of cognitive (e.g., Bandura, 1977a; Meichenbaum, 1977) and emotional (Rachman, 1981a) processes and that these restricted integrations are potentially profitable in research and the therapeutic enterprise (Kendall, 1982d). Indeed, Smith's data indicate the strong trend toward cognitive–behavioral approaches, the dominance of eclecticism, and the move toward integration. While causal analysis of the interrelationships among these trends are not available, I suggest that cognitive–behavioral therapy may represent one successful integration that, unintentionally has paved the way for other integrative efforts.

The veridicality of the above analysis aside, we remain unaware of all of the reasons that lead people to identify themselves as cognitive–behavioral therapists. One hopes that the majority of reasons pertain to some degree of increased therapeutic efficacy, more challenging theoretical and conceptual questions, and more fruitful areas for research. Less optimistically, however, casual conversations hint that one of the motivations seems to be the perception that the new label, as opposed to the behavior therapy label, has thus far been more reasonable in its demands. To be a member of the group marching under the banner of behavior therapy one had to be prepared to conduct naturalistic observations, to eschew all trait notions, and to provide enactive treatment procedures. For the majority of practicing clinicians, these club rules were rigorous and perhaps too demanding. As more and more individual practitioners recognized their limited adherence to the group rules, they were left with a choice: Leave the group or modify the rules. Cognitive–behavioral strategies appeared in time for members to adjust their affiliation without having to leave the club they had come to value highly. By shifting to cognitive–behavioral approaches, practicing clinicians may feel a greater sense of accomplishment with their clients: They are no longer doing their job in a less-than-desired fashion and they are able to value changes in in-session verbal behavior. That is, more logical thinking, more effective problem-solving, and more rational self-talk can be targeted and recognized in the clinician's office. Verbal interactions with clients are viewed as acceptable methods of intervention (compatible with enactive methods) and self-reported "thinking" can be more readily obtained from clients by easily administered questionnaires than observations of "behavior" can be gathered *in vivo*.

With all of its positive forces, the cognitive–behavioral approach may also be having some negative influences on behavioral therapy. First, cognitive therapists may place less emphasis on performance-based procedures—but less enactive interventions are not the desired trend. Second, measures of treatment outcome must be no less rigorous than changes in behavior, but we see too great a reliance on self-reported outcome. The cognitive–behavioral umbrella may be encompassing more people, but not necessarily more proficient people. Perceptions of the hyphenated hybrid as "less demanding" will, in the long run, damage the potential for further true advances. Cognitive-behavioral psychotherapy is no less demanding of demonstrated therapeutic effectiveness, and conducting such interventions should be no less of a challenge.

Several professional publications further evidence the growth of cognitive–behavioral interventions. For example, an entire issue of *School Psychology Review* (Vol. 10, No. 1) was devoted to cognitive-behavioral interventions for classroom and academic behaviors; the first volume of *Advances in Cognitive-Behavioral Research and Therapy* (Kendall, 1982a) provided discussion of theoretical, assessment, and intervention issues for the researcher and practicing clinician; *New Directions in Cognitive Therapy* (Emery, Hollon, & Bedrosian, 1981) offered applied commentaries for clinicians; and a new journal, *British Journal of Cognitive Psychotherapy*, is forthcoming. Perhaps more important, the pioneering efforts of early scholars and researchers have not gone unnoticed. Rather, the pioneers have been witness to the settlers, who, with proper caution are carefully planting and harvesting an encouraging crop.

ACTIVE INGREDIENTS:
DEMONSTRATION AND DISCOVERY

A common theme of sound research programs is the dual emphasis on demonstration and discovery. By this I mean that research efforts profit from the coexistence of (1) efforts to demonstrate that a treatment works or that a variable has an effect and (2) creative inclusion of additional variables such that investigators increase their chances of uncovering an important, but perhaps not identified in advance, finding. Much of the published research is of the demonstration variety, yet discovery assists us in maintaining enthusiasm for our research, for if all we accomplish is to confirm our hypotheses we might soon tire of the demands and attendant difficulties of conducting rigorous research.

As in the general research domain, demonstration and discovery have a place in the study of behavior therapy. When we define the treatment manipulation (e.g., comparison groups) we make explicit the variable that we think will have an effect, and we proceed to conduct the study to demonstrate that the variable we selected to manipulate was indeed an effective component. Can we then discover additional explanatory concepts? Analyses of the *process* of a therapy that has been demonstrated as effective will promote the discovery of active ingredients that might or might not have been hypothesized by the researchers in advance. Replication (cross-validation of these findings) would be required, but the stage for discovery would be set.

Several methodological considerations require careful attention before we begin a process research project. First, when therapy tapes are being reviewed and data are being gathered, either by making ratings or by coding behavioral frequencies, the sheer bulk of tape time must be condensed. For instance, the typical therapy study employs approximately 30 clients and provides about 12 hours of treatment for each. This example results in 360 hours of tapes. Assuming that a modest number of ratings (or codes) are being gathered, say 12, and that the tapes must be listened to 12 times (it is unlikely that the coder can manage to code more than one behavior at a time). Now our total reaches 4320 hours, and without adding training time, this would require 108 40-hour weeks of work, or over 2 years of continuous coding. Assuming that four coders are employed, this still requires 6 months of 40 hours a week!

Selecting and coding (or rating) samples from the therapy tapes provides the highly desirable alternative. If only 6 of the 12 sessions are scored and if three 7-minute segments are taken from the beginning, middle, and end of each of these sessions, then the researcher has a more manageable, yet not overly condensed, sample of in-session process data.

Second, the choice of the codes or ratings to be gathered can dramatically influence the results and, ultimately, the conclusions that are drawn. Accordingly, the selection of codes or ratings for process analysis should be guided by the effort to acquire data on (1) what has been described as taking place in the sessions (conducting a manipulation check of sorts), (2) factors that may help to document differences between the therapies provided, (3) factors that will facilitate theory testing, and (4), again for the purpose of discovery, more speculative hypothesis.

Last, process analyses are not independent of demonstrations of treatment effects. Process analyses should follow methodologically sound and reasonably solid demonstrations of the effectiveness of the treatment. To date we have witnessed an enlargement of the list of treatments that have at least some documented effectiveness, but we have seen all too few studies of process. As in last year's *Annual Review*, I am issuing a call for extended process analyses.

COGNITIVE PROCEDURES

As in last year's *Annual Review*, I have tried to provide a reasonable form of organization to the literature pertinent to cognitive–behavioral procedures. I have let the final organization be determined by the literature itself, thereby not engaging in a procrustean force-fit. I am, perhaps, not dividing the literature as each of my readers might prefer. The categories were identified and employed in an effort to systematize the sheer bulk of relevant research.

The Treatment of Depression

One need only look at the title of articles in any of the professional journals to be struck by the explosion of research on depression. Specific lines of inquiry are varied, but the general thrust of most of the published work has either explicit or implicit relevance for the treatment of depression. Rehm's edited book (1981) on behavior therapy for depression brings together contributions from some of the leading researchers and provides a valuable compendium of reviews and resources.

It became apparent when preparing the present review that research on the treatment of depression falls into two categories. First, several studies are comparative; they compare drugs versus psychological treatment, cognitive versus behavioral strategies, and individual versus group contexts. Second, there has been an apparent increase in the treatment of depressed geriatric patients. These topics and ancillary articles of relevance to these themes are discussed.

PSYCHOLOGICAL TREATMENT VERSUS DRUGS

It is important to recall that until recently there have been no published reports showing that psychotherapy is superior to the effects of antidepressant medications in the treatment of unipolar depression (Hollon & Beck, 1979). With the appearance of the Rush, Beck, Kovacs, and Hollon study (1977) the generalization had to be amended, for the cognitive treatment was shown to have benefits that in some cases surpassed pharmacotherapy. The Rush *et al.* (1977) study compared Beck's cognitive–behavioral treatment[1] and use of impramine. A clini-

---

1. I recognize and accept Beck's tendency to retain his original label, "cognitive therapy for depression," but I prefer, for the sake of clarity, the more felicitous label "cognitive-behavioral therapy" (Franks, Wilson, Kendall, & Brownell, 1982).

cal sample of depressed outpatients was treated, and after 12 weeks, both treatment groups were reported to have improved significantly. Interestingly, the cognitive–behavioral treatment group showed superior improvements on self-report and clinical ratings. The dropout rate for the cognitive–behavioral group was lower than that for the drug group. Follow-up reports indicated maintenance of treatment gains. Because of the rarity with which one sees psychotherapy surpassing use of medication, this finding has stimulated others to research the issue further.

Of the parcel of current reports of the treatment of depression, several include data on the comparison of psychotherapy (of differing definition) and medications. Blackburn, Bishop, Glen, Whalley, and Christie (1981) compared the effectiveness of cognitive therapy, antidepressant drugs, and a combination of the two. Depressed outpatients from either general practice or an outpatient clinic were screened for primary major depression. Blackburn *et al.* thus set out with three main aims: (1) to replicate the Rush *et al.* study and compare cognitive therapy and drugs, (2) to test the effect of combining cognitive therapy and drugs, and (3) to test the treatment on two populations, hospital outpatients and general practice patients. Note also that many of the research reports published to date had been from the United States and the Blackburn *et al.* study was conducted in England.

On the basis of an interview, use of Research Diagnostic Criteria (Spitzer, Endicott, & Robins, 1978b), and Beck Depression Inventory (BDI) scores greater than 14, 64 patients were selected from the 140 patients who were screened. Subjects were then randomly assigned to one of the three modes of treatment. Subjects receiving medication were given the "drug of choice" (usually choosing amitriptyline or clomipramine). Cognitive therapy was provided in groups of unspecified size, and members "usually attended twice a week in the first three weeks of treatment and once a week thereafter" (Blackburn *et al.*, 1981, p. 183). For the hospital outpatients the dropout rate was 18%; it was 38% for the general-practice sample. Three measures of mood were analyzed: the BDI, the Hamilton Rating Scale (HRS), and an 18-item scale designed to assess irritability, depression, and anxiety (IDA). There were variations in the length of treatment (number of sessions) across groups, and there were differences in relevant pretreatment data (e.g., duration of illness, education), which led the authors to employ analysis of covariance for percentage of change scores—a less-than-ideal method of analysis.

The authors report differential outcomes for the hospital outpatients and general-practice patients:

The study has shown that in a group of mildly to moderately depressed *hospital outpatients*, often chronically ill and resistant to previous treatments, cognitive therapy was minimally more effective than paramacotherapy and the combination of cognitive therapy with drugs had an additive effect, bringing about the largest degree of change. In *general practice*, cognitive therapy, alone and in combination with drugs, was superior to drugs alone, the interaction of the two treatments in this group being positively reciprocal, as defined in the introduction section. The effectiveness of cognitive therapy in the present sample of patients argues against the often-voiced criticism that, because it is so logical, it could only be effective in better-educated and more intellectual patients. (p. 188; emphasis in original)

Unfortunately, the Blackburn *et al.* study has serious limitations. Before I discuss these, the strengths of their report deserve to be mentioned. For example, variations in the sample were systematically examined, valid diagnostic criteria were used to select subjects, and the single and combined effects of drugs and psychological therapy were evaluated. Nevertheless, the limitations restrict the degree to which these data offer compelling evidence. First, while they did include both ratings and self-reports, the authors relied entirely on measures of mood, and raters were not blind. The restricted range of dependent measures restricts the conclusions that can be drawn. Second, the authors fail to provide a detailed description of the "cognitive" treatment they provided. This shortcoming is troublesome in all research on the effects of psychological therapies but is particularly problematic in research on depression, where one author's "cognitive therapy" varies substantially from another's.

In an article seemingly on a separate study, Blackburn and Bishop (1981) report data on a comparison of drugs, cognitive therapy, and a combination of the two. Although the authors do not say this explicitly, after reading the report it became apparent that this is the same study discussed above with the inclusion of the number of responders and nonresponders (defined by endpoint scores on the BDI and the HRS) as a new dependent measure. These data indicated that the response rate for drug-of-choice treatment was similar to that of cognitive therapy (77%) and not significantly better than the response rate for cognitive therapy alone (57%). However, the Blackburn *et al.* (1981) results are a relatively more detailed analysis of outcome, and the results reported by Blackburn and Bishop (1981) appear inconclusive without the other analysis.

Roth, Bielski, Jones, Parker, and Osborn (1982) conducted and reported an evaluation comparing self-control therapy alone against

self-control therapy with medication (a tricyclic, desipramine hydro-
chloride). The self-control therapy provided by Roth *et al.* consisted of
a 12-week group program. According to the authors,

> therapy was oriented towards helping patients identify and modify dys-
> functional, self-defeating styles of thinking and behaving. More specifi-
> cally, the self-control model posits that depression is largely related to
> faulty styles of self-monitoring, self-evaluation, and self-reinforcement.
> Each of these three core areas is further subdivided into two postulated
> skill deficits or excesses. For example, dysfunctional self-evaluation tend-
> encies reflect depressogenic attributional biases and/or overly stringent
> standards (see Rehm, 1977). (p. 137)

Although these authors appear to employ a treatment that is "cognitive–
behavioral," they use the title "self-control" therapy. There is nothing
inherently wrong with their descriptive title; in fact, it is apt. However,
because of the semantic dilemma existing in the area of the treatment of
depression (Kendall, 1982b), it is recommended that readers examine
carefully the exact nature of the intervention provided and avoid being
satisfied with treatment titles.

The subjects (9 male, 17 female) in the Roth *et al.* (1982) study were
recruited through advertisements in newspapers and selected based on
three criteria: (1) BDI scores greater than 18, (2) ratings greater than 15
on a 17-item HRS (Hamilton, 1960, 1969), and (3) a diagnosis of major
depressive disorder according to Research Diagnostic Criteria (Spitzer
et al., 1978b). Variations in the selection criteria for studies of the
treatment of depression would be meaningfully reduced if more investigations took such a careful look at each potential client. The
chosen subjects were then randomly assigned to either self-control
alone or self-control and medication combined. Determination of the
effectiveness of the treatments was based on two measures of depression
(the BDI and the HRS), the concepts test (a measure of self-control
beliefs; Fuchs & Rehm, 1977), and the mood related items of the
Pleasant Events Schedule (Lewinsohn & Graf, 1973). The results were
fairly consistent in evidencing significant symptomatic improvement as
measured by the BDI and the HRS, with the improvements maintained
at 3-month follow-up. More rapid improvements on the BDI were
found for the combined treatment. Unfortunately, however, the raters
of the non-self-report data (the HRS) were not blind to subjects' experimental assignments.

Researching the comparative and combined effects of psychological therapies and pharmacotherapies poses new challenges for the
outcome evaluator. Cooperation across disciplines (e.g., with psychiatry) is often central to launching such a project, and balancing both the
clinical and research needs of the different mental health professions

can result in the work of a committee—no one person is totally satisfied with the final product. With these real-world restrictions in mind, Roth *et al.* (1982) are not entirely culpable. However, as the authors suggested, the results would have contributed more plentiful and meaningful information had proper control groups been employed: for instance, a control for placebo medication effects (see also Hollon & DeRubeis, 1981). Inclusion of these controls would have tightened internal validity and eliminated questions of the evanescent quality of depression (that it simply changes over time, with or without treatments).

A social skills training program was compared with pharmacotherapy and psychotherapy by Bellack, Hersen, and Himmelhoch (1981). For their clinical trial the authors treated 72 unipolar depressed women. Subjects were either patients at a psychiatric clinic (60%) or respondents to advertisements on radio or in newspapers (40%). The groups were comparably represented across treatments and did not differ on any of the dependent measures employed. Patients were randomly assigned to one of four groups: (1) amitriptyline therapy, (2) social skills training plus amitriptyline, (3) social skills training plus placebo, and (4) psychotherapy plus placebo. During the initial phase of treatment, clients received a 1-hour session every week for 12 weeks. Patients received placebos in a double-blind fashion. The psychotherapy condition, described as "time-limited dynamic therapy," was conducted according to the therapist's personal style and strategy. Dependent measures included the BDI, the Wolpe-Lazarus Assertiveness Scale (Wolpe & Lazarus, 1966), the HRS, (Hamilton, 1960), a social adjustment scale (Paykel, Weissman, & Prusoff, 1971), the Eysenck Personality Inventory (Eysenck & Eysenck, 1968) and the Hopkins Symptom Checklist (Derogatis, Lipman, & Rickels, 1974). Raters conducted their ratings while blind to the subjects' treatment conditions.

Based on the results of the Bellack *et al.* (1981) report, all treatments were successful. The four treatments were not substantially different from one another. Each produced significant reductions in symptomatology and increases in normal functioning, a finding similar to that reported by Zeiss, Lewinsohn, and Muñoz (1979). However, the treatments produced differential dropout rates. The drug alone condition had a dropout rate of 55.6%, while the social skills plus placebo condition had only a 15% dropout rate. Moreover, when improvement was categorized along a dimension of effectiveness, the social skills plus placebo condition was the only condition in which more than 50% of the patients improved "substantially."

Bellack *et al.*'s report contains many of the methodological niceties that give confidence to the reader of the observed outcomes (e.g., random assignment, blind raters), but because of the cryptic description provided in the journal article, the reader is forced to check another publication or simply to wonder about the exact nature of the social skills training. Although this may be the fault of the style or policy of the journal, additional details of the key features of the treatment are highly desirable.

In a spinoff report, Greenwald, Kornblith, Hersen, Bellack, and Himmelhoch (1981) compared the in-session behaviors of the behavior therapists (those conducting social skills training) and psychotherapists by rating segments of audiotaped sessions of the treatments. Greenwald *et al.* reported that the social skills therapists were more directive, displayed greater initiative, appeared more supportive, and emitted significantly more directive and nondirective statements than the psychotherapists. I suggest that the authors proceed further with their process data and examine the relationship of these in-session process variables to the outcomes reported in Bellack *et al.* (1981).

Another study of the outcome of behavioral and pharmacological treatments of depression was reported by P. H. Wilson (1982). This study, conducted in Sydney, Australia, adds to the increasingly international flavor of the drug-versus-psychological-therapy comparisons. The final subjects were 64 respondents to media advertisements who had BDI scores of at least 20 and a self-reported duration of depression of at least 2 months (and were not seen as having other major disorders). Unfortunately, 97 respondents began the program but only 64 completed. Many dropped out because of unwanted medication effects, thus promoting the likelihood of finding desirable drug effects among the remainder. Using restricted randomization, subjects were assigned to either amitriptyline therapy or placebo and to one of three types of treatment (task assignments, relaxation, or minimal contact). Although minimal-contact subjects were given nondirective discussion for two 1-hour sessions, the psychologically treated subjects were seen individually for seven 1-hour sessions. The task-assignment group received pleasant-events scheduling. In the author's words, this latter therapy was "designed to increase the frequency, quality, and range of activities and social interactions" (p. 175). Subjects in the relaxation-training condition received tension-release progressive muscle relaxation training presented as a self-control procedure, with active coping as part of stress management. These distinct interventions have received deserved attention in the literature and in practice, but it is not clear why muscle relaxation was the chosen treatment for depressive symptoms.

The results of this comparison, when considering BDI scores, for example, were that all treatment conditions led to improvement. These results reflect the general "all improved" interpretation of outcome by the author. It was somewhat surprising to read that there was no evidence to suggest that the events scheduling was superior to relaxation in reducing depression, and one is left to wonder what the results might have been had more objective (as opposed to self-report) data been collected and analyzed. Importantly, P. H. Wilson also reported that 28 clients sought treatment during the follow-up period, with significantly fewer of the subjects from the psychological treatment conditions than from the minimal contact condition seeking outside aid. These data open our eyes further to the methodological need to assess subjects' use of alternate counsel (see also Chapter 2).

In addition to comparing group versus individual cognitive therapy for depression, Rush and Watkins (1981) had a third group of subjects who received individual cognitive therapy with antidepressant medication (tricyclic or lithium carbonate), thus allowing for an evaluation of the treatment context (individual versus group) and a drug-plus-therapy versus therapy-alone comparison. However, no control groups were used. The 44 subjects met DSM-III criteria for major depressive disorder; 28 were assigned to group cognitive therapy, 9 received individual cognitive therapy, and 7 were treated with individual cognitive therapy and antidepressant medication. A maximum of 20 group or individual cognitive therapy sessions (the minimum number of sessions was not given in the article) were conducted over a period of 10 to 12 weeks. The individual sessions lasted 50 minutes, the group sessions lasted 75–90 minutes. Groups consisted of four to six patients and two therapists. Subjects completed the BDI each week during treatment and were rated after treatment by nonblind judges on the HRS. Several subjects took the MMPI before treatment, and all took it after treatment.

Results of the analyses of the BDI data indicated that all treatment conditions resulted in reduction in self-reported depression. This result held when premature terminators were either included or excluded from the analyses. The authors go on to state that there was a trend toward a significant difference for the treatment condition variable, but the p value that they report is far from a trend ($p = .72$). Perhaps this was a typographical error, but the F value was low (2.85). The authors then compare the conditions further and report that group-therapy patients did significantly more poorly than individually treated (with or without medication) patients. Results of the HRS did not evidence differences across the three treatment conditions, and the authors did not report the results of analyses of the MMPI data.

Although the authors tentatively conclude that the efficiency of group treatment was not as great as that for individual treatment, this conclusion may be unwarranted for several reasons. First, the reported "trend" was not significant, and second, differences were not found on the clinicians' ratings. Decisions regarding the relative efficacy of group individual cognitive therapy for depression require, as the authors recommend, a careful replication of the pilot data. At the present juncture, however, one is inclined to accept the merits of group treatment, since several of the studies reviewed here and in last year's *Annual Review* provided "successful" treatment in a group context. Regarding the Rush and Watkins (1981) comparison of individual therapy with and without drugs, the data suggests an absence of meaningful differences. However, this conclusion is based on a restricted data set and is by itself inconclusive.

Summarizing briefly the studies comparing drugs and psychological treatments, I find, albeit with methodological limitations, that psychological therapies for depression seem to fare at least as well as pharmacological treatments and often result in lower dropout rates. It is not necessarily the case, however, that a combined treatment is superior to single components. Instead, the psychological treatment plus placebo was most successful in one of the more carefully controlled studies (Bellack *et al.*, 1981). It is no longer surprising to read that psychological therapy is as effective as drugs in reducing the symptoms of unipolar depression.

A FEW RELATED REPORTS

A select subsample of depressed clients, Puerto Rican women, served as subjects for Comas-Díaz's (1981) comparison of cognitive therapy, behavior therapy, and controls. The 26 women were Spanish-speaking only, had an average of 5 years of residence in the United States, and were receiving government financial aid. The BDI and the HRS were used, along with a depressed behavior rating scale (DBRS) that was completed by a significant other. The DBRS represents an interesting data source and seems worthy of further inquiry. Following pretreatment assessments, clients were matched (e.g., by pretreatment severity of depression) and randomly assigned to conditions.

The cognitive approach followed Beck and the behavioral approach was after Lewinsohn, though Comas-Díaz wrote that there were similarities across the two methods of treatment. This study did however include a therapy manipulation check to determine that the treatments were as described in the manual and distinguishable from one another (a methodological addition encouraged by Kendall & Norton-Ford, 1982). Over a period of 4 weeks, five treatment sessions of 1½ hours each were provided. A waiting-list group served as control for effects of assessments and expectancy. Both treatment groups evidenced a significant reduction in depression, with no significant differences between the cognitive and behavioral approaches. An additional assessment at a short follow-up (5 weeks) revealed support for the maintenance of treatment effects, with a slight advantage for the behavioral approach.

Several of the investigations of the effects of cognitive–behavioral treatments for depression have employed group treatment (e.g., Blackburn et al., 1981; Comas-Díaz, 1981; Roth et al., 1982) and research on encounter groups (Lieberman, Yalom, & Miles, 1973) has identified the importance of leadership style in the outcome of group interventions. An interesting evaluation of therapist characteristics and the relationship of therapist differences to treatment outcome was reported by Antonuccio, Lewinsohn, and Steinmetz (1982). Their intervention was a structured, educational experience, described as cognitive–behavioral. The group met for 2 hours on twelve occasions over an 8-week period. A total of 106 subjects, many of whom met RDC criteria for unipolar depression, were randomly assigned to one of eight five–eight-person groups. The study was conducted in two waves, resulting in 16 groups in total, run by eight different group leaders.

Antonuccio et al. (1982) found significant differences attributable to leaders for measures of participation level, cohesiveness, session length, warmth, enthusiasm, clarity, task activity, and specificity of feedback. However, leaders were not differentially effective with regard to how improved their clients were at the end of treatment. Improvement in this case was based on changes on clients' BDI scores. Thus, although leaders differed, these differences did not affect the positive outcome of the cognitive–behavioral educational treatment. As mentioned earlier, it would be interesting to learn if the observed differences in therapists reported by Greenwald et al. (1981) were related to outcome indices.

In a study by DeRubeis, Hollon, Evans, and Bemis (1982), the ability to discriminate therapies for depression was examined directly. Trained observers rated tapes of two forms of therapy, cognitive–behavioral and interpersonal psychotherapy, and meaningful differences emerged. For instance, one of the factors identified via a factor analysis of the ratings was labeled "cognitive–behavioral technique" and was rated as occurring to a greater degree in the cognitive–behavioral treatment. Also, cognitive–behavioral therapists were found to score higher on the factor that assessed therapist directiveness. It appears, as the authors noted, that naive but trained raters can differentiate at least two types of treatment for depression and that subsequent comparisons of the relative efficacy of these treatments is worthwhile. Given the problems associated with the use of so-called descriptive labels to communicate the details of therapy (titles are not always accurate or very descriptive) and the fact that this problem is particularly pressing in the therapies for depression (Kendall, 1982b), further clarification of the actual differences among and between treatments seems worthwhile.

TREATMENT OF GERIATRIC DEPRESSION

One trend that appears to have burgeoned in the recent past is the application and evaluation of psychological treatments for geriatric patients suffering from depression. Depression has been described as the most common functional psychiatric disorder among the elderly, affecting 7–11% of the population (Gurland, 1976; Mintz, Steuer, & Jarvik, 1981). Moreover, Mintz et al. (1981) point out that depressed elderly people often suffer from physical disorders that complicate or contraindicate drug therapy, thus furthering the need for psychological treatments. Three recent reports illustrate this increasing interest.

Working with 66 Cuban-American elders, Szapocznik, Santisteban, Hervis, Spencer, and Kurtines (1981) evaluated a life-enhancement intervention. Pre-to-posttreatment changes were measured by therapists (the posttreatment assessment was by a different blind therapist). Significant changes were evident on, for example, the Older American Resource Scale (OARS), with the largest improvement on the scale for mental health, and a Subjective Distress Schedule (Spitzer, Endicott, Fleiss, & Cohen, 1970). Additional analyses were conducted on a subsample of 23 subjects who received no medication. These subjects were found to show increases on the subjective distress total score. Unfortunately, the dependent measures were limited in scope and the exact nature of the treatment was not detailed.

Geriatric patients in a nursing home were participants in a comparison of (1) social reinforcement for activity, (2) problem-solving training, and (3) a waiting list control group. This study, conducted by Hussian and Lawrence (1981), preselected 70 patients who were over 60 years of age and not taking antidepressant medication. The 36 subjects with the highest BDI scores were included. Subjects in the treatments were further divided such that groups of six received the treatments in each possible sequence of the two treatments. Treatment covered five sessions, 30 minutes per session, for 2 weeks, with 2-week and 3-week follow-up. The BDI, the Hospital Adjustment Scale (HAS; McReynolds & Ferguson, 1953), and a self-rating scale of depression were the dependent measures. The social-reinforcement-for-activity condition consisted of opportunities for activity, such as crafts, college classes, and artistic activities, with social reward for participation. Problem-solving training followed Goldfried and Davison (1976).

The authors analyzed their data in an unusual fashion. Changes were examined by weeks of treatment (e.g., pretreatment to week 1, week 1 to week 2). This procedure was used to deal with the varying sequences of the two treatments. The results were complicated. After the first week, both treatment groups evidenced significantly lower BDI and depression self-ratings than the waiting-list controls. After treatment week 2, only those in the problem-solving condition evidenced significantly reduced BDI scores when compared to controls. Thus the problem-solving training, described by Hussian and Lawrence as a form of cognitive–behavior modification, was a beneficial component of the treatment of geriatric depression. They speculated that the basis for the effectiveness of the cognitive approach may involve reestablishing control by the subject over his or her own behavior. The lack of change on the hospital adjustment measure (HAS) indicated that while there were reductions in self-reported depression, there were no concomitant increases in hospital adjustment.

Teri and Lewinsohn (1982) have designed and developed modifications of some depression-assessment instruments for use with the elderly. The Pleasant Events Schedule (PES; MacPhillamy & Lewinsohn, 1971) and the Unpleasant Events Schedule (UES: Lewinsohn, 1975) were originally designed to assess the occurrence and subjective report of pleasant and unpleasant events. Because these often-used scales contained items inappropriate for the elderly (e.g., rock climbing, childbirth, fraternity/sorority) and the scales were somewhat prohibitive in length, Teri and Lewinsohn (1982) reduced the 320 items on each scale to 144 items for the PES-Elderly and 131 items for the UES-Elderly. The items were selected only if they met endorsement criteria for the sample of 508 elderly subjects. Sex differences emerged, with women reporting feeling less good about pleasant events and more stressed by more of the unpleasant events. Both new scales were reported to have high internal consistency and concurrent validity (they correlated well with the original schedules). Additional reliabilities, such as test–retest, as well as demonstrated sensitivity to treatment, are areas in need of further inquiry.

Mintz et al. (1981) recognized the increasing interest in geriatric depression and provided a description and discussion of related issues. At the risk of losing some of the richness of Mintz et al.'s comments, I provide the following condensed list of concerns:

1. Uniformity myth—not all old people are alike.
2. Limited representativeness of subjects—inadequate income and reduced mobility limit volunteers.
3. Physical/medical interference—presence of illness (e.g., senile dementia)

4. Treatment modifications—conventional treatment may have to proceed more slowly.
5. Therapist characteristics—attitudes about the aged and the therapist's own age may influence outcome.
6. Assessment modifications—restricted reading ability or failing vision may affect assessments, and there is lack of normative data on the elderly (see Teri & Lewinsohn, 1982).
7. Follow-up difficulties—death or illness may preclude the gathering of follow-up data.

Mintz *et al.* (1981), however, rejected pessimism and indicated that these concerns can be overcome, as their own work with geriatric depressions suggests.

However, before researchers proceed to test the relative effectiveness of behavioral therapy and cognitive–behavioral therapy for depression, we should examine the nature of depression among the aged. Is depression among this group related to cognitive errors similar to the illogical thinking described by Beck? Do these elderly adults experience less contingent positive reinforcement? Are they in the midst of a series of losses of love objects? Are environmental or cultural factors involved in geriatric depression? The list of questions could continue, but these few examples illustrate the need for a more detailed understanding of depression within this group. We needn't go beyond Erikson's theory (e.g., Erikson, 1964) to find that the later years are laced with new and different challenges.

SUMMARY

Research on the psychological treatment of depression has provided documentation for the validity of the claim that medications are not the only effective strategy. Indeed, comparisons between psychological and pharmacological approaches seem to evidence generally comparable outcomes for the distinctive interventions. While this conclusion supports the use of psychological treatment of depression, the typical treatment consists of a complicated package. What appears to be needed are components analyses (dismantling studies) that will aid in the identification of the most salient features of psychological treatment.

In general, the literature has shown a more sophisticated use of selection criteria for studies of depression. Citations to Research Diagnostic Criteria, DSM-III criteria, and so forth, help to ensure that the subjects in one study are in meaningful ways comparable to the subjects in another study. I am troubled, however, by the lack of recognition of the strong correlation between depression and other disorders, such as anxiety. Truly impressive subject-selection (diagnostic) criteria should not only include the key features of depression but also exclude the key features of related disorders. This concern warrants the attention of researchers who are studying the etiology as well as the treatment of depression.

Two final concerns raised in last year's *Annual Review* require restatement. First, there is the need for examination of the process of change resulting from the cognitive–behavioral treatment of depression. We will benefit greatly from a careful look at the in-session behaviors and cross-session cognitions that may be associated with change and maintenance of change. Second, more attention should be paid to the assessment of cognition before, during, and after treatment in order to demonstrate that the targeted cognitions did in fact change. It would also be enlightening to assess a range of cognitions, targeted and not targeted, and determine the generality or specificity of cognitive change. These two concerns are not independent, for as we more systematically assess cognition we are likely to learn more about the process of cognitive change.

Self-Instructional Training

The history of cognitive–behavioral therapy with children has recently been briefly described by Craighead (1982). Three emphases were identified in his analysis: the influence of cognitive psychology (e.g., employment of the cognitive–developmental language literature in self-instructional training, information-processing analysis of modeling effects); the evolution of cognitive explanations of self-control processes; and the interest generated by the writings of Ellis and of Beck. Specific to self-instructional training, the cognitive–developmental language literature and self-control were dominant directives.

Although social problem-solving and perspective-taking training approaches fit comfortably within the working definition of cognitive–behavioral interventions with children (teaching thinking processes; see Hobbs, Moguin, Tyroler, & Lahey, 1980; Kendall, 1981a; Urbain & Kendall, 1980), self-instructional training appears to be the most often used descriptor. One can question the aptness of "self-instructional training" as a generic label, for it is more technique specific than, say, social problem solving, and it does not communicate the complexity of the entire intervention procedure. But fashion often dictates labels, be they euphemistic or accurate. Fashion, however, cannot dictate the results of an evaluation of the effects of self-instructional training, and so we shall proceed to take a careful look at the current literature.

The guest editors of the special issue of *School Psychology Review* on cognitive–behavioral interventions for classroom and academic behaviors have been active in the study of the generalizability of self-instructional training. A review of their work proves most enlightening. Before I proceed, however, it is also interesting to note that Meyers, R. Cohen, Schleser, and their colleagues (e.g., Meyers & R. Cohen, in press; R. Cohen, Schleser, & Meyers, 1981; Schleser, Meyers, & Cohen, 1981) offer an interesting integration of functional and structural approaches. Functionally, these collaborators train children in self-instructional strategies as a means of improving task performance and behavior. Structurally, they assess and take into account the child's cognitive–developmental status, typically via assessments of Piagetian stages of development.

In one of their earlier studies, childrens' cognitive levels (e.g., preoperational, concrete operational) were found to influence level of performance but not to interact with the effectiveness of intervention procedures (Schleser et al., 1981). More recently, however, by adjusting the training to allow the child to take part in the "discovery" of self-instructions, R. Cohen, Meyers, Schleser, and Rodick (1982) reported that cognitive level interacted with the effects of training. Specifically, preoperational and concrete operational children were assigned to either a no-training group, a didactic group, a self-instruction (fading rehearsal) group, or a directed discovery self-instruction group. When performance on a measure of generalization was examined, only the concrete operational children in the directed discovery instruction group demonstrated significant generalization of the training effects. Generalization was measured by assessing subjects' performance on a no-training task and did not include assessments of actual behavior (neither ratings nor observation). Nevertheless, these data are interesting, for they illustrate the key role of level of cognitive development in the effectiveness of self-instructional training (Cole & Kazdin, 1980; Kendall, 1977).

Returning to the earlier Schleser et al. (1981) study, we find yet another set of fascinating data that provide an encouraging replication. Yes, replication. As rare as they seem to be, replications do occur, and Schleser et al.'s (1981) report provided a replication of some of the findings reported by Kendall and Wilcox (1980). Kendall and Wilcox (1980) demonstrated that a conceptual (general) approach to training self-instructions was superior to a concrete (specific) approach in terms of the generalization of the effects of training. Schleser et al. (1981) also found that a general self-instructional approach was superior to a specific approach. Thus, training in conceptual or general self-instructions represents a procedural improvement within the self-instructional paradigm. Accordingly, additional efforts toward refinement seem justified.

In one recent study, the role of the treatment context was examined by comparing individual treatment with treatment provided in a small group context (Kendall & Zupan, 1981). For purposes of evaluation, the two treatments were compared to a control. The subjects were 30 children from grades 3 to 5 (average age 9 years, 9 months), identified by classroom teachers as lacking self-control using the Self-Control Rating Scale (SCRS; Kendall & Wilcox, 1979), who were assigned to treatment conditions using randomized blocks (blocking on initial severity of self-control problem). The 12 sessions of intervention followed the cognitive–behavioral manual developed by Kendall and colleagues and included self-instructional training, modeling, role plays, and behavioral contingencies. The program employed psychoeducational tasks, interpersonal play situations, and personal problem scenarios as the context for training. An earlier criticism of the Kendall program, that it failed to give adequate attention to the emotions of the children (Bernard, 1981), was remedied in this and subsequent research. For instance, affective educational materials became a part of the training.

Results of the Kendall and Zupan (1981) study indicated that there were some improvements for children across treatment conditions (e.g., all children improved their performances on the Matching Familiar Figures tests from pre- to posttreatment). More positive results, however, were obtained from the teachers' blind ratings of self-control. Analyses of these ratings indicated that the group and individual treatment conditions evidenced significant improvements that were significantly better than those of the nonspecific treatment (control) condition. Normative comparisons indicated that the mean SCRS score for both the group and individual treatment conditions was within nondeviant limits (one standard deviation).

In a 1-year follow-up report (Kendall, 1982c) normative comparisons again aided treatment evaluation. It should be noted first that pretreatment-to-1-year-follow-up gains were found for subjects across treatment conditions. In contrast, only the children receiving group treatment were not significantly different from nonproblem children on ratings of self-control, and only the children receiving individual treatment were not significantly different from nonproblem children on hyperactivity ratings. Here the normative comparisons provided an opportunity to determine that the observed changes resulted in children returning to within the nondeviant limits on the measures employed.

Structured interviews were also conducted to determine, for example, if children recalled what they had learned in treatment and if they had used the ideas that were conveyed. Significantly better recall of the ideas that were taught was evident for the individually treated children. Also, the individually treated children produced significantly more illustrations of the use of the ideas. The structured interview data buttress the support for the individual treatment. I am reluctant, however, to draw a firm conclusion that individual training is superior to group training, because in the group intervention, as conducted by Kendall and Zupan (1981), participants performed the training (e.g., self-instructions) one at a time, taking turns. In a sense, this method of operationalizing group treatment fails to take account and make effective use of group process. A potentially more desirable operationalization of group cognitive–behavioral training would use the content of the group process as the content for self-control training. A related treatment manual for use in group training that does incorporate group process is now available (Urbain, 1982).

SOME DATA ON SOME IMPORTANT ISSUES

As noted in last year's *Annual Review* (Kendall, 1982b), in other reviews (e.g., Cole & Kazdin, 1980; Kendall, 1981a; Urbain & Kendall, 1980), and in the discussion section of many of the research reports reviewed here (e.g., Neilans & Israel, 1981), there are several critical issues facing the researcher and therapist involved in self-instructional training. These issues include applying the training with clinical cases, employing a broader range of outcome measures, including more extensive follow-up data, conducting component analyses to determine the active agents that contribute to therapeutic success, comparing the treatment to use of medications, and considering the role of individual differences in predicting treatment response. The studies reviewed in this section address these issues.

Application with Clinical Cases. Several studies have appeared recently in which the application of the self-instructional intervention involves actual clinical cases: in a group home, in the treatment of hyperactivity, and in training two severely hearing-impaired youngsters. Neilans and Israel (1981) compared the effectiveness of a self-regulatory package (with self-instructions in a position of importance) to a conventional token economy system. The clinical cases were 7–13-year-old children referred to a treatment oriented group home. Using the frequency of disruptive behaviors per child and the number of intervals on task as dependent measures, and employing a time-series design, the authors concluded that both the conventional token reinforcement system and the self-regulatory training resulted in desired gains. Moreover, the authors added that "these changes not only were greater while the self-regulation system was in effect but, most importantly, maintained after the withdrawal of teacher controls over the system" (p. 193). Although the maintenance period was brief, the results with "difficult cases" are encouraging.

A hyperactive girl was treated with a cognitive–behavioral strategy that included self-instructional training, modeling, behavioral contingencies, role playing, and social perspective-taking and problem-solving training (Kendall & Urbain, 1981). The client was a 7-year-old girl who had been seen in psychotherapy since age 4. She was reported to have been abused as a child before she was eventually placed in a foster home. Although the child was likable, complaints of severe verbal outbursts, distractibility, and general hyperactivity were evident in her records.

Portions of the treatment were introduced sequentially, following baseline assessment, as the frequency of offensive verbalizations, verbal outbursts, out-of-seat, and off-task behaviors were recorded. Based on a time series analysis of these data, self-instructions on task-related materials had limited effects on behavior. However, when the response-cost component was introduced in conjunction with the self-instructions, the frequency of off-task behavior was reduced. During the next phase of the treatment, when the self-instructions and response-cost procedures were applied directly to the target behaviors (as opposed to the training tasks), there was almost a total absence of the undesired behavior. The intervention continued over a 15-month period, with social problem-solving and social perspective-taking exercises and modeling and role-playing of "thinking before acting" as the intervention strategy over the second half of the treatment. Cognitive task performance and behavioral observation data, as well as ratings of behavior by (nonblind) parents, provided the evidence of treatment effectiveness. At 1-year follow-up, the improvements were found to be maintained. This particular report may be criticized for a less-than-perfect single-subject design (the intervention strategies were stacked onto each other, with no reversal phase), but the report is important because it describes a flexible application of the cognitive–behavioral training, documents the extensive length of treatment necessary for a clinical case, reaffirms the importance of including both cognitive training and behavioral procedures within training, and illustrates the use of cognitive and behavioral assessments to evaluate treatment outcome.

Barkley, Copeland, and Sivage (1980) also reported the use of a self-control training program involving self-instructions with hyperactive children. Specifically, Barkley et al.'s program included self-instructional training, self-monitoring, and scheduling work and play activities. Analyses of frequency data over time indicated that the program improved misbehaviors and attention to work while the children were in their individual seats but not during group instruction.

The severely hearing-impaired youngster has been described as lacking impulse control and the use of self-instructional training has been considered. Often, however, strategic use of modeled self-talk would be undermined by the child's hearing deficit. In a creative application of self-instructional training with three severely hearing-impaired behaviorally disturbed children, Swanson (1982) employed signed self-instructions for math and spelling exercises. Using multiple baselines, Swanson found that signed self-instructions with task-specific information were effective.

Range-of-Outcome Measures. The use of range-of-outcome measures to evaluate treatment has begun to expand. This desired trend is evident in the range of target behaviors observed (e.g., Barkley et al., 1980, Neilans & Israel, 1981), the use of cognitive performance measures (e.g., Cohen, Schleser, & Meyers, 1981; Kendall & Zupan, 1981; Weissberg & Gesten, 1982), achievement tests (e.g., Kendall & Braswell, 1982b), classroom quizzes (e.g., Parrish & Erickson, 1981), and the inclusion of structured interviews (e.g., N. J. Cohen, Sullivan, Minde, Novak, & Helwig, 1981; Kendall, 1981b). Reviews of the various assessments are also available (Kendall & Braswell, 1982a; Kendall, Pellegrini, & Urban, 1981a).

Follow-Ups. Extensive follow-up data remain somewhat sparse, but the trend is toward gathering and reporting follow-ups of at least 1-year posttreatment. In a 1-year follow-up of concrete versus conceptual cognitive–behavioral training, Kendall (1981b) reported that many of the improvements seen at that time were evident for children in all conditions and might be attributed to increased age. As a consequence of the results of the data analysis, though sample sizes hindered the identification of statistically significant differences between groups, it was concluded that long-term effectiveness was somewhat limited (Kendall and Braswell, 1982b, also reported limited effects at 1-year follow-up). However, structured interviews revealed that the children who had received the conceptual training showed significantly better recall of the material they had learned than either concrete-trained or control-group children. By means of normative comparisons it was found that the conceptually trained children were not sufficiently lacking in self-control (as rated by new classroom teachers blind to treatment condition) to warrant referral. Given the support for the general conceptual approach to training described earlier (Kendall & Wilcox, 1980; Schleser *et al.*, 1981), these 1-year follow-up data are somewhat supportive.

Component Analyses. Component analyses are conducted in an effort to determine what aspects of the treatment package are necessary, sufficient, or facilitative for therapeutic change (Kazdin & Wilson, 1978). Component analyses, or dismantling studies, reveal a thorny control problem concerning the number of treatment components provided to different client groups and the need to control for length of therapy. As the number of components given to clients varies, so does the amount of therapist contact time. A reasonable approach to the solution of this problem is to create component analyses that compare key components that are given sufficient and equal time in treatment. Two reported investigations (Kendall & Braswell, 1982b; Parrish & Erickson, 1981) provide data for consideration of the active components of the cognitive–behavioral programs.

Parrish and Erickson (1981) were interested in the application of the cognitive–behavioral package to nondisturbed but impulsive children, and they set forth to do a component analysis to identify the relative effectiveness of two of the facets of the training. Because they intended to work with noninstitutionalized schoolchildren, they hoped to isolate the more efficacious component so that a streamlined intervention could be developed. The authors chose to compare verbal self-instructions and a scanning strategy. The subjects, 24 children who scored "impulsive" on the Matching Familiar Figures (MFF) test, were randomly assigned to (1) scanning strategy instructions, (2) verbal self-instructions, (3) scanning strategy and verbal self-instructions, or (4) control. The findings revealed that both cognitive training components resulted in significant decreases in MFF errors but not in latencies. Contrary to the prediction of Parrish and Erickson (1981), the combined treatment package did not produce significantly greater gains than the two separate components. Importantly, the results documented that "each of the cognitive training procedures led to significant decreases in the total number of classroom quiz errors at posttest. The significant decreases in classroom quiz errors were maintained by the children for at least five weeks" (p. 82). Generalization to classroom behavior was assessed but not identified. The generalization to classroom quizzes but not to classroom behavior is not surprising, since the treatment was focused on training materials such as reading, math, and spelling skills (as opposed to interpersonal behaviors) and the training was limited to six 30-minute sessions. The generalization that was observed was in a context similar to the context of training.

Having personally conducted workshops and institutes on cognitive-behavioral training with children, and having conducted and reported related research, I have on numerous occasions discussed and considered the separate merits of the cognitive component of the cognitive-behavioral treatment package. Until recently, this empirical question was a continuous source of concern. To resolve the issue, a colleague and I (Kendall & Braswell, 1982b) conducted an evaluation of the contribution of the cognitive component of self-instructional training to the total cognitive-behavioral treatment program by comparing a cognitive-behavioral condition (the entire program) to a purely behavioral intervention (the program minus cognitive training). Cognitive strategies were not examined in isolation because of our belief in the fundamental importance of behavioral techniques within the program for management of impulsive disorders. The 27 children who were referred by classroom teachers for problematically low self-control were randomly assigned to one of the two treatment cells or to an attention-control condition. All subjects received 12 sessions of individual therapist contact focusing on psychoeducational, play, and interpersonal tasks and real problem situations. The behavioral condition involved the institution of response-cost and self-reward contingencies and therapist modeling and role playing of task-appropriate behavior; the cognitive-behavioral condition added cognitive modeling and training in verbal self-instructions.

Both active treatments were associated with improvements on teachers' blind ratings of hyperactivity and on such performance measures as cognitive style and academic achievement; however, only the cognitive-behavioral condition yielded improvements in teacher ratings of self-control and on self-report measures of self-concept. Naturalistic observation in the classroom setting evidenced variability, but measures of off-task verbal and off-task physical behavior indicated treatment efficacy. In neither condition did parent ratings of children's behavior at home indicate desired gains.

Gains that were evident in teacher ratings of self-control and hyperactivity were maintained at 10-week follow-up, but a 1-year follow-up study did not demonstrate significant differences across treatment conditions. Normative comparisons suggested that the changes in self-control for the children in the cognitive-behavioral group were clinically significant, for the average of their ratings placed them within (barely) normal limits. Based on these data, it was concluded that the study provided support for the efficacy of cognitive-behavioral treatment and the specific advantage of a combined program over a solely behavioral procedure. However, the interpretation of these results as totally and unequivocally supportive must be tempered by the lack of maintenance of treatment gains at 1-year follow-up and the absence of generalization to the home setting. Kendall and Braswell (1982b) spec-ulated that the intervention might have been too brief and that longer treatment periods with a greater focus on home situations and more in-class interventions may be required before truly satisfactory results can be anticipated. As in other published studies, the attained generalization was limited to and consistent with the nature of the context of training: Our training focused on classroom behavior and we achieved generali-zation to the classroom—we did not deal with home issues and we did not find generalization to the home. The context of training seems essential in understanding and attaining generalization.

Comparisons with Medications: Preliminary Data. Two studies have compared cognitive–behavioral training with use of methylphen-idate in the treatment of hyperactivity (N. J. Cohen *et al.*, 1981; Yellin, Kendall, & Greenberg, 1981). N. J. Cohen *et al.*'s (1981) intervention was an integration of self-instructional training (after Meichenbaum & Goodman, 1971) and the think-aloud procedures of Bash and Camp (1978). The treatment was provided in 20 individual 1-hour sessions. On the positive side, Cohen *et al.* sought a "total push" treatment (after Douglas, Parry, Marton, & Garson, 1976) and therefore informed teachers and parents of the training and its objectives and encouraged them to use similar strategies. On the less positive side, behavioral contingencies were not systematically employed, and I am puzzled by the absence of behavioral contingencies from any "total push" effort. Positive and negative reactions are also appropriate when considering the chosen dependent variables. For instance, use of a global 5-point rating scale for parents to report their perception of the outcome of treatment and the sole reliance on a single rating scale of behavior are weaknesses. More-over, while the inclusion of behavioral observations in the classroom (with nonhyperactive controls) could be said to be positive, only two behaviors of questionable specificity and relevance play behavior and social behavior) were observed and recorded.

In N. J. Cohen *et al.*'s (1981) research design, six children received cognitive behavior modification, eight received methylphenidate, six received both treatments, and four were untreated controls. As the authors noted, the original assignment was random but, due to adverse response to medication, four children had to be reassigned. The average age of these kindergarten children was 5½ years.

Based on the limited numbers of subjects, the relevance of some of the dependent measures, and the restricted cognitive focus (as opposed to cognitive–behavioral) of the training, the meaningfulness of the results must be considered to be preliminary at best. Nevertheless, N. J. Cohen *et al.* (1981) reported that their data did not provide evidence that either of the treatments was more effective than the other, than both in combination, or than no treatment at all. The hyperactive children, in general, became less symptomatic over time. The authors offered a palatable analysis of their lack of effects: "There were relatively few instances of children independently generating and following through on problem-solving strategies. A likely explanation for our findings may be related to the relative lack of cognitive sophistication in all children of this age" (p. 53). As noted on several occasions in the literature the cognitive capacity of children receiving self-instructional training may indeed be a potent individual difference affecting outcome (Kendall, 1977). Moreover, recent evidence underscores the importance of "involvement" (e.g., Braswell, Kendall, Braith, Carey, & Vye, 1983) in training as a predictor of outcome.

The second study to compare cognitive–behavioral training with methylphenidate administration must also be considered very preliminary. Yellin *et al.* (1981) compared five hyperactive boys receiving medications through a child psychiatry service with five hyperactive boys receiving cognitive–behavioral training through a school-based research clinic. Therefore, the children were not randomly assigned to treatments and there were no control conditions. The children in the two groups were, however, matched on initial level of hyperactivity and chronological age. Two ratings scales, the hyperactivity scale of the Conners Parent–Teacher Questionnaire (1973) and the SCRS (Kendall & Wilcox, 1979), were completed by teachers at pretreatment and at 4–6 weeks and 7–12 weeks (for the cognitive–behavioral group these assessments were posttreatment and follow-up; however, the methylphenidate group remained on medication across assessments). Both interventions produced a significant gains on teacher ratings, and although methylphenidate produced slightly larger effects, there were nonsignificant differences between treatment conditions.

The intervention employed in Yellin *et al.* (1981) was that developed by Kendall and colleagues. Thus, unlike N. J. Cohen *et al.*'s (1981) treatment, the Yellin *et al.* treatment included behavioral contingencies modeling and the enacting role plays. While it would be of interest to draw conclusions based on this distinction between the interventions, the methodological limitations of both studies supplant a conclusive comparison and summary. The importance of the question of the relative efficacy of medications and cognitive–behavioral training with hyperactive children merits more careful examination.

The Role of Individual Differences. Individual differences are affectionately referred to as "id's" (eye dees) among those who have a long-standing tradition of studying how variations from the average of a group affect the performances of the individual group members. Perhaps because this tradition is laced through with the measurement of mental abilities and personality traits, behavior therapists have not, until recently, displayed a sincere interest in identifying relevant id's.

Within the arena of self-management, several authors (e.g., Kanfer & Karoly, 1982; Karoly, 1980) have begun to recommend that we be concerned with individual differences. Copeland has provided helpful reviews (Copeland, 1981, 1982, 1983) of ids more specifically related to self-management (often self-instructional) training with children. Although Copeland (1981) documents that the training has been employed across a wide range of age levels, age (a primary variable of concern for any child intervention) does seem to affect the clinician's design of and the child's responsiveness to treatment. For example, Copeland (1981) pointed out that older children can produce moderately effective self-verbalizations, whereas younger children seem to require more specific examples to copy (e.g., Miller, Weinstein, & Karniol, 1978; Toner & Smith, 1977). Furthermore, more concrete self-instructions seemed to be better for younger children (2-year-olds; see Birch, 1966), while conceptual training is superior for older (8–12-year-old) children (Kendall & Wilcox, 1980). Recall also the work of Schleser et al., in which cognitive level affected the generalization of self-instructional training. In terms of the maintenance of treatment gains, a 1-year follow-up (Kendall, 1981b) found that older children evidenced greater maintenance of gains on teacher ratings of self-control. Age of the treated children may have been central in the results of cummulative reviewers: Hobbs et al. (1980) included numerous studies with children under 6 years of age and drew less encouraging conclusions than other reviewers.

Cognitive capacity is another primary individual difference variable (see also Copeland & Hammel, 1981). Authors have pointed out that in several cases, children with higher IQs have responded better to self-instructions than have children who are less cognitively mature (Barkley et al., 1980). Maintenance of gains on teacher ratings of self-control at 1-year follow-up have been reported to be related to the children's IQs (Kendall, 1981b). Copeland suggests that children with lower IQs may need more assistance (see also Pressley, 1979).

Other factors, such as socioeconomic status (e.g., Braswell, Kendall, & Urbain, 1982), medication status (e.g., Bugental, Whalen, & Henker, 1977; Whalen, Henker, Collins, Finck, & Dotemoto, 1979), attributional style (e.g., Bugental et al., 1977), and private speech (e.g., Asarnow & Meichenbaum, 1979) were also reviewed by Copeland. In addition to the potency of age and IQ as ids, Copeland wrote that an internal attributional style was important and suggested that children receiving training be encouraged in that direction.

One final individual difference deserves special attention: type of disorder. Variations in presenting problems are likely to be more important than any other single factor, since, as is true in several of the effective therapies, a logical affinity can be identified between the treatment approach and a particular disorder. One prime example of this is self-instructional training and its association with problems in self-control. This match is scarcely accidental, for it reflects the intention of the design of the therapeutic procedure (Meichenbaum, 1977) to interpose cognitive medication where such processing has been absent (as opposed to modifying existing cognitions; Kendall, 1981a). As a result, target problems such as self-control deficits, where forethought and planning are rare, are precisely the targets of choice for self-instructional training (Kendall, 1977).

With the appearance of research demonstrating the efficacy of self-instructional training for self-control problems it is perhaps not surprising to witness the extension of the procedures to new and different populations. However, inappropriate application of the treatment may lead to inaccurate criticism of it. An outcome study employing cognitive training strategies with isolated children will illustrate this concern. The authors themselves are not being criticized: Rather, I am using some of their work to illustrate a critical point.

Isolated children are said to lack quality peer relations and, based on the predictive relationship between peer relations and adult maladjustment (e.g., Cowen, Pederson, Babigian, Izzo, & Trost, 1973; Roff, 1961; Roff, Sells, & Golden, 1972), are viewed as "at risk" for maladjustment. Recent interest has been directed toward the development and evaluation of interventions to remedy social isolation. Combs and Lahey (1981) used a program based on self-instruction to teach social skills to isolated preschool children in two 1-hour sessions. They failed to find any generalized effect and questioned the utility of cognitive social skills training.

Should self-instructions be expected to be an effective treatment for isolated children? Do isolated children characteristically respond quickly without forethought? Do they behave without thinking? The likely answer to these questions is "no." Thus self-instructional procedures may not be the treatment of choice for social isolates. Moreover, the Combs and Lahey intervention was too brief (2 hours) to be representative of cognitive training, and, as the authors themselves recognized, the subjects were too young (3- and 5-year-olds) and came from an overly disadvantaged background. As discussed earlier, age may be an important moderator of outcome.

Treating social isolates may be a different and more difficult task than anticipated. Berler, Gross, and Drabman (1982), using a behavioral social skills package for socially unskilled children, found training results but an absence of generalization. Self-verbalizations may help children to inhibit behavior, but they are less effective in producing behavior (e.g., Karlan & Rusch, 1982). Before cognitive–behavioral strategies are employed for isolated children, we must examine whether or not cognitive factors play a role in isolation; if they do, we must determine the exact nature of the cognitive errors, excesses, or deficits that require remediation (Kendall & Morison, 1983).

SUMMARY

The literature on self-instructional training has undergone growth and refinement. Studies have evaluated the merits of manipulating various treatment contexts, of employing the treatment with clinical cases, and of various components within the treatment package. In addition, a wider range of dependent variables, longer follow-ups, and a greater interest in individual differences are appearing in publications. Lest the reader assume that all is perfectly well, recall that in several studies the hypothesized outcomes were not always found. For instance, Eastman and Rasbury (1981) did not find desired changes in on-task behavior or academic performance. This outcome, however, is not surprising when one considers that the intervention consisted of only three 20-minute sessions. But even in the more confirmatory reports, the pattern of results are not uniformly positive. Further developments into the classroom and family setting, further considerations of social development and emotional processing, and more psychometrically sound assessments appear necessary.

Problem Solving

Problem-solving approaches to clinical and counseling interventions (e.g., Heppner & Petersen, 1982) have received attention on all fronts, including theoretical (e.g., Kanfer & Busemeyer, 1982); review papers with adults (D'Zurilla & Nezu, 1982) and with children (Urbain & Kendall, 1980); and reports of research on the effects of problem-solving treatments with families (e.g., Blechman, Taylor, Schrader, 1981b), couples (e.g., Baucom, 1982), adolescents and their parents (e.g., Robin, 1981), and children (e.g., Weissberg, Gesten, Rapkin, Cowen, Davidson, deApodaca, McKim, 1981). One of the common features of these problem-solving treatments is their reliance on a multiplicity of clinical strategies in conjunction with problem-solving skills training. For example, Robin's (1981) approach included training in negotiating, communication skills, and cognitive restructuring; Baucom (1982) included communications training and contracting; and Weissberg *et al.* (1981) included affective education, group role plays, modeling, and discussion. The different problem-solving treatments are guided by the principle that the acquisition of skills useful in the resolution of personal conflicts will result in improved adjustment.

Parent–adolescent conflict was treated in 33 families with adolescents aged 11 to 16 by Robin (Robin, 1981). The families had rule and responsibility disagreements, were willing to participate in the research, and were not retarded, organic, or psychotic. Three conditions were compared: (1) problem-solving communication training, (2) alternative family therapy, and (3) a waiting-list control. Treated families received seven 1-hour weekly sessions over a 2-month period. Families receiving the problem-solving communication training were taught a four-step problem-solving model that included defining the problem without accusations, brainstorming alternatives, deciding on a mutually satisfactory solution, and specifying a plan for implementation. In addition, communication training invloved feedback, modeling, and behavior rehearsal. Negative habits, such as interruptions and accusations, were replaced with positive habits, such as active listening and verification of meaning. Four steps were followed as unreasonable beliefs were treated via cognitive restructuring. One doctoral-level and three master's-level psychologists served as the therapists for this condition.

One psychiatrist and four-master's level mental health professionals provided alternative family therapy. These therapists conducted family-therapy sessions in accord with their respective theoretical models (e.g., family systems, eclectic, psychodynamic). In this fashion, Robin's comparison was a specialized form of family therapy against an existing alternate family therapy. The new, specialized twist was the multi-component problem-solving/communication training focus.

Both treatment conditions resulted in significant gains on self-reported measures of disputes and conflictual communication in the home. Only the specialized problem-solving approach, however, resulted in significant gains in problem-solving communication behavior objectively coded from family discussions. Some evidence of maintenance was provided by 10-week follow-up data.

Dropout and delinquency-prone urban high school students were subjects of a research evaluation conducted by Sarason and Sarason (1981), who compared the effects of live models and videotaped models to those of a no-treatment control on five types of dependent measures. The basic training employed modeling and behavioral rehearsal, focusing on both cognitive and behavioral skills. This dual emphasis is clear in Sarason and Sarason's (1981) report:

> The subjects saw demonstrations of both effective overt responses (e.g., how to ask a teacher a question) and the cognitive antecedents of effective behavior (e.g., deciding between alternative courses of action). Repeated emphasis was placed on the links between thought and action. (p. 909)

Before the intervention, interviews were conducted to identify skill deficits. Among the identified needs were social skills, ways to control impulsive behavior, and ways to interact with nonpeers. Pilot studies were conducted to improve role-play scripts and modeling tapes. Based on earlier research (Sarason & Ganzer, 1973) discussion groups were not used.

The actual intervention focused on training the skills that would help remediate the identified problems. The participants were 127 students, and 13 structured classes were provided. Each treatment class included an introduction, live or videotaped enactments, role plays, and homework assignments. Lesson topics included cutting class and asking for help on the job. The dependent measures included self-reports (test anxiety, locus of control, means–end problem solving, alternatives test), an interview, and archival data (incidence of tardiness and behavioral referrals during the year after treatment). Unfortunately, some measures (e.g., means–ends problem solving) were used only in posttest comparisons.

The results indicated that the cognitive and social skills course resulted in an increased ability to think of more alternatives in problem situations and to "handle themselves" in interview situations relative to the control conditions. At the time of the 1-year follow-up, in which 75 subjects participated, the live modeling group had significantly fewer absences and both modeling groups had significantly less tardiness and behavior referrals than the control group. Live modeling was somewhat more effective, but both modeling treatments, which included demonstrations of both cognitive and behavioral skills, were effective.

A dismantling analysis of problem-solving/communications training was reported by Baucom (1982). Earlier research on behavioral marital therapy had endorsed the problem-solving, communication, and contracting components, and Baucom conducted a comparison of some of these components. The subjects were 72 maritally distressed couples (excluding sexual and alcohol problems) who initiated contact with the clinic. Subjects were randomly assigned to either (1) problem-solving communication training plus *quid pro quo* contracting, (2) problem-solving communication training only, (3) *quid pro quo* contracting only, or (4) waiting-list control. Baucom predicted that the three behavioral marital therapy conditions would improve more than controls from pre- to posttreatment. Two therapists, each seeing 36 couples for 1–1½ hours weekly for 10 weeks, were not told the specific research hypotheses. Self-report and behavioral observation data were used to assess outcomes. The Locke–Wallace Marital Adjustment Scale (Locke & Wallace, 1959) and the Areas-of-Change Questionnaire (Weiss, Hops, & Patterson, 1973) were the self-report scales, and a revised version of the Marital Interaction Coding System (MICS; Patterson, Hops, & Weiss, 1975) provided ratings on verbal and nonverbal interactions (obtained from videotapes of problem-solving sessions pre- and posttreatment).

The complete treatment (problem-solving communication training and contracting) replicated the procedures used by Jacobson (1978; see also discussion in Volume 8 of the *Annual Review*). The participants were taught to describe problems in behavioral terms, to discuss alternative solutions, to propose agreements and plans, to avoid being sidetracked or feeling guilty, and to contract to tie together solutions in a contingent fashion (e.g., "If you do ——— I'll do ———."). Homework assignments were also provided, 15 minutes per day (see also Lester, Beckham, & Baucom, 1980). Contracting was introduced in session 6. However, for the subjects receiving problem-solving communication training only, contracting was not introduced; for contracting-only subjects the other components were not provided.

Based on analyses of adjusted posttreatment scores, the results demonstrated that the interventions were more effective than no treatment in alleviating marital distress. However, there were no meaningful differences between the three treatment conditions. While this outcome may be somewhat surprising to some, it is consistent with other controlled research (e.g., Jacobson, 1978; O'Leary & Turkewitz, 1978). Do these data suggest that we should avoid future dismantling studies? I think not. Rather, in this particular area of research we can conclude that of the components studied to date we have yet to isolate one factor that differentially affects outcome. This does not mean that such a factor does not exist. Indeed, future research may benefit from comparisons of other components of problem-solving marital therapy. As Baucom suggested, attempting to alter cognitive factors directly may be fruitful in perfecting the treatment of distressed couples.

Problem-solving training programs are often a part of prevention efforts when employed with school-aged children. Children who are at risk for school and interpersonal problems are identified and given special help in secondary prevention programs, whereas primary prevention programs are designed to help all children develop new skills. Two recent reports deal specifically with problem solving and school-aged children (Rickel & Lampi, 1981; Weissberg, *et al.*, 1981; the reader is also referred to the section on self-instructional training in this chapter and in Volume 8—self-instructional procedures also offer a problem-solving perspective).

Research by the Rochester group (Weissberg *et al.*, 1981) concerned the evaluation of a "52 lesson, class taught, social-problem-solving (SPS) training program for third grade children" (p. 251). The lessons were highly structured, lasted 20 to 30 minutes, and focused on teaching children to (1) recognize feelings in themselves and others, (2) identify (sense) problems, (3) generate alternative solutions, (4) consider potential consequences by thinking ahead, and (5) integrate the new skills in sequence into real-life problems. Participants were 243 children; 122 received training and 121 were controls. As part of the research design suburban and urban schools were examined separately.

In addition to the desirable length and structure of the training, a clear strength of this study was its breadth of dependent measures. Therefore, it is well worth the time and effort to overview all of the assessments. A variety of problem-solving outcome measures were used, including measures of four cognitive problem-solving skills (means-ends thinking, alternative thinking, social role taking, and problem identification/consequential thinking), a behavioral problem-solving test (frequency of problem-solving behavior in a naturalistic task), and a problem-solving interview (see Gesten, deApodaca, Rains, Weissberg, & Cowen, 1979). Measures of adjustment included the Health Resources Inventory (Gesten, 1976), the Devereux Elementary School Behavior Rating Scale (a modification of a scale by Spivack & Swift, 1967), a class sociometric, the trait-anxiety scale of the State–Trait Anxiety Inventory for Children (Spielberger, 1973), and the McDaniel–Piers Young Children's Self-Concept Scale (a modification of the Piers–Harris; Piers, 1969). As mentioned in last year's *Annual Review* the outcome evaluator gains enormously by including multiple method assessments. The measures allow for an evaluation of the impact of the treatment ("Did teachers or peers notice changes?") and of the specific changes that led to the positive impact (scores on specific cognitive and behavioral tests) (Kendall, Pellegrini, & Urbain, 1981a).

Weissberg *et al.*'s results are both encouraging and challenging. They are encouraging because the data documented that the children who received the social problem-solving program improved more than controls on several key problem-solving skills (alternative thinking, more effective solutions). Moreover, based on the behavioral test, some generalization occurred. In Weissberg *et al.*'s (1981) words, "such data . . . suggest that cognitive problem-solving skills acquired through training generalize to relevant behavioral situations removed in time, place, and person" (p. 259). In contrast, role taking, self-esteem, trait anxiety, and sociometric status did not evidence treatment gains. Some positive gains were evident on ratings of adjustment, with the suburban children who received training improving more than the controls on several of the adjustment indices. However, urban children showed decreases in adjustment.

Conceptually challenging results included the reported lack of relationships between the acquisition of social problem-solving (SPS) skills and adjustment gains (Weissberg et al., 1981). A related finding was reported by Rickel, Eshelman, and Loigman (1981): Children who received social problem-solving training gained on measures of interpersonal cognitive problem-solving (e.g., Spivack & Shure, 1974) but teacher blind ratings revealed no significant training effects. The absence of a relationship between the cognitive and behavioral changes reported by Weissberg et al. and the Rickel et al. (1981) call into question the hypothesized mediational role of SPS skills. Future research must seek to determine the role, mediational or otherwise, of changes in social cognitive problem-solving skills. Independent of their results, however, the authors are to be commended for their evaluation of this issue. Although additional work is needed to improve the measures of social cognitive problem solving, several reports document the positive trend of including cognitive assessments as part of the evaluation of behavioral training programs (e.g., Kendall & Zupan, 1981; Sarason & Sarason, 1981; Weissberg et al., 1981).

A program similar to that employed by the Rochester group was initiated in Detroit approximately 7 years ago. In this program, younger (3 and 4 years old) and poorer nonwhite children were subjects. The treatment dealt with these broad areas: learning problems, acting out, and shy or withdrawn behaviors. Reports of the effectiveness of this program have appeared in the literature (e.g., Rickel & Smith, 1979; Rickel, Smith, & Sharp, 1979), and the latest report provides a 2-year follow-up (Rickel & Lampi, 1981).

The methodology of the original studies had several positive features: random assignment of children to conditions, blind posttreatment assessment, teachers unaware of treatment conditions for individual children, and comparisons of high-risk treated children with low-risk control children. The results of the original project were favorable, including significant differences at posttest in favor of the treatment group over the control group on measures of behavioral adjustment and achievement. The Rickel and Lampi (1981) follow-up reported on the results of the program 2 years later using a measure of adjustment (the 11-item AML; Cowen, Don, Clarfield, Kreling, McWilliams, Pokracki, Pratt, Terrell, & Wilson, 1973) and an indicant of achievement (the Caldwell Preschool Inventory; Caldwell, 1970). Teachers were kept blind to whether children had participated by being asked to rate all children at the follow-up period (42 were high-risk children, either treatment or control; 28 were low-risk children).

All high-risk children (treated and controls) improved in adjustment and achievement over time, perhaps because of maturation. However, the low-risk children's performance did not differ significantly from that of the treated high-risk children, suggesting that the intervention moved children in the direction of "comparability in performance to that of children who have not experienced behavioral or learning difficulties" (p. 464). The use of normative comparisons is applauded, whereas the limited range of dependent measures used restricts the conclusions that can be drawn.

Children who were identified as inconsistent in math classwork were identified from 17 second- to sixth-grade classrooms by Blechman *et al.* (1981b). The six most inconsistent children in each class were randomly assigned to one of three conditions: (1) family problem solving, (2) a home-note intervention, or (3) untreated control. The three children from each class with the least scatter served as stable controls. The family problem-solving treatment involved individual 1-hour clinic appointments in which families wrote contingency contracts, engaged in a problem-solving board game, and specified consequences for receipt of "good news notes." The subjects in the home-note intervention condition received good news notes as well, but participants did not receive the 1-hour pretraining. Thus both treatment conditions employed good news notes, with a 1-hour special training session with the family for the problem-solving condition.

Based on a measure of math classwork scatter, both interventions (compared to no treatment) produced significant reductions. In terms of math performance accuracy, only the children who received good news notes plus the pretraining (the family problem solving) maintained baselines levels; classwork of other students became less accurate and less stable. The treated children also evidenced generalization to performance checks on days when good news notes were not attainable. As Blechman *et al.* (1981b) noted, "involvement of the family meant that children produced high quality work even when their classmates' work dropped in quality[2] and that they worked hard even when they expected no reward" (p. 919). However, their performance on a timed math achievement test did not improve. The Blechman *et al.* (1981b) report dealt with math performance as opposed to interpersonal behavior or

---

2. This drop in quality was attributed to the increased difficulty of work assigned as the year progressed.

general adjustment, but nevertheless underscored the increased benefits accrued when family members are fully informed, prepared, and involved (as achieved by their family problem-solving training) in the training of their children.

Rational–Emotive Therapy

In this, my second year as a formal reviewer of the literature on rational–emotive therapy (RET) for the *Annual Review*, I can now more readily recognize the truth of a hunch I ignored years ago. I had speculated that RET generates as much debate, if not more, about its application and philosophical and religious position than it does research about its effectiveness as an intervention strategy. The likelihood that this observation is somehow idiosyncratic to the approximately 1-year period of this review or to me as the reviewer is quite trivial. Others tend to confirm my observation and each year of review provides additional confirmation. My confidence in the accuracy of my observation has risen, but I am no closer to an acceptable explanation for the phenomenon. One potential source of understanding concerns the characteristics of RET practitioners: They are cognitive, in their own heads, analytical, and less behavioral; they evaluate less but debate more. The cognitive activity is laudable, the behavioral inactivity is not.

The praiseworthy nature of the philosophical discourses of RET are perhaps best illustrated in some of the recent printed discussions (e.g., Bernard, 1981; A. Ellis, 1981a, 1981b; Hafner, 1981; Meehl, 1981). Meehl (1981) and Ellis (1981a) come to mind first. No condensation can do justice to these original papers—the following is a humble effort.

Meehl (1981) poses his philosophical concern most clearly when he asks, "Can a therapist, without imposing his personal value commitments on the client, properly 'correct' the client's evaluative dispositions?" (p. 4). Meehl continues by clarifying some terms: "imposing" does not necessarily mean active counterpropagandizing, and "correction" implies an error. With additional substantive clarification, Meehl then concludes that a therapeutic strategy can exist coherently without presupposing that the therapist's values are right and the client's somehow wrong. There can be cognitive errors that are independent of the therapist's personal value system.

Surprisingly to me, Ellis's reply (1981a) largely agreed with Meehl. Ellis stated that he distinctly went along with Meehl's main proposition. However, Ellis also argued that the "shoulds," "oughts," and "musts" that are opposed by RET philosophy are not the consensus "shoulds" that are implied in most ethical postulates but are the absolutistic or over-generalized "musts" that really have nothing to do with ethics.

Ellis argues that whether or not he and his clients have different ethical views is not critical. It is not that one or another point of view is correct but that personal values guide *desired* behaviors, not *required* behaviors. Ellis contends further that he points out the consequences of each client's standards or values, not whether these standards are right or wrong. RET rarely challenges the basic ethics and laws of society in which RET takes place.

From this Meehl–Ellis discussion (and a reply by Rosenberg, 1982) one learns of the philosophical underpinnings of therapeutic efforts, the value of values clarification, and, if nothing else, the analytic skills of the writers. It was, however, a bit disappointing to see a strength of RET—nonabsolutistic thinking—used too often as an argument for the absence of errors within RET. As Ellis noted (1981a), "RET hardly believes in any real absolute, and hence would hold that all moral and ethical rules are relative . . ." (p. 38). Relativity and flexibility are aids in personal adjustment that can be overused in logical argument. Perhaps Ellis is too absolute in his defense of nonabsolutistic thinking.

Sharkey (1981) criticized RET and rational–emotive psychology, and Ellis (1981b) again provided a rebuttal. In Sharkey's view, RET is one of the most philosophically neutral therapies. Ellis agreed. However, Sharkey argued against the condemnation of all religious views that he saw as part of a rational–emotive philosophy. Ellis disagreed, arguing that not all religious hypotheses are negative, only those that are too absolutist.

The restatement and refinement of RET principles and procedures may be of merit and there are philosophical questions worthy of our attention. Discussions or debates are, however, of limited clinical utility unless and until direct treatment implications are provided.

Papers by Hafner (1981) and Bernard (1981) discuss notions relevant to RET (e.g., both subdivide "beliefs" into subcategories) and provide content in the area of treatment methods. Hafner (1981) extends the A-B-C format and describes a problem-solving extension. For instance, the B (beliefs) in A-B-C is subdivided to reflect immediate beliefs (Bi) that the individual is aware of and can communicate, such as self-statements, and underlying beliefs (Bu) that may be less obvious to the individual. C (consequences) is expanded to include outcome consequences (Co) as well as behavioral (Cb) and emotional (Ce) consequences. The outcome consequences are the result of what the client does. After D, *d*isputing the irrational beliefs, Hafner adds E, F, and G:

*e*xpected new realistic goals (E), *f*acilitating methods or actions (F), and goal achievement (G). It is in this second phase of this RET system that the client is taught problem-solving skills. For instance, Hafner (1981) outlines how to address each of the steps with questions for the client. At step E the client is asked "Is this goal based on objective facts of the situation?" At step F the client is told to ask himself or herself "What specifically can I do to reach my goal?" At step G the client is told to put into practice the constructive behavior decided upon at step F.

Hafner also recommends that behavioral strategies be used. For example, when the therapist is setting goals, Hafner encourages the use of observable, concrete goals stated in behavioral terms. When working on goal achievement practice, role playing, graduated tasks, and homework assignments are encouraged. For the practitioner who finds merit in problem solving and RET approaches, the Hafner (1981) paper provides interesting reading.

Bernard's (1981) thesis, that characteristics of clients' thoughts are overlooked in the practice of RET, provides provocative commentary for practitioner and researcher alike. To begin with, Bernard posits that not all thoughts are in the individual's awareness. Many thoughts are partially hidden, and these core beliefs are less accessible. What dynamic therapists have called "resistance" may more accurately be viewed as a result of the "inherent limitations in the way human beings represent experience to themselves in thought" (p. 129). Describing one's personal thoughts is not simply a case of "turning up the auditory stereo channel so that the therapist can hear what the client is thinking" (p. 131). Instead, Bernard argues that characteristics of thought, such as individual meaning and how thought is stored in memory, have a pronounced effect on whether or not clients can access and describe their thoughts. To facilitate the translation of therapeutic instructions into the client's framework, Bernard suggests that therapists have clients expand on their initial thoughts ("What do you mean when you say you thought ——?") and that therapists dig deeper into the client's thinking by "peeling the onion"—seeking hidden irrationality under layers of rationality.

As noted at the outset of this commentary on the current RET literature, RET does not appear to be as compelled to generate as impressive a data base as one would hope. In a sense, this aspect of RET distinguishes it from other cognitive–behavioral interventions in which empirical analysis is sought and highly regarded. In an analysis of the similarities and differences between the various adult cognitive–behavioral therapies, Kendall and Kriss (1983) isolated and examined five dimensions: (1) theoretical orientation/target of change, (2) nature of therapeutic relationship, (3) principal cognitive change agent, (4) source of evidence on which reappraisals are based, and (5) degree of emphasis on self-control. According to this system, RET emerged as most different from other approaches, such as cognitive therapy for depression, stress inoculation, and systematic rational restructuring. RET, as opposed to these other approaches, seeks more philosophical change, is more didactic and confrontive, and is less focused on self-control.

RET remains an enigma. It is a seminal system with important theoretical components and it is an extensively practiced approach with wide-ranging application and acceptance, yet it seems less than mainstream cognitive-behavior therapy. Perhaps limited research efforts contribute to this perception.

Nonassertiveness

Seeing crisp new stacks of *Your Perfect Right* (Alberti & Emmons, 1974) in the window of a bookstore in a major U.S. city convinced me that assertiveness has not passed on. Rumors within the field that "everyone" has been assertiveness trained are, as we realize when we observe subservient and sycophantic behavior, far from true. This year, like past years, provided new data on the effectiveness and relative efficiency of various types of treatment for nonassertive behavior. In large measure the studies were designed to test the separate and combined effects of components (often cognitive and behavioral) of assertion training.

The effects of behavioral, cognitive, and cognitive–behavioral treatments for nonassertiveness were investigated by Valerio and Stone (1982). In addition to comparing treatment strategies, the authors also evaluated the effects of different levels of knowledge about assertive behavior and the interaction of this individual-difference variable with the types of treatment. Of 222 volunteers, 88 women met Valerio and Stone's criteria for nonassertion: a nonassertive score on a self-report test and nonassertive behavior in a role-play test. A hypothetical role-play test (after Schwartz & Gottman, 1976) was conducted under conditions of high demand for assertive behavior, and the data obtained were used to divide the subjects into two knowledge groups (high and low knowledge).

The treatments were similar to procedures described earlier in the literature. For instance, the behavioral rehearsal condition, modeled after McFall and Lillisand (1971), stressed that the way to increase assertion was to learn assertive responses and to practice them. The cognitive intervention was based on Meichenbaum's (1977) coping model paradigm in which the model shares an internal dialogue with some negative thinking and then goes on to generate positive and facilitating self-talk. Subjects in the cognitive–behavioral treatment condition received a combination of these two approaches. Treatment was administered individually via audiotape in four sessions. The control condition was a waiting list.

The pattern of results emerging from this comparison of cognitive and behavioral procedures is different from those reported by Linehan, Goldfried, and Goldfried (1979). Whereas Linehan *et al.* reported greater gains from cognitive–behavioral training, the Valerio and Stone (1982) outcomes indicated comparable gains for all three treatment groups. Although no one treatment was shown to be superior to the others, the data did provide strong support for the efficacy of the three treatments in terms of self-report and behavioral improvements that were maintained at follow-up. The hypothesized interaction between level of knowledge and type of treatment (drawn from Nietzel & Bernstein, 1976) was not found to be significant. Moreover, the observed gains were not restricted to specific avenues of intervention (e.g., the behavioral treatment did not produce greater changes in behavior). The effects of each of the treatments were wide ranging. This outcome is consistent with the evidence for wide-ranging effects from the cognitive and behavioral treatment of depression (see last year's *Annual Review*). Also consistent with extant data, Valerio and Stone (1982) reported significant changes in self-efficacy for the treated clients and found that self-efficacy changes were correlated with demonstrated gains (consistent with data reported by Hammen, Jacobs, Mayol, & Cochran, 1980; and Kazdin, 1979).

Continuing his line of research on covert modeling interventions for nonassertiveness, Kazdin (1982c) evaluated the separate and combined effects of covert modeling and overt rehearsal. A delayed treatment group served as the no-treatment control. On self-report measures, behavioral measures, and self-efficacy judgments, all three treatments resulted in significant gains. Some advantage was seen for the combined procedure at posttreatment and follow-up.

Jacobs and Cochran (1982) compared (1) rehearsal alone, (2) behavioral rehearsal plus a personal rights lecture, (3) cognitive restructuring (an RET-like procedure with self-statement modification) plus personal lecture, and (4) cognitive restructuring plus behavioral rehearsal.[3] The intended waiting-list controls had several dropouts, so no control condition was used. A best-alternative (O'Leary & Borkovec,

---

3. The exact treatment conditions were not clear in the published report, since two groups were inadvertently labeled identically (p. 66).

1978) comparison against behavioral rehearsal was employed. The training lasted 2 hours per week for 8 weeks, with adjustments to allow for extra treatment components. No objective behavioral measures of assertion were obtained, but an *in vivo* self-monitoring procedure (pertinent to individualized training content) served as the outcome index. Based on this index the authors reported support for the superiority of the combination of cognitive restructuring and behavioral rehearsal as opposed to behavioral rehearsal alone. The special efforts on the part of the authors to individualize the training content are to be applauded, yet the limited measures of outcome limit the conclusiveness of their findings.

The literature has witnessed a diversity of outcomes from studies that compare behavioral rehearsal, cognitive training, and combined cognitive–behavioral strategies, and although each treatment has been shown to be effective, the existence of the clear superiority of any single approach cannot be claimed at this time. Searches for individual differences that predict differential treatment outcome are meritorious (cognitive-oriented researches appear to have taken this quite seriously; see Heimberg & Becker, 1981), despite the lack of support for one variable (knowledge) reported by Valerio and Stone (1982). Perhaps, as Bruch (1981) suggests and Heimberg and Becker's (1981) integration endorses, assertion training should continue to give equal attention to both cognitive and behavioral components. However, before we rush to accept this most palatable conclusion, Alden and Cappe's (1981) findings cannot be ignored. These authors reported that among college students, nonassertiveness was associated with negative self-evaluation processes rather than with skill deficits.

Type A Behavior Pattern

With the resurgence of interest in psychological factors and their role in disease, illness, and health, and with the appearance of recent evidence to document the important role of cognitive factors at all points along the health–disease continuum, cognitive–behavioral interventions emerge as a "good fit" within the behavioral-health/health-enhancement perspective (Bradley & Prokop, 1982; Kendall & Turk, in press; Matarazzo, 1980).

The Type A coronary-prone behavior pattern is characterized by intense ambition, continual preoccupation with occupational deadlines, a sense of time urgency, and competitive drive. Type A individuals are also said to perceive challenges where others do not. Several studies have examined psychological procedures for the modification of the Type A pattern (e.g., Jenni & Wollersheim, 1979; Roskies, Kearney, Spevack, Surkis, Cohen, & Gilman, 1979; Roskies, Spevack, Surkis, Cohen, & Gilman, 1978; Suinn & Bloom, 1978).

Thoresen, Friedman, Gill, and Ulmer (1982) reported some preliminary findings from their large-scale recurrent coronary prevention project. Their data offer encouragement to the cognitive-behavior therapist working with Type A clients. These researchers designed their project to answer two questions: (1) Can a behavior-change program reduce the recurrence rate of postcoronary subjects? and (2) Can the Type A behavior pattern be changed and does such a change correspond to reductions in coronary heart disease? Thoresen *et al.* (1982) studied 1035 subjects and conducted a comparison of a behavior-change program, a cardiologist program (with medications, diet, and exercise) and a routine-treatment control. Within the behavior-change program, a cognitive–behavioral strategy (cognitive social learning) was employed. The multifaceted intervention included self-control training, behavioral contracting, and cognitive as well as environmental restructuring. Within the cognitive area, perceptions, beliefs, and self-statements were targeted and specific intervention techniques were included. During the first year, group sessions with 8 to 10 subjects were held weekly and then twice monthly for 90 minutes each. After the first year, sessions were to be held monthly. The preliminary findings discussed here emerged after 1 year of treatment.

For those in the cognitive–behavioral group there was a significant reduction in the recurrence rate, compared to the other groups of subjects. Moreover, the data suggested that subjects in the behavior-change program had altered their Type A behavior pattern. These findings are of interest not only because of the degree of meaningful change achieved but also because of the authors' impression that cognitive factors, such as the personal meaning and individual beliefs associated with Type A behaviors, were of primary importance. The findings reported by Thoresen *et al.* (1982) were described as preliminary, leaving us to wait with anticipation for the appearance of further reports.

Test and Performance Anxiety

There is no doubt that the anxiety disorders and their successful remediation have played an important role in behavior therapy; accordingly, a separate chapter has been set aside to consider the advances and issues pertinent to their treatment. The present section does not pretend to supplant the coverage and discussion provided there. Rather, a few studies that deal specifically with the cognitive and cognitive–behavioral treatment of test and performance anxiety will be covered. Note that in a subsequent section additional anxiety disorders, the phobic disorders, are discussed briefly.

Debilitating test anxiety was the target of two recent treatment outcome comparisons (D'Alelio & Murray, 1981; McCordick, Kaplan, Smith, & Finn, 1981). D'Alelio and Murray examined the effects of different lengths of cognitive treatment for test anxiety by comparing a 4-week program to an 8-week program and to a waiting list control group. These authors employed a group format (7–10 clients) and followed the intervention described by Holroyd (1976). The test-anxious subjects were taught to "identify and challenge the distracting and irrational thoughts that are interfering with performance." Coping and attending self-statements replaced the maladaptive thoughts. Although the subjects were college students, cutoff scores of at least 55 on the Test Anxiety Inventory (Spielberger, Gonzales, Taylor, Algaze, & Anton, 1978) were required. Indices of change were based on a repeat administration of the self-report inventory, a test-taking (analogies) task, and grade-point average. Unfortunately, neither the task nor grade-point average showed any effect of treatment. However, in the subjects in the 8-week treatment condition self-reported anxiety was reduced beyond the change seen in those in the 4 week condition. The lackluster outcome may be the result of the absence of any skill-development program. That is, in addition to identifying and altering distracting thoughts clients may need to be taught more effective study skills (for study-skills training research see Kirschenbaum & Tomarken, 1982). Research by Bruch (1981) documented that math-anxious subjects lack both effective problem-solving strategies and tactics for working math problems, and research by McCordick *et al.* (1981) reported more positive changes and included both cognitive and behavioral training.

McCordick *et al.*'s (1981) study involved self-referred college students who were randomly assigned to one of five conditions: (1) insight-oriented counseling with desensitization, (2) individualized insight counseling and desensitization, (3) insight counseling with test-taking practice, (4) study-skills training only (all other treatments received this as well), and (5) waiting-list control. The individualized insight condition focused on thoughts of being pressured, since 83% of subjects indicated that these types of thoughts were most disconcerting. Self-report and performance outcomes provided interesting data. The insight-oriented counseling was successful, but it was meaningfully improved by making the insight-orientation individualized in the sense of a specific focus on pressured self-talk. Moreover, the authors stated that "a further augmentation results from replacing the desensitization component with situational practice" (p. 176). These conclusions are based mainly on self-reported changes, but they nevertheless contribute to the increasing number of reports evidencing the beneficial effects of combinations of cognitive and behavioral training programs.

Performance anxiety was studied by Kendrick, Craig, Lawson, and Davidson (1982). Subjects were pianists whose teachers referred them for extreme musical-performance anxiety. Although there have been several attempts to date to reduce the anxiety associated with musical performance, the authors' earlier research identified that high-anxious performers were more self-preoccupied and self-deprecating than lower-anxious performers and confirmed the need for further development of cognitively focused interventions.

The study was impressive in its assessments, for not only were there self-reports, behavioral measures, and physiological data, but one of the self-reports was a cognitive assessment—an efficacy measure. The treatment conditions that were compared to waiting-list controls were (1) cognitive–behavioral[4] and (2) behavioral rehearsal. The cognitive–behavioral intervention was well designed, with various components intended for the various facets of the debilitating anxiety. A close look at the intervention seems worthwhile. The pianists met in groups for three sessions, one per week, for 1½ to 2 hours each. First, negative and task-irrelevant thoughts were solicited from subjects. Next, a treatment rationale was presented and negative thoughts were challenged. Attending only to positive thoughts was recommended. A slide tape of a coping model was shown and discussed and home assignments (perform for family members) were given. In the second session the rationale was restated, two slide-tape cognitive-modeling sequences were shown, the therapist played a piece of music and verbalized thoughts aloud, and homework assignments were again given. The third session was similar but added the development of a list of positive self-statements, the cognitive modeling of a pianist in solo recital, subjects' performance of two pieces of music while thinking aloud, and imagery rehearsal. The comprehensiveness of this cognitive–behavioral intervention is perhaps matched only by its astute sequencing of the training tasks. The authors have an insightful grasp on the integration and sequencing of cognitive and behavioral training.

The comparison treatment was a carefully developed behavioral rehearsal condition that provided quality of treatment equal to that

---

4. The authors called this "attentional training" and "cognitively based training" in different portions of their report. My chosen description, cognitive–behavioral, seems quite appropriate.

described in the preceding paragraph. In the behavioral rehearsal condition, subjects received a treatment rationale and discussed performance anxiety. The merits of repeated rehearsal were emphasized. The therapist modeled performance and the atmosphere was intentionally positive and encouraging. Homework assignments were also part of this treatment program.

Compared to waiting-list controls, both the cognitive–behavioral training and the behavioral-rehearsal program reduced anxiety; at follow-up, both reduced visual signs of anxiety and improved quality of play. The cognitive–behavioral condition (attentional training) was superior in reducing visual signs of anxiety and enhancing expectations of personal efficacy. Neither treatment produced desired gains on self-reported anxiety.

Kendrick et al. (1982) provided additional data that are of interest. First, a posttreatment measure of self-efficacy correlated with reduced signs of anxiety and quality of play. Positive thinking (cognitive assessment) was related to reductions in visual signs of anxiety. A performance error count at posttreatment was not related to these gains. Thus, as the authors noted, "cognitive measures appeared to predict follow-up performance better than behavioral measures at treatment termination" (p. 359). Second, therapeutic gains were associated with reductions in negative thinking. These data add to a growing list of studies that support the power of nonnegative thinking (see also Chapter 2, this volume).

The literature on test and performance anxiety has provided some strong evidence that debilitating discomfort can be remedied. However, the relative superiority of one approach over another remains equivocal; cognitive modification plus behavioral rehearsal does seem to offer the most potent one-two punch. Interestingly, based on the Kendrick et al. data, both cognitively and behaviorally focused treatments had desired effects on cognition. Additional efforts to further elucidate the cognitive mechanisms of the change process are encouraged.

Phobic Disorders:
Caution and Research Needed

The recent literature on the treatment of the anxiety disorders is reviewed in Chapter 3; therefore, this commentary is not intended to be exhaustive. However, because of the relevance of recent outcomes concerning the effects of cognitive restructuring on phobic disordered individuals, some mention seems necessary here.

To put the cart before the horse, cognitive restructuring techniques have not been found to be more effective than exposure for the treatment of phobias. Now let us look at some of the evidence. Two reports (Biran, Augusto, & Wilson, 1981; Biran & Wilson, 1981) that compared exposure and cognitive structuring in actual clinical cases produced fairly consistent cautions. In the Biran *et al.* (1981) report, two female clients suffering from scriptophobia (a long-standing phobic avoidance of any situation involving writing in public) received five 90-minute sessions of cognitive restructuring (combining elements of A. Ellis, 1970, and Goldfried, 1979), followed by five 90-minute sessions of *in vivo* exposure (performing a series of behavioral tasks). A third client received only the *in vivo* exposure. The results indicated that repeated assessments did not enhance approach behavior, nor did the cognitive restructuring treatment. In contrast, *in vivo* exposure produced improvement within the five sessions. In the Biran and Wilson (1981) report, clients with simple phobias (e.g., heights, elevators, darkness) were found to show significantly greater improvement in approach behavior, self-efficacy, subjective fear, and physiological reactivity when treated with exposure than with cognitive restructuring.

Since these studies are some of the first to employ cognitive restructuring with a clinical population, the less-than-encouraging outcomes may serve either to dampen enthusiasm or to stimulate further research. I hope for the later. But if the former reaction dominates it should be tempered by a few considerations. First, as the authors noted, the cognitive restructuring condition did not include a behavioral component. If further research is to be done, then it would appear promising to examine the single and combined effects of cognitive and behavioral training. For example, recent data reported by Emmelkamp and Mersch (1982) indicated that for agoraphobics an exposure condition and a combined exposure plus self-instructional training was significantly superior to cognitive restructuring. Nevertheless, there are many facts not yet known about exposure treatment (Barlow, 1981b): Why does it work? What are the basic cognitive and behavioral processes that lead to successful treatment by exposure-based procedures? What role do cognitive changes play in this process? (p. 229).

Second, as Biran *et al.* (1981) suggested, it may have been that "the cognitive restructuring treatment was too brief or too focused on the fear of writing rather than broader social anxieties" (p. 531). Caveats aside, it may be that cognitive restructuring procedures are appropriate for social or interpersonal anxieties but less so for focal phobic anxieties. If we hold true to the quest to uncover the proper match of type of treatment with type of client disorder, then we are encouraged, not discouraged, by more prescriptive recommendations.

ADDITIONAL TOPICS BRIEFLY NOTED

My intention has been to provide some organization for this review by addressing issues within somewhat arbitrary general headings. This effort may be laudable for its organization and comforting to the compulsive types, but there are many strands that have not been woven into our fabric. This is not to imply that individual reports are outside the mainstream of research or less important to the field. Rather, these articles may represent the leading edges of the application of cognitive–behavioral strategies. Garner and Bemis (1982), for example, develop a cognitive–behavioral analysis of and treatment rationale for anorexia and Bowers (1982) proposed that individual differences in hypnotic ability may account for some of the differential outcomes of cognitive–behavioral therapies. Two articles began to examine child abuse (Ambrose, Hazzard, & Haworth, 1980; Wolfe, Sandler, & Kaufman, 1981), with arguments for changing parenting skills and parental attitudes and expectations put forth as necessary cognitive–behavioral treatment components (Ambrose et al., 1980). The treatment of problems associated with recurrent headaches has been reviewed (Holroyd & Andrasik, 1982) and some encouraging data have been reported (e.g., Bakal, Demjen, & Kaganov, 1982). Bakal et al., for instance, used relaxation, self-observation of headaches, and coping-skills training and reported a significant treatment effect in terms of self-reported headaches, headache intensity, and medication use. Hitchcock (1982) also reported on the effectiveness of a coping-skills training intervention for patients undergoing stressful medical procedures. Chronic hair pulling (Bernard, Kratochwill, & Keefauver, 1983) and adolescent unwanted pregnancy (Schinke, Blythe, & Gilchrist, 1981) have also been successfully treated with cognitive–behavioral approaches. A series of studies by Kirschenbaum and his colleagues (Kirschenbaum, Humphrey, & Malett, 1981; Kirschenbaum, Malett, Humphrey, & Tomarken, 1982; Kirschenbaum, Tomarken, & Ordman, 1982; see also review in Kirschenbaum & Tomarken, 1982) have examined study skills. Within this framework, the research has addressed the role of such cognitive factors as plans, different types of plans, and choice on the process of self-control.

CHAPTER

5

BEHAVIORAL MEDICINE

KELLY D. BROWNELL

INTRODUCTION

In a recent commentary on behavioral medicine, Stewart Agras (1982) noted that the field became so popular so quickly because it "was an idea exactly appropriate to the time" (p. 797). This favorable climate exists in both clinical and research settings and has given a field still in its infancy a strong impetus to expand. Last year's *Annual Review* chronicled the major signs of this growing interest. Among these were the publication of journals devoted to behavioral medicine (*Journal of Behavioral Medicine, Behavioral Medicine Abstracts*), publication of numerous texts on the topic, formation of several thriving professional organizations, and the existence of a special Behavioral Medicine Branch within the National Institutes of Health.

The interest is still growing. It is unusual for a field to develop so rapidly that a wealth of new developments takes place from year to year, but such is the case with behavioral medicine. Division 38 of the American Psychological Association has now published the first volume of *Health Psychology*, a peer-reviewed journal for scholarly articles from psychology and the other disciplines associated with behavioral medicine. Health and prevention form one of three major topics for the 1983 convention of the American Psychological Association. The annual meeting of the Society of Behavioral Medicine is flourishing. In December of 1982, the *Journal of Consulting and Clinical Psychology* devoted an entire issue to the topic of behavioral medicine. The Behavioral Medicine Study Section of the National Institutes of Health reviews a great many grant proposals. These are only a few of the signs.

One might speculate that the enthusiasm surrounding behavioral medicine will pass and that the field will lose the same war of attrition that plagues most new movements. For one basic reason, this is not likely to occur. This reason is that the field is becoming institutionalized. The formation of the Behavioral Medicine Branch within NIH, along with repeated calls for increased expenditures for prevention (Breslow, 1979; Hamburg, 1982), have signaled the availability of research and training support in behavioral medicine. With the dramatic cutbacks in federal research and training support, it is not surprising that professionals are flooding into a field that has such great financial promise. Universities, spurred on by student interest, are quick to sieze upon this opportunity. The newsletter of the American Psychological Association (the *Monitor*) now advertises positions for faculty appointments in behavioral medicine and health psychology. This combination of federal and private funding, faculty specialization in behavioral medicine, and tremendous interest among students guarantees a long life for the field. The challenge is not to predict the expansion of the field, but to determine the shape the field will take as it experiences growth.

THE FIELD: EMERGING OR ESTABLISHED?

To understand the future of behavioral medicine, it is useful to examine the history of its development. The fact that this development has occurred so rapidly has given the field a unique character. The character has its positive elements, namely the enormous potential for changes in important human problems. The negative elements involve a need for identity, which is evident in the debate over definitions and terms and in the need for frequent position statements from the leaders in the field. For example, the special behavioral medicine issue of the *Journal of Consulting and Clinical Psychology* (1982, Vol. 5, No. 6) contained 15 articles on specific topics such as hypertension, smoking, Type A behaviors, exercise, and diabetes. Accompanying these articles were four position papers on general issues in the field (Agras, 1982; Blanchard, 1982; Pomerleau, 1982; G. E. Schwartz, 1982). If the field were better developed and more clearly defined, there would not be the need for as many statements of a general nature.

Many of the noteworthy statements in the field of behavioral medicine have included a discussion of its past (Agras, 1982; Blanchard, 1982; Ferguson & Taylor, 1980; Matarazzo, 1980; Melamed & Siegel, 1980; Pomerleau, 1982; Pomerleau, Bass, & Crown, 1975; G. E. Schwartz, 1982). If we examine the various perspectives on the field's development, we may be able to formulate a more precise view of the future.

Blanchard (1982) traced the origins of behavioral medicine to the confluence of three trends that emerged in the early 1970s. The first emerged when reliable procedures were developed to modify overt behavior. The major advances in this regard came from the fields of behavior therapy and applied behavior analysis. The second trend was the birth of biofeedback, a series of procedures that showed that physiological responses could be altered in a reliable fashion. The third trend was the recognition that overt behaviors (personal habits) were important determinants of physiological processes and were therefore implicated in the development of disease.

Agras (1982) has a similar view of the development of behavioral medicine. He notes that the field was a product of several factors: (1) the existence of basic biobehavioral research from the field of psychosomatic medicine, (2) the utility of procedures from behavior therapy and applied behavior analysis, (3) the isolation of risk factors from epidemiology, and (4) the growing interest in prevention.

The views of both Blanchard (1982) and Agras (1982) highlight the interdisciplinary nature of the field. Relating overt behaviors to disease falls in the domain of epidemiology. Understanding the pathogenesis of disease requires a background in medicine and physiology. The technology for understanding, assessing, and modifying behavior has come from behavioral psychology. The implications of proposing and encouraging these changes have been elucidated by specialists in public health. These are but a few of the disciplines involved in behavioral medicine.

The task of identifying and integrating the efforts of professionals in so many disciplines is nothing short of enormous. Differences in training, prestige, accepted roles, and perspectives among the disciplines present formidable obstacles to interaction. Herein lie both the promise and the challenge of the field. Agras (1982) points to this interaction as the key to the survival of behavioral medicine:

> One way to conceptualize the development of behavioral medicine is to regard it as representing an emerging network of communication among an array of disciplines not previously well connected. These disciplines include the behavioral and social sciences and the biomedical sciences and medical specialties. This network is still developing as researchers and clinicians in this active phase of the field's development find relevant work and activities in diverse places. One crucial aspect is the emerging pathway from basic research to clinical application. This is the major strength of the field. (p. 797)

Behavioral medicine will become an established field when the communication pathways between disciplines are operating effectively. Only a small part of this potential has been realized, yet very rapid progress is being made. Two discussion articles in *Science* highlight this progress. In 1980, *Science* carried an article entitled "Behavioral Medicine: An Emergent Field" (Holden, 1980). The article presented behavioral medicine quite clearly as a field struggling for meaning:

> Behavioral medicine is a term that is yet unfamiliar to most people, including many who practice medicine. To some it connotes preoccupation with physical fitness and stopping smoking. To others it is indistinguishable from psychosomatic medicine.
>
> Behavioral medicine is an emerging field which treats mind and body as two ends of the same continuum. The core of basic research in this field is an attempt to locate the specific neurochemical mechanisms by which subjective states—specifically those associated with emotional stress—lead to disease. Ultimately, it is an approach to disease and health that spans everything from research through etiology, diagnosis, treatment, rehabilitation, and prevention. (p. 479)

Two years later *Science* published an editorial by David Hamburg (1982), former president of the Academy of Behavioral Medicine Research and former president of the Institute of Medicine, that discussed the field of behavioral medicine in terms that imply both a strong identity and a powerful repertoire of interventions. He points to a report from the Institute of Medicine (1982) to call for more support for research in behavioral medicine:

> Nowhere are the needs and opportunities for progress in the biobehavioral sciences clearer than in the problems of health and behavior. These matters are documented in a new report from the Institute of Medicine, National Academy of Sciences. Behavioral factors contribute to much of our burden of illness. Half of the mortality from the ten leading causes of death in the United States is strongly influenced by lifestyle. Known behavioral risk factors include cigarette smoking, excessive consumption of alcoholic beverages, use of illicit drugs, certain dietary habits, insufficient exercise, reckless driving, nonadherence to medication regimens, and maladaptive responses to social pressures. (Hamburg, 1982, p. 399).

Hamburg (1982) has presented the problem: Personal behavior is extremely important in the disease process, but altering behavior in the population requires a powerful and concerted effort. The identification of these personal behaviors (risk factors) is one of the factors that led to the birth of the field of behavioral medicine (Agras, 1982; Blanchard, 1982). Hamburg (1982) then goes a step further and states that the technology is now available to modify these risk factors:

> Another opportunity arises from research on learning, a major thrust of psychology since its inception as a science. In recent years, a theory has emerged that clarifies the social context of human learning, is a balanced synthesis of cognitive psychology and behavior modification, and draws

on experimentally verified principles of learning. Such principles are now being used in clinical and field experiments that test ways of changing behavior that affects health. During the past 30 years, epidemiologic studies have delineated objective measures as indicators of the likelihood of developing coronary heart disease and stroke—that is, risk factors such as high blood pressure, tobacco smoking, and obesity. Several large-scale studies have found that many people can diminish their health-damaging behavior and thereby decrease the likelihood that they will develop serious cardiovascular disease. (p. 399)

The field is in need of just such endorsement. The lack of cohesive research support in the field leads to splintered efforts and perpetuates the problems in communication among the disciplines. Hamburg goes on in favor of increased funding:

> The present low level of funding of such research deserves careful reexamination. Broadening of the life sciences in the context of health and behavior can have a profound impact in the remainder of the century. (p. 399)

The key to this movement may well be efforts to synthesize the work of many investigators in many disciplines. The Behavioral Medicine Branch of the National Institutes of Health is a step in this direction. Figure 5-1, taken from Weiss's (1982) Presidential address to

FIG. 5-1.

Areas of research, training, and treatment funded by the Behavioral Medicine Branch of the National Heart, Lung, and Blood Institute, National Institutes of Health. These areas highlight the multidisciplinary effort that will be required for the field of behavioral medicine to advance. (From "Health Psychology: The Time Is Now" by S. M. Weiss, *Health Psychology*, 1982, *1*, 81–91. Copyright 1982, Lawrence Erlbaum Associates, Inc. Reprinted by permission.)

Etiology/Mechanisms
- Psychophysiologic studies of basic relationships between the nervous system and end organs directly or indirectly related to a given disease.
- Studies of mediating mechanisms between psychosocial factors and disease.
- Studies of behavioral factors associated with the pathogenesis of disease.

Prevention
- Psychosocial studies involving the identification and modification of specific risk factors.
- Studies of the modifications and maintenance of health enhancing behavior.

Treatment
- Studies of coping strategies related to chronic illness and pain.
- Behavioral approaches to the treatment of many diseases.
- Studies concerning compliance with medical regimens.

Rehabilitation
- Investigations on psychosocial sequelae of illness.
- Studies of the psychosocial factors involved in rehabilitation.

Division 38 of the American Psychological Association, shows the types of research funded by the Behavioral Medicine Branch. This work will involve many investigators in many disciplines and should help open new lines of communication (Weiss, 1982).

This section began with the question of whether the field of behavioral medicine is emerging or is established. I agree with Agras (1982) that the field must rely on communication between the disciplines, and that in this regard the field is still emerging. However, more and more people in the field are sensitive to this issue, and movement is in the right direction. This movement can only be sustained if the leaders in the field continue to insist on interdisciplinary efforts. Otherwise, the field will follow the tendency that Agras (1982) notes to become more narrow over time:

> Given these previous failures to affect the practice of medicine and the delivery of health care, why should the fate of behavioral medicine be different? One reason for optimism is that the focus of this field is broader than that of previous behavioral science applications to medicine— encompassing the entire spectrum of the etiology, treatment, management, and prevention of disease rather than focusing solely upon understanding the psychological processes leading to specific conditions. These more diverse interests have both emerged from and contributed to the formation of new linkages between the basic and applied sciences. Clearly these links must be strengthened both by increasing contact between scientists working in different areas and by developing more efficient ways to transfer information between them. Here the new societies and journals will help, but only if this aspect of their function is actively fostered. Unfortunately, societies and journals tend to narrow their focus over time. It is not clear how this can be avoided, since one of the factors promoting narrowness is the specialization necessary for the conduct of research and the acquisition of new knowledge. However, we should recognize that the dissociation of basic and applied research will be fatal to the development of behavioral medicine. (p. 799)

Potential Dangers

OVERSTEPPING OUR BOUNDARIES

In last year's *Annual Review*, I noted a trend for investigators and even students to claim some expertise in a subarea of behavioral medicine, say "behavioral pediatrics," "behavioral cardiology," "behavioral epidemiology," or even "behavioral gynecology." This disturbing trend has continued. The professionals using these terms are not from the fields of pediatrics, cardiology, epidemiology, gynecology, and so forth. They are generally from psychology or psychiatry and are risking disenfranchisement by their medical colleagues by bestowing upon themselves labels which imply more than can be delivered. I recommend more cautious use of these terms.

There has been and will continue to be a demand for experts in behavioral medicine to provide services that might potentially influence vast numbers of people. The most immediate applications lie in programs at the work site and opportunities with the media.

Work sites, as discussed in last year's *Annual Review*, provide great potential for research and for testing public health theories about health promotion and disease prevention. Leaders in business and industry find health programs for their employees enticing because of the lure of improved morale, increased productivity, reduced absenteeism, decreased health insurance utilization, and so forth. Interestingly, many business leaders who ordinarily would demand proof that programs will justify their costs, are willing to implement health programs in the hope that benefits will occur. As a result, business is seeking the consultation of professionals in behavioral medicine to develop programs.

Even greater potential may exist with the media. Newspapers and magazines continually seek advice from experts in all areas of behavioral medicine. With the advent of cable television and the development of networks devoted solely to health, the electronic media will need expert advice on a wide variety of topics.

There is great temptation to become involved in these activities. The personal and professional rewards can be appealing. Professionally, activities of this sort can offer research possibilities and can permit the professional to design programs that will affect large numbers of people. The personal rewards include consultation fees and the gratification of designing programs, wide public exposure, and being considered an expert.

These opportunities and rewards present a real problem. Consider the case of a company that asks a health professional to design an exercise program for employees to follow over the long term that will reduce risk for cardiovascular disease. The literature suggests that these aims are rarely achieved—50% of people drop out of exercise programs and reduction in risk factors cannot always be demonstrated (Brownell & Stunkard, 1980a; Martin & Dubbert, 1982; Thompson, Jarvie, Lahey, & Cureton, 1982).

The professional who devises such a program would exceed the boundaries imposed by the data. Several leaders in the field of behavioral medicine have cautioned against this practice. Neal E. Miller (1979) issued a warning in a position statement on the field:

The increasing interest in Behavioral Medicine opens up significant opportunities for research and applications. But there is a danger that overoptimistic claims or widespread applications without a scientific base and sufficient evaluation by pilot testing can lead to failure and disillusionment. Such disillusionment could block the promising developments in this new area for another generation. (p. 5)

Stewart Agras (1982) echoes Miller's sentiment:

Too widespread an application before sufficient research has been done might lead to premature disillusionment with this young field. Moreover, such a development might lead to the widespread application of procedures that are not based on research findings. (p. 802)

Both Agras and Miller use the word "disillusionment" to describe the potential danger of overstepping our data base. The danger here is that the field will promise more than it can deliver. When the time for accountability arrives and the results do not live up to the advance billing, the positive aspects of behavioral medicine may fall victim to the generalizations based on disappointing programs.

This is not a simple issue, and the solution to the problem is not as straightforward as vowing to remain true to the data. Taking the stance that data are needed before a program can be devised raises questions about how much proof is needed and about the different types of proof required for different audiences (scientists, business leaders, media professionals, etc.). If responsible researchers decline invitations to participate in these activities, the void may be filled by irresponsible people. In the case mentioned earlier of a corporation requesting an exercise program, the result of a responsible professional stating that the data do not justify establishing a program would probably be the enlistment of another "expert" to set up a program. The question, then, may reduce to the option of designing an admittedly imperfect program or yielding to someone who may design a program of lower quality.

Unfortunately, there are no guidelines for the solution of this problem. It is clear that professionals should advise consumers about the limitations of the programs they design. Beyond this, I can only suggest that professionals in behavioral medicine remain sensitive to these issues.

A FOCUS TOO NARROW

It is the nature of current scientific and clinical practice for professionals to become specialized. The professional rewards encourage such behavior, and with the overwhelming amount of information available, it is not surprising that professionals find it difficult to keep abreast of the developments in even one field. An example might be a psychologist interested in the use of biofeedback or relaxation for hypertension. For this person to be an expert in just the area of hypertension, he or she would have to follow the medical and pharmacological literatures to learn about pharmacological treatments, to understand the complex physiology of the disorder, and to appreciate the contribution of psychological and environmental determinants of blood pressure. This is no easy task, and this is just the beginning! Consider the importance of epidemiology in establishing the relationship of behaviors to hypertension, of public health in evaluating the cost effectiveness of large-scale screening and monitoring efforts, and of genetics in understanding the role of family history.

There are many advantages to specialization, not the least of which are the rapid advances in research and treatment brought about by workers devoted to a single issue. However, specialization brings unique hazards to a field such as behavioral medicine, which relies on the interaction of people in many disciplines. Agras (1982) sees a split between basic and applied researchers as a likely product of specialization. Such a split would divide the field into many small groups and would rule out any possibility of workers in the field moving as a cohesive unit.

G. E. Schwartz (1980, 1982) has confronted this issue of a broad or narrow focus and comes down clearly on the side of the broad perspective. He has proposed a "biopsychosocial model" for approaching the diagnosis, treatment, and prevention of disease. The model evokes systems theory (J. G. Miller, 1978) to propose that the interaction among factors is the key to understanding health and behavior:

> There are many questions implicit in the biopsychosocial approach to health and illness that are fundamental to systems theory and that need to be investigated empirically. First, the biopsychosocial model proposes that medical diagnosis should *always* consider the interaction of biological, psychological, and social factors in order to assess a person's health and to make recommendations for treatment. The assumption is made that the more information that is collected and the better the information is organized, the better will be the diagnosis. (Schwartz, 1982, p. 1047)

To approach a problem in this way is a challenge, because so much information must be collected and synthesized. There is even greater challenge in designing treatments, but the benefits may be impressive:

The second major prediction of the biopsychosocial model is that *treatments will interact* with each other as well as with the person and his or her environment. Theoretically, by assessing people biopsychosocially, it should be possible to (a) tailor therapies to the individual more effectively, (b) consider diseases not in isolation, but in interaction, and therefore make recommendations that may apply to two or more problems simultaneously, and (c) look for treatment interactions across modalities, that could have additive and possibly synergistic effects. (Schwartz, 1982, p. 1047; emphasis in original)

In the inaugural issue of *Health Psychology*, Stone (1982) viewed the topic of health in much the same multicontextual way as Schwartz (1982) proposes. Stone portrayed his point visually, as shown in Figure 5-2. Stone feels we should "define the health system broadly and direct our attention not only to the individual whose health is at issue, but to the whole complex of institutions and forces within which the pursuit of health takes place" (p. 2).

There is a consensus among people in behavioral medicine that a multidisciplinary effort is required for the field to advance. This necessitates an expanded view of the individual and the role his or her health plays in the broad picture of culture, biology, behavior, and history. Few dispute this notion, but how to accomplish this aim is another matter. As mentioned previously, journals, professional societies, and federal agencies can encourage such activities. However, the issue raises the much more basic question of the quality of professional training. Division 38 of the American Psychological Association has commissioned a group to study models of training for professionals interested in behavioral medicine. Many telling questions await this group.

Currently, people in "behavioral medicine" are trained in the traditional disciplines of medicine, psychology, and so forth. The focus in training, therefore, is not on behavioral medicine per se, but on the study of a discipline. This cannot provide a person with the multidisciplinary background that is needed, but it may at least give a person solid training in at least one area. This raises the age-old issues of what and how much can be incorporated into training and whether basic knowledge in one discipline must precede work on a specific problem.

The next few years will be interesting because these issues of broad training versus specialization and of training within a traditional discipline versus special training in behavioral medicine will be addressed in many ways by many people. The issues are fundamental to the nature of the field and may well determine the character of behavioral medicine and related areas in the years to come.

THE HEALTH SYSTEM

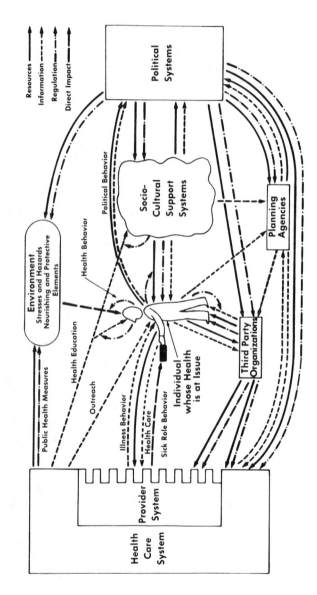

FIG. 5-2.

Some factors and their many interactions which influence the health behaviors of an individual. This conveys the importance of a broad perspective and active communication between disciplines in the effort to promote health and prevent disease. (From *"Health Psychology: A New Journal for a New Field"* by G. C. Stone, *Health Psychology*, 1982, *1*, 1–6. Copyright 1982, Lawrence Erlbaum Associates, Inc. Reprinted by permission.)

THE MANAGEMENT OF CHRONIC PAIN

The management of the patient with chronic pain represents some of the most exciting developments in the field of behavioral medicine. Pain is widely acknowledged to have physical and psychological components, and most researchers now agree that environmental and social factors make a major contribution to the pain experience. Therefore, researchers from many disciplines have been interested in the pain process. As a result, many treatments have been tried, some with limited success and others that appear to exacerbate the problem. These treatments include hypnosis, acupuncture, pharmacotherapy, surgery, biofeedback, and a number of others.

The area of chronic pain is important to the field of behavioral medicine for several reasons. First, the problem afflicts many people and it brings untold distress to its sufferers. Therefore, the problem is socially relevant. Second, it is unlikely that the solution will come from any one discipline or that a treatment based on any one theoretical orientation will help the majority of patients. This provides a challenge for the interdisciplinary model of behavioral medicine now in favor and highlights the importance of communication between professionals with different backgrounds. Third, the pain experience has been studied for many years, most recently in the fields of psychosomatic medicine and behavioral medicine. Tracing the developments in this area gives a picture of how the field of behavioral medicine has matured.

The Scope of the Problem

Chronic pain is defined as pain that endures beyond the normal course of healing for a disease or pain that is associated with a progressive disease, such as arthritis (Turner & Chapman, 1982a). Estimates are that 86 million Americans suffer from some type of chronic pain (Bonica, 1980). The costs of this suffering, independent of the psychological trauma to the patients and others, have been estimated at $60 billion annually; this includes surgery, medication, hospitalization, outpatient treatment, loss of income, loss of work productivity, disability payments, and litigation settlements (Bonica, 1980; Turner & Chapman, 1982a). Bonica (1980) estimates that 35 million Americans suffer from chronic recurrent headaches, 18 million from chronic back disorders, 1 million from cancer pain, and millions more from other chronic pain conditions such as peripheral neuropathies, abdominal pain, temporomandibular joint pain, and pain of central origin.

Chronic pain is one of the most troubling conditions facing medical professionals (Keefe, 1982). It ranks among the leading problems in terms of number office visits and hospitalizations, and amount of disability payments (Nagi, Riley, & Newby, 1973). Patients may appear for treatment after having ten or more surgeries (Black, 1975), so the number of options left to the concerned physician is limited. Chronic pain is a frustrating problem for all involved.

A Clinical Picture of the Pain Patient

By the time most pain patients find their way to a specialty clinic, they tend to have followed a reliable course. The course contains a number of stages, each characterized by particular experiences and behaviors. The end product of these stages is a patient who has had numerous surgeries, may rely on or be addicted to several medications, and is partially or totally disabled (Black, 1975; Keefe, 1982; Turner & Chapman, 1982a). This patient presents a most complex picture that includes psychological, environmental, and physical factors that maintain the condition. To understand the severity of this state, it is helpful to examine the stages leading to the final result (Fordyce, 1976; Keefe, 1982).

Keefe and his colleagues have described the detailed learning history that accompanies the development of chronic pain (Keefe, 1982; Keefe & Brown, 1982; Keefe, Brown, Scott, & Ziesat, 1982). They propose three stages in which the patient progresses from an acute stage, to a prechronic stage, to the chronic stage. The description of the stages that follows is adapted from Keefe (1982).

THE ACUTE STAGE

The early stages of the pain experience are characterized by behaviors that can be considered adaptive: decreased activity and increased use of medication. These, along with muscle spasms, serve to immobilize joints, which prevents further injury. It is common for patients at this stage to be highly motivated to seek treatment and to follow treatment instructions. The length of this stage depends on the nature of the injury or disease and is influenced by a host of psychological and environmental factors. Keefe (1982) notes that healing generally begins to take place 2 to 6 months postinjury, so those patients who continue to experience severe pain after that time are considered to be in the "prechronic" stage.

Keefe (1982) feels that the prechronic stage is the crucial time during which a patient rejects or adopts the behaviors that make the condition chronic. Patients generally attempt to resume their premorbid life style. Some patients will resume normal activities gradually and will remain pain free. Others will be unable or unwilling to resume activity and become a great risk for long-term disability. These patients may attempt to resume their activities abruptly and may experience further pain. They may then resort to behaviors such as bed rest or use of medications. Repeated episodes of this pattern serve to strengthen the pain behaviors, and patients may develop more maladaptive responses:

> Patients may become cautious and guarded in their movements—patterns that lead to a shortening of muscles, increased muscle spasm, and fatigue. Patients may also become convinced that there is little they can do to control pain and may become prone to cognitive distortions—factors that may serve to increase depression. As pain behavior patterns recur, the likelihood that they will lead to positive social consequences is also increased. (Keefe, 1982, p. 906)

It is at this point that social factors become prominent. The family or friends may assume responsibility for activities usually carried out by the patient. These significant others are rightfully concerned about the patient and are likely to become solicitous. At this point, many patients enter the chronic stage.

Many important changes occur as a patient becomes chronically afflicted by pain. Turner and Chapman (1982a) note that "the process of chronicity alters the patient both psychologically and physiologically so that there are complex changes in affect, thought processes, and behavioral patterns that contribute to making painful disorders self-perpetuating" (p. 16).

The chronic stage may become firmly established 6 months or more after the injury, although there is great variability among patients (Keefe, 1982). At this point, underlying tissue damage is absent, minimal, or cannot be detected. The social and environmental reinforcement for being disabled can be powerful. This reinforcement includes attention from the family, avoidance of unwanted work or social activities, and financial compensation. The longer the condition persists, the longer the period of time the patient has to learn maladaptive behaviors.

These stages have been proposed based on clinical experience. A systematic evaluation of the changes in the pain patient and those in his or her environment has never been undertaken. Such an analysis would be difficult, time consuming, and costly, yet it might provide extremely important information about the progression of the chronic-pain syndrome. Keefe (1982) has called for a detailed study of how these changes occur over time by examining patients at increased risk for pain problems. Research of this nature might provide some insight into the important area of prevention.

Assessment

Assessment is important in the treatment of any disorder, but it is particularly central to the area of chronic pain (Follick, Zitter, & Kulich, in press; Keefe, 1982; Sanders, 1979). The complexity of the problem, its detailed development, and the variety of possible maintaining factors must be considered in designing a treatment program. Follick et al. (in press) have noted that pain behavior is the final common pathway for biological, psychological, and environmental variables, so the task of assessment is to determine the relative contribution of these factors.

Keefe (1982) proposes a three-pronged approach to assessment. The three broad categories he proposes are (1) overt motor behaviors, (2) cognitive–verbal behaviors, and (3) physiological factors. A summary of the developments in these three areas is presented here, followed by an assessment scheme for a chronic pain program.

Fordyce deserves credit for calling attention to overt behaviors in the management of chronic pain (Fordyce, 1976; Fordyce, Fowler, Lehmann, DeLateur, Sand, & Treischmann, 1973). He proposed that pain behaviors such as medication intake and time spent in bed should be considered, as should "well" behaviors such as activity, work, or exercise. The method first used to evaluate these behaviors, the behavioral interview (Fordyce, 1976), is still in use today (Follick et al., in press; Keefe, 1982; Sanders, 1979).

A daily activity diary is also used to evaluate overt behavior (Fordyce, 1976). Such a diary might involve a form on which a patient records medication intake and physical activities (usually grouped into the categories of walking/standing, sitting, or reclining). The diaries can be expanded to include associated environmental events, feelings, and so forth. Keefe (1982) notes that the information the diaries provide can be a useful indicator of the direction treatment might take. For instance, patients who spend the majority of their time reclining or sitting may have low levels of strength and endurance and may need physical rehabilitation. Patients whose medications are spaced evenly throughout the day and night may be addicted and may require drug rehabilitation. Recent studies have shown that these self-reports may not be reliable in some cases (Sanders, 1980a) and that patients receiving financial compensation for their disability are most likely to under-report activity (Kremer, Block, & Gaylor, 1981).

Several recent developments in the measurement of overt behavior add a new dimension to the assessment of the patient with chronic pain. These are methods of objectively evaluating physical movements (Keefe, 1982). One such method is an "uptime" clock developed by Cairns, Thomas, Mooney, and Pace (1975). This clock is a device mounted over the patient's bed that records the amount of time spent out of bed. Sanders (1980b) describes a device, a modified electronic calculator worn on the wrist, that records the time spent standing or walking.

Direct observation methods are also being perfected. Kremer *et al.* (1981) developed an observational system for use in inpatient settings. The system evaluates social contact and the physical position of the patient. Interestingly, Kremer *et al.* (1981) reported that the observational code reflected increases in activity and social contact as patients progressed through a treatment program, but the patient's self-reports did not always reflect this improvement.

Keefe and Block (1982) reported four studies on the development and use of a direct observation method for assessing overt behaviors in low-back-pain patients. The method involved the measurement of guarded movement, bracing, rubbing, grimacing, and sighing. Study 1 found that the behaviors could be observed reliably and that the frequency of the behaviors was correlated with the patients' self-report of pain intensity. Study 2 found that the frequency of the pain behaviors decreased during treatment. Study 3 found that the observed behaviors were correlated with naive observers' ratings of the patients' pain. The final study found that the observational system distinguished pain patients from pain-free depressed controls.

The assessment of cognitive and verbal behaviors in the pain patient is also important because of the subjective nature of the pain experience (Keefe, 1982). A number of questionnaire devices have been used to evaluate these factors. The most commonly used device is the McGill Pain Questionnaire (Melzack & Torgerson, 1971). This questionnaire contains a series of adjective pain descriptors that are used to classify pain into three dimensions: sensory, affective, and evaluative. The McGill questionnaire has been used extensively in clinical pain research, but it provides only qualitative accounts of pain (Keefe, 1982).

Several additional questionnaires have been developed to evaluate cognitive factors. Tursky has developed the Pain Perception Profile, which measures sensation threshold, magnitude estimation, psychophysical scaling of pain descriptors, and the relationship of specific behaviors to the descriptors (Tursky, 1976; Tursky, Jamner, & Friedman, 1982). The initial reports on the use of this scale are promising. Another scale, reported by Lefebvre (1981), involves two questionnaires that consist of vignettes reflecting cognitive errors. The questionnaires are reliable and have concurrent and discriminant validity (Lefebvre, 1981). Finally, the MMPI has been used with pain patients (Bradley, Prokop, Margolis, & Gentry, 1978).

The assessment of cognitive factors in pain patients has only been developed in the past few years, so much research is needed in the area. Preliminary results are promising and some of the recent measures (e.g., Tursky et al., 1982) promise to introduce more objectivity. Since cognitive–behavioral interventions are an important component of many treatment programs, assessment of these factors is crucial.

Physiological responses form another important category to consider for the assessment of chronic pain (Bonica, 1977; Keefe, 1982). Both autonomic and muscular responses have been measured. A summary of these studies can be found in the article by Keefe (1982). One of the more interesting developments in this area has been the assessment of patterns of physiological responses under different conditions (Wolf, Nacht, & Kelly, 1982).

TREATMENT IMPLICATIONS

The information described above involves methods for assessing particular aspects of chronic pain. Once these methods have been established, the information must be organized in a coherent way in order to formulate a treatment plan. This is the arena in which clinical insight and scientific knowledge must be combined. Few authors have ventured into this subjective area. Fordyce (1976) proposed some guidelines for developing a treatment plan. Brenna and Koch (1975) developed a classification scheme with two dimensions based on material derived from assessment. The two dimensions are tissue pathology (summed results of physical, neurological, radiographic, and laboratory studies) and pain behavior (activity level, medication usage, and scores on the MMPI and a semantic inventory). Using this system, patients who score high on tissue pathology and high on pain behavior are candidates for surgery, while patients who score low on tissue pathology and high on pain behavior and candidates for a behavioral program.

More recently, Follick et al. (in press) have developed clinical guidelines based on specific assessment methods for determining the course of treatment to be followed for pain patients. Their program is one in which the assessment actually dictates whether a patient enters the program and the degree to which specific program components are emphasized.

The specific measures used in the program described by Follick *et al.* (in press) include a complete physical and neurological exam and a detailed interview with a psychologist. Also included are videotape ratings of the patient's functional limitations (limping, inability to climb stairs, etc.), a daily activity diary, family and marital inventories, the MMPI, a health care utilization inventory, and other psychological inventories as needed.

From these methods of assessment, Follick *et al.* (in press) formulate criteria for inclusion into the program. The inclusion criteria are:

1. The patient's physician must feel that further medical or surgical intervention would not be helpful. If the medical or surgical approaches offer a slight possibility of relief, both patient and physician must agree that a behavioral program aimed at functional improvement is the preferred approach.
2. The physician must indicate that the patient is capable of extensive physical exercise and that there are no medical barriers to restoration or normal physical functioning.
3. The patient must exhibit observable and measurable pain behaviors (pain, grimacing, limping, etc.), which must have environmental consequences that are potentially modifiable.
4. The patient's pain must interfere with life and must prevent him or her from engaging in important physical activities (work, driving a car, etc.).
5. The patient must be able to identify specific goals that are observable and measurable and that are achievable within the time constraints of the program.
6. The patient must be motivated to participate in the program and must indicate explicitly that he or she is willing to learn to live with pain.
7. The family members must be willing to change their behaviors and to help the patient learn to change his or her behaviors.

There are three factors for the exclusion of patients from consideration for the program:

1. The patient should have no litigation pending related to the pain injury that is judged to be important in the maintenance or promotion of continued disability.
2. There should be no serious psychopathology, such as psychosis or organic brain syndrome.

3. The patient should not be addicted to pain medications. If so, detoxification and rehabilitation must precede entrance into the program.

This assessment and treatment scheme proposed by Follick et al. (in press) is not presented as a validated and thoroughly tested approach. The authors themselves note that "its validity and reliability have yet to be determined." The scheme is highlighted here because the authors are sensitive to the many issues involved in the assessment of the pain patient and to the importance of basing a treatment approach on the results of a thorough assessment. The details may change as these investigators and others carry out the necessary research, but this conceptual approach to assessment and treatment will underlie any movement toward the development of a successful program.

Operant Approaches

Fordyce receives credit for the first systematic application of operant techniques for the treatment of chronic pain (Fordyce, 1973, 1974, 1976; Fordyce, Fowler, Lehmann, & DeLateur, 1968; Fordyce et al., 1973). The model used by this group, described in detail by Fordyce in his 1976 book, Behavioral Methods for Chronic Pain and Illness, distinguishes respondent pain, which is caused by physiological distress, and operant pain behaviors, which are learned and maintained by reinforcing stimuli. The approach focuses on overt behaviors such as moaning, taking medication, avoiding work and other responsibilities, and physical inactivity.

The aim of the operant approach is to rearrange environmental contingencies so that pain behaviors decrease in frequency and are replaced by more adaptive "well" behaviors. The most frequently mentioned reinforcers for pain behavior are attention and sympathy from family, friends, employers, and other prominent persons; avoidance of responsibilities, such as work and managing the family; and the opportunity to take medications that relieve unpleasant emotional states such as anxiety and depression.

In the first study of contingency management, Fordyce et al. (1973) reported the results from 36 patients with chronic pain. Nursing staff members and the patients' spouses were taught to use praise and attention to reinforce well behaviors and to withhold these reinforcers when the patients exhibited pain behaviors. In addition, the positive consequences of taking medication were targeted by giving patients medication on a time-contingent basis and by delivering it in a "pain cocktail" in which the amount of active medication was gradually reduced. During the period from admission to discharge, these patients showed significant improvements in physical activity and decreases in medication use. At a 22-month follow-up, the patients acknowledged great improvement during their hospitalization but reported no change from discharge to follow-up.

A number of subsequent studies have tended to replicate the positive results reported by Fordyce and colleagues (for reviews, see Latimer, 1982; Turner & Chapman, 1982b). For example, Seres and Newman (1976) used operant procedures as part of a multifaceted program that included biofeedback, relaxation, education, and psychotherapy. The results were impressive, with patients showing substantial improvements in physical performance; the percentage of patients using pain medication decreased from 87% to 5%. Similar results have been reported in other investigations (Cairns & Pasino, 1977; Cairns et al., 1975; Roberts & Reinhardt, 1980; Swanson, Maruta, & Swenson, 1979).

Relatively few studies have tested an operant approach in the absence of other treatment techniques, so its contribution to the management of the pain patient cannot be clearly defined. The results appear promising, however, in that patients in operant programs, usually in inpatient settings, increase levels of physical activity and decrease use of medication (Turner & Chapman, 1982b). The few follow-up studies indicate that the treatment gains tend to be maintained. However, many questions remain to be answered. The patients for whom this approach is most useful have not been identified. It is not clear when in the course of treatment this approach is best employed. Therefore, further work in this area is needed.

At first glance, it is puzzling why more controlled studies have not been used to test whether operant approaches are effective for pain patients. The evidence could be considered promising (Latimer, 1982; Turner & Chapman, 1982b), but the results are not strong enough to dismiss the need for further research. The techniques have been used since the early 1970s, yet relatively few systematic studies have been done, even in the years when it was so popular to test behavioral strategies against all competition. The answer to this puzzle may lie in clinical intuition.

Most recent articles on the clinical management of the pain patient advocate the use of operant techniques as a component of a larger package (Follick et al., in press; Keefe, 1982; Kerns, Turk, & Holtzman, in press; Turner & Chapman, 1982b). It is apparent from working with pain patients that changes in external contingencies can alter pain behaviors. These changes have a positive effect on the environment, which in turn benefits the patient. The operant techniques may not stand alone as a method of treatment, but they appear to be a necessary part of treatment. The clinical truth of this may be so obvious to many researchers in the area that there is no incentive or perceived need to compare the operant techniques to others.

Biofeedback and Relaxation

Biofeedback and progressive relaxation have been widely used in the management of chronic pain (Turk, Meichenbaum, & Berman, 1979; Turner & Chapman, 1982a). These approaches have been applied to most of the chronic pain syndromes, particularly headache (Blanchard & Andrasik, 1982; Blanchard, Andrasik, Ahles, Teders, & O'Keefe, 1980) Headache pain is an issue that will be covered in more detail in a future volume of the *Annual Review*, so this section will cover the more general issue of whether biofeedback and relaxation are useful for chronic pain patients.

"Biofeedback" is a general term under which are subsumed a number of approaches used with a number of devices, related to many parts of the body, and employed for a variety of pain problems. The aim is to bring physiological processes under a patient's control with the use of feedback about certain internal events (Turk *et al.*, 1979). This is accomplished in a number of steps. The first is to specify some physiological function thought to be associated with the pain experience, the second is to measure changes continually to establish a baseline; and the third is to provide the patient with feedback, usually through an auditory or a visual signal. This allows the patient to learn ways to recognize psychological and physiological cues associated with changes in the feedback. The instrumentation is then changed as the patient learns better control over the response, with the ultimate aim being the voluntary control over the response and the gradual reduction of pain.

The most frequently used types of biofeedback are electromyographic (EMG) feedback, particularly frontalis feedback for headache; electroencephalographic (EEG) feedback to reduce alpha-wave activity; skin temperature feedback; and cephalic blood volume pulse feedback (Turk *et al.*, 1979; Turner & Chapman, 1982a). The EMG feedback has been used most extensively, mainly in combination with some form of relaxation training. There are dozens of case reports, uncontrolled studies, and controlled trials on these approaches. These articles have been reviewed in great detail by Turner and Chapman (1982a) and by Turk *et al.* (1979).

Relaxation training has also been a widely used technique for the pain patient. It is a credible approach to both patients and professionals, and has found its way into most comprehensive programs.

There are many versions of relaxation in practice. The common approach is to tense and relax muscle groups in different parts of the body progressively. The muscle tension is assumed to be implicated in the pain. Some techniques, such as autogenic training and meditation, are thought to have effects similar to relaxation, but it is not clear whether their primary action is physiological or cognitive.

As the treatment for chronic pain has evolved, the use of biofeedback and relaxation has gone through several stages. In the early stages, biofeedback and relaxation were developed independently and were applied mainly to headache patients. The next stage involved a comparison of biofeedback and relaxation, since these were the two most frequently used approaches. At this point, reports began to show the two approaches used in tandem. Currently, relaxation is used in many multifaceted programs, an issue discussed in a following section. However, biofeedback is losing favor.

Two major reviews on biofeedback both conclude that its use with chronic pain cannot be justified by the data (Turk *et al.*, 1979; Turner & Chapman, 1982a). Its popularity has arisen from both historical and clinical origins:

> Physiologically focused psychological interventions have spread extensively throughout the United States and elsewhere in recent years. Partly because it has been promoted aggressively and enthusiastically by commercial equipment suppliers who have worked to both create and meet a demand, biofeedback has become a major tool in chronic pain therapy. This is a matter for some concern considering that its efficacy has been clearly shown only with headache and to some extent with temporomandibular joint pain. (Turner & Chapman, 1982a, p. 16)

Turk *et al.*, (1979) did a careful analysis of the studies on biofeedback for chronic pain. Their conclusions, listed below, lead to a pessimistic view of this approach:

1. No clear relationship has been demonstrated between the pain experience and the physiological responses that biofeedback techniques seek to alter. Therefore, the rationale for altering these responses is not based on confirming data.
2. There are large individual differences among subjects in ability to bring physiological responses under voluntary control. Combined with great differences in the pain experience itself, these differences in the ability to control internal events must necessarily yield a confusing picture when the same techniques are used for all patients.
3. Biofeedback is viewed by many as a unified approach, whereas it actually subsumes many approaches. The main question

must be, "What combination of cognitive, behavioral, and biofeedback approaches would benefit which patients, under what circumstances, and at what expense?" (Turk *et al.*, 1979, p. 1334).

4. Attempts to identify the active components of biofeedback have not been successful. When it works, it is not clear why.

5. The majority of studies have not used adequate controls. These controls are necessary to rule out the influence of placebo effects and to account for the natural history of the pain experience.

6. There is little evidence that effects generated in the laboratory generalize to the natural environment. This is a particularly important issue with biofeedback, because of the highly specific and specialized nature of the setting, in which patients are surrounded by expensive equipment and highly trained professionals.

7. Biofeedback procedures do not account for the situational, psychological, and environmental determinants of pain. Pain cannot be viewed simply as maladaptive physiological responding.

8. The effectiveness of biofeedback depends in large part on the patient's ability and willingness to understand and practice the techniques. For a problem as entrenched as chronic pain, high levels of compliance over long periods of time are necessary. This issue has received very little attention in the biofeedback literature.

9. Patients must learn coping skills for behavioral problems even if biofeedback is effective in teaching voluntary control over physiological responses. This area is generally not considered in biofeedback applications, in which the mechanized aspect of the process is emphasized.

10. Most studies have not considered patients' appraisals of the biofeedback techniques. This information is useful in determining reasons for therapeutic failures.

Are we to assume that biofeedback is not effective? Turk *et al.* (1979) state that "the only conclusion that seems warranted at this time is that one or a combination of the components of biofeedback training is an effective method of pain regulation for some patients in certain situations" (p. 1336). This conclusion might imply that biofeedback may help some people and that it does not carry great risk. This point can be argued.

Current thought is that the management of chronic pain must take into account a variety of factors. Follick, Zitter, and Ahern (1983) attribute some proportion of therapeutic failures to the use of a single technique that encourages the view that pain is a simple and unitary disorder. Turner and Chapman (1982a) feel that biofeedback may actually be counterproductive because of the messages conveyed to the patients:

> We believe there may be a danger for psychotherapists in the use of bio- feedback with chronic pain patients even though these methods seem on the surface to give scientific credence and respectability to psychotherapy. To the extent that preoccupation with physiology leads to ignoring the complex nature of chronic pain problems, the psychotherapist assumes a position little different from that of physicians using nerve blocks, surgeries, or transcutaneous electrical stimulation. One of the generaliza- tions that can be made about chronic pain patients is that they on the whole tend to deny problems of living and to somatize the stress that they experience. The therapist, eager to find problems suitable for biofeedback therapy, may unwittingly collude in the process of somatization by de- livering a physiologically focused treatment that legitimizes the patients' denial of life problems. In the long run this may support rather than weaken pain chronicity. (Turner & Chapman, 1982a, p. 17)

In summary, biofeedback may have limited use for chronic pain patients (other than those with headache), and there are even some possible hazards in using a physiological intervention for a problem with psychosocial consequences (Keefe, 1982; Turk *et al.*, 1979; Turner & Chapman, 1982a). Relaxation, on the other hand, is viewed more positively and is seen as a coping skill to be used as one component for a comprehensive pain management program (Turner & Chapman, 1982a).

Cognitive Approaches

There has been tremendous interest recently in cognitive approaches to the management of chronic pain (Keefe, 1982; Kerns *et al.*, in press; Turk, 1982; Turk & Genest, 1979; Turk, Meichenbaum, & Genest, 1983; Turner, 1982; Turner, & Chapman, 1982b). The cognitive model assumes that attitudes, expectations, and beliefs influence how a patient experiences pain. The implication is that changes in cognitions can help the patient to gain better control over the pain experience and to live more adaptively. Unlike the operant model, in which the pain itself is not emphasized, the cognitive approach focuses on the pain

204 ANNUAL REVIEW OF BEHAVIOR THERAPY

experience and aims to teach the patient to respond cognitively to pain and to the situations that promote pain.

The first application of cognitive approaches was Meichenbaum and Turk's (1976) "stress inoculation." This involved cognitive preparation for the stress of pain by teaching patients to cope with the subjective aspects of the pain experience. The procedures have been improved by Turk and colleagues (Turk, 1982; Turk & Genest, 1979; Turk et al., 1983). The approach can be viewed in three phases:

1. The patient is given a conceptual framework in which to view pain. This emphasizes the influence of thoughts and feelings on the way in which pain is experienced.
2. Patients are taught coping skills to develop specific methods to deal with pain. Some of the techniques used are attention diversion, relaxation, imagery, and relabeling of sensations. The patients are taught four steps in this process: (a) preparing for pain when sensations are mild, (b) confronting pain as the sensations become more severe, (c) coping with feelings that exaggerate pain (e.g., frustration), and (d) administering self-reinforcement for successfully coping with the pain experience.
3. Patients practice their skills, use them in the laboratory and in the natural environment, and plan for the generalization of the skills to situations outside the clinical setting.

Variations of the cognitive strategies have been used in a number of investigations (Hartman & Ainsworth, 1980; Holroyd, Andrasik, & Westbrooke, 1977; Khatami & Rush, 1978; Levendusky & Pankratz, 1975; Mitchell & Mitchell, 1971; Mitchell & White, 1977; Rybstein-Blinchik, 1979; Stenn, Mothersill, & Brooke, 1979; Turner, 1982; Varni, 1981; Wernick, Jaremko, & Taylor, 1981). The results of these studies have been quite encouraging. Two recent studies highlight current work in this area.

Rybstein-Blinchik (1979) assigned 44 pain patients to a control condition or to one of three cognitive treatment conditions designed to give patients a different conceptualization of their pain and to provide them with specific coping strategies. The three cognitive conditions were: (1) somatization—patients were to replace the word "pain" with the words "certain feeling" and to analyze the accompanying feelings; (2) irrelevant condition—patients were instructed to replace thoughts about the pain experience with thoughts about important events in their lives; and (3) relevant condition—patients were instructed to replace thoughts about the pain experience with new thoughts that were to reinterpret the experience (examples are "I feel numb" or "I feel ticklish").

Patients in the relevant condition showed greater improvement than subjects in the control condition and in the somatization and irrelevant condition on several measures. They showed fewer pain behaviors as measured by external observers, and their ratings of pain intensity were lower. They also rated their pain experience as less severe on the McGill Pain Questionnaire. These results are promising, but they do not address the questions of generalization and maintenance (Turner & Chapman, 1982b).

Turner (1982) conducted an impressive study of the outpatient treatment of patients with chronic low back pain. The 36 subjects were assigned randomly to group progressive relaxation training, cognitive–behavioral group therapy, or to a waiting list/attention condition. At posttreatment, the cognitive–behavioral subjects and the progressive relaxations subjects had improved significantly more than the control subjects, but on most variables did not differ from each other. The exceptions were in ratings of participation in normal activities and ability to tolerate pain, where there was an advantage for the cognitive–behavioral group. The results over the long-run, however, seemed to favor the cognitive–behavioral group.

Turner (1982) did a 1-month follow-up on her subjects and then completed a 1½–2-year follow-up via mail surveys. Between the end of treatment and the 1-month follow-up, the progressive relaxation subjects did not show further improvement and reported a significant increase in pain. In contrast, the cognitive–behavioral subjects showed further improvement on measures of pain, depression, and disability. The 1½–2-year follow-up showed that patients in both conditions had a substantial reduction in health care use. The cognitive–behavioral subjects had improved significantly in the time spent working.

The study by Rybstein-Blinchik (1979) and especially the study by Turner (1982) argue both for the effectiveness of cognitive–behavioral procedures in the clinical setting and for the generalization and maintenance in real-life settings. An interesting aspect of the Turner (1982) study was that the cognitive–behavioral treatment gained its advantage during the follow-up period, presumably because patients had been instructed in skills that they were using outside the clinical setting. It is interesting to note that inherent in these studies is the assumption that cognitive–behavioral techniques are effective and that the challenge is to test why they are effective or what version is most effective.

It is important not to lose sight of weaknesses in many of the studies on cognitive approaches (Turner & Chapman, 1982b). Many have not used adequate controls, have not employed multiple measures of outcome, have not evaluated generalization, and have not followed patients beyond a brief treatment phase. However, the evidence that does exist appears positive.

A Comprehensive Pain Management Program

The field of chronic-pain management has undergone tremendous change since the initial reports of behavioral approaches in the 1960s. The early view from the behavioral perspective was that the pain itself could be ignored by the treatment team and that operant techniques could be used to modify the patient's overt pain behaviors (physical inactivity, taking medication, moaning, etc.) (Fordyce, 1976). A similarly unitary view was taken by those interested in biofeedback. The theory here was that maladaptive physiological responses were causing pain and that bringing these responses under voluntary control would reduce the underlying physical sensations that cause pain behaviors. As the view of chronic pain expanded, cognitive–behavioral approaches became popular, and these now form the foundation of many comprehensive pain-management programs.

Chronic pain has multiple origins and is maintained by a complex series of factors. This is the key point that underlies the philosophy of most treatment programs:

> Recognition that chronic pain is a complex neurophysiological, behavioral, and psychological phenomenon has led to the development of innovative treatment programs. These programs share one common assumption: if chronic pain is complex, then a combination of treatment techniques is needed to successfully treat patients. (Keefe, 1982, p. 903)

The primary question, then, is: What techniques form the right combination? There are probably more similarities among programs than there are differences. Common to most programs are operant procedures to modify overt pain behaviors and cognitive–behavioral procedures to alter the pain experiences. As an example of a comprehensive program, Follick *et al.* (1983) employ four treatment approaches:

1. *Behavior modification.* These are the operant techniques described by Fordyce (1976) to reduce the frequency of pain behaviors and to increase well behaviors.
2. *Physical therapy.* The purpose here is to strengthen progressively the muscles that have weakened because of inactivity.

3. *Conjoint marital therapy.* The patient and spouse are instructed in identifying pain behaviors and well behaviors and in manipulating the environmental contingencies accordingly. They are also taught communication skills to enable them to deal better with the treatment process.
4. *Cognitive restructuring.* The patient is taught to take responsibility for the pain experience and to develop coping behaviors to lead a more adaptive life. Follick *et al.* (1983) note that the patient who is searching for the complete relief of pain will seek a "magic treatment" and must reorganize this series of beliefs before treatment can be effective.

A number of comprehensive programs using both operant procedures and cognitive (self-management) techniques have reported good results (Cinciripini & Floreen, 1982; Keefe, Block, Williams, & Surwit, 1981; Painter, Seres, & Newman, 1980; Seres & Newman, 1976; Swanson, Swenson, Maruta, & McPhee, 1976; Turner, 1982). This is gratifying because it provides substance for treatment procedures that can be used in many different settings (Follick *et al.*, 1983; Genest & Turk, 1979; Turk *et al.*, 1983).

Much work is still needed to perfect treatment procedures for the management of the chronic-pain patient (Turk *et al.*, 1983; Turner & Chapman, 1982b). For example, the cognitive procedures differ from setting to setting and their active components have still not been specified. Even though there has been great improvement in specifying techniques to individual patients, there is still the tendency to use the same procedures with all patients. This is due in part to the absence of sensitive assessment procedures to dictate the individual needs of patients. In addition, there is still disagreement on the role of certain procedures. For example, Keefe (1982) notes that biofeedback may be a useful part of treatment for some patients, while Turner and Chapman (1982a) and Follick *et al.* (in press) feel that the very nature of biofeedback encourages the patient to seek a physiological solution to the problem and leads to an unfortunate focus on pain relief.

From a clinical perspective, this is an exciting time in the field of pain management. Important advances have occurred recently and there now exists a treatment package that can be used reliably across settings. The results that do exist (e.g., Cinciripini & Floreen, 1982) on the use of such a program are positive enough to justify immediate and enthusiastic efforts to pursue the conceptual premise underlying the multimodal approach.

New Directions

This section began with a statement that the management of the patient with chronic pain epitomizes some of the major issues facing the field of behavioral medicine. As the chronic pain phenomenon has become recognized as a complex process, there have been calls for multidisciplinary efforts in its management. There is little evidence anymore of controlled studies testing medical against psychological approaches, which of course resulted from interdisciplinary contests as much as from clinical concerns. The interaction between psychological, physiological, and environmental factors is receiving the attention necessary to make real advances in the field. The shape this attention takes and the ability of professionals in the different disciplines to work together effectively may reflect the direction in which the general field of behavioral medicine will be moving in the years ahead.

The evidence discussed here on the assessment and treatment of chronic pain generates many possibilities for clinical work and for research. The absence of enough tightly controlled research makes it difficult to draw conclusions about most aspects of current treatment programs. Studies are now appearing with greater sophistication, a wider range of measures, and longer follow-up periods (e.g., Turner, 1982). This is a positive development.

Some of the directions the field may take in upcoming years are listed here. Many of these are suggested by reviews of the area (Keefe, 1982; Turk et al., 1983; Turner & Chapman, 1982a, 1982b).

1. Greater emphasis needs to be placed on generalization of findings to real-life settings and to the long-term maintenance of clinical gains. Very little is known about the relapse process in pain patients. So little attention has been paid to long-term results because short-term effects were still being sought. However, the picture has now changed, and it is important to evaluate whether the skills that patients presumably learn in treatment, and the changes in environmental contingencies presumably created by the operant procedures, last once the patient leaves the careful supervision of a comprehensive treatment program.

2. The future may bring greater emphasis on the interaction of treatments. An example would be the interaction of cognitive–behavioral treatments and biofeedback. Some authors claim that the use of biofeedback compromises the basic premise of the cognitive approach; that is, that patients may strengthen the already prominent view that relief from pain is necessary for functioning and that "magical" procedures will assist them (Follick et al., 1983; Turner & Chapman, 1982a). This is only one example of the interactions that will undoubtedly

occur as programs become more multidisciplinary in nature and as new techniques are added to the treatment package.

3. Social factors occupy an important place in most treatment programs. Reinforcing and punishing forces in the patient's social environment are systematically manipulated in the operant programs. The family, for instance, is taught to avoid the reinforcing of pain behaviors. Closer examination of these social factors may be instructive in designing programs involving the family. The ideal way to study these factors would be in longitudinal research (Keefe, 1982).

4. Keefe (1982) has proposed a longitudinal analysis of the development of chronic pain. He proposes three stages—acute, prechronic, and chronic—through which patients progress on their way to severe disability. The ultimate aim would be the identification of predictors that would allow for early intervention. The more immediate benefit might be the generation of ideas for treatment.

5. Pain behavior and environmental factors are tied together in a very complex way. Research on these factors would be useful in better understanding the chronic pain process. Keefe (1982), for example, has mentioned several of these interactions. In one study, spouses of pain patients showed increased physiological responding to facial expressions of pain in the patients (Block, 1981). N. E. Miller (1979) reported that pain patients whose financial benefits were time limited tended to show less reliance on medical treatment and tended to return to work more rapidly than did patients with unlimited benefits. These environmental factors may greatly influence the effects of treatment and must be considered in any analysis of the pain patient.

6. Collaborative efforts between treatment centers may provide information that would otherwise not be available. Any one center is unlikely to have enough patients to conduct analyses of important factors such as predictor variables. Relationships among behavior, physiological patterns, and cognitive factors may be possible to study only by using multivariate methods with large numbers of patients (Keefe, 1982). Collaborative studies would permit tests of these factors.

7. There exist many possibilities and needs in the area of assessment. Some of the recent advances have been discussed here. These suggest the need for more research on observational methods, social interactions, cognitive patterns, and a number of other factors germane to the pain experience.

8. Greater attention will probably be given to individual differences in future studies. These differences may explain why all treatments are more effective for some patients than others. Careful assessment is the key to better understanding of the individual.

9. It would be helpful for authors to report the details of their treatment procedures in more detail. Inevitably there are differences in the way investigators employ procedures. A "cognitive–behavioral" treatment may vary enormously from study to study, and these variations may explain some of the discrepancies among studies. More thorough description would facilitate the comparison of studies and would yield valuable clinical information about innovative changes in standard programs (Turner & Chapman, 1982b).

10. Turner and Chapman (1982b) have noted that patient compliance is a key factor in the effectiveness of any procedure in which practice and cooperation are essential. This issue has not been mentioned to any extent in the literature. Future research may turn to methods of enhancing compliance (Epstein & Cluss, 1982) and to methods of assessing whether patients are following treatment prescriptions.

CHAPTER

6

THE ADDICTIVE DISORDERS

KELLY D. BROWNELL

In last year's *Annual Review*, I noted a trend away from outcome research in the area of each of the addictions. This trend has continued during the past year, so that even more is known about the people we are working with and the behaviors we seek to change. In addition, this year may be best known as the year in which we took our programs to the community. The range of applications has been impressive, and the new possibilities are most exciting. These issues and others are the focus of this year's discussion of the addictions.

In the obesity, smoking, and alcoholism areas, there has been increasing interest in public health issues. The most obvious manifestation of this interest is the work in schools; work sites; public settings, such as cafeterias and supermarkets; and the community in general. In the obesity area, some researchers have expanded their work beyond the obese person to an interest in eating patterns in the general population. Smoking researchers have begun to study the prevention of smoking in junior high school students. Behavioral researchers are beginning to collaborate with communications and public health experts in an effort to combine the strengths of several disciplines. The payoff from these efforts should be high.

This year's discussion of the addictive disorders will reflect the tendency for behavioral researchers to expand beyond the boundaries imposed by their training and their need to champion the cause of an emerging field. This expansion will benefit not only behavioral scientists, because of the exposure to other viewpoints; it will also allow the strengths of behavior therapy to be highlighted to other professionals.

OBESITY

Last year's *Annual Review* (Volume 8) noted several trends in obesity research. Several of these trends reflected general movement within the addictions field and others were specific to the area of obesity. The most prominent direction was a shift from outcome research to the study of process variables. This change in emphasis has continued during the past year. Outcome studies still appear in great numbers, but they have been joined by many studies on eating and activity patterns in both children and adults. This is a positive move, because the further refinements likely to result from the traditional outcome studies of behavior therapy are questionable indeed (Brownell, 1982b).

Another major trend is the focus on the long-term maintenance of weight loss. This issue has been discussed in the literature for many years (Stunkard, 1972; Wilson, 1978), but only recently have studies tested specific interventions during the maintenance period (e.g., Abrams & Follick, 1983). This is important, because maintenance remains a difficult problem. However, I noted in last year's commentary that the focus on long-term results carries several risks, not the least of which is overlooking the minimal short-term losses produced by most programs (Brownell, 1982b; Foreyt, Goodrick, & Gotto, 1981; Foreyt, Mitchell, Garner, Gee, Scott, & Gotto, 1982; LeBow, 1981; Wilson & Brownell, 1980). Some researchers have gone back to this issue and have been using more aggressive approaches to dieting—an issue discussed in a later section.

Obesity as a Complex Phenomenon

It is almost trite to say that obesity is a complex problem. Few would disagree, if for no other reason than the frustration they experience in dealing with a problem that is extremely resistant to treatment. I recently gave a lecture on obesity at a medical school and asked the audience whether obesity was primarily a psychological/cultural or a biological/genetic problem. The audience was comprised of equal numbers of medical professionals (physicians, interns, residents, nurses) and psychologically trained professionals (psychologists, social workers). The audience split right down professional lines, but not as one might expect. The medical professionals felt the problem was psychological and the psychological professionals felt it was medical!

I view this interesting vote in a positive light. It may reflect each profession's interest in looking elsewhere for the answer it cannot find on its own, but it may also reveal the tendency to become more familiar with work in other disciplines. This eagerness to leave one's own discipline may be the most positive direction the field has taken in years.

There is clear movement in the obesity field toward conducting interdisciplinary investigations of the problem. Abstract journals like *Behavioral Medicine Abstracts* show that high-quality research on obesity appears in the literatures of many disciplines. Recent papers and books on obesity show this trend clearly (Bray, 1976; Brownell, 1982b; Stunkard, 1980; Wooley, Wooley, & Dyrenforth, 1979). Even more encouraging is the tendency for behavioral scientists to investigate topics usually studied in other disciplines. Included here are the areas of pharmacology (Brownell & Stunkard, 1981a; Craighead, Stunkard, & O'Brien, 1981), energy metabolism (Donahoe, Lin, Kirschenbaum, & Keesey, 1981), nutrition (Beneke, Kohrs, & Paulsen, 1982; Brightwell, Foster, Lee, & Naylor, 1979), lipid metabolism (Brownell & Stunkard, 1981b; Hartung, Foreyt, Mitchell, Vlasek, & Gotto, 1980; Thompson, Jeffery, Wing, & Wood, 1979), and exercise physiology (Brownell, Bachorik, & Ayerle, 1982; Brownell & Stunkard, 1980a; Martin & Dubbert, 1982; Thompson, Jarvie, Lahey, & Cureton, 1982). From these efforts is likely to emerge the best of many disciplines, bringing more hope to a disappointing area.

Specific Topics for This Review

This year's *Annual Review* will cover four main topics: (1) the assessment of food intake, (2) childhood obesity, (3) recent findings with obese adults, and (4) an aggressive approach to dieting. The assessment of food intake will be covered because of the increasing emphasis on studying patterns of ingestion. Many of these studies are based on weak measures. The second area, childhood obesity, is very promising because of the potential benefits of reaching the problem in its early stages. The treatment of adult obesity will be discussed, with the primary aim of defining the proper role for behavior therapy. Finally, a dramatic approach to dieting, very low calorie diets, will be discussed as a means of boosting weight loss.

Assessment

MEASURING FOOD INTAKE

Evaluating food intake is an important step in developing a behavioral program for the obese patient. However, the importance of this measurement issue extends far beyond behavioral programs. Studies on eating patterns in obese and lean persons rely on this type of assessment. Epidemiology studies that relate nutritional practices to health are dependent on the current assessment technology. This may be one of the most crucial applications, because dietary guidelines for the entire country are forged from these studies. The effect of specific nutrients on energy metabolism is particularly relevant to the obesity field, yet surprisingly little attention has been paid to the integrity of the available assessment methods.

Studies on food intake are no stronger than the methods used to measure consumption. Unfortunately, this issue is often overlooked. For instance, one of the classic texts in nutrition, Goodhart and Shils's (1980) *Modern Nutrition in Health and Disease*, contains no mention of the reliability or validity of current assessment procedures. Within the past several years, however, there has been increasing interest in this issue (Durnin & Ferro-Luzzi, 1982; Wadden & Brownell, in press). An entire issue of the *American Journal of Clinical Nutrition* (1982) was devoted to the assessment of nutritional status.

An example might illustrate the critical nature of this issue. There has been great debate on whether obese persons eat more and/or exercise less than thin persons. The studies on energy intake are based primarily on self-reports (food diaries), naturalistic observations, or reports from others. In most cases, obese persons appear to consume no more than their thin counterparts, leading some to believe that energy expenditure is the culprit (Mann, 1974; Wooley et al., 1979). This has obvious therapeutic implications, but what if these studies are based on invalid measures? It is time to investigate the properties of measures of food intake.

Self-Report Measures. Self-report is the most frequently used method of evaluating food intake, and two basic approaches to self-report have been taken. The first and most popular in the behavior therapy literature is the continuous diary of all food eaten. The second is the retrospective recall of food intake, the most popular version of which has been the 24-hour dietary recall. Both approaches have their strengths and weaknesses (Wadden & Brownell, in press).

The continuous food diary would appear to be the most promising method of measuring food intake, yet it has many problems. Patients must comply with the request to record all food eaten, so the diary is subject to distortion from overt noncompliance or from lapses in memory. It is possible that the accuracy of these records varies with factors such as motivation, education, health consciousness, and so forth (Rush & Kristal, 1982).

Use of the continuous diary also assumes that the patient can identify the food being eaten, estimate the amount, and then calculate the calorie values. Lansky and Brownell (1982) displayed ten common foods to obese patients entering a weight-loss program and asked the patients to estimate the quantity and calories in the foods. The average errors were 63.9% for quantity and 53.4% for calories, and 80% of the subjects had recorded calories in previous diets! Furthermore, the errors were not systematic in being overestimates or underestimates. The authors then studied whether these patients would err in estimating calories in their diet diaries. The quantity estimates were assumed accurate (a patient's estimate of 1 cup of cottage cheese was accepted), and the diaries were examined to determine whether the simple arithmetic was performed correctly (if a calorie guide showed that ½ cup of cottage cheese had 120 calories, then the diary should show 1 cup having 240 calories). The patients made many errors in this simple process. Another investigation of this issue also found errors among both obese and lean persons (O'Neil, Currey, Malcolm, Francis, Riddle, & Sexauer, 1982).

Patients could presumably be trained to make accurate estimates of quantity and then to record calorie values correctly. This still leaves the problem of reactivity—the patients might alter food intake because of the recording. This, combined with the factors mentioned above, put the validity of continuous monitoring in doubt. This is an important area for research because so much hinges on the outcome.

The most popular method of dietary assessment in the nutrition field is the 24-hour recall. This measure requires the patient to state types and amounts of food eaten in the previous 24 hours, either with the use of a food list or with no aid. This approach has been used extensively in epidemiological investigations, clinical studies, and nutrition surveys (Beaton, Milner, & Corey, 1979; McGandy, 1982).

A number of studies have examined the validity of the 24-hour recall (Rush & Kristal, 1982; Wadden & Brownell, in press). Some studies show good correspondence between reported intake and actual intake, but others do not. The reliability of the 24-hour recall varies widely among studies and depends on the age, sex, and other factors of the population (Rush & Kristal, 1982). It does appear that the 24-hour recall is best used when readministered two to four times with each individual (Rush & Kristal, 1982).

Self-report is probably the best available method for measuring food intake. Both the continuous diary and the 24-hour recall have problems, but nothing better has appeared. Evaluating the validity of these measures is difficult enough, and improving the validity is even more difficult. For the present time, it is important to acknowledge that studies based on these measures must be viewed with concern.

Naturalistic Observations. A number of studies have appeared on measuring food intake in public locations such as cafeterias, fast food establishments, and other restaurants (Brownell, 1981; Stunkard &

Kaplan, 1977). These studies have been done with both adults (e.g., Stunkard, Coll, Lundquist, & Meyers, 1980) and children (e.g., O'Brien, Walley, Anderson-Smith, & Drabman, 1982). This approach samples an important part of eating behavior, but there are two main weaknesses. First, only a portion of a person's total eating can be studied. Second, "private" eating is not available for measurement, and obese patients often report eating more when they are alone than when they are with others. Krantz (1979) studied obese and lean people in a cafeteria and found that the obese ate more when seated alone that when seated with others.

Controlled Environments. There are some cases in which the food intake of a person can be measured very carefully. This includes persons in hospitals, institutions, prisons, and so forth. The ultimate in precise measurement comes from a patient hospitalized on a metabolic ward. The advantages of institutional assessment are that the institution provides the food and therefore allows great control over availability, subjects can be watched unobtrusively, and the nutritional status of the individual can be evaluated. However, there are ethical problems in research of this type. Also, an institutionalized population may not eat as the rest of society eats, and the special population lends itself to bias (Wadden & Brownell, in press). This approach is probably most useful for preliminary studies of diet and nutritional status.

Childhood Obesity

SERIOUSNESS AND PREVALENCE

Obesity in children has serious medical and psychological consequences. This seems so obvious that one wonders whether it bears mentioning. However, behavioral researchers studied obesity originally because it provided a convenient outcome measure to test self-control strategies (Wilson, 1978). Recent years have brought more interest among these researchers in the disorder per se, so more attention is being paid to the physical, emotional, and social comcomitants of being overweight (Brownell, 1982b). This material will be presented only briefly here. For more detailed descriptions, refer to Brownell and Stunkard (1978, 1980b), Coates and Thoresen (1978, 1980), Collipp (1980), and Foreyt and Goodrick (1981).

Obese children are at risk for carbohydrate intolerance, increased insulin secretion, hypercholesterolemia, elevated blood pressure, and decreased growth hormone release (Brownell & Stunkard, 1978, 1980b; Coates & Thoresen, 1978, 1980). Most troubling is that atherogenic serum lipid disorders may originate in childhood (Kannel & Dawber, 1972) and that adult blood pressure patterns may be predictable from childhood patterns (Zinner, Levy, & Kass, 1971). Furthermore, obesity in childhood tends to persist into adult life, thus disposing an individual to some of the most serious chronic diseases of later life (Van Itallie, 1979). There is evidence that weight reduction in children can remedy some of these problems (Brownell, Kelman, & Stunkard, 1983; Epstein, Wing, Koeske, Andrasik, & Ossip, 1981).

Obese children are also at increased risk for psychological and social problems. Body image distortion is one hazard (Stunkard & Mendelson, 1967). Disturbed family interactions, disapproval from peers, academic discrimination, and poor self-concept are also likely in obese children (Brownell & Stunkard, 1980b). Anyone who has worked with obese children is aware of the deep torment they suffer because of teasing and pressure from peers and family.

The medical and psychological problems would not be a serious public health matter if obesity were a rare disorder. However, estimates of the prevalence of obesity in children range from 5% to 30% of the population (Forbes, 1975; Garn & Clark, 1976). It appears from the available evidence that obesity is more prevalent in girls than in boys and that prevalence increases with age. The precise prevalence is difficult to assess because of variations among studies in populations and criteria for obesity. Even the most conservative estimates reveal a problem of striking magnitude.

ADVANCES IN TREATMENT

The earliest treatment programs for obese children tested dietary counseling, anorectic medications, inpatient starvation, prescribed exercise, and psychotherapy. Several reviews of these programs have shown the approaches to be plagued by small weight losses, high dropout rates, untoward emotional reactions, and high rates of relapse (Brownell & Stunkard, 1978, 1980b; Coates & Thoresen, 1978, 1980). The picture began to improve somewhat when researchers began applying behavioral principles to the problem.

Behavioral programs for children have appeared in two generations. The first involved the application of techniques taken from studies with adults. This was a natural occurrence, because studies with adults preceded studies with children. Some studies used techniques such as contingency management and response cost taken from the classroom management literature. The weight losses in these early studies with children ranged from 4 to 13 pounds (Aragona, Cassady & Drabman, 1975; Gross, Wheeler & Hess, 1976; Rivinus, Drummond, &

Combrinck-Graham, 1976; Weiss, 1977; Wheeler & Hess, 1976). Most studies included very small samples, there was great intersubject variability in weight losses, and little attention was paid to long-term maintenance.

We are now seeing the second generation of behavioral studies with obese children. They employ multifaceted programs with techniques developed specifically for children in addition to those techniques found helpful with adults. The programs have included family involvement, exercise, nutrition counseling, and an array of behavioral techniques (Brownell et al., 1983; Coates, Jeffery, Slinkard, Killen, & Danaher, 1982; Coates & Thoresen, 1981; Epstein et al., 1981; Epstein, Wing, Steranchak, Dickson, & Michelson, 1980). Weight losses have been greatly increased and the maintenance of weight loss has become a key issue.

The Role of Parents. Parents have a great influence on the eating and physical activity patterns of their children (Mayer, 1968). Waxman and Stunkard (1980) for example, found that eating and activity patterns of obese boys differed greatly in the home, outside the home, and in school, suggesting situational control over these important factors. Hertzler (1981) reported that the children who were most successful in a weight-loss program tended to come from supportive families that helped the child develop self-esteem and responsibility. Particularly in younger children, parents control the type and amount of food that enters the house, and via direct or subtle influences, parents encourage or discourage specific patterns of eating and physical activity. It seems, therefore, that parental involvement would be a necessary component of a treatment program for obese children. Despite widespread agreement with this notion, little research has been done on this issue.

The first controlled trial on parental involvement was conducted by Kingsley and Shapiro (1977). Children aged 10 to 11 were assigned to groups in which the role of the mothers was varied: (1) only the child attended, (2) only the mother attended, and (3) both mother and child attended. After an 8-week program, weight losses for those in each of the three groups (approximately 3.5 pounds) did not differ, but all groups were superior to a no-treatment control group. The results were counterintuitive, but they were not challenged until recently.

Brownell et al. (1983) studied the role of parental involvement in obese adolescents aged 12 to 16. The subjects were assigned to one of three conditions of mothers' involvement (the mothers were not required to be overweight): (1) mother and child together—mothers and children attended together and met in the same group; (2) mother and child separately—mothers and children attended together but met in separate groups; and (3) child alone—mothers were not involved.

The groups in which the mothers and children met separately had the greatest weight losses after the 16-week treatment program. The mean loss for adolescents in this group was 18.5 pounds, compared to 11.7 pounds for the mother–child together group and 7.3 pounds for the child alone group. After a 1-year follow-up, the mean weight loss for the mother–child separately group was 16.9 pounds compared to approximately 6.6 pounds for the other two groups. These are among the largest losses reported in studies with obese children.

Figure 6-1 shows the comparison of the three groups in the Brownell *et al.* (1983) study in percentage overweight. This measure provides a more meaningful index of program efficacy in obese children because it accounts for sex, age, height, and growth. (A child might gain weight but show clinical improvement if the gain is less than expected because of growth.) The changes in percentage overweight in this study are significant for two reasons. First, the changes are large enough to be clinically significant. Second, the losses in the most successful group were maintained during the 1-year follow-up. In fact, the mean percentage overweight decreased somewhat during the maintenance period, a most unusual finding.

FIG. 6-1.

Mean changes ($\pm$ *SEM*) in percentage overweight for the three conditions in which the mothers' role was varied in the treatment of their overweight children. (From "Treatment of Obese Children with and without Their Mothers: Changes in Weight and Blood Pressure" by K. D. Brownell, J. H. Kelman, and A. J. Stunkard, *Pediatrics*, 1983, *71*, 515–523. Copyright 1983, American Academy of Pediatrics. Reprinted by permission.)

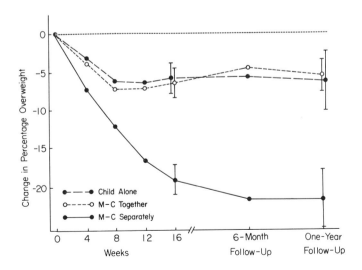

Indirect support for the importance of parental involvement is provided by two studies by Epstein and colleagues (Epstein *et al.*, 1980, 1981) and the paper by Coates and Thoresen (1981). Although these studies were designed to test for variables other than parental involvement, the results provide useful information on this issue. Epstein *et al.* (1980) tested nutrition education versus a behavioral program for obese children (ages 6–12) and their overweight mothers. The behavioral program was more effective, but there was a strong relationship between weight losses in the children and in their mothers when they both wanted to lose weight, they both attended sessions, and they both earned back deposited money for weight loss.

Epstein *et al.* (1981) then evaluated the target for reinforcement when using a deposit-refund contract. Rewards were given when the parent and child lost weight, just the child lost weight, or when attendance met a criterion level. These approaches did not differ in effectiveness for the children, but mothers lost more weight in the group where both they and the children were rewarded for weight loss. Parent and child weights were related at the end of treatment but not at follow-up. Coates and Thoresen (1981) carried out an intensive investigation of three overweight adolescents. Impressive weight losses were found for the children who completed a multicomponent program, one aspect of which was involvement of the family.

Taken collectively, these studies suggest that parents can be instrumental in the weight loss of their obese children. The two studies by Epstein *et al.* (1980, 1981) show the potential benefits of working simultaneously with mothers and children who are both overweight. The Brownell *et al.* (1983) study indicates that the precise nature of the parental role may influence the effectiveness of treatment. This role may depend on the sex of both parent and child, the degree of obesity in both persons, the age of the child, and the developmental issues inherent in dealing with parents and their children.

The uncontrolled evidence of Hertzler (1981) suggests that the parents must exert some control over the child but that it is important for the child to be free to develop self-esteem and responsibility. On the other hand, one recent study found that long-term success in obese children and adolescents was most likely in families with greater parental control (Cohen, Gelfand, Dodd, Jensen, & Turner, 1980). LeBow (1982) also notes that some of these relationship factors are crucial to the success of a program. There is still much to be learned in this important area and there are many fruitful questions to pursue.

Comprehensive Behavioral Programs. The new generation of behavioral studies with obese children are noteworthy for several reasons. First, researchers no longer seem satisfied with small weight losses attained for the sake of answering theoretical questions. Therefore, the treatment administered to the children is far more comprehensive and intensive than the programs used in earlier programs. As a consequence, the average weight losses have increased by a factor of at least three. This may be the most exciting aspect of recent studies, yet this point is sometimes overlooked because the authors focus on the comparison between groups rather than the absolute effectiveness of the treatment package. Second, more attention is being paid to the maintenance of weight loss. There are dangers in this movement if short-term results are given less emphasis (Brownell, 1982b), but this does not appear to be happening in the child area as it is in the literature on adults.

The results of one such comprehensive behavioral program was reported by Coates and Thoresen (1981). An intensive investigation was carried out on the behavioral treatment of two overweight adolescent girls and the nonbehavioral treatment of a third. The two behavioral subjects were 16 years old and 128% and 71% overweight, and the control subject was 15 years old and was 73% overweight. The 10-week program included traditional procedures such as stimulus control, self-monitoring, modification of the act of eating, exercise management, and reinforcement. In addition, parents were trained to support the children, and along with the therapists' twice-weekly meetings with the children, they met five times with the parents.

This study was unique in its careful assessment of behavior change, carried out with time-lagged treatments and a multiple baseline design. Nonparticipant observers monitored the caloric value of foods in the cupboards, refrigerator, and freezer, and during meals they recorded the number of bites and sips per minute, the amount of time utensils were on the table, the amount of time spent talking, and the types of foods eaten. The two behavioral subjects lost 21 and 11.5 pounds respectively, while the control subject gained 5 pounds. The weight loss seemed clearly related to behavior change.

Epstein *et al.* (1980) investigated mother and child weight losses in a program that compared a behavior modification group to a nutrition-education group. The behavioral procedures included modeling and contingency contracting, in which the return of a financial deposit was partially dependent on weight loss for both the parent and the child. The weight loss in the behavioral group (for both parents and children) was nearly double that for the nutrition-education group. The weight losses for parents and children were highly correlated in the behavior modification group but not in the nutrition education group. This led Epstein and colleagues to refine further the role of contingency contracting, the focus of their next study.

The target of contingency contracting was investigated in an impressive study by Epstein *et al.* (1981). Overweight children (ages 6–12) and their overweight parents from 76 families were assigned to one of three behavioral groups: (1) parent–child target—the deposit was returned if both the parent and the child lost weight; (2) child target—the deposit was returned if the child lost weight; and (3) nonspecific target—the deposit was returned for attendance. The program included nutrition education (Epstein, Masek, & Marshall, 1978), self-monitoring, social reinforcement and prompts, therapist support, contingency management (mastery of written materials), and a strong exercise program.

Changes in percentage overweight were equivalent for children in the three conditions. Parents lost the most weight in the parent–child condition. The weights of the children (measured by percentage overweight) were also equivalent at the end of a 13-month follow-up. However, more children in the parent–child group were able to reduce to and stay within the limits of normal weight (less than 20% overweight). Weight losses of parents and their children correlated positively at the end of treatment but not at follow-up.

The decreases in percentage overweight for the children in the Epstein *et al.* (1981) study were substantial (Figure 6-2). The average subject, after starting at approximately 42% overweight, reduced to approximately 25% overweight (close to the normal range). These are clinically significant changes. Even more importantly, significant declines in percentage overweight were maintained during the follow-up period.

There are now four studies with obese children showing both substantial initial losses and promising results over the long run (Brownell *et al.*, 1983; Coates & Thoresen, 1981; Epstein *et al.*, 1980, 1981). This is a very positive development in the field because of the important nature of the problem. We will be fortunate if these results hold up to replication.

Programs in the Schools. The schools offer many advantages as a site for the treatment of childhood obesity: Large numbers of children can be screened and treated, treatment can be both concentrated and continuous, long-term contact with the children is possible, cost to the family can be minimized, children can be reached before their obesity becomes serious enough to prompt referral to a clinic, the social interactions between the obese child and his or her peers and the school staff may help foster weight loss, and obesity may be better approached in an educational rather than a medical or psychological setting.

Seltzer and Mayer (1970) carried out a program in the schools in suburban Boston. Their program consisted of nutrition education,

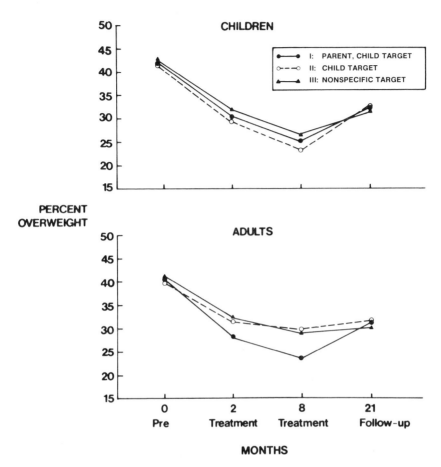

FIG. 6-2.
Mean changes in percentage overweight for children and parents in experimental conditions in which the target of reinforcement was varied. (From "Child and Parent Weight Loss in Family-Based Behavior Modification Programs" by L. H. Epstein, R. R. Wing, R. Koeske, F. Andrasik, and D. J. Ossip, *Journal of Consulting and Clinical Psychology*, 1981, *49*, 674–685. Copyright 1981, American Psychological Association. Reprinted by permission.)

exercise, and psychological support. The program was not a controlled trial, but 76% of the children showed improvement in the ponderal index (height [in]/weight [lb]), indicating decreased degrees of obesity. A study followed in New York City in which schools were assigned randomly to receive no program (controls) or a program consisting of behavior modification, nutrition education, and exercise instruction (Botvin, Cantlon, Carter, & Williams, 1979). In the experimental schools, 51% of the children lost weight, compared to only 15% in the control schools.

Brownell and Kaye (1982) carried out a program for 5-to-12-year-old children in an elementary school in Florida. The program emphasized not only behavior modification, nutrition, and exercise but also social support from family, peers, and school personnel. These authors maintain that the social context in which a program is implemented may be as important to its success as the actual procedures administered. The conceptual framework for the program is displayed in Figure 6-3. This model shows both the importance of social factors and the fact that behavior modification was used as a series of principles to improve adherence to the nutrition and dietary regimens rather than as a group of procedures (Brownell, 1982b).

The results of Brownell and Kaye (1982) were quite positive, given the modest weight losses reported from other school studies. During

FIG. 6-3.

A conceptual model for treating obesity in the schools. The model emphasizes the process by which the program is implemented (social support) as well as the program components (education). (From "A School-Based Behavior Modification, Nutrition Education, and Physical Activity Program for Obese Children" by K. D. Brownell and F. S. Kaye, *American Journal of Clinical Nutrition*, 1982, *35*, 277–283. Copyright 1982, American Society of Clinical Nutrition. Reprinted by permission.)

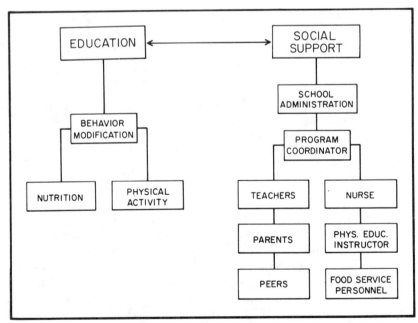

the 10-week program, 95% of the children in the program lost weight, compared to 21% of control children. The mean weight loss for the program children was 9.7 pounds and the average decrease in percentage overweight was 15.4%. The problems with this study are that a true control group was not used and long-term maintenance was not evaluated. The results, however, are worth further investigation.

Work in the schools may be one of the most promising means of dealing with childhood obesity. The initial studies have been encouraging, but much more work needs to be done. Well-controlled investigations are necessary to evaluate the components of a treatment package. In addition, research is needed to identify more clearly the effects of obesity and weight loss on academic functioning, body image, self-concept, and mood. This will probably become a popular topic for research in upcoming years.

Adult Obesity

Studies on the treatment of obesity in adults have continued to appear at a rapid rate. When Wilson reviewed the field in 1978, he questioned whether many behavioral studies had any contribution to make because of the trivial weight losses attained and the insignificant experimental questions being posed. Indeed, many studies of this era merely cluttered the literature and diverted the attention of researchers to manipulations of a treatment package that was only modestly effective. Fortunately, the acceptable standards for publishing research on obesity have become more stringent. As a consequence, the studies now appearing in the literature are more tightly controlled, have better assessment of long-term loss, and are producing greater initial losses. In addition, more investigators are interested in obesity per se rather than in theoretical questions about the process of behavior change. The next few years will probably see the appearance of many studies with greater weight losses, better maintenance, and more careful assessment of the psychological and physiological effects of weight reduction (Brownell, 1982b).

MISSING THE STRENGTH OF BEHAVIOR THERAPY

Behavior therapy for obesity has become known as a group of procedures, and with only modest variation among research groups, the package of techniques is remarkably similar from setting to setting. This has had the positive effect of establishing a treatment package that has been widely used in self-help groups, commercial weight-loss programs, dietary clinics, public health programs, and so forth. However, there are several serious disadvantages to this phenomenon.

Behavior therapy should be viewed not as a group of procedures but as a series of principles of behavior change (Bandura, 1969; Brownell, 1982b; Wilson & O'Leary, 1980). These behavioral principles provide guidance in developing a program of dietary and activity changes, no matter what specific changes are requested. For instance, self-monitoring is the most common technique in behavioral weight-control programs. As a technique, self-monitoring is simply one of many procedures found in a package that produces small weight losses. As a principle, self-monitoring can be applied to any prescribed change in any dietary program; for example, adherence may improve if patients monitor their behavior. Viewed this way, the behavioral package is only the application of the principles to one part of a weight-loss program (altered eating habits).

This conceptual notion has major implications for research and treatment. For research, it is no longer fruitful to compare the behavioral package to other approaches in a contest of disciplines (Brownell, 1982b). This contest approach has served its function of uniting professionals in a developing field, but it is no longer likely to advance our knowledge of the treatment of obesity. Second, it is no longer useful to dismantle the behavioral package to determine the relative contribution of its components. The first step is to understand behavior therapy for what it is and to put this knowledge to work to produce significant short-term and long-term weight losses.

Long-Term Behavior Change. The strength of behavior therapy may lie in its combination with other powerful methods of producing weight loss. There are methods for producing large and rapid short-term losses, but no approach has ever combined these short-term benefits with long-term maintenance. This is where behavior therapy may have a special role in the treatment of the obese patient. This issue was discussed briefly in last year's *Annual Review* and in a recent paper by Brownell (1982b). One new application, the combination of behavior therapy and very low calorie diets, will be discussed in the next section.

The short-term losses attained in behavior therapy programs are not impressive. Numerous reviews have shown average weight losses of approximately 1 pound per week in programs that last from 8 to 16 weeks (Foreyt *et al.*, 1981, 1982; Jeffery, Wing, & Stunkard, 1978b; LeBow, 1981; Stunkard & Penick, 1979; Wilson & Brownell, 1980). Although some patients lose more weight, this average loss of 8 to 16 pounds is insufficient when patients in most programs average 60 pounds or more to lose. This does not mean, however, that behavior therapy is a weak approach. Rather, it indicates that its strength lies in long-term change, not in producing initial losses.

The long-term results of behavioral programs are encouraging. In most cases, the average posttreatment loss is maintained at follow-ups of at least 1 year. Jeffery, Vender, and Wing (1978a) found that the mean posttreatment loss of patients at the Stanford Clinic (12.8 pounds) actually increased to 13.5 pounds at 12-month and 18-month follow-ups. Foreyt *et al.* (1982) reported the results of a very large sample of subjects in Baylor's Diet Modification Clinic in Houston. The average posttreatment loss of 14. 9 pounds in 143 male subjects increased to 16.8 pounds 1 year later. For the 447 female subjects, the posttreatment loss was 9.4 pounds and the 1-year follow-up loss was 11.5 pounds. Wilson and Brownell (1980) reviewed the literature and found that the typical study found good maintenance of the weight losses produced in treatment. Similar findings were reported in reviews by Foreyt *et al.* (1981) and by Stunkard and Penick (1979).

It appears from the available evidence that the changes produced in behavioral programs are well-maintained, at least when the "average" patient is considered. There is, of course, enormous individual variation among patients, but the results from behavioral programs still look very good considering the discouraging long-term results of most other approaches. This suggests that behavior therapy has a contribution to make to the long-term maintenance of weight loss and that the time is ripe for teaming behavior therapy with more aggressive approaches to weight loss.

A Promising Development: Very Low Calorie Diets

The most extreme energy deficit is produced by starvation. The metabolic consequences of starvation have been studied carefully, first because scientists were interested in the effects of imposed food shortages during war of famine and then because the idea seemed appealing for the treatment of obesity (Keys, Brozek, Henschel, Mickelson, & Taylor, 1950). The hazard of this approach is that the body not only metabolizes fat for its energy needs but it also uses lean body tissue—a most dangerous process (Keys *et al.*, 1950; Van Itallie, 1980).

Several research groups began studying whether the supplementation of a fasting regime with protein would spare the body's use of its own protein stores from lean tissue. The diet, therefore, became known as the "protein sparing modified fast," more recently called a very low calorie diet. This approach has been studied most extensively by Apfelbaum in Paris (Apfelbaum, Bostsarron, Brigant, & Supin, 1967), Blackburn and Bistrian in Boston (Bistrian, Blackburn, & Stanbury, 1977), Vertes and Genuth in Cleveland (Genuth, Castro, & Vertes,

1974), and Howard and McLean Baird in England (Howard, Grant, Edwards, Littlewood, & McLean Baird, 1978).

In the midst of the careful scientific scrutiny of the supplemented fast, Linn (1976), in the face of protests from noted scientists, published *The Last Chance Diet*. This book popularized liquid protein and began millions of people using an approach which had not been perfected. The liquid protein diets were associated with at least 60 deaths (Sours, Fratalli, Brand, Feldman, Forbes, Swanson, & Paris, 1981). The deaths were attributed to inadequate medical monitoring, lack of appropriate mineral supplementation, and the use of poor-quality protein of low biological value (Van Itallie, 1978).

New developments have made very low calorie diets (VLCD) a promising form of treatment for obesity (Bistrian, 1978; Howard & Bray, 1981; Vertes, Genuth, & Hazelton, 1977; Wadden, Stunkard, & Brownell, in press). There is still controversy about the amount of protein to be used, whether patients attain nitrogen balance, how much carbohydrate should be included in the diet, and the exact vitamin and mineral supplementation to be used (Bistrian, 1978; Van Itallie, 1980; Wadden *et al.*, in press). These disputes aside, the diet appears to be safe if patients receive adequate medical monitoring. This is based on data from thousands of patients in the clinics where the diet is administered under careful supervision (Bistrian, 1978; Vertes *et al.*, 1977; Wadden *et al.*, in press).

There are two basic approaches to the VLCD. The first is to supplement the fast with 1.5 grams of protein per kilogram of ideal body weight (Bistrian, 1978). The protein is taken in three very small meals each day consisting of approximately 3 ounces per meal of lean meat, fish, or fowl. This regimen is also supplemented with potassium, calcium, sodium, and a multivitamin. The second approach is to provide approximately 70 grams of protein each day from a milk- or egg-based formula that comes in powdered form and is mixed with water and consumed as a liquid diet (Vertes *et al.*, 1977). The supplement that has been used most extensively in research and clinical settings is Optifast[R], a product developed in Cleveland by Vertes and Genuth and marketed by the Delmark Company of Minneapolis. The Cambridge Diet[R] is a popularized version of this approach that is thought to raise questions of safety because of questionable medical supervision and the use of less protein than is recommended by most research groups. Presently, no data exist to recommend a choice between the two approaches to low-calorie diets (the powdered supplement vs. the real food).

The VLCD produces impressive weight losses. In programs using the diet for at least 12 weeks, the average weight losses are in excess of

45 pounds (Wadden *et al.*, in press). The diet and the weight losses it produces have very positive effects on patients with hypertension, diabetes, and hyperlipidemia (Bistrian, 1978; Genuth, 1979). Little is known about the problem of attrition, and few studies have examined the long-term results of the VLCD approach. Genuth *et al.* (1974) found that 56% of their patients had regained at least half of their weight loss at a 22-month follow-up. Palgi, Bistrian, Greenberg, and Blackburn (1982) reported that the average posttreatment loss of 50 pounds had decreased to 15 pounds at a 4½-year follow-up. Lindner and Blackburn (1976) found that a subgroup of their patients regained an average of 14 pounds of the original 46-pound loss from 18 to 24 months after treatment.

The VLCD is a good way to produce rapid and significant weight losses. From clinical experience, patients find the weight losses gratifying and adhere better to these diets of 400–800 calories per day than to diets of 1000–1500 calories per day. Patients attribute this to the fact that no food decisions need to be made and that the absence of a palatable diet suppresses their hunger. There is also the possiblity that diets low in carbohydrates suppress appetite, although the hypothesis that ketogenesis is responsible is controversial (Wadden *et al.*, in press). The major drawback to these diets is the high probability of regaining the weight lost.

One might speculate that the addition of behavior modification to a program of supplemented fasting would bring out the best in both approaches. Presumably the diet would produce large and rapid losses and then the habit change produced by the behavior therapy would aid in long-term maintenance. However, several of the programs that have reported high rates of relapse have used behavior modification (Bistrian, 1978; Lindner & Blackburn, 1976; Plagi *et al.*, 1982). It is possible that the behavior modification could be done better in these programs, but more likely is the possibility that the diet and behavior modification interact in puzzling ways. A major challenge for the next decade may be the therapeutic addition of behavior modification to programs using very low calorie diets.

SMOKING

Lat year's edition of the *Annual Review* contained discussions of the health risks of smoking, the measurement of smoking behavior in individuals, and recent advances in smoking cessation programs. There have been even more advances in these areas in the past year. Researchers have continued to perfect methods for the assessment of smoking behavior. This allows for a more valid evaluation of the effectiveness of treatment programs. On the program side, studies on the group treatment of adults who smoke continue to appear in the literature. One notable development in this area is research on controlled smoking versus abstinence, a controversial topic.

The most evident trend in the field in the past year has been the focus on public health issues related to smoking. As is the case with behavior therapy for obesity, there is increasing sentiment in the smoking area that clinical programs aimed at individuals can be improved only so much, and that expanding the focus to large groups, either for prevention or cessation, may greatly improve cost effectiveness. Public health researchers and educators have been interested in this approach for many years, and it is interesting to see behavior therapists moving in this direction. The potential benefits are enormous, not only because of an emphasis on broad-scale programs or because of the promise of behavioral approaches, but also because this move signals collaboration between disciplines. This openness may increase the effectiveness of treatment and may boost the stature of behavior therapy, because its findings will go far beyond its own audience.

This year's discussion of smoking will cover several public health issues and will reflect this movement toward programs with broader scope. The first issue deals with the health risks to persons who are exposed to smokers. If there are such risks, there may be compelling reasons to limit smoking in public places or to inform smoking parents of the effects they may be having on their children. The second issue is the prevention of smoking in children who are at the age of experimentation with cigarettes. Very exciting data exist on this topic. The third issue is the use of antismoking campaigns to control smoking in the general population. Everyone is aware of both prosmoking campaigns waged by the cigarette manufacturers and antismoking efforts mounted by the federal government and by such agencies as the American Heart Association, the American Lung Association, and the American Cancer Society. What are the effects of these efforts to change behavior? If the antismoking campaigns are effective, there may be major implications for how federal funds should be used to have the greatest impact on public health.

Passive Smoking: The Risk of Exposure to Smokers

The health risks of smoking and the reduced risks associated with smoking cessation are established beyond doubt (USDHEW, 1979). From this we know only that a smoker endangers himself or herself.

However, nonsmokers who are exposed to the products of smokers may suffer as well. Similarly, smokers may place themselves at even greater risk from the smoke they encounter at the hands of other smokers.

This is an important public health issue. The legislation of non-smoking areas in airplanes, restaurants, and other public places may save nonsmokers more than discomfort. Workplaces may become less safe if a large number of employees are smokers. Industrial pollutants are of great interest these days, and the products created by smokers may fall into this category. This amounts to greater responsibility for the smoker now that the health hazards may extend to other persons.

A number of studies have concluded that smokers create "indoor pollution" (Bridge & Korn, 1972; Schmeltz, Hoffman, & Wynder, 1975). Hirayama (1981) found that nonsmoking wives of heavy smokers had significantly increased risk of cancer. Repace and Lowery (1980) claim that "levels of respirable particulates in places where tobacco is smoked *greatly* [emphasis added] exceed levels found in smoke-free environments, outdoors, and vehicles on busy commuter highways" (p. 470). In a study at the workplace, White and Froeb (1980) reported that nonsmokers who were chronically exposed to cigarette smoke had pulmonary function levels similar to those of light smokers and worse than those of nonsmokers in smoke-free environments.

Evidence has now been assembled on the health status of children whose parents smoke. The results are not favorable. Each study by itself does not prove a cause-and-effect relationship between smoking in parents and ill health in their children, but taken collectively, the evidence is convincing.

Pulmonary disorders are the most frequently reported problems in the children of smokers. Several studies have found relationships between parental smoking and acute respiratory illness in children (Bonham & Wilson, 1981; Cameron & Robertson, 1973). Two studies found dose-response relationships between bronchitis and pneumonia in children and smoking in their parents (Colley, Holland, & Corkhill, 1974; Harlap & Davies, 1974), and another found a similar relationship between parental smoking and several indices of pulmonary function in the children (Tager, Weiss, & Rosner, 1979). There is, however, some evidence that does not support such a relationship (Lebowitz & Burrows, 1976).

Two recent studies have examined this issue carefully. Gortmaker, Walker, Jacobs, and Ruch-Ross (1982) present data from two random population surveys, one from an urban county in the Midwest and another from a rural area in the East. In both settings, maternal smoking was associated with a 50–240% increase in risk of asthma and functionally impairing asthma in children. The risk persisted when other factors were entered into the multivariate analysis. Bonham and

Wilson (1981) presented data on 37,000 households from the National Health Interview Survey. Children in families with no smokers had 1.1 fewer restricted activity days and .8 fewer disability days than did children with two smokers in the family. Children with one smoker in the family fell between the two extremes. Acute respiratory distress accounted for the extra disability. These authors found a dose–response relationship between the number of cigarettes smoked by adults and disability in children. The analysis controlled for the age of the child, the number of adults in the family, the education of the family head, and family income; the relationship still persisted.

Most evidence suggests that smokers have a negative impact on the health of people around them. This supports the call for more stringent rules about smoking in public places. The argument against the restriction of smoking (voiced most loudly by Southern politicians) is that the government cannot intrude into private matters simply because people are harming themselves. This argument seems weak when children, spouses, and co-workers of smokers may incur health risks by virtue of contact that cannot be avoided. This fact may add increased impetus for legislation, and it may also provide smokers with an added incentive to quit smoking.

The Prevention of Smoking in Children

EXTENT OF THE PROBLEM

Smoking is a serious problem in children. The Surgeon General's report in 1979 showed that approximately 12% of all children between ages 12 and 18 smoke regularly (USDHEW, 1979). The smoking rates are much higher in certain subgroups. For example, 26% of girls between ages 17 and 18 smoke regularly. The high rates exist despite the fact that 96% of teenagers know that smoking is dangerous; 89% know that smoking can cause heart disease (Gallup Youth Survey, 1977).

There is currently a downward trend in the number of teenage smokers. The trend seems to have begun sometime around 1974–1975. Table 6-1, taken from data presented by the National Clearinghouse for Smoking and Health (USDHHS, 1980) shows these trends.

During the period from 1968 to 1974, the percentage of adult smokers declined from 42% to 33%, but the number of teenage smokers rose almost 30%. The reduction in smoking among teenagers since 1974 has been as dramatic as the rise in preceding years, although the extent of the recent decline is in dispute. A group from the University of Michigan reported recently on smoking rates in a nationally representative sample of 15,000 high school seniors (Bachman, Johnston, &

TABLE 6-1.
Regular Teenage Smokers in the United States

Age group	Sex	Percentage		
		1968	1974	1979
12–14	Male	2.9	4.2	3.2
	Female	0.6	4.9	4.3
15–16	Male	17.0	18.1	13.5
	Female	9.6	20.2	11.8
17–18	Male	30.2	31.0	19.3
	Female	18.6	25.9	26.2
12–18	Male	14.7	15.8	10.7
	Female	8.4	15.3	12.7
12–18	Both sexes	11.5	15.6	11.7

O'Malley, 1981). Yearly trends in smoking rates were monitored from 1975 to 1979. The number of males who smoked at least one-half pack of cigarettes per day declined from 20% to 15% during this period, while rates for females increased from 16% to 17%.

There are many possible reasons for the decline in smoking among young persons (USDHHS, 1980). The hazards of smoking are generally known, although this knowledge alone is not thought to motivate many teenagers to avoid or quit smoking. Many adults have stopped smoking during these years. These include persons who are common role models for children, such as parents, teachers, coaches, doctors, athletes, and media personalities. There also seems to be a general trend for smoking to be considered socially unacceptable. Legislation now prohibits smoking in many public places, and nonsmokers are becoming more forceful in expressing their displeasure with smokers. Finally, many schools have some sort of antismoking campaign. These programs range from educational efforts to prohibitions against smoking on school property.

Whatever the decline in smoking rates, and for whatever reason, too many teenagers smoke (between 12% and 30%). Reduction in these rates may have important public health consequences because the effects of smoking are so catastrophic and because many years of chronic illness may be prevented in each individual by early intervention.

THE IMPORTANCE OF SOCIAL FACTORS

Smoking is strongly influenced by social factors, with the most important sources of influence being the family and peers (Evans, 1979; McAlister, Perry, & Maccoby, 1979). Adolescents who have two parents who smoke are twice as likely to smoke themselves as those whose parents are nonsmokers (USDHHS, 1980). Smoking rates in teenagers are also associated with smoking in older siblings. A teenager with an older brother or sister who smokes is four times more likely to smoke than is a teenager with no smokers in the family (USDHEW, 1976).

There is also a strong relationship between a teenager's smoking behavior and smoking behavior of his or her friends (Evans, 1979; McAlister et al., 1979; William, 1971). The crucial years for experimentation with smoking appear to be during junior high school (Laughlin & Lake, 1970; Palmer, 1970). The first cigarette, which is usually unpleasant, is taken from an older friend in a social setting (Bewley, Bland, & Harris, 1974; Newman, 1970). Teenagers themselves report that peer pressure is the main stimulus for their smoking (Newman, 1970). During these important years, smoking may be perceived as an expression of liberation, self-confidence, and maturity, and it provides the teenager with one means of rejecting authority. The intrigue of smoking is only increased by the risks (William, 1971). Combined with pressure from friends who reinforce experimentation and adventurousness, rebelliousness leads many young persons to smoke (Dekker, 1977; Evans, 1979; William, 1971).

Smoking is related to social class and to several associated factors (McAlister et al., 1979). Adolescents in the lower social classes are more likely to smoke than others, even when parental smoking is held constant (McAlister et al., 1979). Smoking is also related negatively to participation in sports and intent to enroll in college, perhaps because these activities bring peer approval in ways thought to be inconsistent with smoking (Horn, 1960; Johnston, Bachman, & O'Malley, 1977).

The recognition of social factors led several researchers to a new approach to the prevention of smoking in teenagers. Traditional programs focused on the health risks of smoking, including lung cancer, emphysema, and coronary heart disease (Thompson, 1978; Yankelovich, 1974). These programs led to changes in knowledge and attitudes but were not effective in changing smoking behavior (Evans & Borgatta, 1970; Piper, Jones, & Matthews, 1974). The emphasis has now changed to the psychosocial determinants of smoking and to skills training for resisting social pressure (Evans, 1979; McAlister et al., 1979).

SMOKING PREVENTION PROGRAMS

Work on the prevention of smoking in teenagers began with studies by Evans and his colleagues. Evans (1976) first collected information on 130 school children (grades 5-7), their teachers, and their principals. The children believed that smoking was dangerous but the social pressure to smoke was more immediate and powerful. Peers, parents, and the media were the main sources of the influence. Evans and his collaborators then developed a model for smoking prevention and a program to be administered in the schools.

The Evans model was based on the medical notion of inoculation against disease. Social pressure was considered to be the disease and infection by the disease was felt to be preventable by inoculation with a small amount of the offending problem (the pressure). The purpose of this approach was to aid the adolescents in identifying the sources of pressure and in developing specific skills to resist it.

The "inoculation" in this approach takes place in a safe setting (the classroom), where the teenagers are asked to role play appropriate responses to the pressure. The program includes films in which peers are shown encountering and resisting pressures to smoke, discussion of the immediate physiological effects of smoking, and information on monitoring smoking behavior. The students are shown a film that indicates that a saliva test (which they will take every 2 weeks) will be an accurate measure of whether they are smoking. The saliva samples are taken but not analyzed (because of cost). One study found that this procedure increased the accuracy of students' self-report of smoking (Evans, Hansen, & Mittlemark, 1977).

The first controlled trial of the inoculation approach was done by Evans, Rozelle, Mittlemark, Hansen, Bane, and Havis (1978). This group compared monitoring and feedback to monitoring and feedback plus inoculation. The monitoring and feedback reduced the rate of "experimental" smoking to approximately half that of a control group. The inoculation did not improve the results. Since this study, other research groups have made improvements in both the program itself and in methods for studying the prevention of smoking.

Recent Approaches. The most notable research in recent years has come from McAlister, Perry, Pechacek, Telch, and their colleagues, a group that originated at Stanford and now has branched to Harvard and the University of Minnesota (Hurd, Johnson, Pechacek, Bast, Jacobs, & Luepker, 1980; McAlister, Perry, Killen, Slinkard, & Maccoby, 1980; McAlister *et al.*, 1979; Perry, Killen, Telch, Slinkard, & Danaher, 1980; Telch, Killen, McAlister, Perry, & Maccoby, 1982). The program has been labeled the Counseling Leadership Against Smoking Pressure (CLASP) program. The CLASP program includes the components of the Evans approach. In addition, the program differs from traditional health education approaches in five fundamental ways:

1. The program does not emphasize the negative effects of smoking on health.

2. The program exposes students to the social pressures they will face in other situations and teaches them specific skills to deal with the pressures.

3. Teams of high school students teach the junior high school students the skills necessary to resist pressure. The peers are thought to be more powerful models and reinforcers of behavior than adults.

4. Behavioral methods of modeling, behavioral rehearsal, and role playing are the predominant teaching methods, as opposed to the lectures, movies, and worksheets used in other programs.

5. The program is administered in an entire school in the hope that a nonsmoking environment will be created.

Table 6-2, adapted from Coates and Perry (1980), shows the components of the smoking program.

McAlister *et al.* (1980) reported the results of this program in a study with 526 students from two junior high schools in California.

TABLE 6-2.
Components of the Smoking Program

Behavioral sources of influence	
Target behaviors	To identify pressures to smoke and ways to deal with them. To get feedback on own health and learn methods to help others quit or not start smoking.
Behavioral rehearsal	Devise and recite methods to resist advertising and peer pressure.
Behavioral commitment	Indicate verbally to class how to resist pressures and how to help others quit or not start smoking.
Environmental sources of influence	
Models	College and high school students demonstrate biofeedback techniques, with monitoring of session to explain immediate health effects.
Family	Students discussing ways to deal with parental smoking and attitudes.
Feedback	Immediate feedback on students' carbon monoxide levels, pulse rates, skin temperatures, lung capacities, and blood pressures, with smokers and nonsmokers compared.
Personal sources of influence	
	Students learn to identify pressures to smoke, learn the immediate effects of smoking, learn skills to stop smoking, and learn ways to help others quit or not start.

Note. Adapted from Coates and Perry (1980).

The program was administered over a 2-year period and included information on smoking and on drug and alcohol abuse. The students receiving the CLASP program began smoking at one-half the rate of students who received no training. These results are most impressive, but are open to question on the grounds that the effects may diminish over the long run. The authors did, however, follow up on the students 9 months, 21 months, and 33 months after the program (Telch *et al.*, 1982). The results are presented in Figure 6-4. The differences between groups were still evident at each of the follow-up assessments. Interestingly, the differences actually increased over time, so that the students who did not receive the program were smoking at three times the rate of the program students at the 33-month follow-up. Telch *et al.* (1982) note that the 5.1% smoking rate among the students in the program was far below the 12.2% national average.

A study by Hurd *et al.* (1980) tested a similar program in the schools of Minneapolis and St. Paul. The 8-month program was done with 1526 seventh graders. This program added a special emphasis on "personalization" and "commitment" techniques. For the personalization, the students were asked to name three fellow students whose

FIG. 6-4.

Changes in the reported prevalence of weekly smoking from a longitudinal observation of two study cohorts. The experimental school received a smoking prevention program and the control school received no program. (From "Long-Term Follow-Up of a Pilot Project on Smoking Prevention with Adolescents" by M. J. Telch, J. D. Kollen, A. L. McAlister, C. L. Perry, and N. Maccoby, *Journal of Behavioral Medicine*, 1982, 5, 1–8. Copyright 1982, Plenum Press. Reprinted by permission.)

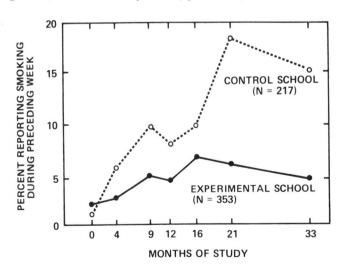

opinions they would most respect. The students with the most votes were then videotaped for the films used to demonstrate ways to deal with pressure to smoke. For the commitment procedure, each student was taped when completing the sentence "I'm not going to smoke because. . . ." The tape was played back to the entire class. In addition, saliva thiocyanate tests were used to substantiate the self-report measures. The program led to substantial decreases in the incidence of smoking in the schools. The authors hypothesized that two components of the program were particularly important. These were the emphasis on the immediate social consequences of smoking and the personalization of the educational materials.

These results are most promising. The programs can be done in an inexpensive fashion and the results are clinically meaningful as well as statistically significant. Large numbers of students can be reached. Most importantly, the long-term results of these programs look very good (Hurd *et al.*, 1980; Telch *et al.*, 1982). This is certainly an area worth pursuing. One important aspect of administering such a program is recruiting students to join. Peltier, Telch, and Coates (1982) compared normal school publicity procedures to person-to-person contact and found the personal contact to be far more effective. These public health issues are very important to investigate.

Some researchers have also studied older children to determine whether smoking cessation can be accomplished through the methods used in smoking prevention programs. Perry *et al.* (1980) used a program similar to the CLASP program with tenth-grade students in California. There was a decrease in smoking rates among students who were involved in the program, but not in control students. Self-reports in this study were verified with carbon monoxide measures. Long-term evaluation of this program is still needed, and a component analysis would help determine which parts of the program should receive more or less attention.

Antismoking Campaigns—A Public Health Issue

Since the early 1960s a tremendous antismoking effort has taken place in the United States, Britain, and some other industrialized countries. British researchers released the report *Smoking and Health* in 1962—a report prepared by the prestigious Royal College of Physicians. The Surgeon General's Report on Smoking and Health appeared in the United States in 1964 (USDHEW, 1964). Since that time a massive campaign to prevent and stop smoking has been urged by many groups, including the U.S. Public Health Service, the American Heart Association, the American Cancer Society, and the American Lung Association.

There is much controversy about these programs, and the stakes are not trivial. Proponents point to the cost effectiveness of large-scale public health campaigns which will influence many people by virtue of their massive audience. Opponents feel that more intensive work with smaller groups is the only way to make lasting changes in behavior. This is an important issue for behavioral researchers. As much from our educational background as from conceptual bias, behavior therapists have focused most of their efforts on small groups or on individuals. If this is not the most cost-effective approach to changing behavior, our reesearch and clinical focus might bear close examination.

These public health campaigns can be aimed at either adults or children. As discussed in the previous section, educational efforts combined with behavioral techniques appear to be effective in controlling experimentation with smoking in junior high school students. Leventhal and Cleary (1980) point to the social underpinnings of antismoking programs and discuss the reasons that intensive programs with individuals may not have the intended effects:

> It is usually assumed that intensive, individual therapy can generate the most significant impact on smoking, but the opposite may in fact be true. Intensive efforts to alter societal, community, and group values and norms might be more effective in producing change in smoking behavior. Restricting smoking in public buildings, requiring nonsmoking sections in airplanes and restaurants, and changing attitudes about the rights of nonsmokers might do more to change smoking habits than intensive procedures aimed at individuals. (p. 381)

SPECIFIC EFFECTS OF COMMUNICATIONS EFFORTS

There have been three main avenues of inquiry into antismoking efforts with discrete groups: small-scale laboratory research on communication, intervention in the schools, and community-wide intervention. These have been reviewed by Leventhal and Cleary (1980), Thompson (1978), and Leventhal, Safer, Cleary, and Gutmann (1980). This area will be covered only briefly here in order to highlight the general nature of the findings.

Much of the laboratory work on antismoking messages has come from Leventhal and colleagues (Leventhal & Cleary, 1980; Leventhal & Niles, 1965). The main emphasis on this research has been on the nature of the message. The primary findings are: (1) Vivid threat messages generated strong intentions to stop smoking but the intentions do not persist; (2) some strong fear messages prompt a person to avoid the message or the threatening situation; (3) messages on personal vulnerability are successful in changing both attitudes and behavior; (4) fear messages must be accompanied by specific action plans to be effective; (5) responses to educational messages are influenced by education and self-esteem (Leventhal & Cleary, 1980). This body of evidence may explain why some educational programs are effective while others are not.

The school programs discussed earlier and the community programs have also investigated educational approaches. One report of an early community campaign in Scotland reported negative results (McKennell, 1968). The Stanford Heart Disease Prevention Program, a three-community study aimed at hypertension, smoking, and diet, used both a mass media approach and an intensive, face-to-face intervention to reduce smoking (Farquhar, 1978; Farquhar, Maccoby, Wood, Alexander, Breitrose, Brown, Haskell, McAlister, Meyer, Nash, & Stern, 1977; Meyer, Nash, McAlister, Maccoby, & Farquhar, 1980). Compared to a 12% increase in the number of smokers in a control community, there was a 5% decrease in smoking in the media-only community and a 17% decrease in the community with both the media and face-to-face interventions. There was a statistical difference between the intensive treatment and control communities but not between the media-only and control communities. A recent study of factory workers in Belgium also show a significant decrease in smoking with a media campaign (Kornitzer, DeBacker, Dramaix, & Thilly, 1980).

Even though these results seem encouraging, Leventhal and Cleary (1980) feel that community programs have had only a minor impact on smoking. An example is the "Cold Turkey" project in Greenfield, Iowa (Ryan, 1973). In conjunction with the filming of the United Artists movie *Cold Turkey*, the Greenfield City Council voted in 1969 to declare Cold Turkey Day, on which smokers signed pledges to quit and the city advertised the hazards of smoking and the benefits of nonsmoking, installed nonsmoking signs, removed tobacco from stores, and had a ceremony 30 days later to honor the quitters. Ryan (1973) interviewed 1385 people 7 months later and found that only 3.9% of the active female smokers and 14.2% of the male smokers had maintained their pledged abstinence. This is discouraging, because it is difficult to imagine a more concerted effort at mobilizing social support for smoking cessation.

Whether these community programs are "effective" depends on perspective. The size of the effects, even in the most powerful programs, are not large. However, the cost per person influenced can be small with such an approach. In addition, there may be synergistic effects of many campaigns, so that the combination may be more impressive than the sum of the components. This possibility is suggested by the information presented in the next section.

GENERAL EFFECTS OF ANTISMOKING CAMPAIGNS

Determining the effects of a social phenomenon, such as the anti-smoking movement, is not easy. Many factors have occurred in conjunction with this movement, including changes in the price of cigarettes, general health consciousness, changes in the demographic characteristics of the population, the introduction of low tar and nicotine cigarettes, and so on. Given this difficulty, however, there have been some attempts to isolate the influence of the antismoking campaign.

Warner (1977, 1981) traced the changes in per capita cigarette consumption throughout the century, with a particular emphasis on the past 20 years. He conducted a time series analysis with a demand regression equation to compare projected smoking rates with actual smoking rates. Per capita cigarette consumption in the United States rose throughout the century until 1964, the year of the Surgeon General's Report on Smoking and Health (USDHEW, 1964). There has been a consistent decline in smoking rate in the intervening years, averaging approximately 1% per year since 1973. Warner (1981) feels that the decline cannot be attributed to specific events such as the Surgeon General's report, but rather that it is the general effect of a widespread social movement.

Figure 6-5 presents Warner's (1981) comparison of actual cigarette consumption and anticipated consumption. Anticipated consumption was used to account for adverse publicity, laws that restrict smoking in public places, per capita consumption, the effect of habit, price, and differences in the smoking population (e.g., changes in the age and sex distribution of the general population). The results show that actual consumption is far below anticipated consumption. Warner (1977, 1981) estimated that per capita consumption would now be 20–30% above its current level if not for the antismoking campaign. Warner also noted that behavior changes lagged behind changes in knowledge and attitudes. To the extent that Warner's equation accounts for competing factors, the antismoking campaign appears to have had a substantial impact on smoking.

The Ban on TV and Radio Advertising. The Fairness Doctrine enacted by the Federal Trade Commission greatly facilitated the communication of antismoking messages. This required television and radio stations to provide public service time for antismoking messages if they chose to air advertisements for cigarettes. This was applauded by

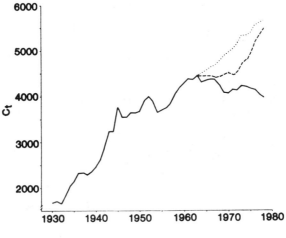

FIG.6-5.

Per capita cigarette consumption (C_t) since 1930. The solid line represents actual consumption, the dotted line is consumption predicted in absence of an antismoking campaign and with an assumed price constancy, and the dashed line is consumption predicted in absence of a campaign but with actual prices experienced. (From "Cigarette Smoking in the 1970s: The Impact of the Anti-Smoking Campaign on Consumption" by K. E. Warner, *Science*, 1981, *211*, 729–731. Copyright 1981, American Association for the Advancement of Science. Reprinted by permission.)

public health experts, and there was a large increase in the number of antismoking spots. In 1971, the ban on cigarette advertising on radio and television took effect. This also seemed a positive move, because it was generally agreed that the advertisements were successful in making smoking more appealing to both children and adults.

The effects of the ban on cigarette advertising may have been counterproductive and were certainly counterintuitive. Along with the termination of cigarette advertising came a great decrease in the time allowed by broadcasters for the antismoking messages. Hamilton (1972) felt that the antismoking advertisements were more effective at preventing smoking than the cigarette advertisements were at encouraging it. This notion should strengthen the conviction of scientists that public health efforts should be evaluated carefully before policies are forged for an entire country.

CONCLUSONS

Public health approaches to smoking reduction appear to be very promising. Warner's (1977, 1981) analysis shows the benefits of large-scale media campaigns, and the community study at Stanford suggests the promise of this approach in conjunction with a more general health campaign (Farquhar *et al.*, 1977; Meyer *et al.*, 1980). The literature is not without negative results, but at the very least the area is worthy of further exploration. This may be an important notion for behavior therapists. Leventhal and Cleary (1980) have noted that specific plans for behavior change are one of the keys to the success of such a communication. This is where behavior therapists can make a real contribution. Collaboration among experts in public health, social psychology, behavior therapy, and other disciplines may be most fruitful.

ALCOHOLISM

The past year has been an important one for the field of alcoholism. One controversy in particular, the debate about controlled drinking and abstinence, has raged with great intensity. At the time of this writing, this issue is dominating the field. Not only has it pitted scientist against scientist, it has captured the attention of the media, thus escalating the already strong sentiment. The outcome of this debate has important ramifications for both research and treatment in the field of alcoholism. It is time to update the discussion of controlled drinking that appeared in last year's *Annual Review* and to identify the sources of controversy.

This section on alcoholism will cover only one topic—controlled drinking versus abstinence. This issue is, of course, not the only topic being addressed by researchers. In fact, very little controlled research is being done on the topic. However, the issue has tremendous importance for the field. What is at stake is the essence of traditional conceptualizations of problem drinking. This emotional debate goes far beyond arguments about theory among academics. The cost of alcoholism in human terms is enormous. On the one hand, if the opponents of the controlled drinking approach are correct, further adherence to the model could lead to the ruin of many lives. On the other hand, controlled drinking may lead to better outcomes for some patients.

It is unusual to cover only one topic in a review of a field, but this is a topic of unusual importance. Next year's *Annual Review* will resume coverage of some of the other developments in the field.

The Furor over Controlled Drinking

In July 1982, an article appeared in the journal *Science* that questioned whether controlled drinking is a viable goal for alcoholics (Pendery, Maltzman, & West, 1982). The article questioned the conclusions reached by Sobell and Sobell (1973a, 1973b) and by Caddy, Addington, and Perkins (1978) that some alcoholics could be trained to drink in a moderate fashion and that the goal of controlled drinking was at least as likely as a goal of abstinence to produce long-term benefits for patients. Such debate is not unusual in science, but the depth of the emotions stirred by this controversy has brought the issue to the attention of both lay and professional audiences.

THE CONTROVERSY

The debate over controlled drinking versus abstinence has interesting historical origins. This history has been outlined in detail by W. R. Miller (in press) and by Sobell and Sobell (1978). It begins with an impetus from both the scientific world and the public arena. The academic impetus came from Jellinek (1960) at the Yale Center for Alcohol Studies. The public impetus came from Alcoholics Anonymous. Together, these powerful sources of influence led to widespread acceptance of the notion that abstinence was without question the only goal for recovering alcoholics.

Alcoholics Anonymous (AA) has touched millions of problem drinkers since its birth in the post-Depression years. Its conceptual model has such popular appeal that people with other problems have formed similar groups, namely Overeaters Anonymous and Gamblers Anonymous. The AA position is that alcoholism is a disease that can be remedied only by total abstinence from drinking. The alcoholic is considered highly sensitive to the effects of alcohol for genetic reasons, and alcohol is thought to have an "allergic" effect on the drinker. There has been a strong and consistent belief in Alcoholics Anonymous that controlled drinking is simply not possible:

> The idea that somehow, someday he will control and enjoy his liquor drinking is the great obsession of every abnormal drinker. The persistence of this illusion is astonishing. Many pursue it to the gates of insanity or death. (Alcoholics Anonymous, 1955, p. 41)

A second quote shows the belief that some persons are allergic to alcohol, so that drinking in any amount is tantamount to complete failure:

> We believe . . . that the action of alcohol on these chronic alcoholics is a manifestation of an allergy; that the phenomenon of craving is limited to this class and never occurs in the average temperate drinker. These allergic types can never safely use alcohol in any form at all. . . ." (p. 4)

The AA model is not surprising given the severity of the disorder, nor is it surprising that divergence from the model is met with such anger. A great number of people who work in counseling for alcoholics are recovered alcoholics themselves, so there is a personal stake in the understanding of the problem. Since alcoholism has devastating social, emotional, and physical consequences, the perceived costs of following an incorrect theory are great. Finally, AA bases its approach in part on religion, so that a Higher Power is thought to be the main source of inspiration for the drinker. The entry of religion into the model greatly increases the emotional impact of the theory on its adherents.

The abstinence model did have and still does have intuitive appeal to both drinkers and nondrinkers. The AA approach, therefore, existed in a social climate in which its tenets were widely accepted. The movement gained momentum with the publication of *The Disease Model of Alcoholism* by Jellinek (1960). Although Jellinek had a broader perspective than he is credited for, and although his model left room for controlled drinking in nonphysically dependent drinkers, his work was used by AA as support for the abstinence approach (W. R. Miller, in press).

Jellinek (1960) proposed five types of alcoholism, the most serious being "gamma" alcoholism which is characterized by physical dependence on alcohol. He hypothesized that alcoholics of the less serious types might return to controlled drinking, and although this phenomenon was more difficult in gamma alcoholics, he did *not* assert that these individuals were permanently subject to loss of control (W. R. Miller, in press). Jellinek was careful to distinguish the types of alcoholism, thus supporting the recent move toward differential diagnosis, and in turn countering the view that any alcoholic cannot drink in a controlled fasion (W. R. Miller, in press).

A Toehold for Controlled Drinking. The possibility that some alcoholics can drink in moderation was based initially on the clinical observation that there were recovered alcoholics who did drink. As early as the 1940s and 1950s, reports on controlled drinking were quite common (Shea, 1954; Wallerstein, Chotlos, Friend, Hammersley, Perlswig, & Winship, 1957). W. R. Miller (in press) noted that studies at these times "unapologetically and routinely reported nonabstinent outcomes as successful." In the 1970s, researchers, mainly behavior therapists, began evaluating controlled drinking in a systematic fashion (Lovibond & Caddy, 1970; Sobell & Sobell, 1973a, 1973b). By the early 1980s, there was general agreement among many noted researchers that controlled drinking, at the very least, does occur for some alcoholics (Miller & Hester, 1980; Nathan & Briddell, 1977; Nathan & Goldman, 1979; Pattison, Sobell, & Sobell, 1977; Sobell & Sobell, 1978, 1980). The opinions range from belief that controlled drinking is a more desirable goal than abstinence for some alcoholics (Sobell & Sobell, 1978, 1980), to the search for which people are most likely to control their drinking (W. R. Miller, in press; Miller & Hester, 1980), to the notion that controlled drinking is a viable goal only for alcoholics who have failed repeatedly at attempts to be abstinent (Nathan & Goldman, 1979).

The controversy flared with the publication of the paper by Pendery et al. (1982) in *Science*. The paper claimed that the subjects studied for 2 years by Sobell and Sobell (1973a, 1973b) and for 3 years by Caddy et al. (1978) had not responded as favorably to a controlled drinking program as the Sobells and Caddy et al. had reported. The Pendery paper brought very strong reactions.

THE EVIDENCE

Pendery et al. (1982) conducted a reevaluation of the status of the patients in the original study on controlled drinking by Sobell and Sobell (1973a, 1973b). These data will be discussed in more detail in a later section, but the essence of the findings was that the follow-up "revealed no evidence that gamma alcoholics had acquired the ability to engage in controlled drinking . . ." (Pendery et al., 1982, p. 174). Pendery et al. were strongest in their exception to the follow-up results of Caddy et al. (1978). The media seized upon this article instantly. The television networks broadcast the findings on the evening news, there were syndicated columns in *The New York Times* and *The Los Angeles Times*, articles in *Newsweek* and *Time*, and so forth. For the most part, the media implied that fraud had been exposed and that controlled drinking was an illusion. Believers in the abstinence model rushed not only to strengthen their position but also to condemn the Sobells for what they saw as an intentional effort to misdirect the field.

It is apparent that this debate goes much deeper than the typical academic dispute over theory. The fact that the media gave the topic so much play is evidence of a strong feeling among the public, and the fact that the media presented the controlled drinking advocates in a negative light is evidence that the public still believes in the abstinence model. What is more discouraging than the absence of objectivity are some statements attributed by the press to members of Pendery et al. (1982). If reported accurately, these statements accused the Sobells of fraud and attacked their personal integrity, a matter that has serious ethical ramifications. It is easy to see why objectivity gets lost in the fray.

The Study by Sobell and Sobell (1973a, 1973b). The study in dispute was conducted by the Sobells at the Patton State Hospital in California in 1971 and 1972. The subjects were 70 "gamma" alcoholics who voluntarily admitted themselves to the hospital. They were assigned to either an abstinence goal program or to a controlled drinking program, a decision made by the research staff. The decision to assign subjects to the controlled drinking goal was made if the subjects: (1) requested limited drinking as a goal; (2) had some history of self-control and ability to control impulsiveness; (3) were expected to return to a supportive environment; and (4) had at some time successfully controlled their drinking at moderate levels.

The 40 subjects in the controlled drinking group were then randomly assigned to the controlled drinker–experimental (behavioral treatment aimed at controlled drinking) or controlled drinker–control (traditional abstinence treatment) conditions. The 30 subjects in the abstinence group were randomly assigned to a behavioral program aimed at abstinence or to a traditional abstinence treatment. The experimental design is shown in Figure 6-6.

The behavioral program for both abstinence and controlled drinking subjects, called "individualized behavior therapy," was administered in 17 treatment sessions. The patients were followed for 2 years after discharge from the program. The program itself is described in detail by Sobell and Sobell (1978), and variations are described by Nirenberg, Ersner-Hershfield, Sobell, and Sobell (1981). Briefly, it consisted of a variety of procedures that were undertaken at a simulated bar in the hospital, including videotaping of drunken behavior, drinking in moderation, aversion conditioning, simulated failure and the development of coping responses, problem solving, education, and a great deal of attention from the program staff.

The evaluation of treatment outcome was discussed at length by the Sobells (Sobell & Sobell, 1973a, 1973b, 1978). The subjects were tracked during the time after discharge and substantiating information was collected from three collateral information sources (family member, friend, etc.) for each subject. The subjects and the collateral sources were given the daily drinking disposition assessment in which they were asked "How many days since our last contact have you had anything to drink and how much did you drink on each day?" (Sobell & Sobell, 1978, p. 110). The responses were recorded verbatim and then classified into five categories: (1) drunk days, (2) controlled drinking days, (3) abstinent days, (4) days incarcerated in jail, and (5) days incarcerated in a hospital. Measures were also taken on general adjustment, vocational status, occupational status, residential status and stability, valid driver's license status, marital status, use of therapeutic supports, possession of the program card, and health status. This was the most extensive evaluation ever conducted on the adjustment of alcoholics after completion of a treatment program. Of the subjects who received the individualized behavior therapy, 98.6% were followed

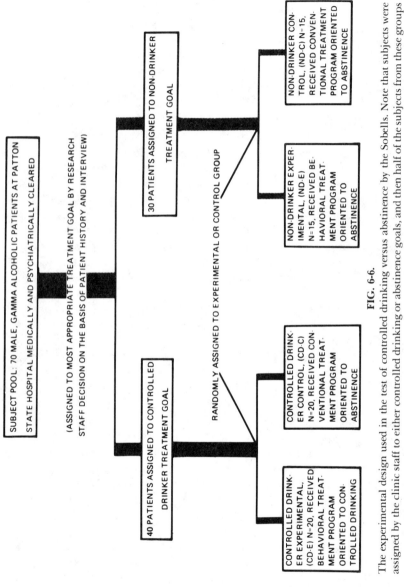

FIG. 6-6.

The experimental design used in the test of controlled drinking versus abstinence by the Sobells. Note that subjects were assigned by the clinic staff to either controlled drinking or abstinence goals, and then half of the subjects from these groups were assigned randomly to receive individualized behavior therapy or standard treatment. (From "Alcoholics Treated by Individualized Behavior Therapy: One-Year Treatment Outcome" by M. B. Sobell and L.C. Sobell, *Behaviour Research and Therapy*, 1973, *11*, 599–618. Copyright 1973, Pergamon Press, Inc. Reprinted by permission.)

248

over the 2-year period—a striking accomplishment given the nature of the population.

The results from the study by the Sobells provided positive evidence that controlled drinking might be the preferred goal for some subjects. Table 6-3 shows the results for the study's primary measures. The first column displays the statistical comparisons of the controlled drinker–experimental and controlled drinker–control groups. The primary measure, the percentage of days functioning well, was defined as the sum of abstinent and controlled drinking days, in contrast to days not functioning well, defined as the sum of drunk days and days incarcerated in a hospital or jail. During both the first and second years of the study, the controlled drinker–experimental subjects had a significantly higher number of days in which they functioned well. There were also advantages for these subjects on the reports from collateral sources and on some of the measures of social adjustment.

An example of the data on experimental and control subjects is presented in Figure 6-7. These data show the contrast in the percentage of days functioning well in the two groups. This visual comparison of the first two 6-month periods reflects the general findings reported by

TABLE 6-3.

Summary of Statistical Analyses Performed between Controlled Drinker–Experimental (CD-E) and Controlled Drinker–Control (CD-C) Conditions and between Nondrinker–Experimental (ND-E) and Nondrinker–Control (ND-C) Conditions

	Groups compared	
Outcome variable	CD-E vs. CD-C	ND-E vs. ND-C
% days functioning well, year 1	$p < .005$	$p < .005$
% days functioning well, year 2	$p < .001$	$.10 < p < .05$
Drinking control index, year 2	$p < .001$	n.s.
CIS evaluations of subjects':		
General adjustment, year 1	$p < .05$	$p < .05$
General adjustment, year 2	$p < .05$	n.s.
Occupational status, year 1	n.s.	n.s.
Occupational status, year 2	$.09 < p < .01$	n.s.
Vocational status, year 1	n.s.	n.s.
Vocational status, year 2	$.02 < p < .01$	n.s.
Residential stability and status, year 1	n.s.	n.s.
Residential stability and status, year 2	$p < .09$	n.s.
Driver's license status, year 2	n.s.	n.s.
Physical health status, year 2	$p < .08$	n.s.

Note. From *Behavioral Treatment of Alcohol Problems: Individualized Therapy and Controlled Drinking* by M. B. Sobell and L. C. Sobell. Copyright 1978, Plenum Press. Reprinted by permission.

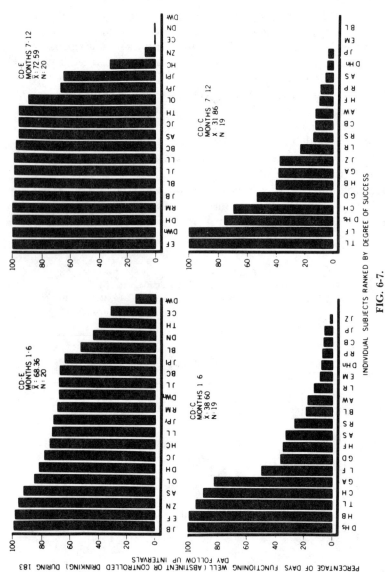

FIG. 6-7.

Percentage of days spent functioning well (either abstinent or controlled drinking) by individual controlled drinker–experimental (CD-E) and controlled drinker–control (CD-C) subjects during the first and second 6-month follow-up intervals. (From "Alcoholics Treated by Individualized Behavior Therapy: One-Year Treatment Outcome" by M. B. Sobell and L. C. Sobell, *Behaviour Research and Therapy,* 1973, *11,* 599–618. Copyright 1973, Pergamon Press, Inc. Reprinted by permission.)

Sobell and Sobell (1973a, 1973b). In summarizing their interpretation of the data, the Sobells made a special point to note that alcoholism is a complex problem and that there are no simple solutions. In light of this cautionary note, they were optimistic about the findings from the controlled drinking subjects in their test of individualized behavior therapy (IBT):

> A quite radical and intensive experiment was performed to test a specific broad-spectrum approach to the behavioral treatment of alcohol problems, and *the experiment was successful.* In particular, *only subjects treated by IBT with a goal of controlled drinking successfully engaged in a substantial amount of limited, nonproblem drinking during the two years of follow-up, and those subjects also had more abstinent days than subjects in any other group.* These findings remain the single most important result of the IBT study. (Sobell & Sobell, 1978, p. 166; emphasis in original)

Caddy *et al.* (1978) did a 3-year follow-up of the subjects in the study by the Sobells. Interviews were conducted by a research assistant and graduate students in psychology. A total of 49 of the original 70 subjects were interviewed; 36 were interviewed in person and 13 were interviewed over the telephone. Caddy *et al.* reported that the controlled drinker–experimental subjects continued their superiority to the control subjects on measures of drinking and adjustment. It appeared, therefore, from data by Sobell and Sobell (1973a, 1973b) and Caddy *et al.* (1978) that the controlled drinking approach was worth further exploration.

The Challenge by Pendery et al. (1982). The Pendery *et al.* group noted that controlled drinking runs counter to conventional wisdom in the field of alcoholism. There is tremendous opposition to the goal of controlled drinking in persons who are physically dependent on alcohol (Block, 1976; Fox, 1967). The fear is that alcohol in any amount is dangerous.

Pendery *et al.* (1982) did follow-up interviews with the patients of Sobell and Sobell (1973a, 1973b) and their collateral sources during the period from 1976 to 1979. These interviews promised to yield important information because they would greatly expand the follow-up done in the earlier studies. According to the authors,

> in order to assess the results reported for these two shorter-term follow-up studies and to determine the long-term effects of the treatment, we located and interviewed as many as possible of the original subjects. . . . One purpose of these interviews was to locate documentary data (such as records of hospitalizations for alcoholism and arrests for drunken driving) that would confirm or refute the evaluations of the original investigators. These data, supported by affidavits and records of interviews, have led us to conclusions that are very different from the conclusions of the Sobells and Caddy *et al.* (Pendery *et al.*, 1982, p. 172)

Pendery *et al.* interviewed 17 of the 20 subjects in the Sobells' controlled drinker–experimental group. Of the original 20, 4 patients had died of alcohol-related causes and 1 could not be located, but the latter's status during the follow-up period was documented from records. From the records, 13 of these patients were readmitted to a hospital within approximately 1 year after discharge. Ten of the subjects were readmitted to Patton State Hospital, the institution where the research took place. These authors also felt that the incarceration records told a tale much worse than the picture presented by the Sobells.

The Pendery *et al.* group took particular exception to the 3-year follow-up data presented by Caddy *et al.* (1978). For example, Pendery *et al.* presented data on the six subjects the Caddy group rated highest (all six were reported to be functioning well 100% of the days). Pendery *et al.* reported that four of the six had appeared engaged in heavy drinking that year. One of the two who appeared to be doing well did so only after three additional hospitalizations for alcoholism and incarcerations in both jail and a road camp. Data for the remaining subjects also showed great discrepancies.

The conclusions reached by Pendery *et al.* (1982) are in conflict with those of the Sobells and are completely contrary to those of Caddy *et al.* (1978). Pendery *et al.* summarize their findings on the 20 subjects by saying that

> only one, who apparently had not experienced withdrawal symptoms, maintained a pattern of controlled drinking; eight continued to drink excessively—regularly or intermittently—despite repeated damaging consequences; six abandoned their efforts to engage in controlled drinking and became abstinent; four died from alcohol related causes; and one, certified about a year after discharge from the research project as gravely disturbed because of drinking, was missing. (Pendery *et al.*, 1982, p. 169)

AN ANALYSIS

There seem to be two main issues here:

1. What was the exact status of the Sobells' subjects after discharge from the program?
2. What can be said about prescribing controlled drinking as a goal for alcoholics?

The first issue, the status of the controlled drinking subjects in the Sobell study, is difficult to settle. Sobell and Sobell (1978) acknowledge the possible weakness of their data because their conclusions were based primarily on self-reports from the subjects and their collaterals.

The Sobells do cite several studies that indicate that self-reports may be surprisingly accurate (see last year's *Annual Review* for a discussion of this topic). They also state that no better measures are available and that some confidence can be placed in the self-reports if they are accompanied by information from multiple collateral sources, unannounced breath tests in the field, official records of arrests and hospitalizations, and periodic liver function tests.

In this regard, the Pendery *et al.* (1982) study is no stronger than the study by the Sobells. Estimates of drinking were based on self-reports from the patients and collateral sources. Official records were used to evaluate hospitalization, incarceration, and so forth, but the Sobells made similar use of these sources. How then could two studies find such different results?

Several explanations are possible. First is that demand characteristics, expectation, and experimenter bias played a role in the responses elicited from the patients. It is not difficult to imagine that the Sobells' subjects, knowing they were part of a novel approach, were prone to bias their responses in the desired direction. Similarly, Pendery *et al.*, at least from the statements attributed to them by the press, believed strongly that the controlled drinking was dangerous. It is possible that these researchers inadvertently biased the responses of the patients. Considering the low cost for lying by the patients, the desire to please the researchers, and the tendency for some alcoholics to distort the truth, it is quite possible that both the Sobells and Pendery *et al.* reported the data exactly as acquired but that the patients gave different accounts to the two groups.

Problems with the demand characteristics can be alleviated in part by reports from the collateral sources. Such accounts were obtained in both studies, yet even these reports disagreed. Perhaps the collateral sources were biased, intentionally or not, by the expectations of the experimenters. What remains, therefore, are the official records of hospitalizations, arrests, and so forth. The discrepancies in this area are puzzling. The data of the Pendery *et al.* (1982) and the Sobell and Sobell (1973a, 1973b) studies are not very discrepant, and differences in the interpretation seem to cloud the picture. However, the Caddy *et al.* (1978) report does differ substantially from the Pendery *et al.* (1982) article, suggesting that one of the two groups is incorrect.

Controlled Drinking Revisited. The most important issue is, of course, whether controlled drinking is a viable goal for some alcoholics. The findings of Pendery *et al.* (1982) have been cited to show that treatment programs should abandon controlled drinking as a goal. However, based on no more than the data from Pendery *et al.* and a conceptual bias, such statements are vacuous. It is not surprising that the Pendery *et al.* paper was published—it raises a very important issue. What is surprising is that the paper inadequately addressed several crucial points. The Pendery *et al.* (1982) paper has three main deficits:

1. The authors do not acknowledge the fact that expectation and demand characteristics might have played a role in the discrepancy in the studies.
2. The paper mentions almost nothing about the many other studies on controlled drinking, as if to imply that questioning the data from the first study (by the Sobells) can settle the question of controlled drinking versus abstinence. Without this presentation, the paper is no more than a dispute over the progress of 20 patients, not a head-on test of whether controlled drinking is useful.
3. The Pendery *et al.* paper was published with no information on the subjects who received the other treatment. Problems among the controlled drinking subjects cannot be interpreted in the absence of data on the other groups. Even if the general outcome among the controlled drinking subjects was unfavorable, it might have been no worse than that of the other subjects. In any group of alcoholics followed for a period of years, there will be many instances of tragic social and medical events. Interpreting these events requires a comparison group.

In the midst of all this controversy, it seems appropriate to examine the evidence not only from the two studies discussed in detail above, but from other studies that relate to this issue. There may be problems in the methods and results of the Sobell and Sobell (1973a, 1973b) study, the Caddy *et al.* (1978) study, and/or the Pendery *et al.* (1982) study, but this does not negate the evidence from many other sources.

THE EVIDENCE ON CONTROLLED DRINKING

A great deal of evidence exists on controlled drinking. These results have been interpreted in many ways by many researchers, and sorting through these opinions can be difficult. Interestingly, even the Sobells, the researchers most closely identified with the controlled drinking model, state clearly that controlled drinking is only applicable for some patients (Sobell & Sobell, 1980). The evidence on controlled drinking was presented in last year's *Annual Review* and has been reviewed thoroughly in other sources (Franks & Wilson, 1979; Lloyd & Salzberg, 1975; P. M. Miller, 1976; W. R. Miller, in press; Miller & Hester, 1980; Nathan & Briddell, 1977; Nathan & Goldman, 1979;

Pattison, 1976; Pattison *et al.*, 1977; Sobell, 1978; Sobell & Sobell, 1978, 1980). This information will be reviewed briefly here and new information will be discussed.

In 1977, Pattison *et al.* reviewed 74 studies in which some alcoholics were reported to be able to control their drinking at moderate levels. More than half of these studies that their subjects were gamma alcoholics (Jellinek, 1960). Sobell and Sobell (1978) cite six additional studies that reported that some alcoholics could return to nonproblem drinking (Armor, Polich, & Stambul, 1978; Harris & Walter, 1976; Orford, Oppenheimer, & Edwards, 1976; Pomerleau, Pertschuk, & Stinnett, 1976; Popham & Schmidt, 1976; Vogler, Weissbach, & Compton, 1977). When the data from these studies were combined, between 12% and 18% of the 11,817 subjects were reported to have engaged in nonproblem drinking, while 10.4% were completely abstinent (Miller & Hester, 1980; Sobell & Sobell, 1978). It is noteworthy that almost all the programs included in this review had abstinence as the goal. The rates of controlled drinking are higher in programs in which abstinence is not the goal (Miller & Hester, 1980; Sobell & Sobell, 1978. One report from the United Kingdom (Robertson & Heather, 1980) and another from Norway (Duckert, 1981) indicate that the goal of controlled drinking may be more commonly prescribed in other countries than in the United States.

The Rand Report, released in 1976, brought the issue of controlled drinking out of the academic world into the general view of the public (Armor *et al.*, 1978). The Rand Report was a national survey of 14,000 patients at 44 federally funded alcoholism centers coordinated by the National Institute on Alcohol Abuse and Alcoholism (NIAAA). The report provided support for the notion that controlled drinking is possible in some cases:

> The improved clients include only a relatively small number who are long-term abstainers. About one-fourth of the clients interviewed at 18 months have abstained for six months . . . the majority of improved clients are either drinking moderate amounts of alcohol—but at levels far below what could be described as alcoholic drinking—or engaging in alternating periods of drinking and abstention. (Armor *et al.*, 1978, p. 98)

A second report by the Rand Corporation was released in 1980 and published a year later (Polich, Armor, & Braiker, 1981). This study involved the tracking of 922 male alcoholics during treatment and 4 years of follow-up. At the 4-year mark, 85% of the follow-ups were completed. Self-reports were substantiated with collateral reports and breath tests. The study has been reviewed by W. R. Miller (1982), so only the highlights will be presented here.

One of the most interesting findings of the second Rand Report was that continuous abstinence was not a useful criterion for success. Fully 28% of the sample had been abstaining for the 6 months prior to the interview, but only 7% had been abstinent for the full 4 years. Furthermore, 18% of the sample had been drinking without the symptoms of alcoholism. W. R. Miller (1982) points out that this is an even higher rate than found in the first Rand Report (Armor et al., 1978), even though more stringent criteria were used for defining controlled drinking in the second report. The second Rand Report also found that abstinence of less than 6 months did not predict success (i.e., subjects abstinent less than 6 months had the same poor prognosis as subjects drinking with symptoms of dependence). W. R. Miller (in press) notes the importance of this finding, as the only evidence for many abstinence programs rely on follow-up periods of 6 months or less.

The Rand Report (Polich et al., 1981) provides new insight into the process of controlled drinking versus abstinence, but the data are only correlational. The report followed the progress of patients who chose to follow the abstinence or controlled drinking route, and only random assignment in a well-controlled series of trials will settle the issue. W. R. Miller (1982) notes this aspect of the Rand Report:

> What the Rand Report does *not* document, of course, is the effectiveness of treatment methods that *intend* to produce moderation. All programs studied had total abstinence as their goal, so that the 18% of clients who became controlled drinkers did so in spite of treatment advice. When treatment programs teach specific methods of *how* to moderate drinking, the percentage of moderation outcomes is much higher. (p. 77).

When all this information is assembled, it simply is not possible to say with certainty whether controlled drinking or abstinence is the best approach for particular patients. Certainly there is enough evidence to warrant the investigation of controlled drinking, and those who advocate its ouster from research and clinical settings seem moved more by well-intentioned belief than objective evidence. It is unfortunate that the current climate will probably deter researchers from pursuing research on controlled drinking.

Current thinking on controlled drinking is that it may be useful in patients with particular backgrounds and drinking histories (Miller & Hester, 1980), although Nathan and Goldman (1979) recommend extreme caution before assigning a patient to such a goal. The Rand Report suggests that controlled drinking may be advisable for nonaddicted drinkers (Polich et al., 1981). This report found that those who were most likely to moderate their drinking were under age 40 and employed, had fewer life problems related to alcohol, fewer dependence symptoms, less heavy drinking, greater disagreement with the disease concept of alcoholism, and increased likelihood of rejecting the label of "alcoholic." Miller and Hester (1980) reviewed the literature on controlled drinking and abstinence and concluded that controlled drinkers do not fit the classic picture of the alcoholic. They are likely to have fewer alcohol-related problems, fewer symptoms, less family history of problem drinking, and more social support. They are likely to drink less initially and are likely to be younger, female, and unwilling to regard themselves as alcoholics.

There is general agreement that abstinence is the most suitable goal for severely addicted drinkers (W. R. Miller, 1982; Miller & Caddy, 1977; Miller & Hester, 1980; Nathan & Goldman, 1979; Sobell & Sobell, 1978, 1980). W. R. Miller (in press), Miller and Caddy (1977), and Sobell and Sobell (1980) have proposed guidelines for choosing abstinence as a goal. Nathan and Goldman (1979) feel that abstinence should be the goal for all problem drinkers but that controlled drinking is worth pursuing if the abstinence approach fails. The important issues to be settled are whether abstinence should be the first goal, whether controlled drinking might be best for some types of patients, and, if so, what characteristics define these patients.

W. R. Miller (in press) completed a careful review of the information on controlled drinking. He feels that the data support five conclusions:

1. Controlled drinking methods produce overall success rates at least comparable to those resulting from studies of abstinence methods at 1- to 2-year follow-ups.
2. Without moderation training, between 5% and 20% of treated cases become nonproblem drinkers.
3. With moderation training, approximately 65% maintain successful outcomes 12 months following treatment.
4. Controlled drinkers are in general no more likely to relapse than are abstainers.
5. Those who successfully maintain control drinking tend to be younger clients with fewer symptoms of alcohol dependence, whereas older and addicted individuals are more likely to achieve and maintain abstinence.

Thus far the debate on controlled drinking versus abstinence has centered on the propensity for the alcoholic to relapse and resume uncontrolled drinking. The main dependent measures in such inquiries relate to how much the person is drinking. There are, however, other factors to consider. One is the physical and psychological status of people at various stages of alcohol use. For example, Wilkinson and Sanchez-Craig (1981) measured changes in cognitive function in problem drinkers who were in a treatment program. Abstinence or very low levels of consumption were associated with improvements in brain function, but moderate levels of drinking were not.

LOOKING AHEAD

This controversy is likely to generate debate for many years to come. If the outcome is a greater focus on controlled research, then the debate will have been worthwhile. The debate will not have been worthwhile if it stirs nothing but emotional charges leveled by one investigator against another. These merely provoke the media and reinforce the public view that there must be a hero and a villain in a battle that must be won (the media need an answer to be able to take sides). This need for an answer is destructive when none may exist, and it destroys public confidence in science. The failing confidence is not surprising in a climate in which one expert proclaims the virtues of some approach and another expert, stimulated by a willing media, is all too eager to condemn the original position.

The challenge of the data of Sobell and Sobell (1973a, 1973b) and Caddy *et al.* (1978) by Pendery *et al.* (1982) cannot be easily resolved. The Addiction Research Foundation in Toronto, a highly respected institution, is supporting an independent investigation (by a blue ribbon panel) of the two studies. The release of the findings from this panel may have a great influence on the field. There is also a possibility that the most respected researchers in the field will comment in a scholarly way about these studies and about the issue of controlled drinking. By the time next year's *Annual Review* appears, the new information which is appearing should broaden our perspective even further.

CHAPTER

7

BEHAVIOR THERAPY WITH CHILDREN AND ADOLESCENTS

CYRIL M. FRANKS

INTRODUCTION: SOME GENERAL TRENDS

The broadening domain of child behavior therapy reflects developments in the field at large. Cognition, systems, and family approaches, although now *de rigueur*, are not without their critics. Some reviewers, for example, conclude that the clinical utility of cognitive procedures with children has not yet been demonstrated (e.g., Hobbs, Moguin, Tyroler, & Lahey, 1980). Other prominent reviewers point to the encouraging results that go along with the methodological short-comings (e.g., Kendall, Chapter 4, this volume; Kendall & Braswell, 1982b; Urbain & Kendall, 1980). I shall try to place these developments in perspective in the pages that follow.

There are many ways to organize the child behavior therapy literature. One could emphasize specific techniques, or, like Harris (1983), survey the field in terms of diagnostic categories. I choose here to focus upon trends, concepts, general reviews, and broad topics rather than procedures, individual cases, or diagnostic categories. Key areas such as assessment, cognitive behavior therapy, and behavioral medicine (behavioral pediatrics) will be given minimal attention, since they form the primary subject matter of other chapters in this volume. Previous section headings will be followed to the extent that there is appropriate new material to report. Certain new sections will be introduced (e.g., the family).

As noted last year, the journal *Child Behavior Therapy* is now called *Child and Family Behavior Therapy*. This year I also note a change in name of the British-based Association for Behaviour Modification with Children to the Association for Behavioural Approaches with Children. There is no comprehensive new text of substance to report this year, and Ollendick and Cerny's (1981) *Clinical Behavior Therapy with Children* remains the new boy in school. As an introduction to theoretical foundations this text is excellent. What it possibly lacks, for the serious investigator, is depth with respect to specific research and, for the practitioner, sufficient detail with respect to techniques. But it is probably unrealistic to expect both qualities in one volume.

A potentially significant series, edited by Steffen and Karoly, appeared in 1982 under the promising title *Advances in Child Behavioral Analysis and Therapy* (Volume 1: *Improving Children's Competence*; Volume 2: *Autism and Severe Psychopathology*). A new biennial edited by Fitzgerald, Lester, and Yogman (1982), *Theory and Research in Behavioral Pediatrics*, interprets the word "behavioral" to mean any research that has a data base. How relevant this series will be to the mainstream of behavior therapy remains to be seen. In this respect, Russo and Varni's (1982) edited text of behavioral pediatrics is more promising. Williams, Foreyt, and Goodrick's (1981) compilation of reprinted articles is of much less value.

Among the bewildering array of practical manuals I single out Herbert's 1981 *Behavioural Treatment of Problem Children*. The notions expressed in this very practical manual are an outgrowth of the author's two more scholarly texts (Herbert, 1974, 1978), already reviewed in this series. As Herbert notes, the problem-solving model that forms the basis of his exposition has been succinctly described by Senn (1959) in the following words:

> The problem child is invariably trying to solve a problem rather than be one. His methods are crude and his conception of his problem may be faulty, but until the physician has patiently sought, and in a sympathetic fashion found, what the child was trying to do . . . he is in no position to offer advice. (Herbert, 1981, p. v.)

It is too bad that these notions had to wait almost a quarter of a century to achieve fruition!

Psychologists have a predilection for writing reviews, and behavior therapists are no exception. There is Harris's (1983) thoughtful, if not very detailed, overview of behavioral developments within certain diagnostic categories of DSM-III. But it is the specialized reviews that are likely to prove more useful to the serious investigator or sophisticated clinician. Rose, Koorland, and Epstein (1982), for example, offer a critically constructive appraisal of applied behavioral analysis interventions for learning-disabled children. Regrettably, most of the studies reviewed by Rose *et al.* stem from investigative curiosity about a specific problem rather than an intent to contribute to a systematic body of knowledge.

Furman and Drabman (1981) offer a comprehensive overview of methodological issues in child behavior therapy. While many problems are common to both child and adult research, there are some that are specific to children. For example, there is the changing developmental status of the child and the fact that children are rarely self-referred. Also, significant others (usually parents or teachers) often play an important part in the child's treatment. The methodology of social skills training for children has received much attention this year (e.g., Conger & Keane, 1981; Green & Forehand, 1980; Lahey & Rubinoff, 1981; Michelson, Foster, & Ritchey, 1981a). Despite a measure of advance, the conclusions reached by Combs and Slaby in their 1977 review still seem applicable: We do not know precisely what skills to train, how to measure them, or how to teach them. Generalization is limited (Berler, Gross, & Drabman, 1982), and performance is all too often related to the method of assessment (Kazdin, Matson, & Esveldt-Dawson, 1981b).

Two other more general reviews merit attention. Doke and Flippo (1981) present a brief and, regrettably, not very original overview of current investigations into selected disorders. Dreger (1981) addresses himself to the difficulties encountered in attempts to classify the emotional problems of children. For those who are adamantly behavioral, classification of behaviors makes little sense. All one has to do is to focus upon the specification of a particular behavior and the pertinent reinforcing contingencies. For those of us who recognize the possibility of alternative strategies, assessment techniques that are both behaviorally and psychometrically sound (Yes, Virginia, the two are compatible!) are very much in order. It is to these individuals that Dreger addresses his review.

Voeltz and Evans (1982) draw attention to the absence of systematic efforts to assess the multiple effects of behavioral treatments undertaken with single target behaviors. Reference to response interrelationships is frequent in the behavior therapy literature, but as yet the construct has had little impact upon either assessment or intervention with children. As these authors put it so well,

> moving beyond the stage of modifying "one behavior at a time" involves affecting far more than single target behaviors or even a series of single targets over an extended time period. While the maintenance and generalization of these single changes across a variety of appropriate stimulus settings is a laudable concern, before we can truly support the treatment validity of behavioral procedures generally, we may need to demonstrate that the targets we select have a larger positive effect upon children's

overall repertoires. While we stop short of recommending that some sort of clinical "cure" is required before intervention may be judged successful, a temporary (or even lasting) change in one target behavior is an unacceptable low standard of effectiveness in behavior therapy. An emphasis upon lawful intra- and interorganism response–response relationships to augment our traditional clinical experimental concern for response–stimuli relationships may save behavioral theory from charges of offering a trivial, equally temporary alternative to the more traditional solutions for deviance. (p. 160)

Finally, in these changing times of child behavior therapy, I will take a look at the rights of children. The American Psychological Association's *Monitor* (Cordes, 1982) recently drew attention to an FBI bulletin with pictures of four fugitives and their children that was mailed to more than 100,000 professionals. The point is made that making these pictures public is a violation of both the rights of these children and the ethics of professional service. In therapy also, the question arises as to who is the client and who has the right to make decisions. Laws pertaining to the rights of children change periodically and vary from state to state. It is sometimes difficult for individual clinicians or even mental health facilities to keep abreast of these enactments. For example, 40% of clinics recently contacted in Virginia were still unaware of a state law pertaining to minors in psychotherapy some 9 months after it was implemented (Melton, 1981). Are we justified in intervening because a boy is showing "excessively feminine behavior," for example, or a girl is "too masculine"? How do we decide whether punishment is appropriate in any particular situation? Who should make these decisions? To what extent should we teach parents how to use punishment procedures as part of management training? Such issues are the subject of much discussion in the recent child behavior therapy literature (e.g., Doke & Flippo, 1981; Harris, 1983; Wood & Lakin, 1982).

The passage of Public Law 94-142, the Education for All Handicapped Children Act of 1975, serves to summarize effectively principles that have been developing in various forms for more than two decades. Virtually every child has a right to appropriate education and the formulation of an explicit plan approved by officials, parents, and all concerned. Furthermore, these specialized programs must be conducted according to the principle of the least restrictive environment (Reynolds, 1982). Unfortunately, as we have often had occasion to comment in this series, this is easier said than done. It is difficult at times to determine what exactly is the least restrictive environment, under what circumstances it is advantageous, and exactly what the determinants of effective management are (Bents, Lakin, & Reynolds, 1981).

Finally, by extrapolation, I draw attention to the rights of all meaningful others who are involved with children. This includes parents, family, teachers, and the staffs of inpatient and outpatient facilities. Kazdin and his associates are increasingly concerned with such matters, which are really part of the problem of social validation, and it is to be hoped that they will become the subject of future investigation (see Kazdin, 1981a; Kazdin, French, & Sherick, 1981a).

CHILD AND FAMILY IN BEHAVIOR THERAPY

Behavior therapists have long been concerned with the impact of the family on the maladaptive behavior of children in settings outside the home. But for the most part their approach to this problem has been fragmented, stressing isolated components rather than multivariate evaluation. For example, Budd, Leibowitz, Riner, Mindell and Goldfarb (1981) developed an effective home-based reinforcement package for the decrease of serious disruptive and aggressive behavior in groups of preschool and kindergarten-age children. In general, their multiple-baseline design was effective in demonstrating the utility of the package. There was even an encouraging 1-year follow-up. But for reasons unknown, the procedure failed fairly decisively with two subjects. This led the authors, not unreasonably, to suggest that, for certain children, their strategy could be insufficient. A well-designed multivariate study might have provided some meaningful leads.

It might be expected that long-term concentration on a narrowly focused problem would lead to methodologically sound research from which valid conclusions could be drawn. Regrettably, this is not always so. For example, the question of whether a child reared by one parent is at great risk for psychological maladjustment has been investigated extensively over the past four decades. This is obviously an important topic, and major social policy could hinge upon the findings. Unfortunately, research has failed to provide conclusive information, and the reasons why this is so are not hard to find. The literature is characterized by major errors in design, unrepresentative sampling, invalid dependent measures, and a variety of conceptual blind spots such as the equating of conventional behavior with healthy behavior (Blechman, 1982).

Blechman's own studies are models of good design. In one project, behavioral family treatment programs in eight geographical locations across the United States collected two years of demographic and other data from some 181 families (Blechman, Budd, Christophersen, Szykula, Wahler, Embry, Kogan, O'Leary, & Riner, 1981a). This study is of significance on at least two counts. First, it is the only one, as far as I know, to employ complex multivariate analysis to assess the impact of family composition on participation in behavioral family treatment. Second, it highlights the need to analyze data relating to external systems and family ecology as well as those obtained from the more limited variables usually employed in such studies.

When parents seek help for a child's behavior problem, three types of family interventions can be considered: parent training, parent–child contingency contracting; and family negotiation, systems, or problem-solving training. Blechman's (1981) algorithm (Figure 7-1) for matching client family and behavioral intervention rests upon four assumptions: first, that the choice of an intervention must be guided by the availability of easily and inexpensively gathered information; second, that it is possible for each of the three behavioral interventions to be provided with equal competence to families concerned; third, that once an intervention is selected, observational data will be collected to chart the course of the intervention and document its effectiveness; and fourth, that systematic evidence about the successes and failures of its component rules will be used to refine the selection strategy.

The algorithm rests on ten questions requiring "yes" or "no" answers. The answer to a question determines if an intervention can be selected or if still another question must be answered. Questions are always answered in the same order, beginning with question 1. The number of questions to be answered in order to select an intervention is variable. When the answer to the first question, "Can the target child be involved in treatment?" is "no," parent contingency management is selected, because it is the only viable approach. Similarly, if the answer to the question "Is the child's behavior life threatening or uncontrollable?" is "yes," then immediate behavior change is demanded. This is best provided by parent contingency management. Similarly, if the answer to the question "Is the target child preverbal or nonverbal?" is "yes," then contingency contracting and problem-solving training are ruled out and contingency management must be tried.

If the answer to the question "Is parental behavior poorly controlled?" is "yes," then it is encumbent on the parents to demonstrate control over their own behavior before they attempt to acquire control over that of their children, and it is necessary for the therapist to work with the parents on this problem first. If marital conflict is severe, then marital cooperation training is indicated as a precursor to any of the prevalent child behavior change approaches. Similarly, if basic life maintenance problems (such as poor physical health, lack of knowledge of how to deal with authority figures, or poverty) remain unresolved, then it is unlikely, no matter how unpleasant the target

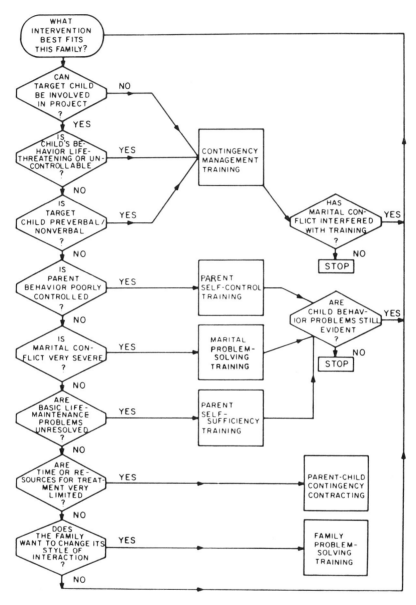

FIG. 7-1.

Strategy for matching client family and behavioral intervention. (From "Toward Comprehensive Behavioral Family Intervention: An Algorithm for Matching Families and Interventions" by E. A. Blechman, *Behavior Modification*, 1981, 5(2), 221–236. Copyright 1981, Sage Publications, Inc. Reprinted by permission.)

child's behavior, that the family will work sufficiently hard at any of the three child behavior-change approaches. Thus, if the answer to this question is "yes," parent self-sufficiency training is advisable.

If the answer to the question "Are time or resources for treatment very limited?" is "yes," then family skill training approaches are ruled out in favor of contingency contracting or contingency management. If the family is interested primarily in alleviating a specific child behavior problem rather than in changing their general style of interaction, then, once again, a skill training approach is inappropriate. The question "Has marital conflict interfered with training?" is usually asked after an intervention has been unsuccessful. When the answer is "yes," marital cooperation training is the strategy of choice.

Finally, there is the question, "Are child behavior problems still evident?" This question is posed after the successful implementation of such strategies as parent self-control training, marital cooperation training, or parent self-sufficiency training. When, regrettably, the answer to this question is "yes," then the search for an appropriate intervention approach begins again.

The array of child-related behavioral family interventions noted here may be incomplete, and Blechman (1981) describes three interventions that can fill the gap under certain circumstances. These are parent self-sufficiency training, geared toward families with basic life-maintenance problems in addition to difficulties with their children; parental self-control training, geared toward parents of uncontrolled, aggressive children who themselves exhibit high levels of such behavior; and finally, marital problem-solving training, geared toward couples who are troubled by their children's behavior but unprepared to cooperate with each other in the correction of this behavior.

Intriguing as this algorithm is, it is helpful only to the extent that it is based upon demonstrably validated research data. Furthermore, as Blechman cautions, there are times—such as when the parents physically abuse the child or when no appropriate day care facility is conveniently available—when there is no alternative to the recommendation of foster care or residential treatment.

Conger (1981) thinks in terms of social systems. The core of a systems orientation is the notion of interdependence. The activities of one element in a system (e.g., the mother in a family or the president in a nation) influences other elements either directly or indirectly and, through a feedback loop, the instigating unit at some later point in time. There is, of course, no reason to limit a systems analysis to intrafamilial events. Bronfenbrenner (1979) stresses the need to regard the family unit as one among many microsystems that are of importance for the developing child. A family must not only be considered as a microcosm within the larger community; each family member must also be studied as a behavioral system in his or her own right.

Until Conger drew attention to these matters, there had been virtually no systematic attempt to relate outside environmental influences to specific patterns of interactions within families. Conger's ecological systems approach is concerned with the reciprocal influences that individual characteristics, family dynamics, and transactions with the outside community have on one another. To study these influences it is necessary to engage in a variety of assessment and intervention procedures at the level of the individual family member, the family system, and, finally, the community.

According to Conger, leading investigators stress one or another level but rarely all three. For example, Patterson and his associates (e.g., Patterson, 1979) describe the complex interactional processes that characterize families in which a socially aggressive child emerges. Forehand and his group have long been concerned with the personal characteristics of the parents (e.g., Forehand, Wells, & Griest, 1980; Rickard, Forehand, Wells, Griest, & McMahon, 1981). The work of Wahler and his colleagues (e.g., Wahler, 1980) provides the framework for Conger's discussion of his third level, the community, as part of a systems approach to family relationships.

It is clear that the problem child is a product of a multitude of variables operating at a variety of levels—individual, family, and community—and that the effects of these different dimensions are reciprocal. For example, parents who are experiencing difficulties within the community are less likely to be able to cope with the demands of family life, and this in turn can lead to continuing deterioration in social and other relationships outside the family. Finally, it seems evident that child-management programs based exclusively upon formal social learning principles may not always be sufficient. Economic, sociologic, genetic, and other biological variables also play their part.

NONCOMPLIANCE IN CHILDREN

In Chapter 1 the focus is on compliance and noncompliance in adults. In working with children, developmental factors assume prominence and it is difficult to evaluate the significance of a specific noncompliance behavior without the benefit of normative data. Even in seemingly simple situations such as mother–son interactions (e.g., Stiffman, 1982), compliance should not be regarded as a dichotomous situation in which one either does or does not comply. As a step in this direction, Roberts and his associates are mapping out the relationships between compliance/noncompliance in small children and specific intervention procedures such as time out (Bean & Roberts, 1981; Roberts, 1982a, 1982b; Roberts & Hatzenbuehler, 1981; Roberts, Hatzenbuehler, & Bean, 1981; Roberts, McMahon, Forehand, & Humphreys, 1978).

Compliance may also be conceptualized as a response class. Bijou and Baer (1967) define a response class as "a group of responses which develop together. All grow strong or weak, even though the environment may be acting directly on only some of them." Compliance may be considered to function as a response class, with reinforcement of compliance to specific requests bringing about increased compliance both to reinforced and nonreinforced requests (Cataldo, Iwata, & Ward, 1982). Based upon this premise, Russo, Cataldo, and Cushing (1981) were able to demonstrate the general reduction of aberrant child behavior in a pediatric treatment facility by means of use of procedures pertaining to adult requests for compliance in areas other than those directly involving the aberrant behavior. Untreated deviant behaviors improved when compliance was increased, even though no direct contingency had been placed on these behaviors. The relationship between untreated deviant behaviors and compliance appeared to be maintained by a different set of events in each of the three children who were the subjects of this study. Further research is indicated.

Child compliance with medical regimens presents a set of problems somewhat different from those encountered when working with adults (see Chapter 1). Masek and Jankel (1982) offer guidelines for research in this problem area. The other area of special concern is that of patient training. Noncompliance is named by parents as one of the most serious of child behavior problems (Chapman & Zahn-Waxler, 1982). Unfortunately, most studies of children's compliance have utilized laboratory, survey, or clinical strategies. Observations of naturally occurring discipline and compliance situations in the home have been infrequent. Moreover, disciplinary techniques have usually been studied as isolated procedures, even though this is not the way most parents function. Study of the relationships between initial misdeed and outcome of disciplinary interactions has been neglected despite research indications that parental discipline can be responsibly modified by appropriate recognition of such occurrences (e.g., Grusec & Kuczynski, 1980).

Explicitly detailed manuals based on systematic observations are rare. A notable exception is Forehand and McMahon's (1981) clinician's guide to parent training, which has special relevance to problems of noncompliance. As these authors note, most child noncompliance behavior is required and maintained within the family setting, and it is unlikely that meaningful change can be brought about out of context.

Equally important, parent training is not effective with all families. Parental depression, low socioeconomic status, and referral by sources rather than self-referral are all associated with poor therapy outcome and high dropout rates in parent training. Fleischman, Shilton, and Arthur (1974) have developed a scale to measure client readiness for parental behavioral training. If it is validated, this scale should assist in the determination of which families are ready for and can profit from parent training.

Forehand's programs, predicated upon almost a decade of research, bring out both the advantages of specific procedures, such as social reinforcement and time out, and the circumstances under which they should be employed. Most important, Forehand and his group recognize the limitations as well as the strengths of their programs. For example, as yet there is no consistent evidence of generalization from home to school. Clinicians involved in parent training are advised to assess child behavior in the classroom so that a separate intervention can be developed in that setting if necessary. Forehand's research also points to the need to assess parent as well as child adjustment and behavior whenever a family is referred for professional assistance. It may be safely concluded that, despite overlap, problems of compliance/ noncompliance in children are not necessarily the same as those encountered in adults. With the increasing sophistication in the parent training research literature, a topic to which I now turn, I hope to find answers to many of the unresolved questions raised to date.

BEHAVIORAL PARENT TRAINING

Introduction

Parent training continues to be one of the most popular research areas in child behavior therapy. A recent bibliography of literature published since 1938 includes 1130 readily available references (Hamilton, MacQuiddy, Brown, Story, Braun, & Johnson, 1983). Child noncompliance as it relates to parent training has been well reviewed by Wells and Forehand (1981) and Atkeson and Forehand (1978). Methodology as related to specific content has not been systematically reviewed since 1978, and it is therefore encouraging to note the attention given to this neglected area by Moreland, Schwebel, Beck, and Wells (1982).

It is apparent from Moreland *et al.*'s critical evaluation that behavior therapists have taught parents to modify a wide range of child behaviors through a variety of behavioral approaches. But there is still a tendency to train parents in a set of procedures and then use the child's behavioral changes as the dependent variable against which to measure treatment effects. Approximately two-thirds of the 43 single-case studies reviewed by Moreland *et al.* include no information whatsoever about changes in the behavior of the parents. Most of the teaching methodologies consist of activities (instruction, reading, discussion, or modeling) to help parents identify the training behaviors to be acquired. Fewer than half of the training programs reported the provision of opportunities for parents to receive feedback about their abilities to perform these skills. Seemingly, investigators devote more attention to the explication of behavioral principles than to the development and assessment of actual parental skills.

Generalization studies of either parent or child behaviors are still rare, and scant attention has been given to the indirect effects of parent training, such as changes in the attitudes of meaningful others as a result of treatment. An issue beginning to receive attention is the prediction of which parents are likely to complete and benefit from what training programs. For example, McMahon, Forehand, Griest, and Wells (1981) found that low socioeconomic status, poor parental adjustment, and command-prone maternal behavior were closely related to failure and dropout. It is also now evident that complex interactions that occur in clinic-referred families are less likely to be present in nonclinic families (Griest, Forehand, Wells, & McMahon, 1980). Other up-and-coming areas include behavioral training for child-abusive parents (e.g., Wolfe & Sandler, 1981; Wolfe, Sandler, & Kaufman, 1981) and for mothers and fathers in the process of divorce, before becoming single parents (Moreland & Schwebel, 1981). Both mothers and fathers may need help in increasing their reinforcing values to their children and in learning how to develop parenting skills that might have been less essential when the parents functioned as a team.

Although assessment is the subject of Chapter 2, I cannot help but note its neglect in the parent training literature. Available procedures tend to rely upon pencil-and-paper tests and self-report rather than direct observation. Two encouraging exceptions are the use of videotape recordings (Berry & Wood, 1981) and Weitz's (1981) expansion of Koegel's five-category code for measuring parental training behavior into eight categories. Unlike Koegel and his associates (e.g., Koegel, Russo, & Rincover, 1977), Weitz reports reliability scores for all categories individually as well as collectively. The major problem with Weitz's code is that its optimal use relies on access to considerable financial and human resources. By contrast, Thorley and Yule (1982) have developed a seemingly reliable, valid, and low-cost direct observation measuring instrument that can be readily applied to the evaluation of both parents and children in a variety of contexts and situations. It may be, as Thorley and Yule note, that codes yield misleading data. Purely quantitative models, especially those using codes, rest on the assumption that parents are performing consistently in all situations. It could be that what also needs investigating is performance in so-called critical situations. Certain interactive occurrences may be more crucial than others.

It is with such considerations in mind that I turn to a selective discussion of recent developments in behavioral parent training.

Evaluation of Specific Programs and Strategies

Components analyses of parent training programs continue apace. Groups such as Sanders and his Australia-based team continue to investigate the effects of instruction, feedback, and cueing (e.g., Sanders, 1982). In terms of cost effectiveness, group training offers obvious advantages, especially if combined with videotaped modeling and the use of paraprofessionals (Webster-Stratton, 1981). Group training also seems to lead to effective generalization to nontargeted behaviors (Adesso & Lipson, 1981; Pevsner, 1982). In the Adesso and Lipson study, families were assigned to one of four groups: mother training, father training, couple training, or a no-treatment control. All participants were shown how to design, implement, and evaluate an appropriate behavior modification program aimed at alleviating their children's problem behaviors. The significant improvement in target behaviors for all treatment groups was maintained at 3-month follow-up. The fact that mothers, fathers, and couples were equally effective is important in view of the ongoing discussion about relative contributions of various parent combinations.

O'Dell, O'Quin, Alford, O'Briant, Bradlyn, and Giebenhain (1982) compared four training methods designed to improve parental reinforcement skills. The 100 parents were randomly assigned either to a minimal-instructions control group or to training by one of four methods: written manual, audiotape, videotape modeling, or live modeling and rehearsal with their children. Outcome was assessed by home observation. While the audiotape manual was significantly less effective than the written manual or live modeling with rehearsal, all training methods were superior to minimal instructions. Parent demographic characteristics and reading levels were significantly related to outcome in the control group and in the groups receiving written or live modeling with rehearsal training, but not in the videotape group. Regrettably, no follow-up was reported.

An interesting question confronting Patterson, Chamberlain, and Reid (1982) at the Oregon Social Learning Center was as follows: How does one evaluate a treatment procedure that continues to change over time? Their decision was to carry out evaluation studies *ad seriatum*. At each juncture, a successful outcome would signify only that the investigator should proceed to the next small complex question in the series. But first it was necessary to demonstrate that appropriately trained and supervised staff members produced reliable changes in the observed rates of deviant behavior.

As an example of this methodology at work, they report upon 19 children among their problem families who were identified as being high-rate social aggressors in the home. Cases were randomly assigned either to a parent-training procedure or to a waiting-list comparison group. After some 17 therapy hours, posttreatment observation data were collected in the homes of both groups. The parent training group showed a significantly greater reduction than the comparison sample in the observed rates of deviant child behavior. Taken in conjunction with earlier studies, the conclusion arrived at was that the achieved beneficial effects were attributable not to the passage of time or to parent expectancies but to specific family intervention processes.

Griest and Forehand (1982) hypothesized that problems within the family system, such as depression or poor communication, may be responsible for occasional failures in parent training. Correlational evidence suggests strong relationships between manifest child behavior problems on the one hand and parental perceptions of this behavior and their own marital status and personal adjustment on the other. According to Griest and Forehand, there is little evidence that parent training efforts directed specifically toward child behavior problems automatically generalize to other problem areas. Few studies have assessed the efficacy of treating a variety of family problems in order to facilitate parent training.

In a multiple baseline study of one child, Kelley, Embry, and Baer (1979) found positive changes in child behavior when parental communication training between spouses was added to the standard parent-training format. Unfortunately, they failed to compare the combination treatment with the effects of parent training alone. More recently, Griest, Forehand, Rogers, Breiner, Furey, and Williams (1982) investigated the efficacy of multimodal parent enhancement in maintaining changes in child problem behaviors and maternal behaviors previously identified as significant to parent training. This study assumes particular significance in view of reported failures in parent training (see Wahler, 1980; Wells & Forehand, 1981; and the discussion of this topic in last year's *Annual Review* [Volume 8]). As expected, a 2-month follow-up indicated that parent training plus parent enhancement therapy was significantly more effective than parent training alone in changing both the deviant child behavior and parental coping strategies. The question that awaits resolution is: Which components of the enhancement package are the more effective?

Working with Special Groups

Understandably, parents of mentally and multiply handicapped children receive much professional attention. Few parents of handicapped children are prepared or equipped to function as home teachers. There is little evidence that any one training method is most effective, and the emerging consensus among professionals seems to be the fashionable belief that a multidimensional, interdisciplinary approach to home training is essential (Stromer & Miller, 1982). Such a broad conclusion says little other than that not much is known at this time.

Hudson (1982) carried out a components analysis of a group training program for parents of developmentally handicapped children. Mothers of 33 children with Down's syndrome, 5 with cerebral palsy, and 2 with a recessive gene abnormality associated with general retardation were randomly assigned to one of four groups: verbal instruction, verbal instruction plus the teaching of behavioral principles, verbal instruction plus the use of modeling and role playing, and a control group. Utilizing multiple outcome criteria, it was found that instruction in general behavioral principles failed to produce any improvement in parental performance. For significant improvements to occur, group shaping techniques (modeling and role playing) had to be employed. In general, other things being equal, group training seems to be as effective as working with the parents individually (Brightman, Baker, Clark, & Ambrose, 1982).

Finally, I draw attention to training programs for foster parents. Noting the mixed results reported to date for this neglected but socially important group, Levant and Slattery (1982) developed a 10-session helping and parental skill training program geared specifically toward inner-city, lower socioeconomic group, minority foster mothers and their foster children. The helping skills consisted of the ability to empathize with the child's experience and be respectful of that experience and to interact sincerely with the foster child. The parenting skills consisted of the ability to plan ahead and structure the situation in order to prevent problems and to present to the child in a caring way the realities of the situation and the available options.

The results were assessed by comprehensive pre- and posttraining comparisons of the foster children of mothers trained in the program with those of a no-contact control group. The children of the training-group mothers improved significantly more than the controls on only one measure, emotionality–tension. Interpretation of these data should take into account the small sample size, the heterogeneity of the children in age and gender, the nonrandom assignment to conditions, and the lack of follow-up.

Problems of Maintenance

The short-term efficacy of parent training programs has been frequently documented (e.g., Griest *et al.*, 1982; Sanders & Glynn, 1981). Substantially fewer data are available concerning long-term efficacy. Furthermore, even over the short term, the majority of studies do not utilize sufficient outcome measures for meaningful determination of effectiveness. Baum and Forehand (1981) examined the long-term maintenance of treatment effects after a standardized parent-training program for 34 mother–child pairs who had completed parent training 1 to 4½ years earlier. The treatment consisted of teaching parents to reward compliance and appropriate behavior and to use a time-out procedure for noncompliance and inappropriate behavior. The assessment of treatment effects included home observation, parental perceptions of child adjustment, and measures of parental satisfaction. Child behavior changes and parental perceptions of change were both maintained at follow-up. Interestingly enough, some parent behavior changes were also maintained as follow-up. In the absence of an adequate control group, it is possible that these treatment effects were attributable to the passage of time or to unspecified environmental factors. It is hard to fault Baum and Forehand on this account. Ethical as well as practical concerns clearly prohibit the placing of clients in a 4½-year waiting-list control group.

Webster-Stratton (1981) obtained highly significant performance-based changes in mother–child interactions immediately posttreatment. In a follow-up study that compared the effectiveness of a parent-training program based on videotaped modeling 1 week after training and 1 year after training, both positive and less-than-positive findings are reported (Webster-Stratton, 1982). Most of the significant behavioral changes noted for mothers and children immediately posttreatment were either maintained or improved 1 year later. The mothers continued to perceive a reduction in the intensity of their children's behavior problems. Nonetheless, at 1-year follow-up mothers reported feeling less confident about their parenting skills than they had immediately posttreatment. Once again, the absence of an untreated control group precludes definitive conclusions, and it is not known what aspects of the treatment were responsible for the reported changes. Furthermore, the sample was limited to highly motivated, mostly middle-class volunteers.

Most parent training studies utilize few families and outcome evaluation periods of no more than 24 months. Until this year, Patterson and Fleischman's (1979) follow-up of 33 families was perhaps the largest sample studied to date. Strain, Steele, Ellis, and Timm's (1982) study is now the model in the field. Some 40 families, each having been exposed to identical treatment procedures, were systematically followed up over periods ranging from 3 to 9 years. The original target behaviors were assessed in the home, together with behaviors predictive of successful performance at school. Additionally, various family and child demographic data were obtained in order to investigate uncontrolled variables that might possibly be related to long-term outcome. Finally, to compare former clients' current behaviors with those of normally developing children, data were collected on four randomly selected same-age and same-sex peers from classrooms in which each former client was enrolled.

Both school and home follow-up led to the conclusion that commands and requests were still likely to be complied with by the children concerned. Social interactions in the home were overwhelmingly positive and behaviorally appropriate, with parental behaviors consistent with child-management skills taught many years ago. Former child clients and randomly selected peers evidenced strikingly similar compliance, on-task, social interaction, and appropriate/inappropriate nonsocial behaviors. There was no difference in teachers' commands, negative feedback, positive social reinforcement, or repeated commands directed toward former clients as contrasted with randomly selected class peers. Of all demographic variables studied, current levels of behavior were related only to the age at which treatment began and to family intactness. Once again, the conclusions are tempered by the lack of a control group.

Generalization across Settings

Generalization can occur across time, person, behavior, or setting. If either child behavior or parental training is effective only within the constraints of the formal instructional setting, it is virtually useless. Thus generalization in all its forms should be viewed as a major explicit objective for all parent training. Accomplishing this objective requires careful planning and implementation (Stromer & Miller, 1982). Only generalization over time for middle-class parents seems well documented. Other classes of generalization (across setting, behavior, and individual) have not been so extensively researched. As Sanders and James (1982, 1983) point out, the predominant strategy within the field still remains "train and hope" (Stokes & Baer, 1977).

A frequently suggested means of dealing with poor generalization is the use of self-management procedures (e.g., Sanders & Glynn, 1981; Stokes & Baer, 1977). In this respect, Sanders and James (1982) critically review the self-management parent-training research and arrive at tentative conclusions:

1. Self-recording seems to facilitate parent behavior change when used as an adjunctive procedure. However, evidence from both classroom and clinical settings suggests that the effects of self-recording alone may be short-lived if not supplemented by reinforcement contingencies, either controlled externally or self-administered. Whether the self-recording is either necessary or sufficient to produce maintenance of parent behavior change remains unclear at this stage.
2. Parental self-reinforcement procedures have yet to be shown to facilitate the acquisition, generalization, or maintenance of behavior change.
3. Multicomponent self-management packages can be used to program for maintenance over time of both parent and child behaviors.
4. There is some evidence to suggest that self-management skills can be used to enhance setting generalization.

One type of generality is behavior change from home to school. According to Forehand, Breiner, McMahon, and Davies (1981), four group studies have demonstrated that treatment of home problems is not associated with significant changes in school behavior. Nevertheless, the results of these studies were sufficiently encouraging for Forehand et al. to take a fresh look at possible predictors of change in school behavior attributable to treatment of home problems. Some 16 clinic-referred children, each with a primary presenting problem of noncompliance in the home setting, served as subjects. The children were observed in the home and at school before and after treatment, which involved parental training in behavior management skills. A stepwise multiple regression analysis indicated that in combination with the pretreatment level of the school behavior, changes in oppositional behavior could serve as significant predictors of changes in school behavior. But their results are far from straightforward, the various analyses revealing a variety of complex relationships.

Sanders and Glynn (1981) argue that, because of competing, conflicting, or otherwise incompatible demands on their time, it is more difficult for parents to apply contingencies in some settings than in others. For example, they found that while changes in parent behavior after home training generalized to an observer-absent home setting (the family breakfast), parents were less effective in applying contingencies in community settings. One solution to this problem might involve the use of stimulus control techniques. A number of studies reported by Sanders and Dadds (1982) suggest that the careful selection and arrangement of activities could be effective both for problem reduction and for increasing social participation, language, and play behavior. Parents could be trained, argue Sanders and Dadds, to rearrange the stimulus environment in "high risk" parenting settings so that the probability of having to deal with misbehavior is reduced. At present, despite some encouraging data generated by Sanders and Dadds, the utility of stimulus control procedures for enhancing generalization effects has yet to be confirmed.

Some Parameters of Parental Success in Modifying Children's Behavior

Although parent training is generally successful, failures are sometimes encountered, and until recently little was known about the possible reasons why this was so. Certain techniques or packages seem to be more effective than others, and even within a particular program, how the material is presented is likely to be related to outcome. And yet, in other instances the method of presentation of information accounts for surprisingly little of the outcome variance (O'Dell et al., 1982).

Family-related difficulties may be responsible for some of the failures that occur in behavioral parent training. When Griest and Forehand (1982) reviewed the literature on the relationships between child behavior problems and their treatment on the one hand and family problem variables on the other, they found outcome to be adversely affected by poor parental adjustment in the areas of personal, marital, and extrafamilial relationships. (Hence the plaintive title of their article, "How Can I Get Any Parent Training Done with All the Other Problems Going On?"). On the more positive side, Griest and Forehand report the occurrence of some generalization from parent training to the alleviation of family problems.

Clark, Baker, and Heifetz (1982) used discriminant analysis to generate simple formulas that correctly predicted both posttraining knowledge of behavioral principles and 14-month follow-through performance for about 70% of the 49 families of mentally retarded children they studied. Social class, income, and mother's education were all positively related to posttraining proficiency, yet none of these variables was related to parental teaching performance during the 14-month follow-through period. For this and other reasons noted by Clark *et al.*, the clinical use of these equations in individual cases would be premature.

Even with these limitations, findings such as these have potential application when trainers are faced with an entire group of parents expected to do poorly in a standard group curriculum. They also have implications for curriculum change. Most parent training programs, for example, traditionally neglect low-socioeconomic-status families. If appropriately alerted, it might be possible to develop a more supervised and intensive training experience for these families. Brightman, Ambrose, and Baker (1980), for example, developed a school-based program in which parents taught children side-by-side with experienced staff members and received close supervision by way of videotaped feedback. The subjects were predominantly low-socioeconomic-status families that had completed a group training program but demonstrated low proficiency. By the end of this additional training, these parents had achieved proficiency levels comparable to those of the average parent in the standard curriculum. Searching out predictors of outcome and then using these relationships as guides for appropriate programmatic change would seem to be a rewarding strategy. When Clark and Baker (in press) extended this research to encompass more families, a broader range of predictor variables, and more comprehensive measures of proficiency, the results were equally encouraging.

As Baker and his group note, the ability to predict which parents are likely to benefit from what training has obvious significance for agencies. Families predicted to do well in groups could be assigned to these relatively low cost intervention programs, whereas predicted lower-benefit families could be offered a more appropriate, if more costly, alternative. Growing knowledge of predictor variables might also be of value in designing training alternatives.

Enhancing Parent Involvement

It is often assumed that parents are sufficiently reinforced by the gains made by their children and that it is therefore unnecessary to develop additional motivators. Perhaps for this reason, little attention has been directed toward the development of programs or procedures to maximize active parent participation in treatment. Unfortunately, improvement in the behavior of the child is not sufficient reinforcement in itself to maintain treatment efforts in all parents (Muir & Milan, 1982).

One solution is to work only with those parents who are most coopera-tive or, as indicated in the preceding section, with those who are predicted to do well. A more constructive approach is to seek out strategies for the enhancement of parental motivation.

Bates (1977) has suggested a variety of tactics for the encourage-ment of parents seeking to serve as effective "therapists" for their children. These include the provision of congenial training settings, the creation of an encouraging and reinforcing environment through telephone calls and gradually attenuated visits, and cash reimburse-ment made contingent upon completion of all assignments. Other investigators have made related suggestions. When Fleischman (1979) compared low- and middle-income families, some of whom received noncontingent monies while others received nothing at all, the low-income group that received money showed greater cooperation than the low-income group that did not. There was no difference between groups for the middle-income families. There is thus growing evidence that reinforcement procedures can be used to enhance parental coopera-tion. But until Muir and Milan (1982) came upon the scene, no experi-mental study had examined the functional relationships between parental reinforcement and improvement in the behavior of their children as contrasted with that of the parents.

Muir and Milan used a single-case method to examine the impact of parental reinforcement for child achievement upon the progress of the children themselves. The parental reinforcement took the form of a lottery in which the parents of three mentally handicapped preschool children in a home-based early intervention project could earn prizes contingent upon the accomplishments of their children. A lottery was used as an alternative to the more usual practice of refunding payments, because the initial payments would have exerted an undue hardship on the families, all of whom lived at or below the poverty line. An ABAB reversal design replicated across the three families successfully demon-strated the effects of the lottery on the children's mastery of language skills. Reinforcing parents for training accomplishments, as evidenced by their children's achievements, yielded significantly more progress in their children than that occurring under the routine supportive prac-tices of the baseline condition. The dramatic gains noted were all the more impressive when the fact that each child had a long history of minimal progress in home intervention programs is taken into con-sideration.

Unfortunately, the discontinuation of the lottery resulted in return to baseline rates of progress for all three children. As Muir and Milan observe, this argues against the notion that improvement in the chil-dren's behavior was a powerful reinforcer for the parents' efforts. Further research is needed to explore the manner in which gains may be maintained in the absence of contrived reinforcements such as those utilized in the present study. All too often, despite the fact that behavioral procedures are demonstrably effective in the short run, the actual implementation of this technology often falls far short of its potential over the long haul. Why is this? What factors cause parents not to use well-developed procedures that are likely to improve their children's behavior?

To answer such questions, O'Dell (1982) mailed a questionnaire to a nonrandom sample of 22 AABT members involved in behavioral parent training and research who had gathered informally together at previous AABT meetings to discuss issues in parent training. Only 16 questionnaires were returned and all information was based upon selective self-report data. The conclusions must therefore be viewed as tentative at best. Within these constraints, it seems that even with the maximal professional dedication to parent training and the most up-to-date research, as many as 40% of families served by the respondents to this survey were reported to have an unsatisfactory response to intervention. Only about 25% were considered as exhibiting high initiative, autonomy, and maintenance of progress.

The question that remains is: What strategies, under what circumstances, are most successful in generating consistent parental cooperation? According to O'Dell, preliminary studies and impressions point to a variety of possibilities. Educational approaches include training designed to provide realistic expectations for the parents, to provide information about normal child development and rationales for treatment methods, and to ensure that parents understand basic social learning assumptions and principles. The problem is that such strategies are applicable only to appropriately educated, and perhaps strongly motivated, parents in the first instance.

Programmatic methods of enhancement recommended by O'Dell include requiring parents to initiate the request for treatment rather than being referred; mutual goal setting with the parent; tailoring the program to the parental situation; providing convenient in-home services; and rapid intervention when parents are in crisis. Behavior management approaches all stress enlisting the support and reinforcement of the parents' social-support system, thereby encouraging parents to attribute treatment successes to their own efforts rather than to some external agency alone. In order of decreasing frequency, the motivational methods judged to be most effective by O'Dell's respondents were as follows: verbal praise, discussing benefits, personal counseling for the parents, frequent telephone contacts, some form of contingency contracting, competency-based training, tangible rewards, and, finally, certificates of accomplishment.

O'Dell cites a limited number of studies in support of these contentions. Thus, Syzkula, Fleischman, and Shilton (in press) report a comprehensive program to maintain parental involvement based on the establishment of close personal contact and rapport with the parents concerned. The program includes training sessions to help educate parents about the program and to set up positive but realistic expectations. Home-based training was provided when transportation was not available or when the parents seemed inadequately motivated. Sessions were often held on evenings or weekends with appropriate "salaries" being provided upon occasion. Cotherapists worked on individual cases to help prevent therapist burn out and to ensure the freshness of the trainer. Under these circumstances, overall drop-out rates were reduced from 46 to 26%.

The measurement of parent involvement in treatment presents a particularly challenging problem. As O'Dell (1982) points out, an ideal measure should be frequent, direct, unobtrusive, and long-term, but this is virtually never obtainable. Regular home observation is probably the closest approximation to this ideal. Most measures of parental involvement are indirect. These include attendance records, number of contracts signed, evidence of completion of homework assignments, pencil-and-paper tests of knowledge, ratings by therapists, and parental self-reports. The validity of many of these measures has not been determined, and there are obvious problems with making inferences from such data about parents' actual use of these skills with their children. Self-report data are particularly suspect in this latter respect. If professionals do poorly (Haynes, 1979, reports that health personnel consistently overestimate patient compliance) one can hardly expect parents to be better.

For reasons that are understandable if not acceptable, parent training programs focus on mothers rather than fathers (Graziano, 1977). There are many reasons for actively involving fathers in all parent-training programs. In terms of learning theory, the durability of changes in child behavior depends in part upon continued delivery of appropriate environmental consequences over time by key members of the child's environment. If only one parent is knowledgeable in child management, then it might be difficult for that parent alone to carry out the procedures consistently once training is over and there is no one to provide feedback or encouragement for effort expended (Budd & O'Brien, 1982).

Fathers tend to be less involved in caretaking responsibilities and more inclined to play with their children than mothers. In distressed families in particular, fathers tend to engage in fewer aversive interactions with their children and to take less responsibility for crisis management (Patterson, 1980). Including the father in parent training might be helpful in increasing the father's role in controlling the deviant behavior of the children. Unfortunately, as Budd and O'Brien (1982) point out, there is little direct empirical support for the assumption that involving the father in training is beneficial to treatment outcome. Budd and O'Brien were able to find only three studies that analyzed outcome as a function of father involvement, and in all three the conclusions were equivocal. There is no study of the frequency of father participation in parent training or of the factors that may make paternal involvement especially important in certain situations.

Two additional points of interest emerge from Budd and O'Brien's overview. First, they conclude from the few and indifferent studies available to them that, at least for families in which the fathers are interested in training and the referral problems are not severe, the father's participation in parent training programs does not substantially increase the effectiveness of training. Second, these findings notwithstanding, virtually all the respondents in Budd and O'Brien's small-scale survey of AABT members engaged in parent training expressed the *belief* that including fathers in parental training was beneficial to treatment outcome. Whether these judgments were founded on expectation or experience remains unclear.

The Hazards of Parent Training

Since Bernal and North's 1978 review of self-help manuals a substantial number of new books have appeared. Regrettably, few satisfy the proposed requirements for such manuals, and many might do more harm than good. The reader is referred to previous volumes in this series for an extended discussion of these matters. As far as self-help texts for parent training are concerned, Stocking, Arezzo, and Leavitt's (1980) new manual is among the best. If followed with care, this book could lead to demonstrable improvement in children's social skills. But it too makes the highly questionable assumption that parents are necessarily in a position to implement such procedures entirely on their own. Techniques that are valid when used or supervised by professionals may not be as effective when used by parents or teachers by themselves. The conclusion that the failure of parents to implement procedures adequately can lead to deterioration rather than improvement has been well-documented in the literature. (See Christensen, Johnson, Phillips, & Glasgow, 1980, for a review of these findings.)

Finally, I draw attention to what Dubey and Kaufman (1982) refer to as the "side effects" of parent-implemented behavior modification. Many parents face difficulties with their children that arise as a result of attempts to implement behavior modification procedures at home. Unfortunately, under certain circumstances, even positive and seemingly benign reinforcement can produce adverse effects. (See previous discussions in the appropriate chapters in this series, especially with relevance to the work of Lepper and Greene (1978) on the hidden costs of reward and the problems involved in the unsophisticated use of token reinforcements.)

Dubey and Kaufman (1981) gave an open-ended questionnaire to 52 parents who had completed one of their 10-week service-oriented behavior modification workshops. The following six statements reflect the essence of the negative comments expressed by their parents:

1. My child tries to beat me at my own game.
2. My child seeks constant attention.
3. My child now wants rewards for good behavior.
4. My other children are now jealous of the attention given to my "problem child."
5. My other children now demand attention rewards for good behavior that they had previously performed without any such reward.
6. My relationship with my child is more strained, as he or she does not necessarily agree with all my efforts.

These conclusions are based on small numbers and selected samples. Furthermore, they pertain to behavioral programs conceived and implemented solely by the parents. It is possible that similar programs designed by professional behavior therapists would have resulted in fewer adverse effects. Nevertheless, there seems to be little doubt that so-called side effects are real, that they need to be recognized as such, and that further investigation is warranted—a point underscored by the failure of Dubey and Kaufman to find significant mention of the hazards of parent training in any of the popular manuals included in their survey.

CHILD ABUSE AND NEGLECT

Child abuse and neglect continues to be one of the pressing problems of our times. In 1982 the Fourth International Congress on Child Abuse and Neglect was held under the auspices of the International Society for Prevention of Child Abuse and Neglect, and the Eleventh Annual Child Abuse and Neglect Symposium was convened. The society's journal, *Child Abuse and Neglect*, is now well established, and a second journal is in the process of development. These developments notwithstanding, there is as yet little agreement about either the definition or incidence of child abuse or its prevention and treatment.

As Isaacs (1982) notes, there seem to be as many definitions of child abuse as there are estimates of its incidence. Three broad approaches seem to prevail: definition in terms of outcome, (e.g., injuries), intentionality to harm, and social judgments or culturally determined labels rather than specific behaviors (Parke & Collmer, 1975). All too often, different studies use different definitions or combinations of definitions, and it is not easy to make meaningful comparisons.

For these reasons, consistency and clarity of definition are of extreme importance. Giovannoni and Becerra (1979) are among the few who use data to grapple with this problem. Groups of professionals were presented with a variety of abusive situations and requested to rate them in terms of seriousness and severity. In a second study, the same situations were presented to members of different ethnic groups. As predicted, different groups arrived at different ratings. All groups were consistent in rating items that involved physical injury or sexual molestation as more serious than those that focused primarily on some form of emotional neglect. Again, as one might expect, different strata in our society, especially black respondents, had different opinions about specific situations. Unfortunately, both studies are marred by a lack of behavioral measures. How the respondents rated various hypothetical situations may not necessarily be the same as how these respondents would behave in real-life situations. This limits the value of these otherwise important studies.

Of equal importance in terms of behavioral assessment is the need to identify the characteristics of specific abuse-prone categories of parents and the reinforcers that seem to motivate them. Isaacs (1981) divides the characteristics of abusive parents, as reported in the literature, into five categories. The first, demographic information (incidences of divorce, unstable marriage, unemployment, inadequate housing, etc.), is often used to describe people who abuse their children. But although they correlate with many abusive parenting practices, demographic variables alone do not necessarily identify a parent as abusive. As Isaacs points out, not all parents who are unemployed or divorced abuse their children. The second characteristic pertains to the personality traits that are believed to characterize abusing parents. Behavior therapists who reject the concept of personality and\point to the frequent failure to validate the presumed relationships between personality traits and actual behavior will find this classification totally unacceptable. Third, there is the parent's child-rearing history. Thus, in a questionnaire designed to predict potential for abuse among 500 mothers from diverse ethnic and socioeconomic backgrounds,

Schneider, Hoffmeister, and Heifer (1976) found that the one item that successfully discriminated known abusers from nonabusing parents was the response that their own parents had used severe physical punishment on them.

Fourth, there are the skills of the abusers as parents. Virtually all investigations lead to the conclusion that abusers have severe deficits in parenting skills. Such parents tend to use high levels of physical punishment, demands, or threats to control their children's behavior. In addition, they tend to be inconsistent in their disciplinary procedures and to make unrealistic demands and expectations. The final characteristic commonly found in abusive families is that of social isolation. There seems to be a high correlation between abusive behavior and isolation. However, as Isaacs cautions, while none of these factors taken alone may accurately predict a person's potential for abuse, in combination these variables provide an impressively well-rounded picture of what to look for in the detection of potential child-abusing parents.

One might expect behavioral intervention programs to be data-based. Out of 20 treatment programs reviewed by Isaacs (1982), 9 presented not even a single datum to substantiate the authors' claims to success. This does not mean that no useful information was provided, but it does point to a disquieting gap between the methods that certain behavior therapists preach and those which they practice (see Chapter 1). While the remaining 11 studies surveyed by Isaacs present varying amounts of data, major methodological limitations make it difficult to arrive at any firm conclusion about the reported findings. In most of the studies reviewed, the focus seems to have been on identifying antecedent stimulus events and the characteristics of the abusive parents or parent substitutes. Little attention has been given to the abusive response or to the contingencies and consequences that control the behavior of either parents or children. Only 9 of the 20 studies reviewed by Isaacs presented outcome data, and even those were methodologically defective.

Few investigators address themselves specifically to what constitutes abuse: in other words, to the question of where discipline stops and abuse begins. Another neglected area is that of the potential consequences of abuse on the future development of the child. The literature abounds with subjective explanations of the alleged fact that the abused children of today become the juvenile delinquents and the child abusers of tomorrow. But as yet the longitudinal data needed to lend substance to these speculations are lacking.

Sandler and his associates give considerable attention to the development of effective child-management programs for abusive parents (e.g., Wolfe, St. Lawrence, Graves, Brehony, Bradlyn, & Kelly, 1982; Wolfe & Sandler, 1981; Wolfe *et al.*, 1981). First, it is necessary to engage in some form of behavioral assessment. This is particularly difficult in cases of child abuse. The characteristic low frequency, privacy, and illegality of child abuse make direct observation difficult, to say the least. The commonly employed strategy of observing more frequently occurring behaviors presumed to be related to a problem behavior presents obvious methodological limitations. Then there are the ethical considerations that restrict the sophisticated investigator who seeks to collect adequate baseline data before beginning treatment. Furthermore, the legal requirement to report abusive interactions observed during either baseline assessment or intervention is likely to confound the experimental design as well as to interfere severely with any attempt to develop a therapeutic relationship with the client. Under the best of circumstances, child abusers rarely come for therapeutic assistance entirely of their own volition.

These limitations notwithstanding, and despite the fact that the causal relationships between parental management practices and child abuse remain debatable, there is ongoing support for the development of training programs for abusive parents. Fortunately, even though the precise parameters are little understood, there is growing evidence to endorse the use of certain behavioral techniques with certain groups of abusive parents (e.g., Denicola & Sandler, 1980). It is unfortunate that few of these studies have given attention to components analysis of the various treatment packages and their potential for effectiveness.

In one of the few exceptions to this generalization, Wolfe and Sandler (1981) utilized direct observation of behavior and a sophisticated family interaction coding system, with follow-up at 3-, 8-, and 12-month intervals, to analyze the specific contributions of parent training and contingency contracting. By and large, their data are highly successful in demonstrating that behavioral training methods with child abusers can substantially reduce the risk of subsequent abuse by the provision of effective child-management techniques. They were able to differentiate between abusive parents, abusive children, and what they term an "abusive partnership," three distinct patterns that may have important theoretical and practical implications. Even though only three abusive families were studied, the sophistication of the methodology used could serve as a model for further investigation. If further studies are done, it will be important to control for care and attention. All three of their families received intensive support and assistance in their homes.

Although it is not necessarily sufficient, providing parents with viable alternatives to physical punishment is a promising strategy. To this end, Wolfe and his associates advocate the use of a variety of standard behavioral procedures: for example, the "bug-in-the-ear" to train overtly hostile and aggressive parents in the utilization of more constructive child-management tactics (Wolfe *et al.*, 1982). Home visits, parental reports, casework data, and other observational procedures all attest to the trainability of at least certain abusive parents by the use of such devices (e.g., Wolfe *et al.*, 1981).

Most important, these investigators are now moving toward more large-scale studies and follow-ups of at least 1 year. The ingenious use of control groups of abusive families who are under continual state supervision and who are receiving the normal services provided to such parents by child-welfare agencies adds to the overall sophistication of their program. If generalization to families other than those investigated by these authors is premature, the findings are encouraging not only in their own right but in the impetus they give to a social learning model of child abuse.

It is reasonable to assume that many parents engage in physical abuse in a futile effort to achieve control or balance in their relationships with their children. Reid, Taplin, and Lorber (1981) postulate that one major cause of breakdown in family harmony is a lack of parental skills both in the teaching of appropriate social behaviors and in coping with discipline problems. Reid *et al.* speculate that this loss of control leads to a feeling in the parent of domination by the child and with it a growing hostility toward the child. It is at this point in the relationship that parents are likely to strike out and abuse their children.

The learning-theory-oriented social interactional approach to the treatment of abusive families developed by Reid and his associates is bidirectional in that both parents and children are regarded as active participants in the process of abuse. The key aspects of these maladaptive parent–child interactions are hypothesized to be lack of parental skill in the effective handling of everyday confrontations and high rates of aversive behaviors emitted by both parents and children. According to Reid *et al.*, there is growing evidence that abusive families display highly aversive patterns of family interaction. It is also suggested that abused children may have more than their share of constitutional defects. Such factors may well predispose abused children to be difficult to raise.

If it is indeed the case that many child-abuse acts are in part the endproducts of defective parental disciplinary and interpersonal skills, then three predictions follow: First, all family members will evidence more aversive behaviors toward one another in their daily lives than members of either nondistressed or distressed but nonabusive families;

second, these abusive parents will demonstrate severe problems in dealing with everyday discipline situations; third, a treatment program designed to teach consistent and nonphysical child-management skills will produce significantly reduced daily aversive behavior in all members of these abusive families.

To evaluate these hypotheses, Reid *et al.* (1981) present impressive data derived from many years of intensive study of distressed families at the Oregon Social Learning Center. Although they are far from conclusive (despite a total of 88 distressed families and 27 nondistressed control families studied), their data tend to support these contentions. One of the most important consistent findings to emerge is that the child is by no means a passive participant in the abuse process. For a variety of little understood reasons, abused children are very difficult to handle. What is common to virtually all these families is recourse to physically aggressive behavior as a primary coping solution. In all families, escalation of parent–child conflicts seems likely to lead to an increased probability that the child will be injured. It is therefore essential that all members of the family be taught nonphysical patterns of conflict resolution; this provides one of the main thrusts of the Oregon program. As Conger (1982) suggests, one of the more important contributions that behavior therapists working in this area can make would be the development of effective programs of child rearing from the earliest years.

Exchange theory offers another behavioral approach to understanding and intervention in this area. The basic assumption of exchange theory that is of primary relevance here is that human interactions are guided by the pursuit of rewards and the avoidance of punishment and costs (Gelles & Straus, 1979). Services offered to another person oblige that person to fulfill an obligation and thus to furnish benefits to the first person. If reciprocal exchange of rewards occurs, the interaction will continue. If reciprocity is not achieved, the interaction will break down. As Gelles (1982) points out, the problem is that most intrafamilial relations are more complex than those studied by traditional exchange theorists. For example, in many parent–child relationships, it is not feasible to break off interaction, even if there is no reciprocity, as this might well lead to anger, resentment, conflict, and even violence on both sides.

To incorporate these complexities into a model of abusive behavior, Gelles has developed an exchange–social control approach that takes into account a variety of additional propositions. Social scientists who seek nomothetic explanations for behavior find difficulty in developing effective programs for application to specific problems. The exchange–social control model developed by Gelles is directly applicable both to general social policy and specific treatment issues. His basic proposition is that people hit and abuse other family members because they can. It follows that the essential goal of treatment is to make it so that they cannot. To accomplish this, a clinician needs to increase the degree of social control exerted over family relationships and to raise the cost of intrafamilial violence to all concerned.

As Gelles soon found out, increasing social control and raising costs is easier said than done. A consistent finding in the family violence literature is that the child abuser typically has a poor self-concept. Thus, even if the cost of family violence were to be raised by directing the offender to accept the label "abuser," one unanticipated consequence might be to undermine further the person's poor self-concept and thus to exacerbate some of the factors causing the abuse.

Recognizing this problem, Gelles developed a series of recommendations for raising the cost of being violent without introducing unnecessarily intrusive social control into the family relationship. Unfortunately, some of his proposal reads more like a social manifesto than a series of specific recommendations, and it is difficult to see what the immediate value is to the practicing behavior therapist. First, Gelles (1982) advocates the elimination of the norms that legitimize and glorify violence in our society. In particular, he draws attention to the need for the reduction of television and other media violence and the passing of laws that prohibit physical violence in schools and other institutions. Second, he draws attention to the economic and gender inequities that permeate our society. Finally, there are the limitations of the criminal justice and child-welfare systems in coping with domestic abuse. Police are often wary of becoming involved in family disputes, and courts tend to treat cases of wife abuse less seriously than other forms of assault. Child-welfare systems have limited resources for rapid and effective response to reports of child abuse.

There would seem to be virtually no instance of child abuse whose determinants are straightforward. Even when the child abuse is relatively specific, as in the case of father–daughter incest, behavioral interventions aimed at the direct modification of the offending behavior have met with limited success (Dixen & Jenkins, 1981). Increasingly, the evidence points to the need for a multicomponent treatment package geared toward the abuser, the victim, and society at large. This is a tall order and we have barely begun to take the first step.

AUTISM

With the possible exception of two edited volumes and a limited number of articles to be reviewed here, the recent autism literature offers little of potential significance. The first book, Steffen and

Karoly's (1982b) *Autism and Severe Psychopathology*, is supposed to reflect noteworthy developments in this area regardless of orientation. Most of the chapters are written by behavior therapists. Can we infer from these two statements that most of the worthwhile research in this area is behavioral? The main thesis of the Webster, Konstantareas, Oxman, and Mack (1980) text is that autism is a result of defects in perception and information processing that emerge as communication deficit. Autism is viewed primarily as a perceptual disorder that is closely related to deficits in communication but that is also to be understood from an ecological or systems perspective. Treatment should therefore reflect all three modalities: perception, communication, and ecological systems theory. Despite a tendency to ignore the more recent work of such seasoned campaigners as Carr, Koegel, and Lovaas (see Volumes 7 and 8 of the *Annual Review*), the explicit recognition of the need to advance the concept of autism to a more societally oriented perspective is a step forward in itself.

Likewise, Harris (1982) draws attention to the need for a family systems approach to behavioral training for the parents of these children. What is particularly interesting is Harris's attention to failures. The failure of certain families to follow through once the group had ended generated a reexamination of existing procedures and a search for new strategies to enhance the likelihood of continued change after formal training was over. It was considerations such as these that led Harris to family systems, the need for training in behaviorally oriented family therapy, and the transition to an interpersonal approach.

The other encouraging sign is the recent opening of the new Autism Research Center at the University of California, Santa Barbara, under the leadership of Robert L. Koegel. Also important in its own context is the attempt by Freeman and Ritvo (1982) to quantify and measure objectively those behaviors considered to be autistic. The array of clinical descriptions readily available is no substitute for objective definition. The ideal assessment tool must be comprehensive, must be able to separate the various subgroups of autistic children, and must discriminate between these children and those with other syndromes.

As Freeman and Ritvo soon found out, all previously proposed diagnostic systems suffer from major theoretical and methodological limitations, and it is not surprising that none has gained widespread acceptance outside its center of origin. There were three major deficits: failure to provide objectively defined and reliable behaviorally based scale items, failure to assess developmental influences on scale items, and failure to develop objective profiles of "normal" and "pathological" states. Although it is not yet adequately validated or submitted to psychometric scrutiny, the Behavioral Observation Scale (BOS) developed by Freeman and Ritvo is a significant step toward the development of an objective assessment device.

It is considered advisable to train autism therapists in the procedural rules of behavior modification as applicable to autistic children rather than to focus either on general principles on the one hand or on a particular treatment program on the other. The outline offered by Schreibman and Koegel (1981) is a good example of this middle-of-the-road strategy. For those whose concern is with the establishment of self-contained classes for autistic youngsters, Handleman (1981) offers a useful series of guidelines. What is interesting about these guidelines is the equal emphasis placed upon empirical data and experiential success.

In all areas of behavior therapy, social validation is in the air, and autism is no exception. Questions are being asked about the extent to which statistically meaningful treatment effects are regarded as of equal importance by the consumers of such treatments (the clients themselves and significant others in their lives). In what may be a pioneering paper, Schreibman, Koegel, Mills, and Burke (1981) report a systematic study of the social significance of objectively observed changes in autistic children before and after behavior therapy. The authors videotaped 13 autistic children in a free-play setting at pretreatment and after 6 months of treatment. Objective measures of behavioral change were obtained from these tapes by trained observers. In addition, the tapes were subjectively evaluated by 182 undergraduates. Three questions were asked: Do naive judges subjectively perceive the same degree and direction of change in treated children as obtained by objective measures? Are the behaviors used by the judges in their subjective evaluation of the children the same behaviors that are observed by means of more objective measures? Are judges more likely to form more favorable global impressions, such as liking the child, after improvement in treatment?

The results of this investigation demonstrate three main types of correspondence between objective assessment measures and the subjective ratings of naive judges. The naive undergraduates did indeed observe changes in the children's behaviors that corresponded to the objectively measured changes and were influenced predominantly by specific behaviors (e.g., appropriate speech). When the children were divided into high and low objective-change groups, these naive undergraduates changed their impressions positively for the high objective-change group but showed essentially no change for the low objective-change group. Such results lend additional support to the prevailing impression that subjective judgments can be used to help evaluate treatment effects. Despite certain limitations, such as the use of college students—rarely direct consumers of the treatment program—as the subjects of the study, these findings point to the need for social as well as traditional validation.

It has been observed both anecdotally and experimentally that many autistic children fail to respond to the multiple cues that are present in all learning situations. This defective response pattern has been called "stimulus overselectivity," thereby emphasizing the overly restricted stimulus control that applies to these children. Stimulus overselectivity has been implicated as one possible basis for the profound behavioral deficits observed in the autistic child and in particular for the failure of these children to utilize traditional prompt-fading techniques.

Based on the premise that prompt fading could be successfully used if it did not require the child to respond to simultaneous multiple stimuli, Schreibman and her associates developed what they term "within-stimulus prompt fading." Continuing this line of investigation, Schreibman and Charlop (1981) reported a comparison of two prompt-fading procedures for teaching difficult visual discriminations to autistic children. Investigations such as these may eventually help us understand the learning characteristics of autistic children, but as yet their practical application is limited.

Despite considerable success in the training of functional language in autistic children, many problems remain. Much of the research in this area has focused on motivating the child to learn. Typically autistic children show a lack of motivation, and the standard approach has been to use primary reinforcers such as food. Unfortunately, reinforcer satiation occurs all too quickly and provides a major obstacle to the continued utilization of that particular motivator. Recently, researchers have begun to examine procedures geared toward the prevention or at least delay of reinforcer satiation. According to Litt and Schreibman (1981), continued exposure to a familiar stimulus enhances satiation, whereas the periodic presentation of novel stimuli increases the effectiveness of specific reinforcers and thereby maintains the behavior. In other words, satiation may be prevented or reduced by any change or variation of sensory stimulation.

As a third example of the development of a specific technique based on some theoretical premise, I draw attention to a study by Dyer, Christian, and Luce (1982) of the role of response delay in improving the discrimination performance of autistic children. A common observation made by teachers of such children is that their students often seem to respond before actually attending to the task. If this is correct, then some kind of response delay requirement is indicated.

To examine this hypothesis, Dyer et al. evaluated the influence of response delay on the correct responses of three autistic children during discrimination training. Two conditions were compared within the context of a multiple-baseline, repeated-reversal design: a no-response-delay condition, in which the child was allowed to make the target response immediately after presentation of a discriminative stimulus; and a response-delay condition, in which the therapist signaled the child to respond 3 seconds after the discriminative stimulus was presented. The response-delay condition produced higher levels of correct responding than did the no-response-delay condition. Furthermore, teachers rated the response-delay procedure as a practical and effective technique that could be readily implemented in a classroom setting. If confirmed, these findings could have important implications for the development of classroom curricula.

Probably the most dramatic advance in this field has been the demonstration that previously nonverbal children can be taught to speak. Traditionally, language training programs for autistic children focused on the development of expressive oral communication skills by means of operant conditioning. Unfortunately, while such programs can be highly successful, acquisition of these skills remains characteristically slow and costly in terms of therapy time. Perhaps for these reasons, researchers have turned to sign language as one possible alternative to traditional oral training and have demonstrated its effectiveness in a variety of situations. The training techniques used in these sign-language studies employ either a total-communication training system incorporating the use of gestural (sign) and vocal (oral) cues or a modified sign-alone system in which gestural cues (signs) alone are used during training and all vocal stimuli cues are eliminated. According to Barrera, Lobato-Barrera, and Sulzer-Azaroff (1980), the total-communication model is substantially superior to either oral or sign-alone training models.

These findings notwithstanding, the question of whether autistic children will benefit more from sign or vocal training is by no means resolved. As far as language training is concerned, it could be that the diverse effects reported in the literature depend on the pretraining characteristics of the child (Carr, 1979). Mute and echolalic children may constitute distinct subgroups, with the former potentially profiting the most from visual language (signing) and the latter from auditory language (speech training).

In a controlled study of the concurrent use of manual signs and spoken words, Carr and Dores (1981) further conclude that there are two subgroups of nonverbal children, each of which exhibits a different pattern of language acquisition following simultaneous communication. Two of the six children in their study acquired receptive signing but not receptive speech; four children acquired both receptive signing and receptive speech. It seems that children with poor verbal-imitation skills acquire receptive signing but not receptive speech, whereas children with good verbal-imitation skills readily acquire both receptive signing and receptive speech. It is evident that the methodology of teaching language acquisition to autistic children is far from resolved.

Teaching speech to nonverbal autistic children is one area where parental self-help manuals can probably do more harm than good if they are utilized without adequate supervision. (See my discussions of this issue in previous volumes of the *Annual Review*.) Parents can be trained to deal effectively with their children's behavior and speech defects, but the extent to which the changes that occur in these children are direct consequences of the procedures themselves remains uncertain. Although ethical issues usually preclude the inclusion of an untreated control group, it is strange that multiple-baseline designs, in which the treatment procedures are applied sequentially to different behaviors or to the same behavior in different settings, are rarely incorporated into the experimental design (Harris & Wolchik, 1982).

This cavalier attitude to methodology is especially curious in view of the compelling reasons in favor of training parents of nonverbal children to act as therapists for their own children. Parents have extensive contact with their children, they control a major part of the environment, and they have access to powerful reinforcers that may be more successful at home than in the classroom or clinic. Parent training could be an effective means of enhancing the probability that skills learned in the classroom transfer to other settings. Finally, parent training is a way of providing treatment for children who are not yet old enough to be enrolled in school programs. Despite the fact that most of their projects were carried out with a selected group of children of highly motivated parents, the numerous training-program studies conducted by Harris and her associates underscore the general significance of these points (e.g., Harris, Wolchik, & Weitz, 1981; Harris & Milch, 1981; Harris, Wolchik, & Milch, 1982).

Among others (see previous volumes of the *Annual Review*), Harris and her associates also draw attention to the need for clinical sensitivity to the anxiety, depression, anger, and other emotional experiences that are likely to arise as the family struggles to cope with the child's handicap. A program that fails to take this into account is likely to be of limited utility. Further research is needed. Another neglected theme is the development of programs that are effective with less educated and perhaps less motivated groups of parents. The other problem noted by Harris, Wolchik, and Weitz (1981) is that progress is too often restricted to the context of group meetings and home visits. Although advances obtained during training are usually maintained, further significant progress is limited or nonexistent once formal training is discontinued. It may be that parents need ongoing consultation or some form of booster sessions to help their children move beyond the point reached at the end of training. A controlled study carried out in Wales by Clements, Evans, Jones, Osborne, and Upton (1982) with preschool and school-age severely handicapped children underscores the importance of long-term house-visiting programs for such children.

HYPERACTIVITY

Debate and inconsistency continue to characterize the intellectual activity of the students of hyperactivity. Hyperactivity (HA) remains a source of contention with respect to etiology, the nature of the syndrome, and its definition, assessment, and remediation. More heat than light continues to be generated, and unanimity is less evident now than it was a year ago.

Three books appeared during the review period. The first, edited by M. Gittelman (1981), contains two interesting longitudinal studies by Hechtman, Weiss, Perlman, Hopkins, and Wener (1981) and Howell and Huessy (1981), together with a much-needed chapter by Pollack and R. Gittelman (1981) outlining some of the practical problems encountered in the behavioral treatment of HA. Regrettably, too many chapters cite outdated references, most begin with a rehash of similar material, there is an absence of cross-referencing, and the editorial selection criteria for the inclusion of papers escape detection.

The second book, by Barkley (1981), pulls together a vast amount of data to generate an informed overview of current opinions on assessment, definition, etiology, and intervention. The numerous scales, forms, programs, and observational systems detailed in the text add to the utility of Barkley's book. Most important, and to be discussed shortly, there is an extensive chapter on parent training that is likely to be of considerable value to the clinician despite the lack of control data. The third book, by Winchell (1981), is an annotated bibliography covering the period from 1974 to 1979. More than 2,000 scattered and diverse HA citations are classified in convenient groupings and cross-referenced under one cover.

For those seeking a superficial overview from a primarily behavioral perspective, there is a once-over-lightly chapter by Stewart and Ashby (1981). Of more substance and significance is a thoughtful review of HA assessment with special relevance to psychometrics, methodology, and practice by Wallander and Conger (1981). Drawing particular attention to the lack of psychometric sensitivity that characterizes this area, Wallander and Conger make cogent recommendations for the development of better assessment tools. What effect this will have upon current investigators remains to be seen.

Meaningful assessment rests upon consistent and operational definition. As yet, consensus in this fundamental area is rare. For example, the American Psychiatric Association's most recent diagnostic system, DSM-III, provides two categories of attention deficit disorder, with and without HA. No assumption about the relationship between these two disorders is made, and no conclusion about the etiology of either condition is drawn. The possibility that the postulation of two distinct disorders is itself an assumption is conveniently overlooked.

With the publication of DSM-III in 1980, the name of this disorder was changed from "hyperkinetic reaction of childhood" to "attention deficit disorder." While this change reflects the prevailing notion that the motor activity symptoms are not the primary ones, supporting evidence and objective criteria are lacking. Although operational criteria are officially specified for the first time, considerable disagreement about the utility of these criteria remains. As Loney (1982) points out, the term "attention deficit disorder" is only partially operational. Studies of the reliability of the DSM-III childhood disorders have been disappointing, and the validity of most of them is still unknown. Under these circumstances, Loney would seem justified, at this stage, in his vigorous defense of the continued use of the term HA. According to Loney, the American Psychological Association has appointed a committee to explore alternatives, and I await with interest the outcome of their deliberations.

Past HA terminology reflects a strong, if not very defendable, organic bias. (Hence such labels as "minimal brain damage" and "minimal brain dysfunction.") Given the increasing agreement that HA can result from several different causes, an etiological focus for describing or defining the disorder would seem to be doubly unrewarding. Wallander and Conger (1981) conclude from their review of the data that hyperactive children are currently best characterized as displaying (1) a motor activity inappropriate to social-situational domains, and (2) a deficient task-approach style primarily observed as difficulty in sustaining attention and/or in controlling impulse responding. Specific problem behaviors, such as low school achievement or aggression, are viewed by these authors as secondary to the primary deficiencies.

What is the relationship between aggression and HA in childhood? Prinz, Connor, and Wilson (1981) studied 109 first-, second-, and third-grade children rated as hyperactive and evaluated by their teachers for

12 consecutive school days on the Daily Behavior Checklist. Daily recordings were made on 11 physically or verbally aggressive acts and on 11 acts of a hyperactive nature. Their findings clearly indicate that, for children rated as hyperactive, interpersonal aggressive behaviors were reported at higher rates for those who exhibited high rates of hyperactive behavior. But it should also be noted that a fair proportion of high hyperactive children failed to evidence high rates of aggressive behavior. For most clinicians, HA and aggression are intertwined and further investigation of their confounding is needed.

Descriptions of hyperactive children typically include an apparently similar and consistent range of diagnostic behaviors. Despite such surface similarities, children labeled hyperactive are heterogeneous. Why is there this heterogeneity among hyperactive children in the face of a seeming consensus with respect to diagnostic characteristics? According to Loney (1980), the heterogeneity could be caused by variations in symptoms, situations, or subjective reports or by variations over time. One possibility raised by Ullman, Egan, Fiedler, Jurenec, Pliske, Thompson, and Doherty (1981) is that the diagnosticians themselves may contribute to this variance. Clinicians may differ on which of various factors to consider and what weight to attribute to these factors when they make the actual diagnoses.

To investigate this possibility, the diagnostic policies for HA used by 16 experienced clinicians were investigated by means of a multiple regression procedure. Individual analyses were made of each clinician's set of diagnoses of children who had been described in terms of 19 cues, including reports of home and school behavior, clinical observation, and test results. Although the clinicians' diagnoses were all intercorrelated, substantial individual differences were obtained both in terms of the cues used and the number of children diagnosed as hyperactive. As Uleman *et al.* correctly conclude, these results cast doubt on the presumption of professional consensus with respect to the behaviors subsumed under the rubric of HA. It may well be that it is the diagnostician who contributes as much to the observed heterogeneity of HA as do Loney's variations.

Given these numerous points of contention, it is not surprising that research advances are less than spectacular. Outcome measures are lacking or inadequate, use of control groups is rare, and investigators tend to compare hyperactive children with normal children rather than with other children in comparable situations. Finally, apart from the comparisons of medication and behavior modification, there has been little work comparing different types of interventions. More controlled longitudinal studies are needed to provide answers to questions about what happens to treated and untreated hyperactive children as they grow up (Hechtman *et al.*, 1981; Howell & Huessy, 1981; Sandoval, Lambert & Sassone, 1981).

Although there is opportunity for considerable improvement, parent training for the families of hyperactive children offers one of the few exceptions to the discouraging conclusions of the preceding paragraph. Barkley (1981) offers an extensive report on his nine-session behavior-management program for parents of noncompliant hyperactive children. Session by session, the clinician is taken through the intricacies of each meeting in sufficient detail for application in his or her own setting. Dubey and Kaufman (1981) report new developments in their time-limited workshops for parents of hyperactive children. Parents are taught that some of their children's behavior problems may have little to do with HA as such and that their children are not as uncontrollable as they have come to believe. Continuing evaluation is an integral component of their program, and some 2,000 parents have been studied to date. Because they are subsidized by a nonprofit organization, the current cost of attending their workshops is $12.50 for the entire 10 weeks for two parents, including the manual!

Finally, I draw attention to Thurston's (1981) comparisons of (1) training parents to use behavior modification procedures to reduce their children's hyperactive behavior, (2) using Ritalin to accomplish the same goal, and (3) no treatment at all. While no long-term follow-up is reported, Thurston's results do suggest that training parents to use behavior modification to decrease behavior labeled as hyperactive is as effective as the use of a central nervous system stimulant. Other things being equal, parent training offers obvious advantages over the extensive use of medication.

Use of Ritalin has been compared to a variety of other treatment modalities during the past year. Cohen, Sullivan, Minde, Novak, and Helwig (1981) evaluated the effects on kindergarten-age hyperactive children of three modes of treatment in relation to an untreated control group. The 3 months of treatment consisted of cognitive behavior modification, use of Ritalin, or the two treatments combined, with a follow-up approximately 1 year later. Regardless of intervention or lack of intervention, all the hyperactive children became less symptomatic over time. What is of perhaps greater concern is the fact that even though the hyperactive children could not be differentiated from normal controls on psychological measures, standardized patient and teacher ratings indicated that they were still perceived by adults as more disruptive than their normal peers. Equally important, the data of Cohen *et al.* confirm earlier reports: While parental global impressions consistently suggest that it is the medicated children who make the most gains, objective indices fail to change as dramatically with these preschool children as with children of school age. A variety of methodological reasons can probably be found to account for these somewhat lackluster findings, but the implications cannot be ignored. Researchers are just beginning to observe empirically that medicating a child sometimes produces changes not only in the behavior of the child but also in the behavior and attitudes of parents and teachers (Whalen, Henker, & Finck, 1981).

With few exceptions, behavior therapy has been reported to be less effective than use of medication (Rapport, Murphy, & Bailey, 1982). The major exception seems to be direct contingency management, which relies on immediate reinforcement for appropriate behavior. Unfortunately, contingency management has major shortcomings. These include unrealistic time requirements, need for high adult–child ratios, and extensive teacher training. To meet these obligations, Rapport *et al.* propose response cost as a viable alternative.

In what is probably the first direct comparison to appear in the literature, a within-subject comparison was made of the effects of Ritalin and response cost in reducing the off-task behavior of two boys diagnosed as having an attention deficit disorder with HA. Several dosages of Ritalin (5–20 mg/day) were evaluated. With free time as the reinforcer, response cost was found to be superior to Ritalin in raising levels of on-task behavior and in improving academic performance. Regrettably, no placebo control condition was used, and because of time constraints, a response-cost-plus-medication condition was not included in the experimental design. Furthermore, although precise measurements were used, only two children were studied. Nevertheless, further investigation seems warranted.

BEHAVIOR MODIFICATION IN THE SCHOOL SYSTEM

Overview

Behavior modification is now firmly established as an effective component of the educational process. For some individuals, behavior modification in the school setting is still synonymous with operant conditioning and applied behavior analysis (e.g., Bijou & Ruiz, 1981). For others, some form of behavioral systems approach is more appropriate (e.g., Douglas, 1982; Suckerman, Hines, & Gordon, 1982). Either way, the mechanistic application of behavioral principles would seem to be at an end. Thoughtful behavior therapists are asking such questions as: What is the purpose of public education? What is the role of behavior modification in the broader social context? While there is no simple or permanent answer to any of these questions, it is encouraging to note that contemporary reviews of behavior therapy within the school system devote considerable attention to discussion of these issues (e.g., Lahey & Rubinoff, 1981).

Kazdin (1982a) draws attention to the need to consider both the social implications of the educational process and those specific parameters geared more directly toward the utilization of behavioral principles in the classroom. The long and short of it is that, at least in principle if not yet in practice, the modern behavior modifier has to be a citizen of the world as well as a competent technician. Sometimes it is difficult to integrate these two rather different themes into a working harmony. The penalties of failure can be either benefits that are short lived or consequences that are untoward.

The use of corporal punishment in the schools and the curious mixture of sociological and learning theory principles adduced by both supporters and detractors in support of their respective positions is a case in point. Regrettably, professional and public opinion alike are shaped by prejudice, hunch, and speculation rather than by data. Thus, despite a lack of solid evidence about the effectiveness of corporal punishment as a long-term behavioral management technique, its continued use in some form or another remains widespread. Rose (1981) makes an intriguing behavioral analysis of the reinforcing events that continue to maintain corporal punishment in the schools despite a lack of demonstrable evidence about its effectiveness. But in so doing Rose himself is guilty of speculation, and he advances no data in support of his theoretical analysis. His position paper is primarily of significance in drawing attention to numerous alternative procedures that have been proved effective for reducing inappropriate behavior in school settings. These procedures include such well-documented techniques as the differential reinforcement of other behaviors, the differential reinforcement of low rates of responding, and response cost.

Lysakowski and Walberg (1981) address themselves to two timely questions: What aspects of reinforcement are most effective for learning, and under what circumstances? What techniques produce optimal results for different gender, race, and socioeconomic-status groups of students? Using recently developed statistical techniques, these authors examine data culled from 39 studies covering a period of 20 years and a combined sample of 4842 students in 202 classes. In general, the effects of specific reinforcement procedures on classroom learning seems to be moderately large, fairly robust, and constant across grades (from kindergarten through college), socioeconomic levels, race, private and public schools, and communities. Tangible reinforcers seem to be slightly more effective than intangible ones, and students in special classes seem to be slightly more amenable to reinforcement than other students.

It is clear that the last word has not been said and that much remains to be investigated. It is with this thought in mind that I turn now to a selective review of behavior modification in the school setting.

Behavioral Contrast and Response Cost

BEHAVIORAL CONTRAST

Relatively little is known about the social validity of token economies, about such seeming intangibles as the influences of token economies on children's attitudes towards their teachers or school work, or about the effects of teacher popularity on the effectiveness of token economies. Although token economies are frequently implemented only in portions of a child's school day and often only in selected classrooms, investigations of the possible effects a token economy may have on the performance and attitudes of children and situations in which the contingencies are not in effect are rare (Kistner, Hammer, Wolfe, Rothblum, & Drabman, 1982).

These effects resemble the so-called behavioral control phenomena of infrahuman research. Although they have been studied extensively in animals, few investigators have examined the circumstances under which contrast effects occur in humans. (For a recent review of behavioral contrast effects, their importance for behavior therapy, and the need to conduct further investigations, see Gross and Drabman, 1981.) A well-designed study by Koegel, Egel, and Williams (1980) examined potential contrast effects in behavioral treatment programs for severely handicapped children. In one environment contingent reinforcement was clearly associated with a decrease in the target behavior in a control setting in which the contingency was not in effect. These authors also found that inappropriate behaviors increased in environments where there was no formal treatment when time out was contingently applied in the therapy setting. Similar findings have been reported within the context of a classroom token economy for profoundly hearing-impaired, disruptive, low-achieving middle school students (Simon, Ayllon & Milan, 1982).

Kistner *et al.* (1982) were interested in the contrast effects likely to occur when a token economy program was introduced in only one part of the school day of six learning disabled children. The token economy was systematically introduced by three teachers, and a multiple-baseline design was used to assess its effects. The dependent measures included two rating forms of teacher popularity and work rates on a programmed reading series. While the token system was effective in increasing productivity, no consistent behavioral contrast effect was observed. Furthermore, the attitudes of the children toward the teachers did not seem to be influenced by the token economy until only one of the three teachers involved in the project was not delivering tokens. At this point, this teacher's popularity declined until she also began to deliver tokens. Thus, at least in this study, the token economy manipulation had a specific, desirable effect on the targeted behavior (work rate) but minimal negative or positive side effects on teacher popularity. No follow-up to see what happened in either situation after termination of the study was reported.

The authors raise a number of methodological possibilities that might account for these discrepant findings. Nevertheless, they have sufficient faith in their data to conclude that the present finding "provides teachers and educators with important additional confirmation of the effectiveness of token systems" and that it should "aid in their planning and implementation of incentive programs in selected classrooms with a larger, standard school curriculum" (p. 95). These generalizations seem premature. What we need to know more about is the circumstances under which behavior contrast effects can and cannot occur and what, if anything, to do about them (Neilans & Israel, 1981).

RESPONSE COST

Response cost involves withdrawing a specified amount of reinforcers contingent upon the production of target behavior that the therapist or teacher is trying to eliminate or reduce. The reinforcers are lost from a positive reserve acquired either through a token economy in which rewards are earned contingent upon desirable behaviors or through a bonus response-cost program in which a predetermined number of rewards are given noncontingently. While response cost is probably effective in eliminating a variety of inappropriate school behaviors, there is little in the literature to help the practitioner decide about the magnitude of the cost and the level of reinforcement most appropriate to any particular situation. Thus for the most part, response-cost programs are forced to proceed on either an intuitive or a trial-and-error basis.

Pace and Forman (1982) systematically exposed four disruptive second-grade students to response-cost programs involving varying initial reinforcements and fines. Somewhat surprisingly, the degree of aversiveness of the procedure did not appear to be related to effectiveness. All treatments were highly effective, with the target behaviors approaching near-zero levels. It is probable that these findings reflect idiosyncratic qualities of the investigation rather than an insensitivity of response cost as a corrective procedure. I draw attention to this study primarily to underscore the need for further research. Given the present level of technological sophistication, it should not be necessary for practitioners to rely upon arbitrary decisions.

Peers as Behavior-Change Agents

With the current movement toward the mainstreaming of handicapped children, the utilization of classroom peers as behavior-change agents assumes increased importance. But the introduction of this seemingly innocuous strategy is fraught with political and emotional as well as methodological problems. A historical perspective is essential for the full appreciation of these matters. (For a more detailed exposition, refer to Strain, 1981, who explores in 366 detailed pages virtually every known aspect of peer intervention. The lack of informed knowledge about the pros and cons of peer intervention and the circumstances under which a specific procedure is best applied is surprising.)

Numerous retrospective reports lead to the conclusion that social withdrawal in childhood can persist into adult life. Inappropriate peer interaction during childhood, including lack of peer interaction, could be a contributing factor in this progression towards adult pathology. There are three classroom-based behavioral strategies for coping with social withdrawal in young children: use of adult prompting and social reinforcement; provision of toys or activities geared toward social interaction; and use of peers both as direct agents of differential reinforcement and social initiation to play and as positive social-interaction models. Strain and his associates are convinced that appropriately designed and monitored peer-mediated interventions can increase the rate of positive social behaviors exchanged between a withdrawn child and other children (e.g., Hendrickson, Strain, Tremblay, & Shores, 1982; Strain & Fox, 1981a). As these authors note, the issue that remains uncertain is whether peers can bring about such changes in any specific child, and, if so, to what degree and under what circumstances. As yet it is difficult to answer such questions with sufficient conviction to provide meaningful advice to the practitioner.

What does seem to be certain is that the mere physical integration of socially competent and withdrawn children has little, if any, positive effect on the social behavior of the withdrawn youngsters. To the contrary, data cited by Strain and Fox (1981a) indicate that, without systematic intervention, withdrawn children can become the objects of verbal abuse and social rejection by their more socially competent classmates.

A vital issue in the process of peer training is the selection of appropriate intervention agents. Although there is no clear-cut formula for the selection of peer trainers, a number of common attributes seem to emerge from Strain and Fox's analysis of the literature. Assuming that the peer trainers are sincerely willing to participate, they must manifest an absence of negative social behavior toward peers, possess the ability to imitate verbal and motor behaviors modeled by adults, and, finally, possess a general tendency to respond in a positive fashion to the social-approach behaviors of other children. Whether all of these characteristics are necessary prerequisites to successful peer-mediated intervention remains unknown. It would seem reasonable to conclude, with Strain and Fox, that the absence of any of these characteristics should lead the investigator to anticipate the need for more extensive and intensive training.

Under some circumstances the possession of certain handicaps by peer trainers might be an advantage, as it might lead to a more empathetic appreciation of the deficits of the target subjects and the problems they generate. Hendrickson et al. (1982), for example, were able to work most successfully with a peer helper who was himself behaviorally handicapped and had a history of negative interaction with peers.

As an example of systematic program research in this area, I draw attention once again to the work of Strain and his associates in unraveling the parameters of teacher-mediated peer feedback in withdrawn and otherwise behaviorally handicapped children. Thus, in an earlier study, Ragland, Kerr, and Strain (1981) showed that peers could be employed as effective feedback agents to increase the levels of appropriate academic and social behavior. But it was not possible to separate out the effects of peer feedback from those attributable to students' performance objectives or to behavioral goals. This deficit was corrected in a subsequent investigation, which systematically examined the relative influences of behavioral goals and behavioral goals plus peer feedback on the negative and positive social interactions of behaviorally handicapped children (Kerr, Strain, & Ragland, 1982). The target subjects were four boys who were described as negative and abusive in their peer interactions. The six peers, all in the same special-education class as the target subjects, were all several years below grade level in all academic areas and had been frequently observed to violate school and class rules.

In general, the findings confirmed the value of teacher-mediated peer feedback in improving the interaction patterns of behaviorally handicapped school-age children. However, considerable caution should be exercised before generalizing from these findings to other client groups and treatment contexts. Whether these effects are maintained across the school day and how they generalize over time once the project is formally discontinued is also unknown. In three well-designed small-scale studies, Lancioni (1982) showed that normal children could be trained to teach social responses to withdrawn mentally retarded peers. But once again the major problem was that of generalization and maintenance. Although there were some indications that the effects of the intervention could spread outside the training setting and continue to grow after the end of the intervention, the details were far from clear.

Behavior Modification in the Education of the Atypical Child

In perhaps the most comprehensive text of its kind published to date, Safer (1982b) discusses virtually every aspect of school programs for disruptive adolescents. To be fully effective, such programs should deal with prevention, antecedents, long-term follow-up, and the general context of the adolescents' life styles, as well as with the presenting problems. At present, investigations tend to focus more upon isolated fragments than on the whole (e.g., Luiselli, Pollow, Colozzi, & Teitelbaum, 1981). Heaton and Safer's (1982) well-controlled evaluation leads one to the conclusion that continued reinforcement programs throughout high school and beyond are essential if progress is to be maintained (see also Safer, Heaton, & Parker, 1981; Trice, Parker, & Safer, 1982).

Behavior modification programs are particularly appropriate for the education of mentally handicapped children, and several good teaching manuals for professionals and paraprofessionals are now available. Popovich (1981) provides an excellent addition to this rapidly growing armament, Luiselli (1982) focuses upon the more general aspects of the evaluation of these programs, and Bijou (1981) presents the perspective of applied behavioral analysis. Suitably trained teachers can apply these procedures to new situations and continue to use them successfully over time. There is even some suggestion that teachers can learn to write limited behavior modification programs for themselves (e.g., Hundert, 1982).

The development of quality education programs for emotionally disturbed adolescents is a challenge that few behavior therapists have taken up. Towns (1981) offers a concise, technically sound and yet very practical introduction to the issues involved. For those who seek to know in detail how to set up such a program, this is probably the most appropriate text available to date. However, readers should be warned that, while primarily behavioral in approach, Towns draws upon key elements from reality therapy, rational–emotive therapy, and a hodge-podge of milieu interventions.

For a variety of reasons, numerous disadvantaged youths, school dropouts, and even high school graduates have not acquired the basic educational skills necessary for independent, gainful adult functioning. Most behaviorally oriented remediation programs focus on process (e.g., paying attention or staying on task) rather than content. What is not often questioned—Kelley and Stokes (1982) excepted—is the comparative efficacy of targeting academic process behavior rather than levels of skill performance.

During the past decade, a variety of approaches to teaching children from economically disadvantaged homes have been studied as part of Follow Through, a large-scale project serving some 75,000 low-income children annually from 170 communities. While the individual programs vary in their conceptual bases, the key units are firmly behavioral (e.g., the University of Kansas's Behavioral Analysis Model and the University of Oregon's Direct Instruction Model) (Becker & Carnine, 1981).

The development of behaviorally based educational programs for the eradication of illiteracy in underdeveloped countries presents a different set of problems. For example, Casalta (1981) makes the important point that, in regions such as Latin America, literacy campaigns all too often result in the civic, economic, and social advancement of those who are already literate rather than in advancement of those "outsiders" for whom the program was designed. Behavioral remediation programs that do not take into direct account the social and political implications of their interventions are unlikely to achieve their goals.

Prevention is presumably more desirable than remediation. School-based behavioral prevention ranges from the specific (e.g., smoking: Jason, Mollica, & Ferrone, 1982) to the highly complex (e.g., Elias, Chinsky, Larcen, & Allen, 1982). Jason and Ferrone (1981) describe a 4-year prevention program for children in inner-city schools. Bry and George (1980) report one of the few controlled investigations of early prevention. In this study, 40 urban adolescents with school adjustment problems were randomly assigned either to a 2-year early intervention program or to a control group. Whereas the attendance and grades of the control students deteriorated significantly, those of the programmed students remained the same. It should be noted that this effect did not occur until the students had been in the program for 2 years. If the data had not been collected over 2 years, these positive effects would not have been documented and the study would have been reported as unsuccessful. Had data not been collected over time, the fact that it was 1 year before the effect of the intervention became apparent would not have been learned. Furthermore, the use of multiple objective outcome measures demonstrates that school failure experience is complex; grades and attendance can deteriorate while tardiness and discipline remain unchanged. Only by use of rigorously designed studies will we eventually be in a position to make meaningful statements.

CONCLUSIONS

Behavior therapy is no longer a traditional one-to-one intervention model transferred into a learning theory framework. Along with a recognition of the limitations as well as the strengths of conditioning and S-R learning theory goes an awareness of new developments in systems theory, environmental and ecological psychology, social psychology, and cognition. Interaction and reciprocity are among the hallmarks of contemporary behavior therapy.

As documented in this chapter, these developments are well reflected in child behavior therapy. No longer is the child viewed as a passive recipient of things to be done to "it." A few investigators still ask undergraduates to rate their reactions to hypothetical treatments for children with behavioral problems rather than relying upon direct observation in real-life interventions (e.g., Kazdin, 1980a, 1980b), but fortunately such reports are rare. Social validation takes into account the feelings, needs, opinions, and responses of the children concerned as well as of meaningful others in their lives. This is not necessarily restricted to problematic situations; it applies to all facets of the educational process. The Krasners, for example, utilized the children themselves to design the architecture of the ideal classroom rather than relying exclusively upon the expertise of adults (Hanley, Houts, Ruzek, Krasner, & Krasner, 1981; Van Wagenberg, Krasner & Krasner, 1981).

All children—all individuals for that matter—are part of a complex ecosystem that includes a variety of modalities, frameworks, and interactions. This requires a radical shift in conceptualization from either a uniquely child- or adult-oriented perspective to a life-span point of view (H. W. Reese, 1980).

When presented with a difficult problem, the struggling behavior therapist may be left at times with a disquieting feeling that the need for objectivity, quantification, and precise delineation of terms, concepts, and strategies that characterizes the behavioral approach is incompatible with the many nuances of the world as it really is. It is my contention that this is not so and that it is possible to adapt the demanding methodology of behavior therapy to conform to these new complexities. The behavioral technology that is beginning to emerge for improving the lives of children and their caregivers needs be neither simplistic nor mechanistic, and those who are in the forefront of these developments are at pains to ensure that this is so (e.g., Fawcett, Seekins, & Braukmann, in press; McSweeny, Freemouw, & Hawkins, 1982; Yates, 1982; Yeaton, Greene, & Bailey, 1981). It is on this encouraging note that I conclude this overview of recent developments in child behavior therapy and look forward with confidence to continued progress in the coming year.

8

CLINICAL ISSUES AND STRATEGIES IN THE PRACTICE OF BEHAVIOR THERAPY

G. TERENCE WILSON

SURVEYS OF TRENDS IN THE PRACTICE OF BEHAVIOR THERAPY

During this past year I seem to have received an inordinate number of requests to complete one or another questionnaire designed to survey my demographics, interests, and activities as a clinical psychologist or behavior therapist. The largely reflexive groan in anticipation of taking the time to comply with the earnest request of the ingestigators usually ends up being reciprocally inhibited by the feeling that surveys of general trends in clinical psychology may yield interesting information (not to mention the nagging guilt of knowingly failing some student or colleague). This behavior was pleasantly reinforced by reading of Smith's (1982) survey of trends in counseling and psychotherapy.

A questionnaire developed to assess the views of clinical and counseling psychologists on current theoretical trends was sent to a randomly selected sample of 800 members of Division 12 (Clinical Psychology) and Division 17 (Counseling Psychology) of the American Psychological Association. The sample consisted of 200 Division 12 Fellows, 200 division 12 members, 200 division 17 Fellows, and 200 Division 17 members. A total of 437 questionnaires (55%) was returned. The demographics of this sample closely approximated those of the Garfield and Kurtz (1976) survey of a much larger number of clinical psychologists, a similarity that Smith takes as evidence that he has tapped a reliable representation of psychotherapists and counselors. Of the sample 85% were male, 65% were above age 45, and 87% had earned a PhD. The proportion of those in university positions was 41%, while 26% were in private practice.

One of the questions in the survey asked about theoretical orientation. "Behavioral," "cognitive–behavioral," and "rational–emotive" were the three labels most likely to be chosen by respondents with preferences for a broadly defined cognitive–behavioral position. The percentages of these categories were 7%, 10%, and 2%, respectively. The largest proportion of respondents indicated that they were "eclectic" (41%). This figure is smaller than the 55% reported by Garfield and Kurtz, and Smith suggests that "several of those who indicated a preference for cognitive behavioral, family systems, or other would have opted for eclectic if the other choices had not been available, as was true in the study by Garfield and Kurtz" (p. 804). Another 11% indicated a preference for "psychoanalytic" and 3% for "Adlerian."

Another question gave respondents a multiple choice of terms descriptive of current trends in the field. Nearly 19% chose "multi-modalism" as the most descriptive term for the present theoretical approaches in counseling and clinical psychology. These were followed by terms such as "creative synthesis" (18%) and "emerging eclecticism" (17%). "Technical eclecticism" related a relatively low 9%, a curious finding given Lazarus's (1981) position as originator on both terms and their inextricable association in his multimodal therapy (see Chapter 8 of last year's *Annual Review* for an analysis of multimodal therapy). Only 2% considered "exclusive schools" to be an accurate descriptor of the field. In view of these findings, it would be hard not to agree with Smith when he concludes that "the trend in psychotherapy is away from the exclusiveness of schools and toward some kind of eclectic system that transcends both the narrowness in schools and the mediocrity of traditional eclecticism" (p. 807).

Respondents ranked the three psychotherapists whom they regarded as the most influential today. Carl Rogers placed first (probably partly a function of the inclusion of counseling psychologists in the sample), while in the top ten, Ellis, Wolpe, Lazarus, Beck, and Meichenbaum placed second, fourth, fifth, seventh, and tenth, respectively. That half the psychotherapists considered to be the most influential were behavioral or cognitive–behavioral in orientation should not go unnoticed. Consistent with this ranking is the finding that among the books considered most representative of the current *Zeitgeist* were the following: Lazarus's (1976) *Multimodal Behavior Therapy* (ranked

2nd); Meichenbaum's (1977) *Cognitive-Behavior Modification* (ranked 4th); Beck, Rush, Shaw, and Emery's (1979) *Cognitive Therapy of Depression* (ranked 6th); Bandura's (1977) *Social Learning Theory* (ranked 7th); Wolpe's (1973) *Practice of Behavior Therapy* (ranked 11th); and Ellis and Grieger's (1977) *Handbook of Rational Psychotherapy* (ranked 13th).

For the behavior therapist, Smith's overall conclusion is most encouraging:

> No single theme dominates the present development of professional psychotherapy. Our findings suggest, however, that cognitive-behavioral options represent one of the strongest, if not the strongest, theoretical emphases today. There seems to be a greater interest at this time in therapy systems that emphasize the integration of affect, cognition, and behavior and stress intervention strategies more than heavily theoretical approaches. (p. 808)

To the extent that this survey is a reasonable representation of what is actually going on, behavior therapy, broadly conceived of, appears to be alive, well, and growing in influence.

In another survey, Gochman, Allgood, and Geer (1982) polled 75 randomly selected AABT (Association for Advancement of Behavior Therapy) members, out of which sample 45 questionnaires were returned, and the final sample consisted of 41 respondents. The results indicate that 63% of the sample considered themselves to be "eclectic" in orientation, 27% considered themselves as strictly behavioral, and 10% as rational-emotive or cognitive-behavioral in orientation. Relatively few details are provided about the characteristics of the respondents, although we are told that 66% had completed graduate training that was behavioral, with the remainder reporting training that was primarily psychodynamic in nature. Of the sample 44% had received personal psychotherapy that was usually psychodynamic in nature. From other terse statements in this paper that could have been more informative than they are, we learn that "behavior therapists tend to rely equally on Wolpe (47%) and Skinner (47%), on Bandura (42%), and on Ellis, Meichenbaum, Lazarus, and Baer (31%)." It is difficult to know what precisely is meant by this observation. Finally, the datum that only 31% of the sample "work with children" comes as something of a surprise. The authors consistently assume that members of AABT are *ipso facto* "behavior therapists," an assumption that is not strictly correct. Whether or not their findings are representative of how behavior therapists view themselves and what they actually do in clinical practice remains for a more detailed investigation to uncover.

PROFESSIONAL ISSUES: MODELS OF TRAINING,
DELIVERY OF SERVICES,
AND THE PEER REVIEW PROCESS

Models of Training

In a recent editorial in *Behavioural Psychotherapy*, Marks (1981b) addressed the relationship between behavior therapy and the behavioral sciences. Within this context he voiced his views about the nature of the training that behavior therapists might ideally receive. He asks what the training is for:

> If we are aiming to produce scientific researchers and teachers, then a broad-based education in the behavioural sciences is essential, ranging from the biological to the psychosocial. However, for those who are mainly interested in therapy rather than in actively pursuing research, less of this detailed knowledge is necessary and much more about the clinical skills needed in therapy. (p. 286)

To clinical psychologists in the United States, adjusting to the new professional model of clinical training (Korman, 1976) and witnessing the explosion of new schools of professional psychology (Peterson, Eaton, Levine, & Snepp, 1980), these sentiments of Marks's have a familiar ring. The commitment to producing therapists with greater clinical skills, unencumbered by "academic" research requirements, has been the rallying cry of proponents of professional degrees and schools. Different professional schools vary in their requirements for research training, but all place distinctly less importance on research activities than do more conventional scientist–practitioner programs. Although it is now a fait accompli, the development of professional schools of psychology has been a continuing source of vigorous debate. The purpose here is not to rehash these general discussions of the pros and cons of professional schools. Rather, the point, as Marks's editorial brings to the fore, is to question whether the professional model of clinical training is an appropriate one for developing behavior therapists.

In 1974, my colleague Cyril Franks asked whether behavior therapy could find "peace and fulfillment" in a school of professional psychology. His immediate focus was the opening at that time of the Graduate School of Applied and Professional Psychology at Rutgers University, but he had the entire professional-school movement in mind. At the end of a lengthy paper in which he set out to answer this question, Franks reached the following conclusion:

> At this stage in our development, it is probably easier to search for the mythical holy grail than for behavior therapy to try to seek peace and fulfillment in any School of Professional Psychology worthy of the name, and it is likely to remain this way for the foreseeable future. (Franks, 1974, p. 15)

Five years later, Agras, Kazdin, and Wilson (1979) discussed the nature of training in clinical psychology from the perspective of behavior therapy as a developing clinical science. They arrived at a conclusion seemingly at odds with that of Franks: "The developing trend in clinical psychology training toward the professional school would seem to fit nicely with developments in behavior therapy" (p. 138). Agras *et al.* hastened to emphasize, however, that the professional schools to which they were referring should

> be part of a university, be located in an area large enough to afford a suitable clinical population, and reflect the relationship between the clinic and science by being closely tied to an academic department of psychology. The faculty should be capable of teaching applied psychology, and the school should offer appropriate courses in related behavioral and biological sciences that are directed to the future clinician and applied researcher. Active programs of applied research should be pursued by the faculty of such schools, as should relevant basic research, thus achieving the vigorous reciprocal interaction between the applied and basic sciences that should be a hallmark of this experimental clinical endeavor. Professional schools of psychology without this close relationship will tend to drift into the dogmatic teaching of therapeutic skills, a tendency already too frequent in the clinic. The majority of students within the professional school will become clinicians. However, a substantial minority should become clinical researchers, and the curriculum should be flexible enough to train both types of professionals. (p. 138)

These criteria, of course, rule out the many free-standing schools of professional psychology that have flourished, particularly in the fertile environment of California.

The question, then, is which of the foregoing views is correct. How has behavior therapy fared in professional schools of psychology? There is no easy answer to these questions. There is even doubt about what data would be necessary to find a useful answer. What can be said is that the absence of research training, or the relative deemphasis on research, should not automatically be interpreted as an a priori guarantee that behavioral training cannot be adequate. As I outlined in last year's *Annual Review* (see Chapter 8, Table 8-1), different levels of scientific/clinical training are needed along the continuum from basic research to clinical practice. Clinical practitioners at level 4 in my framework need not be trained to *do* research. There is no good reason to suppose that well-trained practitioners who are conscientious consumers of research findings are any worse off than well-trained practitioners who have also acquired clinical research skills. And obviously the former are more easily and inexpensively trained than the latter. For this reason, criticism of professional school degrees on account of the reduced or low-quality research training they involve (Garmezy, 1982) may miss the point. The important question is how good the "new-look" clinical training is in these programs, where training is presumably broader and better than that of students trained within the more traditional scientist–practitioner PhD program. This superiority in clinical training is frequently taken for granted, but I know of no evidence to substantiate the assumption, other than the less-than-disinterested testimony of some professional-school boosters. The necessary evaluations of the clinical adequacy of existing and innovative training models should be a priority if rational policy making is to result. In the meantime, a number of other questions might be considered: What is the status of behavior therapy in professional-school programs? How much training is devoted to it? Would the theoretical and therapeutic orientations of graduates from these schools parallel those reported by Smith (1982)? (Of Smith's respondents, 85% held a PhD, and I make the assumption that few if any of these degrees were granted by those professional schools that award PhDs, simply because the schools have not been in operation that long. There was no indication in Smith's report of respondents holding Doctor of Psychology [PsyD] degrees.)

Once again the relevant data are not at hand. An analysis of theoretical preferences along the lines of Smith's (1982) survey does not exist. There are, however, some disturbing signs that we would be unwise to ignore. First-hand acquaintance with the PsyD program at Rutgers University, supported by a limited survey of attitudes and activities of some of its students (Andrews, 1982), indicates that behavior therapy is generally shunned by a majority of clinical students. With varying degrees of conceptual purity these students favor a psychodynamic orientation, and they are likely to pursue careers in private practice and other traditional clinical roles. This relative rejection of behavior therapy training occurs despite the presence of a large behaviorally oriented teaching faculty and the existence of a nationally prominent scientist–practitioner PhD program that is largely, if not exclusively, behavioral in orientation. Whatever the reasons, and different interpretations are possible, on the face of it would appear that Franks (1974) was not far off the mark in his prognostication.

Is the current situation at Rutgers University unique, or does it reflect a general trend in clinical training in other schools of professional psychology? Consoling as it would be to see the fall off of behavior therapy in the Rutgers PsyD program as an isolated instance, it may be that it is reasonably representative of national trends. As crude and unsatisfactory an index as it is, knowledge of the prime movers in the development of professional schools does nothing to discourage this view. For example, of the major representatives of the 28 doctoral programs listed by the National Council of Schools of Professional Psychology, none is a member of AABT.

Assuming, for the sake of argument, that I am correct in my assumption, what if any implications does this state of affairs have for behavior therapy? Some behavior therapists probably would conclude that the outcome was inevitable given the absence of serious research training on which the field is said to be built. Let us hope that this is not the case. Professional schools and the manner of training they represent (the professional model, endorsed at the Vail conference in 1973), seem here to stay. Soon the number of their graduates will surpass those of programs based on the scientist–practitioner model. The political realities are clear. Behavior therapy will suffer seriously if the trend that I have tentatively identified continues. Behavior therapy should feature as prominently in the curricula of professional-school programs as it does in scientist–practitioner training programs. There is no intrinsic reason for behavior therapy not to be an integral part of this new-look training. If we do not train full-time behavioral practitioners, then we are selling the field short, let alone doing an injustice to the people who need the unique services of such full-time practitioners.

Delivery of Mental Health Services

The foregoing discussion of the nature and implications of professional schools of clinical psychology centers somewhat narrowly on developments in the United States. Yet debates about optimal methods for training psychotherapists and delivering mental health services are hardly confined to North America. For example, the past year has seen several discussions about the training and regulation of behavior therapists in the United Kingdom. Marks (1981a, 1981b) has advocated the employment of professionals (e.g., nurses) other than psychiatrists and clinical psychologists, and of paraprofessionals, in the treatment of various neurotic disorders. "It is by no means necessary," argues Marks, "to have a Ph.D or an M.D. to be an effective behavioural psychotherapist, or indeed any other therapist. There is a general tendency for people to work with higher credentials than are needed for their tasks" (1981a, p. 148).

In support of this contention Marks offers his own research on the cost effectiveness of using nurse-therapists to treat agoraphobic and obsessive–compulsive disorders (Marks, 1981c). He also cites Stunkard and Brownell's (1980) report that the group treatment of obese individuals by lay therapists resulted in lower attrition rates than the same treatment conducted by professionally trained therapists. Two often competing trends seem evident in the United States. On the one hand, instead of training the psychological assistants who would provide cost-effective treatment as described by Marks, clinical psychology in the United States seems to be moving toward the alternative policy of meeting mental health needs with greatly increased numbers of expensive, highly trained professionals with doctoral degrees. On the other hand, commercial programs for the treatment of problems such as obesity, cigarette smoking, and agoraphobia (e.g., Ross, 1982) that rely heavily upon the treatment services of individuals without professional degrees who have overcome the specific disorder in question have long been flourishing and arguably achieving impressive results. What, one might ask, is the situation in Britain? How extensive is the use of less-trained workers in the application of behavioral treatment methods?

If the picture painted by Robertson (1982) is accurate (and see the discussion of Yule's [1982] comments in the following section), the British have some basic problems with the regulation and organization of treatment services. "In Britain," states Robertson,

> the mental health services are a mess of confused roles, responsibilities and rewards. It is arguable which form of basic training is the most irrelevant for the practising therapist—six years of medicine, four years of nursing or the three years of experimental psychology—though there is no doubt as to which is the most expensive. (p. 181)

While he applauds Marks's suggestion that treatment services can be shifted from medical training and supervision to more appropriate and cost-effective settings, Robertson warns against overgeneralizing relatively restricted findings showing the efficacy of less-trained nurse-therapists' treatment of specific phobic and obsessive–compulsive cases (Marks, 1981c). Indeed, he might have noted that Marks's example about the treatment of obesity is hardly representative of this area. If anything, some studies have shown that professional therapists obtain superior results to nonprofessional therapists (Wilson & Brownell, 1980). The reasons for being more cautious than Marks appears to be are listed as follows:

> First, behavioural treatments are not panaceas and not all clients recover; we do not know what level of expertise is required to treat those clients with more intractable problems. Secondly, it is essential that these thera-

pists carrying out behavioural psychotherapy are responsive to the empirical findings of current research so that less effective practices are not perpetuated. (Robertson, 1982, p. 181)

As an alternative to Marks, Robertson bravely advocates the radical restructuring of the entire mental health service-delivery system. He calls for a "new . . . professional therapist," one who is trained to cope not only with a small percentage of patients with anxiety problems but also with the full range of psychological disorders. This new breed of therapist would require intensive practical training and would be selected for

> attributes known to be related to therapeutic success and not solely for academic qualities which may be unrelated to—or even inversely correlated with—therapeutic potency. Perhaps under such a system a career structure which promises clinical excellence—rather than administrative or academic prowess—would be more feasible. (p. 182)

The therapist would also be unshackled from the limiting and irrelevant trappings of the medical model and would be better prepared to "understand and tackle the predominant determinants of problem behaviour in the home, the workplace, or elsewhere in the community" (p. 182). Robertson's idealized picture of the new professional looks remarkably like the professional-school product envisaged by Peterson (1976) in the United States. It also conforms to the type of training recommended by Agras et al. (1979) and others. Yet the present-day professional schools do not seem to be realizing this goal, at least not to the satisfaction of behavior therapists. We need to know why and what to do about it.

Accountability and Peer Review

The 1970s witnessed the growing demand that providers of mental health services be made accountable to their clientele and to those who help share the cost of these increasingly expensive services. Closely related to this demand was the growing concern with the protection of the individual rights of patients, particularly those in institutional settings. Behavior therapy featured prominently in discussions and developments in this area. On the one hand, the field of "behavior modification" was attacked, in the early 1970s, as a potential threat to patients' rights (these charges are described and analyzed in the appropriate commentaries and reprinted papers in Volumes 3, 4, and 6 of the *Annual Review of Behavior Therapy: Theory and Practice*). On the other hand, behavior therapists were foremost in attempts to bring the application of psychological procedures to clinical and educational problems under critical scrutiny and to develop guidelines for the humane and effective practice of psychological therapies. Specific efforts toward this end included the publication of a report, *Ethical Issues in Behavior Modification*, by a commission of the American Psychological Association composed largely of behaviorally oriented professionals (Stolz and Associates, 1978; see Volume 6 of the *Annual Review*) and the release, by AABT, of a statement on ethical practice ("Ethical Issues for Human Services," 1977). Like the APA commission, and for similar reasons, AABT decided that there was no need to establish guidelines peculiar to behavior therapy and that a set of questions of importance to the provision of human services in general (independent of the conceptual basis of treatment, the types of clients, and the nature of the treatment setting) would be appropriate.

It is another action of AABT that is the focus of the present discussion. By 1977, no doubt prompted by the events alluded to in the preceding paragraph, AABT began to receive a number of requests for consultation concerning therapeutic programs throughout the country. In order to respond to these requests for assistance, and in view of its fundamental commitment to accountability and evaluation of treatment programs, AABT, in 1978, formed the Professional Consultation and Peer Review Committee, with the mandate to "arrange for consultation, review and testimony by appropriate professionals to provide authoritative interpretation of behavior therapy practice and research." The results of this peer review process, which has been provided free of charge as a professional service, have been described by Risley and Sheldon-Wildgen (1982).

The following six types of consultation have been offered, ranging from the least to the most demanding:

1. Case consultation. Many therapists do not have colleagues with whom to discuss unusual cases or problems with which they lack experience or specific expertise. The Committee, acting as a clearinghouse for information, responds to requests for consultation of this kind by putting the therapist in touch with an expert in that particular area. A Committee member contacts a professional who has the relevant expertise "as evidenced by the professional's publications," and if she or he is willing to consult on the case in question, provides the enquiring therapist with name and telephone number. Roughly 8 to 12 requests are processed each month, and, encouragingly, all professionals contacted thus far have agreed to consult for the Committee. It is always made clear that "the requesting therapist retains sole responsibility for the treatment and that the 'expert's advice' is to be accepted, adapted, or considered at the therapist's discretion" (p. 126). Potentially dangerous or legally complicated problems, such as self-injurious behavior, have been the focus of the majority of requests for consultation.

2. *Providing guidelines for behavioral treatment.* The Committee has collected drafts and publications of different sets of guidelines that have been developed for various problems in certain settings (e.g., May, Risley, Twardosz, Friedman, Bijou & Wexler, 1976). By the end of 1978, 21 different sets had been accumulated and sent to 54 different agencies and professionals.

3. *Review of written materials.* Many administrators of behavioral treatment programs have felt it advisable to have written descriptions of their programs reviewed by AABT. Following the journal review process, a number of competent professionals, particularly those who are especially well informed about ethical and legal issues, are selected as reviewers. The type of issue that is attended to in the reviews includes "identification of the current literature concerning the population being served and the procedures being implemented; comparison of procedures described in this literature with the procedures used by the program; recommendation, where indicated, that new procedures be considered; and specification of potential legal or ethical issues" (p. 128).

4. *On-site reviews of noncontroversial programs.* These involve more formal evaluation than can be provided by written documents. Often administrators of these and other programs have asked for AABT's endorsement of their procedures. As always, however, such a step is beyond the purpose of the peer review process, and AABT currently has an explicit policy that precludes endorsement or certification.

5. *On-site reviews of controversial programs.* Typically these programs involve the use of aversive or deprivation procedures in institutional settings. The programs often receive financial support from a state or the federal government, and the officials charged with regulatory control must rely on qualified professionals to evaluate the adequacy of the procedures used. The Committee requires that four principles be agreed to by all parties involved in the controversy before a specially selected task force is sent to conduct the on-site review. First, the parties of interest in the controversy (e.g., the administrators of the program as well as the state licensing personnel) must agree with the request for review. Second, the members of the reviewing task force are selected by the Professional Consultation and Peer Review Committee to represent a range of expertise appropriate to review the treatment procedures being employed in the program in question. Third, the task

force's functions are to review the program and make pertinent professional interpretations and recommendations. Finally, the reviewing task force's report will be issued only to the relevant parties. AABT does not publicly release any information about its findings, although it will interpret publicly any information from the report that is made public by any of the parties.

The task force has three missions. One is to provide expert information on behavior therapy practice and research. The second is to interpret both general and specific ethical and legal issues as they relate to the issues raised in the controversy. The third is to make recommendations that will facilitate the optimal care and treatment of clients. It should be noted that AABT does not assume responsibility for monitoring the program to ensure that its recommendations, assuming that they are accepted, have been followed. This is the responsibility of the regulatory agency, be it a state or federal agency.

Based on experience gained in conducting these on-site reviews of programs, the Committee concluded that treatment programs that use controversial techniques should establish two committees. The first is a peer review committee, consisting of a group of external, independent professionals who periodically review program procedures. The second is a human rights committee, consisting of laypersons who are aware of the relevant ethical and legal issues. (Suggestions are made about how to help them become aware of the issues.) Such a committee should monitor clients' rights, ensure due process in difficult decisions, and review all aversive or deprivation techniques. These recommendations are in line with previously proposed policies. Risley and Sheldon-Wildgen (1982) go further, however, in urging that this committee also review the treatment progress of individual clients on a regular basis. The following statement deserves emphasis: "It should be incumbent on the treatment staff to demonstrate not only that the type of treatment is appropriate but also that it is the best possible treatment for each particular client" (p. 130). It seems most appropriate that Risley and Sheldon-Wildgen link this function of ensuring the selection of appropriate and preferred treatment methods with human rights. It is insufficiently recognized that one of the most important ethical guidelines in the delivery of mental health services is the use of the most effective (and safest) treatments possible.

However desirable or well-intentioned the establishment of human rights committees for the purposes described above may be, the reality is that they are being saddled with extremely difficult tasks. As Reese (1982) has commented,

clients or guardians and Human Rights Committees are asked to make these decisions without fully realizing what considerations are relevant in making the decisions. They might be told to weigh the effectiveness of a treatment option against its intrusiveness, but what is effectiveness and intrusiveness? (p. 98)

The criteria of effectiveness are not easily agreed upon, as the many, often lively discussions of this topic in the professional literature indicate, and neither are criteria of intrusiveness always straightforward. Toward this end, Reese proposes that the intrusiveness of a procedure be evaluated along three major dimensions: public acceptability, amount of restriction of liberty, and degree of discomfort or stress inherent in its application.

   6. *Involvement with lawsuits or investigations concerned with appropriate treatment.* When AABT is called on for professional advice in mental health–related lawsuits and legal investigations, it again acts as a clearinghouse to facilitate the use of professional knowledge in litigation. The Committee has names of attorneys who are familiar with behavior therapy and mental health issues, and it contacts behavior therapists who can serve as expert witnesses in lawsuits. AABT has also helped to resolve some cases by filing *amicus* briefs that delineate the state of the art and science in the application of behavioral procedures to the case in question.

   Risley and Sheldon-Wildgen (1982) summarize AABT's experience with professional peer review during its early years. The Committee has continued to function and has had to be expanded to meet a growing demand for its services. Currently the Committee, which under the newly reorganized AABT administrative structure is now included as part of the Board of Professional Affairs, receives approximately 20 requests per year for reviews at one level or another.

   Moving across the Atlantic, Yule (1982) presents a disquieting review of attempts to formulate procedures for professional review and to develop ethical guidelines for behavior modification in the United Kingdom. Spurred to action by the death of a patient on a ward operating under the practice of R. D. Laing's notions about schizophrenia, the Department of Health and Social Security in Britain appointed a committee representing the Royal College of Psychiatrists, the Royal College of Nursing, and the British Psychological Society to formulate ethical guidelines for primarily behavior modification (*sic*) programs. The Zangwill committee, as it is known, chose to focus exclusively on token economy programs with chronic mental hospital patients. Yule vents his justifiable exasperation by referring to this extraordinary move as an "audacious non-sequitur" that "diverted attention from the dangerous practices based on Laing's theory" (p. 411).

   Yule points out numerous problems with the report drawn up by the Zangwill committee, problems that make it unacceptable to behavior therapists, including a failure to take the view that choice of therapy should be determined by reference to evidence of treatment effectiveness. Furthermore, the committee reinforces the pernicious professional power struggle that gives psychiatrists "ultimate responsibility" for treatment. As Yule laments, "How can a medically qualified consultant with no training in behaviour therapy be seen to take any form of 'responsibility' for an effective treatment outside his area of expertise?" (p. 412). Fortunately, for different reasons, all three professional societies represented on the committee have rejected the report.

Experimental Study of the Peer Review Process

With the increased demand for accountability and the prominent role that the peer review process is beginning to play in the evaluation of treatment programs, it becomes both sensible and informative to study the peer review process itself. Cohen and Oyster-Nelson (1981) have reported an initial investigation of the peer review process that provides some revealing findings and highlights the many challenges that will have to be faced. The authors view their study of peer review judgment as part of a broader context of research on clinical judgment as it varies across different theoretical orientations. In one of the best known studies of clinical judgment by therapists from contrasting theoretical approaches, Langer and Abelson (1974; reprinted in Volume 3 of this series) had psychodynamic and behavior therapists watch a videotaped interview of a man who had applied for a job. Half of each group of therapists were informed that they were observing a patient, the other half a job applicant. Subsequent questionnaire-based assessment showed that the psychodynamic therapists were heavily influenced by the label assigned to the interviewee. When labeled a patient, the man was described as significantly more psychologically disturbed than when he was labeled as a job applicant. In marked contrast to these labile clinical judgments, the behavior therapists (presumably quite accurately) described the man as well-adjusted regardless of the label. This important finding requires replication and extension. Moreover, Cohen and Oyster-Nelson point out that most of the experimental research on clinical judgment can be criticized on methodological grounds, such as nonrepresentative sampling of therapists and clinical stimuli and reactive measurement. With a view to improving upon methodologies for the study of clinical judgment, Cohen and Oyster-Nelson suggest that the psychological peer review process represents "a natural laboratory" in which to study clinical judgment, entailing as it does "relatively unobtrusive measurement of evaluative judgments of psychopathology and treatment necessity made by a national sample of clinicians, based on their reviews of actual clinical treatment reports" (p. 584).

The peer review process studied by Cohen and Oyster-Nelson was the American Psychological Association/Civilian Health and Medical Program of the Uniformed Services (APA/CHAMPUS) program. The goal of this program is to provide high-quality, cost-effective outpatient treatment. A peer review of adult services occurs automatically after 60 sessions. Treatment reports completed after 8, 24, and 40 sessions may also be submitted for review should questions arise. Three reviewers from the therapist's geographical region, who are authorized to review the service provided (e.g., treatment of adults), provide independent reviews, recommending, among other things, how many of the completed sessions and how many future sessions should be funded. Note that this review system does not try to provide reviewers with the same theoretical orientation as that of the therapist.

Twenty-four APA/CHAMPUS reviewers from each of three theoretical orientations (behavioral, eclectic, and psychodynamic) received one of three treatment reports as part of the regular 60-session review. As Cohen and Oyster-Nelson (1981) comment, it is most improbable that the reviewers would not have assumed that their recommendations would affect the processing of the claim. The treatment reports described long-term psychodynamic therapy for depressed, middle-aged female patients. They were deliberately prepared by three experienced psychodynamic therapists from their own cases. An impressive 97% of the reviewers returned evaluative reports.

The reviewers' evaluations showed a strikingly consistent pattern. Overall, the psychodynamic reviewers, compared with the behavioral and eclectic reviewers, rated the patients as more disturbed and in need of psychotherapy, and they were consistently more positive in their ratings of treatment and more generous in their recommendations concerning the reimbursement for past and future care. These results provide a powerful confirmation of Langer and Abelson's earlier findings and would appear to establish the proclivity of psychodynamic therapists to find greater psychological disturbance than their behavioral counterparts. Conversely, as the authors point out, it might be argued that behavior therapists overlook disturbance. Although this might be the case in the present study, it fails to account satisfactorily for the Langer and Abelson findings. In that study there was no a priori reason to suspect that the individual who was evaluated suffered from any serious emotional disturbance, yet the psychodynamic therapists were quick to find such pathology. Even more persuasively, their judgments of the same "case" contradicted each other flagrantly as a function of an externally assigned label. The ratings of the eclectic reviewers in the Cohen and Oyster-Nelson study often fell between those of the psychodynamic and behavioral reviewers. On several of the evaluative criteria, however, such as adequacy of goals and progress and appropriateness of treatment, the eclectic reviewers were in agreement with those of the behavioral group. The authors pose the interesting question of how eclectic reviewers might evaluate behavioral treatment reports, suggesting that they might then resemble the psychodynamic reviewers more closely because of their rejection of any single approach to treatment. The findings of the Smith (1982) survey, described earlier in this chapter, are consistent with this hypothesis.

The implications of this study for peer review and third-party reimbursement policies are obvious. To put it in a more prosaic perspective, psychodynamic reviewers recommended reimbursement of 37 sessions on average, compared to only 26 and 17 by the eclectic and behavioral reviewers. The data highlight the inescapable reality "that there are discrepant models of psychotherapy characterizing the profession of psychology and that a system of review based on professional judgment must somehow accommodate to paradigmatic heterogeneity among clinicians" (Cohen & Oyster-Nelson, 1981, p. 588). These data provide additional evidence against the view that commonalities among all therapies are known and appreciated by experienced therapists from different theoretical vantage points (Goldfried, 1980).

APPLYING WHAT WE KNOW
AND KNOWING HOW TO DO THIS

In the comparable chapter to the present in last year's *Annual Review* (see also Wilson, 1982c), I pointed out what has been obvious to commentators on the field for some time: that a number of demonstrably effective behavioral treatment techniques for different disorders (e.g., *in vivo* exposure treatment for agoraphobia and compulsive rituals) are not as widely employed in clinical practice as the clinical and experimental literature suggests they might be. The flip side of this record is that many treatment procedures that are routinely used carry no empirical support. In some instances there is reasonable evidence to show that they are ineffective. In short, the recounting of this unsatisfactory state of affairs is simply another expression of the much-discussed failure of basic and applied research to act as a major determinant of what methods are used to treat particular problems. Although part of the solution of this problem requires increased clinical research that is of direct relevance to practitioners (Barlow, 1980; Wilson, 1982c), the development of a broader applied research base, no matter how immediately pertinent to the practitioner's needs, will not by itself suffice to overcome the gap between research and practice. What is required, regrettably, has been bluntly stated by Liberman (1980):

> Implementation, survival, and dissemination of empirically validated interventions require much more than data and journal publications. . . . If we want our work to live beyond a library bookshelf, we will have to jump into the political mainstream and get our feet wet as administrator researchers. (p. 371)

Recall that the Professional Consultation and Peer Review Committee of AABT has recommended that behavioral programs in institutions constitute two separate committees, one of which, the human rights committee, might be asked to take the necessary steps to ensure as far as possible that the treatment each client receives is not only appropriate but also the preferred treatment (Risley & Sheldon-Wildgen, 1982). This call for action beyond the production of more improved research is being voiced by others. Thus Peterson (1981), for one, has stressed the importance of gaining control over the social and political conditions that influence the implementation and dissemination of behavior modification procedures. For another, Stolz (1981) proposes the development of a technology that will ensure the adoption and implementation of the products of applied behavioral research by the different tiers of government.

Restricting herself to applied behavior analysis, Stolz (1981) claims that several effective behavioral procedures have been developed for overcoming different social problems. Yet these methods have not been widely incorporated as part of public of government policy. Instead, the "technologies mostly lie unnoticed in our even-proliferating professional journals" (p. 492). Stolz asks why adoption of these technologies by public policymakers has not occurred, and what it is applied behavior analysts need to do to correct this imbalance between applied research on the one hand and public implementation and dissemination on the other. To shed light on these issues, Stolz analyzes four of the relatively rare occasions when behavioral technologies have been adopted by government agencies.

The first case concerns the fate of the findings from Fairweather, Sanders, Maynard, and Cressler's (1969) "lodge program"[1] as a means of keeping patients discharged from mental hospitals in a constructive community setting. Despite the excellent results of this program, state

---

1. Stolz observes that this study is "not usually identified with applied behavior analysis." Nevertheless, it does seem most appropriate to view the methods of this study as akin to the principles and procedures of behavior modification. (See also Bandura, 1969; O'Leary & Wilson, in press.)

mental hospitals and the Veterans Administration showed no interest in drawing upon Fairweather *et al.*'s innovative strategies to improve their obviously deficient services for coping with posthospital adjustment. Fortunately, the National Institute of Mental Health then agreed to fund a systematic study of Fairweather's program as part of an investigation of the dissemination process. The details of this study were published by Fairweather, Sanders, and Tornatzky (1974), and a brief summary of their procedures and results are in order here. As a start, Fairweather *et al.* (1974) divided the process of implementing the adoption of a new technology into four stages: (1) approaching the target organization, (2) persuading it to adopt the innovation, (3) activating the adoption, and (4) diffusing the innovation to other organizations. In the study the first two stages were combined and operationalized as follows: (1) a brochure describing the program, (2) a workshop presented at the hospital that described the program, and (3) a model program run like the lodge program, but set up in the hospital and using hospital facilities, staff, and patients. One of these three alternatives was offered to each of 225 state and VA mental hospitals. The offer was made in a phone call to a contacted hospital that agreed to accept what was offered. According to Fairweather *et al.* (1974), the brochure and workshop interventions yielded modest and essentially comparable results and both were inferior to the demonstration-ward option.

Stolz faults both the methodology and the original authors' interpretation of the results of this study. She points out that the researcher who made the telephone calls was obviously not "blind" to the experimental procedures and that this might have introduced bias into the results. Of the 85 hospitals that were approached in each group, 4 in the brochure condition, 10 in the workshop condition, and 9 in the demonstration-ward condition subsequently adopted the lodge program. Whereas only 12 hospitals agreed to establish a demonstration ward, 55 submitted mailing lists for brochures, and 58 contracted for workshops. Emphasizing these two sets of data, Stolz argues that contrary to Fairweather *et al.*'s (1974) conclusions, "the workshop seems to be the most cost-effective technique, producing the largest number of adoptions at lowest cost to the adopting hospitals" (p. 496). The third and fourth phases of the study by Fairweather *et al.* (1974) of adoption did not yield impressive results.

Despite its shortcomings, the Fairweather project provides tangible evidence that with the appropriate funding, experimental analysis of the adoption and dissemination process can be conducted.

The remaining three examples Stolz discusses all concerned adoption by state or federal government policymakers of the products of research in applied behavior analysis, namely Stokes and Fawcett's

(1977) trash-packaging program, Azrin's job-finding program (Azrin, Flores, & Kaplan, 1975), and Achievement Place (Phillips, Phillips, Wolf, & Fixsen, 1973). Sifting through these three "case studies" (a most suitable descriptor—the adoptions described were uncontrolled and the data can suggest only hypotheses rather than establish any facts) Stolz generated a list of ten possible key variables that might influence the dissemination and adoption process. They include:

> 1. Research data showed that the innovation was effective. 2. The technology met the continuing mission of the adopting agency. 3. The potential adoptor had a pressing management problem. 4. The availability of the dissemination to the potential adoptor was timely. 5. Potential adoptors were able to view ongoing (model) programs. 6. The adoption was proposed by policymakers, rather than by the researchers who developed the technology. 7. The intervention was tailored to local conditions. 8. Those who would have to implement the program were involved in the preliminary research and in asking for the adoption. 9. Funds were available for dissemination. 10. A key person, trained, enthusiastic, and with significant social skills, persisted through political infighting to protect the program from going. (pp. 498–500)

As Stolz points out, the variables referred to are part of the extensive literature on knowledge utilization, which, she asserts, "cries out for theory, empirical research, and analysis" (p. 501). Applied behavior analysis is invoked as providing an appropriate theoretical and methodological framework. This sounds correct, but there are the inevitable problems. Stolz asks "What . . . can the literature on knowledge utilization offer that would be of use to an applied behavior analyst?" (p. 501). The more appropriate question might be, "What can applied behavior analysis offer the literature on knowledge utilization?" Stolz herself acknowledges that the literature shows that the strongest single factor influencing adoption of technologies is "personal interaction or the influence of the colleagues of the policymaker" (p. 501). According to Stolz, this variable was also crucial in the successful adoptions in the case studies she describes. In other words, "it's who you know, not . . . ," even if we resist the cynicism and reject the remainder of that overdone phrase. There is little to be done here by way of manipulating independent variables. Nonetheless, Stolz gamely speculates about variables that might be grist for the applied behavior analyst's mill, including "involving those same individuals in the request for adoption of the innovation; changing the intervention to suit local conditions; and having potential adoptors view ongoing model program" (p. 502).

Although Stolz's paper does not leave the behavioral researcher with a blueprint for conducting the societally relevant research that will lead to the development of a technology for facilitating dissemina-

tion and implementation of presumably effective behavioral procedures, this is probably too much to ask at the present time. The paper
makes a contribution in raising the question and the possibility of such
a technology. And I remind myself and the reader of my colleague
Cyril Franks's (1981) fondness for quoting Gertrude Stein about the
importance of asking the right questions before worrying about finding
the right answers.

Stolz's (1981) paper comes at a time when a commitment to technology is being touted in some quarters of American psychology.
Fishman and Neigher (1982), for example, reject the view that applied
or technological research derives logically from the application of
principles derived from basic research (Baer, 1978). They declare that a
genuine commitment to technology necessitates a qualitative break
from basic research (science) and cite Azrin's (1977; reprinted in Volume 5 of this series) paper in support of their position. In one of the
year's most sweeping statements, they assert that the

> present reward structure of publication, academic promotion, and research
> grant awards encourages large numbers of ecologically irrelevant, single-
> study experiments with data that are unreplicated, underaggregated, and
> biased (because negative results are generally ignored and not published
> and because the typical criteria of manuscript acceptance are overly sub-
> jective and unreliable). (p. 542)

This extreme position would seem to downplay the advances in applied
behavior analysis that have been made under the existing conditions.
Stolz, for example, is concerned about implementing a technology that
she assumes already exists. Fishman and Neigher seem preoccupied
with the prior step of producing shifts in thinking and publication
policies as a means of facilitating genuinely applied or technological
research. Nevertheless, they would undoubtedly endorse Stolz's call for
the development of a technology to disseminate and implement behavioral interventions (technologies?) aimed at solving social problems.

CLINICAL ISSUES

Resistance: A Behavioral Perspective

No less than other practitioners from other theoretical orientations,
behavior therapists run into the problem of clients who seem to be
ambivalent about therapy, fail to comply with homework assignments,
withhold information, become evasive in response to probes about sensitive material, and so on. The phenomena of "resistance" are an
everyday clinical reality in all forms of psychological therapy. The

literature on behavior therapy has traditionally had relatively little to say about resistance in any explicit fashion. Usually, these phenomena and clinical strategies for coping with them have been included in the all-purpose category of poorly understood but nonetheless important therapeutic processes labeled "nonspecific" treatment variables (Wilson, 1980). A distinction must be drawn between the literature on behavior therapy and clinical practice. Behavior therapists, inevitably, have always had to confront problems of resistance in treatment. They have developed clinical strategies for overcoming such obstacles to effective treatment, and the documented outcomes of behavioral interventions for numerous problems in children and adults attest to the success of those clinical strategies. Nevertheless, it is imperative both for theoretical and therapeutic reasons that we specify what our concept of the phenomenon of resistance is and what can be done to overcome it. To some extent this is occurring. The advent of behavioral medicine as an organized field has focused serious research attention on problems of compliance or adherence with behavioral and medical interventions that are usually designed to change life styles. (See Volume 7 of the *Annual Review*, pp. 367–375, and Chapter 5 of Volume 8 for details on the rapidly developing literature in this area.) Although advances in this field have drawn on knowledge obtained in the more general practice of behavior therapy and have in turn enriched behavioral treatment, much is still to be learned. With this challenging goal in mind, the publication this past year of an edited volume on resistance (Wachtel, 1982) featuring chapters on behavioral approaches is of interest.

Before discussing the factors that influence compliance with treatment and how it may be facilitated, it is useful to take another look at the dimensions of the challenge we face. One of the most central aspects of behavior therapy, regardless of the problem being treated, is the use of homework assignments. Clients are asked to engage in new or different activities (cognitive and behavioral) between therapy sessions, and there is good reason to believe that treatment success often hinges on the degree to which these assignments are faithfully completed. Any behavior therapist will be quick to confirm this view, but is it reflected in the published literature? This is the question that Shelton and Levy (1981b) investigated in a survey of the following journals from 1975 to 1981: *Behavior Therapy, Behaviour Research and Therapy, Behavior Therapy and Experimental Psychiatry,* and *Journal of Applied Behavior Analysis.* Four other journals were included in the survey, starting with the year of their first publication: *Cognitive Therapy and Research* (1977), *Behavior Modification* (1977), *Behavioral Medicine* (1978), and *Biofeedback and Self-Regulation* (1976).

Shelton and Levy coded all articles in these journals for mention of the assignment of homework tasks and for clinical problem treated. Three other measures were made: the number of articles that were explicit in reporting the topography of homework (for example, attention was given to referents regarding the duration and frequency of practice); the frequency of articles reporting compliance with assignments; and a record of the content of prescribed activities. Note, however, that self-recording alone was not counted as a homework assignment.

Not surprisingly, a high proportion (60%) of articles described a reliance on homework assignments to produce therapeutic change. Shelton and Levy found that the treatment areas for which prescribed activities are most prevalent were those involving social skills problems (80%), obsessive–compulsive behavior (79%), and sexual dysfunction (79%). The category with the lowest recorded rate of articles using prescribed outside practice was alcoholism treatment (30%). After self-monitoring alone, the most frequently reported activity, relaxation practice was the commonest homework assignment. Of greater importance and concern, however, are the findings that (1) few details are typically given about the actual clinical implementation of homework assignments, and (2) only 23 out of 330 articles (7%) reported compliance rates. In view of the theoretical and practical importance often ascribed to homework assignments, the absence of this information constitutes a serious inadequacy in the literature. The negative implications for both research and therapy are obvious. Not only does the literature fail to provide necessary clinical details about actual implementation, it also omits serious consideration of problems with compliance (resistance). Here is one of the reasons behavior therapy is often faulted for ignoring fundamental clinical issues. Shelton and Levy (1981b) recommend that published reports contain the following components:

> (1) Explicit reporting of all homework assignments that were part of the treatment strategy including the frequency, duration, and time that these assignments were optimally to occur. (2) Explicit reporting of the setting and manner in which these assignments were given (e.g., by whom, written, taped, repeated, etc.). (p. 14)

CONCEPTUALIZING RESISTANCE

Lazarus and Fay (1982), in their chapter in the Wachtel (1982) volume, provide an incisive analysis of resistance from a cognitive–behavioral viewpoint. One of the reasons the concept of resistance has usually been avoided in the behavior therapy literature has undoubtedly been its identification with a theoretical (psychoanalytic) perspective that is widely rejected. The particular problems with the traditional psychoanalytic conception of resistance are neatly exposed by Lazarus and Fay as they clear the way for presenting an alternative cognitive–behavioral approach. They emphasize, for example, that it

> is necessary to separate resistance as a postulated mechanism explaining a clinical phenomenon (negative outcomes) from resistance as a clinical phenomenon itself. Clearly, it begs the question to speak of resistance whenever positive outcomes are not achieved. Furthermore, labeling all noncompliant behavior "resistance" obscures the essential importance of teasing out specific antecedent and maintaining factors that generate uncooperative behaviors in specific contexts. (p. 116)

The behavioral view, as Lazarus and Fay point out, is that resistance (defined broadly as a client's failure to follow instructions or to show therapeutic improvement) is usually a function of our incomplete knowledge, the limited efficacy of current therapeutic strategies, and idiosyncratic "constraints of our personalities" as therapists. They contrast this conceptualization with the psychodynamic view, in terms of which "resistance" is an inevitable, unconscious, internal reaction against change. The latter, they argue, has all too frequently in the past led to rationalizations of treatment failures by therapists. Lazarus and Fay go on to formulate their view that there are different forms of resistance that are a function of different variables, including the client's individual makeup, the client's interpersonal network, the therapeutic relationship, or the absence of effective treatment methods for particular problems.

In their chapter in the Wachtel volume, Meichenbaum and Gilmore (1982) emphasize a cognitive account in appealing to the scientist model as an analogy in conceptualizing resistance. In therapy they encourage clients to view their cognitions as hypotheses that need to be continually tested and evaluated, in the manner that scientists presumably carry out their investigations. A major goal of this therapy is for clients to adopt a new conceptualization of their problems, and to this end they are prompted to be open to "anomalous data" and to reconsider key beliefs that might be responsible for their difficulties (something akin to a "paradigm shift"). Mahoney (1976) has also put forward essentially the same "personal scientist" model of the therapeutic process. Resistance by clients to new ways of thinking is viewed, "like anomalous data for the scientist," as an additional opportunity "for examining the nature of the client's cognitions, affect, behavior, etc." The strategy for reinterpreting clients' maladaptive cognitions involves careful and planned interpretations. To quote Meichenbaum and Gilmore:

> In the same way that a lawyer carefully lays the groundwork for a brief to be presented to the jury, the therapist collects the data to present to the client. Moreover when the therapist presents the conceptualization it is not presented with certainty, but rather it is offered as reflecting the therapist's current view of what is going on. The therapist carefully checks with the client to see if indeed this view may make sense and will not seem highly unlikely to the client. The therapist may report to the client as follows: "What I hear you saying is . . ." "You seem to be telling me . . ." "Am I correct in assuming that . . . ?" "I get the feeling that . . . , correct me if I'm wrong," "We have covered a lot of territory so far in this interview. Is there anything I said that troubled you? . . . Do you think we left anything out?" Such queries provide the basis for involving the client in the process of collaboration and reconceptualization. (p. 136)

The "behavioral" component of Meichenbaum's cognitive-behavior therapy enters when clients are given specific tasks to do and use these experimental referents as further information for examining possibly distorted cognitions (see Meichenbaum & Cameron, 1982, for a more detailed description of Meichenbaum's position that seems largely indistinguishable from social learning theory).

Meichenbaum and Gilmore's (1982) analogy of the client as a "personal scientist," with the emphasis on testing and changing belief systems, is consonant with current developments in cognitive-social psychology. It is useful to go further into recent research on cognitive processing of information than Meichenbaum and Gilmore do to shed light on the phenomenon of resistance. In their provocative book on human inference, Nisbett and Ross (1980) set out to explain a number of mental phenomena in simple, nonmotivational terms in contrast to less parsimonious, motivational (typically psychodynamic) constructs. One of their examples is resistance. The Freudian position assumes that patients resist (e.g., refuse to accept the therapist's interpretation) because change is threatening to the ego—patients are "well-defended" by protective psychic mechanisms. The alternative view that Nisbett and Ross present does not rely on any unconscious purposive mechanism that can be "uncovered" (i.e., made conscious) through appropriate analysis; rather, people are simply unable to access unconscious material because of inherent limitations in our cognitive machinery.

Nisbett and Ross illustrate the differences between the two conceptualizations of unconscious resistance with the following example. They state that Stuart and Davis (1972) believe that many men gladly accept their wives' obesity because it balances their own inadequacies (e.g., impotence). Any weight loss and hence improvement in the wife's physical allure will therefore be threatening to the husband, whose own psychologically vulnerable status quo is now disrupted. The result? Unconsciously, the husband sabotages the wife's efforts at dieting and weight loss.[2] Nisbett and Ross indicate that the husband will presumably benefit from becoming aware of his unconscious commitment to his wife's obesity. They suggest that the "Freudian view would seem to be that such insight can be accomplished if, and only if, the therapist's assertion makes contact with the client's repressed knowledge of the fact. In our view, there generally is no such knowledge to be 'contacted'" (p. 246). The patient might "resist" when the therapist points out that attempts at weight control by his wife have been regularly associated with actions on his part of undermine her efforts. But rather than interpreting this as "resistance" or "defensiveness," Nisbett and Ross suggest that client views the therapist's interpretation as simply *implausible*. It is implausible because it contradicts the commonly held view that men seek the most attractive women possible as partners. The therapist's interpretation, therefore, is "as odd as it is threatening." Invoking the now-familiar model of the thinking of scientists, Nisbett and Ross comment that the "resistance to [interpretations of this sort] is no more remarkable than the 'resistance' of any formal scientist to unusual propositions challenging a firmly entrenched theory" (p. 246).

By way of advice to therapists, Nisbett and Ross have the following to say:

> Therapists might encounter less resistance to their interpretations if they were to acknowledge that it might be caused by something other than ego defensiveness. A client who is told that he is "resisting" an interpretation only in order to protect himself and that he could "see" the psychological facts for himself if he were willing, seems likely to continue the struggle. He might be less inclined to resist if he were told that, though the interpretation seems unlikely in view of common-sense notions about human behavior, and though his psychological states can no more be "seen" by the client than by the therapist, such an interpretation seems most consistent with the facts available to both the client and the therapist. (pp. 246–247)

This counsel closely resembles Meichenbaum and Gilmore's (1982) tactics of preparing the (cognitive) ground carefully before trying to get the client to develop a new conceptualization of his or her problem.

2. This particular clinical assumption is widely held by nonbehavioral therapists, but it has no empirical support. While some husbands might act in this manner, they are probably relatively rare cases. Most husbands would like to see their wives lose weight (and vice versa). The durability of this clinical stereotype is reminiscent of the unsubstantiated (and probably inaccurate) clinical notions that are espoused in connection with agoraphobia and marital satisfaction (see Chapter 3).

OVERCOMING NONCOMPLIANCE OR RESISTANCE

As noted earlier, the use of homework assignments is an integral part of behavior therapy. Problems with compliance with these assignments are more often the rule rather than the exception, and ways of dealing with these problems serve to illustrate the general approach to resistance in the practice of behavior therapy.

What does the therapist do when a client reports the failure to complete homework assignments? Instead of assuming that this noncompliant behavior reflects purposive resistance, the behavior therapist first considers a number of other more parsimonious possibilities. Some of these are described by Lazarus and Fay (1982):

> 1. Was the homework assignment incorrect or irrelevant? 2. Was it too threatening? 3. Was it too time-consuming in terms of its "cost effectiveness?" 4. Does the patient not appreciate the value of and rationale behind homework exercises? (Is the patient opposed to or unaware of the education, self-help thrust of our ministrations?) 5. Is the therapeutic relationship at fault? (If so, the patient may display passive–aggressive behaviors toward the therapist.) 6. Is someone in the patient's social network undermining or sabotaging the therapy? 7. Is the patient receiving far too many secondary gains to relinquish his or her maladaptive behavior? (p. 119)

Note that there is something of a hierarchical ordering of these alternative explanations for noncompliant behavior along a dimension ranging from the relatively simple mechanics of therapy (e.g., the assignment was unclear), which the therapist presumably can correct, to more complex matters that may include active (and possibly unconscious) opposition by the client. It is only once the simpler alternatives have been ruled out that the behavior therapist is likely to tackle these latter problems.

Several other factors may affect compliance. The complexity and comprehensibility of the therapist's instructions have been shown to influence the degree of patient compliance. Similarly, there is evidence that the therapeutic relationship affects compliance (Garrity, 1981). These issues and the relevant evidence were summarized in Volume 7 of this series, pages 372–375. Noncompliance with some assignments may be the result of the interference of other problems that need direct treatment before compliance can be expected. Depression, for example, frequently complicates treatment of other problems, and one of its negative effects is decreased compliance. In their study of the separate and joint effects of behavioral and pharmacological treatment of obsessive–compulsives, Marks, Stern, Mawson, Cobb, and McDonald (1980) found that the drug clomipramine facilitated compliance with the behavioral treatment. The mechanism for this indirect therapeutic benefit of the drug treatment was improvement in the depressed mood of the patients.

The expectations and goals that clients are given play a significant role in influencing compliance. In social learning theory, both expectations and goals serve as cognitively based sources of motivation that help initiate and sustain behavior (Bandura, 1977b). Expectations should be positive but realistic (Wilson, 1979). Goals should be concrete, well-specified, and short-term, properties that are optimally suited to providing the incentives to carry out the required behavior. Therapeutic assignments that are vaguely described, too general, or too distal will greatly increase the chances of noncompliance. Other cognitive factors are also important in determining compliance, such as clients' beliefs about the nature of their problem, what can be done about it, and what that will mean for future adjustment. Meichenbaum and Gilmore (1982) and Rush (1980) provide informative discussions of these points and how the therapist might cope with them.

One cognitive strategy, for example, is to have the therapist discuss with the client possible reasons for not completing homework assignments in anticipation of doing them. In the following excerpt, Rush (1980) describes this process in a discussion of compliance with drugs, but the term "behavioral technique" could well be substituted for "medication":

> The practitioner would be well-advised to ask the patient to anticipate or imagine what might happen that could reduce adherence. For example, the patient should be asked to concretely imagine the steps involved in taking the medication each day. Where will it occur? Who will be around? Would a schedule change, an unexpected demand, running out of or misplacing the medication, the presence of others from whom the patient wishes to conceal medication taking derail the plan? Would any specific symptoms, side effects or intercurrent illnesses preclude adherence? Would symptomatic remission, opinions of other family members, or any other stimulus to attitude change, modify adherence? Concrete anticipation of various elements that can alter adherence allows the patient and practitioner to plan around or adapt the regimen to the individual. In addition, a detailed focus on these obstacles provides the patient with a metamessage or indirect suggestion that adhering is important enough to be planned for and discussed in detail.

This theme of anticipating difficulties and preparing for them is the essence of what Marlatt (in press) has called "relapse prevention training," and it would seem to be an especially robust clinical strategy.

In sum, there are several cognitive–behavioral strategies for overcoming noncompliance. Aside from those already mentioned, available techniques range from contingency contracting, with its true-blue behavioristic pedigree, to paradoxical methods (e.g., prescribing the symptom), which have been liberally borrowed from nonbehavioral approaches. Reliable evidence indicates that contingency contracting can be effective, as in the treatment of obesity, where its use significantly reduces attrition from behavioral programs (Wilson & Brownell, 1980). It is important to emphasize, however, that the reliance on external regulation of behavior that this method entails is clearly not suitable for most clients or the problems they present. Paradoxical methods rest almost entirely on clinical judgment, and they continue to remain at the periphery rather than the center of behavior therapy (see Ascher, 1979).

The manner in which homework assignments are negotiated is probably crucial in determining compliance. Although full details are beyond the scope of this summary chapter, some key dos and don'ts can be mentioned. Consistent with social psychological concepts such as reactance and attribution, clinical experience has shown that it is important to involve the client in making the assignment. For some oppositional clients who find fault in anything the therapist proposes, a useful strategy is to ask them to suggest a therapeutic homework assignment and to build on this. Therapists are most likely to invite noncompliance if they simply tell the client what to do. Meichenbaum and Gilmore (1982) provide a specific illustration of productive and counterproductive ways of assigning homework tasks. Consider the following three communications:

> 1) "What you are to do is . . . ," "Do the following:," "Do this . . ." *versus*
> 2) "I would like you to . . . ," "I want you to . . . ," "This is what I am asking you to do . . . ," *versus*
> 3) "So what you have agreed to try is . . . ," "As I understand it, you will . . . ," "So you will take responsibility for. . . ." (p. 143)

As Meichenbaum and Gilmore observe, "the client's attributions concerning the change process and therapy are likely to be very different under each of these three message styles, and only the third above can facilitate looking at the resistance to homework that may be experienced while it is being attempted" (p. 143). Lazarus and Fay (1982) voice the same behavioral wisdom:

> Telling a client to relax, imagine scenes, act more assertively, self-monitor specific behaviors, or agree on contingency management is likely to foster some degree of opposition or countercontrol. . . . Asking for the same performance-based responses is less likely to evoke opposition. Thus resistance or countercontrol may be a direct function of the therapist's manner and style. In our experience, at least 80% of patients follow our requests or suggestions without travail. (p. 122)

It is also imperative that the therapist communicate effectively to the client that homework assignments are an integral part of the treatment and that full compliance is expected. Most importantly, all homework assignments must be diligently checked first thing at the following session. Any difficulties the client encountered should be analyzed fully, and alternative strategies should be suggested or the nature of the assignments appropriately modified. Clients are quick to sense that a therapist is not fully committed to regular compliance with assignments and it should come as no surprise if in such cases the therapist finds declining or inconsistent compliance.

Finally, it is a truism that psychological treatment, including behavior therapy, has distinct limitations and cannot help all clients. Although Lazarus and Fay stress that the therapist is largely responsible for clients' improvement, they warn that "it is unrealistic to place the entire onus [of changing the client] on the clinician. . . . There are, in short, people who do not want help, or for whom there could be too many competing factors" (p. 120). The debate over where and how to make this distinction continues.

BEHAVIORAL AND PSYCHODYNAMIC APPROACHES TO RESISTANCE: COMMONALITIES AND CONTRASTS

Given that noncompliance with therapeutic interventions is common in clinical practice, it might be expected that different treatment approaches overlap, at least to some degree, in the management of these problems. This overlap is probably most evident between behavior therapy and other nonbehavioral but directive approaches. One example has already been mentioned: the adoption by behavior therapists of some paradoxical strategies that derive from other theoretical systems. Some other similarities can be seen in the following example, which is drawn from the treatment of sexual dysfunction.

Kaplan (1979) has pioneered what she refers to as "psychosexual therapy" for the treatment of sexual dysfunction. Her approach draws on traditional behavioral interventions, following Masters and Johnson (1970) and LoPiccolo and LoPiccolo (1978), but often integrates these methods within a psychodynamic framework. As with the general behavioral approach to treating sexual dysfunction, Kaplan's methods are directive. Clients are instructed to engage in specific sexual practices with their partners. Noncompliance is a frequent obstacle to therapeutic success.[3] Kaplan provides several informative examples of how she tries

3. Lobitz and LoPiccolo (1972; reprinted in Volume 2 of this series) describe how contingency contracting can be used to enhance compliance with therapeutic instructions in sexually dysfunctional couples. They also indicate ways in which this method is more suited to some clients than others.

to overcome such noncompliance or resistance, and these illustrations are useful in describing the limits of overlap between a behavioral and a psychodynamic approach.[4]

Faced with noncompliance, Kaplan follows standard behavioral practice by first simply encouraging the clients to try again. (Also, at this point the therapist should make sure that the assignment is appropriate, clearly understood, etc.) If noncompliance persists despite encouragement and after a reasonable period of time, however Kaplan assumes that the clients may have a fear of sexual success. Insight into this sexual block is the next goal of therapy, and to this end Kaplan confronts the clients with the interpretation that noncompliance is motivated by fear of success. The following excerpt from her book illustrates how this is done:

> PATIENT: We wouldn't do the pleasuring this week, I had to take work home and by the time we got to bed she did not feel like it.
>
> WIFE: Honey, it was after two o'clock each night. I was tired.
>
> PATIENT: Well, my job is important.
>
> THERAPIST: I am sorry you have to work so hard. Perhaps this is not a good time for treatment. Do you think we should postpone it? (Joining the resistance is often an effective confrontation method.)
>
> PATIENT: No, this is very important. Two weeks ago I had such good erections; I was so encouraged.
>
> THERAPIST: Yes you did, and since then you "haven't found the time" to do the exercises. Do you really think that is the true reason or do you think that your success was a little scary?
>
> PATIENT: No, that is ridiculous. That's why I am here, to be successful.
>
> WIFE: Honey, it always happens when we have had good sex. You always disappear afterwards for weeks.
>
> THERAPIST: It is not unusual for a person to have some anxiety when he starts improving. Let's talk about the week it worked so well.
>
> (Giving the patient "permission" to have success anxiety may help his gaining insight.) (Kaplan, 1979, p. 173)

A useful question to ask clients, before embarking on a behavior change program, is "How do you anticipate life will be when we are successful in overcoming your problem?" Whether the problem is agoraphobia or sexual dysfunction, the purpose of this line of questioning is to elicit the client's expectations about life without the "symptoms." These expectations are frequently unrealistic and require therapeutic attention. Some clients expect improvements in their prob-

4. It goes without saying that there is no uniform psychodynamic approach and that there may be procedural differences among different forms of this therapy.

lems to change their entire lives. Others fear the changed circumstances that will result from treatment. This latter is the "fear of success" to which Kaplan refers.

Kaplan's intervention in the clinical case excerpted above is consistent with what behavior therapists routinely do. "Joining the resistance" can be viewed as a mild form of paradoxical intervention, a strategy that is often employed, as Lazarus and Fay (1982) indicate. Behavior therapists part company with Kaplan when she goes on to assert that for the "more neurotic" clients, simply identifying and confronting resistance as illustrated above is insufficient. These clients, she claims, show resistance that reflects intense conflicts laid down very early (in emotional development). The answer? Long-term psychodynamic therapy that seeks to resolve these early (e.g., Oedipal) conflicts. Here is a clear case of advocacy of psychoanalytic theory of development and psychopathology that leads logically to the traditional psychoanalytic treatment of sexual problems. Behavior therapists reject both the theory and therapy. Neither can be shown to enjoy any acceptable scientific support in the conceptualization of treatment of sexual disorders.

The Wachtel (1982) volume includes comments by the different authors on each others' chapters. The intention was to facilitate something of a dialogue, an exchange of ideas on a central problem. Yet Fay and Lazarus (1982) report considerable difficulty in this respect. Commenting on the chapters written from a psychoanalytic perspective, Fay and Lazarus state that "their basic assumptions about people, about the nature of psychological distress, and about the active ingredients of change (and the barriers to change) are so much at variance with our own clinical perceptions and judgments and meaningful dialogue is virtually precluded" (p. 219). It is important to realize that this impasse occurred with psychoanalytic accounts that seemed rather traditional in nature. For example, Dewald (1982) expresses his concern about a connection between the taking of tranquilizers by an analytic patient and "the wishes and fears regarding oral incorporation of the analyst" (p. 47). Not surprisingly, Fay and Lazarus call this inimitably psychoanalytic notion into question. But it is quite probable that many other psychodynamically oriented therapists, particularly those who take a more "ego-oriented" approach, might also feel uncomfortable with such symbolic interpretations.

In another example, Dewald declares that "in both forms of treatment [psychoanalysis and psychoanalytic psychotherapy] the therapist must recognize that only the patient can modify, reduce, or eliminate a particular resistance" (p. 51). So much for the many strategies available to cognitive–behavioral therapists, as indicated here. Perhaps this is one reason for Dewald reporting that it took 6 months for his patient to disclose a phobia about toilets. These fundamental differences between psychoanalysts and behavior therapists speak not only to alternative conceptualizations of resistance but also, of course, to the recent revival of the argument that the two approaches share major commonalities and that experienced therapists tend to act quite similarly irrespective of their declared theoretical allegiances (see Chapter 8 of Volume 8 of this series for a more extended analysis of this argument). As Fay and Lazarus (1982) put it,

> Despite the fact that within the last decade, phenotypically, behavior therapy has become more cognitive and psychoanalysis more behavioral, genotypically the chasm remains. The need for a better-integrated, comprehensive, and coherent psychoeducational approach will not be satisfied, we feel, by coupling psychodynamic and social learning theories. (pp. 220–221)

The Therapist–Patient Relationship

As has been the case with the phenomenon of resistance, the importance of the therapeutic relationship in behavior therapy has been deemphasized in the literature as one of the "nonspecifics" of treatment. Recognition that important theoretical as well as therapeutic implications follow from an improved understanding of the therapeutic relationship in behavior therapy has been slow in coming. Thus the literature over the past year has reflected limited attention to the topic. A couple of exceptions to this trend are worthy of note, however.

In Chapter 3 of the present volume I make the case that the successful use of *in vivo* exposure as the treatment of choice for agoraphobia involves more than the straightforward and standardized implementation of a conditioning (extinction) procedure. Rather, effective treatment seems to be informed by a broader cognitive perspective that pays careful attention to matters such as compliance, expectations, and appraisals of success and failure. In refractory cases in particular, this dimension of treatment would seem to depend heavily on the therapist's skill. Boulougouris, Rabavilas, Liappas, and Tabouratzis (1982) agree: "From our personal experience in the field and others' findings as well . . . , it has been suggested that the style of the therapist or therapist identity might account for the outcome with exposure treatments or neurotic patients" (pp. 143–144). What is of particular interest here is the assertion of the importance of the therapeutic relationship even in the application of a highly structured behavioral method. In general, it is reasonable to assume that the more structured a treatment method, particularly when applied to a clearly specified target, the less the therapist's personal qualities will influence the outcome.

In an empirical investigation of the therapist's contributions to the use of *in vivo* exposure therapy, Boulougouris *et al.* (1982) assigned agoraphobic or obsessive-compulsive clients to one of two groups of therapists. One group consisted of "experienced" therapists, the other of "inexperienced" therapists. After three preparatory interview sessions and three 1-hour sessions of *in vivo* exposure treatment, the conditions were reversed. Thus clients formerly treated by the experienced therapists now received the ministrations of the inexperienced practitioners, and vice versa. All clients had agreed to this switch as a condition for participating in the program. "Experienced" therapists were

> qualified psychiatrists with previous experience in behavior therapy techniques of at least one year. The inexperienced therapists were trainees in psychiatry or psychologists and did not have any previous experience in any type of psychotherapy but had shown interest in behavior therapy and asked to treat a suitable case. (pp. 145–146)

Assessments were conducted at pretreatment, immediately before the crossover, and at the end of both treatments. The major measures were the typical clinical rating scales developed by Marks and his colleagues at the Maudsley Hospital (see Chapter 3 of this and the previous volumes).

All clients showed improvement from pretreatment, and there were no difference between those treated by experienced and inexperienced therapists. Although the differences were not statistically significant, clients treated by the experienced therapists expressed greater satisfaction with their therapists:

> After treatment, most of the patients reported that both therapists were almost equally effective and in fact they could not differentiate the experienced from the inexperienced therapist. They considered that the therapeutic effect was due to the specific technique employed and not to any particular relationship established with the therapist. However, when asked to choose a therapist to continue the treatment with, most of them made their choice without hesitation. In addition, most patients reported excessive dreaming and even daytime fantasies regarding some of their therapists during treatment. (p. 151)

In apparent conflict with the outcome data showing ratings of behavioral improvement, Boulougouris *et al.* (1982) conclude that the therapeutic relationship may be important in the use of *in vivo* exposure treatments.

The built-in limitations of this study made it very unlikely that therapist effects would have been reflected in outcome. First, treatment was extremely brief—only three sessions with each group of therapists.

The use of a highly structured technique for so few sessions would seem to militate against the effects Boulougouris et al. were looking for. Second, the limitations of their outcome measures must be underscored. It is not at all clear that the 5-point rating scales they used were sensitive enough to pick up actual differences in outcome. Third, it is unfortunate that systematic process measures were not taken. It would be most informative to analyze the process of in vivo exposure treatment in relation to outcome. Finally, it is questionable how experienced the therapists in the "experienced" group really were. We would need more information about their training to arrive at a balanced judgment, but the available data certainly suggest that more experienced therapists should be used in a study of this sort. Whether this would make any difference remains to be seen.

The widely cited comparative study by Sloane, Staples, Cristol, Yorkston, and Whipple (1975) of the efficacy of behavior therapy and psychoanalytically oriented psychotherapy provided some of the most useful information on the actual differences in the behavior of therapists of these two theoretical persuasions. Cross, Sheehan, and Khan (1982) have reported the results of another comparative outcome study modeled closely on that of Sloane et al. They compared behavior therapy to "insight-oriented" therapy and to a waiting-list control. Specific information on the nature of the insight-oriented treatment is not provided, beyond the statement that it was "based on transactional analysis and gestalt principles of change" (p. 105). Patients meeting the same selection criteria employed by Sloane et al. were randomly assigned to one of the two treatment groups. Subjects for the waiting-list control group were recruited through different channels. Three therapists administered each of the treatments for 12 sessions over roughly 3 months. Assessment of outcome and therapeutic process and follow-ups at 4 months and 1 year completed the similarity to the Sloane et al. study.

The results showed that both treatment groups improved from pre- to posttreatment but that they did not differ one another. Treatment gains were maintained over follow-up, with no sign of relapse and with some slight advantage for the behavior therapy group. Although the waiting-list control group was selected according to different criteria, a clear confound, it is surprising that the authors do not mention whether or not the treatments did better in comparison to this group. As Rachman and Wilson (1980) have demonstrated, without a suitable control group results such as these cannot be interpreted usefully. Leaving aside this unfortunate omission, the process data may be considered. These data were derived from measures at the 4-month and 1-year follow-ups. On each occasion, "clients were asked to consider retrospectively the kinds of variables, both primary (e.g., the skill of the therapist) and secondary (e.g., therapist encouragement) that contributed to their improvement" (p. 105). The Questionnaire for Psychotherapy Project (Sloane *et al.*, 1975) was used for this purpose.

The process data reflected differences between the two treatments. Cross *et al.* summarize their findings as follows:

> Clients from insight-oriented therapy predictably tended to place more emphasis on person/relationship variables (e.g., the personality of the therapist and being able to talk to an understanding person), whereas behavior therapy clients attributed more importance to variables associated with treatment itself (e.g., encouraging you gradually to practice facing the things that bother you and encouraging you to shoulder responsibilities by restoring confidence in self). (p. 109)

Nevertheless, the authors also emphasize that the findings show that aspects of the therapist–patient relationship are crucial to behavior therapy, including the role of the therapist in helping clients to achieve better self-understanding. In concluding that "relational factors" may be more important in determining outcome than specific techniques, Cross *et al.* not only go beyond their own data but also ignore solid evidence to the contrary (e.g., Rachman & Wilson, 1980). The repetitive but largely baseless reaffirmation of the overriding influence of the therapeutic relationship, regardless of problem or technique, still ranks as one of the major misleading misinterpretations of the evidence on therapy outcome.

REFERENCES

Abrams, D. B., & Follick, M. J. Behavioral weight loss intervention at the workplace: Feasibility and maintenance. *Journal of Consulting and Clinical Psychology*, 1983, *51*, 226–233.

Adelson, R., Nasti, A., Sprafkin, J. N., Marinelli, R., Primavera, L. H., & Gorman, B. S. Behavioral ratings of health professionals' interactions with the geriatric patient. *The Gerontologist*, 1982, *22*, 277–281.

Adesso, V. J., & Lipson, J. W. Group training of parents as therapists for their children. *Behavior Therapy*, 1981, *12*, 625–633.

Agras, W. S. Behavioral medicine in the 1980's: Nonrandom connections. *Journal of Consulting and Clinical Psychology*, 1982, *50*, 797–803.

Agras, W. S., & Berkowitz, R. Clinical research in behavior therapy: Halfway there? *Behavior Therapy*, 1980, *11*, 472–487.

Agras, W. S., Kazdin, A. E., & Wilson, G. T. *Behavior therapy: Towards an applied clinical science*. San Francisco: Freeman, 1979.

Alberti, R. E., & Emmons, M. L. *Your perfect right: A guide to assertive behavior*. San Luis Obispo, Calif.: Impact, 1974.

Alcoholics Anonymous. *Alcoholics Anonymous: The story of how thousands of men and women have recovered from alcoholism*. New York: AA World Services, 1955.

Alden, L., & Cappe, R. Nonassertiveness: Skill deficit or selective self-evaluation? *Behavior Therapy*, 1981, *12*, 107–114.

Ambrose, S., Hazzard, A., & Haworth, J. Cognitive-behavioral parenting groups for abusive families. *Child Abuse and Neglect*, 1980, *4*, 119–125.

American Journal of Clinical Nutrition. Assessment of nutritional status: Selected papers: Conference on the assessment of nutritional status. *American Journal of Clinical Nutrition*, 1982, *35*, 1089–1325.

American Psychiatric Association. *Diagnostic and statistical manual of mental disorders* (3rd ed.). Washington, D.C.: Author, 1980.

Andrasik, F. Organizational behavior modification in business settings: A methodological and content review. *Journal of Organizational Behavior Management*, 1979, *2*, 84–102.

Andrasik, F., Heimberg, R. G., Edlund, S. R., & Blankenship, R. Assessing the readability levels of self-report assertion inventories. *Journal of Consulting and Clinical Psychology*, 1981, *49*, 142–144. (a)

Andrasik, F., Heimberg, R. G., & McNamara, J. R. Behavior modification of work and work-related problems. In M. Hersen, R. M. Eisler, & P. M. Miller (Eds.), *Progress in behavior modification* (Vol. 11). New York: Academic Press, 1981. (b)

Andrasik, F., & McNamara, J. R. Future directions for industrial behavior modification. In R. M. O'Brien, A. M. Dickinson, & M. R. Rosow (Eds.), *Industrial behavior modification: A management handbook.* New York: Pergamon, 1982.

Andrasik, F., McNamara, J. R., & Edlund, S. R. Brief note: Future directions for OBM. *Journal of Organizational Behavior Management,* 1981, *3*(2), 1–3. (c)

Andrews, J. *Theoretical orientation preferences of Graduate School of Applied and Professional Psychology students.* Unpublished manuscript, Rutgers University, 1982.

Antonuccio, D. O., Lewinsohn, P. M., & Steinmetz, J. L. Identification of therapist differences in a group treatment for depression. *Journal of Consulting and Clinical Psychology,* 1982, *50*, 433–435.

Apfelbaum, M., Bostsarron, J., Brigant, L., & Supin, H. La composition du poids perdu au cours de la diète hydrique: Effets de la supplementation protidique. *Gastroenterologie,* 1967, *108*, 121–134.

Aragona, J., Cassady, J., & Drabman, R. S. Treating overweight children through parental training and contingency contracting. *Journal of Applied Behavior Analysis,* 1975, *8*, 269–278.

Arkin, R., Cooper, H., Kolditz, T. A statistical review of the literature concerning the self-serving bias in interpersonal influence situations. *Journal of Personality,* 1980, *48*, 435–448.

Armor, D. J., Polich, J. M., & Stambul, H. D. *Alcoholism and treatment.* New York: Wiley, 1978.

Arnett, J. L., & Leichner, P. P. Attitudes of psychiatry residents towards psychology. *Professional Psychology,* 1982, *13*, 244–251.

Arnkoff, D. B., & Glass, C. R. Clinical cognitive constructs: Examination, evaluation, and elaboration. In P. C. Kendall (Ed.), *Advances in cognitive-behavioral research and therapy* (Vol. 1). New York: Academic Press, 1982.

Asarnow, J. R., & Meichenbaum, D. Verbal rehearsal and serial recall: The mediational training of kindergarten children. *Child Development,* 1979, *50*, 1173–1177.

Ascher, L. M. Paradoxical intention. In A. Goldstein & E. Foa (Eds.), *Handbook of behavioral interventions.* New York: Wiley, 1979.

Ascher, L. M. Employing paradoxical intention in the treatment of agoraphobia. *Behaviour Research and Therapy,* 1981, *191*, 533–542.

Association for Advancement of Behavior Therapy. Ethical issues for human services. *Behavior Therapy,* 1977, *8*, 763–764.

Atkeson, B. M., & Forehand, R. Parent behavioral training for problem children: An examination of studies using multiple outcome measures. *Journal of Abnormal Child Psychology,* 1978, *6*, 449–460.

Authier, J., Gustafson, K., Fix, A. J., & Daughton, D. Social skills training: An initial appraisal. *Professional Psychology,* 1981, *12*, 438–445.

Azrin, N. H. A strategy for applied research: Learning based but outcome oriented. *American Psychologist,* 1977, *32*, 140–149.

Azrin, N. H., & Besalel, V. A. *Job club counselor's manual: A behavioral approach to vocational counseling.* Baltimore: University Park Press, 1980.

Azrin, N. H., Flores, T., & Kaplan, S. J. Job-finding clubs: A group-assisted program for obtaining employment. *Behaviour Research and Therapy,* 1975, *13*, 17–27.

Babb, H. W., & Kopp, D. G. Applications of behavior modification in organizations: A review and critique. *Academy of Management Review,* 1978, *3*, 281–282.

Bachman, J. G., Johnston, L. D., & O'Malley, P. M. Smoking, drinking, and drug use among American high school students: Correlates and trends, 1975–1979. *American Journal of Public Health,* 1981, *71*, 59–69.

Baer, D. On the relation between basic and applied research. In C. Catania & T. Brigham (Eds.), *Handbook of applied behavior analysis.* New York: Irvington, 1978.

Bailey, K. G., Deardorff, P., & Nay, W. R. Students play therapist: Relative effects of role playing, videotape feedback, and modeling in a simulated interview. *Journal of Consulting and Clinical Psychology,* 1977, *45,* 257–266.

Bakal, D. A., Demjen, S., & Kaganov, J. A. *Cognitive behavioral treatment of chronic headache.* Unpublished manuscript, University of Calgary, 1982.

Bandura, A. *Principles of behavior modification.* New York: Holt, Rinehart & Winston, 1969.

Bandura, A. Self-efficacy: Toward a unifying theory of behavioral change. *Psychological Review,* 1977, *84,* 191–215. (a)

Bandura, A. *Social learning theory.* Englewood Cliffs, N.J.: Prentice-Hall, 1977. (b)

Bandura, A. Self-efficacy mechanism in human agency. *American Psychologist,* 1982, *37,* 122–147.

Bandura, A., & Adams, N. E. Analysis of self-efficacy theory of behavioral change. *Cognitive Therapy and Research,* 1977, *1,* 287–308.

Bandura, A., Adams, N. E., & Beyer, J. Cognitive processes mediating behavioral change. *Journal of Personality and Social Psychology,* 1977, *35,* 125–139.

Bandura, A., Adams, N. E., Hardy, A. B., & Howells, G. N. Tests of the generality of self-efficacy theory. *Cognitive Therapy and Research,* 1980, *4,* 39–66.

Bandura, A., Reese, L., & Adams, N. E. Microanalysis of action and fear arousal as a function of differential levels of perceived self-efficacy. *Journal of Personality and Social Psychology,* 1982, *43,* 5–21.

Barkley, R. A. *Hyperactive children: A handbook for diagnosis and treatment.* New York: Guilford, 1981.

Barkley, R. A., Copeland, A. P., & Sivage, C. A self-control classroom for hyperactive children. *Journal of Autism and Developmental Disorders,* 1980, *10,* 75–89.

Barling, J. Image of behavior modification: A critical analysis. *South African Journal of Psychology,* 1979, *9,* 98–103.

Barling, J., & Wainstein, T. Attitudes, labeling bias, and behavior modification in work organizations. *Behavior Therapy,* 1979, *10,* 129–136.

Barlow, D. H. Behavior therapy: The next decade. *Behavior Therapy,* 1980, *11,* 315–328.

Barlow. D. H. On the relation of clinical research to clinical practice: Current issues, new directions. *Journal of Consulting and Clinical Psychology,* 1981, *49,* 147–155. (a)

Barlow, D. H. A role for clinicians in the research process. *Behavioral Assessment,* 1981, *3,* 227–233. (b)

Barlow, D. H., & Hayes, S. C. Alternating-treatments design: One strategy for comparing the effects of two treatments in a single subject. *Journal of Applied Behavior Analysis,* 1979, *12,* 199–210.

Barlow, D. H., Mavissakalian, M., & Hay, L. R. Couples treatment of agoraphobia: Changes in marital satisfaction. *Behaviour Research and Therapy,* 1981, *19,* 245–256.

Barlow, D. H., & Wolfe, B. Behavioral approaches to anxiety disorders: A report on the NIMH–SUNY, Albany Research Conference. *Journal of Consulting and Clinical Psychology,* 1981, *49,* 448–454.

Barrera, R. D., Lobato-Barrera, D., & Sulzer-Azaroff, B. A simultaneous treatment comparison of three expressive language training programs with a mute autistic child. *Journal of Autism and Development Disorders,* 1980, *10,* 21–37.

Barton, W. H., & Sarri, R. Where are they now? A follow-up study of youths in juvenile correction programs. *Crime and Delinquency*, April 1979, pp. 162–176.

Bash, M. A., & Camp, B. W. *Think aloud program: Group manual.* Unpublished manuscript, 1978.

Bates, P. The search for reinforcers to train and maintain effective parent behavior. *Rehabilitation Literature*, 1977, *38*, 291–295.

Baucom, D. H. A comparison of behavioral contracting and problem-solving/communications training in behavioral marital therapy. *Behavior Therapy*, 1982, *13*, 162–174.

Baum, A., & Singer, J. E. (Eds.). *Advances in environmental psychology* (Vol. 3): *Energy: Psychological perspectives.* Hillsdale, N.J.: Lawrence Erlbaum, 1981.

Baum, C. G., & Forehand, R. Long-term follow-up assessment of parent training by use of multiple outcome measures. *Behavior Therapy*, 1981, *12*, 643–652.

Baum, M. Instrumental learning. In P. Feldman & A. Broadhurst (Eds.), *Theoretical and experimental bases of the behaviour therapies.* New York: Wiley, 1976.

Bean, A. W., & Roberts, M. W. The effects of time-out release contingencies on changes in child noncompliance. *Journal of Abnormal Child Psychology*, 1981, *9*, 95–105.

Beaton, G. H., Milner, J., & Corey, P. Sources of variance in 24-hour dietary recall data: Implications for nutrition study design and interpretation. *American Journal of Clinical Nutrition*, 1979, *32*, 2456–2459.

Beck, A. T., Laude, R., & Bohnert, M. Ideational components of anxiety neurosis. *Archives of General Psychiatry*, 1974, *31*, 319–325.

Beck, A. T. *Depression.* Philadelphia: University of Pennsylvania Press, 1967.

Beck, A. T. *Cognitive therapy and the emotional disorders.* New York: International Universities Press, 1976.

Beck, A. T., Rush, A. J., Shaw, B. F., & Emery, G. *Cognitive therapy of depression.* New York: Guilford, 1979.

Beck, A. T., Ward, C. H., Mendelson, M., Mock, J. E., & Erbaugh, J. K. An inventory for measuring depression. *Archives of General Psychiatry*, 1961, *4*, 561–571.

Becker, W. C., & Carnine, D. W. Direct instruction: A behavior theory model for comprehensive educational intervention with the disadvantaged. In S. W. Bijou & R. Ruiz (Eds.), *Behavior modification: Contributions to education.* Hillsdale, N.J.: Lawrence Erlbaum, 1981.

Bellack, A. S., Hersen, M., & Himmelhoch, J. Social skills training compared with pharmacotherapy and psychotherapy in the treatment of unipolar depression. *American Journal of Psychiatry*, 1981, *138*, 1562–1567.

Bellack, A. S., Hersen, M., & Lamparski, D. Role-play tests for assessing social skills: Are they valid? Are they useful? *Journal of Consulting and Clinical Psychology*, 1979, *47*, 335–342.

Bellack, A. S., Hersen, M., & Turner, S. M. Role-play tests for assessing social skills: Are they valid? *Behavior Therapy*, 1978, *9*, 448–461.

Beneke, W. M., Kohrs, M. B., & Paulsen, B. Nutritional effects of a behavior modification weight loss program. *Behavioral Assessment*, 1982, *4*, 339–345.

Bents, R., Lakin, K. C., & Reynolds, M. C. *Classroom management.* Minneapolis: University of Minnesota, National Support Systems Project, 1981.

Berkson, G., & Romer, D. A letter to a service provider. In H. C. Haywood & J. R. Newbrough (Eds.), *Living environments for developmentally retarded persons.* Baltimore: University Park Press, 1981.

Berler, E. S., Gross, A. M., & Drabman, R. S. Social skills training with children: Proceed with caution. *Journal of Applied Behavior Analysis*, 1982, *15*, 41–53.

Bernal, M. E., & North, J. A. A survey of parent training manuals. *Journal of Applied Behavior Analysis*, 1978, *11*, 533–544.

Bernard, M. E. Private thought in rational–emotive psychotherapy. *Cognitive Therapy and Research*, 1981, *5*, 125–142.

Bernard, M. E., Kratochwill, T. R., & Keefauver, L. W. The effects of rational–emotive therapy on chronic hair-pulling. *Cognitive Therapy and Research*, 1983, *7*, 273–279.

Bernstein, G. S. Training behavior change agents: A conceptual review. *Behavior Therapy*, 1982, *13*, 1–23.

Berrier, G. D., Galassi, J. P., & Mullinix, S. D. A comparison of matched clinical and analogue subjects on variables pertinent to the treatment of assertion deficits. *Journal of Consulting and Clinical Psychology*, 1981, *49*, 980–981.

Berry, I., & Wood, J. The evaluation of parent intervention with young handicapped children. *Behavioural Psychotherapy*, 1981, *9*, 358–368.

Berthold, H. C. Behavior modification in the industrial/organizational environment: Assumptions and ethics. In R. M. O'Brien, A. M. Dickinson, & M. P. Rosow (Eds.), *Industrial behavior modification: A management handbook*. New York: Pergamon, 1982.

Bewley, B. R., Bland, J. M., & Harris, R. Factors associated with the starting of cigarette smoking by primary school children. *British Journal of Preventive Medicine*, 1974, *28*, 37–42.

Bijou, S. W. Behavioral teaching of young handicapped children: Problems of application and implementation. In S. W. Bijou & R. Ruiz (Eds.), *Behavior modification: Contributions to education*. Hillsdale, N.J.: Lawrence Erlbaum, 1981.

Bijou, S. W., & Baer, D. M. Editors' comments for D. M. Baer and J. A. Sherman. Reinforcement control of generalized imitation in young children. In S. W. Bijou & D. M. Baer (Eds.), *Child development: Readings in experimental analysis*. New York: Appleton-Century-Crofts, 1967.

Bijou, S. W., & Ruiz, R. (Eds.). *Behavior modification: Contributions to education*. Hillsdale. N.J.: Lawrence Erlbaum, 1981.

Billingsley, F., White, O. R., & Munson, R. Procedural reliability: A rationale and an example. *Behavioral Assessment*, 1980, *2*, 229–241.

Biran, M. Personal communication with G. T. Wilson, 1982.

Biran, M., Augusto, F., & Wilson, G. T. *In vivo* exposure *vs.* cognitive restructuring in the treatment of scriptophobia. *Behaviour Research and Therapy*, 1981, *19*, 525–532.

Biran, M., & Niaura, R. Unpublished manuscript, Miami University, 1983.

Biran, M., & Wilson, G. T. Treatment of phobic disorders using cognitive and exposure models: A self-efficacy analysis. *Journal of Consulting and Clinical Psychology*, 1981, *49*, 886–899.

Birch, D. Verbal control of nonverbal behavior. *Journal of Experimental Child Psychology*, 1966, *4*, 266–275.

Bird, J., Marks, I., & Lindley, P. Nurse therapists in psychiatry: Developments, controversies and implications. *British Journal of Psychiatry*, 1979, *135*, 321–329.

Bistrian, B. R. Clinical use of a protein-sparing modified fast. *Journal of the American Medical Association*, 1978, *21*, 2299–2302.

Bistrian, B. R., Blackburn, G. L., & Stanbury, J. B. Metabolic aspects of protein sparing modified fast in the dietary management of Prader–Willi obesity. *New England Journal of Medicine*, 1977, *296*, 774–779.

Black, J. L., Keane, T. M., Garvin, R. B., Gross, A. M., & Richter, W. T. *Pyramidal training of ambulatory care nurses in the behavioral interview*. Paper presented at the annual meeting of the Southeastern Psychological Association, Washington, D.C., 1980.

Black, R. G. The chronic pain syndrome. *Clinical Medicine*, 1975, *82*, 17–20.

Blackburn, I. M., & Bishop, S. Is there an alternative to drugs in the treatment of depressed ambulatory patients? *Behavioural Psychotherapy*, 1981, *9*, 96–104.

Blackburn, I. M., Bishop, S., Glen, A. I. M., Whalley, L. J., & Christie, J. E. The efficacy of cognitive therapy in depression: A treatment trial using cognitive therapy and pharmacotherapy, each alone and in combination. *British Journal of Psychiatry*, 1981, *139*, 181–189.

Blanchard, E. B. Behavioral medicine: Past, present, and future. *Journal of Consulting and Clinical Psychology*, 1982, *50*, 795–796.

Blanchard, E. B., & Andrasik, F. Psychological assessment and treatment of headache: Recent developments and emerging issues. *Journal of Consulting and Clinical Psychology*, 1982, *50*, 859–879.

Blanchard, E. B., Andrasik, F., Ahles, T. A., Teders, S. J., & O'Keefe, D. Migraine and tension headache: A meta-analytic review. *Behavior Therapy*, 1980, *11*, 613–631.

Bland, K., & Hallam, R. Relationship between response to graded exposure and marital satisfaction in agoraphobics. *Behaviour Research and Therapy*, 1981, *19*, 335–338.

Blechman, E. A. Toward comprehensive behavioral family intervention: An algorithm for matching families and interventions. *Behavior Modification*, 1981, *5*, 221–236.

Blechman, E. A. Are children with one parent at psychological risk: A methodological review. *Journal of Marriage and the Family*, 1982, *44*, 179–196.

Blechman, E. A., Budd, K. S., Christophersen, E. R., Szykula, S., Wahler, R., Embry, L. H., Kogan, K., O'Leary, K. D., & Riner, R. Engagement in behavioral family therapy: A multisite investigation. *Behavior Therapy*, 1981, *12*, 461–472. (a)

Blechman, E. A., Taylor, C. J., & Schrader, S. M. Family problem solving versus home notes as early intervention with high-risk children. *Journal of Consulting and Clinical Psychology*, 1981, *49*, 919–926. (b)

Block, A. R. An investigation of the response of the spouse to chronic pain behavior. *Psychosomatic Medicine*, 1981, *43*, 415–422.

Block, M. A. Don't place alcohol on a pedestal. *Journal of the American Medical Association*, 1976, *235*, 2103–2104.

Bogat, S. D., & Jason, L. A. *Traditional versus network-building visiting programs among the community-dwelling elderly.* Paper presented at the annual meeting of the Eastern Psychological Association, Hartford, Connecticut, 1980.

Bonham, G. S., & Wilson, R. W. Children's health in families with cigarette smokers. *American Journal of Public Health*, 1981, *71*, 290–293.

Bonica, J. J. Neurophysiological and pathologic aspects of acute and chronic pain. *Archives of Surgery*, 1977, *112*, 750–761.

Bonica, J. J. Pain research and therapy: Past and current status and future needs. In L. Ng & J. J. Bonica (Eds.), *Pain, discomfort, and humanitarian care*. New York: Elsevier, 1980.

Boring, E. G. *A history of experimental psychology*. New York: Appleton-Century-Crofts, 1950.

Borkovec, T. D. Heart-rate process during systematic desensitization and implosive therapy for analog anxiety. *Behavior Therapy*, 1974, *5*, 636–641.

Borkovec, T. D. Facilitation and inhibition of functional CS exposure in the treatment of phobias. In J. Boulougouris (Ed.), *Learning theory approaches to psychiatry*. London: Wiley, 1982.

Botvin, G. J., Cantlon, A., Carter, B. J., & Williams, C. L. Reducing adolescent obesity through a school health program. *Journal of Pediatrics*, 1979, *95*, 1060–1062.

Boulougouris, J. (Ed.). *Learning theory approaches to psychiatry*. London: Wiley, 1982.

Boulougouris, J., Rabavilas, A., Liappas, J., & Tabouratzis, D. Experienced versus inexperienced therapists in the treatment of exposure in vivo. In J. Boulougouris (Ed.), *Learning theory approaches to psychiatry*. London: Wiley, 1982.

Bourdon, R. D. Behavioral analysis and human resources management: An invitation to a wedding. *The Behavior Therapist*, 1982, 5(4), 119–129.

Bower, G. H. Mood and memory. *American Psychologist*, 1981, 36, 129–148.

Bowers, K. S. The relevance of hypnosis for cognitive–behavioral therapy. *Clinical Psychology Review*, 1982, 2, 67–78.

Boykin, R. A., & Nelson, R. O. The effects of instructions and calculation procedures on observer's accuracy, agreement, and calculation correctness. *Journal of Applied Behavior Analysis*, 1981, 14, 479–489.

Bradley, L. A., & Prokop, C. K. Research methods in contemporary medical psychology. In P. C. Kendall & J. N. Butcher (Eds.), *Handbook of research methods in clinical psychology*. New York: Wiley, 1982.

Bradley, L. A., Prokop, C. K., Margolis, R., & Gentry, W. D. Multivariate analysis of the MMPI profiles of low back pain patients. *Journal of Behavioral Medicine*, 1978, 1, 253–272.

Braswell, L., Kendall, P. C., Braith, J., Carey, M. P., & Vye, C. S. *"Involvement" in cognitive–behavioral therapy with children: Process and its relationship to outcome*. Manuscript submitted for publication, University of Minnesota, 1983.

Braswell, L., Kendall, P. C., & Urbain, E. S. A multistudy analysis of socioeconomic status (SES) and the measures and outcome of cognitive–behavioral treatment with children. *Journal of Abnormal Child Psychology*, 1982, 10, 443–449.

Bray, G. A. *The obese patient*. Philadelphia: Saunders, 1976.

Brechner, K. C., & Linder, D. E. A social trap analysis of energy distribution systems. In A. Baum & J. E. Singer (Eds.), *Advances in environmental psychology* (Vol. 3): *Energy: Psychological perspectives*. Hillsdale, N.J.: Lawrence Erlbaum, 1981.

Brehony, K., & Geller, E. S. Agoraphobia: Appraisal of research and a proposal for an integrative model. In M. Hersen, R. Eisler, & P. Miller (Eds.), *Progress in behavior modification* (Vol. 8). New York: Academic Press, 1981.

Breiner, J., & Forehand, R. An assessment of the effects of parent training on clinic-referred children's school behavior. *Behavioral Assessment*, 1981, 3, 31–42.

Brenna, S. F., & Koch, D. L. A "pain estimate" model for quantification and classification of chronic pain states. *Anesthesiology Review*, 1975, 8, 8–13.

Brennan, R. L., & Prediger, D. J. Coefficient kappa: Some uses, misuses, and alternatives. *Educational and Psychological Measurement*, 1981, 41, 687–699.

Breslow, L. A positive strategy for the nation's health. *Journal of the American Medical Association*, 1979, 242, 2093–2094.

Bridge, D. P., & Korn, M. Contribution to the assessment of exposure of nonsmokers to air pollution from cigarette and cigar smoke in occupied spaces. *Environmental Research*, 1972, 5, 192–209.

Brightman, R. P., Ambrose, S. A., & Baker, B. L. Parent training: A school-based model for enhancing teaching performance. *Child Behavior Therapy*, 1980, 2, 35–47.

Brightman, R. P., Baker, B. L., Clark, D. G., & Ambrose, S. A. Effectiveness of alternative parent training formats. *Journal of Behavior Therapy and Experimental Psychiatry*, 1982, 13, 113–117.

Brightwell, D. R., Foster, D., Lee, S., & Naylor, C. S. Effects of behavioral and pharmacological weight loss programs on nutrient intake. *American Journal of Clinical Nutrition*, 1979, 32, 2005–2008.

Bronfenbrenner, U. *The ecology of human development: Experiments by nature and design*. Cambridge, Mass.: Harvard University Press, 1979.

Brown, D. K., Kratochwill, T. R., & Bergan, J. R. Teaching interview skills for problem identification: An analogue study. *Behavioral Assessment*, 1982, 4, 63–73.

Brown, M. Maintenance and generalization issues in skills training with chronic schizophrenics. In J. P. Curran & P. L. Monti (Eds.), *Social skills training: A practical handbook for assessment and treatment.* New York: Guilford, 1982.

Brown, P. Social implications of deinstitutionalization. *Journal of Community Psychology*, 1980, *8*, 314–322.

Brownell, K. D. Assessment of eating disorders. In D. H. Barlow (Ed.), *Behavioral assessment of adult disorders.* New York: Guilford, 1981.

Brownell, K. D. The addictive disorders. In C. M. Franks, G. T. Wilson, P. C. Kendall, & K. D. Brownell, *Annual review of behavior therapy: Theory and practice* (Vol. 8). New York: Guilford, 1982. (a)

Brownell, K. D. Obesity: Understanding and treating a serious, prevalent, and refractory disorder. *Journal of Consulting and Clinical Psychology*, 1982, *50*, 820–840. (b)

Brownell, K. D., Bachorik, P. S., & Ayerle, R. S. Changes in plasma lipid and lipoprotein levels in men and women after a program of moderate exercise. *Circulation*, 1982, *65*, 477–484.

Brownell, K. D., & Kaye, F. S. A school-based behavior modification, nutrition education, and physical activity program for obese children. *American Journal of Clinical Nutrition*, 1982, *35*, 277–283.

Brownell, K. D., Kelman, J. H., & Stunkard, A. J. Treatment of obese children with and without their mothers: Changes in weight and blood pressure. *Pediatrics*, 1983, *71*, 515–523.

Brownell, K. D., & Stunkard, A. J. Behavioral treatment of obesity in children. *American Journal of Diseases of Children*, 1978, *132*, 403–412.

Brownell, K. D., & Stunkard, A. J. Exercise in the development and control of obesity. In A. J. Stunkard (Ed.), *Obesity.* Philadelphia: Saunders, 1980. (a)

Brownell, K. D., & Stunkard, A. J. Behavioral treatment for obese children and adolescents. In A. J. Stunkard (Ed.), *Obesity.* Philadelphia: Saunders, 1980. (b)

Brownell, K. D., & Stunkard, A. J. Couples training, pharmacotherapy, and behavior therapy in the treatment of obesity. *Archives of General Psychiatry*, 1981, *38*, 1224–1229. (a)

Brownell, K. D., & Stunkard, A. J. Differential changes in plasma high-density lipoprotein cholesterol levels in obese men and women during weight reduction. *Archives of Internal Medicine*, 1981, *141*, 1142–1146. (b)

Bruch, M. A. A task analysis of assertive behavior revisited: Replication and extension. *Behavior Therapy*, 1981, *12*, 217–230.

Bruch, M. A., Juster, H. R., & Heisler, B. D. Conceptual complexity as a mediator of thought content and negative affect: Implications for cognitive restructuring interventions. *Journal of Counseling Psychology*, 1982, *29*, 343–353.

Bry, B. H., & George, F. E. The preventive effects of early intervention on the attendance and grades of urban adolescents. *Professional Psychology*, 1980, *11*, 252–260.

Buchwald, A. M., Strack, S., & Coyne, J. C. Demand characteristics and the Velten mood induction procedure. *Journal of Consulting and Clinical Psychology*, 1981, *49*, 478–479.

Budd, K. S., Leibowitz, M., Riner, L. S., Mindell, C., & Goldfarb, A. L. Home-based treatment of severe disruptive behaviors: A reinforcement package for preschool and kindergarten children. *Behavior Modification*, 1981, *5*, 273–298.

Budd, K. S., & O'Brien, T. P. Father involvement in behavioral parent training: An area in need of research. *The Behavior Therapist*, 1982, *5*, 85–89.

Bugental, D. B., Whalen, C. K., & Henker, B. Causal attributions of hyperactive children and motivational assumptions of two behavior-change approaches: Evidence for an interactionist position. *Child Development*, 1977, *48*, 874–884.

Buglass, D., Clarke, J., Henderson, A., Kreitman, N., & Presley, A. A study of agoraphobic housewives. *Psychological Medicine*, 1977, *7*, 73–86.

Burchard, J. D., & Barrera, F. A. An analysis of timeout and response cost in a programmed environment. *Journal of Applied Behavior Analysis*, 1972, *5*, 271–282.

Burger, J. M. Motivational biases in the attribution of responsibility for an accident: A meta-analysis of the defensive-attribution hypothesis. *Psychological Bulletin*, 1981, *90*, 496–512.

Burgess, I., Jones, L., Robertson, S., Radcliffe, W., & Emerson, E. The degree of control exerted by phobic and non-phobic verbal stimuli over the reognition behaviour of phobic and non-phobic subjects. *Behaviour Research and Therapy*, 1981, *19*, 233–244.

Burrows, B. A., Jason, L. A., Quattrochi-Tubin, S., & Lavelli, M. Increasing activity of nursing home residents in their lounges using a physical design intervention and a prompting intervention. *Activities, Adaptation and Aging*, 1981, *1*(4), 25–34.

Burt, C. The inheritance of mental ability. *American Psychologist*, 1958, *13*, 1–15.

Burt, C. The genetic determination of differences in intelligence. *British Journal of Psychology*, 1966, *57*, 137–153.

Burt, C. The inheritance of general intelligence. *American Psychologist*, 1972, *27*, 175–190.

Cacioppo, J. T. Personal communication with P. C. Kendall, February 1982.

Cacioppo, J. T., Glass, C. R., & Merluzzi, T. V. Self-statements and self-evaluations: A cognitive response analysis of heterosexual social anxiety. *Cognitive Therapy and Research*, 1979, *3*, 249–262.

Cacioppo, J. T., & Petty, R. E. The need for cognition. *Journal of Personality and Social Psychology*, 1982, *42*, 116–131.

Caddy, G. R., Addington, H. J., Jr., & Perkins, D. Individualized behavior therapy for alcoholics: A third-year independent double-blind follow-up. *Behaviour Research and Therapy*, 1978, *16*, 345–363.

Cairns, D., & Pasino, J. Comparison of verbal reinforcement and feedback in the operant treatment of disability due to chronic low back pain. *Behavior Therapy*, 1977, *8*, 621–630.

Cairns, D., Thomas, L., Mooney, V., & Pace, J. B. A comprehensive treatment approach to chronic low back pain. *Pain*, 1975, *2*, 301–308.

Caldwell, B. *The preschool inventory* (Rev. ed.). Princeton: Educational Testing Service, 1970.

Cameron, P., & Robertson, D. Effect of home environment tobacco smoke on family health. *Journal of Applied Physiology*, 1973, *67*, 142–157.

Cannon, D. S., Baker, T. B., & Wehl, C. K. Emetic and electric shock alcohol aversion therapy: Six- and twelve-month follow-up. *Journal of Consulting and Clinical Psychology*, 1981, *49*, 360–368.

Carr, E. G. Teaching autistic children to use sign language: Some research issues. *Journal of Autism and Developmental Disorders*, 1979, *9*, 345–359.

Carr, E. G., & Dores, P. A. Patterns of language acquisition following simultaneous communication with autistic children. *Analysis and Intervention in Developmental Disabilities*, 1981, *1*, 347–381.

Casalta, H. C. Illiteracy: Methodological bases for a behavioral approach. In S. W. Bijou & R. Ruiz (Eds.), *Behavior modification: Contributions to education*. Hillsdale, N.J.: Lawrence Erlbaum, 1981.

Catalano, R. *Health, behavior and the community: An ecological perspective*. New York: Pergamon, 1979.

Cataldo, M. F., Iwata, B. A., & Ward, E. M. Community-based interventions for the developmentally disabled. In P. Karoly & J. J. Steffen (Eds.), *Improving children's competence: Advances in child behavioral analysis and therapy* (Vol. 1). Lexington, Mass.: Lexington Books, 1982.

Chambless, D. L., Foa, E. B., Groves, G. A., & Goldstein, A. J. Flooding with Brevital in the treatment of agoraphobia: Countereffective? *Behaviour Research and Therapy*, 1979, *17*, 243–252.

Chambless, D. L., Foa, E. B., Groves, G. A., & Goldstein, A. J. Exposure and communications training in the treatment of agoraphobia. *Behaviour Research and Therapy*, 1982, *20*, 219–231.

Chambless, D. L., & Goldstein, A. J. The treatment of agoraphobia. In A. Goldstein & E. Foa (Eds.), *Handbook of behavioral interventions*. New York: Wiley, 1980.

Chapman, M., & Zahn-Waxler, C. Young children's compliance and noncompliance to parental discipline in a natural setting. *International Journal of Behavioral Development*, 1982, *5*, 81–94.

Chillag, S. Therapeutics in the elderly. In *Communication and compliance in a hospital setting*. Springfield, Ill.: Charles C. Thomas, 1980.

Chiauzzi, E., & Heimberg, R. G. *The effects of subjects' level of assertiveness, sex and legitimacy of request on assertion-relevant cognitions: An analysis by post-performance videotape reconstruction*. Unpublished manuscript, SUNY–Albany, 1982.

Christensen, A., Johnson, S. M., Phillips, S., & Glasgow, R. E. Cost effectiveness in behavioral family therapy. *Behavior Therapy*, 1980, *11*, 208–225.

Ciminero, A. R., Calhoun, K. S., & Adams, H. E. *Handbook of behavioral assessment* (2nd ed.). New York: Wiley, in press.

Cinciripini, P. M., & Floreen, A. An evaluation of a behavioral program for chronic pain. *Journal of Behavioral Medicine*, 1982, *5*, 375–389.

Cipani, E. Social skills training with institutionalized clients: A critical review. *Corrective and Social Psychiatry*, 1982, *28*, 31–38.

Cipani, E., Augustine, A., & Blomgren, E. Teaching profoundly retarded adults to ascend stairs safely. *Education and Training of the Mentally Retarded*, 1982, *17*, 51–54.

Cipani, E., Augustine, A., & Blomgren, E. Teaching severely and profoundly retarded residents to open doors. *Journal of Special Education Technology*, in press.

Clark, D. B., & Baker, B. L. Predicting outcome in parent training. *Journal of Consulting and Clinical Psychology*, in press.

Clark, D. B., Baker, B. L., & Heifetz, L. J. Behavioral training for parents of retarded children: Prediction of outcome. *American Journal of Mental Deficiency*, 1982, *87*, 14–19.

Clements, J., Evans, C., Jones, C., Osborne, K., & Upton, G. Evaluation of a home-based language training programme with severely mentally handicapped children. *Behaviour Research and Therapy*, 1982, *20*, 243–249.

Coates, R. B. Community-based services for juvenile delinquents: Concept and implications for practice. *Journal of Social Issues*, 1981, *37*, 87–101.

Coates, T. J., Jeffery, R. W., Slinkard, L. A., Killen, J. D., & Danaher, B. G. Frequency of contact and contingent reinforcement in weight loss, lipid change, and blood pressure reduction with adolescents. *Behavior Therapy*, 1982, *13*, 175–185.

Coates, T. J., & Perry, C. Multifactor risk reduction with children and adolescents: Taking care of the heart in behavioral group therapy. In D. Upper & S. Ross (Eds.), *Behavioral group therapy*. Champaign, Ill.: Research Press, 1980.

Coates, T. J., & Thoresen, C. E. Treating obesity in children and adolescents: A review. *American Journal of Public Health*, 1978, *68*, 143–151.

Coates, T. J., & Thoresen, C. E. Obesity among children and adolescents: The problem belongs to everyone. In B. Lahey & A. E. Kazdin (Eds.), *Advances in clinical child psychology*. New York: Plenum, 1980.

Coates, T. J., & Thoresen, C. E. Behavior and weight changes in three obese adolescents. *Behavior Therapy*, 1981, *12*, 383–399.

Cobb, J., McDonald, R., Marks, I., & Stern, R. Marital versus exposure therapy: Psychological treatments of co-existing marital and phobic-obsessive problems. *European Journal of Behavioural Analysis and Modification*, 1980, *4,* 3–17.

Cohen, E. A., Gelfand, D. M., Dodd, D. K., Jensen, J., & Turner, C. Self-control practices associated with weight loss maintenance in children and adolescents. *Behavior Therapy*, 1980, *11*, 26–37.

Cohen, J. A coefficient of agreement for nominal scales. *Educational and Psychological Measurement*, 1960, *20*, 37–46.

Cohen, J. *Statistical power analysis for the behavioral sciences*. New York: Academic Press, 1977.

Cohen, L. H., & Oyster-Nelson, C. K. Clinicians' evaluations of psychodynamic psychotherapy: Experimental data on psychological peer review. *Journal of Consulting and Clinical Psychology*, 1981, *49*, 583–589.

Cohen, N. J., Sullivan, J., Minde, K., Novak, C., & Helwig, C. Evaluation of the relative effectiveness of methylphenidate and cognitive behavior modification in the treatment of kindergarten-aged hyperactive children. *Journal of Abnormal Child Psychology*, 1981, *9*, 43–54.

Cohen, R., Meyers, A. W., Schleser, R., & Rodick, J. D. *Generalization of self-instructions: Effects of cognitive level and training procedures*. Unpublished manuscript, Memphis State University, 1982.

Cohen, R., Schleser, R., & Meyers, A. W. Self-instructions: Effects of cognitive level and active rehearsal. *Journal of Experimental Child Psychology*, 1981, *32*, 65–76.

Cole, P. M., & Kazdin, A. E. Critical issues in self-instructional training with children. *Child Behavior Therapy*, 1980, *2*, 1–23.

Colley, J. R. T., Holland, W. W., & Corkhill, R. T. Influence of passive smoking and parental phlegm on pneumonia and bronchitis in early childhood. *Lancet*, 1974, *1*, 1031–1034.

Collipp, P. J. (Ed.). *Childhood obesity* (2nd ed.). Littleton, Mass.: PSG Publishing, 1980.

Comas-Díaz, L. Effects of cognitive and behavioral group treatment on the depressive symptomatology of Puerto Rican women. *Journal of Consulting and Clinical Psychology*, 1981, *49*, 627–632.

Combs, M. L., & Lahey, B. B. A cognitive social skills training program: Evaluation with young children. *Behavior Modification*, 1981, *5*, 39–60.

Combs, M. L., & Slaby, D. A. Social skills training with children. In B. B. Lahey & A. E. Kazdin (Eds.), *Advances in clinical child psychology* (Vol. 1). New York: Plenum, 1977.

Condiotte, M. M., & Lichtenstein, E. Self-efficacy and relapse in smoking cessation programs. *Journal of Consulting and Clinical Psychology*, 1981, *49*, 648–658.

Cone, J. D., & Foster, S. L. Direct observation in clinical psychology. In P. C. Kendall & J. N. Butcher (Eds.), *Handbook of research methods in clinical psychology*. New York: Wiley, 1982.

Conger, J. C., & Keane, S. P. Social skills intervention in the treatment of isolated or withdrawn children. *Psychological Bulletin*, 1981, *90*, 478–495.

Conger, R. D. The assessment of dysfunctional family systems. In B. B. Lahey & A. E. Kazdin (Eds.), *Advances in clinical child psychology* (Vol. 4). New York: Plenum, 1981.

Conger, R. D. Behavioral intervention for child abuse. *The Behavior Therapist*, 1982, 5(2), 49–53.

Conners, C. K. Rating scales for use in drug studies with children. *Psychopharmacology Bulletin* (Special Issue: Pharmacotherapy of Children), 1973, pp. 24–84.

Cook, S. W., & Berrenberg, J. L. Approaches to encouraging conservation behavior: A review and conceptual framework. *Journal of Social Issues*, 1981, 37, 73–107.

Cook, T. D., & Leviton, L. C. Reviewing the literature: A comparison of traditional methods with meta-analysis. *Journal of Personality*, 1980, 48, 449–472.

Cooper, H. M., & Arkin, R. M. On quantitative reviewing. *Journal of Personality*, 1981, 49, 225–230.

Copeland, A. P. The relevance of subject variables in cognitive self-instructional programs for impulsive children. *Behavior Therapy*, 1981, 12, 520–529.

Copeland, A. P. Individual difference factors in children's self-management: Toward individualized treatments. In P. Karoly & F. H. Kanfer (Eds.), *Self-management and behavior change: From theory to practice*. New York: Pergamon, 1982.

Copeland, A. P. Children's talking to themselves: Its developmental significance, function, and therapeutic promise. In P. C. Kendall (Ed.), *Advances in cognitive-behavioral research and therapy* (Vol. 2). New York: Academic Press, 1983.

Copeland, A. P., & Hammel, R. Subject variables in cognitive self-instructional training. *Cognitive Therapy and Research*, 1981, 5, 405–420.

Cordes, C. FBI posters raise furor among child advocates. *APA Monitor*, October 1982, p. 3.

Cowen, E. L., Don, D., Clarfield, S., Kreling, B., McWilliams, S., Pokracki, F., Pratt, D., Terrell, D., & Wilson A. The AML: A quick screening device for early identification of school maladaptation. *American Journal of Community Psychology*, 1973, 1, 12–35.

Cowen, E. L., Pederson, A., Babigian, H., Izzo, L., & Trost, M. A. Long-term follow-up of early detected vulnerable children. *Journal of Consulting and Clinical Psychology*, 1973, 41, 438–446.

Coyne, J. C. A critique of cognitions as causal entities with particular reference to depression. *Cognitive Therapy and Research*, 1982, 6, 3–13.

Craighead, L. W., Stunkard, A. J., & O'Brien, R. Behavior therapy and pharmacotherapy for obesity. *Archives of General Psychiatry*, 1981, 38, 763–768.

Craighead, W. E. A brief clinical history of cognitive-behavior therapy with children. *School Psychology Review*, 1982, 11, 5–13.

Cronbach, L. J. Beyond the far disciplines of scientific psychology. *American Psychologist*, 1975, 30, 116–127.

Cronbach, L. J., Gleser, G. C., Nanda, H., & Rajaratnam, N. *The dependability of behavioral measurements: Theory of generalizability for scores and profiles*. New York: Wiley, 1972.

Cross, D. G., Sheehan, P. W., & Khan, J. A. Alternative advice and counsel in psychotherapy. *Journal of Consulting and Clinical Psychology*, 1980, 48, 615–625.

Cross, D. G., Sheehan, P. W., & Khan, J. A. Short- and long-term follow-up of clients receiving insight-oriented therapy and behavior therapy. *Journal of Consulting and Clinical Psychology*, 1982, 50, 103–112.

Cunningham, T. R., & Tharp, R. G. The influence of settings on accuracy and reliability of behavior observation. *Behavioral Assessment*, 1981, 3, 67–78.

Curl, R. M. Adherence to the legal and ethical requirements of human research. *The Behavior Therapist*, 1982, 5(4), 123–128.

Curran, J. P., & Mariotto, M. J. A conceptual structure for the assessment of social skills. In M. Hersen, R. M. Eisler, & P. M. Miller (Eds.), *Progress in behavior modification* (Vol. 10). New York: Academic Press, 1980.

Curran, J. P., & Monti, P. M. (Eds.). *Social skills training: A practical handbook for assessment and treatment.* New York: Guilford, 1982.

Curran, J. P., Monti, P. M., Corriveau, D. P., Hay, L. R., Hagerman, S., Zwick, W. R., & Farrell, A. D. The generalizability of a procedure for assessing social skills and social anxiety in a psychiatric population. *Behavioral Assessment,* 1980, *2,* 389–401.

Curran, J. P., & Wessberg, H. W. Assessment of social inadequacy. In D. H. Barlow (Ed.), *Behavioral assessment of adult disorders.* New York: Guilford, 1981.

Curran, J. P., Wessberg, H. W., Farrell, A. D., Monti, P. M., Corriveau, D. P., & Coyne, N. A. Social skills and social anxiety: Are different laboratories measuring the same constructs? *Journal of Consulting and Clinical Psychology,* 1982, *50,* 396–406.

Current topics in organizational behavior management. *Journal of Organizational Behavior Management* Special Issue,1981/1982, *3*(3).

D'Alelio, W. A., & Murray, E. J. Cognitive therapy for test anxiety. *Cognitive Therapy and Research,* 1981, *5,* 299–307.

Davey, S. *Animal learning and conditioning.* Baltimore: University Park Press, 1981.

David, T. G., Moos, R. H., & Kahn, J. R. Community integration among elderly residents of sheltered care settings. *American Journal of Community Psychology,* 1981, *9,* 513–526.

Davidson, P. R., Malcolm, P. B., Lanthier, R. D., Barbaree, H. E., & Ho, T. P. Penile response measurement: Operating characteristics of the Parks plethysmograph. *Behavioral Assessment,* 1981, *3,* 137–143.

Deci, E. L. *Intrinsic motivation.* New York: Plenum, 1975.

Deci, E. L. Notes on the theory and metatheory of intrinsic motivation. *Organizational Behavior and Human Performance,* 1976, *15,* 130–145.

Dekker, E. Youth culture and influences on the smoking behavior of young people. In *Proceedings of the third world conference on smoking and health, 1975.* Washington, D.C.: U.S. Government Printing Office, Publ. No. (NIH) 77-1413. DHEW 1977.

Delisle, M. A. Elderly people's management of time and leisure. *Canada's Mental Health,* 1982, *30*(3), 30–32.

Dellario, D. J., & Anthony, W. A. On the relative effectiveness of institutional and alternative placement for the psychiatrically disabled. *Journal of Social Issues,* 1981, *37,* 21–33.

Delprato, D. J. Hereditary determinants of fears and phobias: A critical review. *Behavior Therapy,* 1980, *11,* 79–103.

Demetral, G. D., Gipson, M., Irvin, W., Anderson, W. P., & Catania, P. Improving compliance with psychiatric indication regimens using prompts and reinforcements. *The Behavior Therapist,* 1981, *4*(5), 19–20.

Denicola, J., & Sandler, J. Training abusive parents in cognitive behavioral techniques. *Behavior Therapy,* 1980, *11,* 263–270.

Derogatis, L. R., Lipman, R. S., & Rickels, K. The Hopkins Symptom Checklist (HSCL): A self-report symptom inventory. *Behavioral Science,* 1974, *19,* 1–15.

DeRubeis, R. J., Hollon, S. D., Evans, M. D., & Bemis, K. M. Can psychotherapies for depression be discriminated? A systematic investigation of cognitive therapy and interpersonal therapy. *Journal of Consulting and Clinical Psychology,* 1982, *50,* 744–756.

Dewald, P. A. Psychoanalytic perspectives on resistance. In P. Wachtel (Ed.), *Resistance: Psychodynamic and behavioral approaches.* New York: Plenum, 1982.

DiClemente, C. C. Self-efficacy and smoking cessation maintenance: A preliminary report. *Cognitive Therapy and Research,* 1981, *5,* 175–187.

DiMatteo, M. R., & DiNicola, D. D. *Achieving patient compliance: The psychology of the medical practitioner's role.* New York: Pergamon, 1982.

DiMatteo, M. R., & Friedman, H. S. *Social psychology and medicine.* Cambridge, Mass.: Oelgeschlager, Gunn & Hain, 1982.

Dixen, J., & Jenkins, J. D. Incestuous child sexual abuse: A review of treatment strategies. *Clinical Psychology Review,* 1981, *1,* 211–222.

Dodge, K. A. Social cognition and children's aggressive behavior. *Child Development,* 1980, *51,* 162–170.

Dodge, K. A., & Frame, C. L. Social cognitive biases and deficits in aggressive boys. *Child Development,* 1982, *53,* 620–635.

Dodge, K. A., & Newman, J. P. Biased decision-making processes in aggressive boys. *Journal of Abnormal Child Psychology,* 1981, *90,* 375–379.

Doke, L. A., & Flippo, J. R. Behavior therapy in the treatment of childhood disorders. In L. Michelson, M. Hersen, & S. M. Turner (Eds.), *Future perspectives in behavior therapy.* New York: Plenum, 1981.

Donahoe, C. P., Lin, D. H., Kirschenbaum, D. S., & Keesey, R. E. *Metabolic consequences of dieting and exercise in the behavioral treatment of obesity.* Paper presented at the annual meeting of the Association for Advancement of Behavior Therapy, Toronto, 1981.

Douglas, J. A "systems" perspective to behavioural consultation in schools: A personal view. *Bulletin of the British Psychological Society,* 1982, *35,* 195–197.

Douglas, V. I., Parry, P., Marton, P., & Garson, C. Assessment of a cognitive training program for hyperactive children. *Journal of Abnormal Child Psychology,* 1976, *4,* 389–410.

Dreger, R. M. The classification of children and their emotional problems. *Clinical Psychology Review,* 1981, *1,* 415–430.

Dubey, D. R., & Kaufman, K. F. Training parents of hyperactive children in behavior management. In M. Gittelman (Ed.), *Strategic interventions for hyperactive children.* Armonk, N.Y.: M. E. Sharpe, 1981.

Dubey, D. R., & Kaufman, K. F. The "side effects" of parent implemented behavior modification. *Child and Family Behavior Therapy,* 1982, *4,* 65–71.

Duckert, F. Behavioral analysis of the drinking pattern of alcoholics, with special focus on degree of control in various situations. *Scandinavian Journal of Behavior Therapy,* 1981, *10,* 121–133.

Durlak, J. A. Comparative effectiveness of paraprofessional and professional helpers. *Psychological Bulletin,* 1979, *86,* 80–92.

Durnin, J. V. G. A., & Ferro-Luzzi, A. Conducting and reporting studies on human energy intake and output: Suggested standards. *American Journal of Clinical Nutrition,* 1982, *35,* 624–626.

Dyer, K., Christian, W. P., & Luce, S. C. The role of response delay in improving the discrimination performance of autistic children. *Journal of Applied Behavior Analysis,* 1982, *15,* 231–240.

D'Zurilla, T. J., & Nezu, A. Social problem-solving in adults. In P. C. Kendall (Ed.), *Advances in cognitive-behavioral research and therapy* (Vol. 1). New York: Academic Press, 1982.

Eagly, A. H., & Carli, L. L. Sex of researchers and sex-typed communications as determinants of sex differences in influenceability: A meta-analysis of social influence studies. *Psychological Bulletin,* 1981, *90,* 1–20.

Earls, C. M., & Jackson, D. R. The effects of temperature on the mercury-in-rubber strain gauge. *Behavioral Assessment,* 1981, *3,* 145–149.

Eastman, B. G., & Rasbury, W. C. Cognitive self-instruction for the control of impulsive classroom behavior: Ensuring the treatment package. *Journal of Abnormal Child Psychology*, 1981, *9*, 381–387.

Eastman, C., & Marzillier, J. S. *Theoretical and methodological difficulties in Bandura's self-efficacy theory.* Unpublished manuscript, Warneford Hospital, Oxford University, 1982.

Edgington, E. S. Random assignment and statistical tests for one-subject experimentation. *Behavioral Assessment*, 1980, *2*, 19–28.

Edgington, E. S. Nonparametric tests for single-subject multiple schedule experiments. *Behavioral Assessment*, 1982, *4*, 83–91.

Eelen, P. Conditioning and attribution. In J. Boulougouris (Ed.), *Learning theory approaches to psychiatry.* London: Wiley, 1982.

Elias, M. J., Chinsky, J. M., Larcen, S. W., & Allen, G. J. A multi-level behavioral-preventive school program: Process, problem, and potential. In A. J. Jeger & R. S. Slotnick (Eds.), *Community mental health and behavioral ecology: A handbook of theory, research, and practice.* New York: Plenum, 1982.

Ellis, A. *The essence of rational psychotherapy: A comprehensive approach to treatment.* New York: Institute for Rational Living, 1970.

Ellis, A. A note on the treatment of agoraphobics with cognitive modification versus prolonged exposure *in vivo. Behaviour Research and Therapy*, 1979, *17*, 162–163.

Ellis, A. Is RET ethically untenable or inconsistent? A reply to Paul E. Meehl. *Rational Living*, 1981, pp. 10–11; 38–42. (a)

Ellis, A. Science, religiosity, and rational emotive psychology. *Psychotherapy: Theory, Research, and Practice*, 1981, *18*, 155–158. (b)

Ellis, A., & Grieger, R. *Handbook of rational psychotherapy.* New York: Springer, 1977.

Ellis, N. R. Toilet training the severely defective patient: An S-R reinforcement analysis. *American Journal of Mental Deficiency*, 1963, *68*, 99–103.

Ellis, N. R. Foreword. In J. L. Matson & J. R. McCartney (Eds.), *Handbook of behavior modification with the mentally retarded*, New York: Plenum, 1981.

Emery, G., Hollon, S. D., & Bedrosian, R. C. (Eds.). *New directions in cognitive therapy.* New York: Guilford, 1981.

Emmelkamp, P. M. G. Self-observation vs. flooding in the treatment of agoraphobia. *Behaviour Research and Therapy*, 1974, *12*, 229–233.

Emmelkamp, P. M. G. Recent developments in the behavioural treatment of obsessive-compulsive disorders. In J. C. Boulougouris (Ed.), *Learning theory approaches to psychiatry.* London: Wiley, 1982.

Emmelkamp, P. M. G., & Giesselbach, P. Treatment of obsessions: Relevant vs. irrelevant exposure. *Behavioural Psychotherapy*, 1981, *9*, 322–329.

Emmelkamp, P. M. G., Kuipers, A. C. M., & Eggeraat, J. B. Cognitive modification versus prolonged exposure *in vivo*: A comparison with agoraphobics as subjects. *Behaviour Research and Therapy*, 1978, *16*, 33–42.

Emmelkamp, P. M. G., & Mersch, P. P. Cognition and exposure *in vivo* in the treatment of agoraphobia: Short-term and delayed effects. *Cognitive Therapy and Research*, 1982, *6*, 77–90.

Engstrom-Poulin, C. Support services enable elderly people to remain at home. *Canada's Mental Health*, 1982, *30*(3), 28–29.

Epstein, L. H., & Cluss, P. A. A behavioral medicine perspective on adherence to long-term medical regimens. *Journal of Consulting and Clinical Psychology*, 1982, *50*, 950–971.

Epstein, L. H., Masek, B. J., & Marshall, W. R. A nutritionally based school program for control of eating in obese children. *Behavior Therapy*, 1978, *9*, 766–778.

Epstein, L. H., Wing, R. R., Koeske, R., Andrasik, F., & Ossip, D. J. Child and parent weight loss in family-based behavior modification programs. *Journal of Consulting and Clinical Psychology*, 1981, *49*, 674–685.

Epstein, L. H., Wing, R. R., Steranchak, L., Dickson, B., & Michelson, J. Comparison of family-based behavior modification and nutrition education for childhood obesity. *Journal of Pediatric Psychology*, 1980, *5*, 25–36.

Erikson, E. H. *Insight and responsibility*. New York: Norton, 1964.

Ethical issues for human services. *Behavior Therapy*, 1977, *8*, v–vi.

Evans, I. M. Wanted—A good integrative handbook. (Review of S. M. Turner, K. S. Calhoun, & H. E. Adams, Eds., *Handbook of clinical behavior therapy*.) *Contemporary Psychology*, 1982, *27*, 21–22.

Evans, I. M., & Nelson, R. O. A curriculum for the teaching of behavioral assessment. *American Psychologist*, 1974, *29*, 598–606.

Evans, R. I. Smoking in children: Developing a social psychological strategy of deterrence. *Preventive Medicine*, 1976, *5*, 122–127.

Evans, R. I. Smoking in children and adolescents: Psychological determinants and prevention strategies. In *Smoking and health: Report of the Surgeon General*. Washington, D.C.: U.S. Government Printing Office, 1979.

Evans, R. I., & Borgatta, E. F. An experiment in smoking dissuasion among university freshmen. *Journal of Health and Social Behavior*, 1970, *11*, 30–36.

Evans, R. I., Hansen, W. B., & Mittlemark, M. B. Increasing the validity of self-reports of behavior in a smoking-in-children investigation. *Journal of Applied Psychology*, 1977, *62*, 521–523.

Evans, R. I., Rozelle, R. M., Mittlemark, M. B., Hansen, W. B., Bane, A. L., & Havis, J. Deterring the onset of smoking in children: Knowledge of immediate physiological effects and coping with peer pressure. *Journal of Applied Social Psychology*, 1978, *8*, 126–135.

Eysenck, H. J. An exercise in mega-silliness. *American Psychologist*, 1978, *33*, 517.

Eysenck, H. J. Neobehavioristic (S-R) theory. In G. T. Wilson & C. M. Franks (Eds.), *Contemporary behavior therapy: Conceptual and empirical foundations*. New York: Guilford, 1982.

Eysenck, H., & Eysenck, S. *The Eysenck Personality Inventory*. San Diego: Educational and Industrial Testing Service, 1968.

Fairweather, G. W., Sanders, D. H., Maynard, H., & Cressler, D. L. *Community life for the mentally ill: An alternative to institutional care*. New York: Aldine, 1969.

Fairweather, G. W., Sanders, D. H., & Tornatzky, L. E. *Creating change in mental health organizations*. New York: Pergamon, 1974.

Fancher, R. E., & Gutkin, D. Attitudes towards science, insight therapy, and behavior therapy. *Journal of Clinical Psychology*, 1971, *27*, 153–155.

Farkas, S. M. An ontological analysis of behavior therapy. *American Psychologist*, 1980, *35*, 364–374.

Farkas, S. M. Toward a pluralistic psychology of behavior change. In M. Hersen, R. M. Eisler, & P. M. Miller (Eds.), *Progress in behavior modification* (Vol. 11). New York: Academic Press, 1981.

Farquhar, J. W. The community-based model of life style intervention trials. *American Journal of Epidemiology*, 1978, *108*, 103–111.

Farquhar, J. W., Maccoby, N., Wood, P. D., Alexander, J. K., Breitrose, H., Brown, B. W., Jr., Haskell, W. L., McAlister, A. L., Meyer, A. J., Nash, J. D., & Stern, M. P. Community education for cardiovascular health. *Lancet*, 1977, *4*, 1192–1196.

Favell, J. E., and Associates. The treatment of self-injurious behavior. *Behavior Therapy*, 1982, *13*, 529–554.

Faw, G. D., Reid, D. H., Schepis, M. M., Fitzgerald, J. R., & Welty, P. A. Involving institutional staff in the development and maintenance of sign language skills with profoundly retarded persons. *Journal of Applied Behavior Analysis*, 1981, *14*, 411–425.

Fawcett, S. B., Fletcher, R. K., & Matthews, R. M. Applications of behavior analysis in community education. In D. S. Glenwick & L. A. Jason (Eds.), *Behavioral community psychology: Progress and prospects*. New York: Praeger, 1980. (a)

Fawcett, S. B., Matthews, R. M., & Fletcher, R. K. Some promising dimensions for behavioral community technology. *Journal of Applied Behavior Analysis*, 1980, *15*, 505–518. (b)

Fawcett, S. B., Seekins, T., & Braukmann, C. J. Developing and transferring behavioral technologies for children and youth. *Child and Youth Services Review*, in press.

Fay, A., & Lazarus, A. A. Psychoanalytic resistance and behavioral nonresponsiveness. In P. Wachtel (Ed.), *Resistance: Psychodynamic and behavioral approaches*. New York: Plenum, 1982.

Feldman, M. P. Frame of reference for training: Behaviour therapy. In W. DeMoor & H. R. Wigngaarden (Eds.), *Psychotherapy: Research and training*. Amsterdam: Elsevier/North Holland Press, 1980.

Feldman, M. P. Juvenile offending: Behavioral approaches to prevention and intervention. *Child and Family Behavior Therapy*, in press.

Feltz, D. L. Path analysis of the causal elements in Bandura's theory of self-efficacy and an anxiety-based model of avoidance behavior. *Journal of Personality and Social Psychology*, 1982, *42*, 764–781.

Ferguson, J. M., & Taylor, C. B. (Eds.). *The comprehensive handbook of behavioral medicine* (Vols. 1–3). New York: Spectrum, 1980.

Fisher, E. B. Overjustification effects in token economies. *Journal of Applied Behavior Analysis*, 1979, *12*, 407–415.

Fishman, D. B., & Neigher, W. American psychology in the eighties: Who will buy? *American Psychologist*, 1982, *37*, 533–546.

Fitzgerald, H. E., Lester, B. M., & Yogman, M. W. (Eds.). *Theory and research in behavioral pediatrics* (Vol. 1). New York: Plenum, 1982.

Fixsen, D. L., Phillips, E. E., Dowd, T. P., & Palmer, L. J. Preventing violence in residential treatment programs for adolescents. In B. B. Stuart (Ed.), *Violent behavior: Social learning approaches to prediction, management and treatment*, New York: Brunner/Mazel, 1981.

Fleischman, J. F. Using parenting salaries to control attention and cooperation in therapy. *Behavior Therapy*, 1979, *10*, 111–116.

Fleischman, M. J., Shilton, P. E., & Arthur, J. L. *Client readiness scale*, 1974. (Cited by Forehand, R. L., & McMahon, R. J. *Helping the noncompliant child: A clinician's guide to parent training*. New York: Guilford, 1981.)

Fletcher, R. H., & Fletcher, S. W. Clinical research in general medical journals: A 30-year perspective. *The New England Journal of Medicine*, 1979, *301*, 180–183.

Foa, E. B. Failure in treating obsessive-compulsives. *Behaviour Research and Therapy*, 1979, *17*, 169–176.

Follick, M. J., Zitter, R. E., & Ahern, D. K. Failures in the operant treatment of chronic pain. In E. B. Foa & P. Emmelkamp (Eds.), *Failures in behavior therapy*. New York: Wiley, 1983.

Follick, M. J., Zitter, R. E., & Kulich, R. J. Outpatient management of chronic pain. In T. J. Coates (Ed.), *Behavioral medicine: A practical handbook*. Champaign, Ill.: Research Press, in press.

Forbes, G. B. Prevalence of obesity in childhood. In G. A. Bray (Ed.), *Obesity in perspective* (Vol. 2). DHEW Publ. No. (NIH) 75-708. Washington, D.C.: U.S. Government Printing Office, 1975.

Ford, J. D., & Kendall, P. C. Behavior therapists' professional behaviors: Converging evidence of a gap between theory and practice. *The Behavior Therapist*, 1979, 2(5), 37–38. (a)

Ford, J. D., & Kendall, P. C. Behavior therapists' professional behaviors: A survey study. *Professional Psychology*, 1979, *10*, 772–773. (b)

Fordyce, W. E. An operant conditioning method for managing chronic pain. *Postgraduate Medicine*, 1973, *53*, 123–128.

Fordyce, W. E. Treating chronic pain by contingency management. *Advances in Neurology*, 1974, *4*, 583–589.

Fordyce, W. E. *Behavioral methods for chronic pain and illness*. St. Louis: Mosby, 1976.

Fordyce, W. E., Fowler, R., Lehmann, J., & DeLateur, B. Some implications of learning in problems of chronic pain. *Journal of Chronic Disease*, 1968, *21*, 179–190.

Fordyce, W. E., Fowler, R., Lehmann, J., DeLateur, B., Sand, P., & Treischmann, R. Operant conditioning in the treatment of chronic pain. *Archives of Physical Medicine and Rehabilitation*, 1973, *54*, 399–408.

Forehand, R. L., & Atkeson, B. M. Generality of treatment effects with parents as therapists: A review of assessment and implementation procedures. *Behavior Therapy*, 1977, *8*, 575–593.

Forehand, R. L., Breiner, J., McMahon, R. J., & Davies, G. Predictors of cross setting behavior change in the treatment of child problems. *Journal of Behavior Therapy and Experimental Psychiatry*, 1981, *12*, 311–313.

Forehand, R. L., Wells, K. C., & Griest, D. L. An examination of the social validity of a parent training program. *Behavior Therapy*, 1980, *11*, 488–502.

Forehand, R. L., & McMahon, R. J. *Helping the noncompliant child: A clinician's guide to parent training*. New York: Guilford, 1981.

Foreyt, J. P., & Goodrick, G. K. Childhood obesity. In E. J. Mash & L. G. Terdal (Eds.), *Behavioral assessment of childhood disorders*. New York: Guilford, 1981.

Foreyt, J. P., Goodrick, G. K., & Gotto, A. M. Limitations of behavioral treatment of obesity: Review and analysis. *Journal of Behavioral Medicine*, 1981, *4*, 159–174.

Foreyt, J. P., Mitchell, R. E., Garner, D. T., Gee, M., Scott, L. W., & Gotto, A. M. Behavioral treatment of obesity: Results and limitations. *Behavior Therapy*, 1982, *13*, 153–163.

Fox, R. A multidisciplinary approach to the treatment of alcoholism. *American Journal of Psychiatry*, 1967, *123*, 769–778.

Franks, C. M. Can behavior therapy find peace and fulfillment in a school of professional psychology? *The Clinical Psychologist*, 1974, *28*, 11–15.

Franks, C. M. 2081: Will we be many or one—or none? *Behavioural Psychotherapy*, 1981, *9*, 287–290.

Franks, C. M. The place of theory and concept in a world of practice and doing: A clinician's guide to the behavioral galaxy. In C. M. Franks (Ed.), *New developments in behavior therapy: From research to practical application*. New York: Haworth, 1983.

Franks, C. M. The foundations of behavior therapy and the contributions of W. Horsley Gantt. In F. J. McGuigan & T. A. Ban (Eds.), *Critical issues in psychology, psychiatry, and physiology—A memorial to W. Horsley Gantt*. Baltimore: University Park Press, in press.

Franks, C. M., & Barbrack, C. R. Behavior therapy with adults: An integrative perspective. In M. Hersen, A. E. Kazdin, & A. J. Bellack (Eds.), *The clinical psychology handbook*. New York: Pergamon, 1983.

Franks, C. M., & Wilson, G. T. Preface. *Annual review of behavior therapy: Theory and practice* (Vol. 1). New York: Brunner/Mazel, 1973.

Franks, C. M., & Wilson, G. T. Ethical and related issues in behavior therapy. In *Annual review of behavior therapy: Theory and practice* (Vol. 3). New York: Brunner/ Mazel, 1975.

Franks, C. M., & Wilson, G. T. *Annual review of behavior therapy: Theory and practice* (Vol. 5). New York: Brunner/Mazel, 1977. (a)

Franks, C. M., & Wilson, G. T. Self-reinforcement. In *Annual review of behavior therapy: Theory and practice* (Vol. 5). New York: Brunner/Mazel, 1977. (b)

Franks, C. M., & Wilson, G. T. *Annual review of behavior therapy: Theory and practice* (Vol. 6). New York: Brunner/Mazel, 1978.

Franks, C. M., & Wilson, G. T. *Annual review of behavior therapy: Theory and practice* (Vol. 7). New York: Brunner/Mazel, 1979.

Franks, C. M., Wilson, G. T., Kendall, P. C., & Brownell, K. D. *Annual review of behavior therapy: Theory and practice* (Vol. 8). New York: Guilford, 1982.

Fraser, D. From token economy to social information system: The emergence of critical variables. In E. Kara (Ed.), *Current issues in clinical psychology*. New York: Plenum, 1983.

Frederiksen, L. W. Behavior modification in business and industry: Progress and prospects. *The Behavior Therapist*, 1982, 5(3), 91–94.

Frederiksen, L. W., & Lovett, S. B. Inside organizational behavior management: Perspectives on an emerging field. *Journal of Organizational Behavior Management*, 1980, *2*, 193–203.

Freeman, B. J., & Ritvo, E. R. The syndrome of autism: A critical review of diagnostic systems, follow-up studies, and the theoretical background of the behavioral observation scale. In J. L. Steffen & P. Karoly (Eds.), *Autism and severe psychopathology: Advances in child behavioral analysis and therapy* (Vol. 2). Lexington, Mass.: Lexington Books, 1982.

Fuchs, C. Z., & Rehm, L. P. A self-control behavior therapy program for depression. *Journal of Consulting and Clinical Psychology*, 1977, *45*, 206–215.

Furman, W., & Drabman, R. E. Methodological issues in child behavior therapy. In M. Hersen, R. M. Eisler, & P. M. Miller (Eds.), *Progress in behavior modification* (Vol. 11). New York: Academic Press, 1981.

Gaffney, L. R., & McFall, R. M. A comparison of social skills in delinquent and nondelinquent adolescent girls using a behavioral role-playing inventory. *Journal of Consulting and Clinical Psychology*, 1981, *49*, 959–967.

Galassi, J. P., Frierson, H. T., & Sharer, R. Behavior of high, moderate, and low test anxious students during an actual test situation. *Journal of Consulting and Clinical Psychology*, 1981, *49*, 51–62. (a)

Galassi, J. P., Frierson, H. T., & Sharer, R. Concurrent versus retrospective assessment in test anxiety research. *Journal of Consulting and Clinical Psychology*, 1981, *49*, 614–615. (b)

Galassi, M. D., & Galassi, J. P. Assertion: A critical review. *Psychotherapy: Theory, Research and Practice*, 1978, *15*, 16–29.

Gallagher, D., Nies, G., & Thompson, L. W. Reliability of the Beck Depression Inventory with older adults. *Journal of Consulting and Clinical Psychology*, 1982, *50*, 152–153.

Gallo, P. S. Meta-analysis—A mixed meta-phor? *American Psychologist*, 1978, *33*, 515–517.

Gallup Youth Survey. Associated Press, September 14, 1977.

Garfield, E. Risk analysis, Part 1. How we rate the risks of new technologies. *Current Contents*, August 16, 1982, pp. 5–13.

Garfield, S. L., & Kurtz, R. A survey of clinical psychologists: Characteristics, activities, and orientations. *The Clinical Psychologist*, 1974, *28*, 7–10.

Garfield, S. L., & Kurtz, R. Clinical psychologists in the 1970s. *American Psychologist,* 1976, *31,* 1-9.

Garfield, S. L., & Kurtz, R. A study of eclectic views. *Journal of Consulting and Clinical Psychology,* 1977, *45,* 78-83.

Garmezy, N. Research in clinical psychology: Serving the future hour. In P. Kendall & J. Butcher (Eds.), *Handbook of research methods in clinical psychology.* New York: Wiley, 1982.

Garn, S. M., & Clark, D. C. Trends in fatness and the origins of obesity. *Pediatrics,* 1976, *57,* 433-456.

Garner, D. M., & Bemis, K. M. A cognitive-behavioral approach to anorexia nervosa. *Cognitive Therapy and Research,* 1982, *6,* 123-150.

Garrity, T. F. Medical compliance and the clinician-patient relationship: A review. *Social Science and Medicine, 1981, 15,* 215-222.

Gay, M. L., Hollandsworth, J. G., & Galassi, J. P. An assertiveness inventory. *Journal of Counseling Psychology,* 1975, *22,* 340-344.

Gelder, M. Is exposure a necessary and sufficient condition for the treatment of agoraphobia? In J. Boulougouris (Ed.), *Learning theory approaches to psychiatry.* London: Wiley, 1982.

Geller, E. S. The energy crisis and behavioral science: A conceptual framework for large scale intervention. In A. W. Childs & G. B. Melton (Eds.), *Rural psychology.* New York: Plenum, 1982.

Geller, E. S., Johnson, R. P., & Pelton, S. L. Community-based intervention for encouraging safety belt use. *American Journal of Community Psychology,* 1982, *10,* 183-195. (a)

Geller, E. S., Winett, R. A., & Everett, P. B., *Preserving the environment: New strategies for behavior change.* New York: Pergamon, 1982. (b)

Geller, E. S., Koltuniak, T. A., & Shilling, J. S. Response avoidance prompting: A cost effective strategy for theft deterrence. *Behavioral Counseling Quarterly,* in press.

Gelles, R. J. An exchange/social control approach to understanding intrafamily violence. *The Behavior Therapist,* 1982, *5*(1), 5-7.

Gelles, R. J., & Straus, M. A. Determinants of violence in the family: Toward a theoretical integration. In W. R. Burr, R. Hill, F. I. Nye, & I. L. Reiss (Eds.), *Contemporary theories about the family.* New York: Free Press, 1979.

Genest, M., & Turk, D. C. A proposed model for behavioral group therapy with pain patients. In D. Upper & S. Ross (Eds.), *Behavioral group therapy.* Champaign, Ill.: Research Press, 1979.

Genuth, S. M. Supplemental fasting in the treatment of obesity and diabetes. *American Journal of Clinical Nutrition,* 1979, *32,* 2579-2586.

Genuth, S. M., Castro, J. H., & Vertes, V. Weight reduction in obesity by outpatient semistarvation. *Journal of the American Medical Association,* 1974, *230,* 987-991.

Gesten, E. L. A health resources inventory: The development of a measure of the personal and social competence of primary-grade children. *Journal of Consulting and Clinical Psychology,* 1976, *44,* 775-786.

Gesten, E. L., deApodaca, R. F., Rains, M., Weissberg, R. P., & Cowen, E. L. Promoting peer related social competence in schools. In M. W. Kent & J. E. Rolf (Eds.), *Primary prevention of psychopathology* (Vol. 3): *Social competence in children.* Hanover, N.H.: University Press of New England, 1979.

Gillen, R. W., & Heimberg, R. S. Social skills training for the job interview: Review and prospectives. In M. Hersen, R. M. Eisler, & P. M. Miller (Eds.), *Progress in behavior modification* (Vol. 10). New York: Academic Press, 1980.

Giovannoni, J. M., & Becerra, R. M. (Eds.). *Defining child abuse.* New York: Free Press, 1979.

Gittelman, M. (Ed.). *Strategic interventions for hyperactive children.* Armonk, N.Y.: M. E. Sharpe, 1981.

Glass, C. R., & Arnkoff, D. B. Think cognitively: Selected issues in cognitive assessment and therapy. In P. C. Kendall (Ed.), *Advances in cognitive-behavioral research and therapy* (Vol. 1). New York: Academic Press, 1982.

Glass, C. R., Merluzzi, T. V., Biever, J. L., & Larsen, K. H. Cognitive assessment of social anxiety: Development and validation of a self-statement questionnaire. *Cognitive Therapy and Research,* 1982, *6,* 37-55.

Glass, G. V., & Smith, M. L. A reply to Eysenck. *American Psychologist,* 1978, *33,* 517-519.

Gochman, S. I., Allgood, B. A., & Geer, C. R. A look at today's behavior therapists. *Professional Psychology,* 1982, *13,* 605-609.

Gola, T. J., Holmes, P. A., & Holmes, N. K. Effectiveness of a group contingency procedure for increasing prevocational behavior of profoundly mentally retarded persons. *Mental Retardation,* 1982, *20,* 26-29.

Goldfried, M. R. Anxiety reduction through cognitive-behavioral intervention. In P. C. Kendall & S. D. Hollon (Eds.), *Cognitive-behavioral interventions: Theory, research and procedures.* New York: Academic Press, 1979.

Goldfried, M. R. (Ed.). Some views on effective principles of psychotherapy. *Cognitive Therapy and Research,* 1980, *4,* 271-306.

Goldfried, M. R. (Ed.). *Converging themes in psychotherapy: Trends in psychodynamic, humanistic, and behavioral practice.* New York: Springer, 1982.

Goldfried, M. R., & Davison, G. C. *Clinical behavior therapy.* New York: Holt, Rinehart & Winston, 1976.

Goldfried, M. R., & Robins, C. Self-schemata, cognitive bias, and the processing of therapeutic experiences. In P. C. Kendall (Ed.), *Advances in cognitive-behavioral research and therapy* (Vol. 2). New York: Academic Press, 1983.

Golin, S., Sweeney, P. D., & Shaeffer, D. E. The causality of causal attributions in depression: A cross-lagged panel correlational analysis. *Journal of Abnormal Psychology,* 1981, *90,* 14-22.

Goodhart, R. S., & Shils, M. E. *Modern nutrition in health and disease* (6th ed.). Philadelphia: Lea & Febiger, 1980.

Gormally, J., Sipps, G., Raphael, R., Edwin, D., & Varvil-Weld, D. The relationship between maladaptive cognitions and social anxiety. *Journal of Consulting and Clinical Psychology,* 1981, *49,* 300-301.

Gortmaker, S. L., Walker, D. K., Jacobs, F. H., & Ruch-Ross, H. Parental smoking and the risk of childhood asthma. *American Journal of Public Health,* 1982, *72,* 574-579.

Gottman, J. M., & Notarius, C. I. Sequential analysis of observational data using Markov chains. In T. Kratochwill (Ed.), *Strategies to evaluate change in single-subject research.* New York: Academic Press, 1978.

Grantham, R. J., & Joslyn, M. S. Modeling implications for rehabilitation counseling process and outcome. *Rehabilitative Counseling Bulletin,* 1981, *25,* 342-353.

Grayson, J., Foa, E., & Steketee, G. Habituation during exposure treatment: Distraction vs. attention-focusing. *Behaviour Research and Therapy,* 1982, *20,* 323-328.

Graziano, A. M. Parents as behavior therapists. In M. Hersen, R. M. Eisler, & P. M. Miller (Eds.), *Progress in behavior modification* (Vol. 4). New York: Academic Press, 1977.

Graziano, A. M. & Mooney, K. C. Behavioral treatment of "nightfears" in children: Maintenance of improvement at 2½-to-3-year follow-up. *Journal of Consulting and Clinical Psychology,* 1982, *50,* 598-599.

Green, K. D., & Forehand, R. Assessment of children's social skills: A review of methods. *Journal of Behavioral Assessment,* 1980, *2,* 143-159.

Green, S. B. A comparison of three indexes of agreement between observers: Proportion of agreement, G-index, and kappa. *Educational and Psychological Measurement,* 1981, *41,* 1069–1072.

Greenberg, L. S., & Safran, J. D. Encoding and cognitive therapy: Changing what clients attend to. *Psychotherapy: Theory, Research, and Practice,* 1981, *18,* 163–169.

Greene, B. F. Behavior analysis in the public interest. *The Behavior Therapist,* 1981, *4*(3), 5–7.

Greenwald, D. P., Kornblith, S. J., Hersen, M., Bellack, A. S., & Himmelhoch, J. M. Differences between social skills therapists and psychotherapists in treating depression. *Journal of Consulting and Clinical Psychology,* 1981, *49,* 757–759.

Greenwood, C. R., Walker, H. M., Todd, N. M., & Hops, H. Normative and descriptive analysis of pre-school free play social interaction rates. *Journal of Pediatric Psychology,* 1981, *6,* 343–367.

Greenwood, F. M. Social skills training with handicapped children: A review. *Review of Educational Research,* 1981, *51,* 139–176.

Griest, D. L., & Forehand, R. L. How can I get any parent training done with all the other problems going on?: The role of family variables in child behavior therapy. *Child and Family Behavior Therapy,* 1982, *4,* 73–80.

Griest, D. L., Forehand, R., Rogers, T., Breiner, J., Furey, W., & Williams, C. A. Effects of parent enhancement therapy on the treatment outcome and generalization of a parent training program. *Behaviour Research and Therapy,* 1982, *20,* 429–436.

Griest, D. L., Forehand, R., Wells, K. C., & McMahon, R. J. An examination of differences between non-clinic and behavior-problem clinic-referred children and their mothers. *Journal of Abnormal Psychology,* 1980, *89,* 497–500.

Gross, A. M., & Drabman, R. S. Behavioral contrast and behavior therapy. *Behavior Therapy,* 1981, *12,* 231–246.

Gross, I., Wheeler, M., & Hess, R. The treatment of obesity in adolescents using behavioral self-control. *Clinical Pediatrics,* 1976, *15,* 920–924.

Grossberg, J. M. Comments about cognitive therapy and behavior therapy. *Journal of Behavior Therapy and Experimental Psychiatry,* 1981, *7,* 25–33.

Grusec, J. E., & Kuczynski, L. Direction of effect in socialization: A comparison of the parent's versus the child's behavior as determinants of disciplinary techniques. *Developmental Psychology,* 1980, *16,* 1–9.

Gunter-Hunt, G., Ferguson, K. J., & Bole, G. G. Appointment-keeping behavior and patient satisfaction: Implications for health professionals. *Patient Counseling and Health Education,* 1982, *3,* 156–160.

Gurland, B. J. The comparative frequency of depression in various adult age groups. *Journal of Gerontology,* 1976, *31,* 283–292.

Gurland, B. J., Bennett, R., & Wilder, D. Reevaluating the place of evaluation in planning for alternatives to institutional care for the elderly. *Journal of Social Issues,* 1981, *37,* 51–70.

Hafner, A. J. A problem-solving extension of the A-B-C format. *Rational Living,* 1981, *16,* 29–34.

Hafner, A. J., Hatton, P., & Larkin, F. Spouse-aided therapy and psychiatric nursing: A preliminary report. *Australian Journal of Family Therapy,* 1981, *2,* 143–153.

Hake, D. F. Behavioral ecology: A social systems approach to environmental problems. In L. Michelson, M. Hersen, & S. Turner (Eds.), *Future perspectives in behavior therapy.* New York: Plenum, 1981.

Hake, D. F., & Zane, T. A community-based gasoline conservation project: Practical and methdological considerations. *Behavior Modification,* 1981, *5,* 435–458.

Hamburg, D. A. Health and behavior (editorial). *Science,* 1982, *217,* 399.

Hamilton, J. L. The demand for cigarettes: Advertising, the health scare, and the cigarette advertising ban. *Review of Economic Statistics*, 1972, *54*, 401–411.

Hamilton, M. A rating scale for depression. *Journal of Neurology, Neurosurgery, and Psychiatry*, 1960, *23*, 56–62.

Hamilton, M. Standardized assessment and recording of depression. *Psychiatria, Neurologia, Neurochirugia*, 1969, *72*, 201–205.

Hamilton, S. B., MacQuiddy, S. L., Brown, T. M., Story, D. A., Braun, D. M., & Johnson, T. L. Behavioral parent-training: A comprehensive bibliography: 1938–1982. *J.S.A.S. Catalog of Selected Documents in Psychology*, 1983.

Hammen, C. L. Depression in college students: Beyond the Beck Depression Inventory. *Journal of Consulting and Clinical Psychology*, 1980, *48*, 126–128.

Hammen, C. L., Jacobs, M., Mayol, A., & Cochran, S. D. Dysfunctional cognitions and the effectiveness of skills and cognitive–behavioral assertion training. *Journal of Consulting and Clinical Psychology*, 1980, *48*, 685–695.

Hammen, C. L., & Padesky, C. A. Sex differences in the expression of depressive responses on the Beck Depression Inventory. *Journal of Abnormal Psychology*, 1977, *86*, 609–614.

Handleman, J. S. A model for self-contained classes for autistic type youngsters. *Education and Treatment of Children*, 1981, *4*, 61–70.

Hanley, G. L., Houts, A. C., Ruzek, J., Krasner, M., & Krasner, L. Children as community planners: Report on an environmental design Project 1. *Education*, 1981, *102*, 189–192.

Hanley, I. G. The use of signposts and active training to modify word disorientation in elderly patients. *Journal of Behavior Therapy and Experimental Psychiatry*, 1981, *12*, 241–247.

Harlap, S., & Davies, A. M. Infants' admissions to hospital and maternal smoking. *Lancet*, 1974, *1*, 529–532.

Harrell, T. H., Chambless, D. L., & Calhoun, J. F. Correlational relationships between self-statements and affective states. *Cognitive Therapy and Research*, 1981, *5*, 159–173.

Harris, B. Whatever happened to Little Albert? *American Psychologist*, 1979, *34*, 151–160.

Harris, R. N., & Walter, J. *Outcome, reliability and validity issues of alcoholism follow-up.* Paper presented at the annual meeting of the Alcohol and Drug Abuse Problems Association of North America, New Orleans, September 1976.

Harris, S. L. A family systems approach to behavioral training with parents of autistic children. *Child and Family Behavior Therapy*, 1982, *4*, 21–35.

Harris, S. L. Behavior therapy with children. In M. Hersen, A. E. Kazdin, & A. S. Bellack (Eds.), *The clinical psychology handbook*. New York: Pergamon, 1983.

Harris, S. L., & Milch, R. E. Training parents as behavior therapists for their autistic children. *Clinical Psychology Review*, 1981, *1*, 49–63.

Harris, S. L., & Wolchik, S. A. Teaching speech skills to nonverbal children and their parents. In J. L. Steffen & P. Karoly (Eds.), *Autism and severe psychopathology: Advances in child behavioral analysis and therapy* (Vol. 2). Lexington, Mass.: Lexington Books, 1982.

Harris, S. L., Wolchik, S. A., & Milch, R. E. Changing the speech of autistic children and their parents. *Child and Family Behavior Therapy*, 1982, *4*(3), 151–173.

Harris, S. L., Wolchik, S. A., & Weitz, S. The acquisition of language skills by autistic children: Can parents do the job? *Journal of Autism and Developmental Disorders*. 1981, *11*, 373–384.

Hartman, L. M., & Ainsworth, K. D. Self-regulation of chronic pain: Preliminary empirical findings. *Canadian Journal of Psychiatry*, 1980, *25*, 38–43.

Hartung, G. H., Foreyt, J. P., Mitchell, R. E., Vlasek, I., & Gotto, A. M. Relationship of diet to HDL-cholesterol in middle-aged marathon runners, joggers, and inactive men. *New England Journal of Medicine*, 1980, *302*, 357–361.

Hatzenbuehler, L. C., Parpal, M., & Matthews, L. *Reliability of the Beck Depression Inventory with college students.* Unpublished manuscript, Idaho State University, Pocatello, Idaho, 1982.

Hay, L. R. Teaching behavioral assessment to clinical psychology students. *Behavioral Assessment*, 1982, *4*, 35–40.

Hayes, S. C. Time series methodology and empirical clinical practice. *Journal of Consulting and Clinical Psychology*, 1981, *49*, 193–211.

Hayes, W. A. Radical black behaviorism. In R. L. Jones (Ed.), *Black psychology*. New York: Harper & Row, 1972.

Haynes, R. B. Introduction. In R. B. Haynes, D. W. Taylor, & D. L. Sackett (Eds.), Compliance in health care. Baltimore: Johns Hopkins University Press, 1979.

Haynes, R. B., Taylor, D. W., & Sackett, D. L. (Eds.). *Compliance in health care.* Baltimore: Johns Hopkins University Press, 1979.

Haynes, S. N., Jensen, B. J., Wise, E., & Sherman, D. The marital intake interview: A multimethod criterion validity assessment. *Journal of Consulting and Clinical Psychology*, 1981, *49*, 379–387.

Haywood, H. C., Meyers, C. E., & Switzky, H. N. Mental retardation. *Annual Review of Psychology*, 1982, *33*, 309–342.

Haywood, H. C., & Newbrough, J. R. (Eds.). *Living environments for developmentally retarded persons.* Baltimore: University Park Press, 1981.

Heaton, R. C., & Safer, D. J. Secondary school outcome following a junior high school behavioral program. *Behavior Therapy*, 1982, *13*, 226–231.

Hechtman, L., Weiss, G., Perlman, T., Hopkins, J., & Wener, A. Hyperactive children in young adulthood: A controlled, prospective, ten-year follow-up. In M. Gittelman (Ed.), *Strategic interventions for hyperactive children*. Armonk, N.Y.: M. E. Sharpe, 1981.

Hedges, L. V. Estimation and testing for differences in effect size: A comment on Hsu. *Psychological Bulletin*, 1982, *91*, 691–693.

Heesacker, M., Heppner, P. P., & Rogers, M. E. Classics and emerging classics in counseling psychology. *Journal of Counseling Psychology*, 1982, *29*, 400–405.

Heimberg, R. G., & Becker, R. E. Cognitive and behavioral models of assertive behavior: Review, analysis, and integration. *Clinical Psychology Review*, 1981, *1*, 353–373.

Heimberg, R. G., Cunningham, J., Stanley, J., & Blankenberg, R. Preparing unemployed youth for job interviews: A controlled evaluation of social skills training. *Behavior Modification*, 1982, *6*, 299–322.

Hendrickson, J. M., Strain, P. S., Tremblay, A., & Shores, R. E. Interactions of behaviorally handicapped children: Functional effects of peer social initiation. *Behavior Modification*, 1982, *6*, 323–353.

Heppner, P. P., & Petersen, C. H. The development and implications of a Personal Problem-Solving Inventory. *Journal of Counseling Psychology*, 1982, *29*, 66–75.

Herbert, M. *Emotional problems of development in children*. London: Academic Press, 1974.

Herbert, M. *Conduct disorders of childhood and adolescence: A behavioural approach to assessment and treatment.* Chichester, England: Wiley, 1978.

Herbert, M. *Behavioural treatment of problem children: A practice manual*. London: Academic Press, 1981.

Hersen, M. Modification of skill deficits in psychiatric patients. In A. S. Bellack & M. Hersen (Eds.), *Research and practice in social skills training*. New York: Plenum, 1979.

Hersen, M. Complex problems require complex solutions. *Behavior Therapy*, 1981, *12*, 15–29.

Hersen, M., & Bellack, A. S. (Eds.). *Behavioral assessment: A practical handbook* (2nd ed.). New York: Pergamon, 1982.

Hersen, M., Bellack, A. S., & Himmelhoch, J. M. A comparison of solicited and non-solicited female unipolar depressives for treatment outcome research. *Journal of Consulting and Clinical Psychology*, 1981, *49*, 611–613.

Hertzler, A. A. Obesity—Impact of the family. *Journal of the American Dietetic Association*, 1981, *79*, 525–530.

Hilgard, E. R., & Marquis, D. G. *Conditioning and learning*. New York: Appleton-Century, 1940.

Hirayama, T. Nonsmoking wives of heavy smokers have a higher risk of lung cancer: A study from Japan. *British Medical Journal*, 1981, 282, 163–165.

Hitchcock, L. S. *Improving recovery from surgery: The interaction of preoperative interventions, coping processes, and personality variables.* Unpublished doctoral dissertation, University of Texas, 1982.

Hobbs, S. A., Moguin, L. E., Tyroler, N., & Lahey, B. B. Cognitive-behavior therapy with children: Has clinical utility been demonstrated? *Psychological Bulletin*, 1980, *87*, 147–165.

Hodgson, R., & Rachman, S. Desynchrony in measures of fear II. *Behaviour Research and Therapy*, 1974, *12*, 319–326.

Holden, C. Behavioral medicine: An emergent field. *Science*, 1980, *209*, 479–481.

Hollon, S. D., & Beck, A. T. Psychotherapy and drug therapy: Comparisons and combinations. In S. L. Garfield & A. E. Bergin (Eds.), *Handbook of psychotherapy and behavior change* (2nd ed.). New York: Wiley, 1979.

Hollon, S. D., & DeRubeis, R. J. Placebo–psychotherapy combinations: Inappropriate representations of psychotherapy in drug–psychotherapy comparative trials. *Psychological Bulletin*, 1981, *90*, 467–477.

Hollon, S. D., & Kendall, P. C. Cognitive self-statements in depression: Development of an automatic thoughts questionnaire. *Cognitive Therapy and Research*, 1980, *4*, 383–395.

Holroyd, K. A. Cognition and desensitization in the group treatment of test anxiety. *Journal of Consulting and Clinical Psychology*, 1976, *44*, 991–1001.

Holroyd, K. A., & Andrasik, F. A cognitive–behavioral approach to recurrent tension and migraine headache. In P. C. Kendall (Ed.), *Advances in cognitive–behavioral research and therapy* (Vol. 1). New York: Academic Press, 1982.

Holroyd, K. A., Andrasik, F., & Westbrook, T. Cognitive control of tension headache. *Cognitive Therapy and Research*, 1977, *1*, 121–133.

Homer, A. L., & Peterson, L. Differential reinforcement of other behavior: A preferred response elimination procedure. *Behavior Therapy*, 1980, *11*, 449–471.

Horn, D. Modifying smoking habits in high school students. *Children*, 1960, *7*, 63–68.

Horn, W. F., & Haynes, S. N. An investigation of sex bias in behavioral observations and ratings. *Behavioral Assessment*, 1981, *3*, 173–183.

Horowitz, L. M., Weckler, D. A., & Doren, R. Interpersonal problems and symptoms: A cognitive approach. In P. C. Kendall (Ed.), *Advances in cognitive–behavioral research and therapy* (Vol. 2). New York: Academic Press, 1983.

Horowitz, L. M., Wright, J. C., Lowenstein, E., & Parad, H. W. The prototype as a construct in abnormal psychology: 1. A method for deriving prototypes. *Journal of Abnormal Psychology*, 1981, *90*, 568–574.

Howard, A. N., & Bray, G. A. (Eds.). Proceedings of a symposium on evaluation of very-low-calorie diets. *International Journal of Obesity*, 1981, *5*, 193–352.

Howard, A. N., Grant, A., Edwards, O., Littlewood, E. R., & McLean Baird, I. The treatment of obesity with a very-low-calorie liquid formula diet: An inpatient–outpatient comparison using skimmed milk as the chief protein source. *International Journal of Obesity*, 1978, *3*, 321–332.

Howell, D. C., & Huessy, H. R. Hyperkinetic behavior followed from seven to twenty-one years of age. In M. Gittelman (Ed.), *Strategic interventions for hyperactive children*. Armonk, N.Y.: M. E. Sharpe, 1981.

Hsu, L. M. Tests of differences in *p* levels as tests of differences in effect sizes. *Psychological Bulletin*, 1980, *88*, 705–708.

Hudson, A. M. Training parents of developmentally handicapped children: A component analysis. *Behavior Therapy*, 1982, *13*, 325–333.

Hugdahl, K. Electrodermal conditioning to potentially phobic stimuli: Effects of instructed extinction. *Behaviour Research and Therapy*, 1978, *16*, 315–321.

Humphrey, L. L. Children's and teachers' perspectives on children's self-control: The development of two rating scales. *Journal of Consulting and Clinical Psychology*, 1982, *50*, 624–633.

Hundert, J. Training teachers in generalized writing of behavior modification programs for multihandicapped deaf children. *Journal of Applied Behavior Analysis*, 1982, *15*, 111–122.

Hunt, D. A., & Rosen, J. C. Thoughts about food by obese and nonobese individuals. *Cognitive Therapy and Research*, 1981, *5*, 317–322.

Hunt, D. E., Butler, L. F., Noy, J. E., & Rosser, M. E. *Assessing conceptual level by the paragraph completion method*. The Ontario Institute for Studies on Education, Informal Series #3, Toronto, 1978.

Hurd, G. S., Pattison, E. M., & Llamas, R. Models of social network intervention. *International Journal of Family Therapy*, 1981, *3*, 246–257.

Hurd, P. D., Johnson, C. A., Pechacek, T., Bast, L. P., Jacobs, D. R., & Luepker, R. V. Prevention of cigarette smoking in seventh-grade students. *Journal of Behavioral Medicine*, 1980, *3*, 15–28.

Hussian, R. A. *Stimulus control in the modification of problematic behavior in elderly institutionalized patients*. Paper presented at the annual meeting of the Association for Advancement of Behavior Therapy, New York, 1980.

Hussian, R. A., & Lawrence, P. S. Social reinforcement of activity and problem-solving training in the treatment of depressed institutionalized elderly patients. *Cognitive Therapy and Research*, 1981, *5*, 57–69.

Hygge, S., & Öhman, A. Modeling processes in the acquisition of fears: Vicarious electrodermal conditioning to fear-relevant stimuli. *Journal of Personality and Social Psychology*, 1978, *36*, 271–279.

Institute of Medicine, National Academy of Sciences. *Health and behavior: Frontiers of research in the biomedical sciences*. Washington, D.C.: National Academy Press, 1982.

Isaacs, C. D. A brief review of the characteristics of abuse-prone parents. *The Behavior Therapist*, 1981, *4*(3), 5–8.

Isaacs, C. D. Treatment of child abuse: A review of the behavioral interventions. *Journal of Applied Behavior Analysis*, 1982, *15*, 273–294.

Israel, A. C., Stolmaker, L., & Prince, B. *The relationship between impulsivity and eating behavior in children*. Unpublished manuscript, State University of New York at Albany, 1982.

Ivancic, M. T., Reid, D. H., Iwata, B. A., Faw, G. D., & Page, T. J. Evaluating a supervision program for developing and maintaining therapeutic staff–resident interactions during institutional care routines. *Journal of Applied Behavior Analysis*, 1981, *14*, 95–107.

Jackson, J. L. A behavioral assessment course. *Behavioral Assessment*, 1982, *4*, 47–51.

Jacobs, M. K., & Cochran, S. D. The effects of cognitive restructuring on assertive behavior. *Cognitive Therapy and Research*, 1982, *6*, 63–76.

Jacobson, N. S. Specific and nonspecific factors in the effectiveness of a behavioral approach to the treatment of marital discord. *Journal of Consulting and Clinical Psychology*, 1978, *46*, 442–452.

Jacobson, N. S., Elwood, R. W., & Dallas, M. Assessment of marital dysfunction. In D. H. Barlow (Ed.), *Behavioral assessment of adult disorders*. New York: Guilford 1981.

Jason, L. A. Prevention and environmental modification in a behavioral community model. *Behavioral Counseling Quarterly*, 1981, *1*, 91–107. (a)

Jason, L. A. Training undergraduates in behavior therapy and behavioral community psychology. *Behaviorists for Social Action Journal*, 1981, *3*, 1–8. (b)

Jason, L. A., & Bogat, G. A. Preventive behavioral interventions. In R. D. Felner, L. A. Jason, J. Moritsugu, & S. S. Farber (Eds.), *Preventive psychology: Theory, research and practice*. New York: Pergamon, 1983.

Jason, L. A., & Ferrone, L. From early secondary to primary preventive interventions in schools. *Journal of Prevention*, 1981, *1*, 156–173.

Jason, L. A., & Frasure, S. Monitoring and changing behaviors in supermarket managers and consumers. *Man–Environment Systems*, 1980, *10*, 288–290.

Jason, L. A., & Glenwick, D. S. Future directions: A critical look at the behavioral community approach. In D. S. Glenwick & L. A. Jason (Eds.), *Behavioral community psychology: Progress and prospects*. New York: Praeger, 1980.

Jason, L. A., & Liotta, R. Pedestrian jaywalking under facilitating and nonfacilitating conditions. *Journal of Applied Behavior Analysis*, 1982, *15*, 469–473.

Jason, L. A., Mollica, M., & Ferrone, L. Evaluating an early secondary smoking prevention intervention. *Preventive Medicine*, 1982, *11*, 96–102.

Jason, L. A., & Ziolik, E. S. Characteristics of behavioral community interventions. *Professional Psychology*, 1981, *12*, 769–775.

Jayaratne, S. A study of clinical eclecticism. *Social Science Review*, 1978, *52*, 621–631.

Jeffery, R. W., Vender, M., & Wing, R. R. Weight loss and behavior change one year after behavioral treatment for obesity. *Journal of Consulting and Clinical Psychology*, 1978, *46*, 368–369. (a)

Jeffery, R. W., Wing, R. R., & Stunkard, A. J. Behavioral treatment of obesity: The state of the art in 1976. *Behavior Therapy*, 1978, *6*, 189–199. (b)

Jeger, A. H., & McClure, G. The effects of a behavioral training program on nonprofessionals' endorsement of the "psychosocial model." *Journal of Consulting Psychology*, 1980, *8*, 49–53.

Jeger, A. M., & Slotnick, R. S. (Eds.). *Community mental health and behavioral ecology: A handbook of theory, research, and practice*. New York: Plenum, 1982.

Jellinek, E. M. *The disease concept of alcoholism*. New Brunswick, N.J.: Hillhouse, 1960.

Jenni, M. A., & Wollersheim, J. P. Cognitive therapy, stress management training, and the type A behavior pattern. *Cognitive Therapy and Research*, 1979, *3*, 61–74.

Johnson, B. F., & Cuvo, A. J. Teaching mentally retarded adults to cook. *Behavior Modification*, 1981, *5*, 187–202.

Johnson, D. W., Maruyama, G., Johnson, R., & Nelson, D. Effects of cooperative, competitive, and individualistic goal structures on achievements: A meta-analysis. *Psychological Bulletin*, 1981, *89*, 47–62.

Johnson, S. M., Bolstad, O. D., & Lobitz, G. K. Generalization and contract phenomena in behavior modification with children. In E. J. Mash, L. A. Hamerlynck, & L. C. Handy (Eds.), *Behavior modification and families*. New York: Brunner/Mazel, 1976.

Johnson, W. G., Wildman, H. E., & O'Brien, T. The assessment of program adherence: The Achilles heel of behavioral weight reduction. *Behavioral Assessment,* 1980, *2,* 297–301.

Johnston, L. D., Bachman, J. G., & O'Malley, P. M. *Drug use among American high school students, 1975–1977.* Rockville, Md.: National Institute on Drug Abuse, 1977.

Jones, R. R., Reid, J. B., & Patterson, G. R. Naturalistic observations in clinical assessment. In P. McReynolds (Ed.), *Advances in psychological assessment* (Vol. 3). San Francisco: Jossey-Bass, 1975.

Kanfer, F. H., & Busemeyer, J. R. The use of problem solving and decision making in behavior therapy. *Clinical Psychology Review,* 1982, *2,* 239–266.

Kanfer, F. H., & Karoly, P. The psychology of self-management: Abiding issues and tentative directions. In P. Karoly & F. H. Kanfer (Eds.), *Self-management and behavior change: From theory to practice.* New York: Pergamon, 1982.

Kannel, W. B., & Dawber, T. R. Atherosclerosis as a pediatric problem. *Journal of Pediatrics,* 1972, *80,* 544–554.

Kaplan, H. *Disorders of sexual desire.* New York: Brunner/Mazel, 1979.

Karlan, G. R., & Rusch, F. R. Correspondence between saying and doing: Some thoughts on defining correspondence and future directions for application. *Journal of Applied Behavior Analysis,* 1982, *15,* 151–162.

Karoly, P. Person variables in therapeutic change and development. In P. Karoly & J. J. Steffen (Eds.), *Improving the long-term effects of psychotherapy.* New York: Gardner, 1980.

Kazdin, A. E. Assessing the clinical or applied significance of behavior change through social validation. *Behavior Modification,* 1977, *1,* 427–452.

Kazdin, A. E. Imagery elaboration and self-efficacy in the covert modeling treatment of unassertive behavior. *Journal of Consulting and Clinical Psychology,* 1979, *47,* 725–733.

Kazdin, A. E. Acceptability of alternative treatments for deviant child behavior. *Journal of Applied Behavior Analysis,* 1980, *13,* 259–273. (a)

Kazdin, A. E. Acceptability of time out from reinforcement procedures for disruptive child behavior. *Behavior Therapy,* 1980, *11,* 329–344. (b)

Kazdin, A. E. Implications and obstacles for community extensions of behavioral techniques. In D. S. Glenwick & L. A. Jason (Eds.), *Behavioral community psychology: Progress and prospects.* New York: Praeger, 1980. (c)

Kazdin, A. E. *Research design in clinical psychology.* New York: Harper & Row, 1980. (d)

Kazdin, A. E. Acceptability of child treatment techniques: The influence of treatment efficacy and adverse side effects. *Behavior Therapy,* 1981, *12,* 493–506. (a)

Kazdin, A. E. Drawing valid inferences from case studies. *Journal of Consulting and Clinical Psychology,* 1981, *49,* 183–192. (b)

Kazdin, A. E. Applying behavioral principles in the schools. In C. R. Reynolds & T. B. Gutkin (Eds.), *Handbook of school psychology.* New York: Wiley, 1982. (a)

Kazdin, A. E. Current developments and research issues in cognitive–behavioral interventions: A commentary. *School Psychology Review,* 1982, *11,* 75–82. (b)

Kazdin, A. E. The separate and combined effects of covert and overt rehearsal in developing assertive behavior. *Behaviour Research and Therapy,* 1982, *20,* 17–26. (c)

Kazdin, A. E. Single-case experimental designs. In P. C. Kendall & J. N. Butcher (Eds.), *Handbook of research methods in clinical psychology.* New York: Wiley, 1982. (d)

Kazdin, A. E. The token economy: A decade later. *Journal of Applied Behavior Analysis,* 1982, *15,* 431–445. (e)

Kazdin, A. E., & Bootzin, R. R. The token economy: An evaluative review. *Journal of Applied Behavior Analysis,* 1972, *5,* 343–372.

Kazdin, A. E., & Cole, P. M. Attitudes and labeling biases toward behavior modification: The effects of labels, content, and jargon. *Behavior Therapy*, 1981, *12*, 56–68.

Kazdin, A. E., French, N. H., & Sherick, R. B. Acceptability of alternative treatments for children: Evaluations by inpatient children, parents and staff. *Journal of Counseling and Clinical Psychology*, 1981, *49*, 900–907. (a)

Kazdin, A. E., & Hartmann, D. P. The simultaneous-treatment design. *Behavior Therapy*, 1978, *9*, 912–922.

Kazdin, A. E., & Hersen, M. The current status of behavior therapy. *Behavior Modification*, 1980, *4*, 283–302.

Kazdin, A. E., & Matson, J. L. Social validation in mental retardation. *Applied Research in Mental Retardation*, 1981, *2*, 39–53.

Kazdin, A. E., Matson, J. L., & Esveldt-Dawson, K. Social skill performance among normal and psychiatric inpatient children as a function of assessment conditions. *Behaviour Research and Therapy*, 1981, *19*, 145–152. (b)

Kazdin, A. E., & Wilcoxon, L. A. Systematic desensitization and nonspecific treatment effects: A methodological evaluation. *Psychological Bulletin*, 1976, *83*, 729–758.

Kazdin, A. E., & Wilson, G. T. *Evaluation of behavior therapy: Issues, evidence, and research strategies*. Cambridge, Mass.: Ballinger, 1978.

Keane, T. M., Black, J. L., Collins, F. L., & Vinson, M. C. A skills training program for teaching the behavioral interview. *Behavioral Assessment*, 1982, *4*, 53–62.

Keane, T. M., & Kaloupek, D. G. Imaginal flooding in the treatment of a posttraumatic stress disorder. *Journal of Consulting and Clinical Psychology*, 1982, *50*, 138–140.

Keefe, F. J. Behavioral assessment of chronic pain: Current status and future directions. *Journal of Consulting and Clinical Psychology*, 1982, *50*, 896–911.

Keefe, F. J., & Block, A. R. Development of an observational method for assessing pain behavior in chronic low back pain patients. *Behavior Therapy*, 1982, *13*, 363–375.

Keefe, F. J., Block, A. R., Williams, R. B., & Surwit, R. S. Behavioral treatment of chronic pain: Clinical outcome and individual differences in pain relief. *Pain*, 1981, *11*, 221–231.

Keefe, F. J., & Brown, C. Behavioral treatment of chronic pain. In P. Boudewyns & F. J. Keefe (Eds.), *Behavioral medicine in general medical practice*. Menlo Park, Calif.: Addison-Wesley, 1982.

Keefe, F. J., Brown, C., Scott, D. S., & Ziesat, H. Behavioral assessment of chronic pain. In F. J. Keefe & J. A. Blumenthal (Eds.), *Assessment strategies in behavioral medicine*. New York: Grune & Stratton, 1982.

Kelley, H. H. Attribution in social interaction. In E. E. Jones, D. E. Kanouse, H. H. Kelley, R. E. Nisbett, S. Valins, & B. Weiner (Eds.), *Attribution: Perceiving the causes of behavior*. Morristown, N.J.: General Learning Press, 1972.

Kelley, M. L., Embry, L. H., & Baer, D. Skills for child management and family support: Training parents for maintenance. *Behavior Modification*, 1979, *3*, 373–396.

Kelley, M. L., & Stokes, T. F. Contingency contracting with disadvantaged youths: Improving classroom performance. *Journal of Applied Behavior Analysis*, 1982, *15*, 447–454.

Kelly, E. L. Clinical psychology—1960. Report of survey of findings. *Newsletter: Division of Clinical Psychology of APA*, 1961, *14*, 1–11.

Kelly, J. A., Wildman, B. S., & Berler, E. S. Small-group behavioral training to improve the job interview skills repertoire of retarded adolescents. *Journal of Applied Behavior Analysis*, 1980, *13*, 461–473.

Kendall, P. C. On the efficacious use of self-instructional procedures with children. *Cognitive Therapy and Research*, 1977, *1*, 331–341.

Kendall, P. C. Cognitive-behavioral interventions with children. In B. B. Lahey &

A. E. Kazdin (Eds.), *Advances in clinical child psychology* (Vol. 4). New York: Plenum, 1981. (a)

Kendall, P. C. One-year follow-up of concrete versus conceptual cognitive–behavioral self-control training. *Journal of Consulting and Clinical Psychology*, 1981, *49*, 748–749. (b)

Kendall, P. C. (Ed.). *Advances in cognitive–behavioral research and therapy* (Vol. 1). New York: Academic Press, 1982. (a)

Kendall, P. C. Cognitive processes and procedures in behavior therapy. In C. M. Franks, G. T. Wilson, P. C. Kendall, & K. Brownell, *Annual review of behavior therapy* (Vol. 8). New York: Guilford Press, 1982. (b)

Kendall, P. C. Individual versus group cognitive–behavioral self-control training: One-year follow-up. *Behavior Therapy*, 1982, *13*, 241–247. (c)

Kendall, P. C. Integration: Behavior therapy and other schools of thought. *Behavior Therapy*, 1982, *13*, 559–571. (d)

Kendall, P. C., & Braswell, L. Assessment for cognitive–behavioral intervention in the schools. *School Psychology Review*, 1982, *11*, 21–31. (a)

Kendall, P. C., & Braswell, L. Cognitive–behavioral self-control therapy for children: A components analysis. *Journal of Consulting and Clinical Psychology*, 1982, *50*, 672–689. (b)

Kendall, P. C., & Brophy, C. Activity and attentional correlates of teacher ratings of hyperactivity. *Journal of Pediatric Psychology*, 1981, *6*, 451–458.

Kendall, P. C., & Butcher, J. N. (Eds.). *Handbook of research methods in clinical psychology*. New York: Wiley, 1982.

Kendall, P. C., & Finch, A. J., Jr. A cognitive–behavioral treatment for impulsivity: A group comparison study. *Journal of Consulting and Clinical Psychology*, 1978, *46*, 110–118.

Kendall, P. C., & Ford, J. D. Reasons for clinical research: Characteristics of contributors and their contributions to the *Journal of Consulting and Clinical Psychology*. *Journal of Consulting and Clinical Psychology*, 1979, *47*, 99–105.

Kendall, P. C., & Hollon, S. D. Assessing self-referent speech: Methods in the measurement of self-statements. In P. C. Kendall & S. D. Hollon (Eds.), *Assessment strategies for cognitive–behavioral interventions*. New York: Academic Press, 1981. (a)

Kendall, P. C., & Hollon, S. D. (Eds.). *Assessment strategies for cognitive–behavioral interventions*. New York: Academic Press, 1981. (b)

Kendall, P. C., & Korgeski, G. P. Assessment and cognitive–behavioral interventions. *Cognitive Therapy and Research*, 1979, *3*, 1–21.

Kendall, P. C., & Kriss, M. R. Cognitive–behavioral interventions. In C. E. Walker (Ed.), *Handbook of clinical psychology*. Homewood, Ill.: Dow Jones-Irwin, 1983.

Kendall, P. C., & Morison, P. Integrating cognitive and behavioral procedures for the treatment of socially isolated children. In A. Meyers & W. E. Craighead (Eds.), *Cognitive behavior therapy with children*. New York: Plenum, 1983.

Kendall, P. C., Nay, W. R., & Jeffers, J. Timeout duration and contrast effects: A systematic evaluation of a successive treatment design. *Behavior Therapy*, 1975, *6*, 609–615.

Kendall, P. C., & Norton-Ford, J. D. Therapy outcome research methods. In P. C. Kendall & J. N. Butcher (Eds.), *Handbook of research methods in clinical psychology*. New York: Wiley, 1982.

Kendall, P. C., Pellegrini, D. S., & Urbain, E. S. Approaches to assessment for cognitive–behavioral interventions with children. In P. C. Kendall & S. D. Hollon (Eds.), *Assessment strategies and cognitive–behavioral interventions*. New York: Academic Press, 1981. (a)

Kendall, P. C., Plous, S., & Kratochwill, T. R. Science and behavior therapy: A survey of research in the 1970's. *Behaviour Research and Therapy*, 1981, *19*, 517–524. (b)

Kendall, P. C., & Turk, D. C. Cognitive–behavioral strategies and health enhancement. In J. D. Matarazzo, N. E. Miller, S. M. Weiss, J. A. Head, & S. M. Weiss (Eds.), *Behavioral health: A handbook of health enhancement and disease prevention*. New York: Wiley, in press.

Kendall, P. C., & Urbain, E. S. Cognitive–behavioral intervention with a hyperactive girl: Evaluation via behavioral observations and cognitive performance. *Behavioral Assessment*, 1981, *3*, 345–357.

Kendall, P. C., & Wilcox, L. E. Self-control in children: The development of a rating scale. *Journal of Consulting and Clinical Psychology*, 1979, *47*, 1020–1030.

Kendall, P. C., & Wilcox, L. E. A cognitive–behavioral treatment for impulsivity: Concrete versus conceptual training in non-self-controlled problem children. *Journal of Consulting and Clinical Psychology*, 1980, *48*, 80–91.

Kendall, P. C., Williams, L., Pechacek, T. F., Graham, L., Shisslak, C., & Herzoff, N. Cognitive–behavioral and patient education interventions in cardiac catheterization procedures: The Palo Alto medical psychology project. *Journal of Consulting and Clinical Psychology*, 1979, *47*, 49–58.

Kendall, P. C., & Zupan, B. A. Individual versus group application of cognitive–behavioral self-control procedures with children. *Behavior Therapy*, 1981, *12*, 344–359.

Kendall, P. C., Zupan, B. A., & Braswell, L. Self-control in children: Further analyses of the self-control rating scale. *Behavior Therapy*, 1981, *12*, 667–681. (c)

Kendrick, M. J., Craig, K. D., Lawson, D. M., & Davidson, P. O. Cognitive and behavioral therapy for musical-performance anxiety. *Journal of Consulting and Clinical Psychology*, 1982, *50*, 353–362.

Kent, R. N., O'Leary, K. D., Diament, C., & Dietz, A. Expectation biases in observational evaluation of therapeutic change. *Journal of Consulting and Clinical Psychology*, 1974, *42*, 774–780.

Kerns, R. D., Turk, D. C., & Holtzman, A. D. Psychological treatment for chronic pain: A selective review. *Clinical Psychology Review*, in press.

Kerr, M. M., Strain, P. S., & Ragland, E. V. Teacher-mediated peer feedback treatment of behaviorally handicapped children: An analysis of effects on positive and negative interactions. *Behavior Modification*, 1982, *6*, 277–290.

Keys, A., Brozek, J., Henschel, A., Mickelson, O., & Taylor, H. L. *The biology of human starvation* (Vols. 1 & 2). Minneapolis: University of Minnesota Press, 1950.

Keyser, V., & Barling, J. Determinants of children's self-efficacy beliefs in an academic environment. *Cognitive Therapy and Research*, 1981, *5*, 29–40.

Khatami, M., & Rush, A. J. A pilot study of the treatment of outpatients with chronic pain: Symptom control, stimulus control, and social system intervention. *Pain*, 1978, *5*, 163–172.

Kiesler, C. A. Mental hospital and alternative care. Noninstitutionalization as potential public policy for mental patients. *American Psychologist*, 1982, *37*, 349–360.

Kiesler, D. J. Some myths of psychotherapy research and the search for a paradigm. *Psychological Bulletin*, 1966, *65*, 110–136.

Kiesler, D. J. Empirical clinical psychology: Myth or reality? *Journal of Consulting and Clinical Psychology*, 1981, *49*, 212–215.

Kiessling, J. J., & Andrews, D. A. Behavior analysis systems in corrections: A new approach to the synthesis of correctional theory, practice, management and research. *Canadian Journal of Criminology*, 1980, *22*, 412–427.

King, D. A., & Buchwald, A. M. Sex differences in subclinical depression: Administration of the Beck Depression Inventory in public and private disclosure situations. *Journal of Personality and Social Psychology*, 1982, *42*, 963–969.

King, L. Comment on "Adoption of innovations from applied behavioral research: 'Does anybody care?'" *Journal of Applied Behavior Analysis*, 1981, *14*, 507–511.

Kingsley, R. G., & Shapiro, J. A comparison of three behavioral programs for control of obesity in children. *Behavior Therapy*, 1977, *8*, 30–36.

Kirigin, K. A., Braukmann, C. J., Atwater, J. D., & Wolf, M. M. An evaluation of teaching-family (Achievement Place) group homes for juvenile offenders. *Journal of Applied Behavior Analysis*, 1982, *15*, 1–15.

Kirsch, I. Efficacy expectations or response predictions: The meaning of efficacy ratings as a function of task characteristics. *Journal of Personality and Social Psychology*, 1982, *42*, 132–136.

Kirschenbaum, D. S., Humphrey, L. L., & Malett, S. D. Specificity of planning in adult self-control: An applied investigation. *Journal of Personality and Social Psychology*, 1981, *40*, 941–950.

Kirschenbaum, D. S., Malett, S. D., Humphrey, L. L., & Tomarken, A. J. Specificity of planning and the maintenance of self-control: 1-year follow-up of a study improvement program. *Behavior Therapy*, 1982, *13*, 232–240.

Kirschenbaum, D. S., & Tomarken, A. J. On facing the generalization problem: The study of self-regulatory failure. In P. C. Kendall (Ed.), *Advances in cognitive-behavioral research and therapy* (Vol. 1). New York: Academic Press, 1982.

Kirschenbaum, D. S., Tomarken, A. J., & Ordman, A. M. Specificity of planning and choice applied to adult self-control. *Journal of Personality and Social Psychology*, 1982, *42*, 576–585.

Kistner, J., Hammer, D., Wolfe, D., Rothblum, E., & Drabman, R. S. Teacher popularity and contrast effects in a classroom token economy. *Journal of Applied Behavior Analysis*, 1982, *15*, 85–96.

Kitchener, R. F. A critique of Skinnerian ethical principles. *Counseling and Values*, 1979, *23*, 138–147.

Kitchener, R. F. Ethical relativism and behavior therapy. *Journal of Consulting and Clinical Psychology*, 1980, *48*, 1–7. (a)

Kitchener, R. F. Ethical skepticism and behavior therapy: A reply to Ward. *Journal of Consulting and Clinical Psychology*, 1980, *48*, 649–651. (b)

Klass, E. T. A cognitive analysis of guilt over assertion. *Cognitive Therapy and Research*, 1981, *5*, 283–297.

Knapp, J. R., & Delprato, D. J. Willpower, behavior therapy, and the public. *The Psychological Record*, 1980, *30*, 477–482.

Knight, J. A. The essence of ethical codes and oaths. *Journal of Clinical Psychiatry*, 1981, *42*, 222–223.

Koegel, R. L., Egel, A. L., & Williams, J. A. Behavioral contrast and generalization across settings in the treatment of autistic children. *Journal of Experimental Child Psychology*, 1980, *30*, 422–437.

Koegel, R. L., Russo, D. C., & Rincover, A. Assessing and training teachers in the generalized use of behavior modification with autistic children. *Journal of Applied Behavior Analysis*, 1977, *10*, 197–205.

Komaki, J., Collins, R. L., & Thoene, T. J. Behavioral measurement in business, industry, and government. *Behavioral Assessment*, 1980, *2*, 103–123.

Komaki, J. L., & Penn, P. Better business through behaviorism: Welcome to the real world of preventive maintenance. *The Behavior Therapist*, 1982, *5*(5), 159–163.

Korman, M. *Levels and patterns of professional training in psychology.* Washington, D.C.: American Psychological Association, 1976.

Kornitzer, M., DeBacker, G., Dramaix, M., & Thilly, C. The Belgian Heart Disease Prevention Project. *Circulation*, 1980, *61*, 18–25.

Kraemer, H. C., & Andrews, G. A nonparametric technique for meta-analysis effect size calculation. *Psychological Bulletin*, 1982, *91*, 404–412.

Krantz, D. S. A naturalistic study of social influences on meal size among moderately obese and nonobese subjects. *Psychosomatic Medicine*, 1979, *41*, 19–27.

Krasner, L. Behavior therapy. *Annual Review of Psychology*, 1971, *22*, 483–552.

Kratochwill, T. R., & Levin, J. R. On the applicability of various data analysis procedures to the simultaneous and alternating treatment designs in behavior therapy research. *Behavioral Assessment*, 1980, *2*, 353–360.

Kreitner, R. Managerial reaction to the term "behavior modification." *Journal of Organizational Behavior Management*, 1981, *3*(2), 53–58.

Kremer, E., Block, A., & Gaylor, M. Behavioral approaches to chronic pain: The inaccuracy of patient self-report measures. *Archives of Physical Medicine and Rehabilitation*, 1981, *62*, 188–191.

La Greca, A. M. Children's social skills: An overview. *Journal of Pediatric Psychology*, 1981, *6*, 335–342.

Lahey, B., Green, K., & Forehand, R. On the independence of ratings of hyperactivity, conduct problems, and attention deficits in children: A multiple regression analysis. *Journal of Consulting and Clinical Psychology*, 1980, *48*, 566–574.

Lahey, B. B., & Rubinoff, A. Behavior therapy in education. In L. Michelson, M. Hersen, & S. M. Turner (Eds.), *Future perspectives in behavior therapy*. New York: Plenum, 1981.

Lambourne, R. D., & Wheldall, K. Estimation by microcomputer of interobserver agreement in duration recoding of behavior. *Behavioral Psychotherapy*, 1982, *10*, 48–53.

Lancioni, G. E. Normal children as tutors to teach social responses to withdrawn mentally retarded schoolmates: Training, maintenance, and generalization. *Journal of Applied Behavior Analysis*, 1982, *15*, 17–40.

Landau, R. J. The role of semantic schemata in phobic word interpretation. *Cognitive Therapy and Research*, 1980, *4*, 427–434.

Landau, R. J., & Goldfried, M. R. The assessment of schemata: A unifying framework for cognitive, behavioral, and traditional assessment. In P. C. Kendall & S. D. Hollon (Eds.), *Assessment strategies for cognitive–behavioral interventions*. New York: Academic Press, 1981.

Landman, J. T., & Dawes, R. M. Psychotherapy outcome: Smith and Glass' conclusions stand up under scrutiny. *American Psychologist*, 1982, *37*, 504–516.

Landy, F. J. What have you done for me lately? Review of E. E. Lawler's *Pay and Organization Development. Contemporary Psychology*, 1982, *27*, 282–284.

Lang, P. J. The mechanics of desensitization and the laboratory study of fear. In C. M. Franks (Ed.), *Behavior therapy: Appraisal and status*. New York: McGraw-Hill, 1969.

Lang, P. J. A bio-informational theory of emotional imagery. *Psychophysiology*, 1979, *16*, 495–512.

Langer, E. Rethinking the role of thought in social interaction. In J. Harvey, W. Ickes, & R. Kidd (Eds.), *New directions in attribution research* (Vol. 2). Hillsdale, N.J.: Lawrence Erlbaum, 1978.

Langer, E., & Abelson, W. A patient by any other name: Clinician group differences in labeling bias. *Journal of Consulting and Clinical Psychology*, 1974, *42*, 4–9.

Lansky, D., & Brownell, K. D. Estimates of food quantity and calories: Errors in self-report among obese patients. *American Journal of Clinical Nutrition*, 1982, *35*, 727–732.

La Porte, D. J., McLellan, A. T., Erdlen, F. R., & Parente, R. J. Treatment outcome as a function of follow-up difficulty in substance abusers. *Journal of Consulting and Clinical Psychology*, 1981, *49*, 112–119.

Last, C. G., Barlow, D. H., & O'Brien, G. T. *Cognitive changes during in vivo exposure in an agoraphobic.* Unpublished manuscript, SUNY Albany, 1982.

Latham, G. P., & Sarri, L. M. Application of social learning theory to training supervisors through behavioral modeling. *Journal of Applied Psychology*, 1979, *64*, 239–246.

Latimer, P. R. External contingency management for chronic pain: Critical review of the evidence. *American Journal of Psychiatry*, 1982, *139*, 1308–1312.

Laughlin, T. J., & Lake, F. R. Social-psychological aspects of cigarette smoking. *Canadian Journal of Public Health*, 1970, *61*, 301–312.

Lawler, E. E. *Pay and organization development.* Reading, Mass.: Addison-Wesley, 1981.

Lawton, M. P. Community supports for the aged. *Journal of Social Issues*, 1981, *37*, 102–115.

Lazarus, A. A. *Multimodal behavior therapy.* New York: Springer, 1976.

Lazarus, A. A., & Fay, A. Resistance or rationalization? A cognitive–behavioral perspective. In P. L. Wachtel (Ed.), *Resistance: Psychodynamic and behavioral approaches.* New York: Plenum, 1982.

LeBow, M. D. *Weight control: The behavioural strategies.* New York: Wiley, 1981.

LeBow, M. D. Obstacles to treating obese children effectively. *Child Behavior Therapy*, 1982, *3*, 29–39.

Lebowitz, M. D., & Burrows, B. Respiratory symptoms related to smoking habits of family adults. *Chest*, 1976, *69*, 48–50.

Lefebvre, M. F. Cognitive distortion and cognitive errors in depressed psychiatric and low back pain patients. *Journal of Consulting and Clinical Psychology*, 1981, *49*, 517–525.

Lehrer, P. Rehabilitation and behavior modification. In M. Berkowitz (Ed.), *An evaluation of policy-related rehabilitation research.* New York: Praeger, 1975.

Lehrer, P. How to relax and how not to relax: A re-evaluation of the work of Edmund Jacobson—I. *Behaviour Research and Therapy*, 1982, *20*, 417–428.

Lehrer, P., & Lanoil, J. Natural reinforcement in a psychiatric rehabilitation program. *Schizophrenia Bulletin*, 1977, *3*, 297–303.

Lepper, M. R., & Greene, D. *The hidden cost of reward: New perspectives on the psychology of human motivation.* Hillsdale, N.J.: Erlbaum, 1978.

Lester, G. W., Beckham, E., & Baucom, D. H. Implementation of behavioral marital therapy. *Journal of Marital and Family Therapy*, 1980, *6*, 189–199.

Levendusky, P., & Pankratz, L. Self-control techniques as an alternative to pain medication. *Journal of Abnormal Psychology*, 1975, *84*, 165–169.

Levant, R. F., & Slattery, S. C. Systematic skills training for foster parents. *Journal of Clinical Child Psychology*, 1982, *11*, 138–143.

Leventhal, H., & Cleary, P. D. The smoking problem: A review of the research and theory in behavioral risk modification. *Psychological Bulletin*, 1980, *88*, 370–405.

Leventhal, H., & Niles, P. Persistence of influence for varying durations of exposure to threat stimuli. *Psychological Reports*, 1965, *16*, 223–233.

Leventhal, H., Safer, M. A., Cleary, P. D., & Gutmann, M. Cardiovascular risk modification by community-based programs for life-style change: Comments on the Stanford study. *Journal of Consulting and Clinical Psychology*, 1980, *48*, 150–158.

Levey, A. B., & Martin, I. Cognitions, evaluations and conditioning: Rules of sequence and rules of consequence. *Advances in Behaviour Research and Therapy*, in press.

Leviton, L. C., & Cook, T. D. What differentiates meta-analysis from other forms of review? *Journal of Personality*, 1981, *49*, 231–236.

Lewinsohn, P. M. *The unpleasant events schedule.* Mimeograph, University of Oregon, 1975.

Lewinsohn, P. M., & Graf, M. Pleasant activities and depression. *Journal of Consulting and Clinical Psychology,* 1973, *41,* 261–268.

Lewinsohn, P. M., & Lee, W. M. L. Assessment of affective disorders. In D. H. Barlow (Ed.), *Behavioral assessment of adult disorders.* New York: Guilford, 1981.

Lewinsohn, P. M., Steinmetz, J. L., Larson, D. W., & Franklin, J. Depression-related cognitions: Antecedent or consequence? *Journal of Abnormal Psychology,* 1981, *90,* 213–219.

Lewinsohn, P. M., & Teri, L. Selection of depressed and nondepressed subjects on the basis of self-report data. *Journal of Consulting and Clinical Psychology,* 1982, *50,* 590–591.

Ley, P. Memory for medical information. *British Journal of Social and Clinical Psychology,* 1979, *18,* 245–255.

Ley, P. *Communication variables in health education.* London: Health Education Council Monographs, 1980. (a)

Ley, P. Practical methods of improving communication. *Banbury Report 6: Product Labeling and Health Risk,* 1980, 135–146. (b)

Ley, P. Professional non-compliance: A neglected problem. *British Journal of Clinical Psychology,* 1981, *20,* 151–154.

Ley, P. Giving information to patients. In J. R. Eiser (Ed.), *Social psychology and behavioral science.* New York: Wiley, 1982.

Liberman, R. P. Review of *Psychosocial treatment for chronic mental patients* by Gordon L. Paul and Robert J. Lentz. *Journal of Applied Behavior Analysis,* 1980, *13,* 367–372.

Lieberman, D. A. Behaviorism and the mind: A (limited) call for a return to introspection. *American Psychologist,* 1979, *34,* 319–333.

Lieberman, M. A., Yalom, I. D., & Miles, S. M. B. *Encounter groups: First facts.* New York: Basic Books, 1973.

Lieff, J. D., & Brown, R. A. A psychogeriatric nursing home resocialization program. *Hospital & Community Psychiatry,* 1981, *32,* 862–865.

Lindner, P. G., & Blackburn, G. L. An interdisciplinary approach to obesity utilizing fasting modified by protein-sparing therapy. *Obesity/Bariatric Medicine,* 1976, *5,* 198–216.

Linehan, M. M., Goldfried, M. R., & Goldfried, A. Assertion therapy: Skill training or cognitive restructuring. *Behavior Therapy,* 1979, *10,* 372–388.

Linn, R. *The last chance diet.* Secaucus, N.J.: Lyle Stuart, 1976.

Litt, M. D., & Schreibman, L. Stimulus-specific reinforcement in the acquisition of receptive labels by autistic children. *Analysis and Intervention in Developmental Disabilities,* 1981, *1,* 171–186.

Lloyd, R. W., & Salzberg, H. C. Controlled social drinking: An alternative to abstinence as a treatment goal for some alcohol abusers. *Psychological Bulletin,* 1975, *82,* 815–842.

Lobitz, W. C., & LoPiccolo, J. New methods in the behavioral treatment of sexual dysfunction. *Journal of Behavior Therapy and Experimental Psychiatry,* 1972, *3,* 265–271.

Locke, E. A. The myths of behavior mod in organizations. *Academy of Management Review,* 1977, *2,* 543–553.

Locke, H. J., & Wallace, K. M. Short marital-adjustment and prediction tests: Their reliability and validity. *Marriage and Family Living,* 1959, *21,* 251–255.

Loney, J. Hyperkinesis comes of age: What do we know and where should we go? *American Journal of Orthopsychiatry,* 1980, *50,* 28–42.

Loney, J. Hyperactivity a nonprofessional term? *Contemporary Psychology*, 1982, *27*, 483.

Loney, J., Kramer, J., & Milich, R. The hyperkinetic child grows up: Predictions of symptoms, delinquency, and achievement at follow-up. In K. Gadow & J. Loney (Eds.), *Psycho-social aspects of drug treatment for hyperactivity*. Boulder, Colo.: Westview Press, 1983.

Loney, J., Langhorne, J., & Paternite, C. An empirical basis for subgrouping the hyperkinetic/minimal brain dysfunction syndrome. *Journal of Abnormal Psychology*, 1978, *87*, 431–441.

LoPiccolo, J., & LoPiccolo, L. (Eds.). *Handbook of sex therapy*. New York: Plenum, 1978.

Lovibond, S. H., & Caddy, G. Discriminated aversive control in the moderation of alcoholics' drinking behavior. *Behavior Therapy*, 1970, *1*, 437–444.

Luborsky, L., Singer, B., & Luborsky, L. Comparative studies of psychotherapies. *Archives of General Psychiatry*, 1975, *32*, 995–1008.

Luiselli, J. K. Evaluation of a classroom-based language training program to teach mentally retarded children how to give personal information. *Australia and New Zealand Journal of Developmental Disabilities*, 1982, *8*, 27–32.

Luiselli, J. K., Pollow, R. S., Colozzi, S. A., & Teitelbaum, M. Application of differential reinforcement to control disruptive behaviours of mentally retarded students during remedial instruction. *Journal of Mental Deficiency Research*, 1981, *25*, 265–273.

Luthans, F., & Davis, T. R. V. Behavioral self-management—The missing link in managerial effectiveness. *Organizational Dynamics*, 1979, *6*, 42–60.

Lysakowski, R. S., & Walberg, H. J. Classroom reinforcement and learning: A quantitative synthesis. *Journal of Educational Research*, 1981, *75*, 69–77.

MacIntosh, N. J. Cognitive or associative theories of conditioning: Implications of an analysis of blocking. In S. Hulse, H. Fowler, & W. Honig (Eds.), *Cognitive processes in animal behavior*. Hillsdale, N.J.: Lawrence Erlbaum, 1978.

MacPhillamy, D. J., & Lewinsohn, P. M. *The pleasant events schedule*. Mimeograph, University of Oregon, 1971.

Mahoney, M. J. *The scientist as subject: The psychological imperative*. Cambridge, Mass.: Ballinger, 1976.

Mann, G. V. The influence of obesity on health. *New England Journal of Medicine*, 1974, *291*, 178–185; 226–232.

Marchetti, A., & Matson, J. L. Training skills for community adjustments. In J. L. Matson & J. R. McCartney (Eds.), *Handbook of behavior modification with the mentally retarded*. New York: Plenum, 1981.

Marchetti, B. M., Rusch, F. R., & Lamson, D. S. Social validation of behavioral training techniques: Assessing the normalizing qualities of competitive employment training procedures. *TASH Journal*, 1981, *6*, 6–16.

Margolin, G., & Wampold, B. E. Sequential analysis of conflict and accord in distressed and nondistressed marital partners. *Journal of Consulting and Clinical Psychology*, 1981, *49*, 554–567.

Markman, H. J. Prediction of marital distress: A 5-year follow-up. *Journal of Consulting and Clinical Psychology*, 1981, *49*, 760–762.

Marks, I. Behavioural concepts and treatment of neuroses. *Behavioural Psychotherapy*, 1981, *9*, 137–154. (a)

Marks, I. M. Behavioural psychotherapy and the behavioural sciences. *Behavioural Psychotherapy*, 1981, *9*, 285–286. (b)

Marks, I. M. *Cure and care of the neuroses: Theory and practice of behavioural psychotherapy*. New York: Wiley, 1981. (c)

Marks, I., Bird, J., & Lindley, P. Behavioural nurse therapists 1978—Developments and implications. *Behavioural Psychotherapy*, 1978, *6*, 25–36.

Marks, I. M., & Mathews, A. Brief standard self-rating for phobic patients. *Behaviour Research and Therapy*, 1979, *17*, 263–267.

Marks, I. M., Stern, R., Mawson, D., Cobb, J., & McDonald, R. Clomipramine and exposure for obsessive–compulsive rituals: I. *British Journal of Psychiatry*, 1980, *136*, 1–25.

Markus, H. Self-schemata and processing information about the self. *Journal of Personality and Social Psychology*, 1977, *35*, 63–78.

Marlatt, G. A. *Relapse prevention*. New York: Guilford, in press.

Martin, B. Brief family intervention: Effectiveness and the importance of including the father. *Journal of Consulting and Clinical Psychology*, 1977, *45*, 1002–1010.

Martin, J. E., & Dubbert, P. M. Exercise applications and promotion in behavioral medicine: Current status and future directions. *Journal of Consulting and Clinical Psychology*, 1982, *50*, 1004–1017.

Marzillier, J. S. *Report of the British Psychological Society Working Party on Behaviour Modification*. London: British Psychological Society, 1977.

Masek, B. J., & Jankel, W. R. Therapeutic adherence. In D. C. Russo & J. W. Varni (Eds.), *Behavioral perdiatrics: Research and practice*. New York: Plenum, 1982.

Mash, E. J., & Terdal, L. G. (Eds.). *Behavioral assessment of childhood disorders*. New York: Guilford, 1981.

Masters, W., & Johnson, V. *Human sexual inadequacy*. Boston: Little, Brown, 1970.

Matarazzo, J. D. Behavioral health and behavioral medicine: Frontiers for a new health psychology. *American Psychologist*, 1980, *35*, 807–817.

Matarazzo, J. D. Behavioral health's challenge to academic, scientific, and professional psychology. *American Psychologist*, 1982, *37*, 1–14.

Mathews, A. M., Gelder, M. G., & Johnston, D. W. *Agoraphobia: Nature and treatment*. New York: Guilford, 1981.

Mathews, A. M., Johnston, D. W., Lancashire, M., Munby, M., Shaw, P. M., & Gelder, M. G. Imaginal flooding and exposure to real phobic situations: Treatment outcome with agoraphobic patients. *British Journal of Psychiatry*, 1976, *129*, 362–371.

Mathews, A. M., Teasdale, J., Munby, M., Johnston, D. W., & Shaw, P. M. A home-based treatment program for agoraphobia. *Behavior Therapy*, 1977, *8*, 915–924.

Matson, J. L. Teaching shopping skills to mildly retarded adults with independence training. *American Journal of Mental Deficiency*, in press.

Matson, J. L., & Kazdin, A. E. Punishment in behavior modification: Pragmatic, ethical, and legal issues. *Clinical Psychology Review*, 1981, *1*, 197–210.

Matson, J. L., & McCartney, J. R. (Eds.). *Handbook of behavior modification with the mentally retarded*. New York: Plenum, 1981.

Matson, J. L., & Senatore, V. A comparison of traditional psychotherapy and social skills training for improving interpersonal functioning of mentally retarded adults. *Behavior Therapy*, 1981, *12*, 369–382.

Matson, J. L., Zeiss, A. M., Zeiss, R. A., & Bowman, W. A comparison of social skills training and contingent attention to improve behavioural deficits of chronic psychiatric patients. *British Journal of Social and Clinical Psychology*, 1980, *19*, 57–64.

Mawhinney, T. C., & Taylor, L. *Effects of monetary reinforcers on reinforcement value of task activity*. Paper presented at the annual meeting of the Association for Behavior Analysis, May 1981.

May, J. G., Risley, T. R., Twardosz, S., Friedman, P., Bijou, S. W., & Wexler, D. *Guidelines for the use of behavioral procedures in state programs for retarded persons*. Arlington, Tex.: National Association for Retarded Citizens, 1976.

Mayer, J. *Overweight: Causes, cost, and control.* Englewood Cliffs, N.J.: Prentice-Hall, 1968.

McAlister, A. L., Perry, C., Killen, J., Slinkard, L. A., & Maccoby, N. Pilot study of smoking, alcohol, and drug abuse prevention. *American Journal of Public Health,* 1980, *70,* 719–721.

McAlister, A. L., Perry, C., & Maccoby, N. Adolescent smoking: Onset and prevention. *Pediatrics,* 1979, *63,* 650–658.

McAuley, P. Teaching behaviour therapy skills to social work students. *British Journal of Social Work,* 1981, *11,* 203–215.

McCann, B. S. *Implications of the ethical and epistemological foundations of behavior therapy.* Unpublished manuscript, Rutgers University, New Brunswick, N.J., 1982.

McCartney, J. R., & Holden, J. C. Toilet training for the mentally retarded. In J. L. Matson & J. R. McCartney (Eds.), *Handbook of behavior modification with the mentally retarded.* New York: Plenum, 1981.

McClure, L., Cannon, D., Allen, S., Belton, E., Connor, P., D'Ascoli, C., Stone, P., Sullivan, B., & McClure, G. Community psychology: Concepts and research base. *American Psychologist,* 1980, *35,* 1000–1011.

McCordick, S. M., Kaplan, R. M., Smith, S., & Finn, M. E. Variations in cognitive behavior modification for test anxiety. *Psychotherapy: Theory, Research, and Practice,* 1981, *18,* 170–178.

McDowell, J. J. The importance of Herrnstein's mathematical statement of the law of effect for behavior therapy. *American Psychologist,* 1982, *37,* 771–779.

McFall, R. M. A review and reformulation of the concept of social skills. *Behavioral Assessment,* 1982, *4,* 1–33.

McFall, R. M., & Lillisand, D. B. Behavioral rehearsal with modeling and coaching in assertion training. *Journal of Abnormal Psychology,* 1971, *77,* 313–323.

McGandy, R. B. Methodological aspects of nutritional surveys of young and middle-aged adults. *American Journal of Clinical Nutrition,* 1982, *35,* 1269–1272.

McGovern, H. N., Fernald, C. D., & Calhoun, L. G. Perceptions of behavior and humanistic therapies. *Journal of Community Psychology,* 1980, *8,* 152–154.

McGuire, W. J. Behavioral medicine, public health, and communication theories. *National Forum,* Winter 1980, pp. 18–24.

McKennell, A. C. British research into smoking behavior. In E. F. Birgatta & R. R. Evans (Eds.), *Smoking, health, and behavior.* Chicago: Aldine, 1968.

McMahon, R. J., Forehand, R., Griest, D. L., & Wells, K. C. Who drops out of treatment during parent behavior training? *Behavioral Counseling Quarterly,* 1981, *1,* 79–85.

McNally, R. J., & Reiss, S. The preparedness theory of phobias and human safety-signal conditioning. *Behaviour Research and Therapy,* 1982, *20,* 153–159.

McNamara, J. R. Behavior therapy in the seventies: Some changes and current issues. *Psychotherapy: Theory, Research, and Practice,* 1980, *17,* 2–9.

McNamara, J. R., & Andrasik, F. Behavioral intervention in industry and government. In L. Michelson, M. Hersen, & S. M. Turner (Eds.), *Future perspectives in behavior therapy.* New York: Plenum, 1981.

McReynolds, P., & Ferguson, J. T. *Clinical manual for the hospital adjustment scale.* Palo Alto, Calif.: Consulting Psychologists Press, 1953.

McSweeny, A. J., Freemouw, W. J., & Hawkins, R. P. (Eds.). *Practical program evaluation in youth treatment.* Springfield, Ill.: Charles C. Thomas, 1982.

Mealies, L. W., & Duffy, J. F. Nine pitfalls for the training and development specialist. *Personnel Journal,* 1980, *59,* 929–931.

Meehl, P. E. Ethical criticism in value clarification: Correcting cognitive errors within the client's—not the therapist's—framework. *Rational Living,* 1981, pp. 3–9.

Meichenbaum, D. *Cognitive-behavior modification: An integrative approach.* New York: Plenum, 1977.

Meichenbaum, D., & Cameron, R. Cognitive-behavior therapy. In G. T. Wilson & C. M. Franks (Eds.), *Contemporary behavior therapy: Conceptual and empirical foundations.* New York: Guilford, 1982.

Meichenbaum, D., & Gilmore, J. Resistance: From a cognitive–behavioral perspective. In P. Wachtel (Ed.), *Resistance: Psychodynamic and behavioral approaches.* New York: Plenum, 1982.

Meichenbaum, D., & Goodman, J. Training impulsive children to talk to themselves: A means of developing self-control. *Journal of Abnormal Psychology,* 1971, 77, 115–126.

Meichenbaum, D. H., & Turk, D. B. The cognitive–behavioral management of anxiety, anger, and pain. In P. O. Davidson (Ed.), *The behavioral management of anxiety, depression, and pain.* New York: Brunner/Mazel, 1976.

Melamed, B. G., & Siegel, L. J. *Behavioral medicine: Practical applications in health care.* New York: Springer, 1980.

Melin, L., & Götestam, K. G. The effects of rearranging word routines on communication and eating behaviors of psychogeriatric patients. *Journal of Applied Behavior Analysis,* 1981, *14,* 47–51.

Melton, S. B. Effects of a state law permitting minors to consent to psychotherapy. *Professional Psychology,* 1981, *12,* 647–654.

Melzack, R., & Torgerson, W. S. On the language of pain. *Anesthesiology,* 1971, *34,* 50–59.

Merluzzi, T. V., Glass, C. R., & Genest, M. (Eds.). *Cognitive assessment.* New York: Guilford, 1981.

Meyer, A. J., Nash, J. D., McAlister, A. L., Maccoby, N., & Farquhar, J. W. Skills training in a cardiovascular health education program. *Journal of Consulting and Clinical Psychology,* 1980, *48,* 129–142.

Meyer, D. *The positive thinkers: Religion as pop psychology from Mary Baker Eddy to Oral Roberts.* New York: Pantheon, 1980.

Meyers, A. W., & Cohen, R. Cognitive-behavioral intervention in educational settings. In P. C. Kendall (Ed.), *Advances in cognitive–behavioral research and therapy* (Vol. 3). New York: Academic Press, in press.

Meyers, A. W., Meyers, H. H., & Craighead, W. E. Community behavior change: Practical and ethical issues. *Behavior Modification,* 1981, 5, 147–170.

Michelson, L. Behavioral approaches to prevention. In L. Michelson, M. Hersen, & S. M. Turner (Eds.), *Future perspectives in behavior therapy.* New York: Plenum, 1981.

Michelson, L., Foster, S. L., & Ritchey, W. L. Social skills assessment of children. In B. B. Lahey & A. E. Kazdin (Eds.), *Advances in clinical child psychology* (Vol. 4). New York: Plenum, 1981. (a)

Michelson, L., Hersen, M., & Turner, S. M. (Eds.). *Future perspectives in behavior therapy.* New York: Plenum, 1981. (b)

Michelson, L., & Wood, R. Behavioral assessment and training of children's social skills. In M. Hersen, R. M. Eisler, & P. M. Miller (Eds.), *Progress in behavior modification* (Vol. 9). New York: Academic Press, 1980.

Michie, S. The clinical psychologist as agent of social change. *Bulletin of the British Psychological Society,* 1981, *34,* 355–356.

Milich, R., Loney, J., & Landau, S. Independent dimensions of hyperactivity and aggression: A validation with playroom observation data. *Journal of Abnormal Psychology,* 1982, *91,* 183–198.

Miller, D. T., Weinstein, S. M., & Karniol, R. Effects of age and self-verbalization on children's ability to delay gratification. *Developmental Psychology*, 1978, *14*, 569–570.

Miller, J. G. *Living systems*. New York: McGraw-Hill, 1978.

Miller, J. G. *A preliminary report on disability insurance (Report to Ways and Means Committee, U.S. House of Representatives, May–June, 1979)*. Washington, D.C.: U.S. Government Printing Office, 1979.

Miller, L. M. *Behavior management: The new science of managing people at work*. New York: Wiley, 1978.

Miller, N. E. Behavioral medicine: New opportunities but serious dangers. *Behavioral Medicine Update*, 1979, *1*, 508.

Miller, P. M. *Behavioral treatment of alcoholism*. New York: Pergamon, 1976.

Miller, W. R. Review of *The Course of Alcoholism: Four Years after Treatment*, by J. M. Polich, D. J. Armor, & H. B. Braiker. *The Behavior Therapist*, 1982, *5*, 76–77.

Miller, W. R. Controlled drinking: A history and critical review. *Journal of Studies on Alcohol*, in press.

Miller, W. R., & Caddy, G. R. Abstinence and controlled drinking in the treatment of problem drinkers. *Journal of Studies on Alcohol*, 1977, *38*, 986–1003.

Miller, W. R., & Hester, R. K. Treating the problem drinker: Modern approaches. In W. R. Miller (Ed.), *The addictive behaviors: Treatment of alcoholism, drug abuse, smoking, and obesity*. New York: Pergamon, 1980.

Milton, F., & Hafner, J. The outcome of behavior therapy for agoraphobia in relation to marital adjustment. *Archives of General Psychiatry*, 1979, *36*, 807–811.

Mintz, J., Steuer, J., & Jarvik, L. Psychotherapy with depressed elderly patients: Research considerations. *Journal of Consulting and Clinical Psychology*, 1981, *49*, 542–548.

Mitchell, K. R., & Mitchell, D. M. An exploratory treatment application of programmed behavior therapy techniques. *Journal of Psychosomatic Research*, 1971, *15*, 137–157.

Mitchell, K. R., & White, R. G. Behavioral self-management: An application to the problem of migraine headaches. *Behavior Therapy*, 1977, *8*, 213–222.

Moore, J. On behaviorism and private events. *The Psychological Record*, 1980, *30*, 459–475.

Moos, R. H. The environmental quality of residential care settings. In R. Stough & A. Wandersman (Eds.), *Optimizing environments: Research, practice, and policy*. Washington, D.C.: Environmental Design Research Association, 1980.

Moos, R. H. Environmental choice and control in community care settings for older people. *Journal of Applied Social Psychology*, 1981, *11*, 23–43.

Moreland, J. R., & Schwebel, A. I. A gender-role transcendent perspective on fathering. *Counseling Psychologist*, 1981, *9*, 45–54.

Moreland, J. R., Schwebel, A. I., Beck, S., & Wells, R. Parents as therapists: A review of the behavior therapy literature—1975–1981. *Behavior Modification*, 1982, *6*, 250–276.

Morgan, W. G., & Bass, B. A. Self-control through self-mediated rewards. In R. D. Rubin, J. P. Brady, & J. D. Henderson (Eds.), *Advances in behavior therapy* (Vol. 4). New York: Academic Press, 1973.

Muir, K. A., & Milan, M. A. Parent reinforcement for child achievement: The use of a lottery to maximize parent training efforts. *Journal of Applied Behavior Analysis*, 1982, *15*, 455–460.

Myers, C. W. *The relationship between intensity of maternal punishment and children's interpersonal problem-solving ability*. Unpublished master's thesis, University of South Florida, 1981.

Nagi, S. Z., Riley, L. E., & Newby, L. G. A social epidemiology of back pain in a general population. *Journal of Chronic Disease*, 1973, *26*, 769–779.

Natale, M., & Hantas, M. Effect of temporary mood states on selective memory about the self. *Journal of Personality and Social Psychology*, 1982, *42*, 927–934.

Nathan, P. E., & Briddell, D. W. Behavioral assessment and treatment of alcoholism. In B. Kissen & H. Begleiter (Eds.), *The biology of alcoholism* (Vol. 5). New York: Plenum, 1977.

Nathan, P. E., & Goldman, M. S. Problem drinking and alcoholism. In O. F. Pomerleau & J. P. Brady (Eds.), *Behavioral medicine: Theory and practice*. Baltimore: Williams & Wilkins, 1979.

Neilans, T. H., & Israel, A. C. Towards maintenance and generalization of behavior change: Teaching children self-regulation and self-instructional skills. *Cognitive Therapy and Research*, 1981, *5*, 189–195.

Neisser, U. *Cognition and reality*. San Francisco: Freeman, 1976.

Nelson, R. O. Realistic dependent measures for clinical use. *Journal of Consulting and Clinical Psychology*, 1981, *49*, 168–182.

Nelson, R. O., & Hayes, S. C. Theoretical explanation for reactivity in self-monitoring. *Behavior Modification*, 1981, *5*, 5–14.

Newman, I. M. Peer pressure hypothesis for adolescent cigarette smoking. *School Health Review*, 1970, *1*, 15–20.

Nietzel, M. T., & Bernstein, D. A. Effects of instructionally mediated demand on the behavioral assessment of assertiveness. *Journal of Consulting and Clinical Psychology*, 1976, *44*, 500.

Nietzel, M. T., Winett, R. A., MacDonald, M., & Davidson, W. S. *Behavioral approaches to community psychology*. New York: Pergamon, 1977.

Nirenberg, T. D., Ersner-Hershfield, S., Sobell, L. C., & Sobell, M. B. Behavioral treatment of alcohol problems. In C. K. Prokop & L. A. Bradley (Eds.), *Medical psychology: Contributions to behavioral medicine*. New York: Academic Press, 1981.

Nisbett, R., & Ross, L. *Human inference: Strategies and shortcomings of social judgment*. Englewood Cliffs, N.J.: Prentice-Hall, 1980.

Nisbett, R., & Wilson, T. Telling more than we can know: Verbal reports on mental processes. *Psychological Review*, 1977, *84*, 231–259.

Nord, W. R., & Peter, J. P. A behavior modification perspective on marketing. *Journal of Marketing*, 1980, *44*, 36–47.

Norquist, V. M., & Wahler, R. G. Naturalistic treatment of an autistic child. *Journal of Applied Behavior Analysis*, 1973, *6*, 79–87.

Notarius, C. I. Assessing sequential dependency in cognitive performance data. In T. V. Merluzzi, C. R. Glass, & M. Genest (Eds.), *Cognitive assessment*. New York: Guilford, 1981.

O'Brien, R. M., Dickinson, A. M., & Roscow, M. P. (Eds.). *Industrial behavior modification: A management handbook*. New York: Pergamon, 1982.

O'Brien, T. P., Walley, P. B., Anderson-Smith, S., & Drabman, R. S. Naturalistic observation of the snack-selecting behavior of obese and nonobese children. *Addictive Behaviors*, 1982, *7*, 75–77.

O'Dell, S. L. Enhancing parent involvement training: A discussion. *The Behavior Therapist*, 1982, *5*(1), 9–13.

O'Dell, S. L., O'Quin, J. O., Alford, B. A., O'Briant, A. L., Bradlyn, A. S., & Giebenhain, J. E. Predicting the acquisition of parenting skills via four training methods. *Behavior Therapy*, 1982, *13*, 194–208.

O'Donnell, C. R. Environmental design and the presentation of psychological problems. In M. P. Feldman & J. Orford (Eds.), *The social psychology of psychological problems*. New York: Wiley, 1983.

Öhman, A., Frederikson, M., & Hugdahl, K. Towards an experimental model of simple phobic reactions. *European Journal of Behaviour Analysis and Modification*, 1980.

O'Leary, K. D., & Borkovec, T. D. Conceptual, methodological, and ethical problems of placebo groups in psychotherapy research. *American Psychologist*, 1978, *33*, 821–830.

O'Leary, K. D., & Turkewitz, H. The treatment of marital disorders from a behavioral perspective. In T. J. Paolino & B. S. McCrady (Eds.), *Marriage and the treatment of marital disorders from three perspectives: Psychoanalytic, behavioral and systems theory*. New York: Brunner/Mazel, 1978.

O'Leary, K. D., & Wilson, G. T. *Behavior therapy: Application and outcome* (2nd ed.). Englewood Cliffs, N.J.: Prentice Hall, in press.

O'Leary, S. G., & Steen, P. L. Subcategorizing hyperactivity: The Stony Brook Scale. *Journal of Consulting and Clinical Psychology*, 1982, *50*, 426–432.

Ollendick, T. H., & Cerny, T. A. *Clinical behavior therapy with children*. New York: Plenum, 1981.

Ollendick, T. H., & Hersen, M. Social skills training for juvenile delinquents. *Behaviour Research and Therapy*, in press.

Ollendick, T. H., Shapiro, E. S., & Barrett, R. P. Reducing stereotypic behaviors: An analysis of treatment procedures utilizing an alternating treatments design. *Behavior Therapy*, 1981, *12*, 570–577.

Olson, R. P., Ganley, R., Devine, V. T., & Dorsey, G. C. Long-term effects of behavioral versus insight-oriented therapy with inpatient alcoholics. *Journal of Consulting and Clinical Psychology*, 1981, *49*, 866–877.

O'Neil, P. M., Currey, H. S., Malcolm, R., Francis, W. B., Riddle, F. E., & Sexauer, J. D. Calorie counting by obese and nonobese subjects. *Obesity/Bariatric Medicine*, 1982, *11*, 18–20.

Orford, J., Oppenheimer, E., & Edwards, G. Abstinence or control: The outcome for excessive drinkers two years after consultation. *Behaviour Research and Therapy*, 1976, *14*, 409–418.

Ost, L. G., & Hugdahl, K. Acquisition of phobias and anxiety response patterns in clinical patients. *Behaviour Research and Therapy*, 1981, *19*, 439–447.

Ost, L. G., Jerremalm, A., & Johansson, J. Individual response patterns and the effects of different behavioral methods in the treatment of social phobia. *Behaviour Research and Therapy*, 1981, *19*, 1–16.

Pace, D. M., & Forman, S. S. Variables related to the effectiveness of response cost. *Psychology in the Schools*, 1982, *19*, 365–370.

Page, T. J., Iwata, B. A., & Reid, D. H. Pyramidal training: A large-scale application with institutional staff. *Journal of Applied Behavior Analysis*, 1982, *15*, 335–351.

Painter, J. R., Seres, J. L., & Newman, R. I. Assessing benefits of the pain center: Why some patients regress. *Pain*, 1980, *8*, 101–113.

Palgi, A., Bistrian, B. R., Greenberg, I., & Blackburn, G. L. *Significant weight loss (over 40 pounds) and prolonged maintenance (2–7 years) with medical treatment of obesity*. Unpublished manuscript, Harvard University, 1982.

Palmer, A. B. Some variables contributing to the onset of cigarette smoking among junior high students. *Social Science in Medicine*, 1970, *4*, 359–366.

Parke, R. D., & Collmer, C. W. Child abuse: An interdisciplinary analysis. In E. M. Hetherington (Ed.), *Review of child development research* (Vol. 5). Chicago: University of Chicago Press, 1975.

Parkinson, L., & Rachman, S. Intrusive thoughts: The effects of an uncontrived stress. *Advances in Behaviour Research and Therapy*, 1982, *3*, 111–118. (a)

Parkinson, L., & Rachman, S. The nature of intrusive thoughts. *Advances in Behaviour Research and Therapy*, 1982, *3*, 101–110. (b)

Parrish, J. M., & Erickson, M. T. A comparison of cognitive strategies in modifying the cognitive style of impulsive third-grade children. *Cognitive Therapy and Research*, 1981, *5*, 71–84.

Patterson, G. R. Interventions for boys with conduct problems: Multiple settings, treatments, and criteria. *Journal of Consulting and Clinical Psychology*, 1974, *42*, 471–481.

Patterson, G. R. A performance theory for coercive family interactions. In R. C. Cairns (Ed.), *The analysis of social interactions: Methods, issues and illustrations*. New York: Wiley, 1979.

Patterson, G. R. Mothers: The unacknowledged victims. *Monographs of the Society for Research in Child Development*, 1980, *45* (Serial No. 186).

Patterson, G. R., Chamberlain, P., & Reid, J. B. A comparative evaluation of a parent-training program. *Behavior Therapy*, 1982, *13*, 638–650.

Patterson, G. R., & Fleischman, M. J. Maintenance of treatment effects: Some considerations concerning family systems and follow-up data. *Behavior Therapy*, 1979, *10*, 168–185.

Patterson, G. R., Hops, H., & Weiss, R. L. Interpersonal skills training for couples in early stages of conflict. *Journal of Marriage and the Family*, 1975, *37*, 295–303.

Patterson, R. L., & Jackson, G. M. Behavioral approaches to gerontology. In L. Michelson, M. Hersen, & S. M. Turner (Eds.), *Future perspectives in behavior therapy*. New York: Plenum, 1981.

Patterson, R. L., & Johnson, G. M. Behavior modification with the elderly. In M. Hersen, R. M. Eisler, & P. Miller (Eds.), *Progress in behavior modification* (Vol. 7). New York: Academic Press, 1980.

Pattison, E. M. Nonabstinent drinking goals in the treatment of alcoholism. *Archives of General Psychiatry*, 1976, *33*, 923–930.

Pattison, E. M., Sobell, M. B., & Sobell, L. C. *Emerging concepts of alcohol dependence*. New York: Springer, 1977.

Paul, G. L. Insight versus desensitization in psychotherapy two years after termination. *Journal of Consulting Psychology*, 1967, *31*, 333–348. (a)

Paul, G. L. Strategy of outcome research in psychotherapy. *Journal of Consulting Psychology*, 1967, *31*, 109–119. (b)

Paykel, E. S., Weissman, M., Prusoff, B. A. Dimensions of social adjustment in depressed women. *Journal of Nervous and Mental Disorders*, 1971, *152*, 158–172.

Peale, N. V. *The power of positive thinking*. New York: Prentice-Hall, 1952.

Peele, S. Reductionism in the psychology of the eighties: Can biochemistry eliminate addiction, mental illness, and pain? *American Psychologist*, 1981, *36*, 807–818.

Peltier, B., Telch, M. J., & Coates, T. J. Smoking cessation with adolescents: A comparison of recruiting strategies. *Addictive Behaviors*, 1982, *7*, 71–73.

Pendery, M. L., Maltzman, I. M., & West, L. J. Controlled drinking by alcoholics? New findings and a reevaluation of a major affirmative study. *Science*, 1982, *217*, 169–174.

Perry, C., Killen, J., Telch, M., Slinkard, L. A., & Danaher, B. G. Modifying smoking behavior of teenagers: A school-based intervention. *American Journal of Public Health*, 1980, *70*, 722–724.

Peterson, D. R. Overall synthesis of the Spring Hill Symposium on the future of psychology in the schools. *School Psychology Review*, 1981, *10*, 307–314.

Peterson, D. R. Is psychology a profession? *American Psychologist*, 1976, *31*, 572–581.
Peterson, D. R., Eaton, M. M., Levine, A. R., & Snepp, F. P. Development of doctor of psychology programs and experiences of graduates through 1980. *The Rutgers Professional Psychology Review*, 1980, *2*, 29.
Pevsner, R. Group parent training versus individual family therapy: An outcome study. *Journal of Behavior Therapy and Experimental Psychiatry*, 1982, *13*, 119–122.
Phillips, E. L., Phillips, E. A., Wolf, M. M., & Fixsen, D. L. Achievement Place: Development of the elected manager system. *Journal of Applied Behavior Analysis*, 1973, *6*, 541–561.
Piers, E. V. *Manual for the Piers–Harris Children's Self-Concept Scale (The way I feel about myself)*. Nashville, Tenn.: Counselor Recordings and Tests, 1969.
Piper, G. W., Jones, J. A., & Matthews, V. L. The Saskatoon smoking project: Results of the second year. *Canadian Journal of Public Health*, 1974, *65*, 127–129.
Polich, J. M., Armor, D. J., & Braiker, H. B. *The course of alcoholism: Four years after treatment*. New York: Wiley, 1981.
Pollack, E., & Gittelman, R. Practical problems encountered in behavioral treatment of hyperactive children. In M. Gittelman (Ed.), *Strategic interventions for hyperactive children*. Armonk, N.Y.: M. E. Sharpe, 1981.
Pomerleau, O. F. A discourse on behavioral medicine: Current status and future trends. *Journal of Consulting and Clinical Psychology*, 1982, *50*, 1030–1039.
Pomerleau, O. F., Bass, F., & Crown, V. The role of behavior modification in preventive medicine. *New England Journal of Medicine*, 1975, *292*, 1277–1282.
Pomerleau, O., Pertschuk, M., & Stinnett, J. A critical examination of some current assumptions in the treatment of alcoholism. *Journal of Studies on Alcohol*, 1976, *37*, 849–857.
Popham, R. E., & Schmidt, W. Some factors affecting the likelihood of moderate drinking in treated alcoholics. *Journal of Studies on Alcohol*, 1976, *37*, 868–882.
Popovich, D. *Effective educational and behavioral programming for severely and profoundly handicapped students: A manual for teachers and aides*. Baltimore: Paul H. Brookes, 1981.
Powers, R. B., Duus, R. E., & Norton, R. S. *The commons game: Teaching students about social traps*. Paper presented at the annual meeting of the Rocky Mountain Psychological Association, Las Vegas, 1979.
Presby, S. Overly broad categories obscure important differences between therapies. *American Psychologist*, 1978, *33*, 514–515.
Pressley, M. Increasing children's self-control through cognitive interventions. *Review of Educational Research*, 1979, *49*, 319–370.
Prinz, R. J. A graduate course in behavioral assessment. *Behavioral Assessment*, 1982, *4*, 41–45.
Prinz, R. J., Connor, P. A., & Wilson, C. C. Hyperactive and aggressive behaviors in childhood: Intertwined dimensions. *Journal of Abnormal Child Psychology*, 1981, *9*, 191–202.
Pritchard, R. D., Hollenback, J., & DeLeo, P. J. The effects of continuous and partial schedules of reinforcement on effort, performance, and satisfaction. *Organizational Behavior and Human Performance*, 1980, *25*, 336–353.
Prue, D. M., & Fairbank, J. A. Performance feedback in organizational behavior management: A review. *Journal of Organizational Behavior Management*, 1981, *3*, 1–16.
Prue, D. M., Krapfl, J. E., Noah, J. C., Cannon, S., & Maley, R. F. Managing the treatment activities of state hospital staff. *Journal of Organizational Behavior Management*, 1980, *2*, 165–181.
Quattrochi-Tubin, S., & Jason, L. A. Enhancing social interactions and activity among

the elderly through stimulus control. *Journal of Applied Behavior Analysis*, 1980, *13*, 159–163.

Queiroz, L. O. D. S., Motta, M. A., Madi, M. B. B. P., Sossai, D. L., & Boren, J. J. A functional analysis of obsessive–compulsive problems with related therapeutic procedures. *Behaviour Research and Therapy*, 1981, *19*, 377–388.

Rachlin, H. Self-control. *Behaviorism*, 1974, *2*, 94–107.

Rachman, S. The modification of obsessions: A new formulation. *Behaviour Research and Therapy*, 1976, *14*, 437–444.

Rachman, S. The conditioning theory of fear-acquisition: A critical examination. *Behaviour Research and Therapy*, 1977, *15*, 375–388.

Rachman, S. *Fear and courage*. San Francisco: Freeman, 1978. (a)

Rachman, S. (Ed.). Perceived self-efficacy: Analyses of Bandura's theory of behavioural change. *Advances in Behaviour Research and Therapy*, 1978, *1*, 139–269. (b)

Rachman, S. The primacy of affect: Some theoretical implications. *Behaviour Research and Therapy*, 1981, *19*, 279–290. (a)

Rachman, S. (Ed.). Unwanted intrusive cognitions. *Advances in Behaviour Research and Therapy*, 1981, *3*, 87–123. (b)

Rachman, S., & DeSilva, P. Abnormal and normal obsessions. *Behaviour Research and Therapy*, 1978, *16*, 233–248.

Rachman, S., & Hodgson, R. Synchrony and desynchrony in fear and avoidance: I. *Behaviour Research and Therapy*, 1974, *12*, 311–318.

Rachman, S., & Hodgson, R. *Obsessions and compulsions*. Englewood Cliffs, N.J.: Prentice-Hall, 1980.

Rachman, S., & Wilson, G. T. *The effects of psychological therapy*. Oxford: Pergamon, 1980.

Radloff, L. The CES-D Scale: A self-report depression scale for research in the general population. *Applied Psychological Measurement*, 1977, *1*, 385–401.

Ragland, E. V., Kerr, M. M., & Strain, P. S. Social play of withdrawn children: A study of the effects of teacher-mediated peer feedback. *Behavior Modification*, 1981, *5*, 347–359.

Rambo, W. W. *Work and organizational behavior*. New York: Holt, Rinehart & Winston, 1982.

Rapport, M. D., Murphy, H. A., & Bailey, J. S. Ritalin vs. response cost in the control of hyperactive children: A within-subject comparison. *Journal of Applied Behavior Analysis*, 1982, *15*, 205–216.

Rathus, S. A. A 30-item schedule for assessing assertive behavior. *Behavior Therapy*, 1973, *4*, 398–406.

Raush, H. L. Research, practice and accountability. *American Psychologist*, 1974, *29*, 678–681.

Razran, G. Backward conditioning. *Psychological Bulletin*, 1956, *53*, 55–69.

Reese, H. W. Behavior analysis and life-span developmental psychology. *Developmental Review*, 1980, *2*, 150–161.

Reese, M. Helping human rights committees and clients balance intrusiveness and effectiveness: A challenge for research and therapy. *The Behavior Therapist*, 1982, *5*, 95–99.

Reese, W. G. "Don't count the bricks": Scientific contributions of W. H. Gantt. *Pavlovian Journal of Biological Science*, 1982, *17*, 111–114.

Rehm, L. P. Assessment of depression. In M. Hersen & A. Bellack (Eds.), *Behavioral assessment: A practical handbook*. New York: Pergamon, 1976.

Rehm, L. P. A self-control model of depression. *Behavior Therapy*, 1977, *8*, 787–804.

Rehm, L. P. (Ed.). *Behavior therapy for depression*. New York: Academic Press, 1981.

Reid, J. B., Taplin, P. S., & Lorber, R. A social interactional approach to the treatment of abusive families. In R. Stuart (Ed.), *Violent behavior: Social learning approaches to prediction, management and treatment*. New York: Brunner/Mazel, 1981.

Reinke, B. J., Holmes, D. S., & Denney, N. W. Influence of a "friendly visitor" program on the cognitive functioning and morale of elderly persons. *American Journal of Community Psychology*, 1981, 9, 491–504.

Reitz, A. L., & Hawkins, R. P. Increasing the attendance of nursing home residents at group recreation activities. *Behavior Therapy*, 1982, 13, 283–290.

Repace, J. L., & Lowery, A. H. Indoor air pollution, tobacco smoke, and public health. *Science*, 1980, 208, 464–472.

Repp, A. C., & Deitz, D. E. D. On the selective use of punishment—Suggested guidelines for administrators. *Mental Retardation*, 1978, 16, 250–254.

Revusky, S. Some statistical treatments compatible with individual organism methodology. *Journal of the Experimental Analysis of Behavior*, 1967, 10, 319–330.

Reynolds, M. C. The rights of children: A challenge to school psychologists. In T. R. Kratochwill (Ed.), *Advances in school psychology* (Vol. 2). Hillsdale, N.J.: Lawrence Erlbaum, 1982.

Reynolds, W. M., & Gould, J. W. A psychometric investigation of the standard and short form Beck Depression Inventory. *Journal of Consulting and Clinical Psychology*, 1981, 49, 306–307.

Richardson, F. C. *Theoretical foundation and tacit values of behavior therapy: Some criticisms*. Paper presented at the annual meeting of the Association of Advancement of Behavior Therapy, Toronto, Ontario, November 1981.

Richardson, S. A. Living environments: An ecological perspective. In H. C. Haywood & J. R. Newbrough (Eds.), *Living environments for developmentally retarded persons*. Baltimore: University Park Press, 1981.

Rickard, K. M., Forehand, R., Wells, K. C., Griest, D. L., & McMahon, R. J. Factors in the referral of children for behavioral treatment: A comparison of mothers of clinic-referred deviant, clinic-referred non-deviant, and non-clinic children. *Behaviour Research and Therapy*, 1981, 19, 201–205.

Rickel, A. U., Eshelman, A. K., & Loigman, G. A. *A longitudinal study of social problem solving training: Cognitive and behavioral effects*. Unpublished manuscript, Wayne State University, 1981.

Rickel, A. U., & Lampi, L. A two-year follow-up study of a preventive mental health program for preschoolers. *Journal of Abnormal Child Psychology*, 1981, 9, 455–464.

Rickel, A. U., & Smith, R. L. Maladapting preschool children: Identification, diagnosis, and remediation. *American Journal of Community Psychology*, 1979, 7, 197–208.

Rickel, A. U., Smith, R. L., & Sharp, K. C. Description and evaluation of a preventive mental health program for preschoolers. *Journal of Abnormal Child Psychology*, 1979, 7, 101–112.

Risley, T., & Sheldon-Wildgen, J. Invited peer review: The AABT experience. *Professional Psychology*, 1982, 13, 125–131.

Ritschl, E. R., & Hall, R. V. Improving MBD: An applied behavior analyst's point of view. *Journal of Organizational Behavior Management*, 1980, 2, 269–277.

Rivinus, T. M., Drummond, T., & Combrinck-Graham, L. A group-behavior treatment program for overweight children: Results of a pilot study. *Pediatric and Adolescent Endocrinology*, 1976, 1, 212–218.

Roberts, A. H., & Reinhardt, L. The behavioral management of chronic pain: Long-term follow-up with comparison groups. *Pain*, 1980, 8, 151–162.

Roberts, C. L. A behaviouristic basis for an ethic. *New Zealand Psychologist*, 1981, *10*, 80–85.

Roberts, M. A., Milich, R., Loney, L., & Caputo, J. A multitrait–multimethod analysis of variance of teachers' ratings of aggression, hyperactivity, and inattention. *Journal of Abnormal Child Psychology*, 1981, *9*, 371–380.

Roberts, M. W. The effects of warned versus unwarned time-out procedures on child noncompliance. *Child and Family Behavior Therapy*, 1982, *4*, 37–53. (a)

Roberts, M. W. Resistance to timeout: Some normative data. *Behavioral Assessment*, 1982, *4*, 237–246. (b)

Roberts, M. W., & Hatzenbuehler, L. C. Parent treatment of command-elicited negative verbalizations: A question of persistence. *Journal of Clinical Child Psychology*, 1981, *10*, 107–113.

Roberts, M. W., Hatzenbuehler, L. C., & Bean, A. W. The effects of differential attention and time out on child non-compliance. *Behavior Therapy*, 1981, *12*, 93–99.

Roberts, M. W., McMahon, R. J., Forehand, R., & Humphreys, L. The effect of parental instruction giving on child compliance. *Behavior Therapy*, 1978, *9*, 793–798.

Robertson, I. H. Behavioural concepts and treatment of neuroses: Comments on Marks and Wilson. *Behavioural Psychotherapy*, 1982, *10*, 179–183.

Robertson, I. H., & Heather, N. A survey of controlled drinking treatment in Britain. *British Journal on Alcohol and Alcoholism*, 1980, *17*, 103–105.

Robin, A. L. A controlled evaluation of problem-solving communication training with parent–adolescent conflict. *Behavior Therapy*, 1981, *12*, 593–609.

Robin, A. L., Fischel, J. E., & Brown, K. E. *Validation of a measure of children's self-control*. Paper presented at the Annual convention of the Association for Advancement of Behavior Therapy, Toronto, 1981.

Robin, A. L., & Weiss, J. G. Criterion-related validity of behavioral and self-report measures of problem-solving communication skills in distressed and non-distressed parent–adolescent dyads. *Behavioral Assessment*, 1980, *2*, 339–352.

Robinson, E. A., & Eyberg, S. M. The dyadic parent–child interaction coding system: Standardization and validation. *Journal of Consulting and Clinical Psychology*, 1981, *49*, 245–250.

Rock, D. L. The confounding of two self-report assertion measures with the tendency to give socially desirable responses in self-description. *Journal of Consulting and Clinical Psychology*, 1981, *49*, 743–744.

Roff, M. Childhood social interactions and young adult bad conduct. *Journal of Abnormal and Social Psychology*, 1961, *63*, 333–337.

Roff, M., Sells, S. B., & Golden, M. M. *Social adjustment and personality development in children*. Minneapolis: University of Minnesota Press, 1972.

Romano, J. M., & Bellack, A. S. Social validation of a component model of assertive behavior. *Journal of Consulting and Clinical Psychology*, 1980, *68*, 478–490.

Rose, T. L. The corporate punishment cycle: A behavioral analysis of the maintenance of corporate punishment in the schools. *Education and Treatment of Children*, 1981, *4*, 157–169.

Rose, T. L., Koorland, M. A., & Epstein, M. H. A review of applied behavior analysis interventions with learning disabled children. *Education and Treatment of Children*, 1982, *5*, 41–58.

Rosenbaum, M. A schedule for assessing self-control behaviors: Preliminary findings. *Behavior Therapy*, 1980, *11*, 109–121.

Rosenberg, B. A. Truth and fiction in RET: An addition to Meehl and Ellis' discussion. *Rational Living*, 1982, *17*(1), 37–41.

Rosenthal, T. L. Social learning theory. In G. T. Wilson & C. M. Franks (Eds.),

Contemporary behavior therapy: Conceptual and empirical foundations. New York: Guilford, 1982.

Roskies, E., Kearney, H., Spevack, A., Surkis, A., Cohen, C., & Gilman, S. Generalizability and durability of treatment effects in an intervention program for coronary prone (Type A) managers. *Journal of Behavioral Medicine,* 1979, *2,* 195–207.

Roskies, E., Spevack, M., Surkis, A., Cohen, C., & Gilman, S. Changing the coronary prone (Type A) behavior pattern in a nonclinical population. *Journal of Behavioral Medicine,* 1978, *1,* 201–215.

Ross, J. The role of the family member in the supported approach to the treatment of phobias. In J. Boulougouris (Ed.), *Learning theory approaches to psychiatry.* London: Wiley, 1982.

Roth, D., Bielski, R., Jones, M., Parker, W., & Osborn, G. A comparison of self-control therapy and combined self-control therapy and antidepressant medication in the treatment of depression. *Behavior Therapy,* 1982, *13,* 133–144.

Rothschild, M. L., & Gaidis, W. C. Behavioral learning theory: Its relevance to marketing and promotions. *Journal of Marketing,* 1981, *45,* 70–78.

Royal College of Physicians. *Smoking and health.* London: Royal College of Physicians, 1962.

Royce, J. R. Philosophic issues, Division 24, and the future. *American Psychologist,* 1982, *37,* 258–266.

Rudy, T. E., Merluzzi, T. V., & Henahan, P. T. Construal of complex assertion situations: A multidimensional analysis. *Journal of Consulting and Clinical Psychology,* 1982, *50,* 125–137.

Rusch, F. R., & Kazdin, A. E. Toward a methodology of withdrawal designs for the assessment of response maintenance. *Journal of Applied Behavior Analysis,* 1981, *14,* 131–140.

Rusch, F. R., & Schutz, R. P. Vocational and social work behavior: An evaluative review. In J. L. Matson & J. K. McCartney (Eds.), *Handbook of behavior modification with the mentally retarded.* New York: Plenum, 1981.

Rush, A. J. *Identifying obstacles to health behavior.* New York: BMA Audio Cassettes, 1980. (audiotape)

Rush, A. J., Beck, A. T., Kovacs, M., & Hollon, S. D. Comparative efficacy of cognitive therapy and pharmacotherapy in the treatment of depressed outpatients. *Cognitive Therapy and Research,* 1977, *1,* 17–38.

Rush, A. J., & Watkins, J. T. Group versus individual cognitive therapy: A pilot study. *Cognitive Therapy and Research,* 1981, *5,* 95–103.

Rush, D., & Kristal, A. R. Methodologic studies during pregnancy: The reliability of the 24-hour dietary recall. *American Journal of Clinical Nutrition,* 1982, *35,* 1259–1268.

Russell, J. A., & Ward, L. M. Environmental psychology. *Annual Review of Psychology,* 1982, *33,* 651–688.

Russo, D. C., Cataldo, M. F., & Cushing, P. J. Compliance training and behavioral covariation in the treatment of multiple behavior problems. *Journal of Applied Behavior Analysis,* 1981, *14,* 209–222.

Russo, D. C., & Varni, J. W. (Eds.). *Behavioral pediatrics: Research and practice.* New York: Plenum, 1982.

Ryan, F. J. Cold turkey in Greenfield, Iowa: A follow-up study. In W. L. Dunn, Jr. (Ed.), *Smoking behavior: Motives and incentives.* New York: Wiley, 1973.

Rybstein-Blinchik, E. Effects of different cognitive strategies on chronic pain experience. *Journal of Behavioral Medicine,* 1979, *2,* 93–101.

Ryckman, R. M., Robbins, M. A., Thornton, B., & Cantrell, P. Development and validation of a physical self-efficacy scale. *Journal of Personality and Social Psychology*, 1982, *42*, 889–900.

Ryon, N. B., & Harrell, T. H. *Cognitive-behavioral assessment of depression: Clinical validation of the ATQ-30*. Manuscript submitted for publication, 1982.

Sacco, W. P. Invalid use of the Beck Depression Inventory to identify depressed college student subjects: A methodological comment. *Cognitive Therapy and Research*, 1981, *5*, 143–147.

Safer, D. J. Some factors influencing school misconduct. In *School programs for disruptive adolescents*. Baltimore: University Park Press, 1982. (a)

Safer, D. J. *School programs for disruptive adolescents*. Baltimore: University Park Press, 1982. (b)

Safer, D. J., Heaton, R. C., & Parker, F. C. A behavioral program for disruptive junior high school students: Results and follow-up. *Journal of Abnormal Child Psychology*, 1981, *4*, 483–449.

Salzinger, S., Antrobus, J., & Glick, J. (Eds.). *The ecosystem of the "sick" child: Implications for classification and intervention for disturbed and mentally retarded children*. New York: Academic Press, 1980.

Samelson, F. J. B. Watson's Little Albert, Cyril Burt's twins and the need for a critical science. *American Psychologist*, 1980, *35*, 619–625.

Sanders, M. R. The effects of instructions, feedback and cueing procedures in behavioural parent training. *Australian Journal of Psychology*, 1982, *34*, 53–69.

Sanders, M. R., & Dadds, M. R. The effects of planned activities and child management procedures in parent training: An analysis of setting generality. *Behavior Therapy*, 1982, *13*, 452–461.

Sanders, M. R., & Glynn, T. Training parents in behavioral self-management: An analysis of generalization and maintenance. *Journal of Applied Behavior Analysis*, 1981, *14*, 223–237.

Sanders, M. R., & James, J. E. Enhancing generalization and maintenance effects in systematic parent training: The role of self-management skills. *Australian Psychologist*, 1982, *17*, 151–164.

Sanders, M. R., & James, J. E. The modification of parent behaviour: A review of generalization and maintenance. *Behavior Modification*, 1983, *7*, 3–27.

Sanders, S. The behavioral assessment of chronic pain: Appraisal of current status. In M. Hersen, R. Eisler, & P. Miller (Eds.), *Progress in behavior modification* (Vol. 8). New York: Academic Press, 1979.

Sanders, S. *Assessment of uptime in chronic low back pain patients: Comparison between self-report and automated measurement systems*. Paper presented at the meeting of the Association for Advancement of Behavior Therapy, New York, 1980. (a)

Sanders, S. Toward a practical instrument system for the automatic measurement of "uptime" in chronic pain patients. *Pain*, 1980, *9*, 103–109. (b)

Sandoval, J., Lambert, N. M., & Sassone, D. M. The comprehensive treatment of hyperactive children: A continuing problem. *Journal of Learning Disabilities*, 1981, *14*(3), 1–2.

Sarason, I. G., & Ganzer, V. J. Modeling and group discussion in the rehabilitation of juvenile delinquents. *Journal of Counseling Psychology*, 1973, *20*, 442–449.

Sarason, I. G., & Sarason, B. R. Teaching cognitive and social skills to high school students. *Journal of Consulting and Clinical Psychology*, 1981, *49*, 908–918.

Sarason, S. B. *Psychology misdirected*. New York: Free Press, 1981.

Sarri, R. The effectiveness paradox: Institutional vs. community placement of offenders. *Journal of Social Issues*, 1981, *37*, 34–50.

Sartory, G. Some psychophysiological issues in behavioural psychotherapy. *Behavioural Psychotherapy*, 1981, *9*, 215–230.

Schinke, S. P., Blythe, B. J., & Gilchrist, L. D. Cognitive–behavioral prevention of adolescent pregnancy. *Journal of Counseling Psychology*, 1981, *28*, 451–454.

Schleien, S. J., Wehman, P., & Kiernan, J. Teaching leisure skills to severely handicapped adults: An age-appropriate darts game. *Journal of Applied Behavior Analysis*, 1981, *16*, 513–519.

Schleser, R., Meyers, A., & Cohen, R. Generalization of self-instructions: Effects of general versus specific content, active rehearsal, and cognitive level. *Child Development*, 1981, *52*, 335–340.

Schmeltz, I., Hoffman, D., & Wynder, E. L. The influence of tobacco smoke on indoor atmospheres: An overview. *Preventive Medicine*, 1975, *4*, 66–82.

Schneider, C., Hoffmeister, J. K., & Heifer, R. F. A predictive screening questionnaire for potential problems in mother–child interaction. In R. E. Helfer & C. H. Kempe (Eds.), *Child abuse and neglect: The family and the community*. Cambridge, Mass.: Ballinger, 1976.

Schreibman, L., & Charlop, M. H. S+ versus S− fading in prompting procedures with autistic children. *Journal of Experimental Child Psychology*, 1981, *31*, 508–520.

Schreibman, L., & Koegel, R. L. A guideline for planning behavior modification programs for autistic children. In S. M. Turner, K. S. Calhoun, & H. E. Adams (Eds.), *Handbook of clinical behavior therapy*. New York: Wiley, 1981.

Schreibman, L., Koegel, R. L., Mills, J. I., & Burke, J. C. Social validation of behavior therapy with autistic children. *Behavior Therapy*, 1981, *12*, 610–624.

Schroder, H. M., Driver, M. J., & Streufert, S. *Human information processing*. New York: Holt, Rinehart & Winston, 1967.

Schroeder, S. R., Schroeder, C. S., Rojahn, J., & Mulick, J. A. Self-injurious behavior: An analysis of behavior management techniques. In J. L. Matson & J. R. McCartney (Eds.), *Handbook of behavior modification with the mentally retarded*. New York: Plenum, 1981.

Schunk, D. H. Effects of effort attributional feedback on children's perceived self-efficacy and achievement. *Journal of Educational Psychology*, 1982, *74*, 548–556.

Schwartz, G. E. Behavioral medicine and systems theory: A new synthesis. *National Forum*, 1980, *4*, 25–30.

Schwartz, G. E. Testing the biopsychosocial model: The ultimate challenge facing behavioral medicine. *Journal of Consulting and Clinical Psychology*, 1982, *50*, 1040–1053.

Schwartz, R. M. Cognitive-behavior modification: A conceptual review. *Clinical Psychology Review*, 1982, *2*, 267–293. (a)

Schwartz, R. M. Personal communication with P. C. Kendall, August 1982. (b)

Schwartz, R. M., & Gottman, J. M. Toward a task analysis of assertive behavior. *Journal of Consulting and Clinical Psychology*, 1976, *44*, 910–920.

Seligman, M. E. P. Phobias and preparedness. *Behavior Therapy*, 1971, *2*, 307–320.

Seltzer, C. C., & Mayer, J. An effective weight control program in a public school system. *American Journal of Public Health*, 1970, *60*, 679–689.

Senatore, V., Matson, J. L., & Kazdin, A. E. A comparison of behavioral methods to train social skills to mentally retarded adults. *Behavior Therapy*, 1982, *13*, 313–324.

Senn, M. J. E. Conduct disorders. In W. E. Nelson (Ed.), *Textbook of pediatrics*. Philadelphia: Saunders, 1959.

Seres, J. L., & Newman, R. I. Results of treatment of chronic low back pain at the Portland Pain Center. *Journal of Neurosurgery*, 1976, *45*, 32–36.

Shah, S. A. Dangerousness: A paradigm for exploring some issues in law and psychology. *American Psychologist*, 1978, *33*, 224–238.

Shah, S. A. Legal and mental health system interactions. *International Journal of Law and Psychiatry*, 1981, *4*, 219–270. (a)

Shah, S. A. Dangerousness: Conceptual, prediction and public policy issues. In J. R. Hays, T. K. Roberts, & K. S. Solway (Eds.), *Violence and the violent individual*. New York: SP Medical & Scientific Books, 1981. (b)

Shapiro, D. A., & Shapiro, D. Meta-analysis of comparative therapy outcome research: A critical appraisal. *Behavioural Psychotherapy*, 1982, *10*, 4–25. (a)

Shapiro, D. A., & Shapiro, D. Meta-analysis of comparative therapy outcome studies: A replication and refinement. *Psychological Bulletin*, 1982, *92*, 581–604. (b)

Shapiro, D. A., & Shapiro, D. Comparative therapy outcome research: Methodological implications of meta-analysis. *Journal of Consulting and Clinical Psychology*, 1983, *51*, 42–53.

Shapiro, E. S., Kazdin, A. E., & McGonigle, J. J. Multiple-treatment interference in the simultaneous—or alternating—treatments design. *Behavioral Assessment*, 1982, *4*, 105–115.

Sharkey, P. W. Something irrational about rational emotive psychology. *Psychotherapy: Theory, Research, and Practice*. 1981, *18*, 150–154.

Shea, J. E. Psychoanalytic therapy and alcoholism. *Journal of Studies on Alcohol*, 1954, *15*, 595–605.

Sheldon-Wildgen, J. Avoiding legal liability: The rights and responsibilities of therapists. *The Behavior Therapist*, 1982, 5(5), 165–169.

Shelton, J. L., & Levy, R. L. *Behavioral assignments and treatment compliance: A handbook of clinical strategies*. Champaign, Ill.: Research Press, 1981. (a)

Shelton, J. L., & Levy, R. L. A survey of the reported use of assigned homework activities in contemporary behavior therapy literature. *The Behavior Therapist*, 1981, *4*, 131–140. (b)

Shkop, Y. M., & Shkop, E. M. Job modification as an alternative to retirement. *Personnel Journal*, July 1982, pp. 513–516.

Simon, S. J., Ayllon, T., & Milan, M. A. Behavioral compensation: Contrast like effects in the classroom. *Behavior Modification*, 1982, *6*, 407–420.

Singh, N. N., Beale, I. L., & Dawson, M. J. Duration of facial screening and suppression of self-injurious behavior: Analysis using an alternating treatments design. *Behavioral Assessment*, 1981, *3*, 411–420.

Sinnott, A., Jones, R. B., Scott-Fordham, A., & Woodward, R. Augmentation of in vivo exposure treatment for agoraphobia by the formation of neighbourhood self-help groups. *Behaviour Research and Therapy*, 1981, *19*, 339–348.

Sloane, R. B., Staples, F. R., Cristol, A. H., Yorkston, N. J., & Whipple, K. *Psychotherapy versus behavior therapy*. Cambridge, Mass.: Harvard University Press, 1975.

Smetak, S., & Jason, L. A. Altering the interior design of a nursing home. In M. Gatz & M. Smyer (Eds.), *Mental health programs for adults: Evaluative studies*. New York: Sage, 1983.

Smith, D. Trends in counseling and psychotherapy. *American Psychologist*, 1982, *37*, 802–809.

Smith, J. B., Madsen, C. H., & Cipani, E. C. The effects of observational session length, method of recording, and frequency of teacher behavior on reliability and accuracy of observational data. *Behavior Therapy*, 1981, *12*, 565–569.

Smith, M. L., & Glass, G. V. Meta-analysis of psychotherapy outcome studies. *American Psychologist*, 1977, *32*, 752–760.

Smith, M. L., Glass, G. V., & Miller, T. I. *The benefits of psychotherapy*. Baltimore: Johns Hopkins University Press, 1980.

Smith, R. R., Milan, M. A., Wood, L. F., & McKee, J. M. The correctional officer as a behavioral technician. *Criminal Justice and Behavior*, 1976, *3*, 345-360.

Snyder, M., & White, P. Moods and memories: Elation, depression, and the remembering of the events of one's life. *Journal of Personality*, 1982, *50*, 149-167.

Sobel, H. J. (Ed.). *Behavior therapy in terminal care: A humanistic approach*. Cambridge, Mass.: Ballinger, 1981.

Sobell, M. B. Alternatives to abstinence: Evidence, issues, and some proposals. In P. E. Nathan & G. A. Marlatt (Eds.), *Alcoholism: New directions in behavioral research and treatment*. New York: Plenum, 1978.

Sobell, M. B., & Sobell, L. C. Alcoholics treated by individualized behavior therapy: One year treatment outcome. *Behaviour Research and Therapy*, 1973, *11*, 599-618. (a)

Sobell, M. B., & Sobell, L. C. Individualized behavior therapy for alcoholics. *Behavior Therapy*, 1973, *4*, 49-72. (b)

Sobell, M. B., & Sobell, L. C. *Behavioral treatment of alcohol problems: Individualized therapy and controlled drinking*. New York: Plenum, 1978.

Sobell, M. B., & Sobell, L. C. Nonproblem drinking as a goal in the treatment of problem drinkers. In J. M. Ferguson & C. B. Taylor (Eds.), *The comprehensive handbook of behavioral medicine* (Vol. 3). New York: Spectrum, 1980.

Sohn, D., & Lamal, P. A. Self-reinforcement: Its reinforcing capability and its clinical utility. *The Psychological Record*, 1982, *32*, 179-203.

Sours, H. E., Frattali, V. P., Brand, C. D., Feldman, R. A., Forbes, A. L., Swanson, R. C., & Paris, A. L. Sudden death associated with very-low-calorie weight reduction regimens. *American Journal of Clinical Nutrition*, 1981, *34*, 453-461.

Speltz, M. L., Shimamura, J. W., & McReynolds, W. T. Procedural variations in group contingencies: Effects on children's academic and social behaviors. *Journal of Applied Behavior Analysis*, 1982, *15*, 533-544.

Spetch, M. L., Wilkie, D. M., & Pinel, J. P. Backward conditioning: A reevaluation of the empirical evidence. *Psychological Bulletin*, 1981, *89*, 163-175.

Spielberger, C. D. *Preliminary manual for the State-Trait Anxiety Inventory for children ("How I feel questionnaire")*. Palo Alto, Calif.: Consulting Psychologists Press, 1973.

Spielberger, C. D., Gonzales, H. P., Taylor, C. J., Algaze, B., & Anton, W. D. Examination stress and test anxiety. In C. D. Spielberger & I. G. Sarason (Eds.), *Stress and anxiety* (Vol. 5). New York: Hemisphere-Wiley, 1978.

Spitzer, R. L., Endicott, J., Fleiss, J. L., & Cohen, J. The psychiatric status schedule: A technique for evaluating psychopathology and impairment in role functioning. *Archives of General Psychiatry*, 1970, *23*, 41-55.

Spitzer, R. L., Endicott, L., & Robins, E. Research diagnostic criteria: Rationale and reliability. *Archives of General Psychiatry*, 1978, *35*, 773-782. (a)

Spitzer, R. L., Endicott, J., & Robins, E. *Research Diagnostic Criteria (RDC) for a selected group of functional disorders* (3rd ed.). New York: New York State Psychiatric Institute, Biometrics Research, 1978. (b)

Spivack, G., & Shure, M. B. *Social adjustment of young children: A cognitive approach to solving real-life problems*. San Francisco: Jossey-Bass, 1974.

Spivack, G., & Swift, M. *Devereux elementary school behavior rating scale*. Devon, Pa.: Devereux Foundation, 1967.

Spreat, S., & Isett, R. Behavioral effects of intra-institutional relocation. *Applied Research in Mental Retardation*, 1981, *2*, 229-236.

Staats, A. W. Paradigmatic behaviorism, unified theory, unified theory construction methods, and the *Zeitgeist* of separatism. *American Psychologist*, 1981, *36*, 239–256.

Staples, F. R., Sloane, B., Whipple, K., Cristol, A. H., & Yorkston, N. J. Differences between behavior therapists and psychotherapists. *Archives of General Psychiatry*, 1975, *32*, 1517–1522.

Steffen, J. L., & Karoly, P. (Eds.). *Improving children's competence (Advances in child behavioral analysis and therapy*, Vol. 1). Lexington, Mass.: Lexington Books, 1982. (a)

Steffen, J. L., & Karoly, P. (Eds.). *Autism and severe psychopathology (Advances in child behavioral analysis and therapy*, Vol. 2). Lexington, Mass.: Lexington Books, 1982. (b)

Stein, L. I., & Test, M. A. Alternative to mental hospital treatment I. Conceptual model, treatment program, and clinical evaluation. *Archives of General Psychiatry*, 1980, *37*, 392–412.

Stenn, P. G., Mothersill, K. J., & Brooke, R. I. Biofeedback and a cognitive–behavioral approach to treatment of myofascial pain dysfunction syndrome. *Behavior Therapy*, 1979, *10*, 29–36.

Stewart, M. A., & Ashby, H. B. Treatment of hyperactive, aggressive, and antisocial children. In T. R. Kratochwill (Ed.), *Advances in school psychology* (Vol. 1). Hillsdale, N.J.: Lawrence Erlbaum, 1981.

Stiffman, A. R. Assessing child compliance-noncompliance. *Child and Family Behavior Therapy*, 1982, *4*(3), 141–149.

Stocking, S. H., Arezzo, D., & Leavitt, S. *Helping kids make friends*. Allen, Tex.: Argus Communications, 1980.

Stokes, T. F., & Baer, D. M. An implicit technology of generalization. *Journal of Applied Behavior Analysis*, 1977, *10*, 349–367.

Stokes, T. F., & Fawcett, S. B., Evaluating municipal policy: An analysis of a refuse packaging program. *Journal of Applied Behavior Analysis*, 1977, *10*, 391–398.

Stolz, S. B. Adoption of innovations from applied behavioral research: "Does anybody care?" *Journal of Applied Behavior Analysis*, 1981, *14*, 491–505.

Stolz, S. B., & Associates. *Ethical issues in behavior modification*. San Francisco, Calif.: Jossey-Bass, 1978.

Stone, G. C. *Health Psychology*: A new journal for a new field. *Health Psychology*, 1982, *1*, 1–6.

Strain, P. S. (Ed.). *The utilization of classroom peers as behavior change agents*. New York: Plenum, 1981.

Strain, P. S., & Fox, J. J. Peers as behavior change agents for withdrawn classmates. In B. B. Lahey & A. E. Kazdin (Eds.), *Advances in clinical child psychology* (Vol. 4). New York: Plenum, 1981. (a)

Strain, P. S., & Fox, J. J. Peer social initiations and the modification of social withdrawal: A review and future perspective. *Journal of Pediatric Psychology*, 1981, *6*, 417–433. (b)

Strain, P. S., Steele, P., Ellis, T., & Timm, M. A. Long-term effects of oppositional child treatment with mothers as therapists and therapist trainers. *Journal of Applied Behavior Analysis*, 1982, *15*, 163–169.

Strober, M., Green, J., & Carlson, G. Utility of the Beck Depression Inventory with psychiatrically hospitalized adolescents. *Journal of Consulting and Clinical Psychology*, 1981, *49*, 482–483.

Stromer, R., & Miller, J. Training parents of multiply handicapped/hearing impaired children. In B. Campbell & V. Baldwin (Eds.), *Severely handicapped/hearing impaired students*. Baltimore: Paul H. Brookes, 1982.

Strube, M. J., & Garcia, J. E. A meta-analytic investigation of Fiedler's contingency model of leadership effectiveness. *Psychological Bulletin*, 1981, *90*, 307–321.

Strube, M. J., & Hartmann, D. P. Meta-analysis: Techniques, applications, and functions. *Journal of Consulting and Clinical Psychology*, 1983, *51*, 14–27.

Stuart, R. B. (Ed.). *Violent behavior: Social learning approaches to prediction, management and treatment*. New York: Brunner/Mazel, 1981.

Stuart, R. B., & Davis, B. *Slim chance in a fat world*. Champaign, Ill.: Research Press, 1972.

Stumphauzer, J. S. Behavioral approaches to juvenile delinquents: Future perspectives. In L. Michelson, M. Hersen, & S. M. Turner (Eds.), *Future perspectives in behavior therapy*. New York: Plenum, 1981. (a)

Stumphauzer, J. S. Behavior modification with delinquents and criminals. In W. E. Craighead, A. E. Kazdin, & M. J. Mahoney (Eds.), *Behavior modification: Principles, issues, and applications* (2nd ed.). Boston: Houghton Mifflin, 1981. (b)

Stumphauzer, J. S., Veloz, E. V., & Aiken, T. W. Violence by street gangs: Eastside story? In R. B. Stuart (Ed.), *Violent behavior: Social learning approaches to prediction, management and treatment*. New York: Brunner/Mazel, 1981.

Stunkard, A. J. New therapies of the eating disorders. *Archives of General Psychiatry*, 1972, *26*, 391–398.

Stunkard, A. J. (Ed.) *Obesity*. Philadelphia: Saunders, 1980.

Stunkard, A. J., & Brownell, K. D. Work site treatment for obesity. *American Journal of Psychiatry*, 1980, *137*, 252–253.

Stunkard, A. J., Coll, M., Lundquist, S., & Meyers, A. Obesity and eating style. *Archives of General Psychiatry*, 1980, *37*, 1127–1129.

Stunkard, A. J., & Kaplan, D. Eating in public places: A review of reports of the direct observation of eating behavior. *International Journal of Obesity*, 1977, *1*, 89–101.

Stunkard, A. J., & Mendelson, M. Obesity and body image: I. Characteristics of disturbances in the body image of some obese persons. *American Journal of Psychiatry*, 1967, *123*, 1296–1300.

Stunkard, A. J., & Penick, S. B. Behavior modification in the treatment of obesity: The problem of maintaining weight loss. *Archives of General Psychiatry*, 1979, *36*, 801–806.

Suckerman, K. R., Hines, P., & Gordon, S. B. A multienvironment school mental health consultation: Behavioral skill training for teachers and parents. In A. M. Jeger & R. S. Slotnick (Eds.), *Community mental health and behavioral ecology: A handbook of theory, research, and practice*. New York: Plenum, 1982.

Suinn, R. M., & Bloom, L. J. Anxiety management training for pattern A behavior. *Journal of Behavioral Medicine*, 1978, *1*, 25–37.

Sutherland, G., Newman, B., & Rachman, S. Experimental investigations of the relations between mood and intrusive unwanted cognitions. Cited in S. Rachman (Ed.), Unwanted intrusive cognitions. *Advances in Behaviour Research and Therapy*, 1981, *3*, 87–123.

Sutter, P. Environmental variables related to community placement failure in mentally retarded adults. *Mental Retardation*, 1980, *18*, 189–191.

Sutter, P., Mayeda, T., Call, T., Yanagi, S., & Yee, S. Comparison of successful and unsuccessful community-placed mentally retarded persons. *American Journal of Mental Deficiency*, 1980, *85*, 262–267.

Sutter, P., Mayeda, T., Yee, S., & Yanagi, S. Community placement success based on client behavior preferences of care providers. *Mental Retardation*, 1981, *19*, 117–120.

Swan, G. E., & MacDonald, M. L. Behavior therapy in practice: A national survey of behavior therapists. *Behavior Therapy*, 1978, *9*, 799–807.

Swanson, D. W., Maruta, T., & Swenson, W. M. Results of behavior modification in the treatment of chronic pain. *Psychosomatic Medicine*, 1979, *41*, 55–61.

Swanson, D. W., Swenson, M. W., Maruta, T., & McPhee, M. C. Program for managing chronic pain I. Program description and characteristics of patients. *Mayo Clinic Proceedings*, 1976, *51*, 401–408.

Swanson, H. L. *The use of cognitive behavior modification in the instruction of behaviorally disturbed children's academic performance.* Unpublished manuscript, University of Northern Colorado, 1982.

Szapocznik, J., Santisteban, D., Hervis, O., Spencer, F., & Kurtines, W. M. Treatment of depression among Cuban-American elders: Some validational evidence for a life enhancement counseling approach. *Journal of Consulting and Clinical Psychology*, 1981, *49*, 752–754.

Szykula, S. A., Fleischman, M. J., & Shilton, P. E. Implementing a family therapy program in a community: Relevant issues on one promising program for families in conflict. *Behavioral Counseling Quarterly*, in press.

Tager, I. B., Weiss, S. T., & Rosner, B. Effect of parental cigarette smoking on the pulmonary function of children. *American Journal of Epidemiology*, 1979, *110*, 15–26.

Teasdale, J. D. Personal communication with P. C. Kendall, July 1982.

Teasdale, J. D. Negative thinking in depression: Cause, effect, or reciprocal relationship? *Advances in Behaviour Research and Therapy*, in press.

Teasdale, J. D., & Taylor, R. Induced mood and accessibility of memories: An effect of mood state or of induction procedure? *British Journal of Clinical Psychology*, 1981, *20*, 39–48.

Telch, M. J., Killen, J. D., McAlister, A. L., Perry, C. L., & Maccoby, N. Long-term follow-up of a pilot project on smoking prevention with adolescents. *Journal of Behavioral Medicine*, 1982, *5*, 1–8.

Teri, L., & Lewinsohn, P. Modification of the Pleasant and Unpleasant Events Schedules for use with the elderly. *Journal of Consulting and Clinical Psychology*, 1982, *50*, 444–445.

Test, M. A., & Stein, L. I. Alternative to mental hospital treatment III. Social cost. *Archives of General Psychiatry*, 1980, *37*, 409–412.

Thompson, E. L. Smoking education programs, 1960–1976. *American Journal of Public Health*, 1978, *68*, 250–255.

Thompson, J. K., Jarvie, G. J., Lahey, B. B., & Cureton, K. J. Exercise and obesity: Etiology, physiology, and intervention. *Psychological Bulletin*, 1982, *91*, 55–79.

Thompson, P. D., Jeffery, R. W., Wing, R. R., & Wood, P. D. Unexpected decrease in plasma high density lipoprotein cholesterol with weight loss. *American Journal of Clinical Nutrition*, 1979, *32*, 2016–2021.

Thompson, T. J., Braam, S. J., & Fuqua, W. Training and generalization with handicapped persons. *Journal of Applied Behavior Analysis*, 1982, *15*, 177–182.

Thoresen, C. E., Friedman, M., Gill, J. K., & Ulmer, D. K. The recurrent coronary prevention project: Some preliminary findings. *Acta Medica Scandinavia*, 1982, *660*, 172–192.

Thorley, G., & Yule, W. A role-play test of parent–child interaction. *Behavioural Psychotherapy*, 1982, *10*, 146–161.

Thorndyke, P. W., & Hayes-Roth, B. The use of schemata in the acquisition and transfer of knowledge. *Cognitive Psychology*, 1979, *11*, 82–106.

Thorpe, G. H. Review of *Behavior therapy in terminal care: A humanistic approach* by H. J. Sobel (Cambridge, Mass.: Ballinger, 1981). *Experimental Aging Research*, 1982, *2*, 127–128.

Thurston, L. P. Comparison of the effects of parent training and of ritalin in treating hyperactive children. In M. Gittelman (Ed.), *Strategic interventions for hyper-active children.* Armonk, N.Y.: M. E. Sharpe, 1981.

Thyer, B. A. Behavioral social work: A bibliography. *International Journal of Behavioural Social Work and Abstracts,* 1981, *1*, 229–251.

Thyer, B. A., & Bronson, D. Behavioral training in social work: An update and a program description. *Journal of Behavior Therapy and Experimental Psychiatry,* 1981, *12,* 43–47.

Toner, I. J., & Smith, R. A. Age and overt verbalization in delay-maintenance behavior in children. *Journal of Experimental Child Psychology,* 1977, *24,* 123–128.

Towns, P. *Educating disturbed adolescents: Therapy and practice. (Current issues in behavioral psychology,* Vol. III). New York: Grune & Stratton, 1981.

Trice, A., Parker, F. C., & Safer, D. J. Differing modes of senior high school intervention for disruptive students. In D. J. Safer (Ed.), *School programs for disruptive adolescents.* Baltimore: University Park Press, 1982.

Trower, P. Situational analysis of the components and processes of socially skilled and unskilled patients. *Journal of Consulting and Clinical Psychology,* 1980, *48,* 327–339.

Tryon, W. W. The practice of clinical behaviorism: An overview. *Journal of Behavior Therapy and Experimental Psychiatry,* 1981, *12,* 197–202.

Turk, D. C. Cognitive learning approaches: Applications in health care. In D. Doleys, D. Meredith, & A. Ciminero (Eds.), *Behavioral medicine.* New York: Plenum, 1982.

Turk, D. C., & Genest, M. Regulation of pain: The application of cognitive and behavioral principles. In P. C. Kendall & S. D. Hollon (Eds.), *Cognitive–behavioral interventions: Theory, research, and procedures.* New York: Academic Press, 1979.

Turk, D. C., Meichenbaum, D. H., & Berman, W. H. Application of biofeedback for the regulation of pain: A critical review. *Psychological Bulletin,* 1979, *86,* 1322–1338.

Turk, D. C., Meichenbaum, D., & Genest, M. *Pain and behavioral medicine: A cognitive–behavioral perspective.* New York: Guilford, 1983.

Turk, D. C., & Speers, M. A. Cognitive schemata and cognitive processes in cognitive-behavioral interventions: Going beyond the information given. In P. C. Kendall (Ed.), *Advances in cognitive–behavioral research and therapy* (Vol. 2). New York: Academic Press, 1983.

Turkat, I. D. The image of behavior therapy. *The Behavior Therapist,* 1979, *2*(2), 17.

Turkat, I. D. Social networks: Theory and practice. *Journal of Community Psychology,* 1980, *8,* 99–109.

Turkat, I. D., & Forehand, R. The future of behavior therapy. In M. Hersen, R. M. Eisler, & P. M. Miller (Eds.), *Progress in behavior modification* (Vol. 9). New York: Academic Press, 1980.

Turkat, I. D., Harris, F. C., & Forehand, R. An assessment of the public reaction to behavior modification. *Journal of Behavior Therapy and Experimental Psychiatry,* 1979, *10,* 101–103.

Turner, J. A. Comparison of group progressive relaxation training and cognitive-behavioral group therapy for chronic low back pain. *Journal of Consulting and Clinical Psychology,* 1982, *50,* 757–765.

Turner, J. A., & Chapman, C. R. Psychological interventions for chronic pain: A critical review. I. Relaxation training and biofeedback. *Pain,* 1982, *12,* 1–21. (a)

Turner, J. A., & Chapman, C. R. Psychological interventions for chronic pain: A critical review. II. Operant conditioning, hypnosis, and cognitive–behavioral therapy. *Pain,* 1982, *12,* 23–46. (b)

Tursky, B. Development of a pain perception profile. In M. Weisenberg & B. Tursky (Eds.), *Pain: New perspectives in therapy and research.* New York: Plenum, 1976.

Tursky, B., Jamner, L., & Friedman, R. The pain perception profile: A psychophysical approach to the assessment of pain report. *Behavior Therapy*, 1982, *13*, 376–394.

Tymchuk, A. J. Ethical decision making and psychological treatment. *Journal of Psychiatric Treatment and Evaluation*, 1981, *3*, 507–513.

Tymchuk, A. J., Drapkin, R. S., Ackerman, A. B., Major, S. M., Coffman, E. W., & Baum, M. S. Survey of training ethics in APA-approved clinical psychology programs. *American Psychologist*, 1979, *36*, 1168–1170.

Tymchuk, A. J., Drapkin, R., Major-Kingsley, S., Ackerman, A. B., Coffman, E. W., & Baum, M. S. Ethical decision making and psychologists' attitudes toward training in ethics. *Professional Psychology*, 1982, *13*, 412–421.

Ullman, D. G., Egan, D., Fiedler, N., Jurenec, G., Pliske, R., Thompson, P., & Doherty, M. E. The many faces of hyperactivity: Similarities and differences in diagnostic policies. *Journal of Consulting and Clinical Psychology*, 1981, *49*, 694–704.

United States Department of Health, Education, and Welfare, Public Health Service. *Smoking and health: Report of the Advisory Committee to the Surgeon General of the Public Health Service.* Washington, D.C.: U.S. Government Printing Office, 1964.

United States Department of Health, Education, and Welfare, Public Health Service. *Use of tobacco: Practices, attitudes, knowledge, and beliefs, United States—Fall 1964 and Spring 1966.* Washington, D.C.: U.S. Government Printing Office, 1969.

United States Department of Health, Education, and Welfare (USDHEW), Public Health Service, National Institutes of Health. *Teenage smoking: National patterns of cigarette smoking ages 12 through 18, in 1972 and 1974.* DHEW Publ. No. (NIH) 76-931, 1976.

United States Department of Health, Education, and Welfare (USDHEW), Public Health Service. *Smoking and health: A report of the Surgeon General.* DHEW Publ. No. (PHS) 79-50066, 1979.

United States Department of Health and Human Services (USDHHS), National Institutes of Health. *Smoking programs for youth.* National Cancer Institute, NIH Publ. No. 80-2156, 1980.

Urbain, E. S. *Friendship group manual.* Unpublished manuscript, Wilder Child Guidance Center, St. Paul, Minnesota, 1982.

Urbain, E. S., & Kendall, P. C. Review of social-cognitive problem-solving interventions with children. *Psychological Bulletin*, 1980, *88*, 109–143.

Valerio, H. P., & Stone, G. L. Effects of behavioral, cognitive, and combined treatments for assertion as a function of differential deficits. *Journal of Counseling Psychology*, 1982, *29*, 158–168.

Van Den Pol, R. A., Iwata, B. A., Ivancic, M. T., Page, T. J., Neef, N. A., & Whitley, F. P. Teaching the handicapped to eat in public places: Acquisition, generalization and maintenance of restaurant skills. *Journal of Applied Behavior Analysis*, 1981, *14*, 61–69.

Vandereycken, W. Agoraphobia and marital relationships: Theory, treatment, and research. *Clinical Psychology Review,* in press.

Van Hasselt, V. B., Hersen, M., & Bellack, A. S. The validity of role play tests for assessing social skills in children. *Behavior Therapy*, 1981, *12*, 202–216.

Van Itallie, T. B. Liquid protein mayhem. *Journal of the American Medical Association*, 1978, *240*, 144–145.

Van Itallie, T. B. Obesity: Adverse effects on health and longevity. *American Journal of Clinical Nutrition*, 1979, *32*, 2723–2733.

Van Itallie, T. B. Dietary approaches to the treatment of obesity. In A. J. Stunkard (Ed.), *Obesity.* Philadelphia: Saunders, 1980.

Van Wagenberg, D., Krasner, M., & Krasner, L. Children planning an ideal classroom:

Environmental design in an elementary school. *Environment and Behavior*, 1981, *13*, 349–359.

Varni, J. W. Self-regulation techniques in the management of chronic arthritic pain in hemophilia. *Behavior Therapy*, 1981, *12*, 185–194.

Velten, E. C. A laboratory task for induction of mood states. *Behaviour Research and Therapy*, 1968, *6*, 473–482.

Vertes, V., Genuth, S. M., & Hazelton, I. M. Supplemental fasting as a large-scale outpatient program. *Journal of the American Medical Association*, 1977, *238*, 2151–2153.

Voeltz, L. M., & Evans, I. M. The assessment of behavioral interrelationships in child behavior therapy. *Behavioral Assessment*, 1982, *4*, 131–165.

Vogel, W., Peterson, L. E., & Broverman, I. K. A modification of Rachman's habituation technique for treatment of the obsessive–compulsive disorder. *Behaviour Research and Therapy*, 1982, *20*, 101–104.

Vogler, R. E., Weissbach, T. A., & Compton, J. V. Learning techniques for alcohol abuse. *Behaviour Research and Therapy*, 1977, *15*, 31–38.

Wachtel, P. (Ed.). *Resistance: Psychodynamic and behavioral approaches*. New York: Plenum, 1982.

Wadden, T. A., & Brownell, K. D. The development and modification of dietary practices in individuals, groups, and large populations. In J. D. Matarazzo, N. E. Miller, S. M. Weiss, J. A. Herd, & S. M. Weiss (Eds.), *Behavioral health: A handbook of health enhancement and disease prevention*. New York: Wiley, in press.

Wadden, T. A., Stunkard, A. J., & Brownell, K. D. Very-low-calorie diets: A critical review. *Annals of Internal Medicine*, in press.

Waern, Y. Thinking aloud during reading: A descriptive model and its application. *Scandinavian Journal of Psychology*, 1980, *21*, 123–132.

Wahler, R. G. The insular mother: Her problems in parent–child treatment. *Journal of Applied Behavior Analysis*, 1980, *13*, 207–219.

Wahler, R. G., & Fox, J. J. Setting events in applied behavior analysis: Toward a conceptual and methodological expansion. *Journal of Applied Behavior Analysis*, 1981, *14*, 327–338.

Wallace, C. J., Nelson, C. J., Liberman, R. P., Aitchison, R. A., Lukoff, D., Elder, J. P., & Ferris, C. A review and critique of social skills training with schizophrenic patients. *Schizophrenia Bulletin*, 1980, *6*, 42–63.

Wallander, J. L., & Conger, J. C. Assessment of hyperactive children: Psychometric, methodological, and practical considerations. In M. Hersen, R. M. Eisler, & P. M. Miller (Eds.), *Progress in behavior modification* (Vol. 11). New York: Academic Press, 1981.

Wallerstein, R. S., Chotlos, J. W., Friend, M. B., Hammersley, D. W., Perlswig, E. A., & Winship, G. M. *Hospital treatment of alcoholism: A comparative experimental study*. New York: Basic Books, 1957.

Wampold, B. E., & Furlong, M. J. The heuristics of visual inference. *Behavioral Assessment*, 1981, *3*, 79–92.

Ward, L. C. Behavioral therapy and ethics: A response to Kitchener. *Journal of Consulting and Clinical Psychology*, 1980, *48*, 646–648.

Wardlaw, G. Applied behaviour analysis and crime prevention: Some cautions. *Australian Psychologist*, 1981, *16*, 391–392.

Warner, K. E. The effects of the antismoking campaign on cigarette consumption. *American Journal of Public Health*, 1977, *67*, 645–650.

Warner, K. E. Cigarette smoking in the 1970's: The impact of the antismoking campaign on consumption. *Science*, 1981, *211*, 729–731.

Watson, D., & Friend, R. Measurement of social-evaluative anxiety. *Journal of Consulting and Clinical Psychology*, 1969, *33*, 448-457.

Watson, J., & Marks, I. Relevant and irrelevant fear in flooding: A crossover study of phobic patients. *Behavior Therapy*, 1971, *2*, 275-295.

Watzlawick, P., Weakland, J., & Fisch, R. *Change: Principles of problem formation and problem solution*. New York: Norton, 1976.

Waxman, M., & Stunkard, A. J. Caloric intake and expenditure in boys. *Journal of Pediatrics*, 1980, *96*, 187-193.

Webster, C. D., Konstantareas, M. M., Oxman, J., & Mack, J. E. (Eds.). *Autism: New directions in research and education*. New York: Pergamon, 1980.

Webster-Stratton, C. Modification of mothers' behaviors and attitudes through a videotape modeling group discussion program. *Behavior Therapy*, 1981, *12*, 634-642.

Webster-Stratton, C. The long-term effects of a videotape modeling parent-training program: Comparison of immediate and 1-year follow-up results. *Behavior Therapy*, 1982, *13*, 702-714.

Weisbrod, B. A., Test, M. A., & Stein, L. I. Alternative to mental hospital treatment. II. Economic benefit–cost analysis. *Archives of General Psychiatry*, 1980, *37*, 400-405.

Weiss, A. R. A behavioral approach to the treatment of adolescent obesity. *Behavioral Therapy*, 1977, *8*, 720-726.

Weiss, M., & Stunkard, A. J. Caloric intake and expenditure of boys. *Journal of Pediatrics*, 1980, *96*, 187-193.

Weiss, R. L., Hops, H., & Patterson, G. R. A framework for conceptualizing marital conflict. In L. A. Hamerlynck, L. C. Handy, & E. J. Mash (Eds.), *Behavior change: Methodology, concepts, and practice*. Champaign, Ill.: Research Press, 1973.

Weiss, S. M. Health psychology: The time is now. *Health Psychology*, 1982, *1*, 81-91.

Weissberg, R. P., & Gesten, E. L. Considerations for developing effective school-based social problem solving (SPS) training programs. *School Psychology Review*, 1982, *11*, 56-63.

Weissberg, R. P., Gesten, E. L., Rapkin, B. D., Cowen, E. L., Davidson, E., deApodaca, R. F., & McKim, B. J. Evaluation of a social-problem-solving training program for suburban and inner-city third-grade children. *Journal of Consulting and Clinical Psychology*, 1981, *49*, 251-261.

Weitz, S. E. A code for assessing teaching skills of parents of developmentally disabled children. *Journal of Autism and Developmental Disorders*, 1981, *12*, 13-24.

Wells, K. C., Conners, C. K., Imber, L., & Delamater, A. Use of single-subject methodology in clinical decision making with a hyperactive child or the psychiatric inpatient unit. *Behavioral Assessment*, 1981, *3*, 359-369.

Wells, K. C., & Forehand, R. Child behavior problems in the home. In S. M. Turner, K. Calhoun, & H. E. Adams (Eds.), *Handbook of behavior change therapy*. New York: Wiley, 1981.

Wernick, R. L., Jaremko, M. E., & Taylor, P. W. Pain management in severely burned adults: A test of stress inoculation. *Journal of Behavioral Medicine*, 1981, *4*, 103-110.

Wessberg, H. W., Curran, J. P., Monti, P. M., Corriveau, D. P., Coyne, N. A., & Dziadosz, T. H. Evidence for the external validity of a social simulation measure of social skills. *Journal of Behavioral Assessment*, 1981, *3*, 209-220.

Whalen, C. K., Henker, B., Collins, B. E., Finck, D., & Dotemoto, S. A social ecology of hyperactive boys: Medication effects in structured classroom environments. *Journal of Applied Behavior Analysis*, 1979, *12*, 65-81.

Whalen, C. K., Henker, B., & Finck, D. Medication effects in the classroom: Three naturalistic indicators. *Journal of Abnormal Child Psychology*, 1981, *9*, 419–433.

Wheeler, M. E., & Hess, K. W. Treatment of juvenile obesity by successive approximation control of eating. *Journal of Behavior Therapy and Experimental Psychiatry*, 1976, *7*, 235–241.

White, J., & Froeb, H. Small airways dysfunction in nonsmokers chronically exposed to tobacco smoke. *New England Journal of Medicine*, 1980, *302*, 720–723.

Whitman, T. L., & Scibak, J. W. Behavior modification with the mentally retarded: Treatment and research perspectives. In J. L. Matson & J. R. McCartney (Eds.), *Handbook of behavior modification with the mentally retarded*. New York: Plenum, 1981.

Wiggins, J. S. *Personality and prediction*. Reading, Mass.: Addison-Wesley, 1973.

Wilbur, C. S. The Johnson Live for Life program. *Behavioral Medicine Update*, 1980, *2*, 7–8.

Wilkinson, D. A., & Sanchez-Craig, M. Relevance of brain dysfunction to treatment objectives: Should alcohol-related cognitive deficits influence the way we think about treatment? *Addictive Behaviors*, 1981, *6*, 253–261.

William, T. M. *Summary and implications of review of literature related to adolescent smoking*. Bethesda, Md.: U.S. Department of Health, Education, and Welfare, Center for Disease Control, 1971.

Williams, B. J., Foreyt, J. P., & Goodrick, S. K. *Pediatric behavioral medicine*. New York: Praeger, 1981.

Williams, B. W. Reinforcement, behavior constraint, and the overjustification effect. *Journal of Personality and Social Psychology*, 1980, *39*, 599–614.

Williams, S. L., & Rappoport, J. A. Behavioral practice with and without thought modification for agoraphobics. *Behavior Therapy*, 1983, *14*, 299–313.

Wilson, G. T. Methodological considerations in treatment outcome research on obesity. *Journal of Consulting and Clinical Psychology*, 1978, *46*, 687–702.

Wilson, G. T. Perceived control and the theory and practice of behavior therapy. In L. C. Perlmuter & R. A. Monty (Eds.), *Choice and perceived control*. Hillsdale, N.J.: Lawrence Erlbaum, 1979.

Wilson, G. T. Toward specifying the "nonspecifics" in behavior therapy: A social learning analysis. In M. J. Mahoney (Ed.), *Psychotherapy process*. New York: Plenum, 1980.

Wilson, G. T. Behavior therapy for adults: Application and outcome. In G. T. Wilson & C. M. Franks (Eds.), *Contemporary behavior therapy: Conceptual and empirical foundations*. New York: Guilford, 1982. (a)

Wilson, G. T. How useful is meta-analysis in evaluating the effects of different psychological therapies? *Behavioural Psychotherapy*, 1982, *10*, 221–231. (b)

Wilson, G. T. Psychotherapy process and procedure: The behavioral mandate. *Behavior Therapy*, 1982, *13*, 291–312. (c)

Wilson, G. T. The relationship of learning theories to the behavioural therapies: Problems, prospects, and preferences. In J. Boulougouris (Ed.), *Learning approaches to psychiatry*. New York: Wiley, 1982. (d)

Wilson, G. T. *Cognitive processes and procedures in the clinical use of exposure treatment*. Unpublished manuscript, Rutgers University, 1983.

Wilson, G. T., & Brownell, K. D. Behavior therapy for obesity: An evaluation of treatment outcome. *Advances in Behaviour Research and Therapy*, 1980, *3*, 49–86.

Wilson, G. T., & O'Leary, K. D. *Principles of behavior therapy*. Englewood Cliffs, N.J.: Prentice-Hall, 1980.

Wilson, G. T., & Rachman, S. Meta-analysis and the evaluation of psychotherapy outcome: Limitations and liabilities. *Journal of Consulting and Clinical Psychology*, 1983, *51*, 54–64.

Wilson, P. H. Combined pharmacological and behavioural treatment of depression. *Behaviour Research and Therapy*, 1982, *20*, 173–184.

Winchell, C. A. *The hyperkinetic child. An annotated bibliography, 1974–1979*. Westport, Conn.: Greenwood, 1981.

Winett, R. A. Behavioral community psychology: Some thoughts on current status and realistic expectations. *The Behavior Therapist*, 1979, *2*(2), 14–15.

Winett, R. A. Comment on Matarazzo's "Behavioral health's challenge to academic, scientific, and professional psychology." *American Psychologist*, in press.

Winkler, R. C. The contribution of behavioral economics to behavior modification. In M. Rosenbaum, C. M. Franks, & J. Yaffe (Eds.), *Perspectives on behavior therapy in the eighties*. New York: Springer, 1983.

Winkler, R. C., & Winett, R. A. Behavioral interventions in resource conservation: A systems approach based on behavioral economics. *American Psychologist*, 1982, *37*, 421–435.

Withersty, D. J. (Ed.). *Communication and compliance in a hospital setting*. Springfield, Ill.: Charles C. Thomas, 1980.

Wolery, M., & Billingsley, F. F. The application of Revusky's *Rn* test to slope and level changes. *Behavioral Assessment*, 1982, *4*, 93–103.

Wolf, S. L., Nacht, M., & Kelly, J. L. EMG feedback training during dynamic movement for low back pain patients. *Behavior Therapy*, 1982, *13*, 395–406.

Wolfe, D., St. Lawrence, J., Graves, K., Brehony, K., Bradlyn, D., & Kelly, J. A. Intensive behavioral parent training for a child-abusive mother. *Behavior Therapy*, 1982, *13*, 438–451.

Wolfe, D., & Sandler, J. Training parents in effective child management. *Behavior Modification*, 1981, *5*, 320–335.

Wolfe, D., Sandler, J., & Kaufman, K. A competency-based parent training program for child abusers. *Journal of Consulting and Clinical Psychology*, 1981, *49*, 633–640.

Wolpe, J. *The practice of behavior therapy*. New York: Pergamon, 1973.

Wolpe, J. Behavior therapy versus psychoanalysis: Therapeutic and social implications. *American Psychologist*, 1981, *36*, 159–164. (a)

Wolpe, J. Commentary on the report of the Behavior Therapy Conference. *Journal of Consulting and Clinical Psychology*, 1981, *49*, 604–605. (b)

Wolpe, J. Review of I. Marks, *Cure and care of neuroses: Theory and practice of behavioural psychotherapy*. *The Behavior Therapist*, 1982, *5*(1), 37.

Wolpe, J., & Lazarus, A. A. *Behavior therapy techniques*. New York: Pergamon, 1966.

Wong, S. E., & Liberman, R. P. Mixed single-subject designs in clinical research: Variations of the multiple baseline. *Behavioral Assessment*, 1981, *3*, 297–306.

Wood, F. H., & Lakin, K. C. (Eds.). *Punishment and aversive stimulation in special education: Legal, theoretical, and practical issues in their use with emotionally disturbed children and youth*. Washington, D.C.: Council for Exceptional Children, 1982. (Originally published, 1978.)

Wood, G., Green, L., & Bry, B. H. The impact on behavioral training upon the knowledge and effectiveness of juvenile probation officers and volunteers. *Journal of Community Psychology*, 1982, *10*, 133–141.

Wooley, S. C., Wooley, O. W., & Dyrenforth, S. R. Theoretical, practical, and social issues in behavioral treatments of obesity. *Journal of Applied Behavior Analysis*, 1979, *12*, 3–26.

Woolfolk, A., & Woolfolk, R. L. Modifying the effect of the behavior modification label. *Behavior Therapy*, 1979, *10*, 575–578.

Woolfolk, A., Woolfolk, R. L., & Wilson, G. T. A rose by any other name . . . Labeling bias and attitude towards behavior modification. *Journal of Consulting and Clinical Psychology*, 1977, *45*, 184–191.

Woolfolk, R. L., & Lazarus, A. A. Between laboratory and clinic: Paving the two-way street. *Cognitive Therapy and Research*, 1979, *3*, 239–244.

Woolfolk, R. L., & Richardson, F. C. *Behavior therapy and the ideology of modernity.* Paper presented at the annual meeting of the Association for Advancement of Behavior Therapy, Toronto, Ontario, November 1981.

Yankelovich, D. *The new morality.* New York: McGraw-Hill, 1974.

Yates, B. T. Therapy for human service systems: Five basic steps for measuring and improving cost-effectiveness. In A. J. McSweeny, W. J. Freemouw, & R. P. Hawkins (Eds.), *Practical program evaluation in youth treatment.* Springfield, Ill.: Charles C. Thomas, 1982.

Yeaton, W. H., Greene, B. F., & Bailey, J. S. Behavioral community psychology strategies and tactics for teaching community skills to children and adolescents. In B. B. Lahey & A. E. Kazdin (Eds.), *Advances in clinical child psychology* (Vol. 4). New York: Plenum, 1981.

Yeaton, W. H., & Sechrest, L. Meaningful measures of effect. *Journal of Consulting and Clinical Psychology*, 1981, *49*, 766–767.

Yellin, A. M., Kendall, P. C., & Greenberg, L. M. Cognitive–behavioral therapy and methylphenidate with hyperactive children: Preliminary comparisons. *Research Communications in Psychology, Psychiatry, and Behavior*, 1981, *6*, 213–227.

Young, L. D., & Patterson, J. N. Information and opinions about behavior modification. *Journal of Behavior Therapy and Experimental Psychiatry*, 1981, *12*, 189–196.

Yule, W. Special review of O. Zanqwill: "Behaviour modification: Report of a joint working party to formulate ethical guidelines for the conduct of programmes of behavior modification in the National Health Service." *Behaviour Research and Therapy*, 1982, *20*, 411–413.

Zajonc, R. Feeling and thinking. *American Psychologist*, 1980, *35*, 151–175.

Zeiss, A. M., Lewinsohn, P. M., & Muñoz, R. F. Nonspecific improvement effects in depression using interpersonal skills training, pleasant activity schedules, and cognitive training. *Journal of Consulting and Clinical Psychology*, 1979, *47*, 427–439.

Zettle, R. D., & Hayes, S. C. Rule-governed behavior: A potential theoretical framework for cognitive behavior therapy. In P. C. Kendall (Ed.), *Advances in cognitive-behavioral research and therapy* (Vol. 1). New York: Academic Press, 1983.

Ziarnik, J. P., & Bernstein, G. S. A critical examination of the effect of inservice training on staff performance. *Mental Retardation*, in press.

Zimmerman, B. J., & Ringle, J. Effects of model persistence and statements of confidence on children's self-efficacy and problem solving. *Journal of Educational Psychology*, 1981, *73*, 485–493.

Zinner, S. H., Levy, P. S., & Kass, E. H. Familial aggregation of blood pressure in children. *New England Journal of Medicine*, 1971, *284*, 401–408.

AUTHOR INDEX

SUBJECT INDEX